The ... ...is Myself

'This autobiography is of exceptional distinction and importance. It deserves recognition as a magnificent contribution to international understanding and as a document of how the human spirit can triumph in the midst of evil and persecution'
Economist

'Between modern Europe and the men of the 20th July plot against Hitler there is a gulf . . . This marvellously written book is the first account I have read which brings those men and women and their time to life'
Neal Ascherson, *Observer*

'Nothing but superlatives will do for this book. It tells its story magnificently and every page is worth telling'
Irish Press

The Road Ahead

'Christabel is a very funny writer, but it is the fighting spirit of this remarkable woman, every time she sees an injustice, which really shines through'
Daily Express

'Christabel Bielenberg writes like a dream'
Daily Mail

'Intimate as a quiet talk round a kitchen table, her wonderful story-book writing leaves its readers the more vulnerable to the terrors she exposes'
Spectator

www.transworldbooks.co.uk

Christabel Bielenberg, a niece of Lord Northcliffe, married German lawyer Peter Bielenberg in 1934. Peter was closely associated with resistance circles and was arrested after the failure of the plot against Hitler's life on 20th July 1944. Christabel was interrogated by the Gestapo, but lived through the war as a German citizen, experiencing the horrors of Nazi rule and Allied bombings. In *The Past is Myself*, a bestselling memoir that was adapted for television by the award-winning dramatist Dennis Potter, Christabel presents an unforgettable portrait of this evil time as she writes about her personal experiences, and introduces us to her remarkable friends – whose tragic bravery shines from the book.

The Road Ahead, Christabel's second volume of memoirs, was written in response to the thousands of letters she received from readers begging her to describe her life in the post-war years. As Christabel takes up her story at the outbreak of peace, she does so against the backdrop of a devastated Germany, and a grey and exhausted Britain.

After the war, Christabel was appointed the *Observer*'s special correspondent in Germany and, reunited with her husband Peter (technically an enemy alien), joined the struggle for reconciliation with, and the rebuilding of, a defeated nation. But when Peter suffered a near-fatal accident, the young couple decided to make a fresh start, and began a new life, farming in Ireland.

In 1988, the Federal Republic of Germany awarded Christabel the Commander's Cross of the Order of Merit for her contribution to German–British understanding. Christabel died at home in Ireland in November 2003 at the age of ninety-four.

Appearing for the first time in this volume are two unpublished chapters originally written for inclusion in the books, as well as diary entries and a selection of moving letters from Christabel to friends and family back in England during the war, and later to Peter as they tried to build a life for themselves.

THE PAST IS MYSELF
and
THE ROAD AHEAD

New Updated Edition

Christabel Bielenberg

CORGI BOOKS

TRANSWORLD PUBLISHERS
61–63 Uxbridge Road, London W5 5SA
A Random House Group Company
www.transworldbooks.co.uk

**THE PAST IS MYSELF AND THE ROAD AHEAD OMNIBUS
A CORGI BOOK: 9780552165143**

This omnibus edition first published in Great Britain in 2011 by Corgi Books,
an imprint of Transworld Publishers
This edition copyright © the Christabel Bielenberg Estate 2011

Introduction to the Appendix © Dorothea Depner
Extra chapters, diary notes and letters © the Christabel Bielenberg Estate 2011.

THE PAST IS MYSELF
Originally published in Great Britain in 1968 by Chatto & Windus Ltd
Ward River Press edition published 1982
Corgi edition published 1984
Copyright © Christabel Bielenberg 1968

THE ROAD AHEAD
Originally published in Great Britain in 1992 by Bantam Press,
an imprint of Transworld Publishers
Corgi edition published 1993
Copyright © Christabel Bielenberg 1992

Christabel Bielenberg has asserted her right under the Copyright,
Designs and Patents Act 1988 to be identified as the author of this work.

Addresses for Random House Group Ltd companies outside the UK
can be found at: www.randomhouse.co.uk
The Random House Group Ltd Reg. No. 954009.

The Random House Group Limited supports The Forest Stewardship
Council (FSC®), the leading international forest certification organization.
Our books carrying the FSC label are printed on FSC® certified paper. FSC is
the only forest certification scheme endorsed by the leading environmental
organizations, including Greenpeace. Our paper procurement policy
can be found at www.randomhouse.co.uk/environment.

Typeset in 10½/12½pt Giovanni Book by
Kestrel Data, Exeter, Devon.
Printed in the UK by
CPI Mackays, Chatham ME5 8TD

2 4 6 8 10 9 7 5 3 1

THE PAST IS MYSELF

The future is nothing, but the past is myself, my own history, the seed of my present thoughts, the mould of my present disposition.

Essays of the Road, R. L. Stevenson

CONTENTS

FOREWORD

This account of my life in Germany from 1932 until 1945 was originally intended for my children, and amongst my children I would include my two daughters-in-law, Charlotte and Angela von der Schulenburg, and many other children who came to us in Ireland for their holidays, some of whose fathers had lost their lives because of their opposition to Hitler and to his régime.

Since the war an unprecedented amount of material has been available to historians and to others, enabling them to assess and also to draw their conclusions about the happenings in Germany during those years. I make no claim to be so equipped, but I have one advantage perhaps over those whose knowledge is dependent on documents: I am English; I was German, and above all I was there.

I am grateful to my sister-in-law Elisabeth Burton and to my cousin Cecil King who encouraged me to transform what were originally diary notes into a book. I am also grateful to my nieces Carley Brown and Jill Christie, to Elke Jessett, to Mrs Betts and to Ian Parsons for the help they have given me. Above all I would thank my husband Peter whose patience and unswerving support gave me the courage to write about his country. I would feel the effort to have been worthwhile if it helps to throw new light on what I believe to be for the Germans a still undigested past, and for the English an incomprehensible one.

CHRISTABEL BIELENBERG

1968
Munny House, Tullow
County Carlow

DRAMATIS PERSONAE

Or, some of the people who appear in this book

PETER BIELENBERG. My husband, a Hamburg lawyer, who was arrested after the Plot of July 20th, 1944. He survived, and we now live in Ireland.

NICHOLAS, JOHN and CHRISTOPHER BIELENBERG. Our three sons.

REINHARD VOGLER. My brother-in-law, a judge, now President of Hamburg's High Court.

ULLA WALLENSTEIN (TANTE ULLA). Peter's aunt, whose only son Albrecht Wallenstein was in the German Air Force and was shot down over the North Sea.

ADAM and CLARITA VON TROTT ZU SOLZ. Adam was a Rhodes Scholar, later in the German Foreign Office. He was hanged after the Plot of July 20th, 1944. Clarita, his wife, is now a doctor in Berlin.

BOTHO and MARY VON WUSSOW. Botho was in the German Foreign Office, and now lives in Munich. His English wife Mary died after the war.

CARL and IRMGARD LANGBEHN. Carl, a lawyer, was arrested by the Gestapo in September 1943, and hanged in October 1944.

ELSA VON ROSEN. A school friend of mine whose husband Gustav-Fredrik, Count von Rosen, was Swedish Military Attaché in London during the war.

HELMUTH HIMPEL and MARIE TERWIEL. Our dentist, and his fiancée. Both were executed in 1943 for the parts they played in the Rote Kapelle conspiracy.

LEXI. She was arrested in March 1945, but survived. Lexi later married Richard Weber and died in Spain in 1968.

ELLEN and HANS EICHE. Hans, a lawyer friend of Peter, died in 1961. His wife Ellen lives in Frankfurt.

ARNOLD KOSTER. Survived the war and is now a business man in Munich.

Villagers of Rohrbach in the Black Forest, some of whom still live there, some of whom have since died: Herr Volk, the Mayor; Frau Muckle, proprietress of the *Adler*; Josef (Sepp) Kern, the cobbler; Hans Bausch, the milkman; Pfarrer Kunz, the priest; Lehrer Lorenz, the schoolteacher; and Magd Martina, Frau Muckle's maid.

PROLOGUE

(Autumn 1939)

'I am speaking to you from No. 10 Downing Street. This morning the British Ambassador in Berlin handed the German Government a final note, stating that, unless the British Government heard from them by 11 o'clock that they were prepared at once to withdraw their troops from Poland, a state of war would exist between us. I have to tell you now that no such undertaking has been received and that consequently this country is at war with Germany . . .'

At war with Germany – at war with Germany – the silence was so deep that the precise voice might have had the sitting-room to itself. Adam, who was leaning against the mantelpiece, sighed and turned and glanced at the wireless and Peter and I sat motionless on the sofa, hand in hand. The voice carried on with its message but I was no longer listening. It was as if each of us was away in separate worlds, groping hesitantly towards just what meaning those words would have for us.

At war with Germany. But only a few days back I had tele-phoned to my father and mother (for rumour had been rife that day in Berlin that Hitler had drawn back from the brink, that he had called the whole thing off) and we had laughed together across the miles, and Peter had told my mother that he would be at the Tempelhof Airport to meet her next weekend after all. Could she please bring my Burberry, my watch – as usual, I had left things behind in July. Then just forty-eight hours later Hitler had marched his troops into Poland after all; his 'patience' was at an end. And now? What would happen now if I dialled Continental Trunks and asked for my parents' number? 'I want Hatfield 2014 please.' What excuse would be made by those impersonal voices, who sorted wires and pushed in plugs? German, Dutch, English

15

voices. 'Sorry, we cannot connect you – we are at war.' I tried to listen again to what was being said on the wireless – it was something about conscience – 'We have a clear conscience, we have done all that any country could do to establish peace.'

Two days ago another voice had talked of '*die Ehre des deutschen Volkes*', the honour of the German people, and had also claimed to have done everything possible to keep the peace, but *Ehre* or conscience, *Recht* or right, the result would be the same – War – breaking up homes, separating friends, driving boys to kill each other, Peter and Adam on the one side, my brothers on the other – that would be war.

The room seemed very small, much too small, and I got up suddenly and went out through the french windows into the garden. Peter made a move to stop me, but he seemed to understand, and sat back again and let me go. The air outside was gentle and warm. A pungent smell of pine trees from the Grunewald hung over the garden and it was very dark.

I sat down on the low brick wall which separated our flower beds from the lawn, and stared into the darkness. Ahead of me a narrow shaft of light from the sitting-room window pinpointed my path through the dew, some dahlias beside me, the rough bark, the shadowy branches of an apple tree beyond.

I tried to remember another war, the Kaiser's war, but I had been so small at the time, and the Kaiser just another bogeyman; and although I had been given to understand that the only good German was a dead German, the only real German that I had ever met was Herr Schmidt, the hairdresser, who cut our hair and gave us sticks of marzipan. I had loved him and always mentioned him in my prayers. There was the postcard too of a row of little pigs in brass-spiked helmets, goose-stepping smartly into a pigsty, propelled from behind by the boot of a huge, laughing Tommy, and the time when the sky over the garden was darkened by what seemed to be a giant whale – a huge purring monster which floated above the trees. We had been hustled into the house then and watched from a window as a sudden sheet of flame lit the sky and the monster disintegrated, and human dolls plummeted from the smoking sky, and bits and pieces of flaming monster drifted after them; the last of the Zeppelins had been shot down over Barnet and a cheer went up from the crew of a little gun which had been popping away on the village green.

At war with Germany. Through the crack in the sitting-room

curtains I could see that Adam had moved and was sitting next to Peter on the sofa. They were talking together, leaning forward, staring into the fire, and the flickering flames lit up their faces and threw their dancing shadows on the ceiling. They looked very young, somehow unfairly young to have tried to stem the tide of history.

An electric blue flash from the *S-Bahn* lit up the blacked-out sky, our little yellow house, the billowing curtains of the room upstairs where the children were sleeping. An apple slithered through the branches of the tree behind me and fell with a soft thud on to the flower bed beneath. It was very peaceful and very still in the garden.

THE YEARS BEFORE

Part I: (1932–1934)

At four o'clock in the afternoon of September 29th, 1934, I became a German citizen, when, in a basement office of the German Embassy in London, I exchanged my British passport with its jovial lion and its unicorn and its requirement in the name of his Britannic Majesty that I be afforded every protection of which I might stand in need, for its German equivalent – a nondescript brown booklet with a disdainful looking eagle stamped in black on its drab cardboard cover; the eagle clutched the Swastika emblem in a pair of skinny claws.

Twelve years later in October 1946, in the Lincoln's Inn Fields Offices of a Commissioner for Oaths (who according to regulations put on his bowler hat and buttoned his jacket for the ceremony) I placed my left hand on a bible and raised my right hand in a gesture not unsimilar to the Hitler salute; I swore allegiance to the King and I became a British subject once again. I had been an alien for twelve years; for seven of those years, an enemy alien.

When the German Embassy official handed me my German passport in 1934 and locked away my British one in a drawer of his desk, he made a rather unexpected remark. 'You've not made a very good swop I'm afraid,' he said, and then as he bowed and shook me by the hand, he glanced up at my escort and added with a smile, 'except of course that this handsome fellow is included in the deal.'

My marriage that September morning to Peter Bielenberg, a young law student from Hamburg, had gone off very well indeed, considering that my parents-in-law spoke very few recognizable words of English and my parents' knowledge of German was non-existent. It had been glamorized by the usual turn-out of top hats, morning coats, picture hats and messages of goodwill. At the wedding reception afterwards, my father-in-law, a much respected Hamburg lawyer, made a short and carefully enunciated speech which he had obviously spared no effort to learn by heart. He welcomed me wholeheartedly to his family circle and made no mention of the fact that, by marrying at the age of twenty-two, unqualified as yet to be a lawyer and therefore unable to support a family for some years to come, his only son was breaking with one of the strictest Hamburg traditions, and for that reason it was his considered opinion that the consequences could hardly fail to be dire.

My father replied more coherently, but in similar vein. He did not mention that he had stopped the car on our way to the ceremony and had assured me earnestly that there was still time for me to change my mind. As we drove away on our honeymoon, Peter and I wasted little thought on the warnings, some reasonable some otherwise, which had punctuated the fitful course of our two-year-long courtship.

Peter himself had not escaped his fair share of exhortation and admonishment from his side of the North Sea. For beside the unanswerable objections to our marriage on account of his age, and the only half-completed state of his professional education, there were certain peculiarities about me, due to my liberal up-bringing, which did not conform to the image of a young wife as viewed by worthy Hamburg burghers. Could I cook? Could I mend? Had I any notion how humbly and with what diligence and thrift I would be expected to launch myself into the exacting rôle of a German Hausfrau? Obviously not. I had been brought up in comparative luxury; I had admitted light-heartedly that my cooking lessons had consisted exclusively of weekly expeditions from my finishing school in Paris to the *Cordon Bleu* Institute, where expert chefs had endeavoured to initiate me – along with a dozen other British 'debs' – into the intricate arts of *haute cuisine*, without taking into account that most of us had never even tried our hand at boiling an egg. I had also been forced to admit, and had often enough given ample proof, that I was never quite certain as to how things got done in a house. My parents had made it quite clear that after my marriage I would be financially independent, and this, far from adding to my attractions, introduced another element of doubt as to my suitability as a match. Independence, financial or otherwise, was not a state of affairs to be encouraged in a German woman; it might arouse and set in motion quite a number of disturbing phenomena which had up to date slumbered very peacefully in the German social scene.

If Peter and I had given no heed to these rumbling premonitions, there were other more ominous portents on the horizon which showed signs of affecting our lives, and our future together, more drastically; these, in contrast to many of our elders and betters, we had been unable to dismiss from our minds quite so easily.

During the two years 1932–34 which followed Peter's and my first meeting, Germany ceased to be a democracy and became a dictatorship. The Weimar Republic, which had succeeded the monarchy after the First World War, succumbed without much ado to the demagogy, the bullyragging tactics, and the subtle political manipulations of one man. It became the Third Reich. The countless political parties of the post-war years having finally fought and argued themselves to a standstill, were successfully buried under a muddy brown avalanche: The Nation al Socialist German Workers Party, with Party member no. 7, Adolf Hitler, at its head.

A few weeks before our marriage, the last link with the past was broken by the death of the Reichs President von Hindenburg, and Hitler appointed himself supreme Head of State: Führer and Reichs Chancellor and Commander in Chief of the Armed Forces, whose members would be compelled in future to take their oath of allegiance, no longer to the State and to the Constitution, but to himself, as Leader, personally.

It would have been hard to find any two citizens less occupied by affairs of state than were Peter and I at that time; but these were happenings which we could hardly fail to contemplate without a certain measure of apprehension, more particularly when they began to affect our private lives.

In 1932 I thought I understood just about all I would ever understand about politics in Germany. I could recite the names of half-a-dozen of the innumerable political parties, and recognize the various uniforms of the *Kampfverbände*, which were the armed fighting units attached to these parties. I knew it to be advisable to refrain from taking a stroll through certain parts of Hamburg on a Sunday, because the Monday morning newspapers nearly always carried an obituary of an over-ardent politician, or of some innocent bystander, who found themselves taking part in a political demonstration over the weekend.

I had also learned, by 1932, that no Government in Germany remained in power longer than a few months, because no single party or coalition of parties could ever muster enough votes to enable them to govern.

If I had been anxious for further enlightenment on his country's politics, I soon discovered that Peter was not the man to approach, for he professed himself utterly disinterested in the subject. One good reason for his seemingly indifferent attitude, and one which he shared with many of his Hamburg contemporaries, stemmed from the fact that the city of his birth prided itself on being a free city: one of the earliest and most powerful members of the Hanseatic League, which had governed itself quite independently of its powerful Prussian neighbour for some seven hundred years. The sons of the patrician merchants of Hamburg were not therefore expected to acquit themselves in the Army or the Civil Service, as were those of the Prussian nobility, but served their apprenticeships in far-flung overseas trading posts before returning to occupy comfortable seats on the City Council, and rather less comfortable ones in the massive sombre mansions they had built for themselves around the larger of the Alster Lakes, or along the east bank of the Elbe. There, they were accustomed to live out their lives in frugal solidity, until the next generation grew up to carry on the family business. Sieveking, Amsinck, Brödermann, Kellinghusen: these were the names to conjure with in Hamburg society. The little prefix 'von', significant of some aristocratic blood throughout the rest of Germany, not only failed to cut any ice in Hamburg, but carried with it a faint aura of irresponsibility, even degeneracy, which made it highly suspect. To be 'accepted' was definitely easier if one was English rather than Prussian or Bavarian, and although the goings on in the rest of Germany could not be completely ignored, there were other matters (such as the sugar and coffee plantations in central and south America, or the Corn and Stock Exchanges) which demanded more attention.

Another reason for Peter's lack of interest in public affairs was the result of one piece of paternal advice which, contrary to most others, he had taken to heart. He had not found it too difficult to do so, because among the most vivid of his boyhood memories were those of the inflation period after the First World War, when the value of the German Reichsmark was falling every week, every day, and finally every hour and, as the printing presses all over Germany churned out new paper-money as fast as they could, Peter was sent running from shop to shop lugging a suitcase full of it, barely able to buy enough food to feed the family. Peter's father had impressed on him repeatedly that he should never under any circumstances have anything to do with politics; it was a profession he considered to be shady. Father Bielenberg's view was based on what had hit his family at the peak of the inflation, when a new currency was established and *one billion* paper Reichmarks was made equal in value to one new Tentenmark, and the Bielenberg family funds invested in Government Bonds – supposedly gilt-edged securities – were no longer worth the paper they were printed on.

Peter's father was among those who, during the more tranquil years which followed, set about retrieving his shattered fortunes with great determination. But he sacrificed his health to that end, and when I appeared on the scene he was manifestly only living and working for the moment when, in true Hamburg tradition, he could hand over his flourishing law-practice to his son.

By 1932, whilst studying singing and trying to learn the language, I had had some experience of other German families. I had become quite accustomed to living in an atmosphere of spotlessly clean, worse-for-wear gentility, screened off from the world outside by dense lace curtains and a jungle of potted house-plants. I knew that Germans were considered to be a very musical race, but all the same I had not yet inured myself to the *Musik Abende*: musical evenings at home when friends and neighbours, young and old, surged in with their instruments and filled the air with such an ear-splitting din that I often wondered how any house-plant managed to remain motionless in its pot. Nor could I make out, during the inevitable political discussions which followed, how it was that the gentlemen in jackboots, in flowing capes and headgear covered with spikes or birds-of-prey, should be blamed so little for the painful upheavals which had followed on a lost war. I knew that Germans were by nature inveterate globetrotters, and that they had for financial reasons been confined since the war within the borders of their own country. I could therefore understand something of their surprise that other countries besides their own had suffered from post-war problems; but it was often wearisome, all the same, to be confronted by such dogged determination to be the only sufferers in this world. This discontent with a state of affairs which they considered had been brought about by circumstances quite outside their control was much the same whether or not I moved my lodgings from the modest villa of a Professor of Hamburg University to a charming white house on the bank of a river outside the town, which belonged to a widow who was related to every family of note in the *Hansestadt*.

I was happily ensconced in Hamburg in the autumn of 1932 with an extremely nice family, also come down in the world, but one which did not spend so much time cherishing grievances. Because the only son of the house, the apple of his parents' eye, Hans believed quite sincerely that he had discovered not only the solution to all Germany's ills but also the canker at the root of her troubles. These were respectively: National Socialism and the Jews. Over cups of cocoa, and with picture postcards of Hitler in many different postures pinned to the walls about us, Hans told me why he thought that National Socialism was the only thing which could save Germany from complete chaos. Did I know that the war of 1914 had not been lost by the German soldier at the front, but by the decadent politicians at home? His father had fought bravely for years and had had to see the cockades and epaulettes torn from the uniforms of his brother officers when they returned home to a thankless Fatherland. Had I ever heard of President Wilson's fourteen points? Those terms of surrender, which had persuaded the trusting warriors to lay down their arms, only to be confronted a year later by the Treaty of Versailles, a peace they should never have accepted nor ever could accept? His parents were respectable people, he assured me, and did I think he liked having to see his father go off every morning to his humble job and his mother tied to the kitchen stove? He knew they did it for him, they had great hopes in him, but unless the Nazis came to power there would be no hope of a job for him when he left university, for they had no influential Jewish friends. The Jews living in Hamburg amounted to 3 per cent of the population, but 40 per cent of all doctors, 30 per cent of all lawyers and 10 per cent of all the judges in Hamburg were Jews; the shops, the banks, the businesses – too many of them were run by Jews – and Jews always stuck together. His parents had lost everything they had in the inflation, but not so the Jews; they had flourished since the war.

Hans was by nature a gentle fellow, but sometimes when he really got going he rose to his feet, his face flushed, and struck poses very like those in the postcards on the walls. I never asked him whether he practised in front of a mirror, because I liked him and he was too honest and too earnest to be teased. He lent me Hitler's *Mein Kampf* to read, and I kampfed with four turgid pages before giving up; whereupon he escorted me to some of his Party meetings, which I found far more entertaining, and before leaving we passed down the rows of little tables set up in the side aisles in order to tot up how many new recruits to the movement were queueing up to sign for Party membership.

On one such occasion in the autumn of 1932, by stretching his devotion to the limit, I even managed to persuade Peter to sink his prejudices and come with me. Hitler himself was to speak to an open-air rally, and the venue was – not inappropriately as Peter did not fail to point out – Hagenbeck's Zoo. A huge area had been cordoned off, and rows of burly Storm-troopers wedged the milling crowds into orderly rectangles. Peter survived the community singing, the rolling of the drums, the National and the Party anthems, but his reaction to the usual reverberating start was unequivocal. My ears were hardly attuned to the Leader's Austrian accent, before I found myself being marched out of the enclosure. Up against the giraffe house, well within earshot of and successfully silencing some Party stalwarts in brown pillbox hats who were rattling collection boxes under the noses of luckless late-comers, Peter delivered himself of one of his rare political pronouncements. 'You may think that Germans are political idiots, Chris,' he said very loudly and very firmly, 'and you may be right, but of one thing I can assure you, they won't be so stupid as to fall for *that* clown.'

Three months later on January 30th, 1933, Hitler became Germany's Chancellor. I was in England at the time, and when I read of it in the newspapers I was rather pleased for my friend Hans. I took note that Hitler had only two other National Socialists with him in his Cabinet, and that he was well hemmed-in by such respectable figures as von Neurath and von Papen. Although I was glad therefore that Hans was to get his chance, I was equally certain that a month or so would suffice to bring him speedy disillusionment, and that there would be, as usual, another round of musical chairs, another change of Government.

So I was a little surprised, and also put out, to hear from Frau

Schadow, my singing teacher, that she intended moving her music school to London in the spring. Her letter showed some signs of panic; but as I had not bothered to wonder whether or not she was of Jewish extraction, it did not occur to me that her 'personal reasons' might have something to do with a new political situation. A new political situation: one which would seek to penetrate and control every section of the life of anyone who wished to live within the borders of the Third Reich.

Events in Germany moved very fast after January 30th, 1933. The burning of the Reichstag, the banning of the Communist Party, the last free elections, the passing of the Enabling Laws, the dissolution of the Trades Unions and of all the other political parties – the whole process of what was called 'co-ordination' was over and done with by July of that year. Behind a façade of constitutional legality, it took Hitler exactly six months to manoeuvre himself and his Party to power.

During those six months Peter and I had personal, and there-fore for us more momentous, considerations to occupy our minds. We had become engaged, and Peter's final university law examinations were due to start in the spring; he must stick to his books, whether or not certain texts were becoming out of date faster than he could comfortably digest them.

Almost immediately he was given some warning of what might happen to him. In 1932 he had won an exchange scholarship, and had been looking forward to spending a year in the United States after taking his exams. Early in 1933 he was informed that the American selection committee had decided that they would prefer to welcome a representative of the 'New Germany'. Did he belong to the National Socialist Party, or had he the intention of applying for membership? No? Then unfortunately a member of the Party must be chosen instead.

Peter had a number of Jewish friends, and although some were breaking off their studies and planning to leave while the going was good, most were staying on, unable to believe as yet, and he most certainly shared their disbelief, that the one country in Europe in which they had felt completely at home was about to turn against them.

It was true that bands of rowdy Storm-troopers roamed the flag-plastered streets of Hamburg celebrating their political victory, and that to be seen with a *Judenjunge*, a Jewboy, could start a bout of shouted insults and end in a free-for-all. But Peter was fit enough to be left unharmed and also relatively unimpressed by the occasional street brawl; in fact he got into so many that I wondered if he did not sometimes encourage them, to give himself an opportunity of letting off steam.

It was an incident, which occurred in May 1933, though, that left him disturbed and for the first time apprehensive about the future. He was strolling across the Lombardsbrücke with Ingrid Warburg, a lovely Jewess with something of the looks and carriage of Queen Nefertiti, when there was a sudden commotion on the far side of the bridge, and two small figures came running towards him. They were clutching briefcases, sweating and obviously terrified, darting and dodging like hares in and out through the passing traffic. Several hefty Storm-troopers followed panting on their heels and, as Peter instinctively moved forward to bar their way, Ingrid clutched at his arm. 'Please, Peter, for my sake!' Ingrid's voice was so urgent, and the expression on her face so suddenly tragic, that he stopped for a moment in his tracks, and when he turned again the strolling crowds had folded over the scene like velvet curtains. The Binnen Alster lake sparkled in the spring sunshine and Hamburg's church spires glowed green against a hazy sky. It was as if nothing out of the ordinary had taken place. The evening papers provided the clue to this incident when they carried the news in banner headlines that the Trades Unions had voluntarily placed their fate in the hands of the Führer and that Robert Ley, one of Hitler's particularly nauseating henchmen, had been appointed head of a newly created 'Worker's Front'. Herr Ley had made quite a speech, it seemed, and had declared that he considered worker's institutions to be sacred. Peter remembered that the office of the Trades Unions in Hamburg were situated next door to the Atlantic Hotel, a few hundred yards from the Lombardsbrücke, and that evening he wrote to me in England that if this was the new Germany there would be no place in it for us.

I did not share Peter's unease until a similar incident happened on one of my visits to Germany when we were sitting together in a country inn and three young Jews were drinking their wine and talking together quietly at the table next to ours. The Storm-troopers, who gangled in through the door, stood leaning against the bar staring about them with the truculent bleariness of the very drunk. 'This place stinks,' said one. 'And I know why,' said another. Shades of my Irish father, I knew from the way Peter put down his glass that we were in for trouble. Six drunken Storm-troopers, three not very athletic looking Jews – one a girl – Peter and myself; my state of mind would not have earned me the Victoria Cross. I even found myself placing a restraining hand on Peter's arm, as I glanced about the restaurant, certainly expecting allies. To my surprise there were obviously none. The other citizens present were either gulping down their wine, hurriedly paying their bills or already halfway to the door. 'Silly bastards,' Peter remarked in his best English, using an expression which had become quite a favourite of his. One of the Jews gave him a half smile and called for his bill, which was brought forward at the double. They left the restaurant and Peter had to content himself with guarding their passage to the door, to the accompaniment of roars of beery laughter from the bar.

It was just another incident, and it was not the picture of the drunken buffoons in brown shirts which stuck in my mind, for they were a sight we had got used to; it was rather the hurried scrambling to depart, the jostle of *gutbürgerliche* backsides, the sudden void. It was not the agitation but the acquiescence that shocked me, and made me aware quite suddenly that I was a stranger in the place, born and bred in a country where communal activities and also communal protest belonged as much to a way of life as cricket or Christmas pudding.

It was then that I too had the uncomfortable suspicion that something very nasty indeed might have come to stay.

Part II: (1935–1939)

The history of the years between 1935 and 1938 in Germany could be summarized by a conversation overheard between two Hamburg dock-workers, sitting over their beer in a riverside pub (Hamburg dock-workers are not renowned for their garrulity). 'Ja, ja, ja,' sighed the one, and again after a long pause, 'ja, ja, ja.' 'Listen,' said his friend, gazing mournfully into his beer-mug, 'can't you, for one moment, stop discussing politics?' They were the years when Hitler in Nuremberg promulgated laws for the protection of German blood and German honour, which deprived Jews of their German citizenship; when he occupied the Saar territory and the demilitarized zone in the Rhineland and brought about the *Anschluss* with Austria; when 99 per cent of the electorate in Germany took part in several national plebiscites and went on record as having given virtually unanimous support to his policies. The years of the monster headliners, and of the newsreels showing acres of cheering masses, roaring and *heiling* and swaying like corn in the breeze. They were the years when Peter and I, ordinary young citizens, willing and probably capable of making some useful contribution to the society in which we lived, were being forced to face the stark reality that, although our circumstances appeared outwardly to be ordinary, in truth they were not; for, if we valued our integrity, no normal or natural ambition could find any outlet whatsoever under a régime such as Hitler's.

We could evade making major concessions; joining the Party or taking part in the ceaseless processions and adding our voices to the 'spontaneous' howls of assent, but, as the régime got into gear and spread its tentacles, with germanic devotion to detail, throughout the whole fabric of public life, it became increasingly difficult for us to escape the occasional compromise. By compromising we could learn how each small demand for our outward acquiescence could lead to the next, and with the gentle persistence of an incoming tide could lap at the walls of just that integrity we were so anxious to preserve.

When we returned to live permanently in Germany in the autumn of 1935, Peter still had two years ahead of him before he could take his final law examination, the equivalent in England of being called to the Bar. Legal training in Germany required a law student, after leaving university, to spend some months in each and every department of the judicature, and in one department of the Civil Service, in order to gain practical experience of their functions. Those were his so-called Referendar 'stations', and they lasted some three years in all. After 1933 two rather important stepping stones, or stumbling blocks according to which way one happened to look at them, had been placed in the path of any would-be Assessor. Firstly, as he progressed from one department to the next, a statement as to his political reliability had to be added to the report on his general efficiency by the head of the department concerned; and secondly, he had to spend two months being 'politically indoctrinated' and physically toughened in a semi-military camp for budding young lawyers in Jüterbog near Berlin.

Since political credentials of at least a non-committal nature were essential to the passing of his Assessor examination and it was becoming increasingly difficult to find higher officials willing to compromise themselves on his behalf, Peter found himself having to plan his course with some ingenuity. He chose the German Embassy in London for his Civil Service chore, because he thought he could rely on a harmless political report coming from that quarter. The German Foreign Office had as yet undergone no major purge, and Herr von Ribbentrop had not yet arrived in England to find himself dubbed 'Brickendrop' by mirthful Londoners.

This arrangement we decided would suit us very well, because our first child, due to arrive in the late summer, would be able to claim British citizenship. Our plans indeed worked out perfectly, and I was very pleased with myself when I returned to the Fatherland in the autumn of 1935, to take up residence in a tiny cottage in Reinbek, some thirty kilometres south of Hamburg. What had I to worry about? I had an extremely handsome husband, a healthy British-born son, and a mountain of goods and chattels; I was as brimful of confidence as I was void of know-how in the art of being a *Hausfrau*.

It did not take me long to realize that Hamburg had changed a great deal during our year's absence. Before my marriage I had felt comparatively familiar with the German scene. I was accustomed to the groups of young people with immense rucksacks and rather tight shorts, striding along through the countryside hand in hand singing at the tops of their voices, or to the pale-faced middle-aged couples, padding the streets of a Sunday, like peaceful penguins, hooked to each other, clasping the inevitable bunch of flowers, making their leisurely progress towards mountainous family coffee and cake sessions. These to me were just ordinary people doing things differently, and I only got out of my depth when I discovered that at the drop of a hat, or rather the sound of a voice, they could transform themselves into a roaring jostling mob, with glassy eyes and right arms outstretched. I had only once got myself mixed up in such a hullaballoo and had been frankly scared, until I worked my way to the back of the crowd and found others – few indeed, but a very precious few, who were watching the performance with wary mistrust: a sturdy, silent, but strangely comforting brotherhood.

The change of scene when I returned in 1935 came not only from the fact that my cheerful hikers were now decked out in uniforms of a particularly nauseous colour, that the boys' hair was clipped much shorter and the girls had cultivated rather massive plaits; nor from the fact that small divot-like moustaches 'au Führer' adorned the upper lips of so many of my peaceful penguins; nor indeed because the familiar Rathausmarkt had changed its name to Adolf Hitler Platz, and the hideous Nazi flag fluttered and flapped from every public building. It seemed to me that the change lay deeper. Street fighting, unemployment, fear of civil war, fear of another inflation, had been burning problems when I left; when I returned they no longer seemed to exist. Instead a certain air of modest prosperity pervaded the streets, manners in public (never a very strong point in Germany) had improved beyond recognition. I did not find that everyone I met was enthusiastic about every aspect of the régime, they were not; but most were ready to admit that there was quite a lot to be said for the New Order, and deemed it an improvement on what had gone before. It was considered that Hitler had met his match in the Army, and that, with the murder of Roehm and the eclipse of his Storm-troopers (although the manner in which it had been carried out had not been exactly savoury), the Revolution had to all intents and purposes become respectable. Once everything distasteful had been neatly swept under the carpet, there was something almost touching about the anxious childlike pleasure with which so many tried to share in what they seemed to hope was a newly discovered respectability.

Unpleasantnesses, of course there were unpleasantnesses; but such things, if talked about at all, must be seen in production. There were after all so many more positive aspects of the régime to chat about. Look at young Heini, for instance, with his neatly clipped pate, so purposeful, so different from the long-haired lout who propped up the street corner some few months back; and Father too, there he goes with his Party badge, and his bulging briefcase – 'I'll kill myself working, you see if I don't,' written in triumph all over his face.

What had Hitler provided which seemed to satisfy so many and persuaded them so easily to relinquish their freedom and to turn aside from the still small voice of their conscience? I was ignorant at the time, but later I felt I could venture a guess. Hitler understood his Germans well, or maybe he had just chanced his luck with human nature. There was a titbit for all in his political stew pot. Work for the unemployed, an army for the Generals, a phoney religion for the gullible, a loud, insistent and not unheeded voice in international affairs for those who still smarted under the indignity of a lost war: there were also detention camps and carefully broadcast hints of what might be in store for anyone who had temerity enough to enquire into his methods too closely, let alone openly disapprove of them. He made every move, though, behind a smoke-screen of legality and also of propriety, for he was shrewd enough to know that the spirit of his revolution came from the disgruntled, disenchanted, dispossessed middle classes. He must strike the right note therefore, and he did so by making respectability the quintessence, the irresistible *pièce de résistance*, of all that he had to offer.

In the autumn of 1936 Peter and I moved house from Reinbek to Hamburg. I was expecting my second child, Peter's Assessor examination was approaching fast, Hitler had been in power for three and a half long years, and, although we were becoming accustomed to certain aspects of his régime, we were also beginning to realize that we were living with a dubious dilemma. There was nothing to prevent us from showing our disapproval by our lack of co-operation in as many small ways as we considered possible without risking our necks, and we had learned to watch out for the signs, the subtle signs from others who were doing the same. We could talk, therefore, with like-minded friends and with them register amazement and also disgust. We knew no Nazis at all intimately, since to have done so would not only have been distasteful but also risky. Hitler had not been long in power before a very unpleasant phenomenon appeared on the scene: the informer who was not always a member of the Party, but who was none the less eager to show loyalty by reporting everything he saw or heard.

By consciously disassociating ourselves though from something we did not understand or approve of, we drifted into a way of life removed from the force of the mainstream and were forever being taken by surprise as some further diabolic brainchild was flourished in our faces. The newspapers and also the wireless, controlled by Dr Goebbels and his Ministry for Propaganda and Public Enlightenment, had become a remorseless hammerbeat of superlatives which, for me at least, successfully defeated their own ends. No one person could be so perfect as the Führer, no race so heroic, so long suffering as the German, so idiotic as the British, or so diabolical as the Jewish – I simply gave up.

Peter relied for information on his efforts to read between the lines of the *Frankfurter Allgemeine Zeitung*. It was to me a rather turgid sheet, but one which had the reputation of having developed quite a technique in camouflaged reporting. I began a serious study of the London *Times*, believing sincerely, as I had been brought up to do, that it would convey to me a balanced and objective viewpoint. It seemed that others had been brought up to think likewise, as *The Times* was not always easy to come by in Hamburg. It was sold out unless I arrived at the newspaper kiosk on time.

The homily which was delivered to me daily by the newspaper of my choice could be summed up somewhat as follows: 'If you have reached maturity and are confronted with what may be a delinquent child, obsessed by one or two legitimate grievances, your first duty is to remove those grievances; to be firm but kind, and thus lure him with sweet reason back into the family circle – for the alternative might be the break-up of the home.'

Who was I to argue with *The Times*? Or with the London taxi-driver, for that matter, who gave his views on the German re-militarization of the Rhineland over his shoulder, as he piloted me deftly through the City streets. He didn't much like that Hitler, he said, but if some ruddy frogs had been occupying Devon and Cornwall, he'd feel much the same way. Tell em to 'op it and mind their own business, that's what he'd do.

With all normal channels of information successfully under control, rumour and hearsay took over and ran riot. Hitler was an epileptic, who'd been known to bite chunks out of the carpet when in a rage; he had only a few months to live – someone had it from someone who'd had it from a doctor who . . . Funny stories went the rounds tending to lend credence to such rumours, tending also to reduce the Leader to size: like the one about the assistant in the carpet-store asking politely if the Führer wished to have the rugs he had just chosen sent direct to the Reichs Chancellery, or did he wish to eat them immediately on the premises? Rumour had it that Goering was impotent, or a drug addict, or both, and that Goebbels was a Jew; Ley also – his real name was Levi. Fortune tellers and soothsayers took up residence in the smarter quarters of the town and reported that Hitler was born under the sign of Aries, and that although the planet Mars might hover occasionally rather perilously near his orbit, he would pursue his allotted path and would prevail – without having recourse to war. Since for a time their prophecies coincided so exactly with subsequent events, they did a roaring trade.

It was under such circumstances as these that we learned to believe only such things as we saw with our own eyes or heard with our own ears, and we extended our trust to a few, but only a very few close personal friends. The flashes of insight came to each of us separately, in the privacy of our own experience.

The Nuremberg Laws, for instance, most certainly provided some Jews and also some Gentiles, with just that flash of insight needed to show them that the writing was on the wall and the exodus must begin; they did not do so for me. I could pinpoint no exact date when normal and natural association with Jewish friends became an act of defiance and then petered out, not because the friend was less close, but simply because such a relationship is an unnatural one, mutual embarrassment intervenes. At first we were no less credulous than they. Why should they go? The whole thing was crazy – couldn't possibly last. When was it that credulity turned to doubt, doubt to resignation, and to the unhappy, rather shamefaced admission that you were sorry, you could not help it, you happened to have been labelled an Aryan (whatever that might be), and truth to tell you'd be mighty relieved to know that the good friend was safely off your conscience overseas?

The Nuremberg Laws did not hit me hard until they walked quietly and with dignity across the threshold of my own front door. Professor Bauer looked after our children. He was a dedicated paediatrician and a busy man, although not a rich one, as he had founded a private children's clinic in Hamburg, and had maintained it during the depression years with as much of his personal means as he could spare. I was a little puzzled, and very grateful, that he found time one night to sit with me for long hours at the bedside, while Nicholas, our eldest son, tossed with fever. I watched his delicate handling of my very sick child, and we smiled at each other a little wearily but very happily towards morning, when Nicky lay peacefully sleeping.

Professor Bauer hesitated before leaving the house and then asked me quietly if, after Nicky had been restored to health, I still wished for him to attend my family. Still? Whyever not? I was tired; he had to explain. I knew, doubtless, that he was a Jew, I might not have heard, though, that his Clinic had been threatened with having to close down unless he handed it over to an

Aryan colleague. He had fought the issue for more than a year, but he had given in now in the interest of the patients. Redress? *'Gnädige Frau*, I am no longer a German citizen.' One thing he felt I should know. He had received threatening letters bidding him to keep his hands off Aryan children. If I insisted I might get involved. All right, if I did insist, it might be advisable for me to cease making appointments by telephone.

I called at his flat some weeks later, to find that he was not at home. His wife and I sat together surrounded by packing cases and she told me that he had gone to Holland. No, he had no employment as yet, but something would surely turn up; he was not young of course, nor had they unlimited means, but something would surely turn up. The little housekeeper who brought us some tea was not young either; the Nuremberg Laws forbade Jews to employ anyone below the age of forty-five. She was apparently trustworthy though, because Professor Bauer's wife did not wait until she had left the room before she made her sudden confession that she was afraid. 'He loved this country, you see, Frau Bielenberg, something broke inside him when he had to leave his Clinic.'

The epilogue came two years later, when I found myself standing next to the little housekeeper in a tram queue. The Bauers? She drew me aside. Hadn't I heard? The *Herr Professor* had died suddenly. She shook her head: *'Ne, ne, Frau Doktor*, such things should not be allowed.' Some said it was suicide – but she knew that his heart had been broken. 'They were good people,' she murmured, and she had intended keeping the flat in good order until they returned. – *'Ne, ne*,' she shook her head again and looked at me suddenly, almost pleadingly, as if about to ask me a question to which I might have an answer, since I was, after all, a *Frau Doktor*.

I could have pleaded my cause, the cause of those who should know better. I could have told her that we were not yet thirty years of age and that our elders and supposedly betters – not only in Germany but in Europe and beyond the seas – had not distinguished themselves by giving us a lead. I could have told her that since we were not Jews and there was no capricious higher authority to make up our minds for us, it was easy to bury one's head in the sand, but that we had tried often enough to fumble our way through the confusing fog of fact and fiction. I could have produced some exonerating evidence for her after all, in that

I had been unavoidably confined to the house with a 'cold' when in 1936 I was called upon to vote in my first national plebiscite. We were to approve Hitler's re-occupation of the Rhineland, and voting booths and ballot-boxes had been laid on to give the occasion an air of authenticity. But a rumour spread that certain arrests had been made in the following weeks, because the ballot papers had been numbered with invisible ink. So the next time we were called to the voting booths Peter and I decided we would see for ourselves and record our vote. To make quite certain, Peter volunteered to help count the voting papers in our district.

I was handed a slip of paper and an envelope from a neat pile, and was ushered into an open cubicle by a rotund and smiling party official, who showed me the exact spot where I should place my X, and then stood back a pace, and when I turned on him suddenly I found that the smile had left his face and that he was gazing pointedly at my elbow. I slipped my closed envelope through the slot of a long narrow box, having already decided that I knew enough about the secrecy of the vote, and that, if the worst came to the worst, short sight would have to be my excuse for the illegible hieroglyphic which I had scrawled across the corner of my voting slip. Peter returned home in the evening, quite elated with the result of his count. Quite a percentage of the votes he had counted had been either No's, or destroyed or defaced voting papers, and one doughty fellow had even found the time and courage to scrawl across his slip of paper 'He can lick my arse!'

I could have mentioned how gleefully we had grasped at such straws of sanity, but that when the results were published on the following day, Peter and I had been given to understand that we had shown our approval of Hitler and his policies as surely as if we had gone to the voting booth draped from head to foot in Swastikas.

If I had wanted to get Professor Bauer's housekeeper really muddled I could have told her of the happenings some weeks before, referred to in England as the 'rape of Austria'. For Peter and I had by chance been among the first German civilians to cross the Austrian border after the German troops. A weekend as usual. *'Achtung, Achtung, Extrablatt, Extrablatt, die deutschen Truppen sind in Oesterreich einmarschiert!'* The news vendors parading the platforms of the Augsburg main station before dawn had wakened us with a jolt, and seemed bent on putting a premature end to a much looked-forward-to swastika-free holiday in the Arlberg. Before we had time to dress ourselves, however, the train moved off on schedule and would no doubt have reached its destination with accustomed punctuality if the tracks had not been lined from the Austrian border southwards with *heiling*, smiling crowds, waving makeshift Nazi flags, dancing, laughing, reaching up to grasp us by the hand. Rape, my hat, the whole place was *en fête*. 'Somebody seems to love us anyway,' Peter had murmured as we grinned back inanely, and finally found ourselves returning despondently to our carriage, feeling that the rôle of Nazi liberators might have been spared us.

We were spared nothing, neither the swaggering brown-shirted hooligans, undeniably indigenous, nor the goggle-eyed Führer-worshipping maidens, nor the eye-witness accounts of how the people of Vienna had shown, by their treatment of their Jews and their political opponents, that they could be as uncivilized as anyone anywhere else in the *Gross Deutsche Reich*.

'Swastikas are in the air, you see, people are getting a kick out of Swastikas,' I could have told Professor Bauer's housekeeper, 'and I know no better than you do what we should be doing about it.' But it would have been useless. Explanations and excuses would not have brought back Professor Bauer and so – 'I'm very sorry, just very sorry,' was all I managed to say as I watched her bustle back to her queue for fear of missing her tram.

A short while after that meeting at the tram-stop Peter and I decided at last just what we *were* going to do about it. 'If this is the new Germany there's no place in it for us – or for our children either.' The seed which had been planted in Peter's mind years back on the Lombardsbrücke, and which had been fostered by every manifestation of cant and cruelty, duplicity and dishonesty, and also by the manifest futility of our effort to be obstructive, bore fruit when Peter came home one evening after a day in the Law Courts where he had been defending a poor-law client, a former Social Democrat who had been caught distributing illegal political leaflets. He had managed to get his client acquitted, and they had shaken hands and congratulated each other outside the Court House; someway up the street Peter had turned to wave a final goodbye. He was just in time to see his client being marched away between two uniformed guards and bundled into a green van parked beside the roadway. Before he could run back to the spot the green van and its occupant had rounded a corner and been swallowed up in the passing traffic. He had spent the day making fruitless enquiries in the Law Courts, and taking an equally fruitless stand at Police Headquarters. There had been forms to fill out, of course, but official shoulders had been shrugged. Had he not heard that in the interest of security there now existed such a thing as protective custody? Whatever way it was, Peter's client had simply vanished without trace, and with him any desire on Peter's part to continue his profession as a lawyer.

Our decision to emigrate was not so easy for Peter as it was for me. I had made the move before, I was not so involved; in less charitable moments I could even enjoy myself feeling smug – after all, it was not my rabble which had been roused, not my countrymen who were going so swiftly round the bend. Of Peter it required a ruthlessness towards his past and towards his parents of which he had not as yet been capable. He was an only son, he had shown promise of being a successful lawyer, and he could not escape the knowledge that his father had sacrificed his health in order to hand him over a flourishing law practice. Hamburg tradition, filial duty, eight years of legal training, were they all to be summed up and dismissed as 'a bloody ridiculous performance'? More, to quit meant abandoning a certain cussedness; it forced him to admit that by allowing himself to be pushed around, he had been defeated by Hitler after all.

However, since the world was big and we were young, we were well able to contemplate a complete break with the past and a new start in remote continents. It was not long before we were out-backing in Australia, fruit farming in Africa, lumber-jacking in Canada and finally returning nearer home to arrive at a com-promise. We chose Ireland to be our future homeland. Ireland was in the throes of economic war with England, and the farms there might be going at a price we could afford.

I spent some weeks in the summer of 1938 walking the finest of land, utterly ignorant as to what I should be looking for. I passed through many a fine entrance gate, along many a winding weedy drive, and arrived at many a 'gentleman's residence in need of some structural repair'. No matter that the entrance gates soon gave place to iron bedsteads, or that a 'never failing water supply' signified as often as not a tank on the roof or a well in a field hundreds of yards from the house. I was undaunted – at least there were no Swastikas. Hitler had won many bloodless victories by then, but none greater than that of inducing me to contemplate, with equanimity, the milking of a cow.

We put off the unhappy task of telling Peter's father of our plans for as long as possible. It was not a pleasant prospect; for only a year earlier Peter had at long last joined him in his law practice, and the family joy, the family festivities laid on to celebrate the advent of the new junior partner, had been very moving. Continuity had been assured. Peter's father had even been able to afford a smile at the rocky path which had led to the achievement of this goal; had even allowed himself an extra glass of wine, a forbidden cigar and a knowing nod of the head at the thought that if he had not joined the Party himself, and thus been able to wield some influence, his only son might never have made the grade. What about the time when Peter had walked out of the hall when Dr Rothenberger, Hamburg's Chief Justice, in a moment of exaggerated zeal had demanded that all young Referendars should take an oath of allegiance to the Führer? Or when Hamburg's Public Prosecutor had thought fit to report a conversation he had overheard in the Tennis Club? There had been anxious moments, too, when it had become clear that the sum-total of Peter's political reports was so negative that he could expect to fail in his Assessor examination; when, in fact, a leftover law of Weimar Republic days whereby no member of the armed forces could belong to a political party had to be made use of. Peter had volunteered for the Air Force, and had been granted two days leave to sit for his oral examination. His uniform had not contained a very happy warrior: Airman Bielenberg, Anti-Aircraft Battery VI, but not Party Member Bielenberg, which at the time had afforded us some comfort.

We were so engrossed in our plans during that summer of 1938, and we had become so accustomed to the explosive headlines, that we failed to grasp the full significance of the *Greuelmärchen*, the so-called horror fables, as they progressed from some humble position on the back page of the newspapers to blazing two-inch headlines on the front. 'Pregnant Sudetan German mother pushed off bicycle by Czech subhuman in Ostrava!' 'How long must our patient German brethren submit to such humiliating atrocities?' 'The German people, united as one behind their Leader, can wait no longer—' We'd had it all before, *ad nauseam*.

We decided to tell Peter's father in August just as soon as he returned from his holiday; he would be rested; a particularly tricky case which Peter had on his hands would be wound up. Next week then – but there was to be no next week. Peter's call-up papers arrived by telegram; Lance-Corporal Bielenberg (he had been promoted) was to report to his unit in twenty-four hours.

When the news came through from the Air Force camp outside Hamburg that Peter's unit would be leaving on the following day for Germany's eastern frontiers, I queued up outside the gates with a sorry group of wives and mothers who had also been granted a farewell visit before the menfolk departed. I was only distinguishable from the other doleful ladies in that I was not loaded down with packages and parcels; thick woollen vests, mounds of luscious cakes, yard upon yard of sausage, even a chocolate pudding complete with cut-glass bowl was among the offerings so surely intended to cheer, but so equally certain of being a darned nuisance.

Just how the uproar started would be hard to say. I never found it easy to recognize the overture to an argument in Germany – the quiet non-committal opening cadence, the rapid crescendo, the grand finale with everyone yelling their heads off, shaking their fists and dancing about on their heels. This one came from somewhere near the front of the queue where a lady visible only as a hat like a soup tureen had seemingly inadvertently dropped her cake. '*So eine Schweinerei!*' 'What *Schweinerei*?' 'Can't you see? My cake of course, keep your great hoof off it! What's the use of trying to bake cakes anyway when the butter's like rancid dripping?' 'She's right, indeed she's right, and it's not only the butter that's rancid, that's what I say—' The explosion was upon us; from cakes to Czechs, 'leave me alone with the whole bunch, who were the Sudeten Germans anyway? A lot of lazy good-for-nothing Slavs. It would be nice to see some of the Party Nobs in uniform. Hold your mouth. I will *not* hold my mouth'. We were so 'united behind our Leader' that the sentry considered the time had come to open the gates and let us in.

As we stood herded together with other unhappy pairs in a huge, bare, draughty hall, with Air-Marshal Goering, resplendent in a uniform which looked like a jeweller's show-case, smirking down at us from the wall, Peter assured me that it could not last for long and that it had had to come. Someone, sometime, had had to call Hitler's bluff. We did not mention the rumour that anti-aircraft guns were to be used in the front line against the powerful Czech defences, nor that we knew that an army far greater than Germany's was being mobilized in France, nor that Mussolini, our lone ally, was having a bad attack of cold feet. We talked in hushed whispers of anything but war, except that Peter made me repeat a promise that I would leave with the children for Denmark should things look really black. We parted at the gateway to the camp and I drove away with the owner of the cut-glass bowl, and she and I had a little weep together about it all as we ate up the chocolate pudding in the car.

I judged that things looked black enough when I heard that the British Fleet had been mobilized. I pictured huge grey invincible monsters steaming to their battle stations, and I knew the time had come for me to leave for Denmark. My mother-in-law came with me to the border, and we spent much time assuring each other that I was doing the right thing. Nicky sat between us straight as a ramrod, clutching his large, ragged teddy-bear, and John spent his time being car-sick. The long frontier formalities were quite suddenly behind us, the barrier swung upwards, we were in Denmark and I panicked.

What if there was really going to be a war? What was I doing in Denmark? I surely belonged to the country I had left behind me – my home, the people I loved, Lance-Corporal Bielenberg? I stepped on the accelerator and stared at the road ahead of me so that I need take no notice of the dull, flat, misty, uncommitted countryside. But when I was able to return to Hamburg a few days later, I realized that the farm-houses glowed at me most gaily and the pastures were lush and green, for something prodigious had happened. Chamberlain, a spare Victorian figure and to my mind the dullest of Prime Ministers, had somehow managed to bring about a compromise – never mind what compromise – there was going to be no war.

Nicky chattered gaily of his new tricycle, John was not car-sick more than twice; I'd have to have something done about the brakes, they were pulling a bit to the right. *Na ja*, no matter, so long as the old bus was rolling southwards and we were heading for home. Back to the hurly burly, the laughs and the tears, the ups and the downs and also to my surprise, to what amounted to some reflected glory. England's reputation had soared to the skies. I was told that the Munich agreement had shown beyond doubt that the game of international politics was one that could only be played by the British. Compared with Hitler's foolhardy ravings, Chamberlain's sober sincerity had provided profound relief. Munich had been the answer of a world power to an upstart and no one else could have edged Hitler away from his war.

Far more important than the Munich agreement itself was the fact that Hitler had had to give way; it had been so obvious that he had been far less jubilant than the other signatories – upset because an elderly gentleman, armed only with an umbrella, had got all the applause for once and completely stolen the show. There were cynics – English cynics – 'If at first you can't concede, fly, fly, fly again' – and German cynics who murmured that Hitler's pronouncement about the Sudetenland being his 'last territorial ambition', far from being an honest declaration of intent, would be more suitable as an epitaph over his grave. But who wanted to listen to the cynics? We had all been perilously close to the brink; I was not the only one who had had an almighty fright. On my return from Denmark I found that a new mood had surfaced about me in Germany and, as I shook hands and made my bows all round, I felt certain that the first crack had appeared in the dictator's armour.

The breathing space, the almost stupefied sigh of relief, was short-lived; in actual time, it lasted exactly four weeks. For if anyone had had any illusion as to whether Hitler had been forced by Munich to change his tactics, or had hoped that his ego would have been appeased by the long journeyings of great powers to his doorstep, he provided an answer in the so-called *Kristallnacht*, 'the night of the broken glass', when he interpreted the German people's spontaneous reaction to the murder of a young official in the German Embassy in Paris by a Jew. Synagogues went up in flames, Jewish shops and premises which most people had no idea belonged to Jews, were demolished. It was rumoured that many arrests were made in the night and that there were many dead, and whoever was in town early that morning brought back the news that gangs of young ruffians, obviously working to orders, had systematically moved from shop to shop, smashing windows and hurling the wares into the streets. No passer-by had thought of trying their hand at looting; the glass, the toys, the coats, the shoes and the handbags lay strewn about the pavements until the shopkeepers came out to sweep them aside in the morning.

I was often in town during the following week, in the shops and in the trams; all eyes and ears as befits an incurable busybody. No one to whom I spoke rejoiced in the shambles; on the contrary, those who were supposed to have been spontaneous about it stood around the newspaper kiosks registering puzzlement, perturbation, even disgust, or else they hurried past the hastily boarded-up windows of the Neuerwall with their gaze fixed firmly on their boots.

It was hard for them indeed, for where were their dreams of respectability now? There was no escape, anarchy was back on the streets and there could be no pretending that Hitler perhaps did not know of these things. On the contrary, he was obviously revelling in the whole affair, daily piling insult upon insult, law upon law which would reduce the Jews still living in Germany to the state of pariahs, and which could not fail to arouse the abhorrence, worse still, the contempt, of the whole civilized world. Not only that, he was flaunting the fact that his will was Germany's will, his behaviour theirs. That had been considered all very well when he interpreted their national aims, when he had torn up the hated Treaty of Versailles, and brought about the *Anschluss* with Austria; but now they wished to show disapproval and could only do so by their lack of co-operation, by their shocked silence, or by fumbling individual efforts to succour individual victims. '*Schlimm – schlimm,*' they murmured, sometimes adding, in true Hamburg fashion, that they had heard things had been far *schlimmer* in, for instance, Frankfurt.

As I snooped about I was delighted to discover just how far Dr Goebbels and his Ministry of Propaganda had gone off the beam. It seemed to me that maybe just such a jolt had been needed to debunk National Socialism, and that at long last all but the hard core of fanatics were waking up to the fact that they had put their fate into the hands of an irresponsible madman.

Peter's father died quite suddenly before Peter returned from the Sudetenland. I was sad and yet not sad, because I had become very fond of my father-in-law and was glad that he did not live to see his Hamburg become a bear-garden. I knew that he had seen values which he cherished disintegrate about him, and that he had not had the strength to withstand the storm. Even if he had lived, he would not have had to hear of our plan to emigrate to Ireland, for shortly before Christmas a friend, whom we had not seen for nearly two years, returned from China. Peter visited him in Hesse, and when he returned all thought of turning his back on what I had learned from my *Times* to call 'the German question' had faded from his mind. In fact there was something about the alacrity of his *volte-face* which made me wonder if he had ever really wanted to go globe-trotting at all.

The friend he had been with in Hesse was Adam von Trott zu Solz, who had spent three months in Hamburg in 1935 when we were living in Reinbek. He had come to us on many of his free weekends to get a whiff of country air and to try to get a good night's sleep on our sofa, which, at the time, did duty as spare-room. I remembered him as being something rather exceptional, not exceptional because of his striking good looks and his kindly habit of making everyone he met imagine that they were worth talking to (a habit which kept his private life in a continuous state of upheaval), nor because, like Peter at the time, he was struggling to pass his Assessor examination in the face of calamitous reports as to his political reliability. But exceptional for me because my knowledge of Germans and Germany had been confined almost exclusively to Hamburg and I had not met his kind before.

Adam came from a large and complicated family of landed nobility in Hesse, which for generations had provided the State with a supply of higher civil servants. His up-bringing had been aimed at equipping him to serve his country, and true to tradition he had had no other ambition; the only uncertainty in his mind being in what capacity he should do so. He had won a Rhodes Scholarship and spent two years in Oxford, and if his return to Germany in 1933 had not coincided so exactly with Hitler's coming to power, his career would doubtless have been a straightforward one. But he had found on his return that Government service was barred to him unless he became a member of the Party, and except for a career in business, or a lectureship in some non-controversial subject in a university, there were few openings left for anyone who had no intention of toeing the Party line. His personal predicament did not seem to have affected what I soon discovered to be an infectious optimism, for he did not waste much time indulging in the popular game of blaming the older generation for allowing things to get into such a mess. He seemed instead to regard National Socialism as a passing disease which would ultimately be overcome by the innate sanity of his people. He had seemed confident too that all over Germany, particularly in Berlin, there existed groups of people – some still in prominent positions – who were determined that Hitler's reign should come to an early end.

Peter and Adam became close friends during the three months

of Adam's stay in Hamburg, and after we heard that he had left Germany for America and China, and would not be back for at least two years, we had often in his absence wondered what would have been his reactions to the events which were crowding in on us. We had missed him for what had seemed his natural aptitude for making us think, and remembered that he had done so with such charming expectancy that the exercise had never been too painful.

Adam was now back, Adam had been to Berlin, and the news which Peter brought home with him after his visit was exhilarating enough and also promising enough to have convinced him that we had been wrong to think of leaving Germany at a moment when the tide was on the turn. At long last the isolated dissident voices of some years back had become a chorus; with a possible world war on their hands, the Generals who commanded the only weapon capable of overthrowing the régime were sufficiently alarmed to be ready to act. More, the nucleus of a civilian government capable of taking over after Hitler's arrest was forming. It would be presented with no easy task, for much had happened since 1933, and it would be in need of reliable support in every grade of the Civil Service.

This was heady stuff, and as soon as Peter asked me if I was game to throw all former resolutions overboard and to join in what appeared to be a desperate race against time, I knew that as far as I was concerned the gentleman's residence in Ireland could go to the devil. The thought of being able to do something positive – which we had suppressed for so long – was enough to send our spirits soaring, and I had Hitler behind bars and a new era dawning long before I had started making plans as to how we should move our goods and chattels from Hamburg to Berlin.

Peter went more methodically about the business of abandoning his law practice. He decided to apply for a position in the Ministry of Economics; to do so he would also have to make formal application for membership of the Party. Much documentation as to his and my Aryan forebears would have to be collected before he could be presented with the Party badge, and we could safely reckon that the procedure might take months, even years, as most of my relevant documents had to be extracted from Ireland. By the time he was eligible to wear it in his buttonhole, we hoped it would be comfortably out of date. Adam meanwhile was making tentative plans for getting himself attached to the Foreign Office, wagering with his usual optimism that he would pull it off without having to make any such show of loyalty to the Party.

As I shuttled back and forth in the spring and summer of 1939, dumping the children with my parents in England, house-hunting and moving house to Berlin, I might have been journeying between two diverging planets. I did not find Berlin a beautiful town, but an exciting one; without question a capital city, as different from Hamburg as London from Liverpool. Its particular spell grew on you, so they said, but it had an immediate attraction for me in that the buoyancy of its climate made nonsense of such little indulgencies as 'feeling tired'. I also discovered to my pleasure that the irrepressible Berliners were utterly indifferent as to what impression they or their massive chunks of Wilhelminian architecture made on outsiders. You could take Berlin or you could leave it, from the redolent pine-trees of the Grunewald to the bug-ridden quarter around the Alexander Platz; the inhabitants themselves, the *Ur-Berliner*, could think of no better place in the world to live.

I wanted to live there too, but by making up my mind that, for the sake of the children, I must have a house with a garden, and by deciding rather rashly that Berlin-Dahlem would suit me nicely, I added a private problem to the many others which were keeping my head buzzing. For I also discovered in Berlin that it was not only the sparkling air which differed from the misty haze of the north German seaport; something of the essential nature of the political issues at stake stood out there with a crystal clarity which at first took my parochial breath away.

The old and the new Ministries, the Embassies, the Reichs Chancellery, the Headquarters of the Armed Forces, of the Police and of the Gestapo, all the power and paraphernalia surrounding the dictatorship was concentrated in Berlin, and like a magnet it attracted anyone who still found politics a game worth playing.

Although I had never pretended to understand quite how the rickety old British Empire held together, it was soon obvious even to me that in Germany something had gone terribly wrong with the works. It had become like some prison turned inside out, with the criminals in command, noisy and ruthless, yet also naïve and incompetent, unversed in the complexities of Government and only really capable of appealing to some latent chauvinism which slumbers away in most races, and of waiting timorously on the voice of their master.

Confronting them were the old established administrators of law and order, who, true to the Prussian traditions of loyalty and obedience to the State, had remained at their posts after 1933 and were still firmly entrenched in every branch of the administration. They were surely not by nature revolutionaries, but many of them had been driven by their principles as professionals, and also by repugnance at what was happening to their country, into contemplating just that rôle – for which neither God nor the exacting Prussian state code had prepared them. Considering their limitations, they had not done too badly. The old Ministries had always been exclusive and they had remained so, looking after their own with much ingenuity, in spite of the Gestapo.

No one, it seemed, not even his closest associates, had ever succeeded in penetrating Hitler's curiously intuitive mind. He was a lone operator, which was one clue perhaps to his demonic genius; but, as soon as his intentions emerged and took on the tangible form of instructions and memoranda to his ministers or to the Army, a well established grapevine took over and a flow of reliable information was to hand.

When we arrived in Berlin in February 1939 the message which this grapevine had to offer was specific. Hitler was preparing for war in the autumn. He had hardly put his signature to the Munich agreement before starting to plan for the occupation of the whole of Czechoslovakia; Poland would follow, it would not be long before we would be reading of Polish atrocities, Polish subhumans. The Polish corridor, Danzig, even the rich farmlands of the Ukraine – there were no bounds to his ultimate ambitions. He had not been convinced by what had gone before that if he marched eastwards either England or France would oppose him, and he was being encouraged in this wishful thinking by von Ribbentrop, who was denying him any information which might indicate the contrary. The only ray of light in an otherwise dismal situation was the ever-increasing activity which was developing between some of the Generals and the leaders of the civilian opposition. They were preparing to overthrow the Government and to arrest its leaders, something which I understood had never happened before in German history.

Peter and Adam plunged into the arena with the exuberance of crusaders – there was so little time to lose. If the older generation,

the von Becks, the Goerdelers and the von Hassells, a little die-
hard perhaps but no less Hitler's implacable enemies, were
preparing to break an inherited code of loyalty, then it was not for
the up and coming generation to show itself lacking in initiative
or *élan*. On the contrary, eager and impatient, they must push and
encourage, seek out new allies, further the drive towards cohesion,
add just that extra pep to those revolutionary cogitations, before
it was too late. They were enjoying themselves, too, I could see,
for there were allies enough to be found amongst old friends and
new friends and there was something particularly exhilarating
about banding together to defy Hitler and his gang rule; it was
rather like pitting one's wits against the devil every single day.

Sometimes as I travelled back to England I wondered what in
heaven's name I was at, wandering pop-eyed in a world about
which I knew so little. German Generals, their traditions and their
consciences; Social Democrats, practised undergrounders, who
I understood must be kept informed and encouraged; ordinary
citizens, fat as butter, kidding themselves they were descendants
of Siegfrieds and Sieglindes. Where did I come in? But Peter at the
time was occupying a furnished flat in Berlin with a kitchen like
a matchbox and furniture built for a neanderthaler, feeding the
revolutionary flame on a diet of black bread and sausage, and so
I finally decided that politics or no politics there was probably
still room for someone to cook the odd meal, knock chips off the
hideous crockery, and look for a house with a garden.

In contrast to the hither and thither, the almost desperate
feeling of urgency in Berlin, the atmosphere in England was
that of a calm and peaceful oasis. Not that I found the political
situation less cluttered up with every kind of paradox. Friends I
had considered rather vaguely to be left wing intellectuals, for
whom rearmament had been a dirty word, and the armed forces
objects of derision, had of a sudden become almost bellicose.
Other friends, right wingers who had not found it so easy to
ignore the Russian purges, the treason trials and the rumours of
vast concentration camps set up by Stalin in Siberia to 're-educate'
political prisoners, had their problems as well. In Hitler they had
backed what they considered to be the lesser of two evils, and now
that their recalcitrant child showed signs of becoming a monster
they were in danger of falling between two stools.

Only my father, who seldom became really engrossed in
the morning newspapers until he arrived at the sports pages,

reflected a mood which I found gathered strength every time I arrived back on home ground. My father considered Hitler to be not only a bully, but also an exceptional bore, with just that added unbearable arrogance which reminded him of something – someone, 1914–1918 – Kaiser Bill. My father did not really approve of Churchill, 'too clever by half to make a good Prime Minister', but the fact that Hitler was attacking him so virulently, 'mixing himself into affairs which were none of his business', inclined him to look on Churchill with a more benevolent eye. Taken all in all, and 'after that business in Czechoslovakia', my father supposed that if Hitler made another move something would have to be done about it, and, to prove his point, he risked some indulgent ridicule by constructing an ingenious concrete dug-out in a field near the tennis courts; the children called it the War House, and on rainy days it filled with water and became an exciting underground pond in which to sail their boats.

I talked most earnestly with my father about the opposition to Hitler which was building up in Germany and he listened to me with as big a show of hopeful sympathy as he could muster; but I noticed that a roof went up over his air-raid shelter just the same.

Adam was also in England in June and again in July. His trips were dangerous ones for his audience was far more glamorous than mine and his message had to be more explicit. The opposition to Hitler was in being and gaining strength in Germany. How could it be granted just that little more time, or be given the situation and the support it needed before Hitler's war intervened to arouse national loyalties and thereby blur the issue? Adam talked with Lord Halifax, with Stafford Cripps, even with Chamberlain, and found himself discussing a possible way out of imminent and mutual danger.

He talked with others also, those who had been his friends in Oxford days, all blissfully void of the faintest notion of the perils and intricacies which were part of life under Hitler's dictatorship. He knew England well enough to recognize that, with them, he had been given the treatment; some sympathy perhaps for his own position, but for the rest he had met with a puzzled, polite, almost wordless lack of interest which in true British fashion could only signify, at best, incomprehension.

Meanwhile I had found my house with a garden in Berlin-Dahlem, by paying some very welcome English pounds to a young Jewish couple who, for lack of funds abroad, had found themselves unable to emigrate. It appeared that no country outside Germany, however sympathetic with their plight, had quite managed to bring itself to grant entry visas to potentially destitute Jews. As the summer of 1939 ran its course, day after day the sun shone down out of a cloudless sky, and as the dahlias, the helenium and the Michaelmas daisies took over from the phlox and the roses, I realized that my search for my own little goal at least had been crowned with success.

I needed just such a refuge when I arrived in Berlin in July with the children; for to cross the border into Germany was enough to be caught up immediately in a horrifying atmosphere fraught with impending catastrophe. The strident voice of the propaganda machine was screeching out its abuse of Poland. There were the usual glaring two-inch headlines, and the same old rehashed horror fables, it was just Poles this time instead of Czechs. Partial mobilization was in full swing, and no trained army personnel could leave the country without permission from his unit. According to the grapevine, war in the east was planned to start in a matter of weeks, and von Ribbentrop had successfully persuaded Hitler that neither England nor France would join in. He had not found it difficult to succumb to such persuasion, because he was utterly unimpressed by Chamberlain, Lord Halifax or the British Ambassador Henderson; they were typical of the effete Englishman painted for him by his Foreign Minister.

We heard that behind the scenes several emissaries were hustling back and forth between England and Germany in a last-minute effort to pierce this fog of misconception. One proposal involved such a journey for Peter. Perhaps the British Government could be persuaded to make some dramatic move, to by-pass diplomatic channels and therefore von Ribbentrop, to send some uncompromising figure, such as Lord Gort, direct to Hitler and bearing a message from the King, warning him that by crossing the Polish border he would be launching Germany into a world war. If the visit were to take place in a blaze of publicity, it would convey to the German people exactly what Hitler was letting them in for and might also persuade the Generals to act.

Peter set off for England in mid-August without first obtaining permission from his department or from his unit. For five days I remained in Berlin, half expecting his call-up papers to be pushed through the letter-box any day. I wondered what I would do if they arrived by telegram and Peter did not return in time, and war should break out and the Bielenberg *ménage* find itself pottering about here, there and everywhere, in the wrong places at the wrong time. I need have had no fear, for he returned safely having been unable to make contact with anyone in high places. Parliament had adjourned for the summer recess, no Cabinet Minister was in London, and when I looked at the calendar I reckoned I knew why. It was just one week after August 12th, 'the Glorious Twelfth', opening of the grouse shooting season; I reckoned it would have needed more than an Adolf Hitler to keep them off the Scottish moors.

On the night after hearing that war had broken out between England and Germany I could not sleep, and if I were asked to tell of that night fifty years hence I believe I would remember every detail. The ticking of the clock in the hall, the thin chime from the Dahlem church steeple which sounded every hour, Peter's even breathing from the bed next to mine, the occasional creaking from upstairs as the children moved in their bunks, and then, just before dawn, the muted stirrings and the sudden burst of song from a nightingale in the silver birch tree near the road. I had been told that we had a nightingale in the garden, but had never heard it sing out before. I realized then that I was alone, having somehow landed myself rather precariously straddling a fence. I was not apprehensive, life had been too good to me for that. I knew too that I was blessed with natural optimism, and that my own interpretation of a simple Christian up-bringing had provided me with a sturdy conviction as to the ultimate triumph of good over evil. In national terms, I had the sneaking feeling that by 'good' I had things British in mind, by 'evil' any foreigner stupid enough to dispute the matter. Just the same, in spite of the familiar night noises about me, I sensed that the road ahead might be a lonely one, for nothing would be black and nothing white, and if I wished to travel it with any confidence I would need repeatedly to return to my roots, to re-establish my identity almost, before I could hope to arrive at some tentative conclusion as to how I was to carry on.

The deep violet sky was thinning out to a soft smoky grey when I found myself leaning on the window-sill wondering whether my wakefulness had succeeded in getting me any nearer to whatever truth I had been seeking, guessing that perhaps I would not find the answers because they were not there to find. They say there is a moment just before dawn when the cattle stir in the fields as if in answer to some hidden call, and the birds rustle sleepily in the hedgerows, and the dying breathe more lightly, before giving up the battle for life and slipping away. Perhaps it was not a nightingale, perhaps it was just a very ordinary bird, rather like myself, which had stirred in the branches of the birch tree near the road, and then burst into reckless spendthrift singing.

PART I

Berlin

THE BLOCKWART

(Autumn 1939)

I was sitting on the terrace, doing what I have the face to call my mending, when Herr Neisse came to trim back the vine which clambered in tangled profusion around the french windows of our little house. His rickety old cart, loaded with ladders and garden tools, came to a stop outside the gate. A short buzz on the gate bell and his voice, with its unmistakably Saxon nasal twang, greeted me from across the hedge. 'Neisse, *Guten Morgen*, Frau Dr'.

If it had been a Sunday or one of the numerous Party collection days, the buzz would have been louder and longer, the voice clipped staccato and the greeting 'Heil Hitler'; for Herr Neisse was not only our occasional gardener, but also our *Blockwart*, the Party representative in our immediate neighbourhood. Besides pruning trees, mowing lawns and sweeping up leaves, he collected Party subscriptions, sold emblems for the newly launched Winter Help campaign – postcards, pamphlets, any odd or end which might help to swell the Party coffers. He was also supposed to send reports on the behaviour of his flock to Party Headquarters, so that careful record might be kept of just who failed to hang out their flag and when, or just how much and how willingly so and so had contributed to the Cause.

On weekdays Herr Neisse was friendly, gentle, even a little diffident; a well shaped tree, the herbaceous border, the little dark corner near the garage where the Lily of the Valley needed some coaxing – those were matters for his obvious concern. On Sundays things looked differently. Resplendent then in brown uniform with shining boots and pill-box hat, his moustache trimmed to a neat rectangle, his left thumb hitched into his Sam Browne belt and his right arm raised rigid in salute, he was resurgent Germany – the stocky outward sign of the inward spirit of the Revolution. He was also one of the few cogs in the Nazi wheel known to me rather intimately, for we had a common denominator in the garden.

The story goes that at Hitler's birth three good fairies came to give him their good wishes, and the first wished for him that every German should be honest, the second that every German should be intelligent, and the third that every German should be a National Socialist. An uplifting thought. But then came the bad fairy, and she stipulated that every German could only possess two of those attributes. She left the Führer then with intelligent Nazis who were not honest, honest Nazis who had no brains, and honest and intelligent citizens who were not Nazis. A funny little story, perhaps, but one not too far from the truth; for it seemed to me that those three categories of Germans did indeed live and work together side by side unable, because of the nature of the régime, to maintain more than the most superficial contact with each other.

One did not have to probe far to discover to which category Herr Neisse belonged. I found myself watching him out of the corner of my eye as he removed his homespun jacket, folded it with care and proceeded to prop his ladder up against the corner of the house, to take out then his well-oiled secateurs, and to start clipping the vine leaves away from the grapes, so that the autumn sun might encourage them to ripen. He had assured me that some five years back they had been edible – it was always worth a try. Such a dedicated gardener, such a harmless little bloke, apparently he did not want to be very communicative today; but on other occasions he had not only provided me with invaluable tips on ways and means of overcoming the idiosyncrasies of the dry, sandy Berlin soil, but had also told me much of his story as we pottered about the garden together.

He was the son of a Saxon peasant, hence his slow, pedantic, adenoidal accent. In Germany the Saxons are called the *Plattfüssler der Völkerwanderung*, the flatfooted ones of the migration of peoples, and for some reason or other there is something about a Saxon which is considered faintly ridiculous by the rest of his countrymen. Even the Saxon King had possessed earthy qualities which had endeared him to his people, but not to his more flamboyant cousin the Kaiser. On arriving late for some military parade, he had greeted that resplendent War Lord with the words – 'Na Willem, been sending any telegrams lately?' and this, just after the Kaiser's famous telegram to the Boers, was not considered to be the height of tact. His abdication speech, too, had been short and sweet. *'Also Kinder in Zukunft macht Euern Dreck alleene'*, which can best be translated as 'All right, children, muck around on your own in future'.

I gathered that that was exactly what Herr Neisse, one of his loyal subjects, had been doing, after fighting in the Great War without distinguishing himself in any way, and after returning to the chaos of Berlin, a trifle surprised, as he admitted, at the suddenness and completeness of Germany's defeat. 'You see, Frau Dr, we seemed to be doing all right, we were told indeed of great victories and then suddenly *Schluss*, finish, the Government at home sued for peace – they got their peace and serve them damn well right I say. I came back to Berlin, because my Hilde lived here, and I had promised her when the war was over that I would come back to her. She was waiting, was my Hilde, bless her, she was waiting.'

She must have been a great girl, his Hilde, because she was to wait a further ten years before Herr Neisse had collected together what he considered to be sufficient funds to marry her. He had tried every means of gaining employment after the war. Since he was at heart a peasant, he had decided that gardening was the job for which he was most suited; and every day he had plodded doggedly from garden gate to garden gate, along the tree-lined roads of Dahlem. He did not drink, he did not smoke, he had worked for his lunch and a pittance, and starved for the rest of the day and thus miraculously after some years he had put enough by to consider applying for a little allotment plot on the far side of Dahlem Dorf. Hilde too had saved; she had worked in a meat stall in the Dahlem market. She had her eye on a very special bit of land, next door to her brother's – the house was not much bigger than a rabbit hutch, but it would do just the same.

Herr Neisse had not known quite who had been to blame for the fact that Germany had lost the war, but there was no doubt in his mind that the disaster which befell him so undeservedly in 1923 was the result of some dire and treasonable plot. His savings, Hilde's savings, their plot of land, their humble enough hopes, had vanished into thin air almost overnight. 'The inflation, you see, Frau Dr; suddenly we had nothing. With my savings I was able to buy just one cup and saucer which I gave to Hilde instead of her marriage lines. Funny, wasn't it, that I should be so keen on the saucer?' Not funny really, because when Herr Neisse spoke of those times his voice shook with emotion, and the usual concise movements of his hands became nervous and erratic. The loss of his little bank account had not only shattered whatever faith he might have had in constitutional government, but also struck at the root of his very being, his self-respect, and his right to be respected. The saucer, perhaps there was something respectable about a saucer, perhaps it had been his gesture, his defiant flip of the fingers under the noses of the powers that be.

Unemployment once more had followed on the heels of the inflation as the equally impoverished owners of the Dahlem villas, retired civil servants and the like, could no longer afford the luxury of a gardener. But according to Herr Neisse it was not long before many of them moved away and their houses were re-occupied by a bouncing new class of Jews and shopkeepers. Herr Neisse had definitely never liked Jews, or the others for that matter, the shopkeepers; he called them 'white Jews'. After the war they swarmed in from the east, Lilienbusch and Rosenstrauss, Ipskis and Ovskis, even their names were absurd; but somehow they had managed to wax rich as fast as his savings had waned. He had worked for those new masters – a man had to live – but things were not the same. He found them vulgar and ostentatious, lisping a language he could barely understand, and he could only draw comfort from the fact that although the owners had changed, the gardens stayed the same. He was comforted, too, because slowly but surely with the aid of his thrifty Hilde he could watch his little allotment plot emerging once more from its cloud of might-have-been, into the realm of reality. He was nearing forty years of age the day he married his Hilde, but that had been a day, and they had moved together into an even superior rabbit hutch to the one of his dreams. The one he now occupied, he told me, had a porch.

For two years, such was their combined diligence, that if the year had not been 1929 and had something not happened on the far side of the Atlantic which sent huge repercussive waves rolling over the continent of Europe, leaving a trail of bankruptcies and suicides in their wake, Herr Neisse and his Hilde would have been in a financial position to buy a half share in a vegetable stall, thus raising themselves one small step upon the social ladder. The American depression, the Crisis, the slump to end all slumps, hit the delicately balanced German economy a crippling blow and left no place for an odd-job gardener in its scheme of things. Herr Neisse joined an army of more than six million unemployed, and, although because of his allotment plot he did not actually starve, he was almost back to where he had started, with little food in his belly and plenty of time on his hands.

Although he did not mention it, I imagined that he had also a man-sized chip on his shoulder and a weather eye open for some sort of 'ism. Communism did not appeal to him; he had always worked for the well-to-do, amongst their plants and trees. In some small way he was a creator; he did not want to bust the whole place up, he just wanted to belong somewhere. Nationalism? That was for the gentry, the ones who still had something to lose. National Socialism, that was more like it; he started attending Party meetings. Although he wished he could have had a hand in the floral decorations – he simply did not like pink and blue hydrangeas – Herr Neisse described those get-togethers with a rare show of enthusiasm. The huge beflagged halls, when the lads would slip in one by one, whipping out their pill-box caps, slipping off their raincoats to reveal the forbidden uniform beneath. It was easy to picture him shooting out his right arm and bawling with the rest, his eyes growing moist as the strong male voices broke into the National Anthem, 'Deutschland Deutschland üer alles'.

Then he would listen spellbound as a hush descended on the hall and the deep voice of the master orator boomed through his head, putting so many of his incoherent resentments into words – and what words. Golden words of German blood and German earth ('Blubo' short for 'Blut und Boden' the ribald Berliner was later wont to call those particular golden words) of Germany's rebirth and her need for a place in the sun, of the dishonour forced upon her by the Treaty of Versailles, and of the duplicity and infamy of Germany's postwar politicians, who had betrayed the nation. Then, as the deep voice rose to fanatical screams – the scapegoat: Herr Neisse had been presented with a very satisfactory scapegoat – the evil at the root of all Germany's troubles: the Jews. 'Oh no, Frau Dr, you must not get me wrong, not one particular Jew. Your predecessor, as you say, seemed harmless enough – he was in fact a great dahlia expert. I could not of course work for him after 1933, but I often looked over the hedge as I passed. He spent most of his time in the garden before he left, and I knew what that meant. He had no work and I could even sympathize with him. No, no, International Jewry.' Herr

Neisse included the hedges, the trees, the roof tops and even the clouds in the all embracing circle circumscribed with his garden fork. 'You understand, Frau Dr, International Jewry.'

Once outside the beflagged hall and the range of the golden voice, Herr Neisse, I could believe, had as much difficulty in knowing what he was talking about as I had. He did not join the Party, though, until 1931; he could not make up his mind because Hilde had obviously found the whole performance very silly. A lot of raw boys playing at soldiers, she had declared, and had even showed her solid North German contempt for Hitler's Austrian accent. Herr Neisse hastened to assure me that she was of course converted now – of course. Just the same I frankly wondered, for I knew Hilde to be a Berliner. She belonged to a tough and independent section of the population of a capital city, not unlike the London cockney. She had obviously not tried to discourage his enthusiasm, however, and I had vaguely wondered whether her childlessness had some bearing on her reticence. No German would consider himself to be quite complete without his son, his *Stammhalter* at his side, and because they had married so late in life, Herr Neisse and his Hilde were childless.

In 1933 when Hitler became Chancellor, Herr Neisse, *Parteigenosse* Neisse, was rewarded for his faithful attendance at Party meetings and his regular payment of Party fees by being appointed *Blockwart*. There, on the lowest rung of the Party ladder, he had remained and doubtless would remain, the hardy perennial stooge, watching the Jews and shopkeepers depart in their turn, and the high white brick walls being erected around the new and sumptuous villas of the Party bosses, as they moved in with their large black Mercedes motorcars, with their bulging satin furnishings and their insignificant overdressed wives. Himmler, Ley, von Ribbentrop, we had a fine assortment of Party big-wigs in Dahlem, and it was common knowledge that they lived in conditions of extreme luxury. It was also common knowledge that although we ordinary mortals had been given no air civil-defence instruction whatsoever (Goering having announced that he would call himself Meyer if one enemy aircraft penetrated Berlin's air defence) the big-wigs had been provident enough to arrange for deep and sumptuously appointed air-raid shelters to be dug beneath their homes.

But for all these inconsistencies Herr Neisse had found himself an answer which seemed to satisfy him. It was, quite simply, that Hitler did not know of these things. For Herr Neisse, Hitler was a homely sincere man, who had been a simple soldier like himself and whose sole extravagance was his passionate devotion to Germany and to Germany's well-being. 'He is a child-lover you see, Frau Dr, and dogs – he loves dogs too.' *Schlicht*, modest was the word Herr Neisse and I had agreed upon with which to sum up our Leader's virtues in spite of the fact that I could have thought up an epithet or two which would have filled the bill more accurately.

The particular day I am speaking of was warm, and Herr Neisse was unusually silent as his ladder approached yard by yard along the wall towards me. Clip, clip, like abandoned kites the flat red vine leaves coasted to the lawn beneath him. I had no wish to chat with anyone that day, in fact I was harder put to it than ever to concentrate on my darning. The war was barely a fortnight old. No one had imagined that the German Army could advance into Poland at such dynamic speed. The Poles had apparently no Air Force, and were, with incredible bravery, charging the invincible German tanks with their horse cavalry. And the British – the Allies – what were they doing? As far as I could see, absolutely nothing. What they should have been doing was in truth beyond me. Landing airborne troops? The Fleet? God alone knew what people did when they solemnly went to war to support an ally. I knew that I would have to get used to the headlines in the newspapers, to the accounts of the sinkings of British ships with the loss of thousands of lives, to the exultant war-whoops at the utter impotence of the British warmongers – there was always the chance, anyway, that they were exaggerated, probably not even remotely true. But those other supposedly more reliable voices from outside: the BBC, Radio Beromünster, they too seemed unable to convince one that the state of affairs in the Allied camp was other than one of impotent acquiescence.

I had another reason, too, for feeling deflated. My visit to the Red Cross – my gesture so to speak – had been a singular flop. For after deciding that I could devote about three or four half-days a week to some voluntary service, to rolling bandages, packing parcels – a little vague as to exactly what, but certain that my offer would be accepted with alacrity – I had turned up at their offices in the Domäne Dahlem feeling, I must admit, a trifle virtuous. I was not going to allow the fact that my country was at war with Germany to interfere with my burning convictions as to the all importance of every single human life. I had been greeted, however, by a weary looking blonde, whose patient blue eyes changed their expression from friendly enquiry to one of frank bewilderment on hearing my request. I was married? Yes. I had children? Yes. Then how, if she might ask, had I imagined myself joining the Red Cross?

It was my turn to look bewildered.

'I see. Then there is no room for voluntary—?'

'None whatsoever,' she replied firmly, 'return to your home and to your children, Frau Bielenfeld, that is where you belong.'

She had quite a pleasant face, the lady from the Red Cross, but she also looked extremely tired.

'You look as if you had quite a lot to do,' I ventured.

'More than I can cope with,' she admitted, 'all this paper work—'

I could not say why it was that I had been so particularly depressed by that interview except that there must be something peculiarly wearisome about being in constant opposition. Perhaps I had hoped to be allowed to do something positive for once.

I stuck my darning needle firmly into my finger again, and in answer to my noisy sigh Herr Neisse cleared his throat and stared fixedly at a bunch of rubbery grapes.

'I'm very sorry indeed about this war, Frau Dr', he said, 'it must be strange for you in a foreign land.'

'Well, the way it is, Herr Neisse, I do not feel foreign here, it is my home you see, and I think about the war I suppose as little as possible,' the stock reply. 'Just the same,' I added, 'we hoped things would go differently the last time you were here, didn't we?'

'We did indeed, the Pact with Russia—'

For some reason Herr Neisse fell silent again. Stumping down the ladder he moved it almost roughly a yard or two nearer to my chair, and proceeded to attack the vine with what seemed to me uncalled-for vigour. True, I had caused him some embarrassment on his last visit, which had coincided with the signing of the Russo-German Non-Aggression Pact – a diplomatic *tour de force* and also a political somersault which had caught wiser men than Herr Neisse on the hop. I had asked, on that occasion, what would happen to some of his postcards: lurid pictures of emaciated women and hollow-eyed children, crouching before fiendish looking Jews, armed with whips – the caption beneath which informed whoever might care to send such a greeting through the post that such were conditions in Russian concentration camps. The Russians after all, the Bolshevik rabble, were now, of a sudden, our bosom friends. Herr Neisse had not liked the question. The postcards had been withdrawn it seemed; it was not for us small fry to question such things. Surely not, and we had agreed in parting that the Führer must know what he was doing, and that we would be willing to overlook a lot of things, so long as there be no war.

I do not know why I asked him again about the postcards. Perhaps I wanted to change the subject, maybe because when helping him guide his ladder under the archway to the terrace I had glanced at a brown cardboard box, half hidden by the trowels and balls of twine at the bottom of his cart.

'You have some new postcards, I see,' – the impact of my remark could not have been more dramatic if I had decided to hurl my darning at his head. For a moment it looked as if Herr Neisse would topple off the ladder. He made a wild swipe at the vine and a bunch of grapes came bouncing to the terrace.

'No – yes, I fetched them on my way here. Oh yes, you may look at them if you wish, you will see them on Sunday week anyway.'

I opened the box and flipped absentmindedly through its contents. Glassy-eyed females, glassy-eyed children, glassy-eyed Alsatian dogs, all gazing with devotion at the crummy little figure who was their Leader. Suddenly I came to a stop. Surely I must be mistaken? But no, it was our old friend all right: the women, the children, the whips, the Jews. Only the caption underneath was different. 'British concentration camps in South Africa during the Boer War.' I stared in silence. The secateurs in Herr Neisse's hand fell silent too. I glanced up at him and found him looking at me with an expression on his lined face which was hard to fathom. Supplication? Resentment? Resignation?

'Very similar, aren't they?' I managed to murmur.

'Very similar,' came his reply.

'Almost identical in fact,' I added.

'As you say, Frau Dr, almost identical—' and the way it was, neither of us could bring ourselves to conclude with our usual twaddle about 'us small fry'.

When I took him to the gate, and we shook hands and fixed up for him to come again next week, Herr Neisse could not raise a smile. Poor little blighter, sold down the river again. Life had not shown him much consideration, and those postcards could well have been the ultimate insult. All the more reason, I feared, that his Sunday greeting would, in future, hit us like a clap of thunder.

Before turning the corner at the end of the road, I saw that he had met up with Nicky on his way from kindergarten. They chatted together for a moment or two and then Nicky came skipping along the road towards me.

'I just took Werner home first,' Nicky said when I asked him why he was late, and then: 'Shall I tell you a very very funny story?' I felt like hearing something very very funny, but had not exactly reckoned with what I got.

'Do you know, Mummy, Werner says his mother listens to the radio just the way you do, with your ear right up against it.'

'She does?'

For a moment I held my breath. Since the outbreak of war, listening to foreign broadcasts was punishable by a minimum of five years imprisonment, and the maximum penalty was death. There was always a reason given, however cockeyed – *moralische Selbstverstümmelung,* moral self mutilation, had been the ingenious explanation given for this particular prohibition. As the soldier at the front could be shot for trying to make himself unfit for army service, so it was a crime for the home front willingly to indulge in the destruction of their morale by listening to the lies being spread by the enemy. I had never met Werner's mother, but as from now she and I were bound to each other as if we had committed murder together.

'Well, she's probably deaf,' I said firmly, and before the obvious next question came up, 'deaf as a post in one ear, same as I am.' Nicky looked a bit surprised but made no further comment.

'Herr Neisse says I can go round with him next week selling emblems,' he said. 'Nice of him, wasn't it?'

'Yes,' I said, 'very nice, very nice indeed.'

I'd had enough for one morning, and as I watched him strolling along in front of me, giving each tree that he passed a healthy bash with his satchel, I could only hope that by next Sunday week he would have forgotten his very very funny story.

When I returned to Berlin after the war, early in 1946, I tried to locate Herr Neisse, because I knew by then that my hunch had been a right one. He had done us no harm, passed on no incriminating titbits, such as other zealous informers had thought fit to do. I was told that he had been hanged from a lamp-post soon after the arrival of the Russians, whether by the insurgent troops, or by ardent 'resistance fighters' eager to show their initial paces, was not known. I paid my one and only visit to his little house in Dahlem Dorf, to find it crammed to the roof with refugees, complaining bitterly at their cramped and uncomfortable quarters. No one seemed to know what had happened to Hilde, and I was glad that a layer of snow covered the allotment plot, because I understood from the new occupants that when they arrived there the autumn before, they had found it to be a tangle of untended weeds.

COLD INTERLUDE

Part I: (Winter 1939–1940)

On market days I always had to bestir myself very early indeed, the reason being that I had not lived long enough in Berlin to have my *Quellen* – my sources of supply as they were called; and as soon as food rationing was introduced, everything that was not on the ration cards disappeared like magic from every shop counter and out of every shop window. Unless you were known to some shopkeeper, therefore, some wholesaler or better still farmer, and were able to come to a deal by dint of the ingratiating smile, the tender enquiry after wife and children, cows no longer had livers, hearts, kidneys or tails and hens had vanished off the face of the earth. *'Hamstering'* rapidly became an absorbing occupation, all absorbing for some; for contrary to my expectations (I still took German efficiency for granted) the rationing system in Berlin was chaotic. *Gemeinnutz geht vor Eigennutz* – community welfare comes before self interest. 'German women, your Leader and your country trust you.' Such pious slogans staring out hopefully from every other kiosk, every other billboard, made no impression whatsoever on the agile *Hausfrau* hell-bent on a fruitful scavenge.

My second reason for having to make an early start arose from the simple fact that I was very hard up. To serve the state in Prussia had always been considered an honour needing precious little encouragement financially. Peter's salary at the Ministry of Economics amounted to the princely sum of 486 marks and 20 pfennigs a month, equal to about £30, and when my allowance stopped abruptly on September 3rd, it left a very ominous void in our budget. To have no money was initially quite an adventurous affair, and the children and I would travel all over Berlin on the look-out for a shop or a market-stall where we could buy our wares a few pfennigs cheaper. However, after Peter had explained to me carefully that I was spending far more money on the bus trips than I was ever saving on the odd vegetable or piece of fish bought several miles away, I had stuck to home ground, or rather to home queueing and, as the weeks went by, much of the glamour went out of being poor.

One particular morning I was late, so late that it was hardly worth going to the market at all. We'd had a disturbed night, or rather disturbances had gone on in the house during the night of which we had been blissfully ignorant, but I had had to deal with the aftermath. Our house guest, one Wolf K., wished upon us by Adam, had been scheduled to leave for his new job in Prague on a train due away at 6.30 in the morning. Wolf K. had been a trial from the start. He was a rather limp young man, the more than harmless son of *alter Kämpfer Parteigenosse K.*, head of the personnel department in the Foreign Office and bearer of the Party badge in gold. Such birds were rare, unique in fact in our acquaintanceship, and Adam, having met son Wolf when he was in China, had decided that he must be cultivated. When Adam came to such decisions he was charmingly ruthless, and usually had little difficulty in persuading his friends to co-operate. Four weeks, though, had seemed a long time not to be able to speak openly even within one's own four walls, and I had heaved a sigh of relief when Wolf told us that he was taking a job in Bohemia. It was surely not too soon, for my never very patient Peter had almost ceased bothering to be polite to him any more.

I had set the alarm most carefully for 5 a.m. that morning, and had even heard some faint rummagings in the night which seemed to indicate that Wolf was on his way. No such luck, however, for hardly had we sat down to breakfast before faint hammerings from the washroom upstairs, and a quickly suppressed giggle from my eldest son, warned us that Wolf was still with us. The washroom door was locked. No, he had not locked himself in, the key had been on the outside of the door when he'd entered the washroom at 5.30 a.m. Where was the key anyway? Well, damn it, he'd have to climb out of the skylight window. We were none of us too even-tempered at breakfast time, owing to the National Socialist coffee bean, 'healthy, strength giving, tasty, try it on your coffee guests, indistinguishable from the real thing', indistinguishable except that one produced coffee and the other a nauseating brown mess.

Peter had fetched a ladder – 'Come on, buck up, now heave

yourself up, that's it – oh, wait a moment – ' it wasn't until we discovered that Wolf obviously slept without pyjama trousers that we realized the full extent of his dilemma. Nor was it until after Peter had set off with him for the *U Bahn*, hoping against hope that another train would leave for Prague during the day, that my charming son John solved the mystery of the missing key by rooting under his mattress and handing it back to me with a Mona Lisa-like smile.

I was very late starting for the market, but I did not hurry. The autumn air was so good, so clean, crisp and frosty and the hawthorn trees along the Falkenried quite startling under their smothering of polished red berries. Sign of a cold winter to come, so they say. God always looks after the birds.

I was alone on the road, and imagined that all my neighbours must be home again with a successful morning's queueing behind them. They were glancing through their windows, perhaps, and pitying me maybe, me and my empty shopping net. Frau Dr B., the *Hausfrau* who hadn't made it. The *Hausfrau* who would *never* make it, I reflected rather ruefully as I pushed along through the fallen leaves, and then I dismissed the subject from my thoughts and they returned to a far more engrossing puzzle. The Situation – the War. The war was six weeks old, six long weeks when nothing whatsoever had gone the way we thought it would. We had thought to be bombed by the Polish Air Force, but the Polish Air Force had apparently barely got off the ground; we had faced no danger except that Peter had decided that I should take the children to his mother in Aumühle in case of such air-raids, and I had got myself involved in a motor accident which could have killed all three of us. We had thought that, with the German divisions fully occupied in the East, the French would surely move their huge armies across the western borders of Germany and attack the thinly manned Siegfried Line, but instead they were sitting tight behind their massive fortifications and had hardly troubled to fire a shot. According to hearsay, the atmosphere on the Franco-German border was nothing more nor less than downright matey.

As to our own little outfit, we had thought that Peter would be called up any day and Adam had decided to volunteer for the Army; but Peter's job so far had been considered important enough to keep him at home, and Adam had gone to America. Since we had heard no news, he must have arrived safely, having passed through the Straits of Gibraltar in spite of the British blockade.

As I mooched alone along the road that morning and passed by Nicky's kindergarten, my thoughts only wandered for a moment to the child inside, listening doubtless starry-eyed to cosy little fables of the superiority of his race; they were soon back again at the accustomed churn-about. Will they, won't they, will they, won't they, this year, next year, sometime, never? Six weeks back I had watched through the window from the garden, listened to a precise voice on the wireless, tried to come to terms with a new and unknown situation. Then it had seemed that every effort made to avoid war had failed dismally. But only two weeks later a telegram from America had succeeded in bouncing us successfully even out of that abysmal trough.

The telegram from the States had requested that in spite of war, Adam should be allowed to attend the yearly meeting of the Institute of Pacific Relations in Virginia Beach in November. It had been long and carefully worded and it had mentioned Far Eastern enquiries and a possible scholarship and expressed the hope that Adam's journey could be regarded as his first national service. Peter and I had been fairly convinced that it amounted to a not very subtle invitation to 'scram' if the going was still good, but as far as Adam was concerned, that was a consideration which had merely made him laugh. For him it had been a signal from friends overseas, friends who spoke the same language, who, unperturbed by events, were convinced that there was another Germany behind the one-man voice of official policy, and who were determined to keep open the lines of communication. The ball was in his court, he was to be given another chance to explain the situation and the prospect had released in him an infectious gaiety, a bubbling optimism which had involved us all.

He soon had us persuaded that it was not too late for such a journey, and that the moment might even be auspicious, although time was running out; for the war with Poland was coming to an unexpectedly early end and, according to the grapevine, troops were already being transferred from the eastern front to the west, in order to be ready to take the offensive against France as soon as Poland finally capitulated.

The latest news as to the attitude of the General Staff had admittedly not been too rosy. They were unanimous in their opinion that to cross the Maginot Line would cost the German

Army more than a million men; in spite of their successes in Poland, they were more than apprehensive as to the possible outcome of a war in the West; in fact they believed it could only end in a military catastrophe. But – the usual great big but – they were *not* unanimous in their determination to rid Germany of Hitler, for in spite of their dislike of his régime, and contempt for him personally, some felt bound to him by their oath of allegiance and were still unable to contemplate deposing the Head of State when their country was at war.

Any old excuse is better than none would have been my snap judgement on such shilly-shallying, but I had allowed myself to be persuaded that it was not really quite as simple as that. German Generals were German Generals, brought up in the strictest of traditions, and whether I thought it nonsense or not, as things were we were dependent on them, and they happened to mind about such things as their oath of allegiance.

But Adam had been confident that some soothing formula had been found by those who were hammering away at the concrete consciences of the High Command, for, should Hitler decide against their advice to violate Belgian and Dutch neutrality, to launch in fact into a full-scale war which they believed could not be won, then even the most hesitant would be involved not only professionally but also morally. They would no longer need to feel bound by their code or their oath of allegiance, because Hitler would have jeopardized the very existence of the Reich.

If they were ever going to reach a decision, that would be the most likely moment for them to do so, and all that might be needed to tip the scales in favour of a *coup d'état* would be a clear declaration from the Allies of peace aims, one which would banish for ever the spectre of another Versailles and perhaps lay the foundation for an equitable post-war European settlement. Such a declaration of peace aims would not be addressed to Hitler (in fact a pre-requisite must be that he should first be deposed), but to a government which would take over after Hitler had been arrested.

I soon decided that the task of persuading the neutral Americans to use their influence in bringing about such a *démarche* would be child's play compared to the conjuring tricks Adam would need to perform in order to get official approval for his trip. He might have to join the Foreign Office. In what capacity? Father K. would have to be worked on there. So we must befriend son Wolf.

Secretary of State von Weizsäcker, von Kessel, they would know of course the real reason for his journey and could be relied upon to give it their support. They belonged to the old school, though, so their sponsorship would not be enough; he would have to try Hewel again, Ambassador Hewel, liaison officer between von Ribbentrop and Hitler, he had shown his willingness once and might be persuaded to do so again. To contact Hewel would be an obvious risk, but one which Adam had insisted must be taken. Those had been the moments when we had held our breath.

But Adam had gone about his affairs as gaily as if he were planning a holiday cruise, and a week later I found myself packing a suitcase with a none-too-affluent assortment of clothes and some books for the journey. Adam had his ticket in his pocket, paid for by the German Foreign Office, and a little leather notebook, his faithful companion wherever he went, filled to bursting with a very impressive collection of telephone numbers.

It was the eve of his departure – easy enough to remember – the day when the Russians had hustled into what remained of Poland, a little tardily due to events having moved so fast, but still determined to exact their pound of flesh, their pay-off for the Russo-German Pact. And Adam had been sloping about the room, restless and anxious to be on his way.

'Chris,' he said suddenly, 'would you think there is any danger of England making peace with Hitler after all – after the war with Poland is over, I mean, and as Adolf says, there's nothing more to fight about?' I had almost jumped. 'No,' I said without thinking and quite unexpectedly loudly. 'Why, for God's sake? If you ask *me*, not on your sweet life.' He had caught me off my guard, and feeling that some explanation was needed for the vehemence of my explosion, I added that I thought the British were slow starters, but that once on the move they would never give up, even if it meant losing – well, their Empire as well as their shirts. Adam had smiled at my answer and told me he thought I was right, but that he could see no reason for the British to lose their Empire, let alone their shirts. 'It's a matter of persuading the powers that be that Hitler and all he stands for is as much *our* enemy as theirs and that if it's *Hitler* they are out to destroy, in *that* battle we are on their side,' he had said and added quietly, 'and I don't think we are allies to be ignored.'

It was only afterwards, when Adam had gone, that I asked myself what evidence I had for my so confident overloud pronouncement. I could not have been influenced by the current situation, by England's performance so far, by the pathetic propaganda leaflets dropped from the skies, so hopelessly off the beam, nor by the still somehow ambiguous statements of policy which gave the impression that England had all the time in the world to settle her dispute with Herr Hitler. I came to the conclusion that I had relied purely on instinct. After Munich I had thought to discover in Germany some deep and basic fear of war and its consequences, and later in England, after the occupation of Czechoslovakia, I had sensed the instinctive, spontaneous, almost involuntary closing of the ranks; the slow but certain movement towards a common attitude. They had made up their minds, they had had enough of Hitler, so they supposed something would have to be done about it; exactly what and how was another matter. It seemed almost as simple as that. They had time too, and they had confidence, for they had been brought up, as I had, on memories of victory; whereas the Germans of my generation had been brought up on memories of defeat.

As I strolled along the road towards the market, past the little church on the corner of the Königin Louisenstrasse – Pastor Niemöller's church, filled to overflowing of a Sunday and even more so since Niemöller's arrest some two years back – I wondered whether those folks outside, those folks across the ocean, who were free as the breeze to say what they pleased and do what they liked, I wondered whether they had any notion how complicated life could become. Nothing could be easier if you decided to leave for good – goodbye, and to hell with it all; but if you wanted to return, as Adam did, if you believed that there was something worthwhile in your country, something for which you were personally responsible? It would hardly be much use then if you were met at the border by some gentleman in a black uniform. 'Your passport? Step this way, please.'

I hurried my step. The sun had gone behind a cloud; it was surely going to be a cold winter. Of course Adam had covered his tracks and planned a safe route back. A special adviser attached to the Information Department of the Foreign Office; all expenses paid. It was amazing how he had managed it. He would be away three months, and perhaps the next news we would hear from him would be indirectly via Roosevelt, and when we saw him next, the Generals would have acted.

'*Guten Morgen*, Frau Schmitz, *Guten Morgen*, Fräulein Müller,

Heil Hitler, Frau Professor.' What had happened to the market? There shouldn't have been a cabbage-leaf left, instead the stalls were only half cleared, only the do-or-diers were queueing and the other ladies were standing round in animated groups. As I passed down between the rows, one or two heads nodded smilingly in my direction. It was the baker's wife who enlightened me as she clipped off my bread coupons and recklessly pushed an extra loaf into my old string bag. 'We won't be needing these much longer, Frau Dr,' she said. *'Wieso?'* 'Why, haven't you heard? Peace, they say, peace negotiations are going on at this very minute.' 'What?' I looked across at Frau Schmitz, enthroned behind her vegetable stall, all overcoat and apron, a bulging monument to the peculiar ribald stoicism which characterizes the true Berliner; she would know. *'Ja, Ja, Frau Dr,'* she shouted, nodding and beaming, pushing a bit of felt, bristling with hatpins to the back of her head. *'Ja, Ja. Die Herren haben sich die Sache janz anders überleecht!'* (The gents at the top have completely changed their minds!) She took advantage of the general laughter to tip a few unripe tomatoes into the shopping bag of her pink-nosed customer, a choosy lady whom she usually referred to with all the scorn at her disposal as *So'ne* (one of those). What? Where? How? I was soon the centre of a chattering group, all eager to tell me exactly what was going on. Peace negotiations, oh yes, with the British of course, a special envoy, someone even mentioned the Duke of 'Vintzor'. A little mouse-like figure slipped up to me from behind, shook my hand, whispered 'congratulations' and, as if overcome by her courage, darted back to her queue; I might have been Mrs Simpson in person. No one seemed to know any precise details. Most had got the news from someone who'd had it from someone else; but one thing was certain: everyone, including 'Mrs Simpson', was beside themselves, and our joy reached its peak when the police sergeant, on duty guarding the market, pushed through the crowd and added his voice behind which was all the authority of the law, to our babbling conjectures.

'I understand,' he said, savouring his moment as we stood around him in hushed expectant silence, 'I understand, ladies, that extra police have been drafted to meet a special plane, which is due to arrive at the Tempelhof Airport this afternoon. I likewise understand that the machine will be a British one.' Good God, then it was true! I did not bother to think further of the whys and wherefores. For a moment I had to close my eyes, before breathing a long sigh of relief, before finding myself too shaking hands with a dozen or more happy-faced strangers, including the police sergeant. I hurried homewards on air, feeling well capable of kicking my old shopping net clean over the roof tops. I burst into the house to find no message from Peter. I approached the telephone in a more sober mood. Had he heard any rumours? Yes, he had, nothing definite; he was lunching with someone from the Foreign Office, he would ring me back.

The unctuous voice of Radio Beromünster mentioned nothing unusual in the midday news bulletin. I sat by the telephone until four o'clock in the afternoon, having long since realized that the whole affair, of course, had been quite ridiculous. Peace with Hitler? I had not even the right to contemplate such a thing. Blast everything anyway. There was no danger, I knew, of my being converted by the remorseless hammerbeat of propaganda, but rather of becoming cynical and insensible and of believing nothing any more. Rumour could have this, have that, have many things, some fantastic, some sinister; I should have learned never to believe anything that I had not seen with my own eyes or heard with my own ears from someone – and there were precious few – in whom I had complete trust.

When Peter came back in the evening he told me that the peace negotiation rumour had been circulated by the BBC to test the morale of the Germans. It had been a completely successful hoax. He himself had heard the rumour from the head of his department at the start of an important committee meeting in the Ministry of Economics, who had thought it important enough to postpone the meeting until the following day, when headlines in the newspapers described it as 'Further Insolence from the British Ministry of Lies'. Such absurd reports, said Dr Goebbels, could at most upset the frightened spinsters of both sexes who were domiciled in the London suburbs: but this Germany over which were waving flags of victory never could, and never would, be led from her chosen path by such idiotic and clumsy manoeuvres.

'That's what one gets for being a spinster of both sexes, Frau Dr,' murmured Frau Schmitz the following week, as she wiped the drip from her nose with the back of her hand and popped an extra bunch of *Suppengrün* into my muddy old shopping net. *Suppengrün* was a small and rather nauseous little bundle of vegetable stalks tied together with string which, when plunged into boiling water, supposedly transformed it into soup. Just another rumour; I'd tried it and it didn't.

Part II: (Spring 1940)

The berries were right about the winter; the snows came early and stayed put. Hard icy flakes battered the numbed and exhausted birds up against the window panes. God seemed to give up the unequal task of looking after them, and left it to us humans who were no better fitted for the job. Peter satisfied his childhood longing to be a farmer by setting us up with rabbits and hens, but when we went out one morning to feed our livestock, four rigid furry stones fell out of the rabbit hutch and we were obliged to transfer the hens, who occupied the floor below, to the coal cellar.

Our efforts at stock-rearing did not meet with much approval in the district. 'One might be living on an allotment plot!' Did we understand that Dahlem was a very respectable residential area? One particular lady, referred to by one and all as the '*Frau Baronin*', took time off to give me quite a lecture on the subject. As the thermometer began its descent to unheard of depths, however, and the food rations (cut twice before Christmas) seemed bent on the same downhill path, the sepulchral cluckings from our cellar, which echoed regularly across the hedgetops, made havoc of our neighbours' status qualms. We noticed discreet wooden structures being erected in bushes and behind unused garages, and felt assured that by spring our corner of the smart residential district would greet the dawn as merrily as a busy barnyard.

There was something coldly unreal about those winter months of watching and waiting – watching for the news we hoped would come from America, waiting for the Generals to act. They in their turn, we heard, were waiting for Hitler to attack in the West, he must burn his boats completely before they could be persuaded to make one move to get rid of him. But the expected attack in the West did not come. We were watching and waiting, they were watching and waiting, even Hitler seemed to be watching and waiting – nothing moved. It was as if the bitter, relentless cold had seeped its way into the very fibre of events.

I often found myself staring out of the window into the still opaque greyness of the garden, where the snow had long since been blown into rigid drifts against the bare hedges, and it seemed to me that the whole pattern of our winter was being stamped indelibly on the glassy surface of the lawn. There went the tracks of my old rubber boots, off to the bird bath, past the ice-blue snowman, naked looking since his eyes and buttons had gone into the fire and his nose to feed the hens. John had been disconsolate when our little car had been dragged away 'on Active Service'; those were his tracks, backwards and forwards to the garage, just to see if by chance it could have arrived home again. Closer to the window there was plenty of hither and thither. Friends seemed to prefer to come to the garden door, and if they came often, the enticement was certainly not my spurious coffee. All that I could offer in the way of amenities was a feeling of space around, with no one in the flat above, the flat below or the flat next door. The fact that I seldom had a maid was also a useful asset because maids were as potentially untrustworthy as a connected telephone. It was not long before our telephone had been plugged in and out of the wall so regularly that the cord began to look like an outsize 'hairy Mary'.

I knew, of course, the motive behind their visits: that we were just one of many small heterogeneous groups who were meeting together all over Germany, tenuously joined, each group to the next, by one member whom they could trust. Werner Trott, Curt Bley, Otto John, Teddy Kessel, Haushofer, v. Einsiedel, v. Trotha to mention a few. Socialist, Conservative, Catholic, Protestant, from the civil service, from industry, young officers in the Army; they had no other means of communicating with each other. The enticement then was partly to hear and to report 'the latest', the snag being that 'the latest' was in very short supply. It was not difficult to be aware that Ribbentrop was the warmonger, yearning to avenge his hurt pride, that Goering was perhaps a restraining influence, that Goebbels was the cleverest monkey of the lot, that Generals Beck and von Hammerstein were dedicated opponents of the régime and that von Brauchitsch was a waverer; but the unknown quantity remained – Hitler himself – with his *'unerschütterlicher Wille'*, his unbendable will, his curiously compelling mystique. He kept his counsel, unless he was on a platform, and never seemed to emerge from the shadows.

When will 'it' happen? What would happen afterwards? I did not join in those debates very often, because my footsteps as often as not were dogged by a pair of resolute sons; also I was conscious that my contribution to any discussion as to what might happen after the war would have been short and sweet – I hadn't the slightest idea. Until Hitler was removed from the scene, all talk of the future seemed irrelevant, bubbles of conjecture blown into a vacuum; but then I had to remind myself that the situation might change very suddenly, overnight in fact, the vacuum might have to be filled and that I was listening to a generation of young men who, under ordinary circumstances, would be moving up into positions of high office in their country whose careers had been abruptly cut short in 1933, and yet who would be asked to deal with the aftermath of Hitler's rule.

I listened, then, and I learned a little. I learned that they were unable to contemplate a return to pre-Hitler conditions; that many of the old inflexible barriers, the narrow class and party prejudices, seemed to be melting away after seven years of Hitler's reign. I was touched by their sincerity, the obvious trust they had in one another, the respect they showed for each other's point of view; and it occurred to me that united as they were in a common purpose, something new, classless and non-factional could be germinating under the pressure of a common enemy.

Peter was called up in January. Although every lever at the disposal of the head of his department in the Ministry of Economics was pulled in his favour, the Air Force had priority, and Peter reluctantly donned his corporal's uniform once more. He was only away for four weeks because Freda Winckelmann, who was Furtwängler's private secretary, succeeded where the Ministry had failed. She knew some nice old boy who managed such things for the Berlin Philharmonic Orchestra, she thought it would be worth a try and sure enough twenty-four hours later Peter was back again at his desk. It did not seem to me that his spell with the Air Force had been spent very usefully, for he assured me that he had spent quite a lot of his time crawling around the icy parade ground singing 'the Watch on the Rhine' into a gas mask. This was considered to be some sort of punishment for minor insubordination, but to me the whole episode appeared quite unreal – just another part of a war which was no war.

All the same I liked to imagine, as I stared out of the window, that there must be stirrings beneath the icy surface crust; that in other places there must be other people like Adam who were also determined to preserve the ebb and flow. I had every reason to believe so, for the war had not long started before personal messages began to reach me from the outside world: from Elsa von Rosen and Outram Mott in Sweden, from Jenny Thurneysen in Switzerland; asking could they help, asking could they pass on news. I found such things infinitely comforting, for I sometimes needed assurance that human nature would not allow the freezing up of all emotion, and that it took more than hymns of hate and rattling armour to interrupt the warm and natural flow of human affection.

Adam returned in February, long before the snow turned to slush. He could not add to the tracery of footprints on the still icy lawn, because he could not stay in our house. He had jaundice, caught somewhere on his way home through China and Russia, and when we went to see him we found him not only ill but dispirited, conscious that his odyssey had been a very qualified success. We were unable to give him much cheer, as except for the fact that for some days in November there had been optimistic reports that the Generals were preparing to act, and that our Russian allies' attack on Finland had done nothing to improve the popularity of Hitler's policies, there was little to tell him. Compared with his herculean efforts, we were conscious that our own contribution boiled down to nothing more than rather academic discussions over cups of synthetic coffee.

It seemed that things had gone well enough for him in America at first. It had not been difficult to persuade prominent German emigrés, such as Brüning or Paul Scheffer, competent judges of the German scene, that the civilian opposition was solid enough and also capable of forming a responsible Government, but that because of the very nature of the Hitler régime, only the Army had the power to upset it; that Dr Goebbels' efficient propaganda machine was working overtime churning out the message that the war was being fought for Germany's very existence, and therefore that it was of the utmost importance that the Allies should take the wind out of his sails by promulgating plans for an equitable post-war European settlement; that neutral America was in a unique position to use her influence in bringing about such a declaration of peace aims, to a Germany which had rid herself of Hitler.

Adam had had endless discussions and not only with Germans. He had been received by the Secretary of State Messersmith, and had talked with the British Ambassador, Lord Lothian, twice. He had been confident at first that Roosevelt would lend a receptive ear to such a *démarche* and would not be averse to playing the rôle of peace-maker. Adam had helped draft a memorandum and had been satisfied that it had been rightly channelled and that it would reach the President. But had it? As the days passed and no answer came from the White House, he had been forced to believe that it had met with some obstruction on the way, or that Roosevelt's reaction had been negative. He was inclined to believe the former. Judge Frankfurter? Sumner Welles? He had been followed wherever he went by a couple of what he referred to as 'nice simple cops', obvious as to their identity and easy to shake off, but obscure as to who were their employers, the FBI or the Gestapo. Adam veered away from the thought that there could have been doubts amongst those who knew him as to his personal integrity. Any doubting of his personal integrity always hit him like a blow between the eyes. There had been rays of light though, in that he had been lucky enough to find a trustworthy friend on the British Embassy staff, John Wheeler Bennett, who had many friends amongst the German opposition and with whom he had been able to talk quite openly. Wheeler Bennett had promised to deliver messages to David Astor and had taken a copy of the memorandum back with him to England; another trustworthy messenger had taken a copy to Lord Halifax. So that although Adam had had to leave America, uncertain as to why his endeavours had met with no response, at least he could be certain that prominent Americans and equally prominent Englishmen knew of the existence of a German opposition, of its dilemma and of its needs.

Sitting near the door, as far from the bugs as possible, I watched Adam's yellow face as Peter, supremely confident of his ability to withstand any bug, sat by his bedside helping him compose the report on his journey for the German Foreign Office. They were having some fun with the official jargon. A sudden burst of laughter, 'all right, Peter, if you think so, but isn't it laying it on a bit thick?' 'You can't lay it on thick enough, dear boy.' God, I thought, if they knew what he had really been up to! And then again I wondered why things had gone wrong. I was frankly puzzled, for I could not see that it mattered whether Adam's personal integrity had been in doubt or not; surely things did not depend on personalities. Surely everyone wanted peace, surely everyone wished for the end of Hitlerism. Surely the Allies had nothing to lose, everything in fact to gain, by making every conceivable approach to a possible German opposition. Would it not at least have been worth a try?

It seemed to me that if peace proposals of a kind such as Adam had suggested had been put forward by the Allies, and if they had met with no *active* response on the part of the German Generals, then indeed Adam could have been proved to have been talking nonsense; for the Allies, nothing would have been lost, nothing gained. But if the German Generals had reacted positively to such an Allied *démarche* then it might have meant so much – it might have meant in fact the end of the war.

On May 10th, 1940, the German Armies swarmed across Germany's western borders. The speed of their advance westwards would have needed to be meteoric in order to compare with the agility which was being displayed in the ranks of the stay-at-homes, as the ditherers and the careful ones put out their feelers towards those who might be influential when, as was anticipated, the armoured divisions ground to a standstill before the Maginot Line, and Hitler's prestige suffered a blow from which it might never recover.

As the days passed, however, and Holland capitulated, and the legendary Fort Eben Emael collapsed like a house of cards, and the Maginot Line seemed no more able than the Polish cavalry to halt the advancing tanks, then so much back-pedalling became the order of the day in Berlin, that, if I had felt like being funny, I could have sworn that it was possible to feel the draught.

The incredible had happened. 'I will defeat France in open combat, in a matter of weeks, and then turn my might against Russia,' one of Hitler's 'prophecies' (which had been passed along the grapevine during the winter and always raised a laugh) had been in part fulfilled. True, it seemed that quite a large number of the British Expeditionary Force had managed to scramble back across the Channel, but that could not alter the fact that France had capitulated, in six weeks, in six short weeks.

It was on my birthday, June 18th, with my ear right up against it, as Nicky would have said, that I heard Churchill speak of England's finest hour. I listened, I knew what he meant, and I burst into tears; not so much because our governess had taught me that if ever a hostile power should occupy the Channel ports England sooner or later would be at their mercy, but simply because I wanted to be there. Blessed, cockeyed, ignorant England, quite pleased, I would have said, to be rid of those bothersome continentals and to be on her own.

Adam smuggled out newspapers for me from the Foreign Office and overnight I could read *The Times* from cover to cover. Never the headlines, I was fed up with headlines – just the bits and pieces hidden away inside. 'The Countess of Iddesleigh is staying in Shropshire and will remain there for some time.' 'Mrs Gurowska, wife of the late Captain Gurowska, wishes to be known as Countess Gurowska.' Pictures of laughing soldiers being given a hero's cup of tea and a cheery welcome home, by ladies in hats like blown-up sponge bags. 'Mrs Pleydell-Bouverie regrets that, owing to present circumstances, the exhibition of flowers and dresses by Constance Spry in aid of the Redlands Nursing Home has been postponed indefinitely.' 'A wise precautionary measure in an emergency. Keep a bottle of *Optrex* handy.' Emergency! Present circumstances! A bottle of *Optrex*! It hardly seemed possible.

I would like to think that Churchill's words, steeped as I felt them to be in the very substance of my country's history, and inevitably striking a chord somewhere deep down inside me, immediately quietened all my fears and banished for ever the hideous vista of Hitler's thousand-year Reich stretching away beyond the horizon of my lifetime. But it was not so, because I knew too much. Fighting in the streets, in the fields, on the hills there would surely be, and heroes, many heroes – but there might be others as well. Collaborators, informers, crackpots who believed that Jews were Yids, and Negroes 'nigs', and Italians 'wogs', and that only one race could rightfully consider itself to be the salt of the earth. If such as these were international commodities, I knew there would be no drama about the aftermath. There would be the tramp of marching boots and the loud knock at the door in the night, the creak and rumble of departing lorries fading into the distance of deserted streets; silence then, no drama, just silence, impenetrable silence.

My stiff upper lip, if it did come into its own, would be a purely instinctive reaction, instilled into me by my up-bringing, for at nights I could not stop dreaming of my father, with his back to a red brick wall, hopelessly defiant, defending himself with a golf club – of all things a golf club. Night after night he went down under flailing rifle butts and disappeared beneath a wave of jolting, jerking helmets, helmets like steel-grey tortoises, helmets that I had learned to fear in my childhood – and all the while the roses blossomed profusely in the garden, the lawn needed trimming, the queues lined up in the market place and cherries, lots of them, ripened on the cherry tree above our tool-shed, just behind the house.

A DINNER PARTY

(Autumn 1940)

Someone had been to the country and brought back a load of crayfish, someone knew someone at the Swedish Embassy and had cadged some bottles of aquavit, someone suggested a party. In Berlin life as it had to be lived day by day was singularly void of festivity, and we decided that, in spite of all, we had one very good reason to celebrate. Adam had married Clarita Tiefenbacher in June, and they had found themselves a flat not far from us in Dahlem. Peter and I, as seasoned veterans of six years standing, had approved of the affair whole-heartedly, and we had the added satisfaction of knowing that we were a little responsible, as they had first met in our house in Reinbek. We selected eight special friends to share the crayfish and the aquavit, and others, some forty in all, to join in afterwards; we hoped that they would be laden with extra bottles.

Clarita and I were preparing some rather nauseous sandwiches for their benefit when Freda Winckelmann rang to provide me with another good reason for a celebration. She had been travelling into town on the train from Klein Machnow; there had been soldiers working on the line near the station; she could swear they were Tommies; she thought I might be interested. *Interested*, such were the words we used on the telephone. I hurled a handful of parsley at the dish of sandwiches – on with a hat, my best dress, no coat for it was too hot, and I leaped off the train in Klein Machnow as if about to greet the prodigal son. As the carriages rattled past me out of the station I could see a long line of khaki figures across the tracks on the far side. Yes, Freda, yes indeed, they were Tommies all right. I hurried up the stairs of the bridge crossing the railway lines, and was halfway down on the other side before I realized that I was not quite certain why I had come.

Just to stare at them? Just to see that they still existed? I descended the remaining steps rather more sedately and stood at the bottom feeling a bit foolish. The Tommies were working a little below me, next to the palings beside the track; khaki berets, blue berets, a red beret and one jaunty one from Scotland with a bobble on top. Working would not perhaps be the right word. In fact they were lined up and with much show of effort, were passing a little pile of five or six bricks from one to the other. The stack of bricks at the far end, however, never got much smaller nor that at the near end much bigger, and it was not difficult to see why, since it was always the same little pile of bricks travelling from hand to hand, up the line and down again. The utter pointlessness of this occupation seemed of little interest to anyone, not even to a couple of guards who, with their rifles slung over their shoulders, were strolling up and down behind them, deep in conversation.

I paraded a little uncertainly once or twice up and down outside the palings, feeling increasingly embarrassed, especially when I began to realize from the winks and grins which accompanied my promenade that my thoughts and those of the prisoners of war were running on somewhat similar lines. I decided that I could not face the barrage again, so I waited until the guards were as far away as possible before I addressed the palings with the first words which came into my head. 'We're not beat yet,' I said. The bricks kept on moving, the heads were still bent and the backs were still straining, but the eyes, blue, brown, twenty, thirty, forty pairs of eyes, were looking straight at me. A small, dark fellow who, in spite of the heat, was wearing a huge great-coat, gave me back an answer.

'Might you have been thinking that we were?'

'No, no,' I said and I was surely not consciously lying, 'actually never.'

'Well, darlin' girl, you're right there,' the answer came back as chirpy as could be, and the accent was pure Cork City.

A load of crayfish, three bottles of aquavit, some good friends unused to much alcohol, and one old die-hard fresh from discussing affairs of state with a gentleman from Cork – the party that evening could not help but get away to a good start.

The 'England Committee' from the Foreign Office was well represented and, as I glanced down the table from one smiling face to the next and listened to their chatter it occurred to me that they looked English too, or perhaps it was that they were friends, and I just felt at home with their faces and their voices. I soon gathered, however, that much to their regret they were more than a little doubtful as to whether Peter would stay the diplomatic course much longer.

'If, dear Peter, your immediate superior, your Secretary of State in fact – even if he has never been to England, doesn't speak a word of English, is a perfect fool but thinks he knows all the answers – decides to propound to his underlings his own particular theories on how best to persuade the stubborn Briton of the infinite superiority of the German way of life, you do *not* behave as you did.'

'Well, what the hell *do* I do?'

'You gaze into space, you smile a little perhaps, you wonder what you are going to have for lunch, but you do not, I must repeat do *not* burst out laughing.'

'Well, all right, I'm no good; but when that prize idiot started talking about bombing the East End of London so that the slum dwellers would move to the West End, see how the rich live and immediately go beserk, and then goes on to suggest requisitioning the soap boxes in Hyde Park—'

Poor Peter, I knew that he found his activities on the 'England Committee' quite excruciating, for in spite of our plans before we married he was not made of the stuff needful for a diplomat. Too fiery, too honest, too uncompromising I decided, as I eyed him with much affection, and I then proceeded to take much too large a swig of aquavit, for I was suddenly reminded of how he had given me the fright of my life some months back, when having heard from Teddy Kessel that Colonel Oster of Counter-intelligence was looking for volunteers who were willing to assassinate Ribbentrop, he had treated it as a matter of course that he would be one of them.

The sudden silence which followed my fit of the splutters was broken by Spitzi, who sighed and raised his glass 'Prost, Peter Bielenberg and you too, dear Chris, let's hope that the way things are, we're as near to Hyde Park as we shall ever be.' I understood the sigh because I knew that Spitzi had been engaged to a girl from Cornwall and had had to leave the German Foreign Office on her account, but had been unable to make contact with her since the outbreak of war.

The table had to be cleared, the remains of the crayfish thrown to the hens – there was quite half a bottle left of the aquavit, but not for long. When our other guests arrived, with more supplies, they were greeted with such effusion that they did not take long in pulling the corks and following our good example. At the height of the hilarity Hannes appeared in the doorway. He had borrowed one of Peter's khaki shirts and a black tie and corked his upper lip and pulled his hair forward, in exact imitation of Hitler's famous forelock. He was surely wasting his time in the civil service; he should of course have been an actor, for he took our breath away, so perfect was the impersonation as he flapped his right arm and gazed silently about the room in the recognized fashion, as if seeking the exact section of the crowd at which to direct the start of a tirade. Then he drew a deep breath and, without saying a word, turned on his heel and removed himself, not forgetting to include the unmistakable perky strut.

In the course of the evening I found myself down in the cellar looking for a missing corkscrew with another late-comer. Tall, fresh-faced, very English looking somehow, he suddenly clicked his heels, bowed from the waist, and, giving his head a hearty crack on the ceiling as he returned to the upright, 'Preussen – Prussia,' he said. I gave him a soothing smile of the variety one reserves for those one believes to be less sober than oneself. 'Never mind,' I said, 'Great Britain,' and I bowed in return. He looked a trifle nonplussed and then burst out laughing. 'Now that we have introduced ourselves what actually *is* your name?' I enquired with some dignity. 'Well – er, Prussia – Hubertus Hohenzollern,' he replied, and in the state I was in it took me a moment's hard thinking to understand why I had considered him to be English looking; he must be a cousin of the King and he looked like a taller edition of the Prince of Wales. He was also probably a grandson of the Kaiser. Kaiser or no Kaiser we smiled fondly at each other and found the corkscrew at the bottom of the air-raid bucket.

Meanwhile things upstairs were getting well out of hand. Nikolaus had been persuaded to give his famous version of Goebbels' broadcast to the nation after the *Endsieg* – the final victory. Sitting on the floor, with his hands cupped over his mouth, it was hard to tell that it was not Goebbels who was speaking. 'German men, German women, this is your Minister of Propaganda speaking, your own *Schrumpf Germane*, your Mini German. I am sitting on top of the *Siegestor* and beneath me passes the greatest victory parade of all time, column after column of blonde, blue-eyed giants, filled with one burning desire, which is to gaze for one fleeting second on the face of their Leader. Eagles! As I gaze down the *Siegesallee* I see nothing but eagles to the right, to the left, rows of golden eagles, and I know that you will be pleased to hear that our Leader has declared that as from today the *Siegesallee* has been renamed *Geflügelallee* – the Poultry Boulevard – in honour of those eagles, a title which was suggested to him by a simple Berlin taxi-driver. But wait, who is this resplendent figure who rides beneath me in a motor car, none other I do declare than Party Member Hermann Goering, promoted under the new circumstances, by our Leader, to be *Weltmarschall*, World Marshal Hermann Goering; were it not for the weight of the decorations with which he has presented himself, he would, no doubt, willingly march with the rest. And following behind, who indeed are those four emaciated figures, also car-borne? Ah yes, of course; these, my *Volksgenossen*, are the only four Germans who subsisted solely on their ration cards throughout the war. They can no longer walk, of course, but they too are Heroes of the Nation—'

When was it that we forgot or nearly forgot the time, the date, the place and above all the monstrous set-up which held our fate in its hands? Some time after the carpet had been rolled back and we were dancing, and someone had insisted on turning on the radio and Ambrose's Orchestra was playing from London. The death penalty? To hell with it anyway, let's have some decent dance music! If the Gestapo, or more likely, a zealous informer were stalking the garden, they would make a good catch. I glanced at Peter, wondering if we were not going a bit far, but he smiled back reassuringly. The shutters were closed, four stalwarts were taking turns on the road and around the garden. Aquavit or no aquavit, he had not forgotten his duty as a host.

OUR NEIGHBOURS

(Autumn 1941)

It took us a long time to get to know our next-door neighbours, more than a full year to be exact. Our initial introduction was not too auspicious because our hens, as the nights got warmer, resolutely refused to return to their house at night; they preferred to lodge in the cherry tree which spread its branches between our two gardens. The cock had a strident voice, especially in the early morning, and before returning for breakfast on our side of the fence he and his ladies invariably took it into their heads to descend on the well-weeded flower beds next door. A polite little note therefore, signed Irmgard Langbehn and requesting us to keep the wretched birds off her newly planted salvias, was for many months the only sign of neighbourly life to come our way.

A further, less formal, recognition of our presence did not exactly resound to our credit either, for Nick and John, benefiting from the lack of much supervision, had taken to amusing themselves much as they pleased. I considered they looked like angels and I knew they could behave like demons, but just the same I was frankly a little taken aback when after a violent ringing of the doorbell I was accosted at the gate one morning by a gesticulating lady who was almost speechless with indignation. Did those little boys who were playing up the road belong to me? One dark, one fair? Yes? Well, never in her born days had she had to listen to such language. What had they said? No, she could not tell me – it was just too dreadful, and in front of a man mending the water main. Oh no, Oh yes, *Ach ja – Ach nein! Du liebe Zeit! So was!* She bustled off down the road clucking and spluttering and shaking her head and left me to head rapidly in the other direction.

I found my obviously unrepentant sons laughing merrily with the head and shoulders of a sturdy Berliner who, on seeing me, disappeared abruptly down a manhole. What had happened? *Ach nix!* What had they said? I was finding it none too easy to keep my dignity when talking to a hole in the road. 'Oh well, it wasn't much really. Would have been all right if that old goat hadn't interfered – he had children of his own – anyway they had been giving him a bit of cheek, he had been well able to look after himself, but the lady had stopped and told them that nice little boys didn't say such things.' 'Yes, and—?' 'Well, then the little fellow—' his head came up and he glanced apologetically at John – 'the little fellow had said to the lady "Mind your own business you old bitch".' Needless to say John had made use of a word of similar impact in German, and although swear-words in a foreign language never seem as impressive as in one's own, I realized that the moment had come to be stern. I whisked them back to the garden giving tongue to dire threats, and insisting that they stay there for the afternoon. As I pushed them in at the gate I found myself announcing in clarion tones that if ever I heard them calling people that name again I would send them to bed for the day.

My remark was greeted, more or less neutralized in fact, by a burst of laughter from the far side of the hedge; and I discovered that a little lady with white hair and the face of a spry robin was eyeing me through the branches. 'Excuse me,' she said, 'I should not have laughed, but I have five grandchildren of my own and I assure you your two little boys are not much different from my bunch.'

We chatted then for a while and she told me that she was keeping house for her son, whose wife and children were in Walchensee, near Munich. My children were a bit small to swim in the swimming pool, she imagined, but there were plenty of cherries on her side of the hedge, let them come with their buckets. She seemed a most friendly little person, and from then on we greeted each other occasionally across the hedge or on our way to market; no more, since in the Third Reich neighbours, however friendly, had always to be regarded as potential nuisances, even potential dangers; certainly not social assets. It was not until Peter discovered that the lawyer he had been consulting in some case was in fact none other than the old lady's son Carl, and until his wife (the lady with the salvias) appeared on the scene once more with a pair of rumbustious twin boys in tow, that our passing acquaintanceship ripened into something more cordial.

Again some months passed before we had got along well enough to be asked to dinner. By getting along well enough I would mean that we had made the usual enquiries and they, without doubt, had done likewise. Casual conversations across a hedge, or business appointments, were one thing, a dinner party another. We were fortunate enough to discover that we had mutual friends in the Sarres, who knew Dr Langbehn well. He had seemingly shown his colours way back in 1933 by his spirited defence of some parliamentarian, who had been taken into Hitler's first Cabinet, had proved a nuisance and who, in typically Nazi fashion, had found himself facing some cooked up criminal charge. Since then he had shown an uncanny aptitude for defending other unlucky ones, both Jewish and otherwise; one of his clients had been Albrecht Bernstorff. Puppi Sarre could tell of innumerable occasions where Langbehn had been called to the rescue and we could be sure that he was completely trustworthy. Just the same we knew that when meeting new people, they would probably play the game as we did. The conversation at first would be guarded and non-committal. We knew that we were none of us Nazis, but were we all of us, drunk or sober, also discreet? Had we other mutual friends? Were they real friends or just names dropped to impress? I would find it hard to describe the wary approach, the half-finished sentence, the guarded reference which led at the time to mutual confidence, and to the realization that the air had at last been cleared and all present could sit back and indulge in plain high treason. The procedure was a delicate one, one that had to be carefully learned if we valued our lives, and would trust our fellows sufficiently to put our lives in their hands.

In the case of our neighbours, Frau Langbehn, probably unconsciously, handed out several clues from the start. She was shy and transparently honest, and had possibly been through many an awkward moment with her more ebullient husband. She reminded me a little of a younger edition of my mother and I imagined that when she came clean, so to speak, she would do so with a gentle, but very firm bang. She in fact waited that evening until her mother-in-law had gone to bed, the reason doubtless being that that little personage obviously saw no reason whatsoever to show much reticence. She came of a generation which had grown up in *Kaisers Zeiten*, Kaiser's times, those were the days. As far as she was concerned, the country since then had been run by mountebanks; at present it was Hitler and his 'gang', and she saw no reason to keep quiet about it.

It was obvious when they joined us after dinner that Peter and Dr Langbehn had progressed much faster. They had discovered that their forebears had come originally from much the same part of Germany, north of the River Elbe; in Germany suchlike roots seem to form a rather special tie. Both had studied law, both were fit as fiddles, both radiated a sort of restless energy and I could see that although Langbehn was some years older than he was, Peter had found a man after his own heart. Out of one ear I could hear him telling the older man how he had found it impossible to continue his law practice after one of his poor-law clients had been acquitted and then immediately re-arrested by the Gestapo, and that that had been the moment perhaps when he had known what he had to do; that was why we were in Berlin.

It was thereabouts probably that Frau Langbehn gave up trying to entertain me and simultaneously listen with one anxious ear to the conversation on the far side of the fireplace. 'You must excuse me, Frau Bielenberg,' she said simply, 'but I live in continuous fear that Carl will overdo it. It is as if it were a sport with him, but every time he sets off for the Prinz Albrechtstrasse,* I wonder whether he'll come out again. You see our telephone has been tapped since 1934, and the fact that he has been so successful in his dealings with the Gestapo means that everyone who is in trouble—' Langbehn was sitting back in his chair half smiling as if he were enjoying some private joke.

'My dear fellow, you cannot imagine what luck. Elke, you see, our eldest girl, goes to school with Himmler's daughter, they're about the same age, and Elke was asked to the child's birthday party. Irmgard and I took her along. No, no, they have a summer place on the Tegernsee not far from Walchensee. Anyway, who should turn up at the party but Heinrich himself. I had a couple of tricky cases on my hands, and I guess "know thy enemy" is a maxim always worth following, so when he asked us to stay to tea and then to dinner, we stayed.' 'It was a dreadful evening,' Frau Langbehn broke in quietly. 'I had to make conversation with his wife and out of one ear I could hear Carl telling Himmler of two cases where the SS had made arrests, the victims had disappeared and the next news to come of them had been when their ashes

*Headquarters of the Gestapo.

were returned to their widows without comment. I remember Himmler answered that he did not believe it, and that if Carl could bring him proof he would have the culprits liquidated in their turn—' 'I did bring him proof and those widows at least got their pensions,' Langbehn broke in, and then turning again to Peter he added, 'I also tried to explain to him that arbitrary liquidation of the delinquents was not the proper procedure but that it should be the concern of the law to deal with murder.'

A deep almost unnatural silence had come over the room whilst Langbehn had been speaking. I remembered it afterwards and it occurred to me that radiating quietude was probably not one of his customary habits. I remembered too that if it had not been Langbehn speaking, quietly, soberly without emotion, I would not have been able to believe what he had to say about the SS, what he called a State within the State, and of Himmler who, although he looked like the caricature of any village schoolmaster, was obsessed by an almost sensuous passion for fair-haired Nordic types. Everyone about him, his adjutants, his secretaries, had to be blonde and blue-eyed; his antipathy to dark hair and dark skin amounted almost to physical revulsion. A pervert of course in his own way, only able to function through his SS. 'Meine SS', my SS as he always called them, élite blond knights *ohne Fehl und Tadel*, pure and without blemish, a glowing shield against the powers of darkness, behind which he would willingly sink his own nondescript identity completely. It seemed that as such Langbehn believed him to be approachable, to have some use in fact because he thought he had discovered in Himmler some perverted sense of honour. 'Surely your SS Herr Reichsführer should not consider dirtying their hands with such things?' It was an approach which he had found could serve a purpose.

But what of Himmler's SS? The captains of his shining white knights, Heydrich, Kaltenbrunner, Müller, they were a very different kettle of fish. Cold, clever, utterly ruthless, interested purely in power for the sake of power, they ruled a State within a State, one which had no legal conscience, where the word 'liquidate' had replaced any conception of legality. It would be useless to appeal to their consciences – they had none. It was as if the Chicago underworld of Al Capone and his thugs had been let loose to run the country. He had heard his wife telling me that he had told Himmler some political jokes: old chestnuts, incidentally, which would not have raised a laugh anywhere else any more. He had done so simply to see which ones amused Himmler most, and discovered that he obviously enjoyed those best which were directed against Goebbels. Those were things one had to find out. We knew so little of what went on behind the scenes, what intrigues and counter intrigues carried one or other of those rascals to the top of the ladder, what bound them to each other, where if possible, a wedge could be driven in most profitably. Of one thing he was certain, it was not the miserable party bigwigs, Ribbentrop, Goering, Ley, corrupted as they were by their lust for the trappings of power, who were ruling the country, but Himmler's SS, who were perfectly capable of liquidating anyone who stood in their way – even Hitler, if they felt he had outlived his usefulness.

When Peter asked him did he not think that Ribbentrop's vanity had been responsible as much as anything for the outbreak of war, Langbehn could not agree. For him Hitler was the key figure, Hitler alone, and he leaned forward in his chair and emphasized what he had to say by tapping Peter on the knee. In his opinion Hitler was a lunatic, with none of the normal weaknesses; he was not vain nor interested in sex, neither a glutton nor a drunkard – no approach could be made to him. He was a lunatic, a cunning, dangerous, homicidal lunatic, with some strange but compelling mystique. It was he who still held the whole thing together. Get rid of him and all the others would be at one another's throats.

For some reason I found myself shivering. There was something taut and undisguisedly vital about the athletic figure sitting opposite us, something of the tiger about to spring. I could understand why his wife was often nervous. The colour of his blue eyes might have reassured Himmler, the expression in them at that moment should have made the Reichsführer shake in his black boots.

Suddenly Langbehn jumped to his feet and started pacing the room. 'God, Bielenberg, how I loathe the cynical, derisive contempt with which those bastards ride roughshod over the real and traditional civic rights of the people. We should never have studied law of course, but the distortion, the hypocrisy – "People's Court", "protective custody", "offence against the natural healthy instinct of the people",' he fairly spat out the words. 'What sort of legal terms are those? If the people knew what was being done in their name now, every day, they would never lift their heads again.'

Langbehn came to a stop in front of his wife and me. I did not know about his wife, but I at least was sitting on the edge of my chair as if turned temporarily to not very elegant marble. As he looked down at her his expression changed to a boyish, quite disarming, almost defenceless smile. 'My wife suspects that fundamentally I enjoy the game. She may be right in a way. Perhaps it has become a sort of challenge. One more innocent slipped through the net, one more notch chalked up for the rights of the individual.' He turned to Peter again and added, 'Don't forget though, Peter Bielenberg, that the game if it is one, is very dangerous indeed, not only for us but for our wives and families; that's where the devils have us by the short hairs, and time is running out. If something doesn't happen soon the horrors will close over our heads.'

Peter broke the silence to ask him whether he thought there would be war with Russia. Surely the Generals would not allow themselves to be dragged into that expedition? Langbehn agreed that he could hardly think so either, but from the way he said it I thought I detected an element of doubt in his mind. The Generals? They were of course supposedly the only hope, but their values were the old values, they lived in an era that had passed, they still wanted to consider themselves honourable gentlemen, and he, Langbehn, wondered sometimes if the Generals had any true conception of what they were up against. The SS had been born of National Socialism and was very much of today. The ambitious men who ruled the organization knew exactly what they wanted, and were ruthlessly dedicated to achieving their end which was nothing more nor less than supreme power within the state, and within any other state which fell victim to military conquest.

Peter and I did not feel like going straight home after our dinner party with our neighbours. The roads were dark and deserted and we could walk alone and talk alone – or could we? It seemed strange that after so many years of living with it, I was still unable to gauge the force of evil behind the outward form of National Socialism. In spite of all, life, as it had to be lived, could appear comparatively normal – people could fall in love, the dinner had to be cooked, the children – and then for a moment or two that evening the veil had been lifted on what lay behind, the faceless iniquitous core, man's stark craving to dominate, to wield arbitrary power over his fellow men. The thought left me rather breathless, and feeling young and inexperienced; inadequately armed with nothing much more than a conscience with which to fight such wickedness.

Peter sighed as we arrived back at our gate. 'Well,' he said, 'one thing's certain, if I were in a tight corner that's the sort of man I would like to have around.' I sighed too and found myself staring into the darkness about me. So many human beings, so many patchwork families, all living with their hopes and their fears in their little air-tight boxes, all more or less powerless; but it was good at least to know that our little kingdom had spread beyond its boundary hedges to include the borders of the home next door.

A DANGEROUS TEA PARTY

(Winter 1941)

My late arrival at the ladies' tea party was due to the fact that I first had to get rid of some rather unwelcome guests of my own, who arrived unexpectedly just as I was about to change. The National Socialist Air Defence League. Their visit would not have been so fruitless if our air-raid warden had not been a nice mild little man, very susceptible to a glass of sherry. At our last meeting, I had managed to persuade him, and had foolishly signed a paper to the effect that we had in our possession, or would have in the near future, every contrivance capable of protecting us from possible British bombs.

By July 1941 it had become clear that Goering's boast that he would call himself Meyer if one British bomber penetrated the Berlin air defences could prove an idle one. Rumour had it that the Party bosses had long since built deep shelters underneath their sumptuous villas. Then the order had gone out that ordinary mortals should at least reinforce their cellars, and build emergency exits. We had decided, as had most of our neighbours, that it was all an unnecessary expense. I alone had given the air-raid warden enough encouragement for him to turn up again with the officers of the Air Defence League. They surged into our little hallway: a phalanx of ladies in huge steel helmets and long grey mackintoshes. They shot out their right arms and almost Heil Hitlered me down the cellar stairs as our air-raid warden, somehow managing to ooze his way through the solid block of weather proofing, arrived up in front of me clutching a bundle of papers.

'I'm so sorry to disturb you, Frau Bielenberg,' he said, 'but may I introduce Mrs Colonel X, Mrs Captain Y, Mrs Captain Z, Mrs Lieutenant—' he waved a despondent arm in the direction of several other steel helmets who, for lack of space, had had to stay outside.

'These ladies are officers of the *Luftschutzverein* and they have come to inspect your air-raid defences. I see from my lists that your arrangements are as good as completed.' He shot me a despairing look and I guessed that ours was not the first house he had visited. I felt in duty bound to rally to his cause, so I replied that this was indeed the case, but that unfortunately my husband had the key to our cellar in the office. This brought the stern rejoinder from 'Mrs Colonel' that, in case of an air-raid, the office was not the place for the cellar key. Mrs Colonel, moreover, was not to be out-manoeuvred. She relieved the air-raid warden of his papers and, after flipping through them with a huge leather glove, she came to a stop at the sheet of paper on which I had so jauntily scrawled my name. She turned to her minions and announced that since they could not enter the cellar, she would therefore, with regret, have to confine her inspection to the back of the house, where she understood there to be an emergency exit.

As we moved in a body out into the garden, it was too much to hope that the hens would allow our appearance to go unnoticed. They were family friends after all and, whilst fulfilling their function, they could be sure of warm applause. Geraldine, I think it was, who pranced up the ladder out through the small hole in the cellar wall and greeted our arrival with an ecstatic crow. Why not? She'd laid an egg. The Air Defence League gaped at Geraldine in petrified silence and then retired. Before clanging the gate behind her, Mrs Colonel turned and glared at me from under her helmet. 'I understand you are English born,' she said, and when I nodded assent, 'Well . . .' she said no more, but turned on her heel and marched off, with her Captains and Lieutenants trailing behind her and with her huge mackintosh swirling and slapping about her boots. As I changed for the tea party I wondered what she had wanted to say. Surely nothing pleasant. Stew in your own juice, die under your own bomb. She had looked so fierce that I imagined her being quite disappointed if I failed to do so.

Gräfin B. did not live far away. She was a pretty, rather light-hearted young widow much concerned about her figure; as far as politics were concerned she was as safe as houses. Her parents owned a large country estate in Westphalia, which perhaps accounted for the presence of some of the more serious minded of her guests; they had come for the grub.

Gräfin B. should have known that if her invitation had been accepted by someone who was not politically reliable, it was her duty to warn her other guests, but in this case, she had either forgotten, or considered the lady in question to be well enough known to need no alarm signal.

I received my warning in the cloakroom, where I found myself together with a tall, blonde, very handsome woman, with a pair of large pale blue eyes. She was hanging up her Persian Lamb – which smelled delicately of the occupation of Paris – next to my 'German Forest' (as those garments were called which were made from synthetic fibre) which had cost me half my clothing coupons. I was not casting an envious eye on her coat though, for she had something far more interesting pinned to the collar. The National Socialist Mother's Cross in gold, if my eye did not deceive me. Mother's Crosses had been introduced soon after the outbreak of war, in bronze, in silver and in gold. The more the children, the more glamorous the Cross, but to the credit of my sex they were seldom worn in public, except by those who considered child-bearing to be a service to the State.

'Von something or other,' murmured Persian Lamb, introducing herself as we moved into the drawing-room together. 'Christabel Bielenberg,' I replied, having a quick look around the room to see if there was not an empty chair as far away from her as possible. I also glanced at Gräfin B. in order to catch her signal, but she was far too occupied handing round plates. We pumped hands all round, as was the custom, and by the time Gräfin B. had introduced my companion to whoever did not know her, there were only three adjacent chairs still unoccupied. So there was no escaping having her as my neighbour.

I never found ladies' tea parties even in peace time a cause for much elation. Listening to German women discussing their husbands seldom failed to give me the feeling that some of them felt they were married to inmates of lunatic asylums. Since the war the conversational cycle had been extended to include food – food, via husbands, back to food. Today was no exception, except perhaps that owing to the presence of Persian Lamb the conversation seemed to limp along rather more falteringly than usual, and even the excellent coffee seemed unable to have its usual effect. We were discussing the heavenly pre-war breakfasts provided by the Basle station restaurant, for the second time – those crisp rolls, that black cherry jam, when my neighbour turned her glacier eyes on me, 'You ski, Frau Bielenberg?' 'A little,' I answered, which was already an exaggeration.

'To me, all skiing resorts before the war were ruined by the presence of the English,' she announced, with a curious lilt in her voice which made me wonder whether she was German.

'Oh,' I said. 'Why?'

'I was disgusted by the behaviour of the English women, who seemed to go there for nothing better than to throw themselves at the feet of the handsome ski teachers. I think it was then that I realized just what a degenerate race the British are.'

I glanced across the table to meet the quiet eye of a good friend sitting opposite me.

'Oh,' I said vaguely, 'how interesting, how very interesting.' The next moment the door was flung open and Mary Wussow breezed in. Dear Mary, she was in the best of form, as British as the flag. 'Guten Tag,' she drawled vaguely in all directions, pronouncing the last word as if it were a luggage label and forgetting to shake hands with anyone. Then noticing me, 'Hallo, Chris darling, how are you?' We might have been back in Belgrave Square. 'Well, Mary dear, thank you,' I replied smelling danger somewhere and not knowing for the moment what to do about it. 'You know my neighbour?' 'No,' said Mary, in her best German, 'how do you do?' Persian Lamb shot out her hand and then turned to me. 'You are English?' 'No,' I said, hoping that Mary would take the hint. 'No, I am German now, actually about as German as you are.' It was a shot in the dark, but I thought for a moment that I had discovered where that lilting accent came from; Norway it must be, or perhaps Sweden. Mary sat herself down on the far side of my neighbour and leaned across to me.

'I'm feeling on top of the world, Chris, we've had some wonderful news,' she announced.

'Really,' I said, 'I'm so glad,' and as Persian Lamb had her head turned away from me, and was looking at Mary, I made a face which tried to convey 'For God's sake shut up, she's a Nazi!' I cannot have been very successful, because Mary threw me back an amazed look, as if I had suddenly developed St Vitus' dance.

Meanwhile all the other ladies had rallied to the cause; it was as if the coffee had taken sudden effect. They chatted and laughed and tried to draw Mary away from her neighbour's attentions. But it was useless, for Persian Lamb was on the war path and I heard the words Foreign Office, degenerate ski teachers and more beside. With sinking heart, I had to watch Mary rise to the bait and sail into her, her German becoming more and more dilapidated, shooting, as the saying goes, out of every button hole. The climax was reached when Mary declared in ringing tones that there was not a damn bit of difference between Hitler and Stalin, they were both dictators and only kept themselves in power by terror, and she for one was glad that Stalin was not an ally of the British. There was a deathly silence and then I think Mary suddenly realized what she had done. She shot me a startled look, but it was too late – Persian Lamb had risen to her feet, bowed stiffly all round and was making for the door. Our hostess fluttered out after her. I got up too and met them in the cloakroom.

'We go the same way home,' I said, 'didn't you say you lived in Dahlem too?' I had no idea what I hoped to achieve and she was silent as we pegged along the darkening streets, then: 'Did I understand that woman's name was von Wussow?' 'Yes' – 'And her husband is in the Foreign Office?' 'Yes, indeed' – 'And they are going to be posted abroad? I have never heard of such a thing.' 'Why?' – I felt I was fighting a lost cause, but I had to carry on somehow. 'I don't see anything wrong in that. Her husband is an excellent person and will do a very good job indeed; as for his wife Mary, I know her very well, she's just hot-headed; and anyway, I wonder what you would do if someone made disparaging remarks about your country?' – I still wasn't sure if it was Sweden or Norway.

'Frau Bielenberg,' she said, her mincing lilt more pronounced than ever, 'I still do not think that we should have people like that in our foreign service, and I intend to draw the proper conclusions.'

She must have drawn her conclusions as soon as she got home, and she was in a position to do so, as I learned when I got back with my warning to the not yet abandoned tea party. The family was notorious; her husband's brother – hadn't I known? Hadn't Mary known? – was Hitler's lawyer. His were the little blond children who had been trained to lisp 'Heil Hitler', and present their Leader every year with little posies of wild flowers on his birthday.

When Mary came to see us on the following day she was distraught; her telephone was being tapped and her husband had been requested to stay away from the Foreign Office pending investigations.

How was it then that some months later Botho and Mary left for Portugal? Their safe departure was the result of a natural process, when men and women of goodwill move in to protect a friend against a common enemy – in their case, perhaps the most dangerous, the most iniquitous enemy of all, the common informer. Nothing could seem more natural then than for eight respectable ladies to commit perjury most willingly and to swear that the fatal words complained of were just not spoken. An argument, yes, two foreigners, unable to speak much German, getting in each other's hair, as women sometimes can. But Hitler? Stalin? Impossible! Had such dire remarks been made, no one present had heard them. Persian Lamb had no witnesses.

A HOSPITAL IN BAD AUSSEE

Part I: (Summer 1941)

If I were looking for an exhilarating experience, I would not choose that of lying in bed recovering from the after-effects of a miscarriage. It is not to be recommended in any place or at any time. Should the place happen to be a small country hospital in Austria, and the time, mid-summer 1941, when German armies were pouring across the eastern borders of the Reich into Russia, and if, for good measure, one's only kith and kin within hundreds of miles were two small boys, who had perforce been left behind in a mountain village in the care of a stranger – friendly enough but none the less a stranger – then, as I discovered to my cost, the time had come to call on whatever reserves I might find at my disposal.

I had always thought that I possessed some capacity for looking on the bright side, but this time I found that my usual optimism, when put to the test, could not be relied upon, since I was firmly convinced that those two little boys were the only healthy children I would ever be able to produce.

There were five of us, in all, in that hospital ward: five melancholy mothers-that-might-have-been, two of whom had been there for a very long time indeed. We were not allowed to forget the place, for every so often pink-faced nuns, whose aprons were only clean on Sundays, bustled cheerfully in and out dispensing pills, potions, or God's blessings, whichever remedy they considered most appropriate to the state of our health. We were not allowed to forget the time either, for every fifteen minutes or so a wireless loudspeaker, which was fixed above the door beside a dusty crucifix, burst into hysterical fanfares of trumpets. Ta, tara ta, tara ta, tara ta, tara taaaa! *Achtung! Achtung! Eine Sondermeldung* – a special announcement. Bialystok – Przemysl – Tarnopol –

strange outlandish names, dots on the map until a week before, exploded regularly about our ears, and hung for a second or two on the sultry air before being swept aside, forgotten, obliterated, overrun – *planmässig*, according to plan. We had no map and so could only gather from the supremely satisfied voice of the announcer that once again Hitler's legions were digging daily deeper into enemy territory. I did not notice any sign of elation, any reaction at all in fact on the part of my fellow patients to the noisy hurrahs. Three peasant girls, the wife of a grocer from Bad Aussee and myself, we just lay there quietly, lost in long thoughts of the might-have-been, and our regulation cotton nightdresses, worn back to front and tied with a bow at the nape of our necks, made us look like so many woe-begone dentists' assistants.

Nearly nine months had elapsed since the children and I had left Berlin for the Salzkammergut. This we had done for several reasons, the most pressing perhaps being the advent of British bombers which, towards the end of August, had extended their activities to include Berlin. Since Berliners were looked upon by the rest of Germany as a very cocky lot, who would come to no harm if taken down a peg or two, the RAF were accompanied on their nightly visits by a certain amount of *Schadenfreude* directed at the capital city by the Rhinelanders, and also the citizens of Hamburg, who had suffered under the RAF's attentions for some time.

It had been little use pretending that the British accounts of those raids, recited for us the following day in the smooth unruffled tones of Radio Beromünster – 'Strong forces of RAF bombers attacked selected military targets in the Berlin area, light installations, aero engine factories etc.' – were nearer to the truth than the German reports, which recorded the targets hit as being exclusively morgues, churches or children's hospitals. The damage actually caused, according to market hearsay, had proved barely exciting enough to justify the bus fare for a family outing of a Sunday afternoon, but the significance of the raids lay in the indisputable fact that, night after night, those 'air pirates' gave the lie to the official word that the war was as good as won. Happy as I might have been at such a propitious turn of events, at the same time it was no use my pretending that I had not been scared stiff when, night after night just about bedtime, the haunting wail of the sirens sent me hustling upstairs for the children and downstairs again to the cellar, where for several hours, whilst

Peter slept peacefully on the floor, I would sit enveloped in a rug, trying to amuse the children amongst the buckets, the dish-cloths soaked in water, the stirrup pumps and the hens.

We would crouch there in silence, and I had time to reflect that I ought to be happy that my countryfolk were showing such initiative. My school friend Monica Jordan's husband – who could tell? – might be up there soon, wondering which moment would be the most appropriate for him to drop his load of bombs. Every hour or so distant rumblings would warn us that another handful of high flying aircraft was approaching the outer ring of Berlin's air defences, and I would bestir myself and start away again on my fairy story. By the time the second ring of anti-aircraft guns had opened up, and the rumblings had become thunderings, I had found it most difficult to concentrate on my theme, 'and so the dear little fairy said to the little elf – er – the dear little fairy—' this, or something similar, intoned in a hoarse, fairly well-controlled whisper, had been, as often as not, the prelude to shattering roars, belched forth by the huge anti-aircraft guns which had been placed in the Domäne Dahlem, about one hundred yards from our house. It had not been surprising really that Nicky had condemned the fairy-elf combination out of hand, as being a rotten story and, after a dozen or so such nights I had looked in the mirror one morning and decided I had better get my photograph taken before it was too late.

Our decision to accept Edward Brücklmeier's invitation to go as paying guests to his farm in Austria, where his wife and baby were in imminent danger of being swamped by refugees from the Ruhr, coincided with the end of Peter's career as a civil servant. Peter had come to his decision to leave the Civil Service and to launch into industry with his usual clear-cut reasoning. After the defeat of France he had ceased to believe that the Generals would attempt to overthrow the Government. Since they had found themselves unable to do so before, they would hardly be likely to consider doing so afterwards, when the political climate as a whole was no longer attuned to such a *démarche*. He believed that the war was going to last a long time, and that it would ultimately be lost; it was being fought for a cause that he did not believe in. Although he would never be able to bring himself actively to sabotage Germany's war effort, he would stay out of taking active part in the shooting war for as long as possible. He was conscious

104

that there were certain ambiguities attached to his reasoning, but he was prepared to accept them as being inherent in what appeared to him to be an otherwise insoluble situation.

As I lay in that stuffy little ward in Bad Aussee, staring out of the window, trying to isolate myself from the clatter of victory coming from above the door, and the heavy aura of defeat which hung over the hospital beds around me, I thought that I was beginning to understand, for the first time, something of the irrevocable finality which Hitler's victory over France had brought to the hopes of those who had believed that his régime could be brought to an end from within. Until then it had been possible to imagine that fate could be side-stepped, could even be bent to one's will if you believed in the certain triumph of good over evil – which I just did, since I happened to belong to a generation which had been taught to believe in God.

Adam had been right of course – if I had not seen it clearly at the time at least I did so now – when, at risk of being dubbed an appeaser, he had pleaded for a postponement of war and then again, after war had broken out, had tried to find a possible formula for bringing hostilities to an early end. He had not been the only one; just the one we knew best. Peter had been right, all the others had been right who had joined forces with him on his vain crusade; for I had learned that war had brought with it much horror but also heroism; jingoism but also true patriotism; war in fact had blurred the issue completely.

I had time to ponder on my own patriotism, no longer so straightforward an emotion as it might have been ten years back, but all the same simplicity itself compared to the labyrinthine heart-searchings required of any German patriot who tried to hold the delicate balance between opposition, compromise and corruption. In a régime such as Hitler's, there could be no standing on the sidelines, but there were also no rules to the game; each to his own conscience, that silver thread which must run through people's lives, ruling how far they should go and no further.

Ta, tara ta! Where were they now, those all-conquering legions? Grodno, Rowno, knocking at the gates of a place called Lemberg. It seemed strange that we had known that this war with Russia would come, way back in September of last year, when orders had come through to Peter's department in the Ministry of Economics that priority was to be given to the building of tanks;

not to aeroplanes or landing craft but to tanks. I had wished at the time that I could flash the news across the English Channel, to where church bells were silent and signposts had been uprooted, where ordinary folk must be going to bed wondering what the morrow might bring. 'Sleep on, friends,' I wanted to tell them, 'you've been through the worst, the morrow will bring nothing and soon you'll have allies. Tanks, we're building tanks, you see, Herr Hitler is preparing for a land war, it will be a long war they say, war, you understand, with Russia.'

The sky outside my window turned from deepest blue to sultry orange – a thunderstorm perhaps, it was certainly very hot. It occurred to me that I might have a temperature, a *kleine Sepsis*, a little septicemia, which the doctor had mentioned might be afflicting my fellow patients.

What was it I had been thinking about? Peter's resigning from the Civil Service – his new job. I had to admit to having greeted it with some relief. Although I had learned to live on £30 a month, I had lost sight of whatever virtue might have been attached to doing so when the reason for doing so had gone. I had to leave Berlin and when I heard that Peter's new assignment might mean his being stationed in the north of Norway, where his firm, a subsidiary company of Unilever, was planning to build a fish-meal factory, at least I could be happy that he was not yet in the Army and that we would not be going to Austria as paying guests who could not pay.

The journey to the mountains had had an electric effect on what I had thought to be the children's bronchitis. I had hardly sat down to supper with my hostess, cheerful almost in the contemplation of an undisturbed night's sleep to follow, when an ominous whoop from the children's room upstairs betrayed the true nature of their coughs. Amschi, Edward's wife, had a baby under a year old, an only child; it was clearly too much to expect her to welcome two whooping children. I had known that I would have to go somewhere else, and the following day we took to the roads.

Grundlsee we found to be a humble enough village in Styria. It straggled along the shores of a deep and very beautiful lake, with the snow-covered Totesgebirge guarding the valley's outlet to the east. I had heard that the area, in more splendid days of Empire, had been reserved by the Austrian Court as a shooting estate, and as I wandered in search of accommodation I found it easy enough to believe, from the display of Hapsburg noses, that this had been the case.

The news of my arrival with offspring and with bugs had spread through the village ahead of us like a prairie fire. Our accents, our whoops, betrayed us at every door. Whooping cough? *Whooping cough?* Those savages from Berlin, just the sort of thing a Prussian would inflict on a laughter-loving cousin from the South. Everyone was apologetic, everyone was polite, as was the custom in Austria, but no one had a room free and if they had – *'s'regrettable, Gnädigste'*, they also had children in the house who had not had the disease. I had to be grateful, therefore, when a childless middle-aged couple took pity on us and agreed to give us a room in their chalet way up on the hill above the village. True, they had the reputation of still having some enthusiasm left for the *Anschluss*, but I could not afford to be choosy.

I must admit that in the year of grace 1941, having lived for many years in Nazi Germany, I no longer shared my countrymen's lyrical exuberance where Austrians, or, for that matter, Bavarians were concerned. I no longer entertained a belief that they were more civilized or less vulnerable to the onslaughts of Nazi ideology than were those bogeymen, the Prussians. They were more attractive perhaps, but the fact that they wore flowers in their hats did not alter, for me anyway, the undeniable truth that Munich was the *Hauptstadt der Bewegung*,* that Hitler was an Austrian and that he had recruited some of his foulest minions from amongst the *Küss die Hand*, coffee-sipping, beer-swilling yodellers from the South.

I had even begun to wonder whether, in order to discover truly reliable opponents of National Socialism, I would not have felt more at home in Prussia, alongside a Prussian conscience, rather than with the easy-going, equivocal, God-will-forgive-us Austrian variety. Perhaps being more than half Irish, I knew instinctively how to evaluate charm. Perhaps I suspected that the Austrians were already busy cooking up a convenient little legend that the *Anschluss* with Germany had not been the popular realization of a greater German dream, but on the contrary something which had been forced upon them against their will, which I knew for a fact had not been the case. I reflected that back in 1933 the Germans might not have quite realized what they were in for when 30 per

*Hauptstadt der Bewegung – capital city of the movement.

cent of the electorate voted for Hitler. In 1938 the Austrians had known very well indeed, when more than 98 per cent of them did likewise. Intimidation? I'd heard all about that; 98 per cent was still a tidy figure.

Enough though; perhaps it was the whooping cough and the consequent weeks of isolation which had given me time to think and made me cast such an angry eye on the Austrian carousel. For I had to wait until every child with whom my sons had been in contact recovered from the whooping cough before my neighbours ceased to suspect that I had done it on purpose. I had time to discover, too, that my hosts, who did not deny that they built their hopes on Hitler, were fundamentally just ordinary hard-working people, whose only transgression as far as the village was concerned had sprung from a certain honesty of purpose. Contrary to most Catholics, who were turning moral somersaults trying to have things both ways, they had found themselves unable to serve two masters and had resigned from the Church. It appeared that they were *Deutsche Christen*, German Christians, members of a neo-pagan sect dreamed up by one of the more screwy of Hitler's racial theorists. But since they were also the only adults to come my way for several weeks, I had been most willing some evenings to hear all about their conversion. But I soon had my suspicions that my host found himself equally at sea with his newly adopted religion as he had been with the one he had discarded. It was just a pity that he had had the misfortune to select one which had behind it the impetus of a world power, for he was certainly no demon, had no dreams of world conquest, and incidentally confessed that he had never met a Jew in his life.

His wife too was a kindly soul, never without a rather furrowed brow. She liked my children so I, of course, liked her. I reflected that it would have been so much easier to respect their independent attitude had their house not been so very small and had the living room, the only heated room in the house, not contained the wireless. No more listening with my ear right up against it, no more risking my neck for a short spell of sanity, however complacent, from neutral Switzerland. If I wanted to keep warm, I could take the full treatment, day after day, evening after evening. A gentleman called Dr Hans Fritzsche, the 'intellectual' of the Propaganda machine, patterned his daily homily on Lord Haw Haw, and drawled of England fighting to the last Frenchman. Or worse even, a cosy, folksy little programme depicting a get-together around the Yuletide candle: 'Dear German mothers, come gather round. Yuletide is at the door and we must think of our little ones, but also of course of our purses. Above all, we must think, though, of our Leader, who has dedicated his life to our future and who calls on our spirit of self-sacrifice. Let us think now, dear mothers, let us help you with your choice of a Yuletide gift which will bring a sparkle into the loving eyes of your family and, at the same time, save as many of those precious raw materials so needed by our Leader for the fulfilment of his great task. What about an *Ahnenpass* – a certificate of Aryan ancestry – bound in leather, a splendid gift of lasting value, and, for the little ones, a school satchel for instance, made by mother's loving hand out of her old mackintosh?'

Get soaked to the skin, mother dear, it's all for the good of the cause!

Perhaps it was not surprising, when Peter's letter arrived one morning bringing with it the hardly to be credited news that he had made arrangements for me to visit him in the north of Norway, that my initial reaction was one of undiluted excitement. He assured me that all plans had been made and that he had persuaded a 'very reliable' friend to take on the children for three weeks. But just before leaving I had qualms. A long train journey to Berlin and on to Oslo, an aeroplane from Oslo to Trondheim, and a sea-plane from there to Bodö, suddenly seemed to me to be a very long journey indeed; much too far to be going away from the children. The friend considered to be 'completely reliable', whoever she was, might prove to be exactly the opposite. What about my pious blatherings about a silver thread? Soon I was well on the way to succumbing to quite a respectable bout of guilt-ridden panic, which I only just succeeded in smothering with a tremendous show of joyous anticipation.

Part II: (Summer 1941)

In Berlin the prospect brightened considerably. I found that my journey northwards had been planned carefully enough. I was to travel with Lexi, the wife of Peter's new boss. Lexi was to travel officially as an interior decorator, journeying to Bodö in the north of Norway in order to inspect some new log houses which were being built for the executives there. My rôle, I blush to record, was to be that of adviser on domestic matters. We had been passed by security. Colonel Oster had had his finger in that pie and we did not enquire too closely how he had managed it. He had murmured, with a twinkle in his eye, something about the importance of keeping up the morale of those working in the winter darkness of the far north, and had added that we just had to remember that the place was stiff with Gestapo and otherwise enjoy ourselves.

I had met Lexi once or twice before and had been glad to discover that she seemed a little unconventional. Her flat in the Budapesterstrasse had been partly converted into an office, and on my first visit to pay my respects I found her looking extremely elegant, lying in bed, armed with a toy gun. A board meeting was taking place in the drawing-room next door and she had her gun trained on the connecting door. Should her husband or a member of the Board, for that matter, venture through the doorway, she assured me they would get a rubber pellet between the eyes. She soon admitted to being very bored most of the time, and I was unable to discover whether she took anything or anyone very seriously. She often had an amused glint in her rather sleepy blue eyes. 'My dear, they are all quite impossible,' was her measured opinion of our rulers, and this delivered in a slow, rather world-weary drawl, had suggested the possibility of our becoming good friends. Her husband, on the other hand, I imagined to be a fairly energetic go-getter. On our journey northwards he seemed incapable of separating himself from a bulging briefcase, and, oblivious to the rattling of the train, the bumping about of the aeroplane, or the magnificence of the landscape beneath us, he managed to jot down so many notes, so many business letters in embryo, that I found myself pitying whoever might be his secretary.

Off then to Norway, which the British had had to leave to its fate exactly one year before; where, according to hearsay, beautiful girls, conspicuous for their glorious heads of hair, strode the streets like goddesses, some of them at least having solved the tedious problem of occupation, and the seeming diffidence of their stolid Viking menfolk, by taking a more virile German to their Nordic bosoms. Hearsay of course, but enough to cause much heartache to many a virtuous *Hausfrau* who, left behind in the Fatherland hanging out her flag, whipping up her *Streckbutter** or struggling with her *Sparrezepte†* had not taken too kindly to being asked to accept a fox fur or a tin of herrings as *Ersatz* for an errant husband. In Oslo it soon became clear that danger, if any, would come from my friends rather than from my foes. 'May I introduce Mrs Bielenberg – she's English.' Our host Lyder Sagen, who was working for Unilever, had been quite frank as to which side he belonged, and his wife could not be dissuaded from treating me as if I were some sort of showpiece. At the hairdresser's my cubicle soon filled with assistants, eager to brush up their English. They were soon joined by their clients who, unconcerned at the interruption in their efforts to be beauteous, surged in alongside, only too eager to meet me and shake me by the hand. They chattered like happy starlings above the hum of the driers. 'Mrs Bielenberg, you must tell us what it is like in Germany. It must be horrible; here too, horrible! Quisling, Gott oh Gott! Our King he is gone but he will be back, that will be a great day for Norway.' They took my reticent replies in their stride; I spoke English, that was enough. In a restaurant known to the Sagens the headwaiter persuaded me with urgent signs to lift my plate, and then stood back and watched my amazement from a distance, with a benevolent smile. A minute copy of *The Times*, the London *Times*. 'You will need a magnifying glass, Mrs Bielenberg, magnificent, isn't it?' he murmured as he served me with vegetables. 'Only five days old as you will see. Submarine to fishing boat. *Tak, Tak*, Mrs Bielenberg. It is a pleasure, Mrs Bielenberg.'

What could I do? Smile back of course, put it hastily into my handbag, note from the nods and smiles from the neighbouring tables that the headwaiter and I were not alone with our secret, and hope that amongst those smiling blue eyes there was not one pair whose owner might be waiting to slip away and whisper his message into ears which would find the incident very interesting indeed, and not in the least touching. Oster had warned us that Norway was stiff with Gestapo, and it was certainly unnerving to find myself surrounded by such charming, but alarmingly innocent allies.

By the time our little seaplane bounced down on the Saltfjord and a rearing dinghy landed us in Bodö, Lexi's husband had made

---

*Streckbutter – stretch butter.
†*Sparrezepte* – economy recipes.

enough notes to fill a suitcase, his wife had discarded her booklets on interior decorating and was relaxed and enjoying herself, and I knew that I, too, was rapidly shedding something of the almost claustrophobic caginess which had become a natural part of day-to-day living in the Third Reich. We had flown at no great height beside massive snow-covered mountain ranges, which belched their mighty glaciers into the sparkling sea beneath us. Islands too, there were hundreds of tiny islands, some of them just able to support a patch of green, a tiny white house, and shelter a fishing boat anchored in a rockbound cove. Before leaving Germany I had begun to wonder if there was any place on earth which could escape the tentacles of an ever-spreading evil. It needed those little islands, solitary, remote, blessedly uncompromised, to convince me that I need not have worried.

I found that Bodö itself had not been able to escape involvement. A year before, with some help from the British, it had put up stout resistance to what Herr Goebbels described as being 'saved'; after which it had not taken the Luftwaffe too long to reduce many of its toy-box houses to smoking rubble. It would never have been an imposing township; in fact, compared to the hither and thither on the blue-green waters of the fjord, to the bustle and jostle aboard the sturdy fishing trawlers which nudged each other in their hundreds up against the harbour walls, the town had the air almost of an after-thought. It was early in May and the sun hardly set when I arrived in Bodö. On land, a man could paint his gate at most hours of the night, and football matches could take place at four o'clock in the morning. It was obvious, though, that it was on the sea and on the rich harvests of the Lofoten fishing grounds that the tough leather-faced inhabitants relied for their livelihood. Fish for breakfast, fish for lunch, fish for supper, and if you were in doubt as to what would be their diet in winter, the all pervading smell of clippfish drying on the rocks under a pale cool sun provided the answer.

It was the sea too, no doubt, which had given the fisherfolk their independence of spirit and encouraged them to be some-what fickle employees. For days on end they would work with a will, gutting, cleaning and filleting the fish which poured into Peter's factory across the fjord – then suddenly they would be gone, the harbour deserted. The factory, the cargo boats sent to carry the supplies away, could wait for days, for weeks, perhaps even for months, just so long in fact as the money the fishermen had earned lasted, and the sea remained kindly enough disposed for them to go about their own business out there on their solitary islands. I had been able to sense enchantment, to feel somehow released and free in that clear translucent northern lightness, and I knew, too, that Peter did not need much boosting of morale. He was dealing with a concrete problem, an allotted task, something he could get his teeth into, as far away as possible from evasion and subterfuge.

It was just that independent spirit of the Norwegians and, also, I suppose my nationality again which forced me to decide that I could not stay long in Bodö. I thought I had been careful enough to avoid any friendly glance which might come my way in the dining-room of our little hotel, where one table as often as not was occupied by Gestapo officials, but a visit to the chemist convinced me that I had not been too successful.

'Would you like a cup of real coffee, Mrs Bielenberg?' the lady behind the counter smiled at me shyly and I realized that she was speaking very good English. She opened the door behind her and was ushering me into her parlour before I really had time to decide if I should accept her invitation. 'My sister,' she explained, introducing me to another pleasant-faced middle-aged lady, and then noticing my quick glance behind, she had added, 'Do not worry, we can see who comes into the shop in that mirror on the wall.'

I did not know why it was they told me the things they did, those two gentle-faced women, just like that – over the coffee cups. I did not want to be burdened with more secrets, I had really just wanted to kid myself that I was free. But they insisted on telling me how they had nursed an English officer back to health in a mountain hut above Bodö, and he had left some weeks back, by fishing boat, oh yes, and then by submarine. My husband, he was known to be all right, 'one of us', but he must beware of course, danger did not come only from the Gestapo, there were also Norwegians – one of his engineers in fact. Another, though – Gülbrandsson, he was very all right indeed, only he was in danger, for should some act of sabotage take place, he was next on the list of hostages; he might have to leave suddenly and make his way to Sweden. And now that they had told me enough to show that I could trust them would I not tell them just what it was like in Germany? Was there no opposition, no hope that someone would get up soon and kill that monster?

I did not enjoy being such an obvious disappointment as I faced them over the coffee cups and provided them with trivial scraps of information, which could have been of no comfort to them whatsoever. There was nothing much that I could say except to beg them please to be careful, to accept their resigned shrug of the shoulder, to allow myself to be led out of the backdoor of their house where no windows watched, and to hope that they knew, instinctively, that I was one of them.

Bodö gave me its own kind of send-off before I boarded my little seaplane and flew back southwards. On the day before I left, Peter and I went for a drive over the roughest of tracks along the coast to the north of the town. We stood together on the rocks high above the swirling sea, with our backs to the snow-covered mountains. The air was filled with the sound of rushing waterfalls, splashing down into the foam below us. We might have come to the cold, clear, echoing end of the world, to a point beyond which no man should venture if he valued his identity. Quite suddenly, from somewhere high up on the snow-streaked mountainside, we heard a cuckoo call and call again; we could not tell if it was an echo or an answer. It was hard to believe that a mate had been found up there in those echoing arctic wastelands.

Why was it that such a homely inconsequent song came back to me so clearly as I lay in that hospital bed, staring out at a group of pine trees rigid and colourless in the hazy midday heat? I was very unhappy, and maybe I was thinking of somewhere so different, where trees did not have to crowd together in orderly groups, planted for profit, waiting for the woodman's axe, but could grow, and spread their branches as they wished, out and alone in the middle of rolling green fields; and the day would be warm and pregnant with spring, back there, back home, when there had been no war.

It was lucky that I did not hear until I reached Berlin that Peter's factory had been burned to the ground three days after I left, and that Peter was struggling to prove, for Gülbrandsson's sake, that although it had happened on the anniversary of the bombing of Bodö, it could not have been caused by sabotage. If I had, I would most certainly not have gone my devious ways and pursued a plan which, when studied with some care, and with the help of the Sagens, I found so hare-brained as to be quite irresistible. I discovered that I could fly from Oslo to Berlin, or that I could travel by comfortable non-stop sleeper through Sweden to Berlin;

but I discovered also that I could travel through Sweden, less comfortably, by day, on a train which stopped at every station between Oslo and Trelleborg. This could only mean that it would also stop at Trollhättan, a country town some fourteen miles from Koberg Castle, the home of my good friend Elsa von Rosen *née* Silfverschiöld. Elsa and I had been at school together in Paris, and before the War I had spent many a happy holiday in Sweden. Since her husband was now Sweden's Military Attaché in London, with luck, Elsa might be staying in Koberg with her parents.

I could not resist that train, and as the border guards did not seem to consider my uncomfortable choice unusual, and as once in Sweden we stopped and started, and passengers obviously came and went as freely as could be, I decided that I would chance my luck in Trollhättan. Fortunately I lost my nerve. The platform was crowded with Swedish soldiers drawn up as if on parade, an army band was shuffling itself into position, and I was forced to decide that my credentials might not survive a reception committee of that variety. Gothenburg then, it had to be Gothenburg. Arrived there I drew a deep breath, and suddenly it all seemed so easy. I left my suitcase on the rack and my gloves on the seat, I opened the carriage door, stepped out on to the platform, and mixed with the jostling crowds. I waited beside a newspaper stand until I heard my train give a warning squawk before it moved off smoothly on its allotted journey, minus one of its passengers. I made a little gesture by hustling back to the empty platform and staring in consternation down the tracks. Then I asked an official, in piercing German, what I should do, and noted with much pleasure, from his rude reply, that he was utterly disinterested in my plight.

So far so good. So good in fact that I was a little uncertain how to proceed. I found myself strolling along the lighted streets, goggling into the glowing shop windows, staring at the happy carefree couples, wondering why everyone looked so different, so young, so – somehow abnormal, until I realized with a sudden pang that of course they were normal enough: they were happy and carefree too, and young, and they were not in uniform.

What next? I had no money, not even enough for a telephone call; but I had not quite run out of ideas. I was finding it incredibly easy to adjust, to forget the years between, and to allow the mythical barriers to fall apart. Gothenburg was no mirage but a town that I knew very well. Those were familiar streets and just around the corner was a hotel where Elsa and I had often dumped our parcels. Her father always had a room there, I would not have been surprised if his tall spare figure had greeted me in the foyer – '*Goddag goddag*, Chrees,' 'A little drop in the morning. When you get to London you get a smell of coal smoke' – his English repertoire, he loved airing it. I got a surprise though when the Concierge came towards me, a little puzzled at first, but his expression soon changing to a radiant smile. 'Good evening, Mrs Bielenberg, welcome to Gothenburg,' he said and, when I had given him the satisfaction of looking completely flabbergasted, he added promptly, 'I pride myself on never forgetting a name. You have come to stay? Shall I not telephone with Baron Silfverschiöld, he is in Koberg, oh yes and the Countess von Rosen is staying there at present also' – he could not stop showing off. No, no, not telephone – oh yes I supposed he could, I was in Sweden of course, I had almost forgotten.

From then on a guardian angel took over. A joyous telephone call and Elsa arrived an hour or so later, aboard a motor car powered by something which looked like a huge domestic boiler. She brought the news that her father had alerted the Foreign Office and was trying to get permission for me to stay in Koberg for a few days. It was a weekend, as yet he had not been able to get hold of the required Minister. He had great hopes though.

Elsa's father did not manage to contact his Minister, and although I sent a telegram to England I did not get a reply. Fairy stories cannot go right all along the line and I had known in my heart of hearts that I must not miss another train.

My little suitcase awaited me patiently at the customs shed in Trelleborg, with my gloves neatly tucked through its handle. No one seemed to suspect that it could belong to a possible Mata Hari, nor did anyone seem interested enough to listen to my well-prepared speech about how I had got off the train, hurried to get a newspaper, returned to find the train gone and, oh dear, how worried I had been and, oh dear, how good it was to be back home again on German soil; I could have kept that information to myself. The official who stamped my passport looked half asleep, and did so without so much as a glance at the date of my entry visa into Sweden. Another gentleman who was dozing peacefully beneath a wooden archway trimmed with drooping laurel leaves and bearing the proud slogan 'Willkommen im Grossdeutschen Reich' bestirred himself sufficiently to hand me a small envelope containing ration cards. I was back in Greater Germany again and the electric bulbs were dimmed in the railway carriage, and no gay lights shone out at me from the houses beside the tracks; the darkness everywhere was so deep that I might have been travelling through a long, long tunnel.

I had to pay of course when I arrived back to find that the 'reliable' friend had remained that way until a handsome naval officer had turned up on leave and whisked her off to more exciting haunts than Grundlsee; to find, too, that my children had been neglected and showed signs of having lost confidence in my capacity to provide them with a sense of security; and I knew that I never, never, should have gone so far away. I had to pay too when, strapped to a rusty stretcher I was pushed like a loaf on a tray into a rickety ambulance, and the roar of an antique engine drowned John's plaintive cry, 'Mummy, Mummy, come back please – please.'

I wished it was not so dreadfully hot, I wished they would stop those infernal fanfares, I wished – I wished I could make head or tail of what a fat little nun was twittering about as she patted my cushions and smoothed my bedclothes. 'Mother of God, he's so good looking – come, wake up, Frau Dr, wake up – your husband—'

I do not remember what Peter said as he stood there in his old fishing jersey, looking as if he had just stepped off the fjord. Something about having come as quickly as he could – the company car – he'd driven south non-stop and left the remains of it, devoid of tyres, on the airport in Oslo. I do not remember what it was exactly that I managed to answer. Something about its name, which was to be Anna, or perhaps Stefan, something about Bialystok and the silver thread which must run through people's lives. Something a little incoherent, no doubt, because Peter smiled suddenly and looked at me most gently and, taking my hand in his, he said, 'Now look, darling, I don't know what the hell you are talking about. My mother is downstairs, she is going to take over the children. You're the silver thread in my life if you want to know and I'm going to see you get out of this bloody place as soon as possible.'

A JEW STORY

(Winter 1942–1943)

It happened early in 1943, just after the fall of Stalingrad, when day after day, for page after page, the newspapers were chequered with little black crosses, each one recording the death of a soldier; when the widows and the mothers were being issued with special clothing coupons, which allowed them to purchase their mourning, and when Goering assured us over the radio with a suitable catch in his voice that, in spite of all, ultimate victory had been signed and sealed on the Volga. A thousand years hence Germans would speak of that battle with reverence and awe, he declaimed, and, a few days later he celebrated his 50th birthday by throwing a party of such magnificence that a solid gold diamond-studded reading lamp presented to him by a tobacco tycoon failed to compete with the splendour of the other gifts.

The actual date is immaterial. Enough that it happened a full year after Hitler had decreed that all the Jews still living in Germany must wear the Star of David, inscribed with the word Jew, sewn on to the lapel of their coats, and before the SS decided to present their Leader with the most acceptable birthday present of all time – a Germany that was *judenrein*, free, purified of Jews. 'Submarines' they were called, those Jews who at that time removed their stars and went underground, surfacing here, there, or anywhere, where they might hope to find refuge. They had no ration cards and, every week, Ilse Liedke went the rounds of her friends collecting spare food coupons, which were becoming more and more difficult to provide.

She had a blonde woman with her that morning; rather extra blonde who, after shaking my hand, hesitated on the doorstep and seemed unwilling to come into the house. Ilse, too, seemed satisfied that her companion should stay outside and, after glancing at our telephone to see that it was not plugged in, she explained why. The woman was a Jewess. She had removed her star when the Gestapo had come hammering at the door of her flat, and she and her husband had clambered down the fire escape and had been living in attics and cellars ever since. A safe hairdresser had dyed her hair and, latterly, a priest had housed them in his attic; but some members of his flock, pious Catholics all, had recently been making discreet but pointed enquiries. Since yesterday the good Father had felt himself and his house to be under surveillance. Ilse explained that the priest had not asked his lodgers to leave, but they knew that the time had come, and now they had no place to go. She added that the woman could pass as an Aryan, and would willingly take on any housework, any work at all in fact, which might be useful to me; but that the husband looked so unmistakably Jewish that he would have to live in a cellar and go out only at night.

In the silence that followed Ilse's careful explanation I found myself staring across the garden to the windowed wall of the house next door, which had lately filled with refugees from the Ruhr, unknown quantities in fact. Then over the road to the balcony of the fat professor, who did physical jerks on his lawn in the morning, and beat his small son like a carpet, with sickening regularity, never failing to greet all and sundry with stiff right arm and parade ground 'Heil Hitler'.

It was a little time I suppose before my thoughts returned to the silent sitting-room and I remembered to tell Ilse to ask her companion to come in, because of course I knew that outside the front door, waiting patiently beside the doorstep, was something more than an unknown woman with dyed blonde hair. Whether I liked it or not, prepared or unprepared, the moment had come to me.

We sat on the sofa side by side, the slight neatly dressed woman and I. Her head was bent, the broad dark line of parting in her yellow hair showed that she would soon have to pay another visit to a safe hairdresser. Her thin, nervous fingers never ceased twisting and turning at the wedding ring on the fourth finger of her right hand. She did not seem to realize that every side glance she gave me, every gentle answer to my questioning, was a searing accusation, indubitable proof of the rottenness of the Master Race with which my tip-tilted nose identified me. Had she children? 'No,' then softly, 'thank God.' Where was her husband now? How soon would she want to come? Her need was seemingly immediate. The priest had felt for some days that his house was being watched, and she and her husband could not allow him to risk more for them. They could not and would not go to Ilse as, being half Jewish, she was suspect anyway. As I watched her thin nervous fingers and listened to her quiet voice, I was trying, not very successfully, to calculate just what having her in the house would entail. I would have to send the maid on holiday. The cellar? The children's bikes were kept in the cellar, and Nick was quite proud of his job at the central heating. Well, all that could be overcome, but one thing I had almost forgotten and would have to get straight. Since Peter was away, and seeing that Carl Langbehn and Hans Oster had vouched for me as being no security risk before Peter went to Norway, I would have to ask Carl first.

I found it hard to face the expression in the woman's eyes when I told her that she could stay, but that I could not give her a definite answer about her husband until late that night. The quick flash of relief, the disappointment, the shy emergent hope. 'God bless you,' she said, 'he will be in the roadway after the black-out tonight, he will wait, he knows how to hide.'

She stayed with me all that day, polishing, scrubbing, sweeping and tidying, while I hustled a rather bewildered Louisa off on an unexpected holiday. She told me her husband had been a chemist, his family and hers had been German for generations, her husband had fought in the First World War. They had not believed that Germany would cease to be their home, they had left things too late.

We played a riotous game of snakes and ladders with the boys, when I heard her laugh for the first time. She helped me cook their supper and get them to bed, and soon after she left I pushed through the gap in the hedge to the Langbehns' garden and found Carl at home, luckily alone. Knowing that he and Puppi Sarre were looking after a houseful of Jews somewhere in Potsdam, I do not think that I expected his reaction to my story. It was explosive. I had come to him for advice, well, his advice was quite definite. Under no circumstances whatsoever could I give refuge to the man, or to the woman. I did not know them, I was English, Peter was away, I had no idea what I had contemplated doing. Seeing that Nick was going to school, it could not possibly be long before I would be found out, and the punishment for giving refuge to Jews was concentration camp, plain and simple – not only for myself but for Peter. 'But—' perhaps the expression on my face showed something of a deep and very painful horror which I could feel beginning to take root somewhere behind my ribs – that twisting, turning wedding ring, the husband who knew how to move in the dark. Where were they to go? Was I to be the one to send them on their way?

All of a sudden I had rather a different Carl before me, different at least from the friend I had thought of before as a cheerful extrovert. He drew up a chair and, sitting astride it, took both of my hands in his. 'Listen, Chris,' he said gently, 'I know exactly the way you feel, do not think that I do not know. Why do you suppose I do the crazy things I do? Into the Prinz Albrechtstrasse, out of the Prinz Albrechtstrasse, pitting my wits against those SS bastards, saving the odd one here, the odd one there, but always wondering whether the next visit won't be my last, knowing all the time that single small acts of compassion are not the solution, they are stop-gaps which somehow have to be used if one wants to keep any sort of self-respect. It is little use racking our brains as to how we got into this mess. Believe me, it is the deeper issue, the elimination of the whole filthy régime which must occupy our minds day and night. Now you have come to a crossroads, a moment which must probably come to us all. You want to show your colours, well, my dear, you can't, because you are not a free agent. You have your children, and while Peter is away you are my responsibility. You are British and, in spite of that fact, Hans Oster too has vouched for you, and, believe me, Oster is playing a very big game indeed. By getting yourself into trouble you – you,' he seemed to want to say more, but instead, 'would you like me to meet them outside and give them your decision?' No, I knew I could not allow him to do that if I ever wanted to look anyone easily in the face again. 'No, I'll do it,' I said, and as he took me to the door on to the terrace he told me to come back afterwards, if I felt like it. He would be there.

As soon as I pushed through the hedge again and opened our gate to the road, letting it click back shut behind me, I sensed rather than saw some movement in the darkness about me. 'What is your decision, Gnädige Frau?' The voice, when it came, was quite close to me and pitched very low – it must have belonged to a small man, for I was staring out over his head. 'I can't,' I said, and I had to hold on to the railings because the pain in my side had become so intense that I could hardly breathe, 'at least—', did I hope to get rid of that pain by some sort of feeble compromise? 'at least I can't for more than a night, perhaps two.' 'Thank you,' again just the voice – the little man could not have been much taller than the railings – thanking me, in heaven's name, for two miserable days of grace. I loathed myself utterly as I went back to the house to fetch the cellar key.

The french window to the Langbehn's terrace opened immediately when I tapped on the pane. The spanking lie I had to tell Carl was still ahead, but he took one look at me and asked no questions at all. Moving quickly to the door he called his mother, who appeared in her dressing gown, radiating expertise, bustle and comfort. A colic, gall-bladder? Most likely something I had eaten, not surprising the food we got nowadays, mostly poison – substitute this, substitute that – disgusting. She had some pills though, wait now. I swallowed two obediently, and after a while the hard physical reality of pain seemed to retreat. I would have to go home, to the children; Louisa was on holiday. Carl shot a brief glance in my direction when I volunteered that bit of information, but he asked no further questions. Irmgard was obviously a straighter cup of tea than I was, or perhaps he just felt that I had had enough.

After two days the man and the woman left in the night. They left a little note. I never saw the man, but he must have been nice because the woman spoke of him with such affection. The house smelled of bees-wax, and our bits of silver shone gratefully with unaccustomed glow on the side-board in the dining room. Down in the cellar the camp bed had been folded together and the bedclothes piled neatly beside it on the stone floor. A pot of forsythia twigs had been moved and placed near the barred windows. Someone had told me that if I left them in the warm air, I would have blossom by Christmas, but I had forgotten about them, and they had flowered long since, and the branches were covered with sickly green leaves.

PART II

Rohrbach in the Black Forest

OUR ARRIVAL IN ROHRBACH

(Autumn 1943)

In the summer of 1943, we decided that the children should not go through another winter in Berlin. Our third son Christopher had been born there in 1942, and, although I had become an ardent supporter of the black market, throughout the following year the food situation had worsened month by month. Also when the nights grew longer we knew that we could reckon once more with British air-raids. The damage done by these 'Night Pirates' was not yet great. They usually turned up when the skies were overcast, but when they did so they had a nasty habit of keeping it up bomber by bomber, bomb by bomb, all through the night.

Moreover Peter was very conscious by 1943 that his luck could not last for ever. He had been called up again in the spring, but Carl Langbehn had managed with his usual virtuosity to have him transferred from the Air Force back to civilian life once more. His assignment this time was to an aircraft factory in Graudenz, in West Prussia, where his immediate superior was a Nazi. With Russian Armies advancing slowly but surely toward Germany's eastern borders, he wanted us to live as far to the west of Germany as possible, and, although I put off our leaving home for as long as I dared I knew that when we decided on Rohrbach in the Black Forest, he was right and that I would have to go.

We arrived in Rohrbach in September on board a toy train, which had some difficulty in pulling up the slow incline between Donaueschingen and Furtwangen, and which finally puffed to a stop beside a small, weather-worn, yellow house. *Schönenbach im Schwarzwald*, the name in faded paint was just visible on its shingled wall. Since leaving the lowlands, the locomotive had chugged its way along beside a bouncing little river, banked by high walls of dark green pine trees; any sign of flagging on its part had been swiftly remedied by the engine driver feeding great logs of wood into its boiler. Schönenbach in the Black Forest; the train waited patiently for us to scramble out and collect our belongings before continuing on its laboured journey towards Furtwangen, where it could gather sufficient strength to coast back down to Donaueschingen in the evening. It left us standing on the platform (it was no more than a raised piece of ground), with an assortment of packages and parcels around us, mostly tied with rope. Some of our luggage had not kept up with us, but two suitcases, a trunk, a pram and a cot, some pictures and a carpet had made the journey from Berlin. Thus surrounded by our goods and chattels, Nicholas, John, Christopher and I gazed around us, wondering where and what was Rohrbach, and if there would be a chance of getting there before a glowing red sun sank behind the pine-topped hills.

The children were getting used to being lugged about, and, true to form, it did not take long for Nick and John to discover that there were several red fire buckets on the platform, and also a little pathway which led down to the river. Christopher meanwhile, having tired himself out climbing all over us in the train, seemed content to settle down on one of the softer bundles and await events with the placidity of a small Buddha. The arrival of the train had obviously disturbed the stationmaster at his haymaking. Although his red official cap was impressive, his jacket was spattered with hay seeds and a long wooden hay-rake leaned up against the ticket window. Rohrback? – he pronounced it *Ruhrba* – Oh yes, we could get to Rohrbach, it was two or three miles up the valley, but we would have to wait for the milk cart. 'Bauscher Hans' collected the milk from the various farms and brought it to the station – he would have a load of empty cans, of course, to take back up the valley, but there was surely room for us on the cart as well 'We were going to the *Hilserhof, a wa*'! We had come from Berlin, *so wa*'! Must be very rough up there just now.' I had to concentrate very hard on what he was saying, because he spoke with a dialect I could barely understand.

We had not long to wait before a small wooden cart, drawn by a fat chestnut nag, came rattling down the road and drew up on the station platform. A burly fellow, with some heather stuck through the crown of his green felt hat and with the happy expression of a simpleton in his china-blue eyes, jumped down, took up one of the remaining fire buckets and placed it in front of his pony. He then proceeded, with the aid of the stationmaster, to unload his cans. There were not many of them, five to be exact, but they took some time about it as they had quite a lot to say to each other. They might have been talking Russian for all I could understand, but they glanced at us occasionally with friendly smiles and, as soon as they had the cans lined up on the platform, they disappeared inside the little house, came out with some empties and approached our bundles. Hans Bausch now had a cigar as well as the heather sticking out through the hole in his hat. They stacked our things with some ingenuity, leaving enough room for Nick to squeeze in on the driver's seat and for John, Christopher and me to sit with our legs dangling over the back of the cart.

Hans Bausch was most friendly as we jogged along, peacefully as tinkers, up a rough winding track, heading for what we had decided was to be our home until the end of the war. He let Nick take the reins and pointed with his whip to the scattered farmhouses – the *Jöcklihof*, the *Volksburehof*, the *Spitzehüsli*, the *Untere Beck*, the thatcher Heinrich and the joiner Thoma – and we turned to stare at the great, steeply sloping roofs of weathered pine, at the shingled walls of faded green and yellow and apricot where, surrounded by their fields (Hans Bausch called them mats), and overshadowed by their forests, the peasants housed together with their families, their live-stock, their farm equipment and their winter fodder.

We passed through the village proper, which seemed to consist of nothing much more than a village inn, the *Gasthaus zum Adler*, two little shops, and a large, white, crumbling stucco building, the only one except for the church and the priest's villa which was not built of wood. 'Will I have to go to that school?' John asked me suddenly, his slanting eyes as usual not missing many details. He had obviously spotted a blackboard through the open window. 'Yes, I expect so.' 'Why?' That was indeed a question as far as I was concerned, for somehow, as we continued up that valley and left each meagre sign of civilization behind us, I had become progressively more and more despondent. Why – just why? I knew that I should be overflowing with gratitude for my lot, which was so much better than most, but I also knew that I had long ceased to harbour the slightest romantic fervour for the nomadic life – the inevitable existence of the evacuee. I was tired of living in spare bedrooms, in easily spared bedrooms, of scrounging for my children, and apologizing for my children, of trying to resist the temptation to return home and, as the war dragged on, of sometimes succumbing to the temptation; only to discover that home was no longer home, but was becoming a frail fortress in the front line of battle.

Rohrbach, it seemed to me, would be just another temporary funkhole, taking its place beside all those others; beside that seaside resort on the Baltic Sea, for instance, where all the hotels had been taken over either by *Kraft durch Freude* or by Volga Germans – *Beutedeutsche*, booty Germans, as they were called. Sad groups of black-clad, fur-hatted, slav-eyed, German-speaking peoples from Russia, who had been repatriated, with much sentimental flourish, after the Russo-German pact, and who were eating their hearts out in idleness, making themselves unpopular because they were given extra coffee rations to keep their spirits up, and also infecting the natives with some curious eye disease to which they were themselves immune. *Kraft durch Freude*, 'Strength through Joy'. I could have thought of a more joyful occupation, they too probably, than marching twice a day to the beach, led by an earnest-faced Camp Leader. Old men, old women, young women and children booming, trilling, piping and squeaking the popular lyric of the day: '*Bomben auf Engelland* – boom, boom, boom – whee – boom, boom, boom.' Next on the list had come Austria, gay little Austria, starting with whooping cough and spick and span German Christians, ending in hospital, with anything but immaculate Catholics. Then Swabia, a shabby old castle in Swabia, where the only alternative to sitting in a large and draughty drawing-room listening to the *Wehrmachtsbericht*** crowing stridently of thousands of tons of British shipping sunk at sea, was that of trying to sleep to the sound of worm-eaten shutters squeaking on rusty hinges, as the rain dripped ceaselessly on a few trees around a soggy lawn which the chatelaine was proud to call her garden. And now Rohrbach – the more I thought about it, the more miserable I became.

The sun had disappeared behind the wooded hills and there was a cold nip in the air of the upper valley as our cart turned off the road, wound down a little path past a muddy duck-pond and deposited us in front of what was surely one of the least prepossessing farmhouses of the lot. Peter's aunt Ulla, the staunch companion of my many odysseys, came out to meet us. I could

*Wehrmachtsbericht – German daily war bulletin.

tell from the expression on her face that all was not well, and I soon found out why she looked so distracted. The rooms we had rented and paid for weeks in advance had been occupied by other evacuees, and we were expected to house in a couple of filthy garrets. The better feeding we had hoped for could only prove illusory, since the farm was too poor and could barely support the farmer and his family. Worst of all, the owner of the farmhouse had turned out to have the reputation of being one of the few Nazis in the valley. There was nothing for it, we would have to leave as soon as possible.

The following day we made a despairing approach to the innkeeper of the *Gasthaus Adler*, the inn we had passed in the village, and Frau Muckle, whose village title I learned was the *Adler Wirtin*, agreed to house and also to feed us. She arranged for us to have the *Nebenstube* (the next-door room to the parlour) as our sitting-room. She moved out from her own bedroom above it for me, and provided two little bedrooms across the passage for the boys. Ulla found a room with the priest's housekeeper. The *Nebenstube* was also next door to the kitchen, and I loved it on sight. Its walls were panelled in faded green and it was furnished with a table and some wooden chairs, a hard little sofa and an old spinet. Its tiny windows, with a view far down the valley and a door to the village street, took up the whole of one wall and a green-tiled stove stood in one corner next to a narrow stairway which led to my bedroom above. I soon discovered that real pleasure is just a matter of degree and comparison – no creaking shutters, no beastly coats of mail, no crowing *Wehrmachtsbericht*, no rheumy-eyed Volga Germans – our newest refuge turned out to be comparative heaven.

I soon got used to telling the time of day by the thin chime from the church steeple which called the villagers to prayer, or by the jingling of cow-bells when the long-legged, athletic looking mountain cattle passed our windows on their way to pasture and returned to their byres in the evening, all set to produce a jugful or so of milk from their strict diet of moss and weeds. I even got used to the smell of *Gille*, that all-pervading stench from the cow-house which crept up through the boarded floors and permeated every corner of the living quarters. The sneaking feeling that I was rapidly beginning to smell that way myself left me quite unperturbed. I soon decided too that for such an incurable tram-chatterer as myself, for so resourceful a nose-poker into other people's affairs, there could be few more fitting haunts than a village inn, and that the *Adler* was no exception to the rule. Although the beer was thin and the wine non-existent, every Sunday after Mass, and sometimes in the evenings, the villagers gathered in the parlour next to ours. As I began to understand the dialect, many of the old shingle farmhouses, whose windows on our first trek up the valley had seemed to watch us from behind their window-boxes like so many blind eyes, began to give up their secrets.

I learned that the *Untere Beck*, the Lower Baker, was also the Mayor, a God-fearing man, who was managing to steer his village through troubled times with fortitude and circumspection. The *Obere Beck*, the Upper Baker, on the other hand, was one to be careful of; he also baked inferior bread. The Mayor had a stalwart aide in a man of great physical strength, Joseph Kern, *Kerner Sepp*, the village clerk and also the village cobbler, whose wife kept a little shop near the *Adler*. All day long, except when he was helping out with a calving or giving a hand at getting the hay under cover before a threatened rainstorm, Sepp sat in a small room next door to his shop, with a pile of shoes in front of him, hammering and sewing, and guarding the only telephone in the village. In the evenings he joined the Mayor in the *Amtszimmer** above the school house, where, beneath an oil painting of the Führer, he bashed away on a huge antiquated typewriter. Ration cards and permits for chopping wood, birth certificates and death certificates, faithful if homely accounts of village squabbles, the whole recorded chronicle of the community, jerked out slowly and methodically from under his broad, work-stained fingers. Every Sunday the villagers passed by his workshop on their way from Mass, and if they had a pair of shoes awaiting repair, they would call in on Sepp and, whilst discussing the content of the latest telephone calls, they would endeavour surreptitiously to ease their damaged footwear to the top of the pile. Sepp was a big-hearted and kindly man, a gentle giant and something of a philosopher, and when I knew him better I asked him what he thought about the war. 'The way it is, Frau Doktor,' he said, eyeing me gently over his steel-rimmed spectacles, 'the way it is with me, I don't think that pile of shoes will get any smaller, whoever wins the war.'

Amtszimmer – Mayor's Office.

There were others in the village: Frau Kopp, the *Koppe Wiebli*, who knew all the local scandal almost before any cause for it had been given, and who was not averse to resorting to invention should actuality threaten to become a trifle dull. There was the *Messmer*, or Churchwarden, who was also the midwife for the cows, and who always arrived for this ceremony in a huge blue apron, never removing his battered hat unless he was in church. There was the *Pfarrer* Kunz, a sad-eyed priest, and the schoolteacher Lorenz, who spent his time trying to encourage about fifty children of all ages to read and write, and who occasionally gave up the unequal struggle and sent them to remove the caterpillars from his cabbage patch. For me though, above all there was Frau Muckle herself, a sturdy little widow with thinning black hair and shrewd brown eyes, who soon betrayed her scornful dislike of the Nazis and all their works. To hear her talk of *selle Kerrli*, those rascals, was a lesson in resistance in itself. She fed us and cared for us to the best of her ability, in true innkeepers' tradition, and she soon became my devoted friend. She had not been born in the hill country, but in the comparatively lush farmlands of Würtemberg, and as soon as her son, the *Adler Wirt* Ernst, came back from the war and took to himself a wife, she planned to return to the lowlands and live out her days amongst her own people.

In the meantime she ruled the *Adler* with a thrifty hand and a warm heart, alternatively bullying or mothering her little *Magd* Martina. *Magd* would be a hard word to translate, for there is something feudal about the peasant's relationship to her *Magd*. In Martina's case perhaps the best word would be 'factotum', for Martina milked the cows and fed the livestock, mucked out the cow-house, worked in the fields, washed the dishes and scrubbed the floors; her capacity for work was prodigious. At six o'clock in the morning she could be heard shuffling around in the kitchen, getting sticks for the stoves and preparing for early Mass, and from then onwards until ten o'clock at night, except for when Frau Muckle sat her down firmly at the kitchen table and filled her to the brim with potato soup, with fat raw bacon or with mugfuls of butter milk, she was ceaselessly on the go. She came from the upper valley and was one of ten children. She never bothered much about washing except on Sundays, and she talked of her cows as if they were human beings. She could make simple remarks, but never stupid ones, often hitting the nail on the head with the devastating logic of a child. With her woolly head and stubborn little face, her ragged clothes and interminable rubber boots, Martina was a natural. She, too, was waiting for Ernst to return from the war, until then she would work loyally for Frau Muckle; afterwards she wanted to become a nun.

There was finally Josef, the Pole, whose farm in Poland had been confiscated and handed over to German settlers. He had his wife and children back in Poland and if Frau Muckle had had her way, she would have housed the whole family. For Josef stifled his homesickness by working for her with as much diligence and interest as he would have done had he been on his own farm. Josef's bedroom window looked out over the shingled rooftops to the church and to its steeple, and on Sundays or in the evening when the bell tolled for Evensong, he would kneel in prayer with his elbows resting on his window-sill. Hitler's Reich did not allow people of inferior race, such as Poles, to attend religious services.

That was Rohrbach as I discovered it to be, not even dramatically beautiful, as the Black Forest can be beautiful. There were no precipitous gorges, no breathtaking skylines where layer upon jagged layer of blue-black wooded hill could fade from pale to even paler grey into a far misty horizon. Rohrbach was a little world, an unimportant world, which had no say whatsoever in affairs of state, but still had to carry the burden of Hitler's dreams of conquest. There were no young men in the farmhouses up and down the valley, and every day the little local newspaper, whilst dutifully splashing huge headlines of superlatives on its front page, reserved for the back page the news which affected the villagers most. Alois – Conrad, Smolensk – the Dnieper Basin – my loving and diligent husband – our dearly beloved son – *in stillem Schmerz* – *in tiefer Trauer* – in silent pain – in deepest mourning. Simple records of a soldier dying in a far-off land, his death reverberating back to some lonely farmhouse, where from then on there would be no strong hand to turn the stony sod or wield the axe.

The snows came to Rohrbach in November, driving snows which billowed up the valley and piled the packed flakes up against the doors and window panes. Every morning eight steaming oxen dragged a lurching wooden snowplough past our windows, and the villagers rode the plough, and called out and waved to the children before disappearing into the swirling whiteness. As I stood at the window one day and waved back, I knew that if ever I had been stupid enough to complain of my lot I had been given

132

a well deserved and salutary lesson when I had returned to Berlin before the coming of the snows. I had hoped to retrieve some of our luggage – some trifling, eminently expendable trunks of lost belongings – and I had been greeted with the news that Carl Langbehn had been arrested a week previously. He had gone to *Gestapo* headquarters in the Prinz Albrechtstrasse, having heard that Albrecht Bernstorff had been arrested for a second time. He had hoped to intervene – his mother told me that he had gone just after breakfast and that he had not come back. More, Irmgard and Puppi Sarre had been arrested as well.

Peter, although he did not believe that Carl was in any immediate danger – he was under some special kind of arrest and was allowed food and clothing parcels – looked strained and tired, and had had to leave for Graudenz soon after my arrival. In the two months that I had been gone our house had become just a sheltering roof, nothing more. The furniture stood about, and the pots and pans, and some pictures were on the walls, and friends were there: Arnold Köster and Mabel Harbottle and the Dutch boy, Gerd Dreyers, whom Peter had picked up in a bus shivering with fever, and who had come to us and been nursed back to health, and then his brother Ton and his sister Julie and Carl's secretary in the attic upstairs. I had lodged there but I knew that I did not live there any more.

There was no moon, and there were three air-raids in the three nights that I was in Berlin. The bombs fell indiscriminately on Nazis and anti-Nazis, on women and children and works of art, on dogs and pet canaries. New and more ravaging bombs – blockbusters and incendiaries, and phosphorous bombs which burst and glowed green and emptied themselves down the walls and along the streets in flaming rivers of unquenchable flame, seeping down cellar stairs, and sealing the exits to the air-raid shelters. Carl had had an air-raid trench dug between our two gardens before he was arrested, but he had not had time to cover the tin roof with earth, so every night his mother and I sat together in that trench, listening to the shrapnel splinters bouncing off the roof like vicious hailstones. Carl's mother wore a huge steel helmet during the raids – she looked like a ghost robin, but she would not leave Berlin because she did not wish to be far from her son.

I learned when I was in Berlin that those wanton, quite im-personal killings, that barrage from the air which mutilated, suffocated, burned and destroyed, did not so much breed fear and a desire to bow before the storm, but rather a certain fatalistic cussedness, a dogged determination to survive and, if possible, help others to survive, whatever their politics, whatever their creed.

The driving storm rampages up the valley and the wind drums and roars. Darkness falls quickly in the Black Forest, and the old Inn creaks and groans. The light in the *Nebenstube* flickers rather ominously – but there is nothing to fear from the darkness in Rohrbach. Frau Muckle puts her head round the door into the parlour. She had turned on *d'Engländer* for me some time back – the English news, and I had forgotten to listen and she had gone to sleep behind the stove. *'Gut' Nacht, Frau Doktor,'* she says, *'angenehme Ruh' die Nacht!'* 'Good night, Frau Muckle, may you sleep peacefully too this night – and thank you.'

I watch her through the doorway as she does the last rounds of her domain, as she moves a chair or two and bolts the entrance doorway, as she crosses herself and turns down the oil lamp which flickers before the crucifix in the far corner of the parlour – 'God's corner'. God's oil is on strict rations too. I feel I would like to say something more to her as she draws her shawl close about her before shuffling out into the icy passage-way, but instead we just exchange smiles.

Good night, Frau Muckle, and thank you, thank you for a good deal more than you can possibly be aware of.

THE TERWIEL STORY

(Winter 1943–1944)

When we first arrived in Berlin in 1939, we knew of neither a good doctor nor a good dentist. Both had to be politically reliable because they would be able to talk to the children and could also listen in to whatever one might have to say whilst under an anaesthetic. Mary Wussow told us of a good and reliable doctor. Ellen Eiche advised a dentist, one Helmuth Himpel, who had his practice in the Lietzenburgerstrasse. He came from the Kaiserstuhl and Ellen had known him since he was a boy. He had been engaged for some time to a girl called Marie Terwiel. Helmuth Himpel and Marie Terwiel were devoted to each other, but they could not marry, because in spite of her blonde hair and blue eyes Marie, according to Nazi law, was a *Mischling ersten Grades*, which can only be translated as a first-grade hybrid. Her father, before 1933, had been a senior civil servant and an 'Aryan', her mother was a Jewess. Until her father's death early in the year 1942, Marie's parents had lived in what was called in Nazi terminology 'privileged' matrimony. The children were not yet affected by the full harshness of the Nuremberg Laws. After Father Terwiel died, however, matters changed considerably. Marie, a brilliant law student, had to leave university; her brother Gerd had to change from law to medicine, which study was still permitted. The children lived in constant fear that their mother would be deported and have to follow her many relatives to the ghetto, that limbo in the East from which there was little chance of return.

Helmuth Himpel, when I came to know him, was a tall, gentle, rather delicate looking fellow, quite obviously devoted to his Marie. Marie was made, I could imagine, of sterner stuff. A vivid, passionate little person whose blue eyes blazed with loathing whenever the régime was mentioned. She was fervently convinced that the War would have to be lost, irrevocably lost, before Hitler and all that he stood for could be eliminated; her hatred had deprived her almost of all caution, since she and hers had been hit too close. She had one hope of altering the course at least of her family's destiny: Mother Terwiel would have to be proved half-Aryan, the illegitimate child of her father in fact, and this, according to the racial laws, would automatically transform her into a first-grade hybrid and her children into second-grade hybrids. Second-grade hybrids did not fall under the Nuremberg Laws and Marie would then be able to marry her Helmuth. Above all, her mother would be free of the constant fear of transportation to the ghetto.

Relations and friends of the Terwiels, both Aryan and Jewish, had rallied to the cause and Marie had collected an impressive array of sworn affidavits declaring that the seemingly respectable union of her Jewish grandparents had not been at all what it seemed to be. The documents were lodged with the *Rassenforschungsamt* (Race Investigation Office), the special department in the Ministry of Justice set up to decide on such things. For Marie though, this was not enough. She had to be active in trying to bring about the downfall of a hated régime. She copied and distributed the sermons of Graf Galen, the intrepid Bishop of Münster; she dropped leaflets into letter-boxes; she stuck little stickers on palings and walls and one day she asked Ellen point blank whether her hatred of the Nazis was intense enough to drive her to do more, at greater risk. When Ellen hesitated, she did not mention it again.

The wheels of the *Rassenforschungsamt* moved slowly. They had doubtless many such cases as Mother Terwiel's to occupy their time. In 1942, the case of her legitimacy was still undecided and she could now no longer live in one place for any length of time, for fear of the nightly knock on the door. She went to live with one or other of her children and sometimes stayed with Hans and Ellen. She had to live the life of a 'submarine', a pitiful figure hounded from pillar to post emerging here, emerging there, fed and cared for only by those who were brave enough to risk looking after her.

In 1942 when Ellen's husband's job took him to Strasbourg, she decided to have Marie and her mother to stay with her in Gatow, a suburb of Berlin. For convenience, and for the telephone, Mother

Terwiel became 'Tante Rosa' to all who knew of her presence in Gatow, and it would be fair to add that she was not the only stray 'aunt' to make her appearance in German homes at that time. The evening of their arrival, however, Marie received an urgent telephone call from Helmuth. The telephone call must have been made from the call-box up the road, because three minutes later Helmuth came to fetch Marie; they left together and Ellen never saw either of them again.

When Marie had not returned on the following day, Ellen rang Helmuth's flat in the Lietzenburgerstrasse. The secretary answered the telephone – No, Dr Himpel was not at home; no, he was not expected back that day. Yes, he was away. Thank you. Ellen made for town and found a puzzled patient ringing the doorbell of Helmuth's flat. 'Strange,' the lady said, 'Dr Himpel said nothing to *me* about going away. I made my appointment only two days ago, an emergency one; how very strange.'

It was not strange of course, because Marie and Helmuth had been arrested at five o'clock that morning. I could understand how helpless Ellen must have felt at that time. She knew no one of any influence within the Nazi hierarchy, let alone the Secret Police. She had Marie's mother living in her house; people had been sent to concentration camps for less than that. She was up against the moment which had to come to us all. To whisper, to discuss, to joke even and to hope was not enough; at some time or other we would have to show the courage of our convictions.

It took some weeks before news of Marie and Helmuth began to seep out from behind their prison walls and fit in piece by piece with the rumours which were circulating like wildfire in Berlin at the time. They were in Moabit prison. They were suspected of having belonged to a resistance group called the *Rote Kapelle*, which had been transmitting messages to Russia. One of the transmitters had been found in a suitcase in Helmuth Himpel's waiting room. Only a rumour of course, but, knowing Marie, Ellen could believe that it was not entirely unfounded. Ellen and Gerd did not tell Mother Terwiel of what had happened. They concocted a story about Marie and Helmuth having left suddenly for Switzerland – they never knew whether she believed it or not. After Gerd had been interrogated, though, and had told the interrogator of their mother's ignorance of her daughter's whereabouts, little notes in Marie's handwriting telling of swimming and sunning themselves beside mountain lakes, indicated that the interrogator had at least some heart. Only the drab notepaper did not look as if it came from neutral Switzerland.

Marie and Helmuth were tried by a military court in February 1943 and were condemned to death for high treason. Some weeks after their trial the *Rassenforschungsamt* completed its investigations into the family history of 'Tante Rosa' and ruled that she was undoubtedly the illegitimate child of her father and, therefore, no full-blooded Jewess.

Soon after the trial of Marie and Helmuth a dubious figure reappeared on the scene. A Fräulein Bayer who, some months before their arrest, had answered an advertisement for an assistant to Helmuth in his surgery. I remembered Fräulein Bayer, handsome and blonde, and so blatantly anti-Nazi that she embarrassed me. She talked of 'that scoundrel', adding with a knowing smile, as she hovered about the dentist's chair, 'we all know of course who I *mean*'. Fräulein Bayer wrote asking to discuss a matter of extreme urgency. Smartly dressed, bubbling over with treasonable chatter, Fräulein Bayer unfolded her plan. She professed to have a useful contact and divulged that her influence was such that if the Terwiels provided her with 1,000 Reichsmarks she might be able to effect the release of Marie. Nobody fell for the tale. She was ordered to be gone.

Ellen was now deeply involved. Time was running out for Helmuth and Marie. 'What could I do, Chris? Stop smoking? Send them cigarettes? Send them any food we could? Send them messages of hope through the prison chaplain? God, how helpless can one be. We handed in a plea for clemency. I even went to their interrogator, shaking in my shoes, I may add, and all I took home from the interview was the proof of Fräulein Bayer's rôle in the affair. "Do not underestimate Fräulein Bayer, Frau Dr Eiche," he said, when I told him I thought she was crazy. "Fräulein Bayer would trample over dead bodies."'

Helmuth and Marie languished in prison for more than a full year before they died. Helmuth was in solitary confinement and kept a diary which he gave to the prison chaplain on the day of his execution. Each day began 'Good morning, little Marie' and he filled the pages with imaginary conversations with the girl he loved; for which love, although he never mentioned it, he had doubtless been brought to his death. Marie was allowed to live for eight weeks after Helmuth's execution. When she heard of his death she weakened temporarily and tried to commit suicide.

Gerd was allowed to visit his sister on the day before her execution. There was nothing much left of her except a pair of glowing eyes. She indicated to him that she had been beaten sometimes by the supposedly good-hearted interrogator. The prison chaplain was with her as she walked to the scaffold. She was unafraid and before she disappeared behind the black curtaining which hid the gallows she turned and called out loudly and firmly, 'I know at least of Mussolini's overthrow and that makes my dying easy.'

On that night just before Christmas, when a British land-mine scored a direct hit on her home in Gatow, Ellen had come to our house with her baby, before leaving for Strasbourg. She had come to fetch a few belongings which she had deposited in our cellar and she had been persuaded to stay in Dahlem for the night. She had not left 'Tante Rosa' alone in Gatow, however, because Gerd had Christmas leave from the hospital where he worked. They were in the cellar of course, but, as I mentioned, it was a direct hit. Gerd lived for forty-eight hours after the raid, 'Tante Rosa' was killed instantly.

Ellen joined us in the Black Forest in 1943. She came with her little girl to live across the valley in the house of the joiner Thoma. She told me this story as we sat on some logs in the hot winter sun, watching our children playing in the snow and listening to the wind sighing faintly through the pine trees behind us. She ended as she had begun, like some country parson whose text at the start and the finish has little bearing, as often as not, on the subject of his sermon. 'And so you see, Chris, officially they died as victims of Allied terror, their coffins were draped with the Nazi flag and the town of Berlin paid for the cost of their funeral.'

INVASIONITIS

(Spring 1944)

Spring came slowly and hesitantly to Rohrbach, heralded by a few deceptively mild days which started the icicles dripping from the eaves and little rivulets hustling about beneath the surface of the snow; which turned the pine trees smoky black and speckled the white slopes with patches of brown mush. Then came a fresh fall of snow; out came the skis and the sledges once more and all was white again. Winter loosened its grip reluctantly and did not seem in full retreat until great pancakes of snow and ice broke away from the sloping roofs and came thundering to the cobble stones beneath, and suddenly, almost overnight, the islands of dead-seeming grass were alight with cowslips and wild crocus.

'The suicide season' was how our country doctor cheerfully described that slow transition from winter to summer in the valley, and he doubtless knew what he was talking about; for Dr Guttenberg's rounds, made mostly on skis or an antiquated motor-cycle, brought him to many an isolated farmhouse. His skill as a physician had stood us in good stead since the day of his first visit, when he had removed his goggles, shaken the snow from his anorak, and had stood himself in front of Peter's picture on the old spinet. 'Well, I'll be damned – Peter Bielenberg,' had been his greeting, and he had then explained that he had been with Peter at Freiburg University.

Suicide was not my line, but as winter gave way to spring I found that I was unable to rid myself of an increasing restlessness. The war had gone on for four and a half years, and I was thirty-four. It seemed to me that it might drag on that way for ever, that the spring thaw would come and come again, and that our years, our best years, were sliding past – years which could have been well spent, years that were being thrown away; whispering, cadging, simulating, hating, hoping, stoking away at some inner flame, keeping alive an ever-dwindling faith that somehow, sometime, something would prevail which was good and which was right.

I knew that I should have been glad of the peaceful nights, the good simple food, of the knowledge that Peter was not in Russia, and that my children were safe and healthy in a quiet backwater. I had little excuse, except perhaps that I was mentally a lot alone, that I had had no message from England for nearly three years, and that since one of the trunks which had gone astray had been full of books I had nothing to read but our little local newspaper, or, if we ran out of lavatory paper – the *Völkischer Beobachter*, the Party rag. Day after day the two-inch headlines recorded the dozens of 'air pirates' shot down over Reich territory, the retreats which were vaunted as victories, and the medals for valour which were becoming daily more numerous, monthly more resplendent; the simple Iron Cross of the First World War long since smothered beyond recognition in silver swords, in golden oak leaves, and finally even in precious stones. Then one turned to the inner pages, which so deftly sounded a warning, so slyly, so coyly betrayed the abject poverty. There would be the shocking story of *Volksschädling X*, the parasite who chose to undermine the people's will to victory, who doubted, who listened to foreign broadcasts, or who stole perhaps a jar of lard from an air-raid cellar. Of the patriot who informed the police. A *Sondergericht*, a summary court: in Stuttgart, in Düsseldorf, there was one in every town. Sentence of death, no appeal; *das Urteil ist vollstreckt*, the sentence has been carried out. News perhaps from the East, '*die deutsche Verwaltung im Osten packt zu, die Fragen werden gelöst*', the German administration in the East tackles its task with energy, the problems are being solved – with German diligence and with German thoroughness. What problems? They showed a film in Furtwangen during the winter, Theresienstadt, the 'Adlon* of the Ghettoes'. Anyone who saw it said things looked peaceful enough, Jews going about their household chores, no sign of hunger or ill-treatment, better really, one could believe, than living in the Ruhr; and yet, the rumours that typhoid was rampaging through those ghettoes and that long trains of cattle trucks had been seen shunted into sidings here, there – better not speak too loudly, you remember what happened to the traitor Y?

*Adlon Hotel – the most luxurious hotel in Berlin.

Just the same, what had Ernst the *Adler* host to report when he came home on leave from the Russian front? 'If we are paid back one quarter of what we are doing in Russia and Poland, *Frau Doktor*,' he had said simply, 'we will suffer, and we will deserve to suffer.' Ernst was an honest man, and sad and war-weary, and I had not had the heart to probe further.

They were all there, those words which might mean anything – *entlaust*, *entjudet*, as well as *entzückt*. You could read of de-lousing, of de-jewing, you could also read of delighting. For what could be more delightful than to be able to exchange a kilogram of bones in the *Rathaus* in Furtwangen for a nice little piece of muddy grey soap, or to sample a salad of delicious wild vegetables (subversive to call them weeds), washed down with a mug of raspberry-leaf cordial, or than to provide your little ones with a tasty spread of potatoes and raw onion juice when they came home hungry for tea, trailing that school satchel no doubt made from Mum's old mackintosh or – oh God, I'd had enough.

I found myself taking long aimless walks through the slush, chattering away under my breath, sometimes humming a little tune – always the same haunting little tune, composed I had heard by a French prisoner of war: *Dans un coin de mon pays* – in a corner of my country. I found myself stopping occasionally and addressing some lonely tree, or maybe a wayside crucifix; it didn't really matter much, for the Allies, always the Allies, were the object of my feeble diatribe. 'Listen,' I would start sternly, 'it just can't go on like this. Carl Langbehn has been gone five months and now Helmuth Moltke.' Peter had just said 'Helmuth' on the telephone and 'prisoner of war', and we knew no other Helmuth and I had said how glad his wife must be, and Peter had said surely, and I had said give her my love and Peter had said he would if he saw her, and I wondered if she had been arrested too. 'No, it can't go on like this, if something doesn't happen, if you don't come soon it will be too late, because what with the ghettoes, the air-raids, the summary courts and the concentration camps, there won't be anyone left. You will just find headlines when you come, huge headlines, and maybe a few informers; and ruins, of course, plenty of ruins. But we will have vanished, one by one, the *Volksschädling* X and the traitor *Y*, vanished behind a little paragraph on an inside page of a shoddy newspaper and a curtain of impenetrable silence, and we will not be able to tell you how or why we died. For I must explain to you that you can bomb us for ever; that won't win this war, that's just complicating things, making people bloody-minded, making people forget their politics and what it's all about and rush to help their neighbours. And your unconditional surrender and your Morgenthau Plan: nonsense from start to finish, talk, talk, talk, grist to Dr Goebbels' mill. No you'll have to land in France, but quickly for God's sake! What are you waiting for? You've got half the world on your side.'

My governessy tone never lasted for long, but invariably petered out in a bout of prolonged snivelling. 'Oh come on, please come, please hurry – I'm so sick of it all – this ruddy place is a madhouse – I just want to get back amongst my own people, my own people, do you hear? – *dans un coin de mon pays.*'

I had to get away, I'd ring Peter, he'd think up something. The newspapers at any rate had a word for my disease, for there was no doubt that I was suffering from my own brand of what Dr Goebbels, in his wisdom, was describing as 'invasionitis'.

Peter prepared a great welcome for me in Graudenz. He answered my plaintive SOS with promptitude and managed to wangle for me a sleeper on the train in spite of their being reserved exclusively for those travelling on important missions connected with the war economy. My travelling companion was a lady of uncertain age but of no uncertain politics. I occupied the upper bunk and her Party badge winked at me frostily from a coathanger across the chasm; it did not disturb my holiday spirit, but successfully stifled any animated exchange of pleasantries.

Three whole beautiful days off and I had found myself planning what I would do and see with as much eager expectation as if I were setting out on some safari through darkest Africa. East Prussia, West Prussia, mysterious lands east of the river Oder. Cradle, as I had learned in school, of all that was positively terrifying – the goose-step, the spiked helmet, the shaven head and the cold blue eyes with the screwed-in monocle, cradle of – I whisper it – the *Junker.* Information, let me add, which experience had taught me to mistrust profoundly since I had discovered just what Austria and Bavaria could produce in the way of horrors.

Peter cut my journey short several hours by coming to meet me at Thorn in the factory car. He had also arranged for a wonderful surprise present, which practically covered the bed when I arrived at his hotel. Three beautiful blouses; the owner of the hotel had some swing with a dress shop and Peter had had them specially made. No matter that he had given my size as 62 and the shoulder seams flapped about somewhere near my elbows, that made them into something more of a surprise, not only for me, but also perhaps for the pretty little hotel keeper who may have suffered under the illusion, perhaps even the hope, that I would turn out to be a monstrosity.

No matter either, really, that I saw little of the wonders that I had read up about so diligently. Königsberg and Marienburg, graceful glowing redbrick monuments, I had imagined, to the age of chivalry, when the Crusader Knights of the Teutonic Order had ridden forth officially to spread the faith among the heathen Prussians and unofficially no doubt to feather their mightily fortified nests.

Graudenz as a tourist attraction proved to be a washout, a grey cold city peopled by sullen-faced cloth-capped Poles, wondering doubtless who they hated most – the Germans or the Russians. For me, for us though, it was a bomb-free refuge where for three whole days we could be together, talk together, even try to plan together, and catch up on news which could not be conveyed by letter or by telephone. It was no use pretending that the news was good. True that Helmuth and Dohnanyi and all the other victims of what Peter described as 'another bloody tea party' were still alive and they had seemingly given nothing away. No further arrests had been made. Carl had even managed to pull off one of his ingenious master strokes and telephoned to Peter from Gestapo headquarters. He had asked for some law books and added please to bring brandy as well and Peter had done so and whilst his guards were occupied with the brandy he had slipped Peter an account of his interrogations and told him to take it to Popitz. His mission accomplished, and with the document now safely buried under one of our plum trees, Peter had proof that Carl, at least for the present, was also holding his own. In fact it was not immediate danger which had to be faced, but rather the fact that the nearer we got to the end of the war – and Peter seemed to think it would be over by autumn – the greater was the risk of chatterboxes, scrimshankers and opportunists actively joining the ranks of the opposition. The cry therefore that the opposition should have been broader based had disclosed its own inherent danger, and a menace was abroad which had proved powerless when the opposition had consisted of a closely knit network of friends and friends of friends. There had been some isolated action it seemed, and each one had been dogged by bitter misfortune, nullified by Hitler's incredible aptitude for staying alive. No one knew what action, no one asked, since it was better to know as little as need be, in case of possible arrest. Adam had not quite lost his inborn optimism seemingly and, although I knew that Peter no longer believed in a positive outcome, he would be at Adam's side if he were called. If nothing happened, it would be for the Allies to decide; what would be the upshot of such multifarious victors each expounding their own version of unconditional surrender was hard to guess.

I found that, true to form, I could not contemplate much planning ahead. The manifest, the more adjacent problems were those which concerned me most – those three Gestapo officials playing cards across in the far corner of the smoke-filled dining room of Peter's Graudenz hotel; the one with the smooth white face for instance, and the mouth like a crooked scar, whom Peter described with a shrug as being his own private headache – and then the bombing, always the bombs.

When our three beautiful days came to an end and I'd packed up my three huge blouses and boarded a train for the south, and we'd said 'so long' and 'see you' and neither of us had quite faced up to that word good-bye, I knew that I could work up little interest in what might happen afterwards, to the 'Face of Europe', 'the Grand Design', 'the Fate of Nations', 'the New Order'. All those grandiloquent frothy phrases cooked up and elaborated upon by elders and betters, so that the game of killing and being killed should not be recognized for what it was, by the children who had to play it. We still had six months to go if Peter were right about the war. So let the war end, and let's see what happens then – that was my motto for the moment, and the question whether Peter or I would live to see that day of reckoning was one which I decided should be left firmly out of my calculations.

ADAM

(Spring 1944)

On my journey from Graudenz back to Rohrbach I passed through
Berlin on Sunday. I had a few hours before my train left for the
south so I left my luggage at the station and went round to Adam's
flat on the off-chance of seeing him. Emma, his little factotum,
complete as usual with untidy topknot and crackling white apron,
was laying the table for lunch. Herr von Trott had gone for a walk,
but he would be back – 'No, I must stay, she would lay another
place – Oh, yes, there was quite enough, and Herr von Trott would
eat much better if there were two, he was just eating nothing.
She did her best, and always tried to smuggle her meat ration on
to his plate – old women didn't need meat – but he usually left
half of it, and no wonder he didn't feel well, and got tooth-ache
and rheumatism and the rest!' She bustled about laying a second
place at the table, and then disappeared into the kitchen leaving
me to wander round the sitting-room, which seemed rather bereft
since Clarita and the children had left for Imshausen. I opened
the gramophone and took off a record, and put it absentmindedly
back into its case – Mozart's Requiem in D minor; I sat down and
opened a book which was lying on the table, *The Last Enemy* by
Richard Hillary. I had almost forgotten what it was like to have
an unread book in my hands and I began to turn the pages, and
was far away when I heard Adam's voice in the hall calling Emma.

I heard a faint answer, and then Adam burst into the room.

'Great heavens, Chris! This can hardly be true, how wonderful,
where's Pete?'

I had not seen Adam for more than a year, and had almost
forgotten how handsome he was, or maybe he was so good-
looking that he managed to give me a slight surprise each time
I saw him. Emma was right, though, he did not look well. He

was much too thin, and when he was not smiling there was a certain expression on his face which I could not quite fathom nor remember having seen there before.

It was easy enough to pick up the threads and to slip into an old and happy relationship as we talked of the children and he told me how glad he was that we were in the Black Forest, 'the real Germany, I would get to feel about it, see if I didn't, the way he felt about his Hessian forests', and then of his own little girls and of how he thought Clarita might be having rather a tough time with his family – 'They are rather a formidable bunch as you know,' he remarked, unable as usual completely to smother a none too modest smile. His family, yes I knew, fascinating, infuriating, serenely egocentric and he could never quite escape being proud of them. He glanced at the book I had just put back on the table and told me he had brought it back from Sweden – '*The Last Enemy* – Hillary was a Battle of Britain pilot, he had read it in a night and I must take it with me – no wait, I'd better not, but I could take it home and give it back to Emma later tonight before I left. I would enjoy the offhand way it was written after the blown up rubbish we had to read here. It was the understatement—'

Emma came to tell us that lunch was ready and as we went into the dining room, he put his arm over her shoulder; she looked quite minute next to his rangy height.

'Emma is a marvel,' he said, 'I just don't know how she manages to give me such meals. I have a strong suspicion that she is clearing the district of dogs. I get meat galore—'

'Now now, Herr von Trott,' – Emma reminded me a little of Frau Muckle – 'instead of talking, you just eat it up,' and we sat down to a meal of rather odd looking meat balls, and something that looked like mashed potatoes.

Adam made no attempt to start, but leaned back in his chair and gave me that long, warm, intimate smile which I had told him often enough could only cause complications if he tried it on any unattached woman.

'It *is* good to see you, Chris. Peter was right to send you to the Black Forest. You look so well, with lots of reserves stored up to face the things to come. But I've missed you both badly. I always come back from my walks via the Falkenried, and hope against hope to see one of you around.' Then suddenly rocking back in his chair, so that it balanced perilously on its two hind legs, he added: 'Tell me, Chris, what do you think now?'

'Think about what?'

'Think about the war – think about me?'

I was struggling with Emma's mashed potato. I remembered that kind of question, I'd had it before, not exactly rhetorical, but rather more seeking a sounding board. How did I as an Englishwoman react to this, to that, to the other? At the start of the war, I had been able to answer with much confidence – now I realized that I was no longer so certain of myself. Four and a half years had been a long time and sometimes of late I had felt myself to be wandering in some private no-man's-land. An evasive answer though would not be good enough, for I also knew the drill, and that one of Adam's most compelling qualities was the way he took for granted that he would get an intelligent answer to his question; how he unconsciously put people on their mettle, and drew from them by the very force of his genuine interest an unusual amount of uncustomary scintillation. I also knew that it was only when you knew him really well that you realized just how careful you had to be with your answers, and how truthful, because he had a way of storing them up and fitting them into the uncompleted jigsaw of his political conception, so that an untruth would merely burden him. This natural habit of drawing out the best in people conversely did not always work to his advantage, in that he could estimate too highly, demand too much, involve himself too deeply in situations which, superficially at least, would seem of little import, and thus spend himself, the insoluble drawing him like a magnet, and leaving him no peace.

What did I think about him then, think about the war? The problem which had eluded him through the years, the unsolved problem of his relationship with the Allies, the talking across borders, above the clatter of war.

'Well,' I said carefully, summoning to my aid as much of my rusty mental equipment as I could find, 'let's take you first. You are half German and half American. I think your American blood has given you your optimism, your supreme confidence in the human personality, and a quite puritan inability to avoid the moral issue. Your German side probes the depths, considers the complications, too many complications sometimes, and finally drives you to make decisions. I would like to think that your time in Oxford infused fluidity – no, perhaps better – manoeuvrability into your make-up, because it is neither a German nor an American characteristic.'

148

That sounded to me extraordinarily clever for a start, too clever in fact, I would never be able to keep it up, so I added, 'and the whole, Herr von Trott, combined with your obvious good looks and irresistible charm combines to make you into a decidedly attractive personality.'

Adam gave me a rueful grin. 'Go on, you ass, and China? You have forgotten China and my wish to be buried in Peking.'

'Well now, China.'

I had not forgotten China, in 1938 when he had urged us to come to Berlin, and again in 1940 when he had voiced such bitter disappointment that the resistance to the régime had been making so little progress, and he had had jaundice and we had teased and somehow flattered him that he was beginning to look like a Chinese mandarin.

'I don't know about China, Adam, except that when you came back, you seemed to have acquired a sort of global conception which made us feel rather suburban.'

Emma was making frantic signals from the door that I should make him eat something.

'You'd better get outside those meat balls,' I said. 'I reckon it's a *Führerbefehl*.'*

He picked up his fork obediently, and began poking around on his plate.

'I wish I were as fascinating as you make me sound,' he said. 'But, bother you, you are Irish as well as English. The truth is that I am old and bald, and I get tooth-ache.'

'Oh, for God's sake!' I protested – I had to dispel the gloom somehow. 'You are exactly my age, and I am thirty-four. We've got lots of time ahead of us to get into trouble and muddle things out.'

Adam did not appear to be listening.

'Yes, I owe more to Oxford than I can say, but it's a strange thing. When I decided to come back to Germany in 1933, I would have thought that I did exactly what most of my Oxford friends would have done, if they had been faced with a Hitler in their country. Yet the very fact that I *did* come back, when I suppose I could have stayed away, aroused, I think, nothing but distrust – damaging distrust. I sometimes wonder how many friends I have there now – I mean real friends.'

'Now look, Adam,' I said, and I had to admit that as my brothers

Führerbefehl – Hitler ruling.

had gone to Cambridge, I had a sneaking mistrust of anything but wordy mischief emanating from Oxford, that hothouse of the Establishment. 'I don't know about your friends, but one thing is certain. You are having to live, yes to *live*, what they, at most, can talk about. There's a big difference.'

Adam pushed back his chair, and started pacing the room, and Emma, resigned to the inevitable, removed his half-finished plate, and brought in two little glass dishes of sour cherry compote.

'I don't regret for one single moment that I came back,' he said. 'This is my home, Chris, this is where I have my roots, and I am firmly convinced that any German who wants to help in the reconstruction of a post-war Europe must have experienced – personally, intimately what has gone on here in our country. What made a man a Nazi, what makes men sit tight and do nothing, what it has meant to be in opposition, to oppose, always to oppose. The bust-up hopes, the heroism, and there has been heroism, seemingly useless heroism and then the shame – the paralysing shame. There are things which will need all our strength to unravel – to try to make intelligible after this war is over. Those who left Germany, and may come back afterwards, will be uprooted strangers speaking a different language, and whatever advice they may have to offer, will hardly lure any old dog out from behind the stove.

'I can't believe that they want to create a vacuum here in the centre of Europe – a vacuum fills, and if this bombing goes on, it will fill from the East. Even Stalin has realized that when the Nazis are gone he will have to deal with the German people – even he is making overtures. But the Allies, unconditional surrender, unconditional surrender, like a broken gramophone record, we have to face it, I have to face it, that is the only echo which has come back from across our borders from the West. And yet I know there are people out there who must realize that the Nazis and all they stand for are as much our enemies as theirs.'

I sighed. I wished that I could find some explanation, some answer to the conundrum. Why the distrust? To me, Adam's path had always been crystal clear. I could only feel my way along the dark passages of patriotism. Could it be that for an Englishman to return to his country, to identify himself even with its national aims in times of stress, was easy, an obvious course to take? Whereas to leave it to its fate, as had the German émigrés, would be for a Britisher a more difficult decision, more heroic even. And the demand for 'unconditional surrender', which was perhaps the greatest blow ever delivered to the opposition in Germany, was so superbly ill-timed, coming as it did just after Stalingrad, handed to the wily Dr Goebbels the very weapon he needed to rant and flail, cajole and spur on flagging spirits to fight to the end. How he had revelled in his chance! 'Now at last, the Allies had disclosed their war aim, of which he had told the German people all along – destruction, utter destruction of the German Reich, was all they had aimed for from the start.' How shrewdly had he given to the non-committed, the waverers and the ostriches, a *raison d'être*, a convenient hook on which to hang their miserable consciences, a good reason to endure, to persevere. 'What's the use, we may as well be hung for a sheep as a lamb,' *'wir müssen wohl ausharren.'* How I loathed that dreary, plodding word *ausharren*, a word on everyone's lips after Casablanca. Persevere with what? Persevere with sticking their stupid blond heads still deeper in the mud.

It was incomprehensible to me that the British, that the Americans, had not been able to see that they had nothing to lose, and perhaps months of warfare and thousands of lives to save, by encouraging an opposition to Hitler within Germany. Then again I had so often found myself trying to explain to Germans that, contrary to themselves, for whom the waging of war was somehow still a trade to which no emotion need be attached, the British, as a nation, did not go to war willingly, unless they had worked up a good old hate. The professional versus the amateur. During the First World War, it had been my Uncle Northcliffe's business to do the hate rousing, and he had done very well; so well, in fact, that I was not sure if some of the emotion left over from that other war had not spilled over into this one, and was as deep-seated as the Germans' own genuine resentment of the Treaty of Versailles. I supposed there was nothing very rational about hatred, and I no longer knew just how successfully the British had been taught to hate this time. Perhaps I had caught the bug of trying to find a complicated solution to a simple issue. I could not hate because I knew too much, neither could I be of any more use to Adam, as a mirror. The childish broadcasts from the other side seemed just as footling to me as they did to him, the lack of a serious answer to a serious question just as puzzling. I knew that I would find it hard enough after the war to explain (to whoever wanted to listen) that I sincerely believed that Goebbels had never succeeded in making the Germans hate although he had used methods and arguments quite as ingenious as my uncle. In my opinion he had never aroused the 'seething soul of the people' one way or the other. The Germans had not risen and torn the airmen to bits who were killing so indiscriminately night after night – I had never heard a cheer go up when an Allied bomber came crashing down in flames. But neither had they stirred themselves and cried to high heaven of the things being done in their name. After eleven years of Nazi rule, Germans, it seemed to me, had become an ignorant demoralized insensate mass, and I could only be grateful to the few, the few that I knew, who had shone out reassuringly like beacons, as constant to their principles in defeat as they had been when victory seemed just around the corner.

Adam had ceased pacing the room and had come to a stop by the window. Leaning against the curtain, he was looking out with half-closed eyes over the misty trees, which as yet showed little sign of the coming spring. I could only see his face in profile. Behind his head was an engraving of one of his American ancestors, and I was suddenly struck by the physical resemblance between that American statesman and Supreme Court judge, and his German great-great-grandson.

'You haven't sent John Jay to the country, I see,' I remarked rather irrelevantly.

'John Jay sticks around with me,' he answered without turning his head, and then, 'my secretary was killed out there the other day. Do you remember Fräulein Walter? A nice harmless, very loyal little person. Buried under the rubble of her block of flats, with her mother. We tried our best for hours, but we couldn't get near enough for the heat. It's not always easy to confine one's indignation to the circumstances which bring such things about. I wonder why it was that just she had to pay the price?' And then he added just as irrelevantly, 'You see, Chris, how it is, just why we have to plan ahead, to plan for what will come afterwards. It helps us to keep things in proportion. Nothing can really be solved though, there can be no new start until the guns are silent, and we meet with the Allies, around a table, here in Berlin.'

I sighed again. 'Will this war ever end, Adam? Do you believe the Allies will really land in France?'

'Oh yes, they intend to land, they must land sometime. No one knows exactly when.'

Adam came back across the room and stood in front of me. Somehow his mood seemed to have changed, and something of the old enthusiasm had come back into his voice.

'But perhaps you won't have to wait that long, Chris, not even for the landing, I mean. I don't think that I will be able to go abroad again. The last time I was in Sweden – well, it has become increasingly difficult and dangerous, I guess. I don't know if I could have done more to try and persuade outsiders that there is another Germany, but one way or another I feel that chapter is now closed. I wish I could tell you more, but it's no use burdening you – you'll hear soon enough. We've not been idle, in fact the last weeks, in spite of all, have been positive ones – exciting, in fact. From now on this is a German affair. We must rid ourselves of this régime by ourselves, and believe me if you believe nothing else, it will be done. It will and must be done, before the Allies have to do it for us.'

Adam fetched his bicycle out of the cellar, and came along with me to the Falkenried. He had to go to meet someone, he said, and he wanted to be home again before a possible raid because Emma was scared on her own. We passed some soldiers as we turned into Königin Louisenstrasse; they were not very young, and they did not look very fit.

'You know, Chris, I can't help feeling a heel every time I see old fellows like that in uniform, and here am I, still in my Sunday suit,' he said and I don't know why that remark made me go hot behind the eyes. Perhaps it was because he had told me just beforehand, with obvious pleasure, that he had had a message from the Rhodes Trust just after Christmas, asking after his welfare. So that was the only official recognition he had been able to gather in, after risking his life again and again bearing testimony to 'another Germany'. I was not only nearly in tears, but aroused somehow to impotent anger.

'Blast it all,' I burst out. 'Don't you think you are doing a far more dangerous job than those poor fellows ever dreamed about? Because if you don't think so, I do!'

Adam gave me a remote, quixotic sort of smile.

'Bless you,' he said. 'The incognito, the neutrality of a uniform, orders from above, no more conscience, perhaps it would be a rest sometimes – but I'd make a rotten soldier.'

Outside our gate, he circled the width of the road on his bicycle and came back to my side.

'Mrs B.,' he said, 'one of these days you'll have to write a book – Life Amongst the Huns – what about that?'

'If I do, I'll make a blooming 'ero out of you!' I replied staunchly, and I couldn't help laughing at him, sitting there astride his bike with his hat pushed to the back of his head, looking suddenly years younger, his old self, just a handsome, laughing son of a gun.

'All right,' he said, and put on a great smirk. 'That's a bet. If you make a blooming 'ero out of me, I'll read your rotten book,' – then he added, and the laughter faded as quickly – 'no, wait, perhaps it wouldn't be such a rotten book, Chris B., because I'm beginning to think you understand.' It was only then that I was able to put a name to the expression in his eyes which I thought had not been there before – he looked as if, at some time or other, perhaps more times than one, he had been profoundly hurt.

Before pedalling away around the corner he turned and gave me a cheery wave and cocked a discreet snook in the direction of the house of the Nazi professor across the road. I stood watching the corner long after he had gone – another parting, never an ordinary parting, they were so mighty difficult these days. I put my hands in my pockets as I turned into the gate, and something hard and heavy knocked against my knee – the book *The Last Enemy*, I had not thought it to be such a fat tome. I fished it out and looked again at the title *This Above All*, Frank Knight – I had taken the wrong book. Never mind, I'd read it two years ago, but I could read it again and just now I decided that I preferred the title. How did it go on? 'This Above All – to thine own self be true.' And the other? *The Last Enemy*? I didn't want to read it really any more, for I thought I knew too from where Richard Hillary had got the title for his book. The Last Enemy – 'the Last Enemy . . . is death.'

I looked at my watch and found that I had three hours to go before my train left for the south. I knew that I should be going indoors to rootle about a bit for some possessions which might still come in useful and should be removed to comparative safety. Instead I decided to wander about the garden. It was March after all, and some snowdrops I had planted two years back should be showing some sign of life. They were, they were flowering, and I found a bit of slate and levered a few out of the ground and put one or two in my pocket and replanted the rest next to the Langbehns' air-raid shelter. Then I set off up the road for the station without going into the house.

THE AMERICAN AIRMAN

(Summer 1944)

'Frau Doktor,' I was laying the table for lunch when Hans Bausch's head appeared at the window. His china blue eyes under the fair bushy eyebrows had their usual look of warm and friendly imbecility, but this time there was an urgency in his manner and a very genuine air of pleasurable anticipation. 'Frau Doktor,' he beckoned to me to come to the window and glanced quickly up and down the valley road, 'Frau Doktor, I have something for you.' Bacon? No such luck, I decided. Probably some rather dusty flour or a piece of rancid butter in exchange for one of Nicky's fly-papers. 'Yes, Hans, what is it then?' I went to the window as he looked around him again, in the manner of the true conspirator.

'It's an American, Frau Doktor,' he whispered, 'and if you can guess what he looks like I'll give him to you.'

Sometimes, even a conversation such as this one was preferable to being cooped up with children. However much you loved them, there was something a bit depressing about watching your educative efforts deteriorate to the stage of 'No you can't – well all right yes you can, so long as you buzz off and leave me in peace.' I tried to look duly impressed.

'An American, Hans? How fascinating, thank you very much – now let me see, is he tall?'

'Yep.' 'Dark?' 'Yep.'

I was getting along fine and Bausch's blue eyes were alight with encouragement and childlike admiration.

'Curly haired?' – 'Yep.'

I wanted to please and there was only one caricature of an American which could be known to poor Hans – the American according to the local newspaper the 'Black Forest Messenger'.

'He's wearing a round felt hat, horn-rimmed glasses and he's smoking a big cigar.'

Bausch's face fell. 'No,' he said, 'no, but never mind, you were nearly right. I'll tell you. He's wearing overalls with pockets in the knees, and boots of softest leather lined with fur, and the stuff that his overalls are made of is as smooth as a cow's belly. He's got a watch too, but such a watch. It's got little watches all over its face.'

I looked at Bausch for a moment, but this time a little more thoughtfully. 'Where did you find this American, Hans?' I asked. 'Up in the woods,' he said, 'lying up against my woodpile.' 'And where is he now?' 'He's asleep in my kitchen.'

I asked Frau Muckle to make lunch a little late and followed him up the road and along the winding track which led to his little wooden house at the edge of the woods on the far side of the valley. Bausch hurried ahead of me chuckling away in high spirits. He lifted the latch and pushed open his door, and, shaking with suppressed excitement, he stood back to let me pass. Although it was mid-day, the flower-filled window boxes almost completely blocked the tiny windows, and the little kitchen was very dark. I stood still for a moment in the doorway, and the expression on my face at that moment was most probably no more intelligent than that of Hans Bausch, for stretched on the narrow bench against the far wall, his long legs dangling to the floor, relaxed with a looseness which somehow only Americans achieve most completely, was a tall young figure in blue airman's overalls. He had taken off his fur-lined boots and was using them as a pillow; he seemed fast asleep. As I looked down on him, I do not know why it was that I suddenly realized that the war was inevitably lost for Germany. It was not his unshaven face – a rather typical American face, short nosed, big mouthed, his curly hair close cropped, but just perhaps the general air of health and well-being, of affluence about him; the quality of the stuff his overalls were made of, his boots and the silk scarf which he had tied into his belt, and a soft leather wallet he held in one hand. Suddenly I felt shabby, old, dilapidated and defeated. Everything he had on him was so real: real wool, real leather, real silk – so real and he looked so young. As for me I was bogus – bogus from the soles of my synthetic leather shoes to the brim of my synthetic straw hat, and I was not sure if I would ever feel young again.

'Hi!' I said, giving his shoulder a shake. 'Hi, beautiful!' he answered, without opening his eyes; then he sat up suddenly, very wide awake.

'Say, who are you?' he asked, swivelling around on the bench and letting his feet rest rather gingerly on the floor. 'My name is Chris Bielenberg,' I said, 'and I have just been told by our milkman that he found you propping up his wood-pile.' 'I guess that's just about it, Mam,' he replied with a faint smile. 'How come?' – my wretched habit, inherited from my father, of slipping into the vernacular of whomsoever I happen to be talking with. 'Well,' he said and his drawl was a joy to hear, 'well, I'm sure glad to see you Mam, I guess I have been walking for a long time. Two days and two nights maybe, heading west. We got shot up and baled out over some little town and one of my buddies landed in a tree and I landed near some cover, but when I reached this hill country I realized I'd had it, so when this guy came along I gave myself up, but he's nutty I guess and he brought me here.' 'Have you any idea where you have come from?' I asked. 'No, Mam, no, we just fly nose to tail, nose to tail. I ain't the guy who knows where we're going.'

I tried to remember was it two or three days ago that the huge, high flying formations had last droned over us heading eastwards, streaking the cloudless sky with ribbons of white and making the windows rattle in their frames.

'Well,' I said, 'I don't suppose that matters much now, what is bothering me a little is what to do with you.' 'It ain't no problem, Mam,' he said, 'the war is over as far as I'm concerned,' and from the sudden flatness in his voice I realized he must be very near exhaustion. While we were talking, Hans Bausch was standing beside us eagerly scanning our faces, watching us with the glowing satisfaction of a mother who has given her child a favourite toy to play with.

'If that's the case it's certainly simpler for all concerned,' I said, 'anyway, I think you are right. Your only chance otherwise would have been to get to Switzerland, and you'd have had to cross the Rhein to get there.' 'The Rhein, Mam, what's that?' It was my turn to sound a bit flat. 'Well, it's a river,' I said, 'but never mind—', for suddenly it had flashed through my mind, two days, two nights, Munich possibly or Augsburg, but before that, just a few flying hours before that, of course he must have been in England.

'Tell me quickly,' I said suddenly afraid that someone might come or he might fall asleep again, 'how are things in England, how are they doing, what does it look like?' Perhaps I sounded too urgent, for a wary look crossed his face.

'England,' he said vaguely, 'England, it's a nice enough little place, full of cute little fields and nice flowers.' 'Sure, sure I know, but the war, what are they thinking about the war?' 'Oh the war,' he sounded as if it was the first time that he had heard of it, then he grinned suddenly, 'the war Mam,' he said, 'is in the bag' – equally suddenly he fenced again – 'but why do you ask me so many questions?' 'No reason really,' I said, 'except that I haven't been there for five long years.'

I turned to the window and looked out through the geranium leaves on to the village below us. Things were stirring down there, the drums had sounded their beat and little figures were scurrying about from window to window. There was not much time to lose. It would not be long before rumour took over and knowing my Rohrbach, rumour could quite easily have it that I was having a chat with General Eisenhower.

'You're quite sure you want to give yourself up?' I asked, not knowing quite what I would do if he said no. 'The sooner the better; I'm through,' he answered, taking off his socks and proceeding to massage a pair of very healthy looking feet. 'OK,' I said, 'sit where you are and I will call the Mayor.'

Down in the village everyone was agog. Sepp Kern had left his fields to have a shave, and the Mayor who had been doing his bread round could already be seen urging his nag at an unheard of pace down the hill from the upper valley.

When the Mayor had drawn up to a clattering halt and Kern had returned rather battered from his out-of-season shave, we retired, by mutual consent, to the *Ratszimmer**, a large bare room on the second floor of the school house. The Mayor looked very serious. 'Are you sure he is an American, Frau Dr?' he asked, with an anxious glance at the portrait of Hitler, gazing down at us sternly from the wall behind his desk. 'Oh yes, he's an American all right,' I said, 'he comes from Colorado, and his plane must have been shot down somewhere over Würtemberg.'

'Aha, Colorado, I see, well in that case, Frau Dr, what do you think we should do?' I looked from one to the other as seriously as I could. 'Well,' I said, 'I do not think you have many alternatives. If I were you, I would telephone the police in Furtwangen or in

Ratszimmer – Village Council Office.

Donaueschingen, and ask for instructions.' The Mayor looked most relieved. 'Sepp,' he said, 'Frau Dr of course is right. Come, we will telephone with Donaueschingen immediately.'

We descended the stairs, and proceeded in single file along the road past the *Adler* and up the little path to Kern's shop. Frau Kern had, not unnaturally, an unusual supply of customers standing in front of her bare counter, quite oblivious of her empty shelves. They had not come to shop, and the buzz of conversation died down immediately as we moved on into the little room where Sepp mended shoes and guarded the telephone. No one was going to miss overhearing that telephone call. Just as we were about to close the door, however, the Mayor, the dignity of his office now completely restored, called out sternly, 'I wish to have the shop cleared, do you hear, cleared at once!' And, as Sepp wound the handle and lifted the receiver, we could hear murmurings and shufflings of feet as the disappointed eavesdroppers moved out into the sunshine. Sepp was not having much luck with his telephone call.

'*A wa'*, *a so*, one moment please,' he covered the mouthpiece, and told us there was an air-raid warning in Donaueschingen, no one was answering from the police station, should he try Furtwangen? At first his luck was not much better there. 'Kern here, yes, Sepp, is that you, Johann? Listen, Johann, we have an American here – no, no, an American, he comes from Colorado. What? No, no, he's an airman—' Sepp's good natured face was wreathed in smiles. 'Yes yes, I know, but they found many more over Haslach way, no, but come off it, Johann, I'm serious – wait, I'd better give you the Mayor.' Again he covered the mouthpiece. 'He won't take us seriously,' he said, 'says the only thing as far as he knew which came from Colorado and landed in Rohrbach was the potato beetle.'

The Mayor was fuming with impatience. Apart from the nasty crack about the fact that last year the potato beetle had seemingly made its first appearance in our valley, he was now nervous again and on his mettle. He snatched the telephone from Kern and proceeded to roar down it so loudly, at such speed and in such broad dialect, that I doubted if Johann could have understood had he any ears left to hear with.

'This is the Mayor of Rohrbach speaking, now listen, Johann, if you value your life. We have here a captive American – an American – not a beetle but a man – do you understand you

159

nit-wit, you who spend your miserable life checking whether law-abiding citizens have lamps on the bicycles. Well, we have an American. It is I who tell you, I, the Mayor of Rohrbach. Frau Dr has spoken with him in his own language. Do you hear? He has surrendered to us and if you don't get in touch with the authorities immediately and tell us what to do with him – I will—' Probably the direst threat he could have uttered, would have been that he would never supply poor Johann with that little extra bit of flour on the black again, but he finished by telling him that he would report him for the lazy good-for-nothing bastard that he was. He then shouted Heil Hitler at him and banged down the receiver. 'Well, if that doesn't move him, nothing will,' said Sepp soothingly as we sat back to await results.

We had not long to wait. I was just moving a pair of John's sandals surreptitiously from their lowly position near the floor to the top of the pile of shoes awaiting Sepp's attention, when the telephone rang again. This time it was obviously Johann's superior. 'Yes, Herr Inspector, quite certain, Herr Inspector, certainly, Herr Inspector, we will, Herr Inspector, Heil Hitler, Herr Inspector,' the Mayor, this time, was almost bowing to the telephone. He hung up and turned to the two of us.

'Well, it appears that the whole district is under *Voralarm*,'* he said, 'only reconnaissance planes, but just the same the police and the military are on duty and cannot come here immediately.' He cleared his throat, 'We are, temporarily anyway, to take charge of this American ourselves. He is to be locked up in the Cell.' 'The Cell!' Herr Kern looked genuinely shocked, 'but that's impossible, it's five years at least since – and you remember who was there last, besides I don't think I can find the key.' 'Orders are orders,' said the Mayor, 'the Cell it will be, and if you can't find the key, Sepp, we'll have to break down the door.' 'All right, all right,' Sepp humped out of the room and I could hear him ridding himself of his discomfiture by shouting at his wife and two nice daughters, one of whom appeared, almost immediately, with a huge rusty key.

I had never heard of the existence of this 'cell', although apparently there was one such spot in every village, mainly used in the good old days, when alcohol was available, to accommodate drunks and allow for the cooling off period. I was surprised,

Voralarm – Pre-warning of a possible air-raid.

therefore, to discover that the rusty iron-studded door at the side of the school building was not the coal house, but indeed the Cell. Herr Kern found some difficulty in turning the huge key in the rusty lock, but the blacksmith helped out with an iron bar, and the old door finally creaked open to reveal a tiny cupboard-like enclosure filled with cobwebs and musty hay. The Mayor was now at the top of his form, giving out orders, sometimes conflicting orders to all and sundry. Sepp's daughters were to sweep out and clean the Cell; Fräulein Vohrenbach, the priest's housekeeper, was to fetch bedding, sheets and pillow cases. Frau Muckle was to arrange a meal and I was to be on hand as interpreter when he questioned the prisoner. In the general excitement he had almost forgotten the star of the show and, if the Upper Baker, his rival in the mayoral elections as well as in the bread business, had not pointedly reminded him that if he didn't hurry he probably wouldn't have a prisoner at all, we might have gone on for much longer arranging for our American's comforts. As it was, the Mayor beckoned to me, and we approached Bausch's house as rapidly as possible – with dignity and without trying to look as if we were hurrying. I, for one, was genuinely relieved to find the airman still sitting on the narrow bench leaning against the wall, with a rather morose expression on his tired young face. It had taken me a little time to realize the complications which could have arisen had he escaped. I introduced the Mayor and he got to his feet, towering over both of us, in a casual sort of way. I told him what we had done and that the Mayor wanted to ask him a few questions.

'Go ahead,' he said, 'but I ain't answering any of them.'

It seemed that he, too, had been thinking things over and decided he would communicate no more. Perhaps these were his orders should he be captured, and his earlier lapse had been due to my sudden and unexpected appearance.

'Well, take your time,' I said, 'it can do no harm if you give him your name and number. You told me you were anxious about your mother, and the sooner at least this information gets through, the sooner she will hear that you are a prisoner of war.'

I did not add that possibly, left to himself, the most burning question which the Mayor would have wished to put to him, was what he would prefer for lunch. Anyway, I was suddenly resentful of this tall ignorant boy who had never heard of the Rhein and who flew nose to tail, nose to tail, and did not even know in which town he had left behind a trail of dead and dying. Our artless Mayor in his rough homespuns and square-toed boots, asking his futile questions, and waiting trustfully for me to give him any sort of an answer, was infinitely preferable.

'Well, it doesn't matter much anyway,' I said, when he blocked a very simple question as to how long he had been on the road. I knew the answer and except for the part about England, which I could keep to myself, I could quite easily compose a nice innocuous report for the Mayor.

By the time that the interview was at an end, we found that half the village had arrived in the yard outside Bausch's house and so it was quite a procession which moved down to the *Adler*, led by the tall loose-limbed American airman, who towered above his stocky mountain captors – a head taller than Sepp, who was a big man, he practically obliterated the Mayor. I kept to the rear in order to give the also-rans a true picture of what had happened, since I couldn't risk a garbled story reaching the authorities. Frau Muckle greeted us at the door of her domain. She had on her best apron and Sunday shoes; Martina, hovering in the background, had put a comb through her hair and removed her rubber boots. The Mayor's reserved table in the parlour had been spread with a spotless white cloth, and Nick was waiting behind the chair at the end of the table with a table napkin over his arm and a voluminous blue and white service apron covering his leather pants. Frau Muckle had excelled herself – a splendid joint of roast pork with mashed potatoes and rich red cranberries, with dumplings to follow, feather light and topped with caramelled sugar. Murmuring *'zum Wohl'* Nicky kept the glasses filled with wine which was indistinguishable from vinegar, but which had not been served in the parlour for many a long year.

The American was obviously ravenously hungry and we watched a week's rations disappear at a sitting. Under the influence of the unaccustomed wine, the atmosphere became more relaxed. The airman's morose expression changed to one of slightly bovine puzzlement, and Sepp launched into some rather earthy tales which he insisted I should translate for our guest.

At last we had to leave and, as the tall boy took a last look around him, I noticed that his eye fell on the little bust of Abraham Lincoln in his honoured niche next to the Crucifix. I think this gave him the knock-out blow – and I imagined it providing the climax to a tale he would tell to his grandchildren as he rocked to and fro on his porch years hence somewhere back in Colorado. For he stopped in his tracks obviously dumbfounded, and let himself be led up the road without a murmur until we reached the Cell. Here a transformation had taken place. Nothing could have been done about the size of the cubby hole which went by the name of the Cell, but it had been swept and scrubbed and a strip of red carpeting had been laid on the floor. A narrow mattress had been laid along the bench and a spotless white pillow case, trimmed with lace, peeped out over the bulging white eiderdown. 'Good enough for the Holy Father,' said Fräulein Vohrenbach proudly as she surveyed her handiwork, and seeing that she was the priest's housekeeper, it was clear to all of us that it was to him it doubtless belonged.

Hardly had the huge key creaked to in the rusty lock before I remembered that we had forgotten one important detail. The Mayor had been told to take possession of any papers or belongings our airman might have on him. And we had not even asked him if he was armed. There was a hurried conference; there was no doubt we had slipped up badly. Herr Kern approached the door and knocked politely. 'Yeah?' a muffled answer from inside, and again we had to fetch the blacksmith to help us out with turning the key. The belongings consisted of some identity papers, some pills in silver foil, a silk scarf beautifully printed with a map of south-west Germany, a photograph of a girl and a handful of English money – half-crowns, shillings, pennies; the sheer familiar weight of them in my hand made me catch my breath. He was not armed. We left him the photograph and put the rest into a large envelope. We closed the door and had a peep through the iron grid window. Our airman was already fast asleep.

Early next morning, two middle-aged insignificant little figures in ill-fitting uniforms arrived for breakfast in the *Adler*. They had no ration cards with them, and with little grace Frau Muckle provided them with one or two slices of dry bread and a mug each of synthetic coffee.

A few villagers stopped to stare as the incongruous trio set off down the road to the station. Refreshed and invigorated, towering above his captors, our airman stepped out with long loping strides, his guards having occasionally to break into little runs in order to keep up with him. Then the old continued on their way to early Mass, and the able moved off into the fields shouldering their scythes, impatient to get on with the hay-cut before the dew should leave the grass.

THE PLOT OF JULY 20th

(Autumn 1944)

I wandered slowly up the valley, past the Church and the Schoolhouse and the schoolteacher Lorenz's vegetable patch. The day was cloudless and wonderfully warm. One of those early autumn days in the Black Forest which were worth waiting for through weeks of rain and storm. The hills were clear and near and the trees on their summit a deep purplish black; the only autumn splash of colour a sudden flame of mountain ash or wild cherry. I had an old tin tied round my waist with the coloured rope which Frau Muckle used to tie down the corn cocks. I had told her that I was going mushrooming. I had entered so deeply into the peasant routine that this subterfuge came to me quite naturally and I would have had a guilty conscience about just taking a walk.

I turned up a farm track, which wound uphill away from the road, past piles of neatly stacked logs, across a field, hot and steaming in the morning sun, and I moved into the coolness and silence of the dark woods. Through the trees ahead, like patches of *Pfifferlinge*, pools of brilliant yellow sparkled at me in the half light, and the thought of Frau Muckle's satisfaction if I brought back a free supper made me automatically start to fill my tin. I reached a sunlit clearing and I was glad to sit down – sit down in the warm sun leaning against a fallen tree trunk, breathing in the smell of heather and pine-needles, with the hum of bees around me.

For the last few weeks I had gone through the motions of living, no more. Since that morning, or was it afternoon in July, when the 'Kopp-wife' had come bursting out of her cottage, scarlet in the face, first with the news as usual, shouting 'Turn on the wireless, turn on the wireless, they've thrown a bomb at that Hitler', and

I had stood next to the water trough transfixed, kettle in hand – 'Yes, yes – go on' – I was trying not to shout, 'What happened? – Have they succeeded?'

'I don't know, but it's all being said on the wireless.' Frau Kopp at least had succeeded as never before. I ran through the kitchen to the parlour and she was panting hard on my heels. With my heart bumping I waited for the elderly contraption to heat up and to put me out of my agony. Goebbels was speaking – not Goebbels, it did not matter, the same suave smooth voice – that was enough as soon as I heard the voice, I knew that it had failed. The wireless said that an attempted coup had been made on the life of the Leader by some Generals, whose names I had heard of but did not know; only the name Stauffenberg tolled a bell, a very near bell. Yet even then I could hardly have dared hope that the action was an isolated one, and that those I knew and those I loved were not involved; for without quite realizing what I was doing I pushed blindly through the little crowd of awed faces which had gathered in the kitchen, and made for Kern's shop. Half an hour before I had posted a letter to Adam – I retrieved it – and I was not a moment too soon, for the incoming post had just arrived, and with it a letter from Peter, addressed to Tante Ulla. I tore it open – nearly tore it in half indeed, since my hands were shaking. 'Dear Ulla, I know from Chris that you always take over the children when she is not there, and now I want to thank you for this and to beg you to continue to play substitute mother to our little family. Above all I think it wise to separate up the possessions that we have collected during the years, and to house them with trustworthy peasants. Great changes may be coming in the near future and everything at the moment is slightly unclear. Please look after my family.' The letter was unsigned and I had looked at the date and the postmark, July 14th, posted in Graudenz, and for a moment it was as if my heart had stopped beating and I was held rigid, almost paralysed, in some cold, inflexible vice.

What was it that Hitler said later that night on the wireless, as he rasped hoarsely about Providence having saved him to carry on his task? I could not remember. I had only listened in the faint ridiculous hope that Goebbels' earlier announcement might prove to be untrue. From that moment I had gone about my daily chores as if in a dream, and the sun had risen and the sun had set, as step by fateful step, heralded by sparse announcements over the wireless or in the newspapers, the menace had moved in closer, and the full portent of those happenings gradually beat down upon me.

Some days after that Radio announcement, a week perhaps, they published a first list of 'conspirators'. They were all Army officers and Peter Yorck's and von Haeften's names were amongst those given. No news from Peter. Nicky's birthday – no news. An unsigned postcard on August 8th, from Berlin – 'Adam was arrested on July 25th. I can't imagine why. Love and blessings to you all.' Afterwards – nothing – and four long weeks had passed. I had sent off three letters begging Peter to write, as the air-raids on Berlin were mounting in ferocity. I had sent a telegram asking for money. I had written to Herr Seiler,* Peter's boss – no answer. It was as if there was an echoless void, out beyond the rounded horizon of our hills. Now two days ago they published the names of the main civilian 'conspirators', those who were to have taken over the government when Hitler was dead. Adam's name was amongst the eight – they are to be hanged. Yes, that's what they said – they are to be hanged. I have learned that, just as in physical pain a stage can be reached where the body can stand no more, and becomes unconscious, so too there is a limit to mental suffering beyond which you can feel no more; a sort of numbness takes over which is merciful.

'Failed' – 'failure', wherever I went I could not escape those words and the dreadful meaning behind them. I had read somewhere of some lady in France who had lost a beloved husband and who had not been able to escape the word *seule*. She'd had it embroidered into the coverings and curtainings, woven into the carpets: *seule* – alone, failure – failed: I could not escape it either, even in the silence of the forest.

How had it failed? Why had it failed? Could it be that God, as the German saying goes, is always on the side of the strongest battalions? I sneered away from the thought, but with Adam perhaps already dead and Peter possibly too, and Hitler, the personification of evil, with all his hordes and evildoers about him allowed to live, it was hard to keep faith.

There was no comfort anywhere. The newspaper headlines: 'I will continue with my work since Providence has guarded me.' The telegrams of congratulation – nauseating smirch, 'I

*He was head of the Bankhaus Seiler, formerly Bankhaus Aufhäuser in Munich.

cannot sleep at nights, my Leader, when I think how near the traitor's hand – ' The English wireless – Churchill's ponderous satisfaction at 'Germans killing Germans'; or that jaunty crew from *Soldatensender Eins*, usually good for a laugh, but now like macabre boy scouts gleefully hammering nails into coffins by implicating everyone they could think of in what they called 'the Peace Plot'; or having to stand by and listen when Dr R., a pompous ass whose children were living with Frau Kopp, returned for the weekend from Strasbourg and announced that he had talked with many responsible people there, and all had agreed it would have been a tragedy for Germany if Hitler had died on July 20th.

Why, oh why, had it failed? How *could* it have failed? I supposed there must be some reason why, some reason beyond my comprehension but I could not think, there was nothing to think about; except I supposed that I would have to learn to think again, to adjust, to talk, perhaps even to laugh and somehow to go on living, in a world which no longer held any meaning.

The sun had moved westwards and long shadows dimmed the glow of heather in my little clearing. The autumn afternoon had turned cold. I shivered a bit and picking up my tin of mushrooms, made my way back to the *Adler*. The faint tinkle of cowbells from the cow-sheds as I passed told me that it must be getting late and that it would not be long before the long-legged hill cattle would be let out into the fields. The children must be out of school, lunch must be over long ago.

Nicky was sitting in his corner doing his homework as I opened the door of the *Nebenstube*; his book was propped up by his satchel in front of him. 'Didn't you want any lunch, Mum? We had blueberries and milk and pancakes.' 'No thank you, darling.' I turned to put my mushroom tin on the spinet and saw the letter; letters were a rarity those days. A small square white envelope; Frau Dr Peter Bielenberg, Gasthaus zum Adler, Rohrbach im Schwarzwald. Berlin postmark, August 25th, 1944. I did not recognize the handwriting. I sat on the sofa and slit open the envelope and its contents came almost as an anti-climax, the reiteration of an oft-told tale, read a thousand times in bed at night, on waking in the morning – for the last three weeks I had known it had to come. The handwriting was Mabel Horbottle's. 'Dear Chris, I do not like having to give you this news. Peter was arrested in Graudenz on August 6th. We only heard about it yesterday. We naturally feel certain that he will soon be out again and send you our love and we will let you know as soon as we have further news.'

Nicky's pen scratched along over the rough paper of his copy book, the old wooden clock on the wall ticked off the seconds, some cows passed the window on their way to pasture and the little herd's whip cracked smartly over their backs; a low keening moan beside me made me start. Funny thing, I thought I had been alone with my letter. I had not noticed that Tante Ulla had come into the room and was leaning over my shoulder. 'Oh no, Chris, oh no,' she sobbed, 'first my Albrecht and now Peter, oh no, oh my God no.' I came to life suddenly and glanced at Nicky whose pen had stopped scratching and who was looking at us both with a startled stare, his eyes in his brown face suddenly very brilliantly blue. 'Let's go upstairs, Ulla,' I heard myself muttering, as her sobbing threatened to turn to hysteria, 'let's go upstairs, come—' and I found myself leading her gently up the narrow staircase which led to the bedroom above. 'Look, lie down, my dear, it's not that bad really.' I fumbled through the bottles on my dressing table, trying to find some pill which might help to quieten her – an aspirin, any darn thing. Then I sat on my bed holding her hand, glad to hold her hand, until her sobs subsided and she lay there staring blankly at the ceiling.

Back in the sitting-room, at first, I could not see my son. His head was buried in his arms and his satchel hid his face. As I crossed the room he lifted his head and I realized that I was no longer looking at a child. His face had gone small, very small, almost wizened, and he was struggling with hard, dry, convulsive sobs which shook him, as if with ague. 'Is Daddy dead?' he whispered as I stood next to his table with my hand resting gently on his bony little shoulder. 'No, he's not dead,' I said, 'he's in prison.' He jerked away suddenly and stood up next to me, his head shoulder high to mine. 'In prison? Daddy in prison – but why?' I hesitated for a moment, realizing that the lie I told now was the one I had to stick to. 'Well,' I said rather hesitantly, 'Daddy has an enemy up in Graudenz, an enemy who was out to do him down. He had made all sorts of false accusations against Daddy and has managed to get him into prison.' 'Yes, but what about the police? Daddy's done nothing wrong, so why didn't the police stop Daddy's enemy getting him into prison?' I was not making a very good job of it. A flicker of doubt was dawning behind

Nicky's direct, enquiring, somehow adult look. 'The police, yes, the police. Well, as soon as they find out that the accusations are false, they will, of course, let him out.' With a tact born perhaps of his new adulthood, Nicky averted his gaze, gave a short sigh and turned away. He stood with his back to me looking out of the window. He did not believe my tale and every line of his straight little back told me so. 'Anyway, that's my story, Nick, and I'm sticking to it,' I said as lightly as I could, trying perhaps to make some approach to that lonely little figure at the window. He did not move, but without turning round he burst out suddenly in clear German with no trace of Baden dialect, 'When this war is over I don't want to stay in Germany. I want to go back to England. I want to be English. Mummy, do you hear? I want to be English. In England the police don't let you go to prison for things you haven't done. In England' – his voice was deserting him again – 'In England things are different.'

I, too, was very near the end of my tether and I could think of nothing better to do than to go and stand beside him at the window. Soon I felt a wet, rather inky little hand push its way into mine and we stood together, a truly forlorn pair, gazing out at the green slopes and wooded hills on the far side of the valley. A faint yodel and, 'You'd better go fetch your whip, Nick, Martina will be waiting with the cows.' He clambered through the window and dropped to the grass outside and he rounded the corner of the house without turning back or saying a word.

When I went to tuck the boys in that night it was obvious that John had heard the news. His eyes sparkled at me over the bulging eiderdown. 'I have just heard that Daddy is in prison,' he said. 'Yes.' 'And he has an enemy who has got him put in prison.' 'Yes, that's right.' 'Oh golly, I am just longing to see what happens to Daddy's enemy when Daddy gets out of prison, aren't you, Mummy? There'll be the whale of a scrap. Bang, bang, de dong, de dong – Daddy will make mincemeat of him.' He wriggled in anticipation and punched his eiderdown so smartly that Christopher, who was watching the scene intently through the bars of his cot, simply exploded with laughter.

Later, I was alone in the parlour – alone, except for Frau Muckle, who was sleeping behind the stove. The little nightlight burned in 'God's corner' and the old inn was sleeping too, silent except for the sound of trickling water from the trough outside the window and the flowers in the window boxes tapping gently on the panes, as they were stirred by the wind which came sighing up the valley. Boom, boom, boom – Boom: the English time signal on the wireless; I listened to the ten o'clock news and it was then that I knew what I must do. Boom, boom, boom – Boom, I had not much time to spare, for allowing for every kind of misinformation, there was no doubt whatsoever that the Allies were really on the move. Their tanks were sweeping ahead – Brussels, Antwerp, Verdun. The Rhine might hold them up for a little while, but for an army that had crossed the Channel, it could not be for long. They must know – trust Churchill – yes, they must know because even I knew that they had to reach Berlin before the Russians. What they could not know was that the prisons were full of men, condemned or awaiting trial. Men who would be needed after the war was over, and whose only hope of survival depended on the speed of their advancing tanks. How I wished that I could signal the news to some reconnaissance plane as it hummed over us, aloof and remote – 'There is nothing, just nothing barring your way. There's hardly a Nazi to be seen these days. Most of the voluntary offerings for the last Winter-help clothing collection consisted of brown uniforms. The rats are leaving the sinking ship and your enemies have been reduced to old men and schoolboys. Keep it up, just please keep it up, but before over-running us all, allow me a fortnight, three weeks perhaps, just to get to Berlin and back again to the children—'

For it seemed that the letter, in spite of its dread contents, had succeeded in rousing me to action; it had been perhaps the harrowing uncertainty which had taken all the spirit out of me. Peter, after all, was still alive. Adam, too, for all I knew, and Carl, and Helmuth and the others – but Peter must be got away from Graudenz somehow. The Graudenz Gestapo, those hideous masks seen through a haze of smoke, if he were left in their charge he might be liquidated without trial. I knew that I must go to Munich to see Herr Seiler and then on to Berlin. Perhaps with the war's end just around the corner, the fact that I was English might help rather than hinder. Travelling I had heard was safer nowadays, since the Allies were using all their aeroplanes in France. I was suddenly alive with half formulated plans, and I knew that I had no time at all to spare, but must leave on the morrow for Munich and Berlin.

*   *   *

I did not arrive in Munich until late in the afternoon of the following day. The *Bankhaus* Seiler was no longer so easy to find since the Frauenkirche was an empty shell, and the square around it was mainly a heap of rubble. One such pile, I noticed, was covered with a fine growth of potato plants in full blossom, and I remembered the existence on my last visit of a small vegetable shop. The *Bankhaus* itself was unscathed and neatly sandbagged. I thought the clerk, whose greying hair, for some odd reason, was parted carefully down the back of his head, gave me a particularly friendly look as he led me upstairs and ushered me into Herr Seiler's private office. I could not say the same of Herr Seiler. He did not get up nor ask me to sit down, but sat upright behind his desk, looking rather like my grandmother's chauffeur on his free Sunday. Meanwhile a chinless young man with lank fair hair and germanic cranium fluttered around him, clearing his throat and sorting papers and files. 'What can I do for you? Why are you here?' – the words I was greeted with did not make for a very auspicious start, but luckily, just as I was about to answer, the poor young man tripped over the waste-paper basket and his armful of files shot across the floor; so I was allowed a few moments to collect my thoughts. I knew it to be expedient in Germany always to meet aggressiveness with an immediate counterblast.

'Well, I am here for a very good reason,' I answered with some asperity. 'I want to know why my husband is in prison and why in heaven's name I only heard of it yesterday.'

'I can answer the second question more easily than the first. I had not time to let you know, Frau Bielenberg. As for the reason why your husband is in prison, you probably know it better than I do.' The interview was obviously going to be more difficult than I had thought.

'Well, I don't know how I should know,' I said, 'I've been living in the Black Forest for the last year and a half and we've hardly seen each other.'

Herr Seiler glanced at his watch, 'I have not much time, Frau Dr Bielenberg,' he said and turning to the young man he asked him to go next door and listen to the hourly wireless report on air activity over the Reich. 'I may as well be frank with you,' he said, 'five of my associates are in prison, your husband is one of them. I have no sympathy with any of them. I have some influence, but I cannot possibly testify for them all, neither do I intend doing so.

I will select two and see what I can do. The rest will have to look after themselves.'

I tried to make a quick mental calculation as to whom he might be referring: Peter, Carl Langbehn, possibly Schniewind, Bayer – I did not know who had been arrested and who not.

'Was your husband friendly with any of the main conspirators?'

'Well,' I hesitated, 'yes, I suppose he was – er – Adam von Trott for instance.'

'Von Trott? Well he, of course, has been hanged,' he broke in curtly and again glanced at his watch.

I felt my mouth go dry and for a moment I found myself unable to focus properly. Herr Seiler's nondescript face floated around in front of me and it was only with the greatest effort that I managed to stay on my feet.

'Oh – I see, well, Herr Seiler, I see that you are in a hurry, but before I go there is one thing I would ask you. If you should decide that my husband is to be one of those for whom you mean to testify, I would ask you to use your influence in having him transferred from Graudenz to Berlin. As you probably know, for the sake of proficiency in the aeroplane works he had made enemies with the local Gestapo. As things are at the moment he could – they could—' I was a little doubtful how I should proceed.

Herr Seiler was on his feet tidying the papers on his desk. I noticed that his hands were not too steady and thought maybe he was not quite as hardboiled as he made out to be. 'Highly unlikely, I would think,' he interrupted me, 'but I will see what I can do.'

Did that mean that Peter was to be one of the two? Should I try to tip the scales in his favour and persuade Herr Seiler to desert some other equally worthy candidate? My reply was out before I had time to think, not a reply which would have come from a saint, but rather that of an unprepared mortal suddenly faced with a contest for survival.

'Thank you, Herr Seiler,' I said, 'maybe I shall be able to repay you somehow, after this war is over.'

The chinless young man led me downstairs and left me with an elegant bow on the pavement outside the Bank. It was evening and already dark, and I realized that I had no place to spend the night. I hesitated for a moment, looking about me, and would have tried the Frauenkirche if the great doors had not been boarded up, when I felt a tap on my arm and the nice old clerk was standing there beside me.

'Frau Bielenberg?' 'Yes.' 'My associate and I are on duty tonight in the Bank. It occurred to us that you may have no place to sleep. Would you care to share our air-raid shelter?'

'That is very kind of you, indeed I would,' I said, and he ushered me back into the Bank, and down some stairs to a spotlessly tidy little box of a room sparsely furnished with two bunks, a table and two chairs and a small oil stove. The only picture decorating the walls was a rather worn daguerreotype of the Crown Prince Rupert of Bavaria, heavily bewhiskered, astride a prancing charger; and the only weapons for the defence of the Bank, two enormous pickaxes and a couple of buckets of water.

'One moment,' said my companion, 'I must see the Boss off the premises, and then we can relax a little.'

How friendly and how tactful were those two old men when they came downstairs later and opened their briefcases, spread out their meagre evening meal on the table and removed their collars and ties to put on their carpet slippers and prepare themselves for the night. As soon as we had the Bank to ourselves, they telephoned for me to find out when the next train would leave for Berlin. They also telephoned to Rohrbach, to tell Ellen that I would be passing through Triberg some time in the afternoon of the following day. They turned on the radio and we congratulated each other that there was small chance of a raid that night. Only a few reconnaissance planes were over Reich territory, and if anything major had been thought up for Munich the flocks of night raiders would already have started on their way. After we had finished our meal, we decided that we were still very hungry and it was then that I suddenly remembered the ruins of the vegetable shop next door.

'But of course, you are right, Frau Dr, they may be small, but there must be potatoes underneath.'

My host had temporary qualms about raiding the Bank and making use of the gleaming little brass shovels which to date had doubtless been used solely for marks and pfennigs. His companion was willing to throw caution to the winds, so that having sallied forth *à trois*, armed with rulers and certain air defence equipment, we could return shortly afterwards with two canvas money-bags filled to the brim with shining new spuds. The little oil stove was lit, some water pilfered from the fire buckets, my host's steel helmet did good service as a saucepan, and we all agreed that never had potatoes tasted so good.

Before turning in, I could not resist a last look at the man who had given me his bunk and insisted on dossing down on the floor. I could not fathom how he managed to keep his back parting in place. He slept with a broad linen bandeau round his head, and in the dim glow of the nightlight he looked rather like Suzanne Lenglen in effigy.

*   *   *

The following day the train drew into Triberg punctually at 4.30 p.m. As was usual, the railways functioned normally as soon as they had some respite from raids. Ellen and Nicky were standing side by side on the platform, watching the carriage windows anxiously as they passed. They had walked over the hills from Rohrbach, bringing with them more supplies and the odd extra bit of clothing. While Nicky was stowing away his parcels in my carriage, I told Ellen quickly of the news about Adam; even as I told of it, I knew that I could not be telling the truth. Just the same, Ellen seemed anxious.

'I don't know that you should be going, Chris. Hans arrived unexpectedly yesterday and said they were preparing to evacuate Strasbourg. At this rate the war can't last more than a week or so. I will naturally look after the children as well as I can, but for the moment I can't see what good you can do in Berlin.' Ellen was not far wrong; for the moment I could not see very well either, but the faces of those Graudenz Gestapo haunted me – and I knew I had to go.

*   *   *

Berlin greeted me with a bang, or rather a series of very loud bangs. After a seemingly endless journey of two days and two long nights, the train stopped in Potsdam. It grated to a halt in complete silence, and seemed determined never to move again. We passengers did not look very elegant in the bright morning sunshine, slumped as we were about the carriage as if we had been drugged. The man opposite me, who had been staring blindly out of the window, suddenly tapped me on the knee.

'*Gnädige Frau*,' he mumbled, 'didn't I hear you say yesterday that you lived in Dahlem and that you were in some hurry? Well, if you get out here and take the *S. Bahn* to Zehlendorf, you're no way from Dahlem. You could get a bus or something – even walk. We may be stuck here for hours.'

174

It took me no time to decide. I was suddenly wide awake and, pushing my way down the corridor, I jumped to the platform and came back to our window. My neighbour handed me down my rucksack and I made for the entrance to the Underground. Hardly had I reached the staircase, however, before I regretted my sudden decision, for the train I had left jerked to life, and without warning steamed off down the tracks towards Berlin. Oh well, I had not long to wait for the *S. Bahn*, I thought, and it would not be more than an hour or so before I reached Falkenried; but I had not reckoned with the Americans. As we stopped and started again on the way to Zehlendorf, the passing platforms looked more and more deserted.

'Looks like there's going to be a raid,' said the man opposite me, looking at his watch and glancing at the sky. 'Twelve o'clock, punctual as usual.' He went on reading his paper.

In Zehlendorf, the guard on the platform was using the platform telephone. 'How long? Two minutes? Thank you; how many by the way? Fifteen hundred? Aha, thank you.' He hung up and ran from carriage to carriage – '*Alle aussteigen, bitte. Alle aussteigen* (everyone out please). Air-raid warning imminent.'

I was a little ahead of the crowd, but I had hardly got to the bottom of the stairs before the sirens started wailing and howling about me. Although I knew Zehlendorf well, I could not recognize a single landmark. Since I had been there last, every house, every street had changed its face. Boarded windows, heaps of rubble, walls blown in, blown out, blown away, like open-fronted dolls' houses they disclosed sudden intimate glimpses of furnishings and decorations within.

I sprinted off at right angles in what I thought was the direction of Dahlem, trying to put as much ground as possible between me and the railway track; my footsteps echoed along the silent and deserted streets. I ran until I could hear a dull booming in the distance; the outer ring of anti-aircraft guns, how well I remembered that sound. A louder rumbling, the second ring, and then, above the guns, the high even purposeful humming which I knew so well from Rohrbach – the 'heavies'; only this time, God help me, I was in the target area. The humming became a remorseless roar. An arrow, marked Public Air-raid Shelter, pointed down a side street and I made for what looked like a narrow concrete-sided trench which had been dug out of someone's backyard and covered with a tin roof. At the top of a flight of rough steps I stopped to unhitch my rucksack which was too bulky to get through its narrow entrance. A long drawn out and piercing whistle, a tremendous explosion and a gust of sudden wind from behind – and from that moment I had no idea how I descended the stairs and landed across the lap of a small personage who was trying to keep her balance on a narrow bench inside by pressing her hands and feet against the wall opposite. *'Allmächtiger Gott, Oh Heiland,'* she was moaning, 'and Schnucki is all alone in the flat.' 'I'm sorry, oh God, I'm sorry,' I said, as I tried to get to my feet. Sorry for Schnucki, sorry for having nearly flattened her, sorry indeed that I had come to Berlin. The whole concrete dug-out was rocking about like a dinghy in a stormy sea, and what with the pandemonium of whines and crashes outside, and a certain deafness after the first explosion, I could not hear what my companion was saying. Suddenly, 'Eight', she said loudly and firmly, 'peace now until the next wave comes over.' Sure enough our refuge quietened itself and she removed her feet from the wall opposite. 'Eight? What's eight got to do with it?' I wondered if she had found some magic formula. 'Eight bombs in each bomb cradle,' she announced with professional exactitude, 'and we were obviously in direct line.'

In the dusty half-light I could see that my rucksack was blocking the entrance to our shelter. I retrieved it quickly and came back to sit next to her on her bench against the wall. 'How long do you think this will go on for?' I looked at her with some respect. She was not at all young and was wearing an odd assortment of rather well-cut clothes, topped by the inevitable severe black pork-pie hat with broad green ribbon – *chapeau de rigueur* for the Bavarian gentry, and much to their resigned resentment, *chapeau d'adoption* by Prussians of the same ilk. She looked, in fact, rather like a waxwork figure of Queen Victoria which hadn't been dusted for months. 'Not long,' she said precisely, 'an hour, perhaps two. An American carpet raid. They send over high-flying pathfinder planes which drop lights, they are more easily seen at night. Christmas trees we call them. They drop them at each corner of a large square – one, two, three, four' – she drew a square in the dust on the floor with the toe of her shabby button boot. 'Then, my dear, over come the heavy bombers and drop everything they have into the square. Friendly, isn't it?' Whilst we were talking, the thumping and thudding seemed to have retreated a little, but now the humming roar seemed to be advancing on us again. My companion cocked her ears. 'Yes, here they come again – one, two—' the fifth explosion was so near that the walls about us shivered as if they were about to fall to bits. Suddenly we were in each other's arms, Queen Victoria and I. This was the end – there would be no 'six' for us. Clutching each other as if we were drowning we bent our heads under the hurricane of sound. 'Oh God,' I prayed, 'look after Peter, look after the children, look after—' Six – the trench was still rocking and a cloud of gritty dust had come belching down the stairway. Coughing and spluttering with our heads pressed into each other's shoulders, we heard the thudding retreat once more. We were alive. I was suddenly crying – tears turning the dust to mud on my hands and face. My companion was crying too; I was glad, for she became more human that way. Dreadful, I thought rather hysterically, if she had merely sat there and repeated those famous words of her royal prototype: 'We are not amused.' But no – 'That's the nearest I have ever had,' she said between coughs and sobs, 'the very nearest.' Then, suddenly pulling herself together she adjusted her hat and added, 'An extremely expensive method of trying to kill us, isn't it?'

The rest of the raid was almost an anti-climax. Sometimes it seemed to flow nearer, sometimes further away. The narrow entrance glowed red and yellow and red again as the fires took a hold, but our refuge stayed firmly put. My companion passed the time until the All Clear sounded, cleaning and dusting out the contents of her handbag; an old lady's handbag, filled with odds and ends of junk and memories. She was shaking out a little fur tippet which had fallen to the floor, when she suddenly remembered 'Schnucki'. It was all I could do to persuade her not to leave the trench there and then. 'Who is Schnucki?' 'No, he is not a person, he is my dog; I will never go shopping without him again.' She managed to root out and dust a faded brown photograph of a dachshund sitting at the top of a broad flight of stone steps, leading to an elegant brass-studded doorway. 'Your home?' 'Yes, my home; at least, my home that was. East Prussia, the Russians will be there soon, I suppose. My children thought I should not wait for the Russians. Pure nonsense – it only goes to show that one should never listen to one's children.'

She did not want to communicate further, she was anxious to be off and I had got used to asking no unnecessary questions.

After the final All Clear, when the danger of time bombs was also past, we stood for a moment with our heads above

177

ground, surveying the scene around us, from the blazing sky-line to what must have been a bus depot nearby. It had become an incongruous heap of twisted metal, and the buses had been tossed around like abandoned toys. We shook hands and parted at the top of the shelter steps, and I watched her pick her way through the smoking rubble and around the giant bomb craters. The wind, the unnatural air-raid wind blustered about her, and she had need to hold fast to her tippet and also her pork-pie hat; but she had great dignity that dusty little *grande dame*, and I found myself rather hoping sincerely that Schnucki had survived to take part in further shopping expeditions.

I walked to the Falkenried and, as our garden door was open, I passed around the house and looked into the french window of the sitting-room. Mabel was doing some ironing and jumped as she heard my voice. For a moment she hardly seemed to recognize me, then – 'Chris, my dear Chris.' She put down her iron and still looking at me in a shocked almost embarrassed sort of way, she added, 'Come in, come in and sit down; I did not know when to expect you – come.' She took me by the arm and led me to the sofa; she was treating me like an elderly imbecile. 'Come, let me make you some tea.' She went to the radiator, and removed a bit of paper which was covered in tea leaves. As she went to the door she turned and gave me a scared sort of smile.

I went to the bathroom to wash my hands and when I looked in the mirror a stranger looked back at me – a white-haired stranger with huge black-rimmed eyes and powdered lips. For a moment I, too, was aghast, and lurid tales of people going white-haired overnight flashed across my mind. I looked more closely and then grabbed the hand-shower and watched with some relief as the dust and dirt trickled down the wastepipe.

Back in the sitting-room Mabel was waiting for me with two cups of hot water faintly tinged with yellow. 'I'm sorry, my dear, but the leaves have been used twice before,' she said without looking up. Then as I sat down beside her she glanced at me shyly, and suddenly burst out laughing. 'Gracious, Chris, I am sorry,' she said, 'but you gave me such a fright. I just didn't recognize you. Wherever have you been?'

I told her of the little *entr'acte* in Zehlendorf, and she said thoughtfully that she imagined that that part of Berlin had got the worst of it. She herself had not gone to the shelter but had managed to do all her ironing, having taken advantage of the boost in electric current when the factories closed down for the raid. As we sipped our tea and I watched her worn face, it occurred to me how incongruous it was that we two English-women should be sitting there bomb dodging, and passing the time of day. She even had an English passport, but a German mother, I believed, and had, therefore, somehow evaded being interned. I did not know her very well, but we spoke the same language and so it was not long before I was asking her what she knew of the circumstances of Peter's arrest. She told me first that she did not know much more than I did. He had arrived in Berlin on July 28th and had stayed for several days. Neither she nor Arnold had seen much of him, nor had he spoken much with either of them. He had seemed continuously on the go; he had been arrested immediately on his return to Graudenz.

As her rather barren little story came to an end, she seemed to hesitate and then she quickly put her hand over mine and added, 'It's no use, Chris, I can't hold it back. Two days before he left he seemed to have a high temperature; he was shivering and sweating and I took a hot drink to his room. I don't know if he was delirious or what, but he suddenly burst out to me that he had had some teleprint message from von Trott on July 15th, asking him when he would be in Berlin and that he had teleprinted back that he would be here on the 28th. As you know, there is now a *Führerbefehl* that at least one director must be on the factory premises day and night – the death penalty for all directors if there should be a slip-up. His co-director was away and he was sleeping in the office, so that he could not leave earlier than the 28th; and then he arrived too late to see von Trott before his arrest. He said he was not going to allow Trott to remain in custody. He had found out the exact time of day that Trott was being transported from Oranienburg, I think he said, to the Prinz Albrechtstrasse for interrogation; and that he was going back to Graudenz to collect a machine gun from the factory arsenal and he and another friend were going to shoot von Trott out. He would have the factory car with him and intended taking Trott to the Tucheler Heide, some huge wooded moorland area near Graudenz which is still in the hands of Polish partisans. It all sounded a bit crazy to me, Chris, but these are crazy times. He asked me to tell you if he failed, and he told me he knew that you would understand.'

Her voice was pitched so low that I could hardly hear what she was saying. 'I haven't told Arnold of this,' she went on, 'and you can rest assured that Arnold is doing his utmost for Peter. But I'm haunted at nights wondering whether he was arrested before or after he got those machine guns, or whether he told anyone who was not reliable about his plan.'

The telephone ringing on my writing table made us both jump. I plugged it into the wall and lifted the receiver. An unusual whirring sound greeted me and, seeing my slightly puzzled look, Mabel grabbed a piece of paper. 'TAPPED,' she wrote on it in big letters and pushed it under my nose. 'Oh, hallo—' it was Arnold. 'Is that you, Chris?' His voice sounded brisk and businesslike. 'I must say, I'm glad to hear you've arrived, you took some other train of course. You didn't? But that's impossible, the only train from Munich was bombed and strafed all the way from Schmargendorf to the Potsdamer Bahnhof. Three or four hundred casualties. You were on that train? You what? You got out in Potsdam and came by the *S. Bahn*? My God – well – I'll be home soon. Goodbye.'

Whilst I was talking, I had been idly turning over the papers on my desk. One particular envelope propped up against the inkstand caught my eye; a square green business envelope, the telephone bill or receipt – perhaps, but it was not the typewritten address I was looking at. On the bottom right-hand corner of the envelope was our name written in ink, and the handwriting was Adam's. I put back the receiver and opened the envelope. It had not been stuck down, and inside the bill was a thin slip of paper. 'Love to you both, A.' It was as if I was gripped by a sudden violent pain. I had to stand very still. I think that was the first time I realized irrevocably that Adam was no longer living. I asked Mabel if she knew how the envelope had reached my desk. She did not know. I asked her whether the house had been searched and she said it had not. I asked no more. It seemed that the age of miracles, little miracles at least, had not completely passed.

Arnold arrived about an hour later and the genuine warmth of his greeting made me glad that he was Peter's friend. 'My dear Chris, you shouldn't have come, of course, but now you have, it's jolly good to see you.' He spoke excellent English. 'We have a whole heap to talk about. I am extremely optimistic; but wait 'til I've washed my hands and we'll get down to it. Mabel, what about those tea leaves?' I had forgotten to disconnect the telephone; he tugged it out of the wall and added – 'It's been tapped since Peter's arrest, so we have to be a bit careful.' He came back to the sitting-room, brushed and spruce, and sat down in front of what was now a cup of hot water. I looked at his tough, handsome face and realized that he had changed a good deal since I had seen him last, some two years back. He was thin and fit-looking, but his face had that transparent pallor, particularly about the eyes, which everyone seemed to have who had to live in this beleaguered and bombarded city.

'The age of miracles has not passed,' he said, as if reading my thoughts. I thought for a moment that he must be referring to Adam's note, but his face had gone taut. 'To think that you should have left that train in Potsdam; actually I went down to meet it thinking that you might be on it. I spent the raid in the Underground and came up just as they were taking away the casualties. Rows and rows of stretchers on the platform. Men, women and children, and some people still clutching bunches of flowers hurrying from stretcher to stretcher.' He shook himself, 'I'm sorry Chris, I know we're going to be accused of all sorts of horrors after this war, but for the life of me I can't see where the hell the difference comes in.'

The cup of hot water had gone lukewarm; even Arnold couldn't cope with it. He took a sip and pushed the cup away. 'Well, my dear, let's get down to our Piet' – he used the Hamburg vernacular – 'for the moment I think he is just as well off where he is. He's away from air-raids and he's away from the centre of things so to speak. Before the Courts get round to examining his case' – he paused – 'Chris, I am going to be perfectly honest with you. I do not agree with what happened on July 20th. I think I once told Peter that to try and get rid of this régime would be as foolhardy as to grab hold of a live wire with wet gloves. Anyway I am absolutely certain that Peter had nothing to do with it.' Perhaps it was the quick glance at the telephone, and the way he raised his voice which made me think he could have left out the 'perfectly honest with you' part. For the time being at least one thing was certain, Arnold and I were not going to be able to be perfectly honest with each other, 'I utterly agree with you; we need not even discuss it,' I said firmly, 'but I must disagree on one point and it is for this reason I have come to Berlin. Peter must be got away from Graudenz as soon as possible.'

I went on to describe what I knew of his relationship with the local Gestapo there and at the thought of the brutal face, 'Peter's private headache' seen through the smoky haze of that hotel restaurant, my voice gave way. 'He hasn't a chance up there, not a chance. He will be murdered, if he hasn't already been murdered, before he even comes up for trial.'

'Come, come, things are not as bad as that,' Arnold said as he jumped to his feet, and it was all I could do to stop myself replying 'You know damn well they are.' But from the way he was pacing the room, I knew that my words had gone home. Suddenly he swung round and stood in front of me, equally suddenly he was speaking German.

'Listen, Chris,' he said earnestly, 'you know me and you know what I feel about Peter. He is my friend. I've known him since we were students together and I'm living in his house. You know, too, some of the arguments we've had together, Piet and I. We did not agree but it has made no difference to our friendship. It was my opinion at the time, it still is, that this régime was the last card we had to play here in Germany, and that if we did not back it with everything we had, this country would go communist and a communist Germany would have meant that Peter and I, and you as well for that matter, could look forward to a nice long stay in Siberia, if we even got that far. Believe me, I know the communists. In England, in spite of the miserable conditions I met with in the north, Marxism seemed to me never to get beyond being something of a mental exercise; the lecturers and the talkers, however brilliant, destructively brilliant I might say, could never have succeeded in giving birth to one single communist member of Parliament – well, one perhaps. It was very different here.'

I knew it had been different, and I knew too that Arnold, as a student during the dying months of the Weimar Republic and the early days of National Socialism, had been in the thick of it, in fact in 1933 he had organized a students' march to protest against the arbitrary dismissals of Jewish professors from Hamburg University. As a boy he had belonged to the Nationalist *Jung-Stahlhelm* and had lived in a left-wing district amongst those others – the Red Front, the Social Democratic Reichs Banner, and finally the Nazis – who had felt passionately enough about their various creeds to fight pitched battles in the streets, until Hitler had succeeded in swallowing the lot; rewarding them for their extinction by giving work to the workless, an Army to the militant, and a host of scapegoats on which to focus their manifold resentments – not to forget concentration camps for those who did not approve of his methods. How was it though that Hitler had succeeded with some of the more intelligent ones, with those who still possessed personal integrity, unless he had provided something more, something which had made them long for his leadership to succeed, in spite of the ever more obvious viciousness of his régime? Would it have been that sense of national identity which he could conjure up with such mastery? That awareness of belonging somewhere, which in England just came naturally, but which I believed amongst Germans to be a rare, almost unique phenomenon? Never mind, I gave up. I was suddenly very tired. I knew that Arnold was on my side and as for the rest that was for him to puzzle out.

'Listen,' I said, 'it's no use you and I arguing about the rights and wrongs. I have just been nearly killed by my so-called American cousins, and I'm in a thorough muddle myself. It's just that instinct tells me that Graudenz is not the place where Peter should be. If it is possible to get him transferred to Berlin, I think we shall have to risk the fact that some of our friends were mixed up in that plot of July 20th.' Without looking up or seeming to listen Arnold said suddenly: 'Von Trott came here twice after the 20th, in fact he was here the evening before his arrest.'

'He was – and?' I may have sounded too eager.

'Oh, nothing really. We chatted together for quite a time actually. He hoped to see Peter, I guess.' A slight pause, then he added with a sigh, 'A splendid fellow, I would say. He showed no undue concern, just walked around the room looking at things, then wandered out into the garden and left as he had come.'

Arnold was staring thoughtfully at his tea cup, and for a moment it almost seemed that we were no longer alone in the room. 'You'll have to write a book, Chris – Life amongst the Huns, what about that? I don't regret for one moment that I did not leave my country – we have to solve this *ourselves*, before the Allies have to do it for us – I know there are people out there who speak the same language.'

'Walked about the room, looking at things.' I knew how it had been; past the sofa, up to the bookcase, hesitating at the telephone, leaning against the mantelpiece with eyes half closed and a sudden young, very personal smile; asking, probing, suggesting, listening attentively, and unconsciously weaving his spell. Determined, in spite of every rebuff and at great risk, that the threads which bound friend to friend, like-minded to like-minded, should hold fast and survive the storm. With Hitler's armies stretching from the Bay of Biscay to the Crimea, purposefully considering a Europe not dominated by one man, but united in mutual respect. As the concentration camps filled, confident in the intrinsic saneness of his people, and the rôle they could play holding the delicate balance between East and West, in a post-war world dominated, as he believed it would be, by Russia and America. Even persuading me, old dyed-in-the-wool Britisher that I was – 'British to my Irish core' was the description – that 'Pax Britannica', the British Empire, Sea Power, all the cornerstones of my rather woolly political faith, would hold no longer after the warring nations returned to their peaceful occupations. 'Nothing can be the same after this war. Don't look so blue, Chris. Your little island will just have to change its rôle. It won't be so important, it may not be so smug. It will have to loosen the reins, cease exploiting and start to educate, and allow those pink blobs on the map to change to any colour they please. I could believe it will be done gracefully; England is a pastmaster at seeing the light just in time, and I could believe, too, that she will be helped by all the richer countries having to provide massive support to the poorer ones in order to help them to their nationhood. No charity about it; it is dangerous as well as unethical to be rich in a poor world.'

'Walked about the room looking at things.' I felt I was beginning to understand why Arnold looked thoughtful, and also why Peter had felt compelled to try and rescue Adam regardless of the consequences, forgetting me and forgetting the children. Living close to death I knew to be heightened living. More than a friend, Adam had become a symbol, a clear and shining symbol of the possible, of the might-have-been; he had been our future in some way and also our conscience. It was something therefore in himself perhaps, which Peter had tried to save, something on which we had pinned our hopes, something which at all costs must not be lost. There had to be a purpose, which gave us the right to live and there had to be the hope, in spite of any outward compromises we had made with a foul régime, that when the great moment came we would be found staunchly on the side of the angels.

I must have been very tired, for without my noticing it Arnold had taken up his tea cup, gone out of the room and closed the door. Without my noticing it darkness had fallen, and without my noticing it I was quite alone.

In the short five days that I was in Berlin, Peter's brother-in-law Reinhard Vogler came down from Hamburg bringing with him a breath of immensely comforting and respectable fresh air. He had decided to try his luck by putting in a good word for Peter at the Ministry of Justice. I knew that as a true Hamburg citizen he felt like a fish out of water in Berlin, but after his brush with officialdom when he was given a rude rebuff, he assured me that although he was a judge, he felt even less at home in the atmosphere of his Ministry.

Other friends were still around, though precious few: Hannes, Freda, Werner Traber, Lexi, but I knew they must be on the danger list and could do without a compromising visit from me. Racking my brains to find someone who was politically innocuous, I suddenly remembered von Brösigke, a handsome, lighthearted officer in the Cavalry SS, who had joined the set-up, I could swear, because the uniform suited him so admirably. Nazis and anti-Nazis, to him, were all just good chaps. In spite of his uniform he was the type who couldn't believe ill of anyone, a great man at a party, as innocent, one might say, as a new-laid egg. His good-heartedness had led him to help many who were in trouble, and many of his interventions had succeeded because one just couldn't disappoint such a sincere and likeable fellow. I rang him up and his reaction was true to form. Oblivious of the tapped telephone, he was loud in his indignation.

'What, Peter in prison, impossible! Good gracious, what the hell is going on. I've never heard such rot. Is there anything I can do? Wait, *Gnädige Frau*, we must meet.'

He told me that he was busy redecorating a little hunting lodge which he had inherited, somewhere east of Berlin. He asked me to come out and see it with him and help him perhaps with ideas.

With the Russians just outside Warsaw, hurtling westwards at incredible speed, I could think of many more fruitful ways of spending an afternoon, but he sounded a valuable ally and when I arrived, the little baroque hunting lodge was so lovely, and von B.'s enthusiasm so infectious, that I found myself offering suggestions which I realized later would have turned it into a very typical English manor house.

We were fetched from the station by a pony trap drawn by a pair of spanking cobs. An elderly coachman handed over the reins, covered our knees with a heavy fur rug and we bumped busily along through the flat, misty countryside. We wandered through the chilly, dusty rooms and an old manservant, obviously delighted at having the young laird home again, pulled back the heavy curtainings, brought out the silver and served us with tea and sandwiches in front of a blazing log fire.

Von Brösigke was a charming host and later brought out photograph albums to show me pictures of his family: faded picnic parties, posed about a table-cloth laden with eats, ladies in voluminous hats, and young men in boaters with heavy watch-chains adorning their waistcoats. Pickel-helmets galore and more of the old house as background to hunting scenes; portly hunts-men grasping their guns, and stag and wild boar stretched out in rows on the drive. A later volume showed wedding scenes, a smiling Hitler mixing with his guests. 'What a happy occasion that was,' von B sighed nostalgically, 'the Führer was in such good form,' and sure enough the bride looked lovely, the husband fond, and the groups of wedding guests well satisfied with themselves, as they toasted each other in doubtless French champagne. I looked at the date and place – Ober-Salzberg, 1943 – the trees were in blossom, it was springtime I could see, it was also therefore – incredible as it may seem – a very short while after Stalingrad.

Before taking me to the station von Brösigke promised he would visit Peter as soon as he was transferred to some prison nearer Berlin. 'Such unheard of nonsense,' he repeated, 'Peter in prison. What the hell is happening anyway? Tell you what I'll do. I'll visit him in uniform. That'll show 'em. I can assure you, it will be a pleasure, *Gnädige Frau*, I'm allergic to policemen.'

Somehow I thought he would keep his word, for as he spoke his handsome face glowed with innocent zeal.

I only just got back to Rohrbach in time, for as I trudged up the valley road from the station I was overtaken by a motorcycle and sidecar. Such an unaccustomed sight made everyone pause in their work in the fields, and follow its progress down the track which led to the Mayor's house. There may have been nothing particularly menacing about the stiff figure in the green Homburg hat who climbed out of the sidecar and disappeared into the darkness of the Mayor's best front room, but there was certainly something most urgent in the manner in which the Mayor came running out of his doorway, grabbed his bicycle and started pushing it up the steep track to the road. There was also some embarrassment and at the same time a measure of relief in the look he gave me as he pedalled past and murmured, '*Grüss Gott, Frau Dr*, so you're back?'

I had not gone much further along the road before he returned posthaste, with Sepp pedalling behind him as swiftly as his ancient contraption could cover the ground. Yes, most certainly there was something up, for hardly had I reached the *Adler*, to be greeted with shouts of joy and hugs and kisses by my family, before Sepp passed the window on his way back to the shop. He was sweating profusely and did not stop to give us his usual cheery greeting.

In the evening though, he appeared at the window. 'May I talk to you a moment, Frau Dr,' he said, his kindly furrowed face looking unhappy and disturbed. 'Why of course, come in.' 'No, I won't come in,' he replied, 'it's easier said outside,' and when I joined him on the step, he moved away from the inn, down the road a little, to where there were no watching windows and only the misty fields stretched away to each side of us. 'I am going to tell you something which the Mayor and I think you should know,' he said. 'That fellow on the motorcycle came from Donaueschingen. He belongs to the Secret Police. He put you in our charge – you are under what he called "house arrest", Frau Dr, which means you must not leave the village. He asked us all about you, whether you had talked politics with us at all, and I can assure you we gave you a great reference. I told him how you worked with the peasants collecting stones off the potato patches, and your children helped with the herding, and how you felt almost more German than English. *Grosser Got*, we gave that little townsman a real earful.' 'That was good of you, Sepp,' I said, 'very good of you indeed. He didn't, I suppose, mention why my husband was in prison?' 'No – no,' he hesitated, 'just high treason was all he said it was – which reminds me, Frau Dr, he did say we were to give you no details as to what he had said to us,' he gave a short laugh, 'as if half the village didn't know at least who he was as soon as that motorcycle of his turned up the valley road. Anyway he told us that if we told you anything except that bit about house arrest we would be shot. The poor lower Baker got a bad fright when he said that, but we talked it over after he left and decided it was none of his business who we told. Stupid lowlander! Anyway, that's the way it is, and just don't tell anyone we have told you, and if you want to go to Furtwangen or any place to do some shopping, just let us know. Goodnight now, Frau Dr. And by the way, my wife told me to tell you there might be some white flour on the ration cards tomorrow, if you care to look in, and John's shoes – I'll try and have them ready for tomorrow too.'

RUSSIAN INTERLUDE

(Autumn 1944)

The snows came early in 1944 and soon after the first heavy falls came the Cossacks. Suddenly they were there, short, straight figures in bushy round fur caps, riding their lively ponies with long stirrups, their rifles held across their saddle bows and their cartridge belts slung crosswise over their tunics. Like Vlassov's army of the Ukraine – they were typical of those Russians who in 1942 had thrown in their lot with the Germans, hoping for better things under Hitler than under Stalin. Their German officer riding ahead of them, and only distinguishable from them because of his peaked field cap, raised his right arm and the long grey column came to a halt outside the *Adler*. A bugle call rang out and immediately pandemonium broke loose. Clattering, dismounting, shouting, laughing, stamping their feet in the snow they seemed to be everywhere; requisitioning fodder for their ponies, billets for their riders. Our thrifty peasants were soon given to understand that this was no circus. There were to be eighteen in the *Adler*. Frau Muckle was in tears; she could not spare the hay. Since I too was still a greenhorn in these matters I went to look for their officer to plead her cause. I found him already housed in Frl. Vöhrenbach's best front bedroom. *'Gnädige Frau,'* he said quietly after asking me to sit down – and I noticed that without his cap he looked much younger and also very tired – *'Gnädige Frau*, this is war. My boys have been with me since they joined us in the Crimea. When the German armies retreated, their homes were burned I believe, and their families were sent to Siberia. I have fought with them in France and to three of them I owe my life. Now we are being transferred back to the Eastern Front. They know and I know what awaits them there. No prisoners will be taken. They must have warm billets and fodder for their horses and I am here to see they get it.' He gave me a weary smile. 'You understand?' Yes, I understood and as I got up to leave he added, 'Only one thing, *Gnädige Frau*, if you have any influence in this village, see that they don't get a drop of alcohol. I love these boys, they are brave and loyal companions, I'm the only German amongst them and they respect me. But alcohol, if they get alcohol, they could go beserk and I can take no responsibility for what might happen.'

Back in the *Adler* I told Frau Muckle to lock her cellar. Cellar was an exaggeration – she gave me the key and I locked the door on what looked like some cases of empty lemonade bottles. When I returned to the kitchen great cauldrons of steaming soup were already bubbling away on the stove, and Martina was looking quite coy, flanked by two sturdy Cossacks who were helping her carry in the wood and the water. The children were in the *Gaststube* watching with fascination as the soldiers unrolled their bedding and stacked their firearms up against the wall, whilst Christopher, surrounded by admirers, was astride the knee of one laughing fellow who had obviously already taught him his first word of Russian. To every question he was asked Christopher was answering firmly *'Da'*, and a roar of laughter greeted him every time he said it. I thought it best not to risk a guess as to what sort of questions were being put to him.

The Cossacks were with us for three days and we soon got used to the clatter and to the sudden piercing whoops and shouts as they urged their sure-footed ponies in sharp staccato gallop past our windows and up the icy lanes, with as often as not a laughing, rosy-cheeked child wedged firmly in front of their saddle bows. Then, like a flock of migratory birds, just as they had come, they were gone. They were preparing to leave and were standing around the porch of the *Adler*, when one of them brought out a mouth organ and started to play a gay, jigging, humming little tune. Two of his fellows immediately leaped forward to dance and before our eyes and in spite of their heavy boots and rough uniforms, the one became a bashful girl, the other her lovesick swain. It was sheer artistry and it was all there: the eager approach, the sharp rebuff, the hurt retreat, the coy invitation to approach again and, as the music quickened faster and faster to the whirling finale, arm in arm, waving their caps they squatted and leaped, sending the snow flying beneath their heavy boots. A bugle call interrupted our applause, and one of them who could speak a few words of

German came forward, panting a little, and took Frau Muckle's hands in his. 'Little mother,' he said, 'we go now, as we go we sing for you our Song of Farewell.' Again the bugle call and they were on their horses, their officer saluted and the long grey column moved off down the road. As they passed the Volksburehof their magnificent voices, in perfect harmony, rang out strong, clear and nostalgic in the frosty air; as they rounded the last bend in the road one or two turned to wave, and their song of farewell echoed back to us up the valley like the humming of thousands of bees.

It was quiet in the *Adler* that evening, after the Cossacks left. The Mayor came up for a game of Old Maid and the *Lehrer* Lorenz and his wife sat quietly in the corner of the *Gaststube* sharing a bottle of lemonade. Martina was unusually silent, and would doubtless have stayed that way if somehow the conversation had not turned to the subject of milk deliveries. The poor Mayor had had to go the rounds some days before, trying to urge his unwilling flock to send more milk to the creamery, and Martina had resolutely refused to send another drop. What with Sylvie calving in a month's time and Bemi with a swollen udder, Martina had aired her views at the time and was still sore at his lack of consideration. 'Well, Martina,' said the Mayor, shuffling and dealing the sticky cards, 'what about that milk, eh?' and I added unwittingly, 'I think Hitler himself wouldn't get a drop more out of her cows.' Martina was silent, looking fiercely from one card to another and then suddenly, 'If that rascal Hitler came around here, I'd put him down the lavatory and put the lid on him.' There was a deathly silence. Frau Muckle and I stifled our laughter and the Mayor, visibly shocked, glanced over his shoulder at the Lorenzes who were eyeing their lemonade bottle with a faraway look as if they were about to be seasick. They left the parlour quietly and the Mayor packed up his cards and did likewise. Oh dear, how crazy it all was, the aptest remark of the day and we all had to behave like a lot of guilty schoolchildren.

Frau Muckle and I hurried through the kitchen and found the Mayor standing irresolutely in the snow outside the back door. He cleared his throat. *'Adler Wirtin,'* he said, 'I did not hear what Martina said just now, but I trust you will impress on her never to say such things again.' A brave decision, the manner of conveying it just a little Irish perhaps.

Back in the parlour I found Martina scrubbing the tables as if her life depended on it. 'Martina,' I said as sternly as I could, 'we none of us heard what you said tonight, but if you say it again and in front of others you might get into terrible trouble. You might be taken away to prison and no one would know where you were and you might never come out.' Martina did not look scared or repentant. 'All right, Frau Dr,' she said, 'if you say so; but I can think what I like, can't I?' Yes, yes, little Martina, you can think what you like, but it won't get us far, it hasn't got us far, this thinking business.

I knew what she had felt about those Russians who had teased her and laughed with her and treated her as one of their own, and as I watched her give a last ferocious swish with the cloth before she disappeared through the door to the kitchen, for some reason or other I nearly burst into tears.

A JOURNEY TO BERLIN

(Winter 1944)

On December 24th, 1944, I set off on a second journey to Berlin. Arnold had rung me five days previously to tell me that the Gestapo had given permission for me to see Peter in Ravensbrück, a concentration camp somewhere north of Berlin. With the sound of the tape recorder buzzing in the background, he had naturally given me no reason for this sudden decision, but he had urged me to come, and I figured there could be actually only two possible causes for such an unusual show of philanthropy. Either I was to be allowed a last farewell visit, or Arnold had pulled every string he could think of, and the Gestapo had granted the interview in a fit of idle curiosity. Let's see what his English wife looks like, an unusual specimen perhaps. I had little doubt in my mind that the first alternative was the most probable, and although they tried to cheer me, I knew that Sepp and the Mayor shared the same fear, for although they at first felt that they should await written instructions or at least communicate with Donaueschingen, of a sudden they changed their minds, cast caution to the winds and decided to allow me to travel on their own responsibility.

On the morning I left Rohrbach Frau Muckle's alarm clock woke me at 3 a.m. It performed its usual little dance on the bedside table and then subsided growling on its back. A glance out of the window showed me that it was not snowing. The sky was clear and starlit. I climbed into as many of my warm clothes as were still holding together, pulled on my skiing trousers, gathered up my rucksack and anorak and, with my boots in my hand, I went out into the passage. At every step the old wooden house creaked and groaned. I stopped for a moment outside the children's room, then opened the door quietly and went in. Nick and John were lying sprawled on their backs, their thick thatches of hair like haloes around their heads. One dark, one fair. Nick turned in his sleep and murmured something. I covered him gently and went to the cot in the corner. Only a wisp of hair was to be seen of Christopher, above the bulging red and white check eiderdown. It flashed through my mind that I had meant to cut their hair before I left. That didn't matter now. Their chests were bursting out of their nightshirts which were far too small for them; their funny little snub-nosed faces were brown and glowing with health. Peter's and my long separation, and much bleak loneliness had been worthwhile, if only for that. If they had to go on without us, they had at least this splendid health to build on.

I closed the door quietly and went down to the kitchen. To my surprise the little round figure of Frau Muckle was standing over the stove. She had thrown a black shawl over her flannel night-dress and a wispy black plait of hair stuck out over the top of it. She slipped in her teeth as I came in and started slicing bacon into the pan.

'You really shouldn't have done this, dear Frau Muckle,' I said, 'it's not good for your rheumatics at all to be standing about in the cold.' 'Pouf my rheumatics, you're not going off on that long journey without something inside you.' To my horror she began to break one egg after another into the pan. She had an infinite faith in the power of food to help you over any difficulties. 'And what's more, I have been to the tin,' she gave me a sly look; 'just a few little beans, Frau Doktor, I think a little cup of coffee – just the two of us.' 'The tin' played quite a rôle in our social life at the *Gasthaus Adler*. Every Sunday afternoon four or five coffee beans, remnants of my efforts on the black market, would be ground ceremoniously and added to our usual brew. This had the effect of turning an ordinary occasion into a real party. We would sit around the old kitchen table and chat and laugh and go quite gay, and Frau Muckle would recall racy stories of village scandals and afterwards we could never close an eye for half the night.

She bustled around, scolding and talking and laying the table as I sat and laced up my skiing boots. She was trying very hard to make it seem like an ordinary occasion, but almost without seeming to realize it she had laid out the best cups with the flowered border, and the four fried eggs swimming in bacon, the loaf of homemade bread, an unheard of extravagance, showed me that she knew, as I did, that there was a possibility of our never seeing each other again.

'You have my letter to my parents, Frau Muckle?' I asked. 'Yes, indeed I have, dear Frau Doktor, and I have hidden it well in Ernst's room behind the wall boards. No one will find it. I had everything hidden in there in the last war, safe as can be, and their address is in the cocoa tin under the third red-currant bush on the left.' She recited her piece like a schoolgirl. 'And I got you this little parcel, too, to take with you. Ernst's favourite sausages. I was saving some for when he came back. You have to have good teeth to eat those, perhaps you will be able to give some to Herr Doktor,' she looked at me gently with her old, wise eyes, 'and give him my greetings, please, and tell him that I am an old woman and that I am ashamed – but perhaps you won't be able to say that.'

I was trying hard to eat the eggs she had swept on to my plate, but after struggling with two I had to give up. 'Frau Muckle, perhaps you will give the rest to the children for breakfast. I'm afraid I just can't – but I feel wonderful now and the coffee was a terrific idea.'

I got up and slung on my rucksack and pulled on my cap and gloves. Now that the time had come, I was almost eager to be off.

Frau Muckle was standing in front of me and I realized that her chin was trembling and that she had tears in her eyes. I took her in my arms and kissed her and said, 'Now, don't you cry, dear Frau Muckle. I shall be back. I just cannot tell you what it means to me to be able to leave the children in your care. It is something I shall never forget.'

Just as I was leaving the room she darted away to the sideboard and with much grumbling at Martina, 'that stupid codfish,' she came back with a beer bottle. She asked me to bend my head and she wetted her finger and made the sign of the cross on my forehead. I turned to wave as I rounded the corner of the vegetable patch, and I saw her standing framed in the lighted doorway with her beer bottle of holy water in one hand, the other raised in a gesture of unconscious benediction.

The air was cold and hard and the snow squeaked and crunched under my boots. To the right and left of the winding valley road the white fields rose steeply to the woods. The valley was silent, deeply silent, the only sound an occasional pluff, as some snow slid quietly from a roof or a branch on to the road. The huge outline of the *Duffnerhof* with its steeply sloping roof loomed up beside me. A light was burning in one of the upper windows, and

I remembered that Frau Duffner was expecting her third child any day. A pair of skis leaned beside the doorway. The doctor must be there already. I hesitated a moment and almost felt like going in to ask how she was getting along, but I had to stifle the wish. Those things somehow already belonged to yesterday.

As I passed the old school-house with its rickety bell-tower, the clock gave a little cough which I knew meant it was 4.15. From there the road made a swinging bend to the left. I turned back to have one last look in the direction of Rohrbach. I knew the view so well that it was easy to imagine it sleeping there in the folds of the white hills; the huge crouching houses with their deeply sloping roofs, sometimes almost touching the ground, the delicate church tower, the ribbon-like road winding up into the hills beyond. A light was still burning in the *Adler* and I could imagine Frau Muckle sitting in the kitchen finishing up the coffee. For a moment my thoughts wandered upstairs to the three beds and the three little heads under the huge red and white check eiderdowns. They did not stay there long. I had said my goodbyes.

As I strode along I began to glow warmly and the clear cold air and unaccustomed coffee seemed to make me wonderfully clear headed. It was a real relief to be doing something after weeks of helpless worry, when only the unexpected arrival of a censored note in his handwriting first from a Berlin prison and then from a concentration camp, had conveyed to me that Peter was still alive. Now my plans were laid and my mind made up. When I reached Berlin I hoped to find out a little more clearly how things lay, and if they were as bad as I thought they might be, I would put my plan into action and ask for an interview with *Kriminalrat* Lange, Peter's chief interrogator. Sepp and the Mayor had told me that the Gestapo believed that I had very influential relations in England. I would play on that. Without in any way admitting Peter's guilt, I would convey to Lange that I believed the war would soon be over and, that being so, I might be able to strike a bargain with him. He to mislay, subdue, or at least postpone a decision on Peter's file, I to see what I could do for him after the war. It seemed simple and worth trying – although there was a certain chance that Lange might think fit to arrest me too.

Strangely enough, in spite of the fact that the Allied armies were poised on the Rhine, I had not found it too difficult to leave air-raids, war, the ebb and flow of armies threatening separation for the children, out of my calculations. I was not brave enough to face up consciously to more than one danger at a time. God had to take care of some things, and the only aspect of my plan I did not like was that by going to Berlin I was breaking a solemn promise to Peter, never, whatever happened, to leave the children.

I reached the station with ten minutes to spare and sat down on the bench outside. The Stationmaster was busying around his kitchen at the back of his little wooden house. He came out when he saw me. A fine smell of bacon wafted out through the door. 'Grüss Gott, you're early, Frau Doktor,' he said, 'but you have a long journey ahead of you. To Berlin, I hear—' Since I was officially under house arrest and the Mayor had taken on himself the responsibility of providing me with a travel permit, my journey was supposed to be almost a state secret; but as usual, news moved fast in Rohrbach. 'Well, you can tell them up there,' he went on, 'that if they don't stop this war soon there won't be a train running between Furtwangen and Donaueschingen.' He laughed and stamped his feet. 'No fuel, no anything; when she was pulling up the slope between Vöhrenbach and Schönebach yesterday everyone had to get out! What a business; well, well, here she comes now – goes better downhill.'

He nipped behind his little hatch and handed me a ticket for Donaueschingen, 'That's as far as she goes,' then heaved my rucksack through the door of a carriage, proudly marked with an I; it was no different from any of the others. As he shut me in, he leaned towards me. 'Pretty rum bunch they are in Berlin as far as I hear tell – don't know when they are beat – but for goodness sake don't tell my wife what I just said, she still believes in Father Christmas!' He hustled back into his kitchen, giving the frying pan a shake as he passed the stove. Then he returned, resplendent in his red cap, and grasping his baton with the red and green light. I let down the window and leaned on the sill. The carriage seemed a bit hot and suddenly I was not feeling very brave at all. So easy just to open the door and slip off up the mountain road back to the peaceful life of all the yesterdays. The Stationmaster was at the window. 'Gute Reise and good luck, Frau Doktor,' he said, then he stepped back, raised his baton, shouted Abfahrt, and with much squeaking and snorting the little train trundled off down the valley and out into the world.

In Tuttlingen I had to change for the Berlin Express coming through from the Bodensee. It had been indefinitely delayed, however, because of raids and repairs up and down the line, so

I wandered up into the clean, gay little town. No bomb craters here, anyway. The streets were thronged with people dressed in their best and carrying neat little parcels tied with silver string. Although food was scarce and there had been nothing to buy on the clothing cards for months, the crowds, mostly women and children, seemed neatly and warmly dressed. I was always rather overcome by the efficiency of German women and their infinite capacity for making do. They would darn and redarn, turn and patch, and the end product was a monument to their ingenuity and skill. Although my up-bringing had not really been haphazard, I could never quite rid myself of a seemingly inborn Irish inclination to look quite fatalistically on holes in clothes. They always seemed to me to be phenomena which you couldn't do much about, except put up with them until they became annoying, or even embarrassing, and then Glory be – throw them out. As the war years dragged on I had improved a bit, but had never approached those heights when every garment looked clean and respectable until it fell to bits.

It was late afternoon and everyone seemed to be hurrying somewhere. Of course, it was Christmas Eve. We had celebrated a day early in Rohrbach – a long time ago yesterday. A little wooden toy carved by our Pole Josef for Christopher, and for Nick and John two precious penknives sent by Outram through the Swedish Embassy, and saved up since last March. A tree too, brought down from the woods by Nick, and decorated with the silver foil which strewed the fields after the Allied bombers had droned over us, bound for Munich or Augsburg. We were told it was meant to disturb radio communications. Maybe it did that too, but it certainly came in useful at Christmas.

It was not yet time for the blackout, and through the gaily lighted windows I could hear the music and watch the busy Christmas preparations.

I amused myself trying to imagine what kind of people lived in the houses, by looking at their Christmas trees. That was usually not too difficult, because in Germany Christmas trees are very individual affairs and seem to reflect the special character of the family that decorates them. The austere tree, all white and gold; the traditional tree, hung with carved wooden figures and faded baubles, handed down from generation to generation, and only beautiful because of the memories they held of other Christmases; the children's tree, covered with sweets and rosy apples; the tidy, symmetrical, almost pernickety tree; the messy tree; but never, I think, the vulgar, gaudy tree such as we often have in England. Beside each tree the lighted crib. True, I was in Catholic Germany, but even so it was reassuring that Hitler had seemingly not yet succeeded in banishing that symbol from so many homes.

But now, as I looked closer, even the trees had a more uniform look. Odd length candles, left-overs from other years. No sweets; the lametta, except for where the Allied silver foil had come to the rescue, ragged and tarnished; the presents not very numerous and not much to write home about either.

It was a rather lonely business, however, just being outside of it all, and as the shutters closed one by one I began to feel a bit sorry for myself. I made my way back to the station waiting room. A scraggy-looking Christmas tree had been rigged up in the corner and the waitress, who was standing behind an empty counter, surrounded by empty glass shelves, had turned on the wireless which was playing slow sentimental Christmas music, 'O Tannenbaum – Süsser die Glocken nie klingen – Stille Nacht.' A large, highly-coloured oil painting of Hitler – the work, no doubt, of some local Velasquez – hung on the wall beside the wireless and stared down morosely at the coffee urn.

The only other occupant of the waiting room was a soldier who seemed fast asleep, sprawled across the table, with his head on his arms. The paraphernalia of war were strewn about him: his rucksack, rifle belt and steel helmet, and what seemed to be an assortment of tins and mugs.

The programme of music was interrupted to tell us that a few planes were over West Germany. The soldier looked up and said: 'They don't even leave us alone on Christmas Eve, the —s.' He seemed to be addressing no one in particular, but the girl behind the counter surprised me by answering: 'Well, Christmas Eve isn't Christmas for them, is it?'

'No, I don't think it is,' I said.

'Going far?' She moved her elbows along the counter. 'Don't mind him,' she added in a low voice, 'he's going to the Russian front, his leave was up today of all days, poor chap. Wife and three kids at home. *Ach so*, you are going to Berlin? I'm glad I'm not you. It must be an awful place.' She looked thoughtfully at the radio. 'I wish they would stop this war, don't you?' 'I don't know,' I said cautiously, 'perhaps they have a wonder weapon, after all, which is going to change everything. What do you think?'

'I don't know either,' she answered, 'but I never have trusted those Berliners – too blooming smart altogether.'

'Yes, but it's not only the Berliners who are running the war.'

'Maybe not, but the Government is there, isn't it?'

Our conversation was interrupted by the crackling of the loud-speaker over the door – '*Achtung, Achtung*, the Berlin Express is drawing into Platform 4.' I gathered up my belongings and paid for my cup of soup, or perhaps it had been coffee – there wasn't much difference in the taste these days. The dreadful picture of Hitler seemed to be eyeing me as I pushed towards the door; I decided he looked as if he had acute indigestion.

The express steamed in with its engine and carriages caked with snow. The carriages at the end of the train seemed to be unheated, for the windows were white with hoarfrost. Some of them, too, were broken so I wandered to the front and climbed into the first carriage behind the locomotive. The only disadvantage of being in the front half of a train was the danger from the 'Jabo'* point of view. Some of the Allied pilots had brought engine-busting to a fine art. A whining dive, a burst of fire, and the punctured steam kettle drew slowly to a forced stop, the steam whistling out through the bullet holes. Others could make several bosh shots and the passengers in the front carriages then had to jump for it, darting backwards and forwards across the rails and crouching for protection behind the train. However, I reckoned I was safe for the night anyway; I was tired, the carriage was warm, and I was asleep in my corner before the train left the station.

In Stuttgart there seemed to have been a raid, and several houses were still burning. Whilst I had slept, the carriage had filled, and the corridor, too, seemed packed with soldiers. Ours was probably the only heated carriage on the train. The fug was stupefying. I pushed off down the corridor to the lavatory, only to find two soldiers asleep against the basin. One of the soldiers in the corridor shouted 'Hey, Franz, *eine Dame*,' a lady, and the two boys turned their backs without seeming to waken. When I got back to my compartment my place had been taken by a woman who must have come in from the corridor. She looked completely exhausted and was already half asleep. I was feeling very fresh again and I realized that, compared with the others, I was brown and abominably healthy looking. So I decided to sit down in

*Jäger-Bomber – fighter-bomber.

the corridor. One group of soldiers were playing *Skat*,* chalking up the score on the panel of the door, and further up a chirpy Berliner was sitting on his rolled-up great-coat, regaling all and sundry in his unmistakable dialect, with a riotous description of his part in the retreat through France. 'Run – run,' he was saying, 'I have never run so fast in my life,' he turned to me, his face wreathed in smiles. 'Sit down, Fräulein – no, wait till I pat up the cushions and dust the sofa.' He jumped to his feet; every bit of his uniform, from his scruffy little cap to his clumsy boots, seemed too big for him. German army clothes are not just off the peg, but look as if they came off any old peg; only the officers are inclined to dress up like peacocks.

'You've never seen an army on the run, I bet – well it's the funniest sight on God's earth. Once an army gets running, nothing can stop it. First we threw away our drinking bottles, then our helmets, belts and ammunition – finally our rifles. Then we just bolted!' He burst out laughing. 'I can see them now, chasing us, just as we popped over one hill they got to the top of the one before. Americans, mind you, a fairly easy lot, every time we shouted "*Scheisse*", they stopped and sent for air cover. They get sore feet like poor Jup here – hey, Jup—' he nudged a cherubic-looking figure who was sitting astride his gunny sack, perspiring gently and leaning against the door. 'But we made it, didn't we old friend?' Jup smiled down good-naturedly and nodded; he seemed half asleep.

It was obvious that the little Berliner was the wit of the party, and that he was also probably laying it on a bit thick for my benefit.

'Where are you off to now?' I asked, feeling rather bewildered. 'I haven't a clue,' came the answer, 'we have to report in Magdeburg. But one thing I can tell you, Fräulein, I'm not trying for an Iron Cross; and I'm going to see I don't get a wooden one either. I've got this far and when the war is over I'm going to be back in Berlin with my missus, running my vegetable stall.' His voice had changed and I looked at him quickly. He looked back at me with an expression of sudden defiance on his otherwise nondescript face. A spark of what I thought to be complete understanding flashed between us. I knew what he meant, that little Berliner. We were both being kicked around, surely we were, caught up in

Skat – German card game.

a ruthless uncontrollable machine, but by God it wouldn't get us – not if we could help it.

I remembered that I had a bottle of Kirsch in my rucksack. It had been meant as a present for Arnold, but this seemed the moment. I climbed back into the carriage and came back with it under my arm – a whole litre. I had traded it for a silver tea-pot on a rather foolhardy expedition to the Rhine one day. At the sight of it, our little group miraculously increased in number, even the *Skat* game seemed to peter out. Someone produced a pen-knife and dug out the cork and handed me back the bottle with a bow. '*Zum Wohl, Gnädigste.*'

'Here's to next Christmas,' I said ' – at home,' and I spluttered a bit after the first gulp. It was good, strong Kirsch all right, straight from the farm home-brewed and far stronger than any ordinary branded variety. As the bottle did the rounds, they wiped it on their sleeves and murmured '*Heimat – Weihnachten,*' and after Jup had had his turn he fumbled in his pocket and brought out a mouth organ. He banged it on his knee and pursed his lips, and the first reed-like notes of that most haunting of all German soldier-songs vibrated hesitantly at first, and then seemed to gather volume and strength above the rumbling of the train. '*In der Heimat, in der Heimat, da gibt's ein Wiedersehen.*'

We hummed it gently, each of us lost in our separate worlds. Peter in Ravensbrück, the Black Forest, England – where were my brothers? – my sister in Canada? A fair boy in the background slipped naturally into alto harmony. 'In the homeland, in the homeland, there we shall meet again.'

I was sorry to lose my friends at Magdeburg. We had talked through the rest of the night and into the morning and emptied the bottle of Kirsch. At one time Jup, who had been a waiter in Munich, had turned to me and told me confidentially that one could see that a lady was present by the way the boys were watching their language. As their every second word seemed to me to start with an F, I wondered rather fuzzily what it would have been like had I not been there.

They could have been a cross section of any army, anywhere, that little group of soldiers. Blown about by the whims of higher authority, to the East, to the West, and now back again to the East. They had no particular hates, no resentments, no particular ambition, except to stay alive and get back to their families – although some of them had no idea where their families were.

Heini, the little Berliner, could easily have been a London cockney, with his *Galgenhumor*, as the Germans call it; a tough, cynical, chirpy, unabashed sense of humour which seems to thrive only in big cities.

As he left, he squared his small shoulders, clicked his heels, raised his right arm and said: 'Well, whoever still wants to listen, *Heil Hitler*, etc., etc.' In one absurd gesture he somehow managed to caricature the whole rotten business.

After Magdeburg I moved to the back of the train, unheated, but safer. Every station we passed was crowded with refugees; patient groups of old people and of women and children, with their possessions in bundles and sacks around them. They seemed to be waiting for trains going West and South. In spite of a clear sky, there seemed to be no planes about and late in the afternoon we arrived in Berlin. The gaunt, grey ruins of that huge, indomitable city closed in around us. Were there more piles of rubble than in September?

'If they want to hit more targets, they'll have to bring them with them,' my little Berliner had said. I could see what he meant.

BERLIN

(Winter 1944)

It was late in the afternoon and already dark when I reached the Falkenried. The dimmed street-lamps lit up the grey snow, and the villas behind their garden fences were dark and remote. I could not make out whether some of them were not missing altogether. Our gate was swinging and creaking to and fro on un-oiled hinges. There was probably no one left to mend the electric mechanism which operated it automatically from the house. So I felt my way along the garden path and knocked on the front door. There was a fairly long pause – no one opened up too quickly those days – and then a voice, Mabel's voice from inside, 'Hallo, who's there?' 'Chris!' The door swung open immediately, a shaft of light flashed across the snow as she pulled me in and closed it quickly behind me.

'Chris, my dear, how welcome you are. Come in, come in, we were just wondering when you would turn up.' The door to the sitting-room opened and Arnold came out into the hall and closed the door behind him. 'Welcome, Chris, it's good to see you.' He came forward, grinning boyishly, and gripped me by the hand. For a second he put his other hand over his mouth and shot me a quick look, then hurried on, 'You must be tired, you've had a tough journey, eh? Well, come in and sit down and have some coffee, real coffee. Or would you rather go to your room? We have turned everyone out of it and it is your room again. Wait a moment.' He took my rucksack and led me along the passage and flung open the door to our bedroom. Clean and tidy, warm and cosy, with even a little azalea on the dressing table. It was our own room, as Peter and I had left it.

I washed and tidied a bit and dug my rather meagre offerings out of my rucksack. A loaf of home-made bread, a pound of butter, a piece of smoked bacon. I felt rather mean about the bottle of Kirsch, and glancing at the azalea added two of Frau Muckle's little sausages to the humble pile.

Back in the sitting-room I found them all sitting round the coffee table in front of a blazing fire – Mabel, Arnold and Arnold's nephew, a fair, lanky fourteen-year-old.

They jumped to their feet when I came into the room and I sensed a slight embarrassment. I, for my part, was anxious to put them at their ease, for they were friends and I was glad of them. 'So the house is still standing, how marvellous,' I said, 'not a window broken. What do you think of my spy service? I have a special line to Bomber Harris of course, but, jokes apart, however have you managed it? Not a window broken as far as I can see.'

'Well, we do our best, Chris, the double windows are padded with cushions as soon as the sirens go, and there's always someone watching out for incendiary bombs.'

They told me that so far only one had hit the house and it had come through the roof and attic, made a hole in the ceiling and landed on the sofa. Unfortunately it was the explosive kind, and just as Ton, who was on watch from the trench, was scuttling across the lawn with a sack, it had exploded and blown holes in my writing desk and punctured the radiator, and the water had run out all over the floor and somehow seeped underneath the parquet flooring. Hence the extraordinary hummock which I could see near the door. I had heard of that exploding incendiary before: a particularly despicable kind of weapon, which had obviously been devised to kill or maim the foolhardy citizen who tried to save something of his wordly goods from the holocaust, and which suggested in its own way that the Germans did not hold a monopoly on calculated cruelty. 'Better the old writing table, than Ton,' murmured Arnold's nephew gruffly, and I felt that Ton, of the forced-labour force from Holland, had a sturdy champion in Arnold's nephew who went to a *Napola* school.

I placed my offerings on the table and was almost ashamed at the clamorous applause they received. 'Real bread, real butter. Oh, it's not true, and bacon – when did I last see bacon!' For some reason or other I suddenly remembered a small pot of Tiptree's Little Strawberry jam, which I had hidden in a bucket in the cellar several years ago, at the outbreak of war. 'Wait a moment,' I said, and I hustled down to the cellar stairs, past the absurd air-raid shelter equipment, and came back triumphant. 'Now,' I said, 'let's eat the lot.' It was fun watching them stuffing, especially the boy. The coffee tasted very much as it did in Rohrbach – three or four beans to a gallon of water – but it all helped a little to ease our embarrassment. The conversation had been limping along with everyone talking at once or else silence, but after the coffee it flowed smoothly enough, although always evading the main issue – the reason that I had come to Berlin at all.

When every crumb of the bread had been eaten and we were awash with coffee, and the jam pot was empty, and a huge dent had been made in the butter, Arnold gave the signal that the table should be cleared. His nephew slipped out of the room and I heard him running upstairs to the children's room, where I supposed the Dutch boys were still camping. Mabel cleared the tea things and the door closed behind her and I turned instantly to Arnold, who was sitting opposite me in Peter's wing chair, staring into the fire with an odd expression on his face. 'Funny, isn't it,' he said in English, 'I am doing everything I can think of for that boy. He's the only living relative I have in the world. He's a weak sort of a chap, but I expect you know that I have even managed to get him into a *Napola* school.* Only the best can get in there, and I thought it might help to make a man of him. But when he's here he wants nothing better than to spend his time with those blighters upstairs. What they teach him, the Lord only knows.'

Arnold's English always reminded me of some British army colonel's. 'But what am I doing,' he looked at me with a smile. 'I know, I know, Chris, you can hardly wait.' He crossed the room and disconnected the telephone – 'You want to hear how things stand with Peter, of course you do.' He hesitated a moment and then went on, 'I might as well tell you from the start, I am not too happy about things. In fact, I am glad you are here. Now don't get unnecessarily bothered,' he added quickly, 'nothing very definite has happened or is happening. Actually, that's what bothers me.' He leaned back in his chair and stuck out his chin, half closed his eyes and went on in perfect English. 'Now as I told you the last time you were here, I know that Peter had nothing whatever to do with this July 20th business. After you left last time, rightly or wrongly I used what influence I had to get him transferred from Graudenz to Berlin. He is now in the hands of experienced interrogators and they are out for one thing. We cannot escape

*Special boarding-school.

205

the fact that he had friends, many friends, who were up to their necks in it, although they are most of them dead now, which is fortunate.' I glanced at him in an effort to find out whether he was serious or whether he was just sticking to the rules of the game as he intended to play them. As his face was inscrutable, whichever way it was, I guessed I could play along.

'Now, in my opinion,' Arnold went on, 'the police have nothing specific against Peter, but I would take a bet that they dislike him personally. I wouldn't say he has done too well in his interrogations. Heavens, Chris, he is too big, too good looking and too arrogant to appeal to them.' He gave me a quick smile. 'I can see him sitting there, treating them all like dirt, can't you? Well, they won't like that. The second thing, which may be making his interrogations more difficult for him, is the fact that he probably does not know that Trott and Langbehn are dead, he may be trying to shield them in some way.' I had not heard about Carl's death before, nor was I seasoned to such things. I wanted to say something, to ask if he was certain, if this could be true – but no words came. A vision of a little frightened old lady, in a huge steel helmet, rose before my eyes, 'Muttl', who had braved the raids and stayed near him to the last. Irmgard, tall, dark, reserved, her gaiety and warmth behind her shy mask of passivity.

Arnold seemed to sense my questioning. 'I would not be telling you these things if I did not know for certain,' he said. 'As I say, Peter may be trying to shield them in some way, and this is where you come in. By the way, you have to be in Ravensbrück at ten o'clock on the 28th, that is the day after tomorrow. You will only be able to talk to him for about ten minutes, but during that time you must see that you convey to him very definitely that his friends are dead. They cannot speak against him, and they do not need protection.' 'I will do my best, Arnold,' was all I could manage to say and I thanked him then for all that he had done.

He rose to stretch his legs and I watched him curiously, wondering what was in his mind. He was far too bright not to know that Peter was 'up to his neck' in this thing too. He crossed to the telephone, but before plugging it in he turned and looked at me very gently, 'I don't like shirkers,' he said. 'I'm not a shirker and I don't think you are either.' He went to the door and called out to Mabel, then he looked at me and smiled. 'Now we are going to have a little drink. Mabel, the glasses. We will drink to the time when we have Peter amongst us again,' he slipped into Hamburg dialect, '*Der gute Schunge*, I miss him very much.'

Before going to bed I went upstairs to the children's room to see the Dutch boys. I was given a tumultuous welcome. Ton pumped my arm up and down until it hurt and Gerd bowed and kissed my hand. They were no longer alone, and introduced me to their sister-in-law and another little one who was, officially at least, a cousin. The room looked like a glorified gypsy caravan. Not quite, though, because a network of complicated wires festooned the walls, and seemed to connect one very expensive looking piece of electrical equipment to another. A cooking stove stood in the corner, with the chimney sticking out of the window. Next to the stove stood a large sack of what looked like brown beans. They looked well fed, better actually than the ones downstairs, and when I asked Ton about the wires he joyfully informed me that practically everything in the room had been swiped from the UFA.* 'It's nothing to what we have in the trench,' he said, 'we have telephones and sound detectors, lights, of course, and air conditioning. If the war goes on much longer, we'll have a private cinema.' I was amazed at his ingenuity as an electrician, and also as a thief. Some of the equipment seemed too bulky to carry about, but he told me he had smuggled it out piece by piece and spent his evenings re-assembling it. I congratulated them, too, on the fact that the house was still standing and in such good shape, and Gerd answered that it was the end of the road for them if anything happened to the house. 'Who knows what the guards will do to us in camp when the end comes?' he said and then seeming to realize that his remark had come rather near the knuckle, he added rather shyly, 'Ton and I and the boys at the camp are not much good at praying, but if prayers do help at all, I can assure you, Dr Bielenberg will come out safe and sound.'

Downstairs again I went to fill my hot-water bottle and whilst the kettle came to the boil on the tiny gas flame, which seemed to have no pressure behind it at all, I wandered back once more to the sitting-room. I did not turn on the lights, but went to the french windows, drew back the curtains and pulled up the black-out blinds. It was snowing outside, big white flakes that melted when they touched the windows. It was all so unreal. Behind me, in the sitting-room, that Christmas tree should not be standing

*UFA – German film company.

bulkily in the corner, covered with cotton wool, but right in the middle of the room, covered with sweets and lametta and gyrating slowly, a trifle jerkily, on its little silver stand, which had turned the tree when Peter's grandfather was a boy. The room should not be tidy and smelling of cigar smoke, but strewn with Christmas paper, and the air should be filled with the pungent smell of gingerbread and candle grease, which every German child associates only with Christmas.

I remembered a special scene – in 1941 – when the star present had been Peter's old railway. The Christmas dinner had not been such a success that year, because some months earlier, Peter had made a trip to the country and returned with three goslings. They had eaten all my cabbage plants and messed up the lawn, but also become an integral part of the family circle, greeting us through the french windows every morning at breakfast. When the time had come for one of them to die, Peter had put off the evil moment until the last, until in fact his dignity was at stake. Having smoked nearly a packet of cigarettes, armed with a hatchet, pea green but determined, he had stalked to the back of the house and done the deed. The children had been got out of the way at the time; and Clarita and I did not feel our Christmas dinner, crisp and brown, stuffed with apples and surrounded by red cabbage, bore much resemblance to the companion of the week before. But Nicky was not to be deceived. He had controlled himself until it reached his plate and then, flinging down his knife and fork, he had burst into tears and rushed from the room crying: 'You just can't eat friends.' We had none of us felt too good after that, but the train had restored the equilibrium. Peter and Adam spreadeagled on the carpet, vying with each other in ingenuity at the laying out of the rails, whilst the boys watched intently. John with raised eyebrows and half closed slanting eyes, squatting over the engine in trancelike concentration, and waiting, as I knew, for the coast to be clear for him to pull every rail apart and fix things up his own way. Clarita and I on the sofa, a trifle cowlike. We were expecting Adam's son and Peter's daughter in March and May of 1942. Babies which had turned out to be a daughter for Adam and Clarita, another son for Peter and me – momentary disappointment, ultimate complete satisfaction – oh God those memories.

Later, Peter and Adam, their long legs stretched to the fire, relaxed, replete and content. A huge belch from Adam (a trick he had learned in China, where, he always assured us, it was the height of manners after a good meal) and which, much to his joy, never failed to get a rise. Clarita: 'Adam, really.' Chris: 'Oh, shut up, Adam.' Peter: 'Adam, you are an incurable swine.' And the tales we had told of other Christmases, way back; a little Adam wandering alone through his snow-covered Hessian forests, looking for Father Christmas; Clarita and Peter, the children of worthy Hamburg burghers, silent and entranced at midnight carol services in the Michaelis Kirche, or taking part in vast family eating sessions – carp and horseradish sauce, goose and red cabbage. The night I heard unmistakable rustling outside the night-nursery door and my suspicions were at last confirmed, when I heard my father's unmistakable whispers, 'I hope to God they're asleep, Girl, because I want to get to bed.' No more Father Christmas, but the magic of that limp weight at the end of the bed, which rustled when prodded from under the bedclothes, did not wear off for many years after.

The snow was falling faster now, soft flakes crowded up against the windows, melted, trickled down the panes and away into the darkness of the garden. I turned to the fire and stirred the ashes with my foot, a faint glow and then darkness, too. The room was too alive with memories, and I could be with them no longer because I could not face the thought that perhaps, after all, it was just part of a play. The scenery and the props had remained the same, but the players had changed, and it just happened that I was the only one left of the original cast.

LEXI

(Winter 1944)

The following day I went to see Lexi. Mabel had told me she thought that she was still living in the Budapesterstrasse, although she could not imagine where, as the whole area around the Zoologische Garten was more devastated than any other part of Berlin.

The Falkenried looked fresh and clean under its coat of freshly fallen snow, and the air-raid shelter in the Langbehn's garden sparkled like a friendly igloo. The sky was overcast, but the magic air of Berlin was cold and bracing.

I crossed the road to avoid the Langbehn's gate. It would have to come, but I could not face little Mother Langbehn yet.

The anti-aircraft guns in the Domäne Dahlem had on their nose caps and were covered with tarpaulins; they did not seem to expect trouble today. Two lads in blue-grey uniform, with the red lapels of an anti-aircraft regiment, were waiting at the bus stop. They seemed incredibly young, fifteen perhaps, not more, one of them still having some trouble with his voice when he laughed.

The old M. Bus (Emma to her regulars) skidded to a stop in the slush and trundled off with us, down the Caecilienallee, past Adam's flat, closed and shuttered, with the snow hiding the dead flowers in the window boxes around its balcony. Clarita had been very proud of her window boxes, I remembered, and when she had left with the children for Imshausen, Adam had religiously deluged the poor things with water once a week.

When we reached the Halensee, past the old ruins and the new ruins, I decided to get out and walk down the Kurfürstendamm. Perhaps after all I would go to the hairdresser before seeing Lexi and, tomorrow, Peter. I was rather tired of looking like an outsize reproduction of Joan of Arc. Besides, I would like to see my nice Fräulein Lydia again, and find out how her marriage plans had worked out. She was such a pretty, positive little bird, and although her Jürgen had been in the thick of the fighting on the Russian front, and his leave had been postponed three times, she had been certain that he would get through all right. Frl. Lydia's sister was married to an Englishman, also a hairdresser, who had his salon somewhere near London. 'Shorrerdish' she called the place and we had felt rather close to each other back in 1940, when the bombs had been falling on London, and had exchanged many a hurried word of sympathy under cover of the roar of the drier.

Fräulein Lydia had been badly overworked when I had seen her in September, since Herr Walter, the proprietor of the hair-dressing establishment, had been struck by a psychosis which had affected quite a number of Germans. With their driving urge for efficiency and, to my mind, almost uncanny ignorance of many of the simplest rules of human behaviour, an air-raid warning system had been devised whereby anyone who so wished could find out just how many enemy planes were over German territory at any given time, in what direction they were flying, and which township therefore was likely to be in for an air-raid. Rumour had it that the huge approaching formations could be located and even numbered as soon as they left the English coast behind them. Information as to their whereabouts could be obtained by tuning in to a certain wavelength on the wireless, and by listening to gay dance music being interrupted every so often by an air-raid announcement. *'Achtung, Achtung. Eine Luftlagemeldung!* One hundred – two hundred – one thousand – two thousand heavy bombers are now crossing the North Sea.' This piece of news only became of interest to Berliners if the announcer went on to inform his listeners that the spearhead had reached the north of the river Elbe, and that the bombers were heading in a south-easterly direction; for although their target might still be Hamburg or Hanover or any other town which lay in their path, it might also be Berlin.

I seldom felt like availing myself of such a golden opportunity to prolong the agony of waiting; and if I did so I was embarrassed to find myself heaving an involuntary sigh of relief should it turn out that some town other than where I happened to be, was being blown to bits.

Herr Walter, however, had caught the bug badly and remained

glued to his radio most of the day. He had huge maps of *Gross Deutschland* pinned to the wall of the cubbyhole behind the cashier's desk, and he followed the course of the planes with little coloured flags. Sometimes when the airspace over the Reich was not so occupied, the spare flags got mixed up with the curling pins and cotton wool in his little box of tricks; on other occasions his map was ablaze with colour. Herr Walter had been prevented by stomach ulcers and a long and lurid list of internal complaints from joining the Army. Perhaps his behaviour gave him some sort of compensatory satisfaction. At any rate, '*Meine Damen*, you must hurry,' he would rush in and announce in stentorian tones, guaranteed to penetrate the sound of the driers, which were soon to be reduced to a gentle hum through lack of electric current. 'One thousand heavy bombers are approaching our city and, unless they decide to drop their load on Hamburg or the *Leunawerke*, we are in for two lively hours. Hurry, *meine Damen*, hurry.' He certainly showed more interest in the war in the air than in the nerves of his clients, some of whom might be firmly attached to a permanent wave apparatus. A rather tense silence would follow as we waited for the advance warning. Frl. Lydia would bustle about quietly and efficiently, padding the windows and giving quiet instructions to the two scared apprentices, whilst we ladies sat in rows, like cottage loaves, the rather fatuous expressions of critical self-satisfaction wiped abruptly from our faces as we wondered whether we would have any luck with our hairdos this time. It was all of course a rather chancy business, why did we go to the hairdresser at all? Part of the illusion that life must go on as usual; for if the powers that be had decided that 'our city' was to be the target of the day, then, of course, we all had to descend to the cellar, permed, half-permed, dyed, half-dyed, as we might be, and, as often as not, the cellar would soon be full of dust and when we got upstairs again, Herr Walter and Frl. Lydia and the two scared little girls could start on us all over again.

On one never-to-be-forgotten occasion the cubicle next to mine had been occupied by a large teutonic vision, with sumptuous blonde plaits coiled high on her head. Frl. Lydia had not betrayed those plaits, but had enveloped her client's head in towels for the descent to the cellar. On our return, though, the cubicle curtains had blown open to reveal those glowing braids, hallmark of her Germanic womanhood, suspended like smoked eels from the drier. Frl. Lydia and I had collapsed in helpless laughter as the mortified Valkyrie had grabbed her crowning glory and stalked from the salon, never I could imagine, to return. 'She was an old *Narzisse*,* anyway,' had been Frl. Lydia's remark, and we had agreed that there were few things on earth quite so nauseating as a fake blonde plait.

Lost in my thoughts of Frl. Lydia, her Jürgen, Herr Walter and his flags, I came to a halt in front of the façade of No. 175. I stood in the doorway and gazed upwards at the gaping empty shell and the sky. As if to prove some identity, I could even make out the pink silk walls and twisted curtain rods of the third floor. A neat wooden cross on the piled up rubble in front of me told its own tale – there were bodies buried beneath.

Had Jürgen got his leave? Had he come back to this? I closed my eyes for a moment before turning away. All the threads that had been woven into the pattern of my life seemed to be snapping around me. So many human stories broken off just like that, when there seemed so much more to tell. A flash, a crashing roar and a wooden cross on a pile of rubble. Perhaps quite soon the main thread, too, would break and I would have left the scene, for there seemed no particular reason why my special personal anecdote should survive to its conclusion.

When I reached the Gedächtnisplatz and passed the truncated Gedächtniskirche, I was surrounded by a frozen sea of shattered ruins. I had never seen bombing like it before. In the Budapester-strasse house after house was an empty shell, not one single building had survived. The rubble had been neatly stacked to the gaping windows of the first floors. A thin powdering of snow, which covered the pavements, muffled my footsteps and had only been disturbed before me by the wandering tracks of a dog. The centre of Berlin. Capital of Hitler's mighty empire which, he had boasted, would last a thousand years, and I was alone in a silent ghost town.

I went as far as to what had been the Hotel Eden before I realized that, of course, it was impossible that anyone could be living there. I retraced my steps and stood uncertainly in the shadow of the Gedächtnikirche, wondering what to do next. It was hard to have to give up hope of seeing Lexi as I needed her companionship badly. Across the square, I spotted a battered

Narzisse (daffodil) – Slang word for a female Nazi.

telephone kiosk and the telephone inside it seemed intact, so for no particular reason I crossed the square and reached inside and dialled her telephone number. To my surprise, I seemed to be making some sort of connection as I could hear it ringing out and, a minute or two later, a sleepy voice, unmistakably Lexi's, came along the line, 'Hallo, who's that, who's speaking please?' 'This is the Dahlemer Laundry,' I said, 'I am speaking from a call box, would you mind coming down and fetching your washing as I cannot find my way to your house.' 'Well, it's the third pile of rubble from the corner,' she still sounded bored and sleepy, 'but wait a moment, I'll come down and fetch it.'

Back again, down the Budapesterstrasse, I counted the piles and tried to imagine where had been the entrance to Lexi's flat. From the other side of the road I examined the third pile rather more carefully and imagined that I could almost detect a faint track leading upwards. A few minutes later, a long slim leg, encased in a large felt army boot, swung over the window-sill of the first floor and Lexi came sliding and scrambling down the pile. She crossed the road to where I was standing. She was wearing a beautifully tailored Hungarian sheepskin coat, and with her long easy stride, she managed, in spite of the boots, to look extraordinarily graceful and elegant. As she approached, her face became completely expressionless. 'Good morning, Frau Dr Bielenberg,' she said and gave me a quick wink. *'Heil Hitler, meine dame,'* I answered, going one better. 'Would it be possible for us to have a word together?' 'Of course, of course, I know what you have come about. That suitcase of clothes which your husband left in our cellar. Well, as you see—' she glanced quickly up and down the road – 'as you see, he has not had much luck, but you can come in anyway.'

Although there was not a soul about, we continued our absurd conversation as she piloted me up the heap of stones and mortar. 'I'm sorry you have to come this way, Frau Dr Bielenberg, it's actually my short cut to the Bunker in the Zoo,' she waved her arm in the direction of a huge windowless concrete block which stood out square and stark beyond the splintered tree-stumps of the shattered Zoologische Garten. 'The state entrance is round by the Kurfürtstenstrasse,' her drawl became more pronounced, 'such a bore the whole thing, isn't it? Bombs and aeroplanes I mean, they must have mistaken us for a military target, but they say it will not be long now before our Leader has another brainwave. Some sort of wonder weapon, don't you know. Spiffing, that's what it'll be – spiffing.'

We climbed through the window and slid down the slope on the other side. Radiators hung drunkenly from the walls and bits of furniture were strewn around us, but Lexi steered her course unerringly through doors and windows until we came to a courtyard. It was her courtyard all right, I could recognize the misshapen faun in the snow-filled fountain in the centre. The heavy oak doorway on the far side looked solid and intact. Lexi shoved it open and hurried up the dark stairway, I was close on her heels. Then she flung open her door, went to the telephone and pulled out the connection, and turned to me with a joyous smile – 'Chrislein, darling, this is just too good for words, this is wonderful! I could hardly believe my ears when I recognized your voice on the telephone. Where have you come from? Oh God, this makes me feel years younger.'

She flung her arms around me and I hugged her and then we stood back and looked at each other through a mist of sudden tears. She fished a handkerchief out of her boot, wiped her eyes and handed it over to me. 'Come,' she sniffed and took my hand, 'I must hear what you have to say to my apartment. This is the hall of course, you recognize it, that's the sitting-room with windows and here's my bedroom without windows, and if you go through that door you fall straight into the cellar. But it's pretty good, isn't it? Nice and near the bunker too. I'm scared stiff of air-raids. Isn't it warm, too? I have a grand stove which I found in the porter's lodge when that went up in smoke and plenty of old bits of furniture for fuels. Helmuth's old files burn well, too. Crazy about the telephone, isn't it? It broke down the other day, so I got on to the breakdown service and they came round and mended it. I don't think it's even tapped, you see, no one believes that anyone lives here, but I really love it. Oh God, Chris, I'm talking too much, but it is good to see you and you look so well, so brown, really disgracefully well. How do you think I look? Lousy, eh? It was clever of you not to see anyone when you were last in Berlin. I only heard about it after you left, but I said to Werner Traber, by the way, Werner is still around, how damned clever it was of you. We can't resist seeing each other, we few who are left. It would be inhuman not to.'

I had been watching her as she chattered on, tense and at random, like someone who is a lot alone. She did indeed look changed, very thin, very pale under her obviously hurriedly applied make-up. But in spite of her pallor, with the skin drawn tightly over her cheekbones, I realized for the first time that she was beautiful, bone beautiful. Her usual look of slightly bored sophistication had left her and she had a completely new expression in her sapphire eyes.

'No, I don't think you look lousy; in fact, I actually think you look beautiful,' I said. 'But you don't look as if you had enough to eat.'

'Oh, I don't need much,' she answered, 'and anyway, I have so many to look after. Father is in Moabit, Helmuth in the Lehrterstrasse. Albrecht Bernstorff, "Hänschen" Oster, and a dozen others, are there too. I have to help feed them all.' When I asked her how ever she managed to get food to them, she laughed and shrugged, and gave me the old Lexi look from under her lashes, part amused, part just dead pan. 'Well, Chrislein, there are ways and means, but you, my dear, are far too young to know them. Be that as it may, I know the prison doctors, the Protestant priest, the Catholic priest, and a lot of the warders. The warders are not all Gestapo, you know, some of them are regular police, some conscientious objectors, some even petty criminals who happened to be doing time when the flood started. I spend a lot of time in the prisons and make myself useful where I can.' As she spoke she led me into the room which had been Peter's office, and now seemed to be her bedroom. The windows were broken, but the frames had been filled with brown paper. She switched on the light and we sat down on a narrow bed covered with rugs. It was good and warm. A small black iron stove, with an odd assortment of firing stacked around it, stood in the corner roaring merrily.

'And now, dear Chris, tell me about Peter, he's in Ravensbrück I believe. He was in the Lehrterstrasse for a short while, but before I got wind of it he had been transferred. The food is better up there and there is less chance of raids, and I think Puppi Sarre has managed to get herself a job in the reception office there, which is surely a help. But my dear, here I am talking away and I haven't even asked you why you are here.' She shot me a sudden, straight look. 'No special reason, Chris? Peter is all right, I suppose, I haven't—'

'Oh yes,' I said quickly, and felt I knew at least one reason why she had talked so much and so fast. 'He is all right – at least, I mean, he is still in Ravensbrück. I am here—' and I told her the whole of our story as far as I knew it. Of the postcard which Peter's aunt had received from him on July 18th, of his visit to Berlin at the beginning of August, of his talk of shooting Adam out, of his arrest as soon as he got back to Graudenz, and of how Arnold had managed to wangle his transfer to Berlin. I told her too of Arnold, whose politics had been different to ours, but who I believed to be a real friend, and I told her, of course, that I was to travel to Ravensbrück tomorrow to see Peter.

She listened in complete silence, and when I had finished she sighed and said quietly: 'One thing is certain, that Arnold of yours is worth his weight in gold. A good friend and still with some influence, such people hardly exist. You cannot, of course, trust him completely. Even good friends – the ones who are still around – may be arrested any day, and then come the interrogations. Some can take them, some can't. Every time that certain people are interrogated there is a wave of new arrests, whereas others, and I could imagine Adam and Carl Langbehn are amongst them – take their secrets with them.' I asked her who was still alive and she told me Helmuth Moltke, 'Hänschen' Oster, Albrecht Bernstorff, Schlabrendorff, Gerstenmaier and some others. The courts were so full that they could not cope with the cases, but that Helmuth's case would be coming up any day. I also asked her whether she had seen Adam after his arrest and she said she had not, but that a girl from the Foreign Office had had to take some documents to the prison and had passed him in a passage. It was some time after his trial. He had looked, she had said, withdrawn and unapproachable, 'as if he already belonged to another world'.

I got up and went to the door. It was stifling in that little room. Lexi got up and stood beside me. 'It's no use, Chris,' she said, 'we are all living so close to death these days. If you want to keep sane you have to keep your mind on the living – wait a moment, stick another table leg into the stove and I'll get some coffee.'

She came back with two steaming cups of the real thing and put them on the floor. 'Now, my dear, you have to be in Ravensbrück tomorrow, you say. Well, you must take advantage of this. Your Arnold has told you that you must convey to Peter that most of his friends are dead, and can no longer give evidence against him. He is right; of course you must. What he may not have added is that the stinkers are fully capable of showing him fake implicating documents, with counterfeit signatures. Part of my own job, I'll show you afterwards, is to collect bits of given evidence and pass them round. You see, it's so important that evidence tallies. And remember, these Gestapo are not all wise and all knowing. Why, if you can believe it, I got permission to see my father after he had his last heart attack, on the pretext of wanting him to make his will, and whilst he dictated his will, I wrote down what he should know for his interrogations and gave it to him to read and sign and hand back to me. Those oxen of jailers sat there at their desks, reading, and hadn't even the sense to search me on my way out!'

I looked at her in amazement. For sheer cool nerve this seemed to me about the height of things. But Lexi was staring ahead of her with half-closed eyes, sipping her coffee with an odd, half smiling, almost cat-like expression on her face and it occurred to me that she was somehow in her element. 'Of course, Father is a hopeless case,' she was saying, 'you know, he had his first heart attack soon after he was arrested, and dumb-bell that I am, I thought he might not be able to stand any more interrogations, so with some difficulty, I might say, I got a loaf of bread to him with a phial of poison in the middle of it. A few days later I got a note from him, telling me to send more bread if possible, but to leave out the ridiculous stuffing as he had had some difficulty in disposing of it.' Lexi's father, whom I had only met once or twice, was certainly a rather quixotic character. He had fiddled around in politics in pre-Hitler days and had a fund of amusing and sometimes hardly credible stories in his repertoire. When called up as a Reserve officer and asked to sign the oath of allegiance to Hitler, he had refused. 'An Alvensleben doesn't sign such things' had been his parting shot. No one quite knew why he had not been shut up years ago: *Narrenfreiheit* maybe – a sort of fool's freedom. But time was passing and I could not allow my mind to wander far. In my Black Forest hideout I knew that I had lived a relatively protected life during the last eighteen months. In Rohrbach the ever-recurring theme of birth and life and death and birth again, the rising and setting of the sun, the sowing, the reaping and the harvesting, and the long winter whiteness had, in spite of all, provided a peaceful, rhythmical background to my living. There was so much I had to learn about this world outside of the law, a world of *kassibers* and tapped telephones, of midnight arrest, and unnatural death, and who could tell me of it better than Lexi, who was facing up to it every day and had been doing so for months.

'Lexi,' I burst out, 'perhaps you don't realize just how little I know. I last saw Adam in March, and Peter in June, and since then I have just lived on newspapers, the odd prison note and my imagination. I did not see anyone in September and you think it was wise, but listen, my dear, it left me ignorant. I am not really anxious that I will not be able to lie and act up as well as anyone else, but somehow I must know where I am. How could it have gone wrong? What happened? Why didn't Adam, why didn't any of them make off when they knew things had gone wrong, while the going was good?'

Lexi leaned back against the wall behind us and closed her eyes. 'I cannot tell you much, dear Chris,' she added, 'nor do I think, the way things are, that I should tell you even as much as I know. It was such a hot and beautiful summer day, July 20th, hot and still and normal really – at least as normal as any other day. Maybe later I will be able to pretend that I had some particular premonition, but now I don't think it would be true. There had been so many false alarms before, and just as many disappointments – and then, well, you see these ruins as they are today, but whilst it's all happening, the bombing I mean, it's so hard to think of much else really – just cleaning up, trying to live again, wondering whether it's all worth while because maybe the next day – or the next . . .

'But July 20th, the 20th, oh yes of course the tension did build up during the day, in fact I think it had been building up for weeks before. It was not what certain people said, but what they didn't say – there was no more hearsay, no more gossip, and yet an atmosphere not exactly of excitement, perhaps more of watching, of waiting as if everyone was holding their breath – I don't know, I can't describe it. And then on the 20th as the day progressed there seemed to be troops, more troops than usual in the streets, and they seemed to be marching to places as if they had a purpose, and there were people hurrying along the pavements; in spite of the heat they did not stand and watch the troops march by. And then during the afternoon there were rumours – rumours that the Wilhelmstrasse, that the Government buildings had been cordoned off by troops, no one seemed to know why, or what troops, until rumours began to spread, rumours that something tremendous was afoot, rumours that Hitler had been wounded, was perhaps even dead. Where do rumours come from, anyway? How do they spread? I don't know, but all I can say is that the streets were suddenly deserted, not a soul about anywhere, and

219

everyone must have been sitting by their wireless sets listening, listening for news, and I remember staring out over the trees towards the Brandenburg Gate – there were trees left then and I prayed, Chrislein, I just prayed – me mind you – since I knew and yet did not know what was going on there on the other side of the Brandenburg Gate.

'Then came the news, there had been music, then the news, you heard it too perhaps, and you tried not to believe it any more than I did. There had been a foul attempt on Hitler's life, some Army officers, but Hitler had survived – just a few scratches. I just didn't believe it, that he had survived, I mean – I just couldn't, until he spoke after midnight, and then of course I knew, no one could fake that voice – and then—' Lexi's voice faded away. I waited a moment to see if she would go on. There were so many more questions to ask. How had it been possible that Stauffenberg's bomb had not killed Hitler, had it not been powerful enough? Even if he had survived, could not something more have been achieved? A revolt, a rebellion, a revolution? How had it been possible for Goebbels to broadcast? Remer to play his fatal rôle? Why had there been such faulty links in the chain? When I turned to look at Lexi, though, all those questions, utterly immaterial, just faded from my mind. What did it matter? Why should I need to know? 'And then—' Lexi seemed about to go on, but instead she got slowly to her feet and put her half empty coffee cup back near the stove. She squatted down in front of it and I could not see her face.

'Chris,' she said, 'thank your stars, every day of your life, that you do not belong to my rotten, yes my rotten, unhappy and accursed race.' 'Listen, my dear.' I tried to speak quietly, to give her some comfort in a way, and also my thoughts had wandered for a moment to a little wooden cross on a pile of rubble just up the street at No. 175 – 'I don't know that I have so much reason just now to be so mighty proud of my race—' but she did not seem to be listening, instead she shook her head and held up her hand in front of her eyes as if to shield them from the glowing fire. 'Chris,' she said simply, 'they hanged them slowly one by one from meat hooks – and they filmed them whilst they were dying.'

An hour or so later we struggled back together over the heaps of rubble, and before I climbed through the last window Lexi wished me luck for tomorrow and reminded me to watch out for the microphone and to sit next to Peter if possible, in order to hold his hand and give contact signals when conveying news. She turned and gave me an encouraging wave, as she stood for a moment, a slim and valiant figure, framed in the doorway of what might have been someone's drawing-room. I waved back. Not so slim or half as valiant, but at least equally determined to keep my mind on the living, come what may.

A VISIT TO RAVENSBRÜCK
CONCENTRATION CAMP

(Winter 1944)

'Enemy' aircraft and the weather were kind to me. A peaceful night and I slept. A long, dreamless sleep so deep that when the alarm clock woke me at six o'clock I thought for a moment it was the church bell in Rohrbach, calling the villagers to matins. But this was not Rohrbach, this was Berlin and the sounds from the kitchen must be Mabel getting me breakfast. I was suddenly very wide awake. This was the day. It was still dark outside and the electric light bulb from my bedside lamp was doing duty in the kitchen, but I had learned to move easily in the dark and I had laid out my clothes on Peter's bed the evening before. I had discarded my skiing pants and rooted through my wardrobe for my best. A fur coat and my fur Cossack hat; somehow I wanted to go in with flags flying. Mabel had done her very best with my breakfast. A huge plate of porridge, a cup of strong rather musty tea, and as she opened the front door to let me out into the icy greyness and asked me to give Peter her love, I felt almost gay and light-hearted. Incredible but true, come hell and high water, I was going to see him today.

It was bitterly cold. When I reached the station, little scuffles of grey snow whirled along the platform ahead of me. But inside the train it was warm and comfortable. The only other occupants of the carriage, a woman and two little girls. The woman rather typical of her kind, an antiseptically clean, worried-looking *Hausfrau*, with allegiance to duty written all over her nondescript face. She was dressed from head to shoes in beige and couldn't have looked smart if she tried. She was wearing white cotton gloves and was already immersed in a book covered in a neat linen cover. As I pushed my way into the carriage she looked up, murmured '*l'Hitler*', glanced at the children, and returned to her reading. I may have been mistaken, but a quick movement of her right hand might have been the start of a Nazi salute. Aha! '*Heil Hitler*' I replied firmly, as I took off my coat and retired to my corner. The two children were incredibly plain, with pale, pudgy faces, mousy fair hair and beady blue eyes. They were dressed in bright red tartan dresses and long white stockings. Why a popular get-up for children in Northern Germany should be bright red tartan, preferably Cameron or even Royal Stuart, I do not know. Bearable, even stirring perhaps to some, when swinging over a pair of knobbly knees on some Scottish moor, but a sure killer as party best on a small, pale child.

Normally maybe, in spite of their unprepossessing appearance, I might have started up some conversation with those two little girls as they sat there watching my every move with unwinking curiosity; but today I was glad to be left in peace in my corner, staring out through the frost-free porthole I had rubbed in my window, at the endless flat North German plain as it slipped past, featureless and white.

I was a bit worried. Lexi had groomed me well, but just the same I was not sure what I had to expect, and had made no plans ahead. I felt I should be planning something instead of sitting there, filled with a bubbling elation I could not suppress. Although I have lived so long in Germany, where everything from a picnic to a *coup d'état* had to be planned down to the smallest detail, I knew that I had remained an incurable compromiser, inclined to plunge into a situation, flap around, see what was cooking, hope for the best and, as often as not, with God's help, come up smiling. A characteristic which alternately infuriated and fascinated my poor Peter between whose sense of right and wrong was drawn a clear white line; a glorious friend, an implacable enemy, he moved swiftly and surely, or stayed put like a Red Indian, still and withdrawn.

As the train trundled along, stopping occasionally at some wayside station, snatches of conversation from the seat opposite slipped in and interrupted my thinking. The two girls had soon lost interest in me and had fetched themselves down two large bags of biscuits and sweets. From then on they had not stopped talking and munching, and Mama, who was still trying to read, had only shot the occasional rather absentminded reply at their

223

endless questioning. I felt almost sorry for the whole party, when I heard one of the little girls – she was really unbelievably plain – ask her Mama why was it that Papi had to go away to be a soldier. 'Because the Fatherland needs him – don't talk with your mouth full, Edeltraut' was Mama's short reply. Of course, Edeltraut, she would be called Edeltraut – one of those hideous Germanic names, so popular after 1933. The other little brat was probably called Kriemhilde, and serve her damn well right, I thought, as I watched her poking round in what seemed an inexhaustible bag of eats.

It was not exactly snowing when I reached the halt for Ravensbrück, but the small wooden station dumped down in the midst of nowhere, creaked and groaned under the blast of an icy wind from the east which was whistling across the plain, whirling the fallen snow ahead of it like desert sand.

A large, black Mercedes limousine was parked outside the station, the only vehicle of any kind in sight. Although the flags on the front mudguards were hidden by canvas coverings, it was obviously an official car, the chauffeur in SS uniform. Any nascent sympathy I might have felt for my travelling companions evaporated as I watched them climb into it and drive off in a scurry of snow.

My Cossack hat was about the one part of my equipment which was not out of place in that bleak emptiness, and I wished I had not been so rash as to leave my skiing pants behind, but as I stood there watching the car disappear into the distance down the one straight road leading from the station, a dramatic picture which had hung in our nursery at home flashed across my mind. Captain Oates, of Scott's Antarctic expedition, leaving his tent to go out into the blizzard and to die, so that Scott could live a short while longer on the rations that remained. I had always been very impressed by that picture, and so with my head bent to the wind – watch your step, Mrs Oates – I set off along the tracks made by the tyres of the Mercedes.

It seemed a long trek before a high wire fence, topped again with barbed wire, loomed up beside me out of the driven snow. Higher again was a wooden tower, surmounted by a small wooden hut and by what, from the distance, looked like a giant tea cosy. As I passed underneath I glanced upwards, and realized that it was the guard in his sheepskins and what might have been the spout of the tea pot was a tommy gun aimed very accurately at my head. It was not a very comfortable sensation, although the face above it, looking out between the flaps of an enormous fur collar, grinned broadly as I passed. Had the wind been blowing away from the camp instead of towards it, I had the feeling that the German equivalent of a wolf whistle might have come my way.

I passed several watch towers and what seemed like hundreds of yards of barbed wire before I reached the red, white and black barrier and was shown into a long narrow wooden hut at the entrance. The hut was stiflingly hot and airless and seemed full of people coming and going. I waited for a bit for my face to unfreeze, and then joined the queue at the far end of the hut where two huge flags, the Swastika and the regimental colours of the SS, covered the wall, and a mild-faced elderly man behind a desk seemed to be coping with enquiries. In front of me was a tall, very handsome lad in the uniform of the regular Army. We both carried parcels, mine with Frau Muckle's sausages and a photograph album, his looked like cigarettes. The man behind the desk was looking up at him with a gentle, almost fatherly, expression on his face. 'Your father is a prisoner here you say, and you have no appointment to visit him? I'm afraid I cannot help you.' 'But – ' the young soldier hesitated, 'you see, I have to leave for the eastern front tonight, I only want to say goodbye, there must be some means—' The man behind the desk shrugged helplessly. 'Wait a moment,' he said, 'I will telephone, although I don't think it will help much. Take a seat, will you?' He turned to me, 'And you?' 'I have an appointment to see my husband, Peter Bielenberg, at ten o'clock.' The guard or porter or whoever he was, looked almost relieved. He went to the telephone and returned. 'Take a seat,' he said, 'you will be called.' A row of chairs stood along the wall, and I sat down next to the young officer. He was leaning forward with his elbows on his knees, his cap and gloves and his parcel on the chair beside him. Capless, he looked very young. Although I could see he was a lieutenant, he had not needed to shave much yet, and I felt he should have still been in school. The expression on his face was quite tragic, a mixture of deep sorrow and impotent rage. 'Can't you get permission somehow?' I asked him, under cover of the general noise. 'I've not had time,' he answered, 'only three days leave, you see, and I have to go back tonight.' 'Couldn't you miss the train and sit it out?' I asked, 'some official might come through and give you a permit after all.' It seemed so crazy that I, an Englishwoman, should have permission whilst this lad, who was giving everything he had, should be refused. 'Miss the train? But my leave is up.' He looked at me in childlike, almost shocked bewilderment. 'No – yes – I see,' I murmured. It was no use, I did not see, but how to explain? Tomorrow he would be on his way back to the front, fighting for a régime which would probably kill his father and would not even allow him to bid him farewell. My name was being called from the door and I had to go. The boy jumped to his feet and we shook hands. He managed to give me an encouraging smile: 'Hals- und Beinbruch! Good luck to you, Gnädige Frau,' he said as we parted, then he hesitated a moment and added, 'I assure you it is no penance to go back to the front. The air is cleaner there – but I would have liked to have seen my father before I went.' As I turned away it flashed through my mind that I would like my sons to have his look about them when they reached his age.

The guard who had called my name led me across the square to another wooden hut, on the far side of the compound. I was rather at a loss to discover what this place actually was. It did not seem to be a concentration camp as I had imagined it to be, but rather more some military encampment with SS army personnel. Groups of SS were marching briskly about, and some seemed to be doing physical jerks. Sharp staccato commands rang out in the frosty air, and in a far corner of what seemed to be a parade ground some rows of dolls in shorts and singlets jumped and marched with the wooden movements of marionettes. The wind seemed to have dropped or perhaps the buildings gave us some protection. A pale pink, wintery sun was trying its best to temper the cold.

We were challenged twice, but the guard showed my pass and we were allowed to continue on our way past a row of rather better built houses – the black Mercedes was parked outside one of them – to the far end of the compound. Ahead of us once again was the high wire fence and on the far side of it more huts, and some sort of factory with two high chimneys smoking energetically. Only two more huts separated us from the fence. The guard, who had not opened his mouth since taking me in tow, stopped at the last of these, pushed open the double doors, ushered me in, then still without uttering he went out, closing the door firmly behind him. I stood and looked around me. The hut was very like the one we had left except that it was empty, and instead of wet uniforms it smelled strongly of carbolic. I glanced out of the window to see if the guard was well out of the way and then went about my business fairly systematically.

At one end of the hut was a desk and at the other a table flanked by benches on either side, there was also another door opposite me. The walls were decorated with large photographs of Himmler, Heydrich, Kaltenbrunner and other heroes I did not recognize, all in the black uniforms with the silver facings of the SS. Some were more smothered in decorations than others. Himmler carefully posed, that the light should not reflect in his pincenez, and full justice could be done to the deceptive mildness of his pale, beady eyes. Heydrich, killed in Czechoslovakia a day or two before Christopher was born. His picture was adorned with a large black ribbon, to signify mourning, no doubt. Mourned by whom, I wondered. As I went the rounds of this rogues' gallery I examined each one in a slightly myopic way, and lifted each picture carefully on its hook, as if interested to discover who had taken the photographs – no microphone there anyway. I opened my bag and clumsily emptied my purse, so that the *marks* and *pfennigs* rolled all over the floor, underneath the radiators, desk and table. I had to go down on my knees to collect them. The microphone was under the bench against the wall.

I had hardly settled myself down to wait before the door opened and a tall, dark, very dapper young man appeared. He was in the dark green uniform of the Security Police and was carrying a bulging briefcase. He introduced himself politely as *Kriminalkommissar* John, hoped that I had had a pleasant journey, told me please not to bother to get up and that I would not have too long to wait. He asked me what was the book I had in my hand and when I told him it was a photograph album, he asked politely whether he might look at it. I handed it to him, with the little parcel of Frau Muckle's sausages, and he took it to his desk and began idly turning the pages. We might have been two passing acquaintances in a dentist's waiting room.

A few minutes later the door to the square opened again and I felt my throat go tight. A party of six or seven men trudged past me and went out through the door on my right. Three obvious prisoners and the remainder guards. The prisoners all seemed elderly men, pale and thin, their crumpled suits hanging around them in folds. All three were clutching their trousers and shuffling one foot in front of the other; they had neither braces nor shoelaces. I glanced at Herr John as the door closed behind them, but he did not look up from his study of the album.

A few more minutes passed in silence when a tall shadow passed the first window to my left. I could hear my heart thumping as it passed the second window and I knew that it was Peter. Herr John had risen to his feet and come towards the door, which was pushed open from outside. First came a short, fattish guard and after him, limping a little, the tall, erect figure of what I knew at that moment to be the only bit of Germany I had any interest in whatsoever. I jumped to my feet as Peter came towards me with hands outstretched. An urgent look crossed his face as we stood there face to face and holding hands, and I realized that he was pressing a small, hard, square object into my right palm. I turned my back on Herr John and the guard and went to the table to retrieve my purse. Under cover of fishing out a handkerchief to wipe my eyes, I dropped the object into a side pocket. It was a matchbox. This had all happened incredibly quickly. I turned back and glanced at Herr John and the guard, but they were not looking at us and had obviously noticed nothing unusual. I could only hope and believe that some remnant of natural tact had made them look away when Peter and I had greeted each other.

The guard motioned to Peter to sit down on the bench against the wall and I immediately moved in next to him and took his hand, according to plan. After a moment's hesitation the guard sat down opposite us, and Herr John, after handing me back the album and the parcel, returned to his desk at the other end of the room. So far so good, there we were together, Peter and I, so close, hand in hand – a tenuous link indeed, when barbed wire, stone walls and all the rigid paraphernalia of a ruthless régime was bent on tearing us apart.

I looked at Peter as he sat beside me. I was surprised, I don't know why, to see how normal he looked. I don't know what I had expected, but in his green tweed jacket and grey flannels, with even a scarf tucked into his open-necked shirt, he did not look like a prisoner. He was very thin, his face rather puffy and grey looking and – a shock this – the first few strands of silver streaked his dark hair, but otherwise – he never wore braces or shirts with detachable collars, so he had been spared the degradation of the men who did. He had changed in some way, but for the moment I was not certain how.

There was no time to lose, fifteen minutes was all we had and

I had to give my message. As usual when nervous I found no difficulty in talking. I said that I hoped he would tell *Kriminalrat* Lange how grateful I was that he had given me permission to come here as there were so many family matters I had to discuss with him; matters that really could not wait until he was freed. At first Peter hardly seemed to be listening. Holding my hand in a painful grip with the pulse in his wrist thumping against mine, his eyes were fixed on the album of photographs. I realized later that, coming as he was from his solitary cell, he must have been taking the brunt of the shock of our meeting. Perhaps he had not even known that he was going to see me. 'There is so much to tell you, Peter, that I don't really know where to start,' I said, undoing my coat so that the flap covered our clasped hands, and at the same time taking one of his fingers and forcing it to point downwards under the bench. For a moment I wondered whether he would understand my rather crude manoeuvre; but I need not have worried, for suddenly he looked at me and I noticed then where the change in him lay – it was in his eyes. The boyish direct look had gone from them and they were wary, watchful and inscrutable.

He had understood about the microphone and he would get my message all right. 'There is so much, too, that I am longing to know, Chris,' he said, 'but tell me how are the children?' 'The children are marvellously well,' I said, 'they are skiing every day, and Christopher now talks with the most wonderful Baden accent—' and I proceeded to tell him anecdotes of their escapades, whilst racking my brains as to how to convey to him the news about Adam and Carl that Arnold had said he must know. I could sense in him an alertness and watchful waiting. 'And Frau Muckle,' he said, 'is she well?' 'Oh she is very well,' I answered and suddenly, with an intense wave of relief, I knew my course. 'Only there is sad news from down the valley,' I said, 'Frau Muckle's sister, you remember? The one who had four sons in the Army or rather three in the Army and one in the Air Force—' I squeezed Peter's hand quickly once – twice— 'well, the eldest one, Carl, and the third one, Arnold – Adolf – what was he called?' I dared not say Adam because it was an unusual name, but a quick responding squeeze from Peter told me that he knew who I meant. 'Adolf, I think,' he said, 'and?' 'Well, she had news this autumn,' I hurried on, 'they were killed on the Russian front.' 'Killed?' he asked, 'or just reported missing?' 'No, definitely killed,' I said as firmly as I could, 'killed in action.' There was a moment's silence, then Peter drew a short sighing breath. 'Their poor mother,' he said, and again, 'their poor mother.' 'Oh, I think in many ways she must be proud,' I thought I ought to remark, for *Kriminalkomissar* John's ears and for the microphone, 'she loves her country and they have died for it.' Poor little Amalie of Gutmadingen, pride was surely the one emotion she had not felt when told that her fourth and last son was missing – the son in the Air Force, shot down over France – and she had hoped that by asking me to light a candle in the village Church and to pray with her that he might prove to have been taken prisoner by the British.

A quick pressure of Peter's hand and his quiet voice saying: 'Have there been many casualties in the valley otherwise? I do not hear much news here, but the Western front seems to be holding, thank God.' 'Oh yes, there have been many casualties,' I said, 'little Hel – ger' a quick signal, 'little Hel – ger from over Triberg way seems to be one of the few who is still writing letters home, but of course the post is a bit topsy turvy with the front so fluid at the moment. Things will get better when it settles down.' Our clasped hands, a veritable life-line functioning as smoothly as any secret transmitter. Now I had even been able to tell him of Helmuth Moltke. I had almost forgotten what had been the official reason for my visit. What was it Arnold had said? Oh, yes, monetary matters, lack of funds. Now that I had delivered my message the strain of talking and saying nothing was becoming intense. I had exchanged my fund of stories about the children and yet did not dare stop talking for fear that the interview would be terminated. I could see that Peter, too, was suffering under the same strain, as he started to explain to me slowly and carefully how I should ask Seiler to advance me money for the rent, or if necessary borrow from Arnold, whom he would repay as soon as he was freed. Like the tension which builds up when taking someone to a train, someone beloved who is leaving on a long journey. All has been said, there is no more to say, the carriage doors are slamming shut, the guard's whistle is somehow almost a welcome relief. I glanced at my watch and saw that we had already sat together for at least twenty minutes. It could not be long now before prison walls would close around him again, and I would go my way and we would be worlds apart.

Like the crack of a whip Herr John's chair scraped back along the boarded floor as he rose to his feet. The guard got up, too, and took his stand next to Peter, 'I'm sorry,' Herr John said, 'but you have already had a longer time than is officially allowed.' 'That was kind of you,' I managed to mutter and then: 'Goodbye, dear Peter, see you soon again, very soon, I hope – don't forget the album and the sausages.' 'No I haven't forgotten,' he was on his feet now too. 'No, I haven't forgotten,' he said and he gathered them up. Before leaving he turned and gave me a long, slow, extraordinarily gentle smile. 'Bless you, darling,' he added in English and made for the door without turning back. He strode out, limping slightly again, but his step was firm and light and I noticed that his shoes were neatly tied with two little pieces of hemp. Somehow those improvised shoelaces gave me great courage. No bloody power on earth was going to make him shuffle. They were so typical of him, those little flags of freedom.

I asked Herr John politely if he would be so kind as to give me a pass out of the camp, or perhaps even send someone with me as I was afraid I might not find the way. As I turned to pick up my bag from the table I suddenly remembered the matchbox. Herr John seemed bent on acting the gent. 'Most certainly, *Gnädige Frau*,' he said and handed me a docket. Then he took me to the door and hailed a passing guard who was carrying his tin mug and a plate and seemed to be going to his lunch. '*Heil Hitler, Herr Kriminalkommissar*, and thank you,' I said. '*Heil Hitler, Gnädige Frau*, it was a pleasure,' he answered and bowed and clicked his heels.

The guard seemed a harmless fellow, eager to chat. He told me that there would not be a train leaving for Berlin before the late afternoon, but that there was a cosy pub up the road, 'where we all go', and I could wait in there. Talking away, he led me smoothly through the various check-points and left me with a friendly smile back on the long white road to the station. The cosy pub turned out to be a stuffy little dump, and 'we all' a milling crowd of SS guards and army personnel who gazed at me as if they had not seen a woman for a very long time. One in particular, pale and scarred, had one of the most brutal faces I had ever seen in my life. He had a leather-covered whip stuck into his belt and I decided that my matchbox and I would feel happier at the station. I hardly dared open my purse as I sat alone in the waiting room next to the Stationmaster's office, but found myself clutching it tightly as if the small square object inside might take wing. In the carriage later, though, I was again by myself and could wait no longer.

So, shaking a little, I slit it open, emptied a few matches onto the seat beside me and took out a small, rolled-up scrap of paper. It might have been lavatory paper or perhaps a strip off the side of a newspaper. On it was written in clear script, unmistakably Peter's, a string of words which at first seemed almost meaningless. The writing was so tiny that I had to stand up and read it close to the lamp. In its way a miniature work of art and so untypical of my impatient Peter. 'Self non-political have conceded nothing Adam close friend Hamburg days Clarita childhood Langbehn neighbour only Chris Irish Moltke lawyer together professionally wife hen-food Peter Yorck—' one word followed the other, name after name, information snippet by snippet, until there was one word in the bottom corner, one word which I could not decipher.

So that was it – a little post-script to our meeting; I folded it up and put it back into the box. I almost had to smile to myself. Peter was not renowned for long effusive letter writing, but this one was surely the shortest and most concise note that I had ever had from him.

When I got back to Dahlem the door of the Falkenried opened immediately and Mabel and Arnold were waiting for me in the doorway. They could hardly wait to hear how I had fared and I was hardly allowed to take off my coat before being dragged into the sitting-room. Arnold was lavish in his praise of how I had managed to convey the messages to Peter. His jubilation was so genuine that I decided to tell him about the matchbox. He looked at me in amazement, and then burst out laughing. 'Oh no – this is too good for words – trust Peter – but he really is the limit.' Suddenly he became serious. 'But, Chris, it really makes me shake to think about it. You might have been searched. Come, show me that paper—' He took it to the light and studied it in silence for some minutes, then: 'Short and sweet,' he said in English, 'a résumé of his interrogations; the particularly sweet part is where he writes "that he has conceded nothing", not that there was anything to concede,' he added quickly. 'Exactly,' I murmured, looking at the floor. There was a rather awkward silence and Arnold went over to the fireplace and leaned with his head on his arm against the mantelpiece, staring into the fire. 'One thing puzzles me, Chris, and that is why did he do it? Why did he give you this note? It put you in such danger. Had you been searched, you would not be standing here now. It's unlike him somehow. But I guess we shouldn't judge. He has been long in solitary confinement. The temptation to reach the outside world must be great. Still, I don't know – it's unlike him somehow—'

I was too sleepy to bother much about the whys and wherefores, but in the middle of the night I was suddenly wide awake, with Arnold's words ringing in my ears. Why did he do it? Why did he give me that note? I switched on the light of the bedside table and stared at the little matchbox, standing there so sturdily between my alarm clock and a glass of water. Of course, of course, the answer was now clear. Peter had given me the message in case I should be interrogated – our evidence must tally. I hadn't been interrogated yet, but perhaps, I still could be. The second part of my plan could function if I rang *Kriminalrat* Lange and asked to be. I felt like jumping clear out of the bed and ringing him there and then. Instead, I went to the sitting-room and fetched a shovel. I found myself staring for some time at my matchbox, even holding it to my head for a moment or two; then I put it on the shovel and burned it and its contents with one of its own matches. I knew its message off by heart, I could not afford to be sentimental and it had given up its secret. It only seemed to me extraordinary that I had not thought of it before.

INTERROGATION IN THE PRINZ ALBRECHTSTRASSE

(Winter 1944–1945)

I made my appointment by telephone with *Kriminalrat* Lange for January 4th. My brother John's birthday, perhaps a good omen. He sounded surprised at my rather unorthodox offer of help to him in his investigations, but finally agreed to see me at 11 a.m. in the Prinz Albrechtstrasse, headquarters of the SD (*Sicherheitsdienst*).* Arnold was scandalized when I told him of my plan. He may have been accustomed to more docile ladies, for it took me some time to persuade him that he was dealing with a member of the species who was an exception to the rules as he knew them. He used every argument: the possibility of my arrest, of my being ill-treated, injected with some drug, my duty to my children, my flaunting of Peter's express wishes. He painted such a lurid picture of what could happen to me that it was hard not to throw back at him why in God's name he had ever seen any sense in such a régime. But I knew he meant it rightly and I think in the end he was persuaded that if all went well I might do some good. Lexi was quite emphatic – she thought it an excellent idea.

To pass the time of waiting, I decided to make a trip to Hamburg and visit my mother-in-law in Aumühle, and in the short time we had together we came closer to each other than ever before. She had aged considerably during the past months, but there was a stoicism about her and a warm, quite selfless sympathy which moved me deeply.

On New Year's Eve I made the mistake of visiting some half-Jewish friends who lived not far away. There was quite a gathering and the discussions turned mainly on whether it was

---

**Sicherheitsdienst* – Security Police.

or was not still worth while investing money in the occupied territories. A soya bean factory in Poland – interesting from an investment point of view perhaps. It occurred to me that the expression *verhinderter Nazi*, frustrated Nazi, had some aptness after all; that some Jews, in fact, would have made potent Nazi material had they not been barred from joining in for racial reasons. At 10 o'clock the master of the house insisted that the wireless should be turned on. Hitler was to make his usual New Year's broadcast. Maybe, who knows, he might still have something up his sleeve. *'Die Wunderwaffe'* the wonder weapon (already dubbed the 'Wu-Wa' in Berlin and dismissed out of hand) was discussed seriously and deliberately as a possibility which might change the whole course of the war. With part of their city walled off to prevent typhoid, so complete was the ruin, so numerous the half-burned mutilated corpses beneath, the merchants of Hamburg were clinging, it would seem, to their old shibboleth 'business as usual' – the last to join but also the last to leave the Nazi bandwagon. As the trumpets sounded and a hush descended on the gathering in the drawing-room, I got up and left the house without saying goodbye. I almost forgot to fetch my coat from the cloakroom. *'Deutsches Volk! National-Sozialisten! Meine Volksgenossinnen!'* God, that sickening Austrian accent. Small comfort that the words were slurred and the hoarse voice hardly recognizable, he was alive and, seemingly, still able to cast his diabolical spell.

Back in Berlin the few remaining days dragged slowly past. It was not easy to maintain my original calm. I could not sleep too well and I was glad when the figure three on the clock on the sitting-room mantelpiece, which showed the date as well as the hour, seemed about to slip away and the four to move into its place. January the fourth. Acting on Lexi's instructions I dressed myself very carefully for the part I hoped to play. She had assured me that in spite of their warped mentalities most Gestapo officials were essentially middle-class and conventional in their tastes. *Spiessig* was the word she used, it would be hard to translate. After a day's work they would clear their desks, put their whips and knuckledusters neatly back in the drawer and return to exemplary family lives, their misdeeds locked away with their files. They preferred their womenfolk to be neatly and tidily dressed rather than smart, with very little, if any make-up. Long hair with a large bun at the back and, if I had been able to sew decently, even a neat darn in one of my gloves would, I felt, have made the picture more convincing.

Lexi was an artist in these things. When I stopped in front of the mirror in the hall before I set out, I thought I had made quite a good job of myself. My best black coat, a simple black hat, my grey-blue dress, slightly the worse for wear but otherwise clean and neat, my last pair of ladderless stockings and black flat-heeled shoes. I did not possess an *Einkaufstasche*, that capacious handbag, which hangs like a pavingstone from the arm of every German housewife worthy of her salt, but the get-up oozed respectability and abstinence from black marketeering. The face wasn't too bad either; round eyes, turned up nose, unmistakably Aryan, and I was glad to see that I no longer looked so aggressively healthy. Amongst other things, a diet of synthetic foods – curious dishes which tasted invariably like curried sawdust – had taken their toll.

The headquarters of the Gestapo in the Prinz Albrechtstrasse I found to be a huge, gloomy edifice partly destroyed by bombs. As I climbed the wide stone steps I realized that I had made one mistake in my eagerness to play the part. My coat was made of synthetic wool, a new discovery since the war, material made from wood. It looked like wool and felt like wool and might have been cotton netting for all the warmth it provided. I began to shiver a little as I paused at the top of those wide stone steps. This was it. It was here that the green padlocked vans drew up daily and disgorged their victims. Peter, Adam, Carl Langbehn, Helmuth Moltke, Haeften, all those others, they had all mounted those stairs, hoping – hoping, hoping against hope. I shivered again and hurried inside. A mild-faced porter came out of his office and asked me what I wanted. Room 525, Herr *Kriminalrat* Lange. He told me to go up the stone staircase to the third floor, along the passage and that it was the fourth door on the left.

When I reached the third floor I was out of breath and numb with cold. My knees were knocking together and my hand on the marble banisters was shaking as if with ague. At each floor, I passed the padlocked doors of a huge lift shaft, which descended into the darkness of the cellars. The atmosphere of the place was horrifying, silent, echoing and cold, deathly cold. A long, dimly lit corridor stretched out ahead of me, No 527, No 526, No 525 *Vorzimmer Kriminalrat* Lange. I knocked at the door and after a short wait the door was opened by a uniformed SS man. *'Heil*

Hitler, you have an appointment?' 'I have.' 'Your name please?' 'Frau Bielenberg.' 'Come in and sit down,' he said.

I moved into the room and was glad to sit down. My heart seemed to be thumping somewhere in my throat and my legs were behaving in an extraordinary way, they could hardly carry me. I had never in my life felt anything like it before and I dimly realized that I must be going through a stage of utter and complete panic. I sat for some time with my eyes closed, seeing nothing, thinking nothing – nothing, just nothing, until from somewhere far back in time and deep down within me I came upon the escape route, a habit which I had learned so well in childhood, when nebulous fears, indefinable horrors seemed too close to be dealt with. Think of something else, Chris, insist, insist, think of something else. Come now, it is easy, the garden at Nast Hyde and the path through the orchard which leads past the broken seesaw to the fields beyond. It is spring and the orchard is carpeted with daffodils, let's watch them nod and bend in the wind, let's see how much blossom there'll be on the apple trees and hope that there'll be no late frost, and – it was working, that habit of mine, the panic was subsiding, jerking still a little erratically, my heart seemed to be back in its place and except for an occasional twitch, my knees seemed to belong again.

The room came slowly to life and I found I was sitting up against a wall in a long, dimly lit hall, and opposite me were two high doors and to my right three large windows partly boarded up, looking out over a sea of ruins. Near to the window were four yellow desks with typewriters and behind the desks with their backs to the windows sat four women. Opposite the women four men, whose faces somehow looked alike, lit up as they were by the grey light from the windows. They were sitting in awkward positions, one upright, one slumped forward and as my glance wandered down the line from one figure to the other, I saw that they were chained hand and foot. They were all talking in low voices to the women behind the typewriters, except for the man nearest to me who was reading some typewritten sheets of foolscap. Behind each of the chairs stood a still figure in ordinary police uniform.

'Did you hear what I said?' I jumped, all childhood moonshine ends on some such note, but the strident voice was very near and the young, hard-faced blonde sitting at the desk nearest to me, was speaking German.

'Have you finished at last?' she snapped at the chained bent figure nearest to me and he glanced up from his reading and answered quietly, 'No, not yet, but nearly.'

'Well, hurry up for goodness' sake, I can't sit here all day.'

'You must excuse me, but this happens to be very important to me,' he said, 'I don't like signing papers I haven't read.' 'Do you suppose for a moment that I have taken down anything you have not dictated to me?' She looked truculent. He did not look up but again answered quietly, 'I wouldn't know.'

Quite suddenly a truly fiendish look crossed her face and with a quick movement she leaned forward and slapped his face. 'That is an insult.' Her rasping voice had risen to a screech. The man did not change his position, but glanced at the guard behind him who moved slightly and seemed almost to resent her behaviour. 'Let him be, Fräulein,' he said, 'he won't be long.'

During this little altercation the typewriters at the other tables had not ceased their clatter and the low voices continued their dictation. No one had moved, no one had looked round, nothing out of the ordinary seemed to have happened.

I found myself staring aghast at the woman sitting there so near to me. She was calmly covering her typewriter and tidying her desk, whilst the man collected his papers slowly and methodically and started to sign each page. I longed to read the signature because I thought I might be able to tell someone outside that I had seen their husband – brother. I almost planned in my mind the dismal lie I would tell about how well he was looking; but his chains hid the paper as he wrote. He stacked them together neatly and handed them back to the girl and as he lifted his head, the red mark of her hand showed plainly on his pale face. 'Thank you, Fräulein,' he said and, glancing at his guard, 'May I go now?' The guard nodded and he got to his feet with difficulty. He was so chained that he could hardly move one foot in front of the other. He had no shoe laces in his shoes and as he turned to get up, he nearly fell. I made an involuntary move to help him but was motioned back by the guard. I looked up into his face as he passed my chair and tried to show him how I felt. I tried to show him actually how proud, how humbly grateful I was that a human being could behave with such dignity in such circumstances. Too much to hope that he would understand, but for one moment he did look back at me and then with a short sigh he started for the door. Shuffling one foot in front of the other, he made slow progress but finally the door closed behind him.

I looked back again at the woman who by now was preparing to leave too. She had removed her black sateen sleeve protectors and had a large shiny black bag on her lap. She was powdering her nose and patting her hair, eyeing herself with some satisfaction in a small pocket mirror. Now I knew very well what I was feeling. I was snaking again, but this was different, this was cold deadly hatred such as I never hope to have for any human being in my life again. I hated her, every living bit of her, and the fact that she was a woman made this hatred if possible more intense, for I think it was mixed with impotent rage and deepest humiliation that I belonged to her sex. Perhaps something of what I felt showed on my face because she gave me an odd, almost scared look before she gathered up her belongings and left the room. After she had gone I did not find that my anger abated, on the contrary if possible it increased.

How could such things exist? How dared the Gestapo, how dared anyone behave that way to another human being? And allow me to witness such behaviour, as if, since I could do nothing to prevent it, my bearing witness, my puny conscience did not count? Why was I being made to sit there surrounded by such horrors? An hour, two hours, how long had it been? Had they devised some primitive, hamhanded means for undermining my resources? Perhaps the intensity of my fury came from the fact that they had so nearly succeeded. I dimly realized the depth of gratitude that I owed to the unknown prisoner and even to his tormentor, for had it not been for them I might have been in very poor shape. Now I knew that I was no longer afraid. Writing this down, back in the protection of my white hills, I would not want to convey that because I was not afraid, I would consider myself essentially a brave person. I am not. No one knows how they are going to behave in real danger until they are faced with it. Not to be afraid is just something to be grateful for and, in this case, in my case, because of the things I had seen, another, equally primitive emotion had taken the place of fear.

'Frau Dr Bielenberg.' One of the two high doors at the end of the room opened and a shaft of brilliant light streamed across the long room and lit up the wall behind me. My anger carried me past the row of chained prisoners – the one at the far end was oddly enough smoking a cigar – and I came to a dead stop inside the door. For a moment or two I was completely blinded. The room seemed smaller, it was warm and airless and all I could make out was the vague shape of a writing desk in the corner. Arc lights seemed to be fixed behind the desk, somewhere near the ceiling, and they were focused on the door; something that I rather foolishly had not anticipated and instinct told me that I would not be able to stand those lights for very long.

'*Heil Hitler*, Frau Bielenberg, will you take a chair?' a high-pitched voice with a slight Saxon accent addressed me out of the void of light. It was now or never.

'*Heil Hitler, Herr Kriminalrat*, I would take a chair with pleasure if I could find one, but with these lights blazing at me, to tell you the truth, I can see nothing at all. My eyes are not very good anyway. Be kind enough and turn them off.' Rather to my surprise the last sentence came out more as a demand than a request. There was a moment's complete silence, then I heard him push back his chair, the click of a switch and the lights were out.

The turning off of the lights reduced him to size. No longer just a dismembered high-pitched voice, he came into focus as a short, thick-set, youngish man with a head shaped like a pear. He had a high, narrow forehead topped with dark thinning hair, rather pudgy cheeks and a small, red, full-lipped mouth. He was surely not beautiful on any count, but it was the expression in his eyes which gave him the distinction of horror. They were set close together, very small, very blue, very cold and they were staring at me with unwinking intensity. Strange, I thought for a moment as I moved the chair a little so that I would not be directly facing the window, strange, for a moment I thought I had seen those eyes before. 'Thank you, that was kind of you,' again to my surprise my voice sounded more than businesslike. He said nothing, so I sat down and looked back at him across his leather-topped desk, cleared except for a tray of coloured pencils each sharpened to a perfect point.

Being rather short-sighted, I have never found any difficulty whatsoever in staring back at people with great directness. The childhood game of staring someone out always left me an easy winner, since the object of my stare was never quite in focus. I had been led to believe by infuriated nannies, governesses and school mistresses that the impression given could be one of candid truthfulness itself.

Kriminalrat Lange did not seem to want to speak, so to break the silence which was becoming a bit oppressive, 'I owe you gratitude, Herr *Kriminalrat*,' I said, 'it was good of you to give me some of your valuable time and also I must thank you for allowing me to visit my husband. I found him looking well.' He made a slight movement with his head and continued to stare at me. Careful – careful – my tone was still not at all what I had planned it to be – far too aggressive, far too overbearing. My simple words had sounded almost like an insult. In the average German home it is Papa who does the bossing and this was not the time or place to take a chance on the reversal of rôles. So I went on in what I hoped was a more conciliatory voice to assure him how glad I was that he was dealing with Peter's case. From the moment I had learned that Peter had been transferred from Graudenz, I had been confident that it could not be long before an experienced man such as he, *Kriminalrat* Lange, would discover that Peter's arrest had been a mistake and that he would be freed. He broke his silence at last to ask:

'How is it that you know and have such confidence in my capacities, *Gnä' Frau*?'

'Two friends of my husband's,' and I gave him the names, 'have both told me that my husband could not be in better hands,' I answered simply. I do not know if it was wishful thinking, but I thought I could detect a slight relaxation in his manner. There was a faint hope that he was vain.

I hesitated a moment trying to find the right tone, just the right words which would lead him on to putting me through the whole drill.

'Herr *Kriminalrat*, I want to be very straight with you,' I said, 'you may have been surprised at my telephone call, at my asking to see you, but one thing which has been bothering me more than a little since my husband's arrest is the fact that I am a foreigner. True, I have the greatest confidence in you, as I have in fact in German justice, but I find it so difficult to understand why my husband is not yet freed. Would it be possible—' I hesitated again – 'would it be possible that the very fact of his being married to me could be weighing against him?' I looked down at my feet to give myself a rest from those little blue eyes. 'You see,' I said, 'I have to feel my way in these things. I think that if this had happened in England and I were German, this might be the case and, if so—' now in spite of his unwinking stare and sphinxlike immobility, this I reckoned was the moment to turn on as much

241

charm as my sedate rig-out would allow. I looked up again – 'and if so this would be a burden which I could hardly bear and for this reason alone I would have come to you. You see, Herr *Kriminalrat*, I have always felt that my husband and I were united beyond the borders of nationality. Our different nationalities have never made any difference to our happiness. I have married a German and Germany is now my homeland, I have learned the language as well as I can and it is here that I wish to bring up our sons.' I was warming to my theme – 'Why,' – a lie, but a good one, I thought – 'even our wedding cake was decorated with the English flag and with the Swastika and – we may have been foolish, but sometimes we have even felt that by uniting our two countries we put into practice one of the *Führer*'s dearest wishes. I can assure you that when war broke out between England and Germany our sense of frustration was unbounded. I followed the *Führer*'s speeches word for word when again and again he held out the olive branch to my people, and again and again he met with nothing but rebuff.' The *Völkische Beobachter* was coming into its own. 'I can assure you that had it been for me our two countries would be as united today as my husband and I are united.'

A curious change came over his flabby face. It was as if it had been disturbed by some subcutaneous eruption. There was a possibility that he was trying to smile.

'That was a very pretty speech, Frau Bielenberg, quite moving in fact,' he said, 'but I have yet to meet an Englishman or Englishwoman for that matter who, when it comes to the point, does not feel in their heart of hearts, right or wrong my country.' The old quote which turned up like a bad half-penny at many an argument on nationalism – only he pronounced it in such an extraordinary way that I had some difficult in recognizing it.

'A very apt quotation, Herr *Kriminalrat*, I did not realize that you speak English' – I tried to smile too . . . tinged even with admiration, 'but in a way it does not quite apply to me and this is perhaps one reason that I do not find my attitude difficult to maintain; you see, I am not completely English, in fact by blood I am Irish – and blood does tell.'

For a moment I thought he looked a trifle surprised. It was possible that he was acting too, but more likely the complexities of the Anglo-Irish relationship were no clearer to him than they were to me or to most of the Anglo-Irish for that matter.

'I understand you are a niece of Lord "Bayarferbrook",' he said. I had been wishing he would not bring that one up. The one word which had not been written quite clearly on Peter's note. Had he written 'thinks Chris niece Beaverbrook' or '*thought*'. Had he left Lange in his error or had he corrected his mistake? There were advantages in claiming relationship with either one or the other. Lord 'Bayarferbrook' was Minister of Aircraft Production in England and if I had to offer Lange post-war help in exchange for the destruction of Peter's file, then the Beaver would be the better bet. On the other hand my uncle Rothermere was a candidate of some merit. He had visited Hitler in the early thirties, had been immensely impressed and had for some time insisted on holding high the *Daily Mail* banner on the wrong crusade.

Better of course if I could adopt them both, but what was it I had said! Blood will tell. I settled for Rothermere and, in my eagerness to please, I almost pronounced it Rozzermere. I added a suitable touched up résumé of his political slip up.

'And how is it you consider yourself Irish?'

'My mother's family came from Ireland,' I said, rattling along at some speed. 'Lord Rothermere was actually born outside of Dublin and my father came from County Clare in Ireland, my grandfather and grandmother and, in fact, all my ancestors back a long way, they all came from County Clare. They were great patriots. My father's great-aunt was called Barbara Fitzgibbon, I always thought it a lovely name. Anyway, she wrapped the Union Jack about her and swam out beyond Ireland's Eye (that's a little island in the Irish Channel) to remove the hated flag as far as humanly possible from Ireland's shores and she let it sink there or, wait a moment, I think she was drowned even. Anyway, my father was very proud of his great-aunt Barbara Fitzgibbon. My sister is called Barbara after her. It's just that I was brought up in England – and in Ireland, too, of course.'

'Then your father was in the Irish Army?'

'Oh no, he was in the English Army naturally – in the First World War anyway, but then you see he is Irish. My uncles on my father's side were also in the English Army naturally, but stationed in Ireland. They felt very Irish too. They could not bear to live anywhere else but in Ireland. I also have cousins in England, in an Irish regiment of course.'

Now I certainly had him looking dazed. Irish English, English Irish, I was getting a bit muddled myself, so I paused to draw breath and thought I ought to add soothingly, 'It's actually not as complicated as it sounds.'

'What language do they speak in Ireland?' he managed to ask. 'Irish,' I answered firmly. I think it must have been the word 'naturally' which had had him worried, and I pressed on with my advantage.

'Herr *Kriminalrat*, don't let's bother about the Irish. I am really here to help you. I know you are only trying to discover the truth. Can we find no possible way of my being able to help you do this? You see, my husband and I had no secrets between us and, to me, his case is such a clear one. He has never been interested in politics in his life. His character is not nearly complicated enough. But wait, perhaps I have an idea. I wonder – what would you think? Why not question me? Maybe that would help. My husband and I after all, as I said, never had a single secret between us. I would be very willing in fact eager, to answer any questions you want to put to me.'

He took a moment sorting out his face, gave me a long look and picked up one of his perfectly sharpened pencils. Then he opened a drawer to the right of his desk, took out a bulging file and said:

'All right, Frau Bielenberg, I will ask you a few questions, but I warn you that if you do not answer truthfully you are playing a very dangerous game indeed.'

Quite suddenly his manner changed, he leaned forward and his eyes became so blue that they almost hurt.

'Your husband is a nitwit,' he said, 'a great big slob of a nitwit who has betrayed himself at every turn. You see this file, it is surely thick enough; well, I can tell you that there is not one page which does not contain some evidence of his idiocy and guilt. I open it at random; ah yes, here he goes to the house of one of his clerks, a true patriot who has, hanging in his sitting-room, the text *"Der Führer hat immer recht"* (The leader is always right). What does your husband say to this clerk? He says, this paragon of a husband of yours, "However could you frame and hang up such rubbish?"' I felt my wretched knee beginning to twitch again – the change had been very sudden. Just exactly what Peter would say. I remembered that clerk, Miksch was his name, and also why Peter had gone to his house. Miksch's wife had had to go to hospital and Peter had fetched her in the factory car. It seemed incredible that Miksch, not even a member of the Party, had had nothing better to do after Peter's arrest than to scurry round to

244

the Gestapo and add his twopence worth of condemnation to the growing file of evidence. Just another common informer, the foul backbone to a régime such as this, without which it could not survive and perform its despicable function.

Lange was fingering through the pages. 'You too, *Gnädige Frau*, in spite of the fact that you profess yourself to be so germanophile, here I see you visit your husband in Graudenz – what does he do? To save you travelling a mere extra two hours in the train, he takes the car, yes, the factory car and drives some forty miles to the mainline station, eating up precious petrol which the Fatherland can now ill afford. A pretty patriot!'

I was trying to control my anger and also some anxiety, but a sudden flash of memory came to my rescue. Now I knew where I had seen those eyes before. Two incredibly plain little girls in the same carriage on my journey to Ravensbrück. There was an unmistakable family likeness. *Papi* was going to the Army, of course now I knew who *Papi* was and also why he was going to the Army. The field-grey uniform of the ordinary soldier would surely be less embarrassing after the war than the dark green and black one of the SD.

'I do not agree, Herr *Kriminalrat*, that such trifles need be a sign of lack of patriotism,' I said. 'When I travelled to Ravensbrück to see my husband, your wife and two little girls were in the same carriage. They were fetched from the station in a black Mercedes. I remember well, because I had to walk. You are the boss there, as my husband was in Graudenz. I can see nothing wrong in what either of you did.'

I thought maybe that I had gone too far and found myself waiting for the next onslaught, but instead, he laughed and suddenly relaxed again. He was certainly something of an actor, probably a much better one than I was trying to be.

'You are not a stupid woman,' he said almost gently, 'although you would have me believe you are guileless. I have here a list of your friends, every one of them traitors, Trott zu Solz, Moltke, Yorck von Wartenburg, Langbehn, Haeften, Trotha, Einsiedel and so on. You are not going to sit there and tell me that when you met in their homes, or they came to you, that you had no political discussions with them of any kind. Be careful with your answers, we have records of your telephone calls and your husband in his stupidity has told us much.'

Oh blessed piece of paper. It seemed photographed on my

mind. Now it was coming into its own. It was almost as if Peter were sitting there beside me jogging my memory and leading me steadfastly along. 'Have denied everything – Self politically uninterested – Adam close friend, Langbehn neighbour, Yorck didn't know well' and so on.

'You may think it extraordinary', I answered, 'but this is exactly what I am going to tell you. I am not and never have been and never will be interested in politics, and men and women who discuss politics make me very tired. My husband felt the same. I am a simple person and with me patriotism is a simple emotion. It seems to me madness that at a time like this when every able-bodied man should be defending his country, my husband should be sitting in jail doing nothing. That is why I came here, but if you ask me to discuss politics I am quite useless to you. I would not know how to start. You ask me about Adam von Trott – well, I would say that my husband considered him to be his best friend. We have many ties. His wife Clarita comes from Hamburg, they first met I think in our house there and my husband is godfather to their eldest child, but that has nothing to do with politics. Perhaps it is sometimes a relief for intelligent people to come in touch with simple folk like us.'

'You think that Trott was intelligent?' He almost spat it out. All the venom of the little man condensed into the few words.

'Oh yes, I do, I—'

'He was a traitor, Frau Bielenberg.'

'Yes,' I answered sadly, 'it appears so, I would never have thought it. But who else was it you wanted to ask me about? Dr Carl Langbehn? Well, of course the Langbehns are neighbours of ours in Dahlem.'

'More than neighbours according to your husband.' 'I don't quite know what you mean.' 'Well, I have records. Without even taking into account what your husband and of course Langbehn has told us, I have records of telephone calls between you and Dr Langbehn's mother, sometimes daily calls.'

Poor little Mother Langbehn. I had been a bit apprehensive about those telephone calls. I had cut them short rudely often enough and slipped through the hedge and begged her to desist. But she came from another age. In 'the Kaiser's time' telephones just weren't tapped and such 'miserable creatures' as Gestapo officials did not exist.

'Herr Lange, this is perhaps something you would find hard

to understand. You are a man, I am a woman and also a mother. Whatever my sons would do and however much I might disapprove, I would find it impossible to cast them out. I would not cease to love them. Frau Langbehn is also a mother and I do not think it strange that she rings me often and hopes for sympathy. I think you should ask your wife about this, as from what I saw of her face in the train, I think her reaction would be the same as mine.'

If old Mother Earth can improve on that, I thought, she is a better woman than I am – and I began to wonder, were my thoughts not becoming a trifle incoherent.

The short winter afternoon seemed to be darkening to night. Daylight was fading in the window and the odd street lamp came to life and flickered across the sea of ruins. There is a certain blank here in my memory. I think I must have become light-headed, partly hunger, partly effort and partly due to the close airlessness of the room. He was asking about Moltke and I gave him the automatic answers. I did not know him well but found his wife very nice indeed; we had swapped hen food for plums which grew in abundance in our garden. I found myself asking him earnestly if he kept hens and he answered that he did and there followed quite a lively discussion on the difficulty of feeding them. Perhaps the stuffy room was having its effect on him too. Rhode Island Reds *v.* White Leghorns; if the argument had gone on much longer, I might have found myself giving him the address of an excellent black marketeer in Zehlendorf, where he could have got all the hen food he wanted – at a price. But he returned to the point.

'Your evidence has been interesting,' he said, 'interesting because it does not coincide in any way with the evidence given by your husband.'

The bloody liar; that remark at least roused me from my temporary torpor. 'Then indeed, Herr *Kriminalrat*,' I said, 'I was foolish to come here, but I am not a good liar and I cannot change what I have said.' I collected my last bit of strength to look him directly in the eye.

'If you really want to know what I think,' I added with all the conviction I could muster, 'it is that you and not I should be sitting in my chair. I, after all, have gone my way, lulled in the belief that the *Führer* was in safe hands. But it has needed a bomb, and a bomb in the air-raid shelter of the *Führer*'s headquarters, before the *Gestapo* discovered that there were enemies in the camp. A terrifying thought. Does it terrify you as it does me, Herr *Kriminalrat*, because if it doesn't, it should.'

Herr Lange sprang to his feet and came towards me, '*Gnädige Frau*, the interview is at an end. I have volunteered for the Army, but before I go I promise that I will deal with the case of your husband. I cannot tell you what the outcome will be, but I will see that the matter is settled before I go.'

I thanked him and assured him that that was everything I could wish for. He nodded his head and had turned his back before I reached the door.

The mild-faced porter at the bottom of the stone staircase told me to hurry home as it was getting late and the Tommies would be along soon. I looked at my watch. It was hard to believe that I had been in that building for more than nine hours.

The air-raid warning must have sounded when I was in the Underground, because when I reached the Podbielskiallee tube station the big anti-aircraft guns in the Domäne Dahlem were already hammering away. I could hear the shell splinters pinging on the roadway, but I could not hurry, it was as if I was walking in my sleep. I pushed open the door of our house and went and sat down on my bed near the window, which had been propped open with cushions. The house was empty, everyone seemed to be in the air-raid shelters. Some phosphorous bombs must have fallen nearby, because a weird, rather beautiful green glow lit up the garden occasionally. One of the Dutch boys came out of his shelter and dodged back again quickly. Minutes, perhaps hours, passed, I do not know. I did not hear the All Clear but some time or other the boys came out of their shelter again, smoking and laughing and dragging their suitcases. They burst into the room and made for the windows, but stopped short when they saw me. I think I must have looked a bit odd, sitting there on the bed with my hat on, staring out into the garden, because they closed the door quietly behind them and went away upstairs.

RETURN TO ROHRBACH

(Winter 1944–1945)

Berlin's Anhalter Bahnhof had become a symbol of disintegration; its huge domed roof, once glassed in, stood out like a skeleton greenhouse against the sky. Along the platforms the propaganda posters hung unnoticed in red and black tatters from the shrapnel-pitted walls. *'Führer* we thank you', 'To Victory with our Leader', 'National Socialist Order or Bolshevik Chaos'. Every day the windowless trains trundled in and out in the few hours left for living between the American mass daylight raids and the sporadic British night attacks; they carried a rudderless crowd of soldiers, civilians, refugees and evacuees along diverse routes to uncertain destinations.

The day that I left Berlin to return to Rohrbach was no exception. The platforms were jammed with people, shuffling along through the blackened snow and broken glass. An incomprehensible loudspeaker seemed to keep the grey crowds on the move. Down the stairs, through the tunnel, up the stairs to Platform 3, down the stairs, along the tunnel, up the stairs again, to Platform 5, down the stairs – it seemed to know as little about when a train would come in, and where, as did the shuffling crowds. No one spoke, the expressions on our faces did not change, only our clothes gave us some vestige of individuality. I passed a chocolate machine on my journeys up and down the stairs and thought that I recognized one of the set grey faces in the broken mirror. The next time I passed, I realized in a disinterested sort of way that it was my own.

Back on Platform 5, for the second time, I took my stand against the loudspeaker. It so obviously knew no better than I did what was in the mind of the railway authorities. There was as much chance of the train coming into one platform as any other,

I decided, and I found a luggage barrow underneath a dim lamp, pulled off my rucksack, and sat down to wait.

As the crowds pushed by me, trudging aimlessly along, this way that way, I began to recognize some faces as they passed. The tall Mongol in the fur hat and his little wife in her black shawl – perhaps some Russian collaborator, with revenge hard on his heels; a bustling Party official, still in his brown uniform, who tried to keep order when pushing started from behind, and whose commands petered out to futile mutterings when confronted by the silent, hostile gaze of his neighbours; the straggling group of silent children, with labels round their necks, shepherded by a thin, anxious woman in Red Cross uniform; the soldiers in their shapeless uniforms, some of them mere boys; the rather helpless woman, wearing her Mother's Cross in silver, who had asked me if I knew whether trains were still going to Leipzig – two of her children had been evacuated there with their school and she was hoping to find them before the Russian wave went over them.

I found myself battling with black despair. Any spark of elation which I might have allowed myself, any surreptitious back-patting as to the manner in which I had acquitted myself during my interrogation, had certainly fizzled out in the days which followed when once again impenetrable silence had covered the whole episode. I could do no more, I could feel no more except that I was utterly alone, a stranger, an outsider, for in spite of the face in the chocolate machine I knew that I did not belong to the defeated people about me. A people who had always known in their heart of hearts that they would be defeated, but who had been led to believe, for some splendid months, that they might pull it off this time. Victory had come so near; but they had failed and were now past caring, with nothing left to them but the urge to get home, to get together with their families, and to face what the end would bring.

There would be few to pity them, for the wheel had turned full circle, as deluded by piffling ambition, bent on taking revenge for their failure, they were now slaughtering everything that was best in their own country. No nation could afford such extravagance, there was no excuse, no pardon, for such things. This was the punishment, ruins, ruins and more ruins, and as the hours passed and darkness fell, even the stars glinting through the twisted girders looked down upon them like malevolent spikes. When I married Peter ten years ago, I mused wearily, I did not realize that I would be binding myself to the fate of the whole of this unhappy race. The 'Master Race' that was, which was falling apart as soon as the rigid bonds of dictatorship began to lose their grip. The Southerners hating the Prussians and the Prussians despising the South, and the people of Hamburg's Free City disdaining the lot. What sort of a nation was that? Not one as I knew it. How easily had the Wickham Steeds and Lindley Frazers, the so-called experts, been led astray by the roll of drums, the flags, the marching feet. German nationalism, I had learned, was a tender plant, continuously having to be nourished by success. It had nothing in common with the warm, comfortable, take-it-for-granted feeling I had for my own country. Maybe I was the true nationalist in that I never felt I had to make a noise about it. When the Germans stood poised on the northern coast of France, and the air-raids on London were at their height, I had listened with my ear close to the radio to Churchill's stirring speeches, 'We stand alone' – 'we shall fight on the beaches'. We – us, social and personal, fish and chips – that was where I belonged.

On one of those days, back in 1940, Adam had brought me along a copy of the *Daily Mirror* with a full front-page picture, and a headline 'Doing the Lambeth Walk'. Four costers arm in arm, dancing along a ruined street. A large, fat lady in the middle, with her hair in curl papers and an expression of indomitable cockiness on her face. 'May I introduce you to your spiritual sister,' Adam had said with a grin. He had shown it to me to cheer me up and he had succeeded. I straightened my back and had to smile a little in remembering.

'Excuse me, *Fräulein*, are you English?' I jumped so violently that the book I had on my lap slid to the floor. I had been reading until it got too dark to see, *The Song Celestial*, a translation of the Vedas by Matthew Arnold, as good an escape route as any.

'Yes – no – well, not exactly,' I instinctively tried to cover my little book with my foot. A small, round man with a *loden* coat was standing beside me, beaming benevolently. He had a large flat check cap on his head, was carrying two neat suitcases, and had obviously been trying to read over my shoulder. He was quite unabashed.

'Oh, don't worry,' he said. 'Look, I was just saying to myself that you were the only sensible person in the whole of what's left of the Anhalter Bahnof. You do not move. Then I noticed your face, for a moment the only happy expression in the Anhalter

Bahnof. So, I thought, I must look and see what makes you look so happy, and I look close and I read the English words "The Sonk something or other". Then I think, of course, that is it, English, so sensible, so still. We Germans are always hurrying about, especially if someone gives the command,' he gave me a quick look, 'just now it is the loudspeaker.' He hurried on to assure me that he could not really read English, 'hemendeggs' was as far as he went, oh yes, and of course his cap. He put down his cases and whisked it off his head and showed me the ticket inside. 'English style – *Vorkriegsware,* pre-war quality. Ah yes, the English with their grey top hats, their green lawns, so safe in their tradition. But you say that you are not English, at least not exactly?'

I was watching him carefully as he chattered on in the lilting dialect of the Rhinelander. Instinct told me he was harmless, but he was fattish, he certainly didn't live on his ration cards – 'Behind the kindly face of the ordinary citizen – lurks the SPY', a propaganda poster, which glared from every street kiosk, flashed across my mind. I knew I had every reason to be cautious, I knew I should not be talking to anyone at all, not even to a fat, innocent looking little fellow in an absurd 'English style' cap. The risk was too great, however much I might long for human contact.

'My parents are Irish,' I said. 'I was brought up in England, I have a German husband,' and I moved along the barrow to give him room to sit down. 'Your husband, he is at the front?' 'No, he is in a concentration camp.' It was out now and he could leave me if he wanted to. He was silent for a moment and then suddenly he jumped to his feet, clicked his heels, bowed from the waist and shot out his hand.

'Allow me to introduce myself, my name is Lemke. Helmuth Lemke,' he said. An odd, almost heroic expression crossed his face, and I wondered if by that gesture he had somehow defied his past. 'My name is Bielenberg, Frau Bielenberg.' I stood up too. 'Lemke – Bielenberg!' We shook hands without a smile and both sat down again on the barrow. He broke a slightly embarrassed silence to ask me if I had children, and when I told him three sons, and that they were in the Black Forest, and that I was trying to get to them, he immediately fumbled in his pocket for his briefcase, and produced two glossy photographs. A look of immense pride came over his face as he passed them over to me. A rather surprised looking little girl in the inevitable tartan dress, with short horizontal plaits, and a boy of about fourteen in Hitler

252

Youth uniform, his hair cut so short that his ears stuck out like door knobs, Lieselotte and *Klein*-Helmuth. I knew that we had now reached the second stage in German social relationships of this kind – the exchange of children's photographs. I fished around in the pocket of my rucksack and found two rather crumpled pictures. I discarded the nicest one of Nick and Christopher, because John had rather spoilt it by putting on a squint and sticking out his tongue. I handed him one of the three sitting on the bench outside the *Adler*, where Nick and John laughed up at me as the wind ruffled their hair, and Christopher sat sturdily between them, staring into the camera, with his finger in his nose. I surely looked as proud as Herr Lemke, who studied the snapshot in silence and handed it back with a sigh. 'It will not be long now and you will be able to take them back to England. They will not need those leather pants there, but you will put them into top hats and cutaway coats, and they will be able to become true English gentlemen.'

I glanced at him to see if he was joking, but he was not smiling; instead, a faraway, almost wistful look had come over his cheerful face. All right, that clinched it, I just decided he was a dear little man and I even wondered if it would be worth while trying to explain to him that I felt the age of the top hat had been passing before the war, and if it had not gone completely after this upheaval, my faith in England and her mission would be truly shaken. I could tell him perhaps of Durham, with its drab rows of houses, stinking privies at the end of dirty backyards, and in the centre of the town the huge padlocked iron gates of the Londonderry estate, munificently open to the public once a year, so that the lesser breeds might not forget what a blade of grass looked like. I could tell him that because after all that, too, was England.

'Listen, *Gnädige Frau*,' he tapped my knee and spoke very slowly and clearly. Either he had realized that I was tired, or else begun to wonder if I was not very stupid indeed. 'A train for the South has been due some five hours ago. If it comes at all before the Tommies' raid, we have small chance of getting on board – just look at these crowds. If we want to reach our children we must plan, do you hear, PLAN. We have some advantages. You are tall, I am small, but, thanks to my morning exercises, I am strong. We have a barrow. We will push the barrow to the edge of the platform and place the suitcases and your rucksack upon it. When the train comes in, I will make a rush for the door and the compartment opposite the barrow. You will then climb on to the barrow and hurl the luggage through the window and climb in after it. In this fashion not only will we be in the train, but we shall have seats.' He adjusted his cap, cleared his throat and looked quite napoleonic, and I hardly liked to ask him what he intended doing if the train should come in somewhere else. A wall of faces across the tracks showed us that the crowd was waiting patiently on a far platform, but as we watched they seemed to be on the move again, and a few stragglers came up the stairs on to our platform. Amongst them, for the first time, I noticed one or two station officials. It looked as if we were in luck. I became suddenly very wide awake. We moved our barrow firmly to the edge of the platform and took up our stations none too soon, for in a matter of seconds the huge engine moved past us in a cloud of steam. The train jolted to a halt, and immediately pandemonium broke loose as everyone pushed and scrambled for the doors. I remained a lonely pinnacle on my barrow, and watched the crowd surging about me. Herr Lemke gave me a cheery wave before being propelled at some speed through the door, one of the first.

'*Gnädige Frau*, Frau Bielenberg, the luggage, quickly. *Himmel*, I am losing ground.' I was jerked to life by an agonized yell. A heated argument flowed out through the darkness of the window in front of me. A typical German argument, rising in crescendo to shouts of rage, and falling to furious mutterings of *Unerhörts* and *Vollidiots*. 'I come,' I called, and I heaved my rucksack over the sill and into the darkness. Herr Lemke's neat suitcases must have had something to do with it. I peered into the carriage and, as my eyes got accustomed to the dim light, I could make out the figure of my fat friend. He had lost his cap, but miraculously managed to retrieve his suitcases and with one under each arm, he was battling to keep two places free.

The space between the dark cavern of the window and the barrow seemed very wide but, spurred on by the sight of Herr Lemke, I somehow heaved myself over the edge and landed in a heap on the floor of the carriage. '*Donnerwetter*, what is the world coming to,' a gasp in my ear, but I dragged myself up and a moment later I was sitting beside Herr Lemke on the bench. We gazed at each other triumphantly and shook hands. His plan had worked perfectly, we agreed that he had every reason to be proud, but our joy did not last long. For a moment time stood still, before a rush of wind seemed to sweep through the open carriage window and the dread banshee wail of the air-raid sirens scythed up out of the darkness. There was a sudden quiet as the dim lights went out on the station platform, and as we waited for the sirens to breathe out their last haunting moan. Then pandemonium broke loose once more. 'To the bunkers.' 'Come.' 'Where's Hansi, HANSI,' a woman's shriek, a child whimpering. 'The best place is the underground. We've only ten minutes if it's the Tommies? Has anyone heard the radio? Will it be a big one?'

The carriage was emptying, but Herr Lemke sat quietly in his place. 'Listen, dear *Gnädige Frau*,' he said, 'I've been in lots of these raids, as you know I come from the Ruhr. We just can't bother about raids there any more. Take it from me, however much they think they can, the Tommies can't hit special targets at night and we're as safe in this train as anywhere. There may be a chance, too, of the train leaving the platform before the fireworks start. Engines are scarce these days and they cannot afford to lose them. My advice is to behave English and stay put.' His voice came reassuringly out of the darkness, with its lilting accent which might so easily come from Wales. I would never be surprised if Rhinelanders ended their remarks with 'look you'. As for me, I was really too tired to decide what I should do. The fight had gone out of me again, and I was more than willing for Herr Lemke to take over.

We sat together in the deathly quiet which always seemed to descend before an air-raid; an involuntary, almost reverent silence, a tribute, a fleeting prayer for those who were about to die. An occasional dull booming was the only sound to be heard, and Herr Lemke whispered out of the darkness that he thought it was not anti-aircraft as yet, but the Russian guns from the Eastern front. My countrymen were taking longer than usual to arrive this time, I thought vaguely; sometimes they did seem to wait around for a bit before coming in to the kill. Slowly then, one after another, the searchlights soared up into the darkness and began their ritual dance across the clear starlit sky; the reception committee – it could not be long now.

Then, quietly, without warning the train began to move, slowly, almost hesitantly at first, clanking over the points, out from under the domed roof it began to gather speed. Herr Lemke was jubilant. 'What did I say, you see, *Gnä Frau*, what did I say? A combination of German planning and English calm and Irish luck could run the world. Oh dear, I must laugh. How pleased Mutti will be when I tell her this story. "Papi," she will say, "I knew you would get home somehow." But this calls for a little celebration. Wait now, I must find the glasses.'

He was on his feet, fussing about, feeling for his suitcases, seemingly quite oblivious of the fact that we were still in the target area. He seemed to be taking off his boots and I could almost imagine him putting on his bedroom slippers – carpet slippers, I'd be bound. A rustle of paper, either the promised glasses or a neat packet of sandwiches – a smell of smoked ham – it was sandwiches.

Suddenly a blinding light filled the carriage. A searchlight sweeping upwards from just beside the track, shone for a few fleeting seconds straight through our window and threw our small world into brilliant relief; every detail stood out as in a flashlight photograph. Papi Lemke's stockinged feet resting neatly side by side on a folded newspaper, next door to his opened suitcase. My rucksack, and above it hanging from the rack, the usual yellow and black notice, 'Achtung Feind hört mit' – 'Beware an enemy may be listening'. Helmuth Moltke had had such a warning hanging in his library, Freya had pinched it from somewhere and given it to him as a joke. On the rack to the right of this one, though, lay a black peaked army cap, decorated with the skull and crossbones, a Sam Browne belt too, and in the corner next to the window opposite, staring straight at me, sat a tall figure in black uniform, motionless as a statue. I had time to register fair short-clipped hair, a pale, long, rather handsome face, even a curious twitch in one cheek, once – twice, it forced him to wink with one eye and it was the only sign he gave of being alive. Then the searchlight swung away from the train and the picture faded slowly into darkness. I slid back along the seat and nudged Herr Lemke, and told him perhaps we should tidy our luggage as we were not alone in the compartment. In case he should not have seen the cap on the rack opposite, I drew the sign of the Swastika on his knee with my finger. I need not have bothered. Poor Herr Lemke, he had seen it all right and, no doubt, the forked lightning insignia on the uniform as well. He kept clearing his throat and I could almost sense his sitting to attention. 'Gestatten Sie, excuse me – Sir – would you allow me to offer you a sandwich?' 'No – I would not,' the answer came in a slow, insulting drawl. 'A little cognac perhaps?' 'No.'

This was terrible, I could hear my friend shuffling about in his corner – finally 'But you, *Fräulein, Gnädige Frau*, perhaps you would give me the pleasure?' I would have liked to come to his rescue, as I knew he was suffering, wondering desperately if he had said anything he shouldn't have, and wishing to goodness that he had closed his suitcase with the forbidden brandy. But I dared not help him out. I had eaten practically nothing all day and something told me I might need a clear head, 'I'm sorry, Herr Lemke, but I don't think I will just now.' That settled it. He cleared his throat again and murmured something about having left his bedroom slippers in the hotel. I heard him fold up his sandwich paper and his suitcase slicked shut. Then he slid open the door to the corridor and shut it firmly behind him. He returned some minutes later to grab his other suitcase, moving so quietly that I supposed he must be carrying even his carpet slippers. In his agitation he even forgot to say goodbye.

The silence was broken by a short laugh from the opposite bench. 'A brave little fellow, our erstwhile travelling companion.' The voice was quiet and cultivated, with an accent I could not locate. 'I expect he wanted to stretch out in a carriage to himself.' In truth I felt a bit deserted, but it seemed only fair to try and rustle up some remnant of loyalty.

'With his bottles of loot, no doubt.'

I did not answer, hoping that he would leave it at that, but no – 'You are travelling far, *Gnädige Frau*?' 'Far? Well, not so far really, it all depends what one calls far—' the old technique, an answer and no answer.

'It's very cold in this compartment, isn't it? Would you care to have my army coat over your knees? I don't need it as I have my sheepskin affair.'

'That's very nice of you, but actually I have on my skiing clothes and I am fairly all right as yet.'

How I wished he would leave me alone; I was so tired, I was finding it so hard to concentrate, but his next question had me wishing sincerely that I had followed Herr Lemke's good example and left the carriage.

'Would you mind my asking where you come from?'

I supposed I had made some mistake with my German, but there was a chance that the question was put quite innocently, so I told him I didn't mind his asking a bit, but wondered could he guess. After a moment's pause he said he did not know. Sweden?

Holland, perhaps? But then a little while back I had made some remark in unmistakable Black Forest dialect. 'I am living in the Black Forest at present, with my children,' I said. 'I am neither Swedish nor Dutch. By the way, where do you come from?' In order to evade a straight answer I knew that I was getting drawn into a wretched conversation, but I was too tired to think up a way out.

'Me? Aha!' he gave a short rather brittle laugh. 'I come from Riga. Do you know Riga? It is very beautiful. We Latvians are what is called a border people, which means that we have been "liberated" very often. You know, perhaps, the story of the Alsatian boy who was recruited for the German army in 1942 and he was asked which side he thought would win the war. He answered that his great-grandfather had fought in 1870 for the French and lost, and his grandfather in 1914 for the Germans and lost, and his father in 1940 for the French and lost, and now he was going to fight for the Germans and he didn't really know what to think. It was much the same with us, sometimes we were "liberated" by the Poles, then by the Swedes, just lately by the Russians, and then lastly by the Germans. We were glad, very glad, for the Russian occupation had been very hard. My father was killed by the Russians and my mother died of grief – I think it must have been. Our people baked cakes and stood by the roadside and gave them to the German troops as they marched through our villages. The troops looked splendid, crack German regiments, and each soldier had a flower in his cap, and as I watched I knew that I had only one wish in the world and that was to get into uniform as soon as possible and to march with them. You see, I felt that this would be the only chance to take my revenge for what the Russians had done to my home. So I volunteered and, as my head had the correct Aryan measurement – my shoulders, my chest, the shape of my nose, truly Aryan, also I hadn't flat feet – I had the particular honour of being recruited for the SS.'

His slow voice had quickened, and I could hear him move in the darkness. He seemed to be leaning forward for his voice sounded nearer as he asked suddenly: 'But where *do* you come from, *Gnädige Frau*? Are you German?' 'No,' I said, 'I'm not, my people come from Ireland.' 'Ach, now I understand, the Irish, they are musical, hence your voice. You have a very sympathetic voice, *Gnädige Frau*. Perhaps it is because of your voice that

I'm telling you these things – that and the funny expression you had on your face as you stood on the barrow outside the window. Then perhaps you can understand a bit the feeling. Your country, too, was occupied by the British. Your people were insulted, starved, murdered – but where was I – oh yes, my Aryan contours, my hopes for revenge. Well, they told us that we could revenge ourselves on our enemies and they sent us to Poland. Not to fight the Poles, oh no, they had been defeated long ago – but to kill Jews. We just had the shooting to do, others did the burying,' he drew a deep sighing breath. 'Do you know what it means – to kill Jews, men, women, and children as they stand in a semicircle around the machine guns? I belonged to what is called an *Einsatzkommando*, an extermination squad – so I know. What do you say when I tell you that a little boy, no older than my youngest brother, before such a killing, stood there to attention and asked me "Do I stand straight enough, Uncle?" Yes, he asked that of me; and once, when the circle stood round us, an old man stepped out of the ranks, he had long hair and a beard, a priest of some sort I suppose. Anyway, he came towards us slowly across the grass, slowly step by step, and within a few feet of the guns he stopped and looked at us one after another, a straight, deep, dark and terrible look. "My children," he said, "God is watching what you do." He turned from us then, and someone shot him in the back before he had gone more than a few steps. But I – I could not forget that look, even now it burns into me.'

The window I had climbed through would not close properly and a numbing cold seemed to be creeping upwards from my feet, but the voice, just a voice in the darkness, went on and on, sometimes pitched so low that I could hardly hear it above the creaking and rumbling of the train, sometimes raised to a note of near hysteria. He told me that he had resigned from the Death Commandos and joined the *Waffen SS*, the fighting SS units, and he told me of how he had tried to be killed, but his comrades had fallen around him and each time, by some miracle, he had lived. The ones with the photographs in their wallets, the frightened ones, and the ones with the dreams of the future, they were the ones who got killed, he said. Only those who didn't care, got the Iron Crosses. Now he was going to the front, to his unit if he could reach it, otherwise anywhere, *anywhere*, did I hear, where he would be allowed to die.

During his story I had found it increasingly difficult to listen. I had eaten practically nothing all day and the cold in the carriage was intense. As I fought wave after wave of exhaustion, my head kept falling forward and only the most startling points of his story penetrated the fog of sleep. The little fair-haired Jewish boy – the old Rabbi. Oh God, was it for these that Adam had done penance and maybe now, Peter, too?

Some two years back I had been in a tram with Nicky when an elderly lady, with the Jewish star pinned to her coat had got up from her place so that my Aryan eight-year-old son could sit down, I had got up too and the three of us had stood silently looking at the empty seats. I had felt quite proud of my little gesture at the time. How utterly feeble it seemed now. Too much – too much. 'You are silent, *Gnädige Frau*? You are horrified at my story?' He seemed very near. 'No – no,' my own voice from somewhere far away; it seemed no longer my own. 'I am not horrified, I think I pity you, for you have more on your conscience than can be absolved by your death.'

And suddenly, for a second in time, the fogs cleared and it was as if Adam's and Carl's dying and Peter's imprisonment seemed a splendid, glowing, real thing, absolutely necessary and right. 'But others have died and may have to die for you,' I heard myself murmuring. I do not know if he heard, as I was already nearly asleep. The train rumbled rhythmically onwards into the night. Totteridge, where I was born – a village church – a small Chris collecting her weekly text at children's service. Miss Osborne at the organ. 'He died that we might be forgiven. He died to make us good. He died – He died—'

I awoke twice before reaching Tuttlingen. Once, when the train jerked to a stop at a half-lit station, I realized that I was warmer and that my head was resting on something hard and uncomfortable. The man had moved and was sitting beside me, his greatcoat was over my knees and my head had fallen on to his shoulder. His SS shoulder tabs had been pressing into my cheek. In the half light I saw his face for the second time: perhaps I had been mistaken about that twitching nerve; it looked peaceful enough now anyway, almost childlike. His hand, with the signet ring of the SS, was resting on mine, and as I moved it closed with an almost desperate grip and then relaxed. I put my head back on his shoulder gently, so as not to waken him, and I slept again. The next time I woke, the carriage was empty and the train was moving. A grey, cold dawn lightened the window. I glanced involuntarily at the sky and the low snow-clouds scudding past. It was not going to be a very good day for an air-raid I thought, and so there was a chance that I might be home in my valley before evening.

PETER'S RETURN

(Winter 1945)

How did the day start? I must try to get it all quite straight. Things were not ordinary because Nicky had tonsillitis and I had brought him into my room. It was warmer there and would save me having to run along the icy passages at night. He was on the mend already, sitting up in bed in the daytime with a thick woollen stocking round his neck looking a bit peeky, but no longer feverish and beginning to get a little bored.

But the start, the never to be forgotten start. 'Frau Doktor! Frau Doktor!' It was still dark outside when Sepp's voice from below my window was followed by a huge lump of snow hitting one of the panes and nearly demolishing it. 'Frau Doktor!' I stumbled out of bed, for Heaven's sake he mustn't wake Nicky. I managed to get to the window and open it in time to stop Sepp firing another cannonade at the *Alder*. 'Come down, come down, Frau Doktor, I have good news.' Sepp's voice was shaking with excitement. I dragged on my pants and a jersey, I couldn't find my boots, but retrieved my skiing socks from under the washstand and, forgetting poor Nick's much-needed sleep, I stumbled down the stairway to our sitting-room, through the kitchen out of the back door and into the snow. Sepp was waiting by the door to the cowbyre. Martina was already at the milking and the dim light from inside the shed was enough to show me that Sepp's get-up was as haphazard as mine. Bedroom slippers, a pair of old pants and what looked like a striped flannel nightshirt. He came towards me out of the shadows, and as long as I live I will not forget the look of simple glowing goodness which shone out at me as the light from the kitchen behind me lit up his homely unshaven face. 'I am the bearer of great tidings—' no – 'Herr Doktor rang up in the night,' he said, 'all the way from Berlin, he is free.' There was a moment's silence and then 'Sepp! Sepp!' I do not know how it was that we found ourselves wrapped in each other's arms, but I know that I was crying and laughing and behaving very much as people do in novels and Sepp was beating me on the back as if I had swallowed a fish bone. I could hardly breathe because I was pressed so tightly against his scratchy old nightshirt. When I asked him to come into the kitchen, I could not move because the cold was so intense that my socks had frozen to the snow.

'No, Frau Doktor,' he said as he chipped the ice from under my feet, 'I must get back to the milking – don't slip now, I'll tell you all about it after breakfast.' I went back into the kitchen and sat down near the freshly lit stove. Except for the cracklings and splutterings of the fir twigs, the clanking of buckets and Martina's soothing murmurings from the cow shed, the *Adler* was incredibly silent. I had not woken Nicky and Frau Muckle was probably at early Mass.

Free – Peter was free. Free as the wind, what a wonderful word – free. They had had to let someone free. I was completely dazed. Why Peter? Why me?

Martina came clattering through the door bringing with her a pungent whiff of the cow house. '*Grüss Gott*, Frau Doktor,' she said, as she poured a bucket of milk into the separator and started to wind the handle. She did not seem in the least surprised to see me about so early.

'Martina,' I said, staring dazedly at her sturdy back-view, 'I have just had some wonderful news. My husband is free, he has been freed, he is free.' I could not stop using the word. Martina did not turn round but kept on swinging the handle rhythmically with one hand.

'I know,' she said, 'I heard – and about time too is all I have to say to that.'

She was frowning ferociously, a sure sign that she was impressed, as she plunged a saucer into the milk bucket with her free hand, put it down on the floor and pushed it across to the stove for the cat.

The next two days passed in a whirl of organized pandemonium. I took to tidying the place up. It would have disconcerted me if I had allowed myself to wonder whether the German male was casting his shadow before, so I decided that my urge to bring some semblance of order to my shambles of drawers and cupboards must come from a wish to indulge in some practical form of thanksgiving. I had been given so much, I must turn over a new leaf. In the course of my rummagings I found a host of odd things, which I had forgotten existed, and often wondered later how a knife and fork and a perfectly good bicycle pump got themselves inside the old spinet. I was sweeping the crumbs of many a meal out from under the sitting-room mat when I was drawn into a conversation which I was to be reminded of the following day. Nick was downstairs on the sofa and John had taken advantage of my state of elation to persuade me to allow him to take my gramophone to pieces. He wanted to turn it into a gadget for winding wool – I would willingly have allowed him to transform it into a moon rocket. The conversation went something like this:

NICKY: If I can keep rabbits again this spring, Mum, I think I'll stick to females because then I can have heaps of baby rabbits and sell 'em or do some good swops.

ME: All right, darling, you can have the females and Johnny the buck rabbit.

JOHN: No, I want to have females, too.

ME: Well one of you must have a buck otherwise you won't get any little rabbits.

NICKY: Why?

ME: Well because there must always be a daddy and a mummy in every family.

NICKY: Why?

JOHN: (*Fiddling away with my gramophone and not looking up*) Oh you know, Nicky, it's because of the covering business, same as the Mesmer's bull. The buck must cover the female otherwise there can't be any little rabbits.

His summing up seemed to satisfy everyone and I went on with tidying-up.

The sun was shining out of a clear blue sky and every hour the air-raid report announced fresh batches of Allied planes over Reich territory. My thoughts, truth to tell, were with a train somewhere between Berlin and Rohrbach – a train, please God, making steady uninterrupted progress southward.

On the following day as evening came, cold and clear-skied, and the afternoon train to Schönenbach had failed to bring Peter, I began to get jittery. What was it Kern had said about able-bodied men not being allowed to leave Berlin? The last stand and what not? He had not been very communicative, almost surly in fact when I had gone to his shop to hear more details of his telephone call with Peter. Perhaps his formidable wife had watched our early morning embrace and drawn some dire conclusions. The evening train should have arrived in Schönenbach at seven o'clock and now it was half-past eight and still no sign. The children all dolled up in clean pyjamas would have to go to sleep. I was tucking them in rather absent-mindedly when Nicky asked me a question over the eiderdown – a very direct look from his blue eyes belied his off-hand manner.

'About those rabbits, Mum,' he asked, 'how does it work with people?'

'People?'

I stopped short in my tracks – God help me, not because the question had cropped up for which I suppose all parents prepare themselves with emotions ranging from trepidation to dire determination. It was not that, but unless my ears were deceiving me I had heard a very faint sound; hardly a sound even, more a break in the silence carried on the wind. I dashed to the window and flung it open and, staring into the darkness, I strained my ears to hear if it would be repeated. There it was again, I had not been mistaken, there was no doubt about it from somewhere far down the valley I had heard a yodelling call 'Haaaiti Laaaus Pu'. Peter! How often had I heard that wild yahoo as he came streaking down some ski slope, bubbling over with joy at the speed and ease of his descent. I closed the window gently and turned back into the room. Nicky, still a little deaf from his illness, had obviously heard nothing and his expression had turned to one of mild surprise, wondering perhaps if it had been his question which had propelled me to the window with such suddenness and if, by staring into the darkness, I had hoped for an answer from God.

'Listen, boy,' I said as calmly as I could, 'I'll have to tell you another time. I think I just heard a yodel from down the valley and I think it may be Daddy.'

PETER'S STORY

We were still in the *Nebenstube* at seven o'clock the next morning. The stove had gone cold and between us was an empty dish, a couple of empty glasses and Frau Muckle's largest coffee pot. Soon after Peter's arrival and after the children were back again in bed she had appeared with a huge sizzling frying pan. Ten eggs floating in monstrous piles of bacon and a jug of very sour wine, not exactly a diet which any doctor would have prescribed for someone who had been half starved for months. But Peter had put away nine eggs and most of the bacon and rounded it off, to no ill effect, with a reckless midnight raid on the coffee beans. We were both wide awake. All through the night Peter had paced the room, limping a little, and never deviating from a dead straight line. Four short paces to the door, a turn on the heel, four paces back to the sofa, the exact measure of his prison cell. All through the night he had talked and talked, his voice pitched low as if unaccustomed to a hearing, his sometimes seemingly disconnected anecdotes building up one upon the other to become a saga of fearful magnitude. I had listened, wrapped in a rug, almost mesmerized by his regular pacing, knowing intuitively that I would probably never hear his story in such detail again. I never have. Here it is.

'Yes I got a teleprint from Adam on July 16th just asking me to let him know when I would next be in Berlin. Oh yes I knew what it meant of course although I didn't know what date had been decided upon – I couldn't leave immediately – had to wait until my co-director came back from Czechoslovakia. It was just another case of the death penalty if a factory was left without a director and there were only two of us. I was due to be in Berlin on the 28th though so I wired Adam to let him know. Then came the 20th and I heard the news over the wireless – yes – the news over the wireless just like that as I was sitting having a cup of something or other in the canteen. I don't know what I thought but when I got back to the office I found I had put the pepper pot in my pocket and I kept it beside my bed after that – futile really but I did – I didn't need it and I left for Berlin on the 28th – Adam had been arrested three days before. I went of course immediately to the Foreign Office to see if I could get some news – there weren't many left in the Information Department – Alex Werth – Leipoldt – Richter – they were doing what they could. The last they had seen of Adam was through the canteen window – one of those semi-basements with the top of the window just above pavement level – he had been with them a few minutes before and the telephone had called him back to his office. Then they heard the clink of marching boots on the pavement – they had listened to them coming nearer and they had watched as they passed the window – two pairs of boots they told me and between them Adam's long stride – Adam's suit – of course when they got back to the office he had gone. But they had found out where he had been taken to – Oranienburg, you know Oranienburg – of course you don't, how could you – outside Berlin with quite a bit of quiet countryside to pass through before you get there. And they'd found out too that he was being brought to the Prinz Albrechtstrasse in a limousine every morning for interrogation – nine-thirty every morning. Bismarck's secretary knew because she had to take papers to the Prinz Albrechtstrasse and she had hung about keeping her eyes open – there was only one guard and the driver in the car. When I first got to Berlin they seemed to think things were not going so badly with Adam – he was defending himself superbly but I guess the evidence was piling up and three or four days before I was to leave again for Graudenz things were not looking so good. There seemed only one very obvious thing to do and I had to hurry – the arsenal up at the factory was full of machine guns and I had the key – I had a car and plenty of petrol and not far from Graudenz only about seven kilometres say was the Tucheler Heide, a huge boggy area. Plenty of trees and scrub and full of Polish partisans – probably still is – the army had made several small forays into it but had usually come out with a thick ear leaving ammunition and provisions behind them – or just not come out at all – amazing place really. I reckoned Adam could hold out there for some weeks at least –

no one thought the war was going to last longer – I had to have a driver of course and was relying on Sybille's half brother – you remember – looks like a Siegfried and is actually half-Jewish – I got him up to Graudenz when things were getting a bit hot for him in Berlin – a grand fellow I felt he would play. But it wasn't to be – it just wasn't to be. I hadn't been in my office for more than a quarter of an hour before two Gestapo fellows arrived and asked me to go with them to Gestapo headquarters down town – they wanted to discuss something about security in the works. I thought it a bit odd when they told me I needn't take the car – they would drive me back afterwards – but I don't think I really realized what was up until I arrived in their office and they closed the door behind me and I found myself looking down the barrels of a couple of revolvers – they searched me for arms and took me downstairs and pushed me into a cell and that was that . . .

'There are moments I guess which last for an hour, for a day, possibly for a lifetime – I think the moment when that door slammed shut and the key turned in the lock and I was alone in that tiny cell was one of those moments – just that cell with nothing in it but a bucket of water – no bed, no stool, just four stone walls, a bucket of water, Peter Bielenberg and the silence – yes – the silence. I was sure of course that my plan had been betrayed – Alex – Leipoldt Richter – it wasn't either of them – must be Bismarck's secretary. For some reason or other I started to shiver – shake and shiver – I can hardly describe what it was like – I had never known what it was to be frightened before you see – something to do with my size perhaps – just dead scared – you know yes then I needn't describe it – I guess we know. I don't know how long that darned shivering went on – for a day – a night – two days – anyway quite suddenly it stopped I mean the shivering stopped. I was sitting in the corner of my cell and it was dark. What was I scared of – Death – Torture – I spelled out the words slowly and started thinking about them – torture and death, pain, annihilation – I considered them all in quite considerable detail and quite suddenly I stopped shivering just like that – and I was no longer afraid. It must have been early morning, because the rising sun always shone through my cell window – just a pencil of light moving down the stone wall and gone before it reached the floor. It was lucky that I was not interrogated during those first four days – they would have enjoyed themselves – as it was I discovered that they knew very

268

little – one of the clerks had tried his poor best to record some nonsense and my secretary had not been exactly helpful – a tiresome old maid who hoped for something more exciting from her boss than dictated letters I guess. I had been wrong about Bismarck's secretary though – my plan was not mentioned – they asked me about Adam of course and I told them he was one of my best friends – besides being the truth, there seemed a small chance of saving time for him that way – we might be confronted with each other – anything to save time . . . I don't know how long I was in that cell alone – some weeks anyway . . .

'I didn't get much to eat – a piece of bread and a mug of water in the morning and again in the evening – that was all – and then I got pleurisy or something – a dry sort of cough and a pain in my side – the stone floor was not quite dry and I had to sleep sometimes. I told the fellow who came with my bread and he seemingly reported it but he told me in the evening that I wasn't in a sanatorium which was true enough – but it cured itself anyway. Then one day they threw another prisoner into the cell – poor chap – a Pole from our factory – he had been condemned to death by one of those Summary Courts – he spoke good German and I shall never forget – we were given a load of beans to shell he and I – they came from the garden of one of the guards. Oh I forgot to tell you I could see the guard's garden through the slit in our cell window – at least I could see some inches of it – some radishes and lettuce and the start of a row of onions – I can't remember how many radishes but I knew at the time. He was very keen on his garden that guard – spent all his free time in it – I could hear him scuffling between the rows and sometimes his boots passed the window and sometimes his hands pulled a radish or two – I never saw his face. But the beans, it wasn't the beans we were interested in except to tot up how many we could eat without spoiling the look of his bloody crop. You see the beans were wrapped up in newspaper and the newspaper had news – the Allies had occupied Paris – they had passed Paris and were nearly in Verdun. He could hardly contain himself that little chap – Paris – Verdun – he jumped to his feet – we have won he shouted we have won – he looked so happy – *wir haben doch gesiegt.* A day or so later they took him away and the guard who brought my supper told me he had been shot. I would have to go back to my cell and count the scratches I made on the wall if I wanted to know just how long I was in Graudenz – five – six weeks perhaps – I know I was beginning to wonder how long a fit man can hold out on bread and water – the weather had turned colder and I had to move about a bit – I couldn't save my strength all the time. It seemed to be taking the Allies the hell of a long time to get to Berlin. Then they came one day and fetched me out – I was shaved and chained hand and foot and when I got to the top of the stairs I was hoping that I wouldn't have to walk much further. If you try to escape you'll be shot in the back said one of the guards – I almost felt like laughing. We travelled in the night train to Berlin – yes in an ordinary carriage – oh yes there were others in the compartment – no I can't remember any astonishment but I do remember the wooden bench feeling extraordinarily comfortable in spite of the chains. We walked from the Lehrterstrasse Station to the Lehrter Prison – it's not far of course but it took a bit of time because I could only move one foot in front of the other very slowly – some procession – the guards walking behind me in case as they said I should try to escape – makes me want to laugh even now. My cell in the Lehrterstrasse Prison was paradise compared to Graudenz – actually it was filthy, it had walls splattered with squashed bed bugs but it had a wooden bunk, a straw mattress some sanitary affair in the corner and I got three meals a day – soup as well as bread – sometimes there was even a bit of meat floating in the soup. I got my first news from outside too, three cigarettes and some glucose tablets from Arnold, bless him – he sent lots more apparently, but three were pretty nice. I met up with Schniewind too – met up is good – I saw him through the little trap door they opened when they pushed in our food or watched us at night – we had to sleep with our hands above our heads you see – in case we tried to knock ourselves off. Schniewind, he didn't look too good coming as he was from an interrogation – he had a cell opposite mine and I sent him across a glucose tablet, he seemed mighty pleased – funny, a glucose tablet. I had my first interrogations with Lange too – he gave me a cigarette and even some brandy on the first day – I thought I wasn't doing too badly but then he got down to business. If I met Lange today I would kill him – I know I would have to kill him – kill him slowly – the way he killed others. Most interrogations were at night in the Prinz Albrechtstrasse those who could walk afterwards, well they walked back – the others were carried back to their cells in rugs and – just dumped.

'You said a moment ago that when certain prisoners were

interrogated everyone outside trembled because their interrogations were always followed by a wave of new arrests. No one outside can be a judge of such things because they don't know what means were used to drag out information – I know of some, not all – and I couldn't possibly tell you. Lange was no beginner as an interrogator – he knew what to ask and how to ask it but I guess my legal training came in useful for the first time since 1933. I spent hours memorizing his questions and my answers this way, that way, my answers always had to be the same – it was hard work after the interrogations – hard work to keep awake, I mean. There were air-raids of course, plenty, and the warders went to the cellars – a strange feeling being locked in a cell on the fourth floor of a prison bang next to a railway line – but one gets used to most things really. One day the warder who brought my lunch told me I was to be released – he wasn't a warder by trade – just one of the petty criminals transferred to warder's duty – he caught me napping though – I believed him and only realized how he'd fooled me when the *Grüne Minna** was heading out for the country. Schniewind must have been pleased though because before I left him I sent him across the rest of my glucose tablets and a cigarette.

'There were others with me in the van and I knew them all – three professors from Freiburg University – Lampe Dietz and Ritter and a little man I didn't recognize at first – Max Unz, you remember how dapper he was with his rose in his button-hole stuck into a little phial behind his lapel, yes Max Unz that's who it was. We arrived at Ravensbrück sometime in the evening – my cells were on the up and up, this one had a hot-water pipe running through it and the bunk had a blanket – cell No 13. There was a nice old lady next door – wife of a Colonel Staehlin – can't imagine why she was there – she was dead scared of raids anyway, even the siren sent her into a panic. So I would tap out songs on the heating pipe and she would tap back – during the alarms, I mean – *Hänschen klein ging allein* and back would come *in die weite Welt hinein* – nursery songs. Christmas songs we got quite good at it and it kept her occupied – she died, I'm afraid, at least I heard she died – I was upstairs in cell 54 then – upstairs in cell 54, next door to the guardroom. Did I tell you that the building we were in was the punishment block for SS guards – what they had

Grüne Minna – Black Maria.

271

to do wrong to get a punishment is beyond me seeing that they committed every sin in the book – but there it was, surrounded on all sides by this concentration camp for women – and by pulling myself up on my arms I could look through the air vent out on to the camp. Some of those women had beautiful faces – many of them came from the Polish aristocracy – even when their heads had been shaved because of lice – beautiful faces. But under my window was a wall – some sort of punishment wall and all day long in the bitter cold women who had been beaten until they could hardly stand were made to lean against that wall. My cell was never silent all day long and sometimes at night I listened to the crying, the moaning and the whimpering of those beaten women – like animals in pain . . . you'd think you'd go mad but you don't. One day I was given permission to read – the usual tactics, one day blow hot, one day cold – at one interrogation friendliness and light permission to read extra rations – at the next rough stuff, bread and water – anyway I had permission and was allowed to take a book from a little collection in the hall-way – you'll never guess what I found – *Pickwick Papers* in English – what a find – I read it through word by word – but more I found myself laughing. I laughed out aloud – I didn't hear the sounds outside my window, I couldn't have, because I laughed out aloud more than once – you see you don't go mad, you adjust, you adjust. There was one particular wardress – not a wardress really but an inmate who had been promoted to Camp police. *Kapo*'s they were called – she was a sort of fiend, looked more like a butcher than a woman – never without a whip. One night I heard screams and thuds coming from the courtyard and then this bitch's voice talking to a man – I couldn't stand it – stop that ruddy noise at once, I yelled, hoping they would think it came from the guardroom next door to my cell – it seemed to work. I heard that Kapo creature say, pity I would have liked to give her a few more and the man laughed and their voices faded in the distance – the moaning stopped soon afterwards too. Then, on Christmas Eve, I was woken by a different sort of music, a choir from the camp singing Christmas carols. Beautiful voices – *Stille Nacht* – Puppi, that good girl, had sent me a candle, a little fir twig and a packet of cigarettes and I listened to that music by candle-light. They sang again, those women, on Christmas Day, outside their barracks and, believe it or not, that Kapo bitch was leader of the choir – had a voice like a bell. But I also saw great deeds of courage under my window – women who came to comfort and bring water knowing they would be standing there themselves the next day *Bibelforscher* – Quakers, I think you would call them – incredible courage.

'How did I find out these things – it's a strange place a prison, Chris – of course I didn't know it all to start with, but Puppi, she had been there for months – more than a year and she had got herself some job in the secretariat – I had hardly been in the place for more than a few hours before she sent me a message telling me to watch out for forged confessions. She knew which guards were bribable, she knew her way around – God I hope that girl gets out, she made use of every chance. There were ninety-six cells in the block and there were only four prisoners I didn't know or know of – we were given exercise once a day, round and round the courtyard, and I got permission to overtake the others. Behind my handkerchief, in passing, I could talk – we could all talk without moving our mouths – you learn pretty fast. There was one woman there incidentally whom I did not know – she seemed a lone bird and once when I passed her she asked me in English why I was there – I took her for a stool pigeon – she had a funny accent so I asked her on the next round why she was there and she told me she was married to a nephew of Churchill – Odette she told me was her name – she sounded French actually – I wonder – maybe she was telling the truth. Another chap, van Husen he was in a bad way he couldn't stand the interrogations – who could – he was always on the verge of giving himself away. I spent hours wondering what could be done to keep him going, we had lots of time to think of these things – I made him a little pair of shoelaces like mine – he wore them for a couple of days, they seemed to do him good but then he disappeared and Puppi heard he had been condemned to death by the People's Court. Then there was Wilmovsky, how he managed to look dignified under the circumstances amazed me but he did – handsome and dignified – and old Schacht of course, perky as ever in a fur-collared coat. His cell was opposite mine and when they opened the trap doors to give us food there he was – old Schacht – he tried to cock up some signal language with his hands but it became too complicated, we never had time to signal more than a few letters. Funny thing though, on the whole women, seem to stand these things better than men. Of course we all looked pretty dreadful shuffling around that courtyard unshaved and the fellows who had no braces or shoelaces – but the women, they made all sorts of efforts those women. I was lucky I had visitors – Arnold came first, he proved a sterling friend all right, without him I guess I wouldn't be here – then Heino* yes he came along too bless him, treated all the guards like dirt, presented me with three packets of cigarettes which were nabbed as soon as he left and told me to let him know what he could do for me. My mother too – Arnold got permission for her to come on my birthday, I do not think she should have been allowed to come but she behaved wonderfully – then after Christmas you came along. Yes, darling, I knew I was going to see you, the fellow who shaved me told me so and I thought of course that you had been arrested too. I always tried to have that piece of paper on me, it spent the rest of its life in the mattress and I put it into Puppi's matchbox, the one she gave me for Christmas – it was a risk of course but a smaller one I thought than you giving different evidence. My God I never thought of you asking to be interrogated – only you, sweetie, could come up with a crazy idea such as that – but it helped, oh yes of course it helped – I would think it probably tipped the scales – you made the whale of an impression on Lange and he told me some days later that he couldn't imagine how a nitwit like I was had come by such an intelligent wife. No I don't think it was your dotty get-up or just one ardent hen keeper about another, he meant it because he surely loathed my guts as much as I loathed his. I just couldn't make myself get up or anything when that bastard came into my cell – everything was so bloody humiliating – even when he came to tell me that in spite of the fact that he didn't trust me he was going to advise my release – I just had to lie there on my bunk staring at the ceiling as if he didn't exist. But a few weeks later the miracle did happen – I left that cell for good – Lange told me he was discharging me to a *Bewährungskompanie* in the Army – what's a *Bewährungskompanie* – well a sort of punishment squad having to run about over minefields clearing up the place, doing jobs with not much risk of survival attached – it sounded like a holiday to me and I didn't believe him. Suspicious as a rat, that's the way you get – I don't think I believed him until I got out of that train in Schönenbach and no one got out with me – the train steamed out and there was no one standing behind it – I walked up the road and there was no one following me.

*Heino von Brösigke.

'Anyway – there it is – four days ago I was given back my watch and the odd things I had had in my pockets when I was arrested. I was taken to a little office – there were two others being released at the same time. I heard them giving their home addresses to a clerk – somewhere in Silesia and when my turn came I said Donaueschingen. How long would I take to get there – I said five or six days and the clerk handed me a fistful of ration cards – a release warrant and a travel pass to Schönenbach. Why not to the *Bewährungskompanie*, I don't know, darling, I just don't know. One of those cases where the organization slipped up or else I was in the hands of one organization, the SS, and was being released to another, the Army – and that little clerk had no rulings in the matter so he did the usual and sent me home first. Needless to say I didn't try to enlighten him. I've no doubt that my regiment has been informed and it won't be long before another invitation comes my way – but we'll deal with that when it comes along. I haven't even started asking myself why I am here and not the others – Arnold helped, Heino helped, you bless you helped but above all the ones who won't come back helped because they never gave me away. It doesn't seem right though, I'm not any sort of hero – nothing extra special – and it just doesn't somehow seem right. But I can't think any more – in fact, Chris, I've talked too much – I've told you things tonight that I never want to tell again.'

Peter stopped his pacing, and kneeling on the hard, little sofa, he reached across and flung open the window. A gust of icy air rushed into the room. He leaned far out on the sill, breathing deeply. 'I'm here, Chris,' he said, 'and here I stay, and if I live, nothing, nobody on God's earth will make me leave this valley.'

I went and knelt beside him on the sofa. The stars were fading. The forests on the far horizon were just a faint etching on the first pale glow of the morning sky. The lights were going on in the cow-byres up and down the valley. They did not flicker. It was going to be another glorious day.

THE END

(Spring 1945)

The war is over, and I must write of a time far back in history – a week ago? Two weeks perhaps? When the final hurricane swept over us, it left us strangely unimpressed. I do not know what I had expected – nothing much. I had not seen myself marching at the head of my villagers, like some dishevelled Britannia, waving the Union Jack and trumpeting, 'Do not fire, we are friends,' but I had surely imagined something a little more dramatic than to be standing alone at the crossroads in Schönenbach, standing quite alone, staring at a screwed-up packet of Lucky Strikes, and saying to myself, 'So that's it. It's finished – the war is over.' The Luckies had been dropped at the side of the road, and I knew that Allied troops must have passed by.

Unfortunately, there had been many things on God's earth that determined that Peter should not stay in the valley. Hardly had his health improved enough for him to move without pain before a communication arrived from his regiment, informing him that he was to report for duty in Mariendorf, east of Berlin, immediately. The letter had taken ten days to arrive, and after a decent interval Peter replied that he was ready to comply, but that he was without funds. Would they kindly send him a travel permit? His answer must have taken wing, because a fortnight later he was told peremptorily to apply for a travel permit to the Army railway station patrol. Peter seemed to think he might get away with one more procrastination, and replied that the railway station in Schönenbach unfortunately had no Army patrol, and that he awaited further orders. By then we had come to the middle of March, and although the Rhine had been crossed at Remagen, and also somewhere near Mainz, we were still living within the boundaries of the Third Reich, and summary shooting was the order of the day for deserters and stragglers, and for those who could give no valid reason why they were not with their units; we knew therefore that he could not go on stalling for ever. Meanwhile the war, too, was coming daily nearer to Rohrbach, not only the familiar war from the air, terrifying enough in itself, but the war of the *Wehrmachtsbericht*,* the soldiers' war, the still unknown quantity. The Cossacks had been the outriders, there had been a lull when Hitler had thrown his last reserves into the Battle of the Bulge, but there was no denying that the tide was now in full flood, and some time or other, very soon, we would be plunged under a great wave of conquest, and have to try our best to rise up once more, Phoenix-like, on the other side. Under the circumstances I found myself unable to react any more to the larger issues. The local newspaper gave up the ghost after a barely legible fanfare of exhortation to fanatical resistance, which seemed to come from another world. No more paper, no more ink, possibly no more editor, anyway no more 'Black Forest Messenger'. The wireless still reminded us that, somewhere out there, a German Government was still performing its function.

The diatribes from Britain – Wickham Steed and Lindley Frazer and some fruity gentleman who seemed to revel in what was happening to the German devils – merely made me want to laugh. I went to ground emotionally and mentally, and found myself only able to concentrate on the business of survival. I'd had my shining hour, my family was alive, very much alive, and as far as I was concerned they were going to stay that way, even if I had to scrounge, steal, lie, and commit any other sin which might be required of me.

The village gradually changed its appearance, although hardly its character, for the peasants did not allow the approaching vortex to disturb the steady rhythm of their lives. In spite of the sudden whining roar of the fighter bombers, and the distant thunder of guns, the little church bell still drew them to Mass. The fields had to be tilled, the cows milked, and the cattle fed. In deference to the bombers a few trenches were dug beside the roadway, which soon filled with snow and slush, and no one seemed seriously to consider taking a leap into an icy bath. They carried on regardless, the only sane element in an insane world, and the clatter and noise, the hustle and stir of arriving and

Wehrmachtsbericht – News bulletins from the front.

departing soldiery, seemed just passing theatricals against such a backcloth of eternal reality.

We had a *Sanitäskompanie*, an Army Medical Unit, billeted in the village when the final telegram arrived from Peter's regiment, telling him that unless he reported for duty immediately he would be considered a deserter and treated as such. We had failed to appreciate the activities of the *Sanitäskompanie* to date, because after carpeting the fields with Red Cross flags they had fetched fine fir saplings from the woods, and proceeded to camouflage their transport. Since their transport was painted white, and also covered with large red crosses, we could see small reason for this manoeuvre. Our scepticism merely showed how much we still had to learn about the dismal stupidity of an army in action. The lunch hour was at twelve, and the orderlies were summoned by bugle. Come what would – even one or two thousand heavy bombers accompanied by hundreds of fighters *en route* for Munich, Augsburg or Vienna – that bugle sang out at midday, and the Company lined up in the village and marched off in brisk single file to the cookhouse in the *Gasthaus zum Löwen*, situated about half a mile up the road. They were able to enjoy their luncheon break exactly twice without being disturbed, on their third expedition to the cookhouse their progress had obviously been spotted from the air and bombs fell in the upper valley. They did no serious damage, for they fell beside a great wooden farmhouse which, instead of collapsing like a pack of cards, behaved much as would an insulted broody hen; it shook itself disdainfully and settled back once more on its age-old foundations. Nicky could have been killed, though, by some fighter planes which returned seemingly to make a further check. They swept down the valley below tree level, and caught him out of cover. Peter yelled 'Drop!' and he fell to the ground like a stone, and the planes respected the Red Cross flags and did not fire; but ironically the incident sufficed to dissipate any goodwill that we might have had for the Army Medical Corps.

The arrival of the telegram, however, sparked off some revival of interest, for it was then that Peter knew he had only one card left to play. In spite of the fact that he looked extremely healthy again, he had decided to be ill and unable to travel even if it meant breaking his leg. To lend credence to such an affirmation he need-ed a sickness warrant signed by an Army doctor. We soon had our eye on a likely candidate who was fat and extremely comfortable looking, who had obviously come through his war quite nicely, and who had confessed to Hans Eiche over a game of *Skat* and a bottle of brandy that he had civilian clothes in his luggage and had no intention of being taken prisoner by the French. Peter and I spent a long evening discussing what disease Peter could suffer from, trying also to evolve some fool-proof method of breaking a leg, but decided then to consult Dr Guttenberg, who, after a little thought, came up with the answer. Malaria – he would give him a malaria injection which would, for a few hours at least, send his temperature rocketing. When at its height, the army doctor must be summoned and if he were possessed of any goodwill he would perhaps sign the sickness warrant.

It had been a touching bedside scene after Peter returned early the next morning from Furtwangen, having pedalled as fast as his bicycle would cover the ground, in order to arrive back in Rohrbach before the fighter bombers and the malaria injection got busy. Ellen and I had hovered over him like ghouls, taking his temperature and applauding every rise. A hundred and one, a hundred and two, a hundred and three – four – five. Much to our joy with the thermometer nigh on 106° he was becoming delirious, and that seemed a suitable moment, I thought, to fetch the doctor. 'The best laid schemes—' however. After much searching I found him as usual playing *Skat*, and although I considered that I looked sufficiently distraught, he did not seem very impressed. Yes, he would look in, not now though – later. Later? I had no idea how long the wretched fever would last, and my worst fears were confirmed when I got back to the *Adler*. Peter was still tossing about in a most encouraging manner, but he was beginning to sweat. An hour later he was still sweating, his temperature was 104° again, and the doctor was still playing *Skat*. With every sign of improvement in his condition, Ellen's and my hearts sank, and there was no doubt that I would have to make another effort with the doctor. I soaked my handkerchief in water and pressed it against my eyes, before bursting in hysterically on the peaceful card players. 'Please, please, Herr Doktor!' I sobbed, 'I must beg you to come now, my husband is so ill, so very ill!'

I could have added, quite truthfully, that I did not know how long he would last, but I only thought of it afterwards. I always found it more gratifying if, amongst all the lies I told these days, one or two at least happened to contain a small grain of truth. *Skat* is a serious game, not easily to be interrupted, but the players had just finished a round of what is called *Doppelbock*, a suitable moment to call it a day, and the doctor reluctantly rose to his feet. 'All right, *Gnädige Frau*, I'll come along.'

He drained his glass, and put on his cap, buttoned his jacket and fixed his belt and seemed to slow-motion out of the door. I hurried down the road ahead of him, entertaining him with the occasional noisy snivel, to find Ellen in the kitchen and the kettle in one hand and a hot-water bottle in the other, preparing to use our last defence and heat up the thermometer. 'A hundred and three,' she whispered in despair.

The fat doctor looked into Peter's throat and ears, and tapped his chest and took his pulse. He shook down the thermometer most carefully, and stuck it under Peter's arm, afterwards examining it with a slight frown. Then he cleared his throat, and eyed the patient over his spectacles. Finally, 'What is it you want?' he asked, puzzled, I could see, but still stern enough to give me a twinge of alarm. Peter, doubtless still lightheaded and never much of an actor, looked him squarely in the eye.

'I was released from a concentration camp some weeks back,' he said, 'and I have to go back to a *Bewährungskompanie*.* I have had a telegram telling me that if I don't turn up immediately in Mariendorf, east of Berlin, I will be considered a deserter. I want a sickness warrant, signed by you, saying that I am unfit to travel.'

There was a long moment of complete silence. The doctor looked once more at the thermometer, and began tapping it gently against his teeth. Ellen gazed out of the window, and I found myself staring fixedly at a ball of fluff which had blown out from under the bed. Had we, or had we not, backed the right horse? The doctor put back the thermometer slowly, oh so slowly, into its case. He unbuttoned the breast pocket of his tunic, brought out a pad of forms, and proved he was a winner.

'All right,' he said. 'What is your full name and rank?'

A few days of grace, but from then on we knew that Peter had to disappear for good. Ever since his regiment had shown signs of being interested in his whereabouts, he had gone about planning his hideout in the woods. He moved at night. Logs, sacks, blankets, food; we had known the moment would come when he would be on the run, and we had made our plans. Our own General Staff, consisting of Peter, Ellen, Hans, Frau Muckle,

Bewährungskompanie – Punishment squad in the Army.

Martina and myself, had discarded the idea of making a break for Switzerland. We had little chance of crossing the border with the children. We had also turned down the idea of building some sort of a redoubt in the mountainside to protect us from possible artillery fire. Martina had put the kybosh on that one, and had somehow taken the wind out of our sails by repeating fiercely over and over again that when the shelling started she was going to her cows, as they might be frightened. We had come to the conclusion that only Peter should take to the woods, somewhere above Hans' and Ellen's quarters, so that if it got too cold he could come down at night and sleep in their hayloft. The Mayor had to be told, with an assurance that when the war was over we would see that a benevolent eye was cast on his Party badge; and the inimitable Sepp, of course, was a certain ally. We also decided to tell the two elder boys; and we had every reason to be glad that we did so, for they co-operated in our subterfuge with a natural enthusiasm, which did not speak too well for my efforts at up-bringing. Children have their own underground, and Nicky had transferred his interest in village affairs to the *Wehrmacht.* It was quite a revelation to watch my sons setting off on their missions, threading their way amongst the soldiers, *Grüssgotting* here and *Heilhitlering* there with unerring discrimination. Breaking away innocently across the fields, then watching the skies in case of sudden attack, and slipping unobtrusively into the woods at some point far from their goal.

The only time I accompanied them nearly ended in disaster, for when we were crossing the fields, carrying a basket with Peter's lunch, I noticed some Allied fighter-bombers idly circling over Furtwangen. Halfway up the slope I realized that they were forming into line and heading in our direction. We made for a stack of logs, which seemed the nearest form of protection, and dropped to our knees behind it gasping – at least I was gasping – as a splatter of machine-gun fire opened up directly above us. The food basket upset as we crawled round and round the log pile in a sticky trail of warm pea soup, and the planes whined down to another and yet another attack. I made the mistake of imagining that my little John, at least, must be as scared as I was. I pressed his head against my side in an effort to spare him some of the din, and true enough he let out an agonized howl. The more he howled, the harder I pressed, and it was only when it was all over, and the planes had danced disdainfully away over the hilltops, that I realized that my leather button had been pressing into his jaw, and his howls had been not only of pain but of frustration at being unable to see what was going on. As we clambered to our feet Nicky remarked that he thought they must have been having a bash at the anti-aircraft gun emplacement which had been set up some days before on the hill above the Mesmers' cottage. While the boys began to lick the pea soup off their sleeves we all agreed that in future I should mind my own business.

My own business was wearing enough, cooking up tasteless concoctions from ever depleting rations, minding the children, cleaning up the mess left by our unwanted guests. Ordinary living was slowly grinding to a standstill. No soap, no flour, needles but no thread, no pencil, no paper, pens but no ink – just as simple as that. Privacy, too, was a thing of the past. Weary soldiers stumbled daily unannounced into our sitting-room, lay down on the mats and slept: exhausted boys in outsize uniforms, armed with lethal weapons they had not even the sense to handle with care. There was as good a chance of finding a *Panzerfaust*, a tank buster, on the breakfast table as there was a mug of milk. Chased from pillar to post, escaping from one encirclement after another, only able to travel at night, unable to understand why they were not allowed to capitulate, they were indeed a different army from that which had fanned outwards over Europe so confidently five years back.

A grey-faced, red-eyed sergeant looking down at his sleeping charges, touched me suddenly one night by bending down and covering one or two with their greatcoats. 'Those swine at the top have committed many crimes,' he said, 'but none greater than sending these babies in to fight. One could almost believe the Americans could pity us when they see them.'

Frau Muckle, too, was over-tired, complaining ceaselessly of rheumatics in her *Arschbacken*,* and Martina did not ease matters by carrying on as if her cows were the hub of the universe. She took our last soapflakes for washing their tails with, and I had to stop Frau Muckle from crowning her with a bucket. Christopher even managed to cause his own little flutter by informing a young officer, in bell-like tones, that his Daddy was up in the woods.

'Ha! Ha! the woods!' I gave a hollow laugh, and whisked him out of the room; but the lad was shaving, he gave us a vague and

*Arschbacken – her behind.

weary smile through the mirror; he was obviously past listening to anybody.

Before the final cataclysm we were granted a few days of comparative peace, when all but rumour was quiet. We saw nothing, and we heard nothing, except a dull thudding to the north and south, to the east and again to the west. We were, it would seem, surrounded on all sides, and the reason that we heard so little, according to our World War I vintage military experts, was because the artillery was now shooting over our heads. Hans Bausch, our village simpleton, on the one hand was certain that we were already American; on the other hand the pig controller who, for some reason known only to himself was still doing his rounds, was of the opinion that the moment had come when the wonder weapon would be used, and the war would go on for another two years at least, before Hitler's final victory was assured. Both Herr Bausch and the pig controller were wrong, the thudding from the west proved to be from German guns. There was still some game left in the cornfield, and the fates had decided that they were to choose our valley through which to attempt a last getaway.

After a stormy night, filled with the familiar clamour of rumbling wheels and shouted commands, the curtain went up next morning on a scene I shall find hard to forget. Overnight the village had become an armed camp. Every farmhouse had some army vehicle, ingeniously camouflaged with logs and firs, nestling under its protective eaves, and under cover of a cloudy, windswept sky, more and ever more grotesque monsters rolled up the valley. The heavy artillery pieces were drawn by horses and even oxen, and with their great gun barrels like giant smoke-stacks draped in protective shawls of netting, they had some air about them of elderly inquisitive titans as they lumbered across the fields and nosed their way into the forests. Their attendants followed on bicycles, in farm carts, or in small stretcher-like con-veyances drawn by Alsatian dogs. Some trudged along on foot, not looking to the right or to the left, not even when two large Mercedes cars, carrying the heroes of the act, forced them with peremptory hooting to stumble on in the ditch.

The cars drew up outside the *Adler*. '*Jawohl, Herr General, sofort Herr General.*' Click click, zack zack, three stiff figures, their faces almost hidden by the huge fur collars of their greatcoats, climbed out of the cars. Flashes of scarlet braid and highly polished boots, and they disappeared inside the door to the *Gaststube*. Why was it that I always had to recall some ridiculous story whenever I looked at such jumping, heel-clicking marionettes? How did it go? The general sees an old cigarette stub tarnishing the otherwise glossy polish on the floor-boards of his quarters. The war is nearing its end, cigarettes are scarce. 'Who does that stub belong to?' he roars, and the trembling adjutant clicks his heels, and answers, 'To you, *Herr General*, you saw it first.' But I did not laugh, I just stared at them and their entourage with the same sullen indifference as the passing troops, and my heart sank abruptly to my well-patched boots.

Back in the kitchen, Frau Muckle was in much better form. '*Echter Kaffee*, Frau Doktor, real coffee,' she whispered, and I could see from the sparkle in her eye that she had already been sampling it. Coffee, not by the bean but by the sack, meat and smoked sausage, bacon and flour, the kitchen was stacked with provisions, and a sturdy batman was already preparing a tray of cups and saucers from Frau Muckle's best china. 'Coffee for the *Herren Generäle*,' said Frau Muckle, placing the huge jug amongst the tea cups with as much reverence as if she were proffering the Host. She could not quite subdue a hint of pride in her voice that such distinguished guests had chosen the *Adler* in preference perhaps to the *Löwen*, but I felt that her exaggerated air of veneration was caused as much by the quality and quantity of the coffee as by the presence of three gentlemen in her *Gaststube*.

'They'll need coffee if they're going to get us out of this mess,' grinned the batman, before composing his face and moving off down the passage.

Frau Muckle and I were left with the chipped enamel, but the coffee was good, and Martina had been careful to skim the milk before sending it in to our guests, so it was not surprising that such a brew had the same effect on me as if I had drunk half a bottle of whisky. 'This mess', he had called it a mess, that chirpy batman with his shaven cranium, but the radio had another word for it. 'A pocket of resistance', a last pocket of resistance – a disquieting thought kept buzzing through my head. What did they do with pockets of resistance? They defended fanatically, if you were listening to the *Deutschlandsender*, or they wiped them out, cleaned them up and wiped them up, if you preferred listening to the BBC. The thought of being wiped out with those three Generals made me panic. '*Jawohl, Herr Gott, sofort Herr Gott.*'

What if I had to join a heavenly choir, adding my voice to an everlasting chorus of *Jawohls*? The coffee of course was much too strong, my heart was going like a sledgehammer. I lost my head, I knew that I had to see Peter. If we were to be wiped out, we must be wiped out together – together with the children, under a cloudless sky, with the springing turf beneath us and the smell of pine trees around us. That, to me, was a possible thought – the other could not be contemplated.

I glanced through a window at the racing clouds, and took the children by the hand. I hated to be separated from them these days, even by the width of the valley. They slept in my room, and we moved around together in an inseparable group. We picked our way past piles of ammunition and great steel drums of rubber tubing. The *Adler*, festooned with telegraph wires, was beginning to look like a spider in a web. We climbed the hill opposite, and I was surprised to find how relatively quiet it was up there, even at such a short distance from the village. Little streams bounced merrily about through the meadows, and the wild cowslips came back into their own.

'Go up to Daddy, Nick,' I said, when we arrived at Ellen's house, on the edge of the woods. 'Tell him I *must* see him, not today, but tomorrow. Tell him what's going on in the village, and that he's on no account to move, except at night. I will be back here tomorrow morning again – so long, that is, as the clouds don't clear.'

I watched him slip away past the woodpile, pause for a moment at the water trough, looking casually about him, and I watched as he made for the rough path above Bausch's cottage and disappeared behind the sheltering fires. I waited an hour before I heard a cheery yodel from much further up the valley.

'He'll be along tonight, Mum. Sorry I was so long, but there's guns and things in the woods. It's sort of scary.'

I regretted my hasty decision as soon as I got back to the *Adler*; it did not make sense. Peter had been unwary enough since taking to the woods, for after Ravensbrück he simply could not get used to the fact that danger could lurk in a Black Forest village. Ellen and Hans had spent hours playing *Skat* with him, when he turned up unexpectedly at any time of the day or night. If Ellen ever had to play *Skat* again after the war, she had declared, she would go clean off her head. He was secure up there, and if the clouds broke we could always join him without my having to make such a footling rendezvous.

Ellen came down in the night though, to tell me that Peter had arrived, and that he could sleep in their room. The troops billeted on them were harmless chaps who slept like logs, and were never there during the day.

I took Nicky along with me the next morning, and Peter was waiting for me in Ellen's sitting-room. As usual he calmed my panic and lulled my fears. He assured me that he had no intention of passing out under a cloudless sky, adding that as my 'springing turf' was soaking wet, we were more likely to get rheumatism than anything else.

'. . . but if the clouds clear—'

'Daddy!' Nicky was keeping watch at the window, and I saw him stiffen. 'Daddy, the Mayor is coming up the hill, and he has two soldiers with him.'

Peter made a bound for the kitchen at the back of the house, and I hurried to the window, and looked out over Nicky's head at the approaching party. With my bad sight I could hardly yet pick out the Mayor, but Nicky had his face pressed to the window pane, and his eyes were slits. He looked up at me suddenly, white and taut.

'They're not soldiers, Mummy, they're military police.'

'Sure?'

Nicky knew his stuff. 'Yes, sure, I can see the facings on their uniforms.'

Oh, no, it couldn't be true. So this was it, we had held on so long, crossed so many hurdles, only to . . . and all my fault, my own bloody, bloody fault.

'Run and tell Daddy, pet,' I said. 'He may have to run for it; and keep an eye on the back door. I'll keep them talking as long as I can.'

Poor little lad, he was only nine; I was asking as much as he could take. He ran out of the door, and I heard him clattering upstairs to the loft. I went to the door, and stood leaning up against the heavy oak upright; my legs were a bit unsteady. I watched the trio climb the winding pathway, and wondered should I invite them in or receive them outside in the porch. There seemed advantages and disadvantages either way. I had time to glance round the corner of the house, and saw that Nicky had taken up his post by the back door. He looked as if he were about to be sick, and I tried to give him an encouraging smile. The Mayor came up to me, puffing noisily, and looking nervous and embarrassed.

'*Grüss Gott, Frau Doktor,*' he said, 'excuse me for the inconvenience, but these two gentlemen want to speak to the *Herr Doktor.*'

'But, *Herr Bürgermeister,*' I said, staring at him as stonily as I could, 'you know that my husband is not here; can I be of some help?'

'Yes – no,' the Mayor was floundering. 'The trouble is they want to speak to the *Herr Doktor* personally. It is a matter of importance.'

'Well, if he is not here, they obviously can't, can they?' I was trying to stop my voice sinking to an almost inaudible whisper.

'No – well – '

I cleared my throat, and turned to the two silent figures standing in the doorway. 'Can I perhaps be of help to you gentlemen? I'm sorry about my husband, but he is not here, he is away.'

One of the policemen, who was carrying a leather briefcase, removed his glove and fumbled with the catch. Now it was coming, how would it be? 'I have a warrant for the arrest of your husband on the charge of . . .' but the Mayor had recovered his equilibrium.

'Well,' he said, looking anxiously from one to the other of his attendants. 'I suppose *Frau Doktor* would do as well.' He turned to me. 'You see, these gentlemen have been ordered to requisition bicycles, and *Herr Doktor,* I think still has . . .'

'Bicycle?' I stuttered. 'Bicycle? Oh, I see, yes, bicycle.' I had been preparing myself for I don't know what, and now I had to back-pedal as hard as I could.

'My husband's bicycle! Why, of course,' I heard myself saying, 'it is down in the *Adler.*' I nearly added, 'under the hay, same as all the other village bicycles,' but I stopped myself in time. I also stopped myself flinging my arms about them and telling them they could have my bicycle, Tante Ulla's bicycle, the children's bicycles and a *schnapps* into the bargain, if they would care to come in. Instead I told the Mayor to ask Martina for it, as she knew where it was. The policemen seemed most relieved, suddenly they did not look so fearsome at all. I was left in no doubt that ours was the first bicycle they had located so far.

'Thank you very much, *Frau Doktor,*' they chorused. 'Sorry to have bothered you. Shall we give you the receipt, or leave it in the *Adler?*'

A receipt? Oh yes, we would claim compensation, of course,

after the *Endsieg*, after Hitler's final victory – so that was the little block of papers he had had in his briefcase.

'Please leave it in the *Adler*,' I said, as the trio turned away, and went sliding and scrambling together down the bank to the path-way. Halfway down the path the Mayor left them and returned up the hill. I was still standing in the doorway.

'I'm sorry, *Frau Doktor*, I'm so sorry.' He looked tired and strained too, 'I don't know what came over me – there's so much going on, I just can't keep pace.'

'Never mind, Herr Volk, never mind. You're not the only one. I did the same – lost my head. Perhaps it's not surprising, really,' and suddenly remembering Peter and Nicky, I started to laugh, a high-pitched, breathless, off-key sort of laugh. Then I stumbled back into the house.

'Peter, Nick, come on down! They've gone, they wanted your bicycle. Oh God, no, they only wanted your bicycle?'

Peter slipped silently into the sitting-room in his stockinged feet, and Nicky came slowly up the stairs from the back door. He was shivering, and I was shivering, and it was my turn to feel suddenly and violently sick. We held each other tight, the three of us, and Peter said quietly, 'As I was saying, if the clouds clear, you come up here with the children. I will join you, and we'll go through the last bit together.'

Back in the *Adler*, two more days passed slowly under cloudy skies. Messengers astride sputtering motorcycles roared up to the inn, and departed again on unknown errands. The Generals murmured together in the *Gaststube*, and I was not allowed into our sitting-room next door in case I should overhear the outcome of their ruminations. The wireless, too, was in with the generals, so we knew nothing and heard nothing, except for the odd scraps of news brought to us by the batman, or occasionally one of the adjutants.

Skat was the order of the day. Nero fiddled while Rome burned, Hitler's legions played *Skat* whilst his Thousand Year Reich collapsed about his ears; and occasionally a would-be English phoenix, whose eyebrows, through overdoses of coffee, were arched in an almost perpetual expression of surprise, would join them at their card-playing. When in doubt play *Skat* – for all we knew, the generals were at it in the *Gaststube*, there were three of them after all, and their card-playing would not have seemed out of place in such a grotesque charade.

We were to learn one evening, though, that we were taking part in no mummery when the once so proud *Wehrmacht*, a now degraded, dishonoured, and dying monster, chose to bare its fangs. Two silent figures were led past the kitchen door, and on into the *Gaststube*; a boy in a ragged uniform, and a peasant in his Sunday best. The *Skat* cards were held unnoticed in our hands as we sat in silence around the stove, dimly aware that something dreadful was afoot. The back door was pushed open, and Sepp joined us. He was as white as a ghost.

'My wife's cousin from Triberg,' he said, his voice cracking hoarsely. 'The electrician, Alois, they sent him an order to come and help them with the telephone wires, and he refused to come. Said he wouldn't work on Sundays. Oh merciful Heaven, he was always a stubborn man, but pious and hardworking. He has a wife and three sons, young Hans is fighting somewhere, and the others . . .'

Sepp sat down at the kitchen table, and buried his head in his arms, and his huge shoulders shook with sobs.

'And the other? The boy?'

'A deserter, I think.'

We had not long to wait before the door opened again, and the electrician Alois was pushed, not really roughly, into the room. He looked like a sleepwalker, almost fainting, and a batman caught him by the arm. One of the guards with him said gruffly, 'Fetch the priest,' and Sepp stumbled out of the room.

'Do you want anything, old one?' A pale young soldier touched him gently on the sleeve. 'Can I do anything for you?'

'No – no,' Alois looked completely bewildered. 'Well, perhaps I would like a cigar.'

Someone hurried to the pile of provisions, and took out one from a wooden box. Alois did not seem to know what to do with it, and the young soldier lit it for him, and stuck it in his mouth. The door opened again, and Father Kunz stood hesitantly on the threshold, a small, slight figure, in his faded cassock. He glanced round the kitchen, and then went up to Alois, and took him by the hand.

'Come, Alois,' he said, 'they are waiting for you outside. I will go with you on your way.'

We stood in deathly silence, as the stir of rifles and the stump of marching boots faded into the distance. A spiral of smoke rose lazily from the stove, and curled upwards to the rafters;

Alois had left his cigar. A sudden crack of rifle fire from above us near the woods, a second salvo, and one of the batmen, hardly seeming to know what he was doing, pressed out the cigar, pressed and pressed, screwed and pressed, and then threw it in the flames.

Late that night the priest called again. He was looking for volunteers to dig the graves and bury the dead in consecrated ground. It seemed to me that something of the agony of Christ on the Cross had been stamped on his gaunt, ascetic face. But he was no Christ, just a simple village priest looking weary and defeated in his shabby cassock.

'They will have to pay for this,' he said, and closed his eyes as if trying to shut himself off from what he had seen, 'they will have to pay. The boy died crying for his mother, and Alois just said nothing – nothing at all.' I could see that he was no more able than I would have been to add at that moment. 'Father, forgive them, for they know not what they do.'

I would like to think that it was the sheer, stark hatred of the whole village, the shocked, concentrated condemnation, penetrating the closed windows, seeping under the doors, being served up to them with their meals, which finally drove those Generals from our valley. Martina was quite prepared to add rat poison to their stews, and I found myself in feeble revulsion, decorating their mashed potatoes with Swastikas, every day, every meal, three neat, green chopped parsley Swastikas.

Our little kitchen community, which had developed something of the camaraderie of the servants' hall, changed its atmosphere overnight. We no longer spoke to the soldiers, ate with them, played cards with them. It was not fair of course, but their uniforms identified them with the deed, and when the signal came for them to depart we showed no emotion other than relief. It appeared that the gap on which they had relied for their escape had been closed; they were to try another route. This decision by their overlords meant for us a reprieve but, as we learned later, for them the almost total annihilation of their ranks.

The stir started in the night, and by morning the muddy green river was flowing down the winding road to Schönenbach. The oxen, the horses, the heavy artillery, the bicycles, the farm carts, and the sledges. All the motor transport had been pushed into the fields, tipped up and abandoned, since the last drop of petrol had to be saved for the Mercedes.

There were ominous breaks in the clouds, patches of sunlight sped up the valley, and high overhead again the reconnaissance planes, like hovering hawks, floated and turned, floated and watched, unopposed and undisturbed. They had no reason to hurry, they could wait, watch and wait, before sending out their signals that the moment was ripe to pounce.

Before the Generals left, when their two huge motorcars were already drawn up outside the *Adler*, a young adjutant slipped in to say goodbye. He knew that I was English. 'Goodbye, *Gnädige Frau*,' he said, 'good luck. It won't be long now before you are home again. That'll be the day!'

'I hope you'll be home soon too, back to your studies, perhaps,' I answered. He had wanted to be a biologist, but had had to go into the army straight from school. The boy shrugged, and gave me a very old smile from such a young face. 'Not very likely after this assignment,' he said. We shook hands, he saluted, and was gone. By evening the soldiers had left us too. The last to leave disentangled the *Adler* from its network of wires, and flung hand grenades and lighted torches into the abandoned motor transport.

I had packed the children back into their rooms, and was ready to go up the hill to Peter when, passing through our sitting-room, I noticed an odd object lying on the table. It was giving out strange crackling noises, and seemed to be breathing stertorously. I picked it up, and found it to be a pair of earphones, and a cone-shaped mouthpiece. It was attached to wires, which snaked along the floor, under the door, and up the staircase to my room above. The breathing came from the earphones, and I slipped them over my head.

'Well, well,' I said into the mouthpiece, and the breathing stopped for a moment, to be replaced by John's joyful stutter.

'Hey, Mum, is that you, can you hear me?'

'Yes, I can.'

'Hey, Nick, Nick, she's listening, she can hear me!' His exultant shout nearly broke my eardrums. 'Wait, Mum, I want to see if the branch line is working. I'll hand you over to Nick.'

There was another series of earsplitting cracklings, and Nicky came on the line. 'Hallo, hallo, who is there? This is Colonel Bielenberg speaking . . .' This witticism was so self-appreciated that he dissolved in a fit of laughter which came through like a clap of thunder. A little overcome at the speed with which they had gone souvenir hunting, I addressed the absurd tube without the faintest hope of being obeyed.

'Look here, you two,' I said, 'I'm going across the valley. You're not to get out of bed, or wake Christopher, and you're to get to sleep as soon as possible.'

'*Jawohl, Herr General, sofort, Herr General.*' Another explosion of laughter; Nicky, the natural mimic, talked it through his nose, and pronounced it '*Jawoll*'.

I did not have to go as far as the woods. Halfway up the pathway, and clearly visible in the light of the fires which flickered and flared as far as the eye could see, stood a tall, still, lonely figure. I climbed up and stood beside him. The valley was alive with dancing shadows, some of them unmistakably human; silent and secretive, carrying bulky sacks, slipping from house to house, from bonfire to bonfire, the scavengers were already at work. At the mouth of the valley, a huge white flag flapped dully against an improvised flagpole; the carpenter's wife had been mending that sheet for weeks.

'Isn't that a bit premature!' I whispered, unable to raise my voice in that uncanny silence.

'Oh, I don't know, I wouldn't think so. They say they're in Furtwangen. The French, they say. Those chaps won't come back. Strange – I begged one or two of them to stay behind, I told them it could not last longer than a day or so – I could have looked after them, but they wouldn't stay. Just said they'd got so used to toddling along with their outfit, and one of them even thought that there might be something in the wonder weapon . . .' Peter sighed, and slipped his arm through mine. 'It had to come, Chris. Thank God it's over, but I just can't stop thinking of those poor devils who left today.'

The eye of the storm, the motionless centre. Where had I read of such unnatural quiet? The sky beyond the hills flashed pale, as if with summer lightning, and the flickering bonfires threw strange shadows on Peter's brown face. Motionless and withdrawn, he looked like the image of some Indian god behind a sacrificial fire.

'They won't come back,' no, they can't come back, nor the plans, the hopes, the friendships. This longed-for moment, and I could not rejoice, but just stood there silently, watching the bonfires as they dimmed, glowed red, and went out, one by one, up and down the valley.

*   *   *

292

It took all of forty-eight hours for the village to pick up the reins again and to decide that life had to go on, that the early potatoes had to be planted, whether we were French, American, or living in some strange no-man's-land not yet allocated to anyone by the powers that be. The only visible indication of some confusion in our ranks came from the disorganized fashion in which we tried to convey our burning wish to capitulate, and our failure to make up our minds whether or not we were still German, with all that such tribal brotherhood entailed. The carpenter's wife soon regretted her precipitate decision and withdrew her sheet; other equally over-hasty ones immediately followed suit. From then on tea cloths, towels, and occasional white aprons blossomed or faded according to the rumour of the moment. In and out, out and in, like bashful wraiths, they performed a bizarre little ballet of their own, which was most distracting. I had to discard an idea to paint a large Union Jack on a piece of paper and stick it on the door of the *Adler*, mainly because I had no chalk, but also, to my shame, because I could no longer remember which crosses went which way, on what.

At night the village was a hive of industry. There was so much to scavenge. Provisions, cigarettes, fine leather straps, axles, tyres and wheels, much that could come in useful and must be stored beneath the hay. Straggling remnants of German troops came down from the woods, after dark, begging for food and civilian clothing, and departed before daybreak, hoping under cover of the woods to get a few miles nearer home. I could not picture them getting far, clad as they were in a strange assortment of ill-fitting cast-offs; morning coats and knickerbockers, Peter's remaining suits and shirts of Frau Muckle's deceased husband, rubber boots and Homburg hats – they looked more like circus clowns than law-abiding citizens. We had not much to give, but we wished them God speed, for they told us that they were all that remained of the troops which had left us two days before. And they brought news of their last stand: the final idiocy, when our three Generals had decided to force their slow-motion caravan through a narrow gorge seven miles long, and Allied guns and Allied planes had waited patiently for them to be well and truly caged before opening up a carefully prepared barrage and annihilating them. Their fleeting passage, however, resolved any doubts that we might still have had as to the timing of our capitulation. The next morning spotless white drapery fluttered and flapped from every farmhouse, and it was as if we had all taken part in some stupendous communal washing day.

I went across to the *Ratszimmer* in the evening, since the light was on, and it was possible that Sepp and the Mayor were at their desks. They were indeed, and I was glad to see that their manner towards me had not changed, they were no less friendly, and no more respectful – I was one of them. It was some time, however, before I had the uncanny feeling that something – or could it be somebody – was missing from the room. Behind their desks, above their heads, was a large, square, clean, and empty patch on the wall, and for the first time I noticed that the grubby wall-paper had been a patterned one. Sepp and the Mayor seemed to sense what I was looking at, for they became very busy with their papers.

'Where is he?' I asked, after rather a long pause.

Sepp did not look up, but nodded his head towards a huge iron contraption, which was roaring away in the corner, giving out a powerful heat.

'In the stove,' he said.

'What – right now?' For some reason, I felt almost shocked.

'No, yesterday.'

'Yesterday? Wasn't that a bit early on?'

'No, we thought not.'

I gazed at them in fascination, and suddenly a silly story flashed through my mind. Equally suddenly, I realized that it did not have to stay in my mind but that I could tell it out loud to anyone, shout it from the hilltops, write it in a letter, do what I liked with it.

'Did you ever hear the story of Hitler looking at his portrait,' I asked, 'looking at it and saying, "I wonder what will happen to you and me after the war's over," and the picture answering back, "I don't wonder, I know. You will be hung, and I will be unhung – *aufgehängt, abgehängt*".'

There was a moment's silence, and then from somewhere near Sepp's top fly-button there erupted a growling rumble which exploded into a great roar of laughter. Banging his knees, and rocking backwards and forward, Sepp threatened to break the back off his chair. The Mayor, with whom habit obviously died harder, glanced carefully first to the right and then to the left, and finally managed to join him in a nervous titter, which soon developed into a high-pitched squeal of merriment. I, for my part, was laughing so much that the tears were streaming down my face. It wasn't such a funny story really, but God, how we laughed! Every time that we seemed to be petering out through sheer exhaustion, something started us up again. Whatever were we laughing at? Surely that old chestnut of a joke could not possibly be so hilarious? It was as if some spring within us, tense and taut through the years, had all of a sudden been released. We had got out of control – and were instinctively, impulsively bent on hurling to the winds the deception, the evasion, the cant, the dreadful pressure, in one convulsive storm of near-hysteria. I had to open the window for fear that Sepp might become apoplectic.

'By the way,' he gasped, 'someone told me they heard on the radio that he snuffed it yesterday, fighting to the last breath was how they put it. I was too busy to listen . . .' Too busy? Of course he had been too busy! I knew what he had been doing yesterday evening, the old fox. The lorry which had lain prostrate in his field had taken him hours and hours to dismantle completely.

I was still laughing as I climbed back down the rickety stair-case. I was mopping my eyes and blowing my nose and had quite forgotten why I had climbed up it. In the village street I almost ran into a large, square, sturdy figure, who was staring upwards with a half-smile on her face, listening to the ebb and flow of laughs and coughs which still flowed out through the open window of the *Ratszimmer*. She had a dead hen under one arm, and was bursting out of the seams of several satin blouses. She appeared to have been quick off the mark, for she was also sporting a couple of watches and a glossy handbag.

'Brrrrr!' I said, glancing at the window, sticking a finger in my one ear, and winding an imaginary handle round the other, which was a habit of the children when they wanted to convey that someone was right off their heads. 'Brrrr! Mad!' I said.

'*Ja ja*,' she agreed, flashing her silver teeth at me in a huge grin, obviously not understanding a word, but as friendly as could be.

'Russki?' I asked. I had seen many of her kind, less glamorously attired, working faithfully alongside the peasants, and only distinguishable from them by the massive strength of their physiques. '*Ja ja*,' she smiled and nodded, and pushed a large, square finger at my anorak.

'*Du?*'

Me? That was a pretty pertinent question. I could, I suppose, have given her at least two answers, both half truths, neither of which could she have possibly understood. One, that after many long years I was no longer a stranger to these parts, and that I therefore could not compliment her on her second watch, her dead hen, or her layers of satin blouses. On the other hand, I could have introduced myself quite formally with: 'How do you do? An ally, I presume?'

There was enough madness in the air and so instead 'Me?' I replied, 'Oh, *Ingelski* – or something,' and this pleased her well enough for her to grin again and to take my hand and shake it in a grip of iron.

Little explosive spasms of laughter sputtered up out of me still as I made my way back to the *Adler*. There was something about such laughter, I knew, that was closer, indeed, to tears. She laughed until she cried, did Chris Bielenberg. In fact, come to think of it, she nearly died laughing. It was thus, with her joy indistinguishable from her grief, that on May 2nd, 1945, she celebrated her liberation.

THE END

THE ROAD AHEAD

Writing is sometimes a curiously lonely occupation, and I am very grateful to my husband, Peter, and also to my now much extended family, all of whom gave me encouragement to carry on. I would also like to thank my publishers for their patience and Antonia Till, whose sensitive editing helped me to finish my self-appointed task.

CONTENTS

INTRODUCTION

The decision to write a sequel to my original account of my life in Nazi Germany before and during the Second World War came about because, after the publication of *The Past is Myself,* I received numerous letters – in all some four thousand – among which were many expressing disappointment that, after having become involved with my family and its story, my readers were left in the air so to speak, wishing to know what happened to us all afterwards.

I am conscious that some who pick up our story for the first time may find themselves confused as to how and why the Bielenberg family, a German husband, his British wife and their three little boys, aged ten, nine and three at the time, ended the war in Rohrbach, an isolated little village in the Black Forest.

For them the explanation would be that, after the failure of the bomb plot to rid Germany of Hitler which happened on 20th July 1944, Peter, my husband, was arrested and spent nearly seven months in Ravensbrück Concentration Camp. He was released in February 1945 and assigned to a punishment squad in the Army. He escaped to Rohrbach, where our sons and I were evacuees from the air-raids over Berlin, and remained there in hiding until the war was over.

In retrospect I am certain that he, perhaps all of us, would never have survived but for the goodness and integrity of those Rohrbach villagers to whom I dedicate this book.

CHRISTABEL BIELENBERG

1992
Munny House, Tullow
County Carlow

PART I

Germany

'In der Heimat, der Heimat, da gibt's ein
Wiederseh'n'
(In the homeland, in the homeland,
there we shall meet again)

German soldiers' song

Chapter One

On 20th April 1945 Hitler celebrated his fifty-sixth birthday; ten days later he was dead.

The news reached us as we sat around the stove in the *gute Stube* of the *Gasthaus Adler* listening to the wireless, which was our only remaining link with the outside world.

Since the arrival of the French in our little local town of Furtwangen, the Adler had recovered something of its pre-war repute and become once more a rallying point for many bewildered Rohrbach villagers, eager to pick up the latest rumour, eager if possible to hear the latest news, although Frau Muckle's ancient contraption gurgling and whistling away in the corner seemed sometimes as confused as we were as to quite which programmes we were listening to. Allied? German? To which side did all those voices at present belong? Which version were we supposed to believe, as day by day more and more German townships, further chunks of German land were overrun, changed hands and passed under the control of American, British, Russian and French armies?

This time the wireless seemed certain of its message. (There had been plenty of rumours, but this was a certainty.) It gave no details as to where, how and when, but just crackled out something about Hitler (the Führer), having first appointed Admiral Dönitz to be his successor, had made up his mind to die a hero's death and had done so.

A sudden stillness came over the room as the message petered out, along with the usual mechanical convulsions. Perhaps even the death of a devil casts a certain spell, for by force of habit some crossed themselves while others just stared at the stove, some took the odd sip from one of the lemonade bottles which Frau Muckle had managed to provide for our entertainment, others puffed on pipes filled with tobacco left behind by the departing German *Wehrmacht*. Only the measured clacking of the cuckoo clock on the wall behind us interrupted the silence.

'*Na, ja*', – so that was it; he was dead. Although Allied bombers still droned occasionally overhead, reminding us that some parts of Germany still had to pass through the final ordeal, he, Hitler, was gone. It could not be long now before the *coup de grâce*, the final knock-out blow, was administered to his mad dream of creating a Thousand Year Reich, empty of all but pure-bred Germans; round, blond heads, glowing blue eyes, Aryans one and all – oh dear.

But we, Peter and I, our three sons and the good friends around us were alive, we had outlived him. He had not managed to drag us off with him to some preposterous make-believe Valhalla. So perhaps it was for that reason that the silence was suddenly broken and we found ourselves glancing at each other, pushing back our stools, starting to our feet and moving eagerly from one to the other in order to hold hands, to embrace, to celebrate, one survivor with another.

The day that an armistice was finally declared and hostilities ceased was the first of a sequence of spring days, clear, warm and glorious. The sun shone over the Black Forest, the sky remained blue and cloudless, and, as the last snows retreated, the dark trees standing sentinel on the hilltops took on a softer, misty quality and overnight the cowslips spread over the pastures like carpets of gold.

Until then such cloudless days had been looked upon with misgiving, but now the blue skies held no menace and it was as if the whole creation was giving thanks that the killing was over, was bent on giving us a reassuring reminder that life must and would go on.

We were surely in need of such reassurance when Father Kunz, the village priest, arranged for a Mass of Thanksgiving to be held in the village church. Some old men long past their prime, some quiet, sad-eyed women and the children; these were the remains of his flock. He doubtless meant it well, but I could not believe them capable as yet of showing much gratitude.

Months had passed since news seeped through from the battlefields. Until then it had been a scribbled note, at most some official flowery account of a brave warrior killed in action

308

whilst defending the Fatherland. But of late the post had brought simply a brief communication telling that a husband or a son was *vermisst*: missing somewhere in those blazing infernos of the eastern or the western battlefronts. At Father Kunz's Mass of Thanksgiving, therefore, those who were 'missing' could only take their places in the side chapels as faded, dog-eared, candle-lit photographs, asking dumbly for a prayer that the *barmherzige Gott*, the merciful God, might take pity, and send them home again.

We still had to learn that war loosens its grip only with reluctance. After the *Wehrmacht* left us, no more than three days passed before a little boy in his Sunday best, returning from Mass, spotted a hand-grenade, carelessly discarded by retreating soldiery and wedged into the bank of a tinkling rivulet.

He knew something of warfare, that little boy; his brother was somewhere in France. 'All you have to do is pull the cord and it flies like a butterfly – bangs like a bird scarer!' His name was Hans and he was a schoolfriend of our older sons, Nicky and John, who, along with their other schoolmates, were called to stand guard beside his coffin.

From then on we barely had time to bother about military occupation as we combed the hills, collecting similar lethal trinkets of war from the woods, the streams and the haybarns and stacking them by the roadside. But Peter's dire warnings and even Sepp the cobbler's heavy hand, guaranteed to administer swift punishment to any child failing to give these dumps the widest of berths, could not prevent four further such accidents in the valley.

Our first contingent of liberators consisted of a regiment of French engineers. They were armed to the teeth, but seemed content to rattle through the village by jeep and truckload at breakneck speed, yelling, *'Sale Boche!'* at anyone who did not leap for the ditches and doorways with sufficient alacrity.

When they screeched to a halt, it was only to nail placards to the trees informing us of the deeds of valour performed by La Grande Armée du Rhin et du Danube, under the inspired command of General Lattre de Tassigny, and to threaten us with the dire fate which awaited us should we descend to looting, consider disobeying an order, or move further than one kilometre from our homes. We were also instructed to wear white armbands in case we should forget that we had capitulated.

For relaxation, the *Ingénieurs* fished the streams with hand-grenades or took pot-shots at the porcelain caps on the telegraph poles, thereby destroying whatever remained of the communication system.

These were followed by the Spahis and then by the Goumiers. The Spahis turned out to be bearded Moroccans in white turbans and flowing capes, looking most glamorous and dignified when astride their Arab ponies; but when evening fell they roamed the countryside on foot, searching for food, but, above all, for women. Their first preference was definitely women, but close behind came pigs and also chickens.

The Goumiers were small, bow-legged, bearded and slit-eyed. They were dressed in what looked like corduroy dressing-gowns, with ferocious knives stuck through their belts. They moved with uncanny silence on sandalled feet, and they hunted in packs. As far as goals and priorities were concerned, those of the Spahis and the Goumiers were identical.

The sturdy little peasant girl who had carried the post and who still considered it her duty to report with her empty satchel every morning at Sepp the cobbler-cum-postmaster's shop, was the first victim in our valley. She was discovered lying by the roadside, having been raped so many times that the villagers thought it best to take her to hospital in Furtwangen. Her departure under village escort was the prelude to innumerable sorties which reached their climax when the *Fuchsfallewirt*, an old man living in a remote farmhouse in the upper valley, was shot dead when trying to protect his sixty-seven-year-old wife from a similar fate.

I could not say whether the comparative immunity of the Adler was due to a somewhat unorthodox Union Jack which I chalked on some cardboard and stuck up in the window, but it certainly came from no other form of communication, for these scavengers could speak little French. When, therefore, a terrified squeak from Frau Muckle summoned me to the kitchen door, the resulting conversation was limited.

'You – husband?'

'*Ah oui*, me, big, big husband.'

'Where husband?'

'Husband with *Commandant. Comprenez-vous*, you blighter! *Commandant.*'

A wide sweep of the arm in the direction of Furtwangen and it seemed I had found the magic formula, for thereafter, except for the loss of the odd hen or two, I could reckon on their dejected departure.

News of my successes soon spread up the valley, so that although she could provide nothing to eat or drink, Frau Muckle's *Gaststube* was seldom empty of apprehensive ladies, old and young, seeking the protection of the British flag. Some brought their knitting, some their mending; so that except for the hens which accompanied them in boxes and baskets wherever they went, and were inclined occasionally to lay eggs on the floor, and also the fact that conversation turned mainly towards how best to barricade bedroom doors, we might have been taking part in some pleasantly sociable, non-stop Mothers' Meeting.

Only the official news which reached us over Frau Muckle's ancient wireless reduced us to complete silence, as it told us that Allied troops were overrunning one concentration camp after another, and finding there nothing but half-demented, ghostlike caricatures of human beings, together with mounds of neatly stacked skeletal corpses. It also told us of the possibility that not thousands, but hundreds of thousands of Jews, gypsies and dissidents had been systematically put to death in gas chambers.

We were not accustomed to believing a single word delivered to us by the wireless, but this, after all, was no longer Nazi stuff: it was official Allied information. Could it be possible? Any more possible than the unofficial reports brought to us by-passing refugees that the Russians were taking their revenge? Raping, looting, burning, driving the fleeing population before them like cattle?

Then all eyes would be turned to me, the *Frau Doktor*, the only possible representative of an Allied power they knew and believed to be trustworthy. I could not be of much help because I, too, was confused, conscious that in my ignorance I had expected far too much, prattled far too confidently of what would follow, of some kind of super-millennium reflecting all the long-lost virtues of liberty and justice. Now that I was confronted with reality, the sheer relief at having survived with my entire family gave way all too rapidly to disillusionment and mounting anger.

Yes, I supposed, these news bulletins, no longer cooked up by Dr Goebbels and his Ministry of Propaganda, but authorized by the Allies, could, certainly should, be authentic. But, as one enormity followed another, such as a camp overseer amusing herself by making lampshades out of human skins, preferably tattooed skins, I began to have serious doubts.

It was the murder of the *Fuchsfallewirt*, a friendly old man trying to pit his feeble strength against the iniquity of power, which succeeded in shaking me out of a mood which was nearing despair. For some reason or other it also roused in me something which in retrospect I could only believe to be a severe attack of rampant chauvinism. I felt myself becoming daily more British; fiercely, uncompromisingly, die-hard British. So much for liberation and all that rubbish. We had merely exchanged the National Socialist German Workers' Party for La Grande Armée du Rhin et du Danube; neurotic Germans for neurotic Frenchmen. As for the French, they had always been, and would always remain, a bunch of egocentric frog-eaters; wogs begin at Calais, a plague on these confounded continentals. Such things were simply not done.

I decided that as I could speak adequate French there must be someone in authority somewhere whom I should contact without delay. To blazes with the General Lattre de something-or-other. Orders or no orders, the time had come for me to get moving, to take to the roads, take to a bicycle, take to any old bicycle – it might even have to be Sepp's bicycle, the only village bicycle about the place since my own and all the others had left home with the *Wehrmacht*.

My departure for Furtwangen was not particularly dignified because Sepp's bicycle had its own ideas on how best to cover the ground. But I managed to concoct another, rather more accurate, facsimile of the Union Jack which I fixed to the handlebars. I was also heartened by assurances from Peter – who did not really approve of the expedition – that if I had not returned by late afternoon, he would take a short cut through the woods, meet me on the road as near to the town as possible and escort me and my virtue safely back home again.

I need have had no fear of meeting up with some prowling Spahi on the main road from Schönenbach to Furtwangen, nor had I time to pay much heed to my dignity nor that of my cardboard flag. The narrow winding highway was alive with traffic. Huge army vehicles and chunky rattletrap jeeps, all 'Made In America', were being driven along with Gallic enthusiasm, at breakneck speed. Some private cars, too, requisitioned by the French or else stolen by Russians and Poles freed from their labours, were keeping pace as best they could, although many were being driven in first gear and some had tyres, some had none. There were plenty of bicycles, too, which must have been handed over to freed Russian farmworkers, most of whom had obviously never ridden on such a contraption before. The result was that parties of cheerful ladies, in a bewildering assortment of scavenged clothing, wobbled perilously towards me from all directions before collapsing in laughing heaps all over the road. I had to laugh with them often enough as I extricated myself from one pile after another of arms and legs and tubular steel for, quite oblivious of the peril they were in, they were enjoying themselves with the infectious abandon of children.

Furtwangen itself resembled a fairground. The pavements were crowded with dazed-looking townsfolk, all obediently wearing their white armbands. The houses in the main street had obviously been taken over by the Russians because each window framed a row of beaming moonlike faces. Radios also facing outwards to the street and, turned on full blast, saw to it that passers-by could be entertained by the resulting ear-splitting din. The hotels, whose decorated walls and flower-bedecked balconies had been a feature of many pre-war travel brochures, were reserved for the Moroccan lady camp-followers. It would seem that, much to the relief of the locals, this most colourful consignment of silks and veils had arrived by the truckload the previous day. Wooden shutters were hastily improvised, they quickly set up shop, and – 'Jesus Maria' – were obviously doing good business behind the unlikely façades of the *Gasthäuser zum Bären, zum Hirsch* and *zum Stern*.

My obvious goal was the *Gasthaus zum Löwen*, the largest and most prominent of inns in the town square. It was draped from gable to ground with Tricolours, the Stars and Stripes and a Union Jack quite as bizarre as my own. A few French soldiers armed with tommy guns, and smoking cigarettes, were lounging about in the sun on the stone steps before the entrance.

Brandishing my version of my national flag, and shouldering Sepp's bicycle, I pushed past them up the steps. I had to think of the anxious eye with which Sepp had watched my departure from Rohrbach, and decided to stow his old bicycle under the stairs before approaching the *gute Stube*, the dining-room, where the door was adorned with a picture of General Lattre de Tassigny, several more Tricolours and the announcement that it

313

was now the office of the Military Commandant. Having got so far, I thought I might just as well push open the door without knocking, and so I disturbed a dark handsome young man in uniform who was examining some papers at one of the tables. The only other person in the room was a well-made blonde who appeared to be his secretary.

'*Bonjour, monsieur,*' I announced rather breathlessly, finding it awkward to slip into a language I had not spoken for years. 'Please excuse the interruption, but I happen to be English, and I feel that I have things to report which could be of interest and some concern to you.'

The young man got to his feet politely and offered me a chair. 'But certainly, madame,' he said, and added, 'this is my secretary, Fräulein G.'

'She speaks French, monsieur?'

'A little.'

I found myself staring intently at Fräulein G. I knew why, and I soon reckoned that she did also. There was no need to go by the book or the badge. After twelve years of Hitler's rule, I would have had to be an imbecile not to recognize a Nazi when I saw one. This specimen oozed National Socialism from the top of her neat blonde head to the toe of her patent-leather shoe.

'You learned it in Paris, I suppose?' I remarked mildly, and when she nodded, I added very nastily, 'During the occupation, I suppose? You must have had great fun in Paris, during the occupation, I mean.'

That remark seemed to me so good that I decided to repeat it, nice and slowly, in French.

Capitaine C. was not only handsome but he had an intelligent, sensitive eye, and I was not too surprised when he agreed to speak with me alone.

During the two hours that we sat together that day in the *Gasthaus zum Löwen*, I became aware of many things, and sensed my rising resentment for our liberators beginning to subside. I even had hope that some of his detestation of *le sale Boche* did likewise. Capitaine C. listened patiently to my accounts of the excesses taking place in his district; he made no denials nor excuses. The colonial troops were splendid in battle, but they lacked experienced officers. He came from an army family. As a cadet in St Cyr, when the German hordes were swarming through his country, he had taken part in that hopelessly heroic cavalry charge on the advancing German tanks, after which there were few left alive to form the nucleus of an officers' corps.

'We behaved as if on parade, wore our white cockaded caps, sheer madness, but we felt at the time we would rather face an honourable death than defeat in dishonour.'

From his father's or grandfather's point of view, the present troops were no French army as they had known it, but an undisciplined rabble, partly genuine Maquis, partly those who joined the bandwagon when they saw which way things were going. Occupation, he believed, corrupted entirely; corrupted the occupiers as well as the occupied. The *Wehrmacht*, the German front-line troops, had behaved well enough at the start in France, but what came after? There were some unsung heroes to be sure, but also secret police, informers, collaborators. '*Ce n'était pas joli, madame – pas joli.*'

Before parting, I asked him whether he thought that the news reaching us by wireless could possibly all be true, and he confirmed my worst fears, telling me simply that after his experience in France, he personally could believe anything.

Capitaine C. helped me down the steps with Sepp's bicycle and we shook hands in parting. I do not think he resented the fact that I had possibly deprived him of a secretary, for he also gave me a permit which allowed Madame Bielenberg to '*circuler à bicyclette*' with the blessings of the Military government, and asked me to report to him should I be in need of any help.

As I wove my way homewards deep in thought, hardly aware of the crazy circus going on about me, I tried to come to grips with new unaccustomed emotions.

We had opposed; we had lost. The French had lost also; so maybe they had to compensate, had to show now what heroes they were – *La Grande Armée* – clad, fed and set in motion by the Americans or the British. But grandiloquence was in vain for, white armband or no white armband, behind the innocent blue eye of every German man, woman or child they must read or think to read the fateful message: six weeks, it had taken six short weeks to occupy their beloved Paris. They could insult, plunder, rape, even murder – it would take long years, probably a new generation, to wipe out the bitter memory of those six short weeks.

And as for Germany? She had surely lost far more than a war. Millions of her people, her land, her heritage, her honour. With her cities and townships in ruins, it would seem she had lost even her identity. What country could afford such profligacy? Chasing after a myth, a perverse preposterous pie-in-the-sky?

A soft evening mist was rising from the fields as I left the main road behind me and pushed up the hill towards Rohrbach. My bout of chauvinism having subsided, I found myself drained dry, dead weary of this monotonous chorus of failure. I felt no sympathy, no hostility, but just a dull longing to get home. I was merely a pseudo-German and home for me was not Hamburg, not Berlin, not even Rohrbach, but a warm, glowing, sheltered place, miles away, on an island where I belonged.

A cheerful yodel from near the tree line brought me swiftly back to reality. I had been away over-long. Nicky and John had been sent to keep look-out while Peter prepared to set off for Furtwangen on the short cut through the woods.

In spite of the delight expressed at the successful outcome of my journey, I knew something of the character of my own particular German, and had to wonder whether there was not a slight air of disappointment at my trouble-free, unmolested home-coming. For if he had been called to my rescue, Peter could have jettisoned so much bottled-up energy, such mounting frustration in one glorious, quite legitimate punch-up with whichever liberator happened to come his way.

In truth, since the inevitable defeat of his country, the daily round had proved almost more difficult for Peter than for me. He could speak no French, so that when army patrols were around rooting out deserters and possible prisoners of war, he was confined to dodging about inside the four walls of the Adler; into the attic, under the hay; the initial thrill of the game could not last for ever. True, he had his release document from Ravensbrück Concentration Camp, but rumour had it that there were so many forgeries in circulation that the Allies were beginning to pay little heed to such things.

I at least could kid myself that I was doing something about it all; he was able to do so only once, when three rugged figures came trudging up the valley and sat themselves down on the bench outside the kitchen door. They could speak little German and wanted to talk with the Bielenberg who was a doctor, and 'oh ja', if need be they could wait all day. When Peter appeared and sat down with them, after coming back into the kitchen to fetch his bag of *Wehrmacht* tobacco, I felt no shame at listening in to their voices through the open kitchen window above their heads. They were Poles freed from some prison camp near Triberg and they had been told by the authorities that in due course they would be repatriated. But with the passing of the months and the years they had taught themselves to trust no one. They hoped that they still had wives and also children at home, and they wanted advice. Should they wait, or should they scram and risk the long journey back to Poland on their own?

When I heard Peter ask them how it was they trusted him to give them an answer, how indeed they knew his name, they chuckled amongst themselves as a cloud of cigarette smoke drifted past my window. Hadn't he been through the same thing, hadn't he escaped from camp and been hiding in the woods for the last six weeks? There was not a Pole, nor for that matter a Russian, in the district who did not know of it. Who else should they come to but to a fellow fugitive? Peter gave them the best advice he could think of, which was to stay put a little longer as his country was in such turmoil that a journey homewards over hundreds of miles on foot could possibly end in disaster.

It was only after they got up to leave and Peter went with them to the bend in the road and they were shaking hands all round, talking and laughing up at him as they stuffed their pockets with the remains of his tobacco, that it occurred to me that I had learned of a different breed. They had their own secret lines of communication; they had known of Peter's whereabouts, but it had not occurred to any of them to betray him. This was a new kind of brotherhood, with a simple moral code, essential for the survival of those who were up against an unpredictable authority, those who were perforce on the run.

As we sat on the hillside and passed my precious permit from hand to hand, the importance of my being allowed to circulate on a bicycle was not as yet quite clear to any of us. The boys seemed to contemplate with much merriment the possibility of their mother pedalling about the countryside in ever-decreasing circles, whereas Peter and I were not sure whether Sepp's bicycle could make a further trip without collapsing altogether.

In fact my humble slip of paper held other advantages. It signified that I could speak French and had been granted special privileges, however limited. With the privileges also came responsibilities, for as soon as the news spread up the valley, a special village bicycle appeared from nowhere and was put at my disposal, nor was it long before Frau Muckle's *gute Stube* was promoted to becoming some kind of miniature Court of Appeal. 'They've taken my last pig, *Frau Doktor*!' – 'I'm down to one hen!' – 'How am I supposed to feed the cow, with no hay left until the harvest?' – these were problems I could not solve, but when Hans Bausch's wife came hotfoot to tell me that Hans had been taken away in the night and that as far as she could understand it had something to do with America, it was easy enough to put two and two together. For it had been simple Hans the milkman who had found an escaping American airman sleeping in the woods and had taken him home, and had come to me suggesting I might like to have a chat with him.

My journey to rescue Hans took me as far as Tuttlingen, where I finally found him sitting on the hut floor of what was seemingly a collection point for major war criminals. He was crying like a helpless child and told me he thought that they felt he had mur-dered a *ganzen Haufen* – a whole heap of Americans somewhere between Furtwangen and Villingen.

When he returned home and came to give me some bacon for my pains, I think he still had little idea of the fate which could have befallen him, any more than he or I could have known at the time what had happened to our American airman who, having decided he could run no further and had little chance of crossing the Rhine, was fed and cared for by the villagers and left us under police escort *en route*, as we were still naïve enough to believe, for a prisoner-of-war camp.*

But there were also days when I wished I could not speak French. Days when a truckload of assorted 'civilians' would draw up and grind to a halt before the Adler, and an interpreter was needed to sort out the genuine civilians from those who were deserters from the *Wehrmacht* and destined for prisoner-of-war camps.

It was always the same. A row of tired war-weary faces, their expressions alternating between hope and resignation. A cursory inspection could have passed them off as ordinary, somewhat eccentrically clad citizens in ill-fitting clothing, which I knew had been provided by good-hearted householders who had given

*He and his escort were ambushed by storm-troopers between Furtwangen and Villengen and he was shot by order of the local Kreisleiter (Party Boss) who was later condemned to death as a war criminal for five other similar offences.

them temporary refuge. The command to undress never had to be followed further than the shirt or jacket, for underneath was always the rough, grey, woollen army-issue vest, and that vest sealed their fate.

Perhaps soldiers find it hard to discard their few possessions, for once only was I successful in getting my message across: 'Please remember that I am merely here to interpret,' I would pronounce with much solemnity. 'The French officers here can speak no German, and it's your underclothes, your *Unterwäsche* you understand, that they are interested in.' On this one occasion the words were hardly out of my mouth before a skinny little individual in an outsize overcoat, doubled up suddenly clutching his stomach. '*Frau*,' he screamed, his face contorted in pain. '*Frau, ia muess scheisse!*' (I must shit). Bavarian, I could gather and not too easy to translate. But when I explained as best I could to one of the guards that I thought we might be in trouble, as it looked as if this one was going to fill his pants any minute, I met with understanding and he was allowed to retire to our outside lavatory, which was directly above the cess-pool under the dung heap.

When some weeks later the pool was drained to spread its contents on the meadows, it did not really surprise anyone that the pipes were almost choked with what still resembled a vest, some long underpants and a pair of woolly socks.

The true significance of my visit to Capitaine C. in Furtwangen emerged only later when a vehicle drew up outside the Adler, and there was a knock on the front door. Peter for the hayloft, ladies beware, hens away, I went to open up prepared to recite my usual dogmatic gibberish: 'Big, big husband, *Commandant*, *Angleterre*, *Allez! Allez!*' Whenever I think of the sight which met my eyes when I opened that back door, it comes back to me with all the vividness of divine revelation.

The uniform was British, the beret was British, the short leather-covered swagger-stick stuck under the arm was British, and the words, 'Excuse me, Captain Register's my name, SHAEF British American liaison 6th French army. Sorry to bother you, but I heard over in town there was a British woman living here somewhere, and we thought – we might – we could . . .'

We? I glanced behind him to where two further archangels were clambering out of an army jeep flying the Tricolour and also a real Union Jack. "Ullo, Mum,' said one; and, 'Good day, missus,' said the other as they came towards me. Came towards me and came to a dead stop, as well they might, because the 'British woman living here somewhere' had found nothing better to do than burst into a torrent of uncontrollable tears.

When Captain Register and his companions drove off three hours later, awash with watery coffee and well supplied with the hunks of fat bacon which Frau Muckle insisted was absolutely necessary to keep soldiers on the go, they left us with many valuable gifts, perhaps the most priceless being the careful and sympathetic heed they paid to our story and the effort they made to understand.

I could write my first letter to my parents in six years, telling them of our survival and begging for news. Peter could unburden himself of at least some of the confused emotions fermenting in his mind: his certainty that it would not be long before hunger spread disease, and that the children and I should be spared; his own helplessness in a zone where he could not speak the language of authority; the sense of responsibility inherent in having survived and his own wish to be of use somewhere in his demoralized and defeated country.

As for the children – manna from heaven! They could be introduced to two oranges, one banana and three whole bars of Cadbury's chocolate.

Captain Register's parting gift was a singularly unconventional document, written in ink on one of my remaining pieces of notepaper, wherein he, Captain Register of British American 6th Army group, SHAEF, introduced Peter Bielenberg of German extraction and his wife, British born, the daughter of Lieutenant-Colonel Burton of the British army and requested assistance for them in any way possible.

He handed it over to us with a grin, saying that it might help, but he wished he had had some kind of a rubber stamp with him as in any army there were few things so useful as a bloody impressive-looking rubber stamp.

Although we did not realize it, he was providing us with the equipment needed for the start of a long odyssey which would include our bidding farewell to Rohrbach and would end . . . Well, where would it end? We had no idea at the time but when we parted they left behind a miniature hive of industry and ingenuity. Did someone mention something about the occupation corrupting? What about that Citroën which must have been requisitioned by the *Wehrmacht* in France, and abandoned in the ditch before being rescued and hidden in the village bowling-alley before the French arrived? It probably only needed petrol to get it on the road again and with a bit of luck some of those wrecked hulks of *Wehrmacht* lorries lying about in the fields might still have a few cupfuls of fuel in their tanks. All that was needed was a hammer, a nail and a bucket, and Peter and the boys would soon find out.

Had Captain Register not mentioned something too about rubber stamps? What better than that of the Military Governor of the district? We'd have to drive to Villingen, twenty-eight kilometres, on one bucket of petrol. There would also be military patrols on the road, but Peter and I both had green-grey anoraks, not dissimilar to those of French army issue and being as brown as a berry from the waist up, at least Peter could be mistaken for a deaf and dumb Frenchman or even a Moroccan. What I could be mistaken for would be anyone's guess!

Our journey was completely successful. We dodged past three patrols, saluting smartly and stepping equally smartly on the accelerator, and arrived in Villingen to discover that Capitaine Robert was an extremely civilized, very confused, Military Governor. His father had been a diplomat in London and he spoke excellent English. Due to the antics of the *Ingénieurs* with the telegraph wires, he was also extremely isolated, and showed his gratitude for the information we could give him about his district by providing Captain Register's document with two quite splendid rubber stamps. Our world was expanding by the day. We could now travel by any means at our disposal to Stuttgart *et retour*. Although the means at our disposal were one stolen motor car and one decrepit bicycle, Peter decided blithely that nothing less than a motor bicycle would suit his requirements.

As communication by post or telephone was prohibited for German citizens, he must get to Hamburg and reassure his mother that he was still alive; he must get himself a job; he must look for Clarita, the widow of Adam von Trott, a great friend of ours, who had been cruelly executed after the failure of the 1944 Plot against Hitler's life. Peter wanted to see if he could be of help to her. His spirits were high and his plans were boundless; all he needed was that motor cycle. Rumour had it that there was a warehouse packed with requisitioned vehicles somewhere on the other side of Furtwangen so, armed with our document, off he went through the woods and returned in the evening astride a magnificent machine which looked as if it had barely left the assembly line.

He threw caution to the winds and wasted some of our precious petrol careering about the forest tracks with the boys riding pillion before setting off on what must have been a unique journey: from our south-west corner of what remained of his country, through all three occupied zones across the River Elbe to Hamburg. He returned three weeks later, his mission accomplished, having proved Captain Register's theory to be correct, for our ridiculous document now had a collection of rubber stamps fit to be framed.

Before the war ended a joke was doing the rounds about a citizen saying to his friend that when the war was over he intended to make a bicycle tour all round Germany, and his friend replied by asking him what he was going to do in the afternoon!

In fact no one seemed to know exactly what would be left of Germany, what indeed had been decided in Yalta when Churchill, Roosevelt and Stalin had divided the spoils and carved out the territories over which they would hold sway when victory was theirs. In Hamburg it was known that to the east, in Schleswig-Holstein, huge prisoner-of-war camps were being run with much efficiency by officers of the German *Wehrmacht*. Why? Could it mean that at least the British had woken up to the fact that although the Nazi menace was now behind them, the barbarous advance of the Russians into Europe might not bode too well for the future?

But for us in Rohrbach it was the present which occupied our minds. Peter had found his family alive; hungry, but well. Clarita, also, had been freed from prison, but was not yet reunited with her children who, after Adam's death and her own imprisonment, had been removed from their grandmother's care and placed in a Nazi children's home.

Frankfurt had become the headquarters of the American zone of occupation, and because of his clean sheet politically and his newly found ability to communicate, Peter had found himself a job in the recently established Chamber of Commerce. He must leave again at once, for there was even the possible chance that two or three rooms in a little house in Kronberg, just outside the town, might be put at his – at our – disposal.

After he left again, I was overtaken by increasing restlessness, persuading myself that there was little more I could do to help.

Lush weeds and wild raspberry canes were beginning to camouflage the rusting war machines which still littered the meadows; one such monster had been taken over already by a little bird, busy building its nest in the exhaust pipe. There would surely always be the odd crisis but life in the valley would go on, could go on, without me.

I was also unhappy as I had had no reply to my message to my family. Perhaps Frankfurt would be more central, perhaps I should try from there. Indeed I had sent off two messages into the blue, the second by way of a gay Irishman who appeared on the scene not only bent on having a good time but, seeing that he was in the logging trade in Canada, also to cast a curious, perhaps even covetous, eye over the acres of massive conifers known as the Black Forest.

'You will have to leave us one day, *Frau Doktor.*' Frau Muckle gave a loving glance at Christopher who was sitting on her lap having his supper. She had become as devoted to *Christofli* as to a grandson. 'You will have to leave us and I – we – will wish you Godspeed, but we will miss you here in the valley.'

So it was to be. A further trip to Frankfurt riding pillion on Peter's motor cycle, a cursory inspection of some small empty rooms in a little house in Kronberg, and a return journey to Rohrbach at the wheel of an elderly motor car, the registered property of the Frankfurt Chamber of Commerce.

On the eve of our departure, I could hear unusual stirrings in the *gute Stube* next door to our little sitting-room, which looked strangely forlorn after I had taken down our two pictures and rolled up the rug. At breakfast Frau Muckle had mentioned rather over-casually that some of the villagers might want to drop in that evening to say goodbye, for if I was leaving at dawn the following day they might be held up at home with the cows and so on.

When Sepp's two daughters joined her and Martina in the kitchen though, to spend the afternoon bustling back and forth at her bidding, and I also heard her rummaging about in the chimney where she hid the smoked meats, I had to suspect that something rather out of the ordinary might be afoot.

I was packing all day, trying to figure out which of our few possessions we could discard in order to cram children and dire necessities into the motor car, so that dusk was moving up the valley before I glanced out of the window to see Sepp and his wife emerging from their shop and approaching the front entrance to the Adler. They were both dressed as if for Mass and Sepp had his hat on. A further glance down the road and I could distinguish the mayor's bread-van approaching from the direction of Schönenbach and across the valley quite a few black-clad figures seemed to be converging on the inn.

I had a dress somewhere in one of the bundles and hurried upstairs to drag it out. The boys were over-excited and had been a nuisance all day, but at least they should be clean.

Frau Muckle was quite pink with excitement when she came to call us, and she had every reason to be so for the *gute Stube* was a festive sight. Many of the tables were spread with white table-cloths, two candles were lit before the statue of the Virgin and Child in the *Herrgottseck* – God's corner – and there were jam-jars of wild flowers in the windows. There had surely been nothing like it since we entertained our American airman.

The Rohrbach villagers were standing about in silent groups, not yet quite at ease wearing their Sunday best on a weekday, and as we were ushered in, the mayor stepped forward, clearing his throat as if to make a little speech. He seemed to change his mind when the *Lehrer* Lorenz and his wife, closely followed by Father Kunz, slipped through the heavy curtainings which covered the front door.

I thought I knew perhaps why. Only three weeks before, I had managed to persuade the Military Governor in Villingen to reinstate him as Mayor of Rohrbach in spite of the fact that he had been a member of the Party; a privilege of which he had made no use whatsoever. However, since his world at present was standing on its head, he might have wondered whether the priest should take precedence on such an occasion.

The silence which followed his hesitation could have become oppressive if Martina had not saved the situation by getting a splendid fit of the giggles. She was reprimanded as usual most vehemently by Frau Muckle and as usual took no notice whatsoever, so that our festive array and the mayor's speech were quickly forgotten and we all started talking at the same time before turning our attention to the feast which had been prepared for us.

Something untoward might prevent Frau Muckle from ever entertaining on such a scale again, but now she was bent on doing us proud: two great tureens of steaming noodle soup, a mound of fat smoked bacon and dozens of bottles of fizzy lemonade. We guessed that the three giant loaves which occupied a table all to themselves were a contribution from the mayor's bread-van.

As the meal progressed and we had drained the soup tureens and were well on the way to demolishing the mountain of fat bacon, Sepp made sure of the success of my send-off by telling his daughters to fetch over a bottle or two of his homemade red-currant schnapps known far and wide to be delicious and quite lethal. As most of us through necessity had become unaccustomed to alcohol of any kind for years, a thimbleful of this heady brew was enough to have us all laughing and talking at the tops of our voices. Hardship and the sorrow of parting were temporarily forgotten as earthy jokes and way-out stories did the rounds in a dialect which became increasingly incomprehensible.

Frau Muckle was asleep behind the stove with Christopher curled up in the log-basket at her feet when the cuckoo clock on the wall told us in staccato style that it was midnight. The last to leave took their plates to the kitchen where Martina was already busy tipping the remains into the pig bucket.

'Goodnight, *Frau Doktor*!'

'God bless you, *Frau Doktor*!'

'Come back soon, *Frau Doktor*!'

'Oh, I will, I will, very, very soon – I promise.'

As I stood in the doorway and watched them disappear into the darkness, although I knew in my heart that a chapter of my life had come to a close, I do not think that I was consciously avoiding the truth.

At five o'clock the next morning, when the summits of the black hills were already outlined against a soft yellow glow and a mist hid the lowlands, we climbed into our little motor car which was barely recognizable beneath the bags and bundles tied to its mudguards and the bulging rug strapped to its roof.

A slight hold-up, and it was fortunate that three sturdy villagers were already up and about, for we had to be pushed for several hundred yards before the engine sprang to feeble life.

Then we were off: Frankfurt, England, here we come! I could not wave goodbye as I needed both hands on the steering-wheel to keep us on the road, but the boys kneeling on the back seat told me that they could still see two white handkerchiefs fluttering bravely, before we rounded a bend in the road and the village hidden behind the morning mist was no longer in sight.

Chapter Two

Nearly four months passed before a Royal Air Force plane of Transport Command took off from the United States air base Frankfurt/Main – 'Operation Woman and Child' – and Nicholas, John, Christopher and I were airborne *en route* for England.

During those four months we became crafty and self-centred, no different from any others who were being classified by Americans, re-educated by the British, conquered – however belatedly – by the French, while our sole interest lay in planning where the next meal, the next lump of coal, might come from.

Our journey from Rohrbach had taken us many long hours, mastering what remained of Germany's road network. Our maximum speed was a sedate twenty-five kilometres an hour, as, with more skill than sense, I managed to avoid mighty bomb craters which could have swallowed us altogether, and to get ourselves sucked along in the wake of one of the huge army vehicles which seemed to be the only other form of transport on the move. Jeeps and trucks, tanks and gun carriages; when they thundered past us these juggernauts covered us with dust, loosened the ropes and played havoc with the bundles tied to our roof and mudguards. But our little motor car survived and reached its destination, although towards the end of its ordeal it looked no better than a junk heap on wheels.

I had not known Frankfurt before the war, but could imagine that the old part of the town sloping down to the River Main and known as the *Goethe Stadt* might have been beautiful before it was obliterated by bombs. The best of the city, where it was still intact, seemed merely a faded monument to past prosperity and lack of taste, and the pot-holed streets and pitted pavements did nothing to improve its image.

A large residential area had been cordoned off and the houses requisitioned for occupation troops. It was carefully guarded with a high wire fence and numerous military check-points in order to keep out possible intruders and also disease, about which the Americans seemed to have an almost pathological horror. It was known to the liberated as the 'Ami Ghetto'.

The American GIs, some black, some white, were fine-looking, loose-limbed young fellows who seemed to spend much of their day squatting on the kerbside chewing gum and casting longing eyes in the direction of any presentable but officially unavailable *Fräulein* who happened to pass by. *Fräuleins* were officially unavailable because after hostilities ceased, the Allies, in their wisdom, had promulgated various directives in the simple hope of solving the immediate problem of how to deal with a race of defeated Germans who had committed unspeakable crimes and yet, to meet with, seemed so helpful, so eager to please, so wishful to learn whatever language was required and to insist that, of course, they had never been Nazis and had known nothing of what had gone on during the twelve long years of Hitler's rule.

The only relics of an army which had rampaged through Europe and penetrated deep into Russia were now lonely, silent figures in tattered uniforms, leaning on makeshift crutches or propped up in sheltered doorways. These were the *Schwerkriegsverletzten*, the severely war wounded. The fact that they were legless, armless or blind was surely proof enough, but the rough message chalked on cardboard and the begging bowl on the pavement before them told passers-by that they were also penniless and hungry.

Non-fraternization, a ruling ignored by the Russians and the French, stipulated that unless on official business, no Allied personnel must communicate in any way with a German civilian; no greeting, no word, no smile must be exchanged with any remnant of the once all-conquering Master Race. Every possible contingency had been considered and provided for in order to impress on the Germans that this time they had been truly defeated, and that their behaviour had been beneath contempt. But one all-important factor had not been considered and that was human nature, so, in spite of the presence of quantities of military police, it was not long before a flourishing black market developed in the red-light district near Frankfurt's main railway station; a hive of clandestine activity where alcohol and cameras, fountain-pens and *Fräuleins* could be bartered for cigarettes and petrol, candies and cookies. Anything for anything, indeed, in a world where life had been reduced to the basics.

We were luckier than most in not having to join the long queues for housing, because Peter had managed to rent three rooms for us in the tiny house in Kronberg, a suburb of Frankfurt. He had also rustled up four beds, a table and some chairs. We had a kitchen with a sink and a stove, and an outside lavatory of the chain-pulling variety. A saucepan, which unfortunately had a habit of turning somersaults, completed the picture. What more could we want? ('Count your blessings, dear' was one of my grandmother's pious maxims if, as children, we ran to her in the belief that life had given us a particularly hard knock.) All right, there was of course much more to want, and there were moments when I almost succeeded in understanding that satisfaction with one's lot is purely a matter of perspective, of comparability. In the Black Forest, there had been times of loneliness, and of despair. I also had to admit to moments of intense boredom when, lying in bed at night, listening to the wind howling over the hills, I sensed with dull resignation that life was passing me by. But we had been sheltered there, cared for by good and simple people and we had also been safe from the bombs. Here in Kronberg we were falling over each other, making do, shuffling along in endless queues for food by day, confined by the curfew to our cramped quarters at night. But, unlike so many others, we were alive, healthy and together, and we had a roof over our heads.

The rumour of that roof over our heads soon spread, so that homeless friends appeared out of the blue, certain of welcome and a chance to sleep somewhere on a nice dry floor. Freda Winckelmann was one of the first to arrive and became a permanent fixture. I was delighted to see her because though I longed to leave for England, I suffered an occasional twinge of conscience as to what would happen to Peter after I had left, and here was one of my closest friends who would be the perfect candidate to take my place.

Freda and her husband Hannes Winckelmann were long-standing friends from Hamburg. We had married in the same year, but they were both older than ourselves and, much to Freda's sadness, they had no children.

Hannes was by profession a not very successful lawyer, by temperament probably an academic. His purpose in life seemed to revolve around some thesis on the subject of Max Weber, an eminent sociologist, which, with the years, was becoming a huge tome. He had also been a friend of Dr Goerdeler, former Mayor of Leipzig, one of the senior members of the Opposition, at whose request he had found himself appointed to a minor post in the Ministry of the Interior in Berlin in order to establish contact there with others of like mind. Needless to say, he was a dedicated anti-Nazi, but if I were to be honest, anyone who cared nothing about Herr Max Weber could find Hannes something of a bore.

Freda came from an estate in East Germany and unlike most other Prussian nobility whose female offspring were driven to learn the art of housekeeping the hard way, her family, the von Rechenbergs, had never insisted on her doing anything at all except enjoy herself, until they lost all their possessions after the First World War. She then had to do something about earning her living and had battled along fairly successfully as a secretary, until finally employed by Furtwängler, the conductor of the Berlin Philharmonic Orchestra.

The longer our friendship lasted, the more certain I became that her success as a secretary was due more to her personality than to her skill with a typewriter. If I needed convincing I only had to go with her to one of the orchestra's rehearsals, and see for myself how she seemed to take each one of those magnificent musicians, including their conductor, under her wing.

Freda was small and wiry, with blue eyes which were inclined to glance at you occasionally with the sparkle of a bright-eyed bird. Her capacity as a listener was limitless, and such was her sympathetic involvement in the affairs of others that if the occasion arose she could burst with laughter, but also, with equal facility, shed a sudden tear.

Just before the Russians arrived in Berlin, a *Luftmine* – an air mine – landed in the Winckelmanns' garden, and successfully flattened their little house in Gatow. She and Hannes had miraculously survived in the cellar, but, homeless and destitute, she had been persuaded to leave for Bavaria with Furtwängler and his orchestra, who seemed unable to come to any decision without her. Hannes, still hopeful of the earlier arrival in Berlin of the Americans or the British, preferred to stay at his post in the Ministry. When she heard about our 'roof' in Kronberg she decided to trek westwards and arrived on our doorstep with the remains of her possessions strapped to her back in a rucksack – a few pieces of jewellery, some bundles of old curtains and an equally elderly bedspread which seemed an odd collection until she explained with a confidence which might have been bravado that, since she had no money and no one had much to wear these days, she had decided to turn her hand to dress-making.

Dear Freda! Neither Peter nor I could remember her being able to darn a sock, or fry an egg for that matter, but even if the mind boggled at the thought of her brave venture into the world of *haute couture* – picturing the trail of chintz and damask sacks liable to fall to pieces at any moment that she might have left behind her *en route* – we had not the heart to dampen her spirit.

Freda was followed by two eminent but rather tiresome professors of Philosophy, mutually good friends until they had to decide who was the more eminent, who indeed deserved the only blanket we could provide for their comfort. The argument as to their respective scholastic merits went on into the early hours until Peter decided that the children were not quite warm enough and removed the blanket, leaving the eminent professors to argue themselves to sleep on two very uncomfortable chairs.

I soon learned that in circumstances of need, certain minor moral principles can no longer be relied upon and finally slip away altogether. It was, for instance, surprising how rapidly I switched from being slightly shocked to being simply delighted when the children turned up for lunch waving a piece of chocolate or a banana which could only mean that they had been begging outside the local GI encampment.

Nor did a conversation with my neighbour in one of the food queues in any way reduce my suspicion that the German *Hausfrau* belonged to a very special breed, possibly more dedicated, indomitable and tenacious than the whole of the German and Allied armies rolled into one.

'It was all because of the sugar for the preserves,' she remarked suddenly, as her eyes followed a group of GIs who happened to be passing by.

'*Ja, ja,* of course, the sugar for the preserves . . .' I had no idea what she was talking about but decided that under the circumstances any sort of conversation would do.

'It's the bottled plums,' she went on. 'The syrup, you understand, it needs so much sugar to get them right.'

'Surely,' I said, still well out of my depth until she added, 'He

330

was a nice gentleman, could not speak much German, not black of course, and he never left without paying – a kilo of sugar, sometimes even two – a most satisfactory arrangement.'

My neighbour did not look promiscuous: homely in fact, but also determined and rather pleased with herself.

'Yes, I guess it was a very good arrangement,' I replied as we moved a few steps nearer to the grocer's shop, and for some reason or other I felt myself to be rather inadequate, a truly feeble votary to the goddess of the store cupboard.

It was perhaps this cosy chat which drove me to embark on an expedition which could have ended in disaster. A good friend, the doctor's wife, pretty, respectable, devoted mother to her children, came by with the proposition. She had bicycled to the country with a piece of jewellery and returned with six bottles of wine; not very good wine, she assured me, but she'd heard the *Amis* didn't know the difference. She had also learned that the going rate for wine was two bottles for one jerrycan of army petrol. She had done some reconnoitring and discovered that the guards who took over at our local army camp at night were very partial to the odd bottle of wine. There had to be two of us though, one to keep the guards happy and the other to fetch the petrol from the huge army storage compound some two miles away. Think of it, two whole jerrycans of petrol! Who knows where we could go from there: petrol to cigarettes, cigarettes to butter, butter to – we could end up living on beefsteaks for weeks, and just in case I might be disturbed by anything resembling a still small voice, she added that it need not mean only food, for we might also pick up some unobtainable medicines *en route*.

The whole expedition had obviously been planned most carefully, for as soon as we arrived at the camp and my friend had jumped out of the car with far more confidence than I knew she possessed, a uniformed figure emerged from under some trees and climbed in beside me. He was bulky and black. 'Howdy, ma name's Louis,' he whispered in an accent coming from well south of the Potomac.

'Howdy, mine's Chris,' I replied and, 'Get going, honey' came his swift reply.

So get going I did, out onto the main road, heading for a glow on the skyline which I knew to be the floodlit petrol compound. Louis was friendly and chatty and it was obviously not the first time that he had set off on such an expedition, for just before we reached the high wire fence topped with barbed wire he told me to stop, waited for two cars to pass us and then—

'Now, Chris, honey, sharp to the right and turn out the lights.'

'Honey' by this time was ready for anything; sharp to the right, the lights were out, and she could see nothing whatsoever. As far as she was concerned we might have been taking a dive into the ocean. But it seemed we had landed on a well-worn trail, and my little motor car had dropped into two deep tracks which allowed no room for manoeuvre. Onwards for about three hundred yards, then Louis patted my knee, told me I had done fine, ordered me to stop and said he would be back in about five minutes.

The five minutes seemed rather long, because although a high bank topped with some kind of a hedge hid the glow of the arc lights to my left, to my right must have been an open field and I could not understand how the headlights from the cars passing along the main road and temporarily lighting up the surrounding countryside did not include me in their vision. A certain amount of rustling and grunting, and Louis was back, dragging two splendid jerrycans of petrol which he stowed on the back seat and we set off on our return journey; in reverse this time, but the tracks still held us on course.

All was going well, in fact I was beginning to enjoy myself when, after we had covered about a hundred yards, a gasp and then a moan from Louis told me that something was definitely not in order.

'Ma Luger, doggone it, ma Luger, ah've left it in the hedge,' he wailed, and when I turned to look at him, he was no longer the cheerful, confident guide, but a heap of misery with nothing much to be seen of him but the whites of his eyes.

'Couldn't we leave it there?' I murmured, not quite certain whether a Luger was a pistol or even a machine-gun.

'You jes don't know Uncle Sam,' he replied, and before I could say more he was out of the car, stumbling off back down the track and had disappeared into the darkness, leaving me crouched over the steering-wheel, woefully considering the extent of my misdemeanours and totting up the inevitable consequences. The minutes ticked away, as the headlights from the main road, so much closer now, flashed and faded over my head. It was too much to hope that a passing vehicle would not be alerted: brakes would be applied, huge headlights would swing around and a jeep most likely loaded with military police would draw up behind me and my cargo of contraband loot.

Caught red-handed abroad without permission after curfew, in possession of two jerrycans of stolen army gasoline. With luck, poor Louis crawling about in the hedgerows looking for his Luger might make a getaway, otherwise the two of us could look forward to spending part of our lives behind bars, getting to know Uncle Sam.

I had lost count of time when the car door was wrenched open and Louis was back again, sweating and breathless.

'Sweet Jesus,' he gasped as he flung himself down beside me. 'Sweet Jesus, Chris honey, ah found it, ma old Luger, ma dear li'l ol' Luger.' The words were hardly out of his mouth before our little car started shaking as if overtaken by an earthquake, for Louis had his Luger, Louis was a man again, rocking back and forth in a giant fit of uncontrollable laughter.

The remainder of our trip was comparatively uneventful, except that when we arrived back at the camp I could see that my poor friend had not had an easy time either.

'Heavens, Chris!' she exploded as she jumped for the car. 'Whatever happened to you? I reckoned on half an hour at the most, and you've been gone more than two hours – oh dear, what's the English for *hau ab* anyway?'

'Buzz off,' I obliged, and as we headed for home and family, I told her and she told me and we both decided that we were not the stuff of which gun-runners are made. As far as we were concerned, once this consignment was used up, our children could go on eating groats for every meal and our husbands go about their respective businesses on foot.

It was here though, in our little house in Kronberg, that my spirits soared sky-high, for a message reached me from UNRRA (United Nations Relief and Rehabilitation Agency) that my family in England were all alive and well. My brothers Basil and John had survived the African campaign, although for the last two years John had been a prisoner of war, captured after the landing in Italy. My sister and her family had spent the war in Australia and then in Canada. All were heading for home and my father was pulling strings and making arrangements for us to join them as soon as possible.

The silence from the other side was broken; somehow one or other of my many messages must have slipped through the dense wall of censorship. My family had our address and the strings being pulled must have been considerable because close upon that first message followed an invitation from General Morgan of UNRRA for Peter and me to join him for dinner in Kronberg Castle, which was now Allied Command Headquarters. Out with my pre-war blue, my one remaining glad rag, and we were fetched by an army driver in a real motor car, later to dine off real plates and be served real food by real batmen in white jackets. There was silver, there was glass, and the port did the rounds under the cool, indifferent eyes of former Princes of Hessen assembled about us in portraits on the walls. But Peter and I knew that what we needed, above all, was the sympathy we received and the interest shown, and the fact that we could take part in serious discussion as to how, after the devastations of war, new structures for Europe must emerge, ensuring that the peoples, currently buffeted about like human driftwood, could reach home, some longed-for harbour, and be allowed to start life anew.

Two evenings later we were paid a surprise visit by several more junior members of General Morgan's staff. They came because they had felt we were of similar age, that British or German we had all perforce grown up under the threatening shadow of an impending world war and it was up to us, to our generation, to see that it never happened again. There was so much more to discuss and they felt we had not reached enough conclusions in the more formal atmosphere of Kronberg Castle.

They knew of our children and, besides three bottles of whiskey, had brought with them a bulging rucksack filled with unheard-of delicacies: chocolates and fruit, sweets and biscuits, even some chewing gum, so we decided that the boys should also have their party. 'Eat yourselves sick,' I chirruped recklessly as they dragged the rucksack back to their bedroom, and when in the early hours of the morning we settlers of the world's ills staggered in to bid them good night, it was obvious that they had taken my advice. Orange peels and banana skins, half-eaten chocolate bars and sweet papers were strewn all over the room with riotous abandon and our sons had passed out, their night-clothes and their peaceful faces smeared with chocolate and aglow with what I hoped was not violent indigestion.

My last official encounter before we left for England was less encouraging. In a way it was brought about by the visit of the UNRRA officers, for the evening had revived so many memories, of times with friends who were no longer alive, of the plans we had made, of the things that must be done. This left me with a guilty conscience, telling myself that in times like these, counting my blessings and cursing the somersaulting saucepan were useless occupations and that I could and should do better. Now that Freda was installed and could look after the children, I was free to take on some kind of job, perhaps as an interpreter. I could, after all, speak three languages fluently and had learned when living in the French zone how the language barrier can impede progress. Here in the American zone many of the officials in the Press and Information and also Intelligence Departments were German-Jewish emigrants who, as Peter had discovered, could speak better German than English, but whose attitude, policies and behaviour understandably made for little positive collaboration. A neutral interpreter then, that's what was needed, and I decided with much confidence that I was made for the job.

The four stalwart guards who stood sentry outside the entrance to the British Liaison Office were easy to deal with, the pre-scribed rigidity of their facial expressions relaxing immediately to become broad grins on being spoken to by a civilian whose accent they could recognize as the genuine article. From there I progressed from one office to the next and thought I was doing very well until I reached the top, where the interview was short and not very sweet.

'You are British born, I understand, and married to a German – Bylenberg I note – and you wish to enter Allied employment, is that it?'

The gentleman was not very tall, he had a rather steely eye beneath bushy black eyebrows and what remained of his face was hidden behind an outsize moustache.

'Yes, well, I suppose it is – er . . .' I got no further.

'Well, I can tell you right away, Frau Bylenberg,' he snapped, 'you have not got a hope.' Whereupon, drawing himself up to his full five foot six, looking almost as if he was about to blow his moustache at me, he added, 'It is my considered opinion that you were a poor fool to marry a bloody German anyway, and . . .'

Whatever he wanted to say next was aimed at a closed door, but fate was to decide that we should meet again under very different circumstances, of which I must tell later.

Down at the entrance the four guards were anxious to know how I had got on, and when I told them that I had been given the thumbs down in no uncertain terms, they were most sympathetic.

'The trouble is that little men never really like tall girls very much,' I found myself confiding rather miserably.

'You look all right to me, miss,' one of them remarked, and seeing that they were all well over six feet, we found ourselves bursting with laughter together, which did much to cheer my dejected frame of mind.

At last the day arrived when an official-looking document required us to report at the air base, prepared to take off for London.

We had made two false starts before, and twice taken tearful farewells of Peter at the air base entrance checkpoint, only to spend the rest of the day stuffing doughnuts in a canteen, to be sent home again in the evening like unwanted cargo. On this occasion though, we had barely said goodbye when a loudspeaker crackled out our names and we were hustled along several narrow passageways out onto the wide expanse of tarmac. A short jeep ride and we were dumped beside a huge silent grey-green monster. A monster for me, as I had only seen its like before when, together with hundreds of its kin, it winged its way high above the Black Forest *en route* for Augsburg or Munich – towns already shattered, but doubtless preparing to batten down again and dig in once more, awaiting its arrival.

The only other passenger in the same category as ourselves was a pale-faced German girl clutching a brand new British passport and holding a sleeping baby on her lap; the baby was jet black. She could speak no English, and she was scared, she came from near Leipzig and had married an African prisoner of war. The Russians, you see, and, oh yes, he was very kind and had given her food and cigarettes. Did I know Africa? Would he come to meet her? He had not yet seen his son.

As she unburdened herself in obvious relief at finding someone who spoke her own language, my eye wandered from one to the other of my own children. Nicky was holding tightly to a small cardboard suitcase containing the remains of his favourite possessions, Christopher to a coloured handkerchief to which he had become attached, and John had a canvas camera case slung round his neck. It contained my old Box Brownie camera, a birthday present, and I had only been able to keep a flicker of interest in it alive by telling him of the wonderful pictures he would be able to take in England as soon as he could get a film for it.

One of the soldiers was making himself popular by showing them how to inflate their life-jackets, and when they turned and laughed back at me over their bulging rubber waistcoats, looking for all the world like three bright-eyed coconuts, I decided Peter and I had reason to be proud, for they looked healthy enough in spite of those last months spent in Frankfurt.

'I'm hungry,' Christopher announced at the top of his voice in broad Black Forest dialect. I knew this could not be the case, because even in the short while we had spent in the PX canteen, the Americans had been generous in plying us with food, milk and coffee.

'You'll have to wait until we get to England,' I said firmly, wondering in fact just how long that would be as we were so obviously still rooted to the ground. But Christopher knew better. He eyed John's camera case expectantly, while John, with a slow secret smile, started fiddling with the clasp and finally slipped back its canvas cover. The case no longer housed my Box Brownie and I could only think it had been left on the counter of the PX canteen, for instead, squeezed in most carefully without a square inch to spare, were three neat rows of golden-brown doughnuts.

Seated to my left was a boy who did not seem inclined to join in the general high spirits. Instead, after apologizing and pushing along the bench to give me more room, he sat there beside me, elbows on knees, quietly reading a book.

Perhaps it was the contrast between the clamour about us and his stillness which made me look at him more closely. Although his trousers were airforce blue, he was not wearing battle-dress, but an old tweed jacket, a blue open-necked shirt and some kind of a silk scarf which did not look like army issue. His face, too, seen in profile, was of a type which I had not seen for many years. My mother, with true British reasoning, always insisted that Germans were pale because they slept with their windows shut. Be that as it may, it was not the fine head, the short straight nose, the crop of curly fair hair, but the rosy freshness of his complexion which made me come to the conclusion that he could not be anything but British and that he was really much too young to have taken part in any war.

Now, as if conscious of my attention, he straightened suddenly and putting aside his book turned to me and smiled. 'Sorry,' he said, 'but you have me puzzled – what nationality are you?'

I had been asked that question many times before. The last

time was nine months earlier – it seemed a lifetime ago – on a long train journey back from Berlin to the Black Forest after seeing Peter in Ravensbrück Concentration Camp. The question had come from a pale-faced SS officer, who had slaughtered Jews, who could not forget and who wished in his turn to die. What nationality was I? There was something rather shy and very engaging about my neighbour's smile which made me smile back.

'Well, officially I think I must be a Kraut,' I said and watched his smile broaden immediately.

'I see,' he said, and then with his eye on a poker game which had established itself with much ingenuity amongst the baggage in front of us, he added, 'and your husband, he is still . . . ?'

'Oh yes, he's alive,' I answered quickly, 'he's still in Frankfurt,' and I found myself adding, 'alive – just one of the few.'

I do not know if something in my voice struck a hidden chord, but it was as if a shadow passed across his face. I had been mistaken, it was no longer so young. Handsome, yes, fresh-cheeked, just not so young any more. 'I know what you mean,' he said simply, and then added with a smile which immediately recaptured his youth, 'at least you have three very nice little Krauts to show for it.'

I hesitated a moment, and am not sure if I would have spoken more. It was the sudden change in his expression, his knowing what I meant by being 'still alive' which made me wonder. But the moment, if there had ever been one, was lost – when a cheerful face barely visible behind a huge moustache was thrust round a trap door to the front of the plane which presumably led to the cockpit.

'OK, lads, get ready for take-off.' Order was established immediately with military precision. The poker game faded out in seconds, safety straps were adjusted, life-jackets donned and inflated and, as the giant engines sprang to life one after the other with ear-splitting roars, we were all lodged in our places as rigid as robots.

The din did not lessen after the bumps and jolts gave place to pitching and rearing, so that except for an occasional nod and smile, and one fruitless mouthing to the children to go slow on the doughnuts, conversation ceased and I was left with my own wandering thoughts, which I found I could not focus properly yet on an England I had not seen for more than six years. Instead they seemed bent on drifting back to Rohrbach, to my people there, unable to speak French, unable to communicate with their masters, still waiting in hope that their missing menfolk would return. Alois, young Sepp, Friedl, Frau Muckle's Ernst. The second hay-cut would be finished now and the cattle back in their sheds, but soon would come the snows, and the potatoes must be dug from the ground and stored and those giant logs dragged down from the forests. Maybe it was easier to think of the Rohrbach villagers for there was something in the rhythm of their lives which was certain of survival and I had not yet the courage to think too long of those others – Adam, Carl, Helmuth, Claus Stauffenberg – whose dreams and plans had come to nothing, their potential recklessly sacrificed. Lexi who had told me of those meat-hook hangings after 20th July after the plot that failed – where was Lexi now?

Far away, lost in my thoughts, I had barely realized that the shudders, the dives and the jerks of the plane had become noticeably more pronounced, but the door to the cockpit opened once more and the appearance of the cheerful gentleman with the whiskers brought me back from the past. This time he struggled down the length of the cabin, to shout at us in sparkling humour that due to adverse weather conditions we would be unable to land near London, that he was not certain where exactly our 'ditching' would take place, but we were to cheer up as, ha! ha!, he did not expect much flak.

I glanced at the children, who in spite of the racket seemed fast asleep, as were the little German war-bride and her baby. My neighbour, too, his book dropped to the floor, was sleeping. But I could not sleep for whenever I closed my eyes they floated in from the mists, those shadowy faces, faces I loved and had left behind, faces of some still living, faces of others I would never see again.

The dim lights in the cabin snuffed out suddenly, and as the plane plunged on in the darkness, the fleeting images became blurred and faded out, and I, too, must have fallen asleep, only to be woken either by the sudden silencing of the engine roar or by Nicky's anxious thumping on my life-jacket.

'Oh, *Mami*, come on, wake up.' What? – Where? He was pointing to the back of the plane where an open hatchway let in a shaft of light and his voice was shaking with excitement. '*Mami, um Gottes Willen!* For God's sake, look!' he said. 'It's England.' I do not know if I had expected Big Ben to be there to greet me, but 'England' turned out to be a deserted airstrip, a few Nissen huts, a smell of the sea and an airforce bus which was to dump us in front of a railway station.

As I clambered out into the pale sunshine and looked about me, I had a strange feeling that I had done all this before. The railway station was unnamed, or rather its name, which I felt should have been proclaimed in bold lettering above the entrance and along the platforms, was covered over with green paint. A tactical measure I had been told, used everywhere in order to mislead the Germans should they decide to land on British soil. There was something else which struck me as unfamiliar about my surroundings in that everything around me seemed so very small. Like Alice in Wonderland, had I grown bigger and bigger? The station which should have been huge and imposing was not very remarkable at all. Now I had it – Westgate-on-Sea, it could try to fox the Germans, but it could not fox me, for when I was a little girl I had spent two not very happy years at boarding-school in this place. Beginning of term, end of term, helpless home-sickness, bubbling excitement; the years had passed, but that little Victorian railway station had not changed, only apparently shrunk.

It had a further trick to play, however, when I approached the ticket-office. 'One single and three halves, please, to London.' 'That'll be ten and six and fifteen bob, twenty-five shillings and sixpence in all' – but I had no money.

'Well then, you and the kids can't travel to London, mum, can you now?' 'Could I telephone?' – Yes, if I had sixpence – but I hadn't sixpence either.

A wary look came over the man's face in the ticket-office, as he turned his attention to the next passenger in the queue. It was his obvious opinion that the lady in front of him was probably not dishonest, but just plain daft.

I was indeed non-plussed, for this was an absurd predicament which I could not have foreseen. 'Operation Woman and Child' – the RAF had fulfilled its duty on landing, and, mission accomplished, was no longer involved.

There was a train standing on the far platform and for a moment I thought of gathering up the luggage, alerting the children and making a dash for it, but I had to discard the idea as being over-ambitious, and was wondering just what I could do when I recognized a welcome voice beside me. It was that of my neighbour on the plane and he was asking me whether I was in trouble and if he could be of any help. Could he help? Oh, certainly he could. He gave me a rather curious look when I took down his name and address in order to repay the five pounds he lent me, but his name, George Millar, did not ring a bell. I heard only later that the boy I had thought too young to be a soldier was a distinguished war-hero, who had been dropped into occupied France dozens of times, contacting the Maquis underground, helping prisoners of war and other dissidents of Hitler's régime to escape across the Channel. He was also one of the few who had survived.

As the train puffed along through the Kent countryside I felt the rising tide of excitement, no different from what it had been years before. Beside me I could hear Nicky patiently teaching Christopher his first words of English. 'Hallo, Granny, I am a little German boy. No, no, not Tsherman, Stophi, J-J-J-Jerman. Now, try again.' Not exactly a very appropriate start I supposed, but never mind, Nicky's accent was still excellent and anyway the clatter of points told me the track was widening – the train was slowing down – we only had another ten minutes to go, I knew it all.

The platform at Victoria Station was crowded with eager, anxious faces expectantly scanning the carriage windows as they passed. A crowd with a difference in that huge moustaches seemed the rage. One particular young man in uniform and similarly equipped seemed to have seen his loved one as he ran along beside our carriage, dodging and smiling and waving his cap. When the train jerked to a stop, to my surprise he flung open the door to our compartment, jumped on board the train, gave me a big kiss and announced happily, 'Well, well, I'm the lucky one,' and then he added, with a laugh, 'don't look so dazed, darling, it's just me, your little brother John.'

It was then his turn to look somewhat taken aback when my elder sons filed out after me and with due respect to his uniform clicked their heels and bowed, and Christopher, not to be outdone, intoned his message of greeting, 'Hallo, Granny, I am a little Tsherman, *nein, nein,* Jerman boy.'

But John took it all in his stride. 'We've all been rushing around from station to station,' he said. 'No one seemed to know where you were landing, but Dad's been alerted and he's on his way from Paddington now.' And even as he spoke I could see another tall figure pushing through the jostling, joyous crowds. Unchanged by the years, it was my father. 'God in heaven, Chriskin,' he said as I rushed forwards and flung my arms around him. 'Dear God, it's wonderful to see you.' And as he held me tightly in a well-remembered hug, I knew that I had come home.

Chapter Three

In the year 1945, after the killing ceased, all of Europe's uprooted and scattered peoples seemed to be heading for home. Some for homes no longer to be found under the rubble, others for a haven, an ultimate goal – some promised land in which they could build up their lives all over again.

It was a time when the concept of Home took on almost transcendental qualities – 'There's a long, long trail awinding to the land of my dreams'; 'In der Heimat, der Heimat, da gibt's ein Wiedersehe'n'; 'Dans un coin de mon pays'.

I was one of the privileged few, able to head for home in a country where sixteen miles of water and an island people defending themselves with dogged determination had resulted in most homes remaining intact.

Six long years, and again I was lucky for I found that my father, my mother, my sister and two brothers, all of my close family had survived. Not everything was quite the same: because of the proximity of a military air base and resultant bombs in the grounds, my parents had sold our home near Hatfield and were living in less luxury in Codicote, a Hertfordshire village near Welwyn.

My mother only once confessed to a further reason for leaving her home which was that after listening to the thundering overhead as the heavy bombers left for Germany and, mission accomplished, returned again in the early morning, neither she nor my father had been able to sleep all night.

Instead of a flock of retainers, my mother's household now consisted of one faithful and much loved relic of the old days, and two daily ladies who whisked about the place with much enthusiasm, busy in the limited hours at their disposal at what they called 'clearin' up'.

Nor, of course, had we ourselves remained unchanged. My eldest brother Basil, much loved because of his mindfulness as to my well-being when I was doing my first 'season', had married a very beautiful, but somewhat temperamental Russian girl soon after he came down from Cambridge, and it had not been long before they parted company. When war broke out their little son Richard was being cared for by my parents, and my brother, although he should have been dealing in antique furniture for which he had a unique flair, was for some reason or other trying to write a book. Now he was a full-blown colonel, having survived several years of desert warfare in Africa, which I considered some achievement as I could well remember him returning from an OTC (Officers' Training Corps) camp when still at public school, declaring that as far as he could make out the first order to be given to troops if they found themselves in some awkward military situation would be to 'dig latrines'.

My red-headed sister Barbara, whose escapades at boarding-school had not always been much appreciated by a supposedly responsible elder sister, had married a glamorous Australian air-man, an Imperial Airways pilot whose base was to become New Zealand. In 1939 she had left with three children and a retinue of nannies and undernannies for the other side of the globe.

When the Japanese entered the war and there were fears of a possible Japanese invasion into New Zealand, her husband, by then an officer in Transport Command, had packed his family into a bomb cradle and flown them to Canada. She had remained there until Transport Command also flew her back to England some weeks before my arrival. She had anticipated the situation by collecting bunk-beds from deserted air-raid shelters and installing them wherever she could find space in my parents' house. As for her tour of the globe, she was heard to declare that as far as she was concerned the inside of a sink looked much the same anywhere in the world.

My younger brother John had been called to the Army when his medical studies were only half-finished. A gay young fellow then, much loved by ladies of all ages, he had been taken prisoner after the landings in Italy and found himself appointed as sole medical officer to a huge POW camp in Germany. It was filled with Polish and Russian prisoners, many of whom should have lived but were doomed to die because suitable medical supplies were either insufficient or non-existent. Doomed to die, sometimes in much pain, because he, the doctor, had no pill or potion with which to keep them alive or ease their going. He was quiet now and rather serious, sometimes staring into the fire as if his thoughts were far away.

My sister's and my children had been little more than toddlers when we left; they were bouncing seven to ten year olds when we returned. The Australian contingent, two girls and a boy, were splendid specimens, equipped with a repertoire of expletives, some of which I had never heard in my life before. This did not deter their German cousins who, although unable to compete, seemed only too willing to learn. An exception was my youngest son, Christopher, aged three, who obviously considered anyone who could not understand the Black Forest dialect to be so dense that they were not worth talking to at all.

Now we were back, and in spite of the initial disappointment at the change in surroundings, I was only too ready to allow the long years of separation to drift away, at least temporarily, into a mist of forgetfulness. I was among my own again, a listener to familiar voices, catching up with a particular family idiom, suddenly overcome by half-remembered smells. Banish the years, I was home, young once more with no responsibilities and there were flowers on the mantelpiece in my bedroom.

The fantasy could not last, for it was not very long before it became clear to my sister and to myself that our mother had nobly bitten off a good deal more than she could chew.

She was a natural home-maker, firmly believing that a home did not consist of merely a roof and four walls, but also of what she called 'those extra bits and pieces' which was her uncomplicated way of describing a certain ambience, a safe and changeless rhythm, generated by both of my parents, which had helped us to grow up and face what was to come, from a background of total security. But although my father, who did not have to suffer it all day, seemed to enjoy the hubbub, I doubt if she had ever dreamed of her orderly home being turned into a multilingual beargarden.

In fact she was already beginning to talk about having to build another house when my sister and I realized that we must stir ourselves and do something about it instead of sitting around talking our heads off over endless cups of tea.

We must learn to accept that not only home conditions, but that England, too, had changed. In Germany I had become accustomed to trying to get around every rule in the book. In post-war England everyone seemed so law-abiding, so virtuous. In Berlin, queue-busting had been one of my favourite pastimes. It was quite a simple game which could start perhaps with a box of fresh spinach or anything unusual in front of a foodstore. Such a delicacy hardly needed to be put on display before a queue of determined *Hausfrauen* seemed to erupt out of the ground and start automatically on the slow shuffle towards a chancy meal. When the shopkeeper's supplies were diminishing by the minute, it was time for the game to start with a discreet murmur to the lady ahead of or behind me: 'Do you remember last week trying to get near those carrots – and we'd hardly arrived up at the front when that black Mercedes rolled up and the chauffeur got out and swiped the lot – I wonder where they went?' If the response to this opening gambit was positive – the neighbour in front or behind murmured back, 'I don't wonder, I know' or perhaps, *'Unerhört'* or, with luck, even, *'Schweinerei'* – my morning was made, for I knew that, with a little encouragement, the solos could become a chorus, shopping bags potential weapons. A horde of steely-eyed housewives were ready to go on the rampage and should a glittering Mercedes dare to draw up anywhere near the foodstore, the driver in his black uniform would be lucky to get away with his life. Meanwhile, she who started the rumpus could stroll forward and collect whatever it was she had been queueing for.

In England there was so much to learn – or unlearn. No black market; no scrounging for that little bit extra on the ration card; queues, however long, must be treated with respect. It started at the bus-stop, where instead of the frantic pushing and shoving in order to get on board that I was used to, civilized behaviour meant waiting in a queue. Wait, now wait, until the conductor's bugle call sounded 'Full up', to put you dutifully back again in your place on the pavement.

It was when standing immobile in such an orderly procession, with my feet getting colder by the minute, that I found myself trying to make out just what had happened to my country. England had won the war, the boys were coming home again, the bells should be ringing out, everything should be so joyous, and yet it was so very dull. I could only come to the conclusion that maybe the effort had been so great that now everyone was simply tired out.

With Christmas around the corner, the newspapers excelled themselves predicting one catastrophe after another waiting to engulf us. The coming winter was to be the coldest in living memory; an influenza epidemic of dire proportions was also on its way; due to a state of near-starvation in Germany, the rations in England could not be kept at the same level for much longer.

There was no official way of communicating with Germany until the victorious powers made up their minds about a Peace Treaty. I knew that cigarettes were hard currency in the Fatherland, so that all I could do about 'near-starvation' was to beg anyone in uniform who happened to be travelling that way to take with them as many cigarettes as they could stuff into their duffel bags and give them to Peter. The lack of any message in return seemed to indicate that they had not arrived at their proper destination.

The day arrived when my mother and I were seated alone at the breakfast table dissecting a pat of butter into minute portions destined to last the family for the day. I knew that we were both thinking about my sister. She was with us yesterday, why not today? The opening door gave us the answer as she stood there shivering and shaking, her cheeks about the colour of her hair. The 'flu epidemic we had been warned about had arrived on our doorstep a week earlier, and now it was only for the coldest winter in living memory to follow suit in order to complete the newspapers' predictions.

'It's a sort of ten green bottles situation – then there were only two,' remarked my mother rather wearily as she packed my sister off to bed to join the rest of the household in awaiting the arrival of an over-worked doctor whose sole prescription consisted of bustling from patient to patient telling them in breezy tones to 'Cheer up'.

Left on my own at the breakfast table I found myself staring disconsolately at the tiny blobs of butter lined up in front of me and I knew that my usually fairly dependable spirits were sinking so fast that it could not be long before they reached rock bottom.

So this was the home that I had dreamed about. No matter how often I reminded myself that I was privileged and surely ungrateful, it had to be faced that I had wasted a great deal of time longing for something which could never return. It was nobody's fault but my own that I could not adjust to a new situation. I was a survivor, oh yes, but I was branded by Hitler, by war, by failure, almost by the fact that I had not ended in a gas chamber. To add to my troubles I was very likely to get the 'flu.

If you have been given an almighty fright make a rush for the nearest lavatory; when in trouble go for a brisk walk. Two oft-repeated axioms learned in the nursery flashed across my mind and I decided to leave the family rations to look after themselves – they could melt if they felt like it – but I would head for the garden.

I pushed back the curtains, opened the french windows and stepped out, to be greeted by a blast of ice-cold air which nearly took my breath away. The lawn was no longer green and welcoming as it had been yesterday, but stretched out before me, cold, rigid and white as a deserted ice-rink. Not to be deterred I stomped over to the low wall which overlooked the main road to the village where muffled figures in army greatcoats were busy removing the remains of some lumps of concrete. These, I had been told, were intended to protect Codicote from an invasion of German tanks; the war, including its absurdities, was still with us. Back then past a bed of dahlias, ablaze with colour yesterday, but which had suffered an overnight defeat, and were now jet black. Some roses seemed to have survived the sudden winter onslaught, but this was not surprising seeing that they had also managed to outlive the mis-kicked footballs of our children.

By the time I passed through the vegetable garden and arrived at the plot where my parents, determined not to go under, had decided to build a small house for my sister, I realized that this relatively straightforward cure for low spirits was beginning to make itself felt. After all, things were not altogether hopeless. In our efforts to lessen the burden on our parents, my sister and I had decided that our boys at least must go to boarding-school. We had found one in Pyrford where the headmaster, a Mr Pooley, faced the prospect of trying to educate two little Germans and one Aussie with complete equanimity, assuring us that he found the prospect not only interesting, but exciting. He would have no difficulty with Nicky, who was British born and since his arrival had slipped into the scene as if he had always belonged.

I was not so sure about my middle son, John, as he still referred to Berlin as home and when his English was challenged or laughed at was inclined to reply with his fists. As for Christopher, a sturdy three year old, we could perhaps persuade Madi, a former governess, to take charge.

Briskly now, Chris, briskly. Once more round the garden and by the time I was back near the house I was practically running, glowing all over from the crisp cold air and a newly discovered sense of purpose.

Up the stairs with the breakfast trays, and it was almost as if several nebulous hopes and half-cooked plans were already on the road to possible achievement.

Gently, now gently, one thing at a time. Firstly, I decided that I must do something about regaining my British nationality. I was fed up with being German, and the law of the land now allowed me to do so. Then, I would try to communicate with someone whom I had not seen since before the war when Adam brought him to our house in Berlin and described him when we met for the last time, as possibly the only real friend he had left in England: David Astor, a son of Nancy Astor whose parliamentary forays, according to an uncle of mine, were guaranteed to liven up the place. I could remember David as tall, fair haired and boyish looking, whose shy, almost diffident manner belied not only a shrewd knowledge of the political scene, but an instinctive understanding of the situation in which we found ourselves. It was July 1939 and his visit had done us all good, lifting for a while a sense of helplessness and isolation, as Hitler's war crept up on us, nearer and nearer, day by day. I had reason to believe that Adam had made contact with him during the war; as I galloped up and down the stairs with those breakfast trays I made up my mind to do likewise.

A telephone call, and two days later the Green Line bus rattled me off to London and deposited me back in Codicote in the evening. The hours between passed quickly for Adam's friend had hardly changed, except that he had since married and was now Foreign Editor of the *Observer*. The same boyish good looks. The same shy, almost self-effacing, manner, but, above all, when it came to problems, I was to meet with a unique sense of personal involvement and an immediate searching for some solution. I could well understand why Adam considered him to be someone very special.

I considered that I had plenty of problems. How was I to relieve my parents' household? Get back to Germany even temporarily? In moments when I felt extra privileged, I had even wondered about trying to do something for the widows and children of the 20th July Plot, some of whom were in dire straits. But what was the use? How could one launch into such things? David Astor seemed to take all such matters in his stride. I must of course first regain my British citizenship, after which he managed to persuade me with infinite tact that his newspaper was in dire need of a correspondent with knowledge of the German scene who could also speak the language fluently. He was even willing to tackle the problem of helping the 20th July widows, which he considered to be a splendid idea. The British were compulsively generous; they just did not know that there had been a Germany other than Hitler's. Such a venture could become a bridge, bringing English women, possibly also war widows, together with Germans who were likewise having to face up to life alone. It must be a Trust Fund with charitable status. Victor Gollancz, who had founded the charity 'Save Europe Now', would be the man to give us advice as to the setting up of such a Trust. We must have a Patron, and Lady Cripps, wife of Sir Stafford who was now Chancellor of the Exchequer, would be the ideal person. Both she and Sir Stafford had known and always trusted Adam during the war, and a letter to *The Times* signed by her would be just right to get things started. He knew of another girl, Diana Hopkinson, who would be only too willing to help. An address? We could use the *Observer*.

I had little to offer in return beyond giving him as clear a picture as possible of the life we had led since our last meeting, and as the daylight faded and the London lights came to life (not quite as brightly as in days gone by), he listened to me in complete silence, not stirring, just glancing at me now and again with an expression on his face as if he were having to go through some of these things himself.

As I lay in bed that night random thoughts passed through my mind, one almost making me want to laugh aloud. As an Official Correspondent for the *Observer* in Germany, I would have to wear a uniform; my brother John had already offered to lend me his battle jacket. Non-fraternization was the order of the day in Germany though and it was strictly forbidden even to smile at a German, let alone embrace one. What in God's name would be Peter's reaction at having to meet up again with his lawfully wedded wife dressed up in such singular fashion? But I had relearned today that problems were there to be overcome, no more useless moaning, no more uncertainty. I was back on course again and I turned on my side and was soon fast asleep.

Chapter Four

The plane which transported me back to the Fatherland some weeks later was much the same as that which I had boarded with the children many months previously. Transport Command, no comforts provided, everyone in uniform, including myself. Our destination was Hamburg and I had been careful to pack an extra supply of cigarettes in my duffel bag in the hope of dumping them with Peter's mother who lived in Aumühle. To judge from the shape of the boxes and bundles strewn about by my fellow passengers, their contents were not dissimilar. I was a little unsure about my get-up, except for my beret with its golden 'C' badge on a green ground which I thought rather smart. The rest of my rig-out was borrowed, and at the last minute my elder brother, who had never felt warm since leaving the desert, had insisted on my taking along his army greatcoat which was far too big and troubled me with the thought that the whole ensemble made me look rather like Hermann Goering. But on this, my first journey back to Germany, I had a good deal more to think about than my appearance.

True, after my first bus trip to London when David Astor had picked up the pieces of my shattered morale and launched me on this unusual expedition, I could be glad that things on the home front seemed to be sorting themselves out. Perhaps the elements had something to do with it, for, as if trying to compensate for the atrocious weather served up during the winter, spring had burst upon us quite suddenly; an English spring bringing with it all the warmth, life and colour which I had so often dreamed might come my way again one day.

As the weather picked up, the congestion in my parents' house and the temper of its occupants improved likewise. It had not taken too long before my elder boys, who had been going to the local day school, were able to speak quite passable English and, with the language barrier behind them, they were teaming up and becoming good friends with their cousins. They all now had bicycles provided by my long-suffering but also cunning parents and seemed willing to sacrifice their footballs and depart on long trips around the countryside. They had also set up a putting green on the lawn which gave my father much pleasure as he was a superb golfer and, far from flailing each other with golf clubs, they, particularly Nicky, seemed eager to learn the game.

My indefatigable mother, in spite of her moral principles, had managed to bypass building regulations and obtain permission to build what she called an 'experimental house'. Nobody knew exactly what was to be experimental about it, but before I left, the foundations were already laid and there was plenty of activity going on at the far end of the vegetable garden.

My sister's and my plan to send our school-age sons to boarding-school had also worked out well, and a fortnight before my departure, they, too, had left for Dane Court, a prep school in Surrey, wielding their brand-new tuck-boxes and looking surprisingly British after exchanging their leather pants for grey flannel suits and round, rusty-red school caps. A subsequent telephone call had assured me that they were 'settling well', whatever that might mean, but I could also gather from their accounts that the atmosphere in the school was such that they had met up with no national prejudice whatsoever. That left only Christopher – and here I had been lucky too when I managed to persuade our former governess Madi to come along, at least temporarily, in order to keep an eye on him. In my young days she had been supposed to teach us French but, as she came from the Alsace, she also spoke some German and, since she had never put the wind up any of us, I had to hope that all would go well.

I had applied to become British once again and although I had no passport yet, the fact that I could travel in uniform on a Control Commission pass seemed to indicate that I had already been welcomed back to the fold.

So far so good, but ever since I had accepted the *Observer*'s original offer with alacrity, a small, but increasing cloud was looming on the horizon. I had been fairly confident that my successful arrangement with Madi would survive even if I were not always there to give her a hand. But I had forgotten that in the meantime Madi, too, had grown older and was much less mobile, and even on my short trips to London I could sense my now four-year-old son had got her measure. Warning bells sounded ominously whenever I returned, giving me to understand that much though she loved us, it would not be long before she would find herself forced to depart from sheer exhaustion.

At David Astor's suggestion I turned up as frequently as I could at the *Observer*'s offices in Tudor Street in order to get some idea as to how a newspaper functioned. I always tried to be there on Thursdays, as that was the day when they held their weekly editorial conference. This rather splendid title proved to be a congenial get-together presided over by the editor, Ivor Brown. It took place in a small, dimly lit room around a long narrow table smothered with an assortment of books and papers.

The editor himself appeared to me at first to be a pillar of silence who, should he decide to interrupt the general chatter at all, would merely ask rather gruffly such questions as, 'Well now, what about Spain?' or, 'All right, let us turn to Africa'. As a raw recruit, I sometimes found myself wondering how on earth any newspaper, let alone one so prestigious, could possibly appear in thousands three days later. It needed quite a few such sessions before I realized how privileged I was to be among a team of young journalists who were already well on their way to becoming stars in their profession.

After a cup of rather wishy-washy tea which usually terminated the proceedings, I only had to climb a few flights of stairs in order to take part in a hive of activity of a different nature: the 20th July Memorial Fund which, like many another charity perhaps, had come to life by way of random thought; ours had been simply to try to find a way of diffusing the post-war atmosphere of hatred and mistrust which existed between Britain and Germany. We hoped to cross a divide by bringing English families together with German counterparts who had been widowed or orphaned after the failure of the 1944 Bomb Plot to rid the world of Hitler. When Lady Cripps and the Bishop of Chichester agreed to become our patrons, and an appeal signed by them had been launched in *The Times* as well as the *Observer*, the response had been overwhelming. So here, in an even smaller room which looked out towards the dome of St Paul's, I could find Diana Hopkinson battling with a typewriter she had not made use of since she was an Oxford student, and also Gritta Weill who had been seconded by the *Observer* to give us much needed help with the flood of letters and parcels which were arriving daily on the newspaper's doorstep.

There is something nice and exhilarating in doing what my mother would have called 'good works', so that, perched high above the city roof-tops, we certainly enjoyed ourselves trying to cope with the unexpected avalanche of good will. Even the return trip to Codicote no longer seemed so cheerless for, after reading some of the letters and sorting through the parcels, I was convinced that beneath the humdrum, clothes-coupon-clad exteriors of at least some of my fellow travellers, there must surely beat hearts of gold.

It was after one Thursday session that David told me that news had reached him which might mean my leaving for Germany as soon as possible. Political life there was seemingly beginning to stir, with some Germans already trying to start up new political parties, and he was thinking of having more permanent representation over there. Post-Nazi Germany was still practically an unknown political territory and as I could speak the language and knew the country so well I could surely be of help in providing reliable and trustworthy contacts. He was also concerned about Adam von Trott's family since, because of the postal censorship, he had had no news from them for some time.

So it was that in May 1946, all dressed up in khaki, I was air-borne, making my way towards Hamburg. In spite of the roar of the plane's engines, and my real joy at the thought of seeing Peter again, the sound ringing in my ears was Christopher's cry of 'Back soo, Mami, *bitte, bitte*, back soo' as he was led away by gentle enough guardians who in my eyes had suddenly become determined wardresses.

A message had been sent off to Peter telling him of my possible arrival, but I had no idea as to whether or not he had received it. It so happened that he had done and, with faithful Freda in tow, had managed to scrounge an old Volkswagen, and they had driven from Frankfurt since dawn in order to be in Hamburg on time.

The shock when we did meet was not too shattering as, not knowing of my outward transformation, he failed to pick me out of the khaki torrent which poured off the plane, and was about to leave the airstrip when Freda, not easily thwarted, spotted my pseudo-military presence, rushed up and flung her arms around me, greatcoat and all. Chatting away nineteen to the dozen, she danced along ahead of me towards the retreating figure of my unsuspecting husband and when we caught up with him we all simply burst out laughing.

We had not left all complications behind us however, as Peter, who had been up since dawn, was beginning to feel the strain of dodging behind giant military transport in a Beetle which had seen better days, and it seemed that both he and Freda had to be off the road by curfew time. So we decided that we would have to find some place to stay the night.

We had not yet quite realized the implications of our situation, so it was a bit disconcerting when we stopped before the entrance to an estate somewhere near Hanover which had obviously been requisitioned by the Allies. After much telephoning back and forth, the sentry at the gates informed us that I would be welcome to spend the night in the castle itself, whereas my 'chauffeur' and my 'secretary' could only be accommodated in the sergeants' quarters which were situated somewhere in the stables.

My first night back in Germany therefore was spent in much luxury. Shades of my 'deb' days! Here was I toasting the King and chatting with fresh-faced, glossy-haired boys who, in spite of their immaculate uniforms, seemed equally overwhelmed by the elevated circumstances in which they found themselves.

Peter and Freda, for their part, enjoyed a far livelier evening, being fed to bursting with sausages and scrambled eggs, washed down with strong, sweet tea known as 'army brew' and later, after Freda had wisely retired to her quarters, with gallons of good strong ale. Such were the festivities that the following morning Peter could only remember rollicking out songs which repeatedly referred to some place called Blighty, and a final decision arrived at by one and all that it would not be long before they would all be marching together against the Russians.

On the following day we set off for Frankfurt and as our route brought us near to Imshausen, Adam von Trott's family home, we decided to make a slight detour and look in on Adam's widow, Clarita. It was a joy to find her reunited once more with her two little girls and also doing her best to come to terms with life without him.

After the failure of the 20th July Bomb Plot, Clarita had been imprisoned and the children removed from the care of their grandmother, given false names and transported to a camp for children on the North Sea coast. Rumour had it that Hitler had demanded that the offspring of such 'traitors' should also be wiped out. But there must have been some remnants of humanity left in a few of his underlings because the order was never carried out, and luckily for the little von Trotts, the sister-in-charge had carefully noted down all the real names of the children in her care. So shortly after hostilities ended, Elsa and Ilse could become Verena and little Clarita once again. Indeed, a few days before our visit, one of the guards who had fetched them away had returned to Imshausen to apologize for his deed. Adam's mother was a majestic figure and he confessed that he could not forget the look of utter contempt that had come over her face at the time, and her telling him that she had not thought that she would ever have to admit to feeling shame at being a German.

In Frankfurt I found myself billeted in the Press Camp which had been a former hotel and was near the main railway station. It was an important part of the city because it housed the black market which had become one of the busiest in post-war Europe. I had known of its existence before, but now it was just around the corner and from my window I could watch GIs by the dozen bargaining with the native Germans, mostly women, who turned up every day with their wares – jewellery, cameras, watches. If necessary, they included themselves in the deal in order to stock up with coffee, sugar, alcohol and, above all, cigarettes. Every so often an army jeep manned by military police would patrol noisily up and down the street and the crowd disappeared into doors and alleyways, only to reappear as soon as the crisis had passed.

I had found it difficult to conform to the orderliness of law-abiding post-war England, but now I was being confronted with another side to the picture, and could see for myself that when certain circumstances prevail, civilized behaviour can easily be cast to the winds.

In the Press Camp I could listen to an otherwise congenial fellow, willing to treat the Germans fairly, eager to show them what democracy was all about. But then there was the problem of that outsize cuckoo clock he'd found hanging on the wall of the flat allotted to him. His kids would go wild about it, but Uncle Sam would have to provide him with a crate to ship it home when he next went on leave to the States. He was not the only one to have problems, for according to allied directives non-fraternization was still in force. Peter could therefore not cross the threshold of the Press Camp which was off-limits to civilians while I, being part of the Allied Forces set-up, could not go home without an official permit to do so. Peter still lived in our little house in Kronberg looked after by Freda, as were other homeless refugees. She herself was awaiting the release of her husband, Hannes, who, although he had been one of the noisiest of our anti-Nazi friends, had been arrested by the Allies because of his rank in the Ministry of the Interior.

There are certain situations so absurd that no rule or regulation, however strictly enforced, can hope to be obeyed. It is then, I guess, that human judgement must come to the rescue. In our case humanity triumphed when Pat Nicholson, Dick O'Regan and Betty entered our lives.

Dick was a restless, go-ahead young journalist working for Associated Press, willing to jump a train, hitch a ride, barge in anywhere to pick up a good story. It was therefore heart-warming to see how much time he spent 'interviewing' Peter at just about lunchtime in the Press Camp or in the evenings when the bar was crowded and multi-coloured, lethal-looking concoctions were doing the rounds. Betty was working freelance, although instinct told me it would not be long before she became Mrs O'Regan. Pat Nicholson was a lovely-looking girl, whose dazzling white teeth and slim legs stamped her unmistakably as 'Made In America'. She held the rank of captain and a key position in the administration of the Press Camp, for she ruled over the office which dispensed passes in and out of the premises and could thus control where anyone happened to be at any given time.

'Gee, Chris, why that's a real laugh!' she remarked after hearing my unusual tale and, although otherwise scrupulous about her work, she proceeded to hand me out a travel permit whenever I needed one to wherever I wished to go; she also managed to provide transport whenever she had a jeep to spare.

From then on both Peter and I, motorized as often as not and armed with necessary travel permits, could move around as we wished, and naturally I headed immediately for our little house in Kronberg, where some of my civilian clothes were still hanging in the cupboard.

In Kronberg the house itself appeared to have become more like a transit camp than a home. Except for Peter and Freda's rooms, which actually contained beds, further furnishings in passage-ways and the attic seemed to consist of a jumble of mattresses and sleeping-bags, the odd chair and a lamp. The kitchen downstairs was the centre of a household where Freda, an enthusiastic but atrocious cook, spent much time dishing out curious messes which I could now augment with tins of US army rations. Thank goodness my love for Freda did not depend on her cooking. 'People come and go, you see, Chris, it's a roof and sometimes even quite warm and they don't mind a bit what they get to eat,' she would announce cheerfully, although even she had to admit that once, having boiled up some old fish bones and presented the result as *Bouillabaisse à la Rechenberg*, Peter had tried one spoonful and emptied the rest out of the window. 'So you see, your old pan with the somersaults came in useful after all!' she concluded with supreme lack of concern.

The only addition to the household and now part of the kitchen equipment was a rusty old sewing-machine which she told me she had picked up outside one of the requisitioned villas up the road. It had certainly seen better days and took up a lot of room, but I could not help feeling glad of it because it signified that in spite of our dire predictions, Freda had not given up her venture into dressmaking.

Chapter Five

My first assignment as a War Correspondent, if I can call it that, was intended to last some three to four weeks, after which I was due back in England for the boys' summer holidays. It did not take long before I began to feel extremely uncomfortable in my phoney rôle.

I was conscious that my main reason for coming back to Germany had been to see Peter, to discover how he was faring and, if possible, to plan with him some future for ourselves and our family. I could not type and had no idea how to manipulate the stops and wires which carried any useful piece of information back to the newspaper. True, unlike most other representatives of my adopted profession who had to pick up their material from informants able to speak their language, I could speak fluent German, and had some experience of the twelve years which had gone before. This should have been an asset; I did not find it so.

In fact as I travelled between the comparative comfort of the 'Ami Ghetto' and the underprivileged world outside, I found myself becoming increasingly confused and angry, and was probably not being fair to anyone.

On the one side were my American cousins, glowing with health, touchingly friendly, possibly lonely, but happy enough it would seem, so long as the *Fräuleins* were willing and the plumbing functioned smoothly wherever they were billeted. If they thought at all of the rôle they had been forced to play in reconstructing a new and democratic Germany, they had a further national obsession to call upon – 'classification'. How could you recognize a Nazi if you saw one? How to separate the wolves from the lambs? Quite simple really, Uncle Sam had the answer, classify the lot and proceed from there—

On the other side were the left-overs of the defeated Master

Race, drowning in self-pity, for whom a sympathetic ear in allied uniform was a chance not to be missed. I did not know Frankfurt well as a town, except that it had been the centre of Germany's huge chemical and leather industries, and having to watch the dismantling of their mighty empires must have been hard for some of its citizens to take. All the same, the ceaseless wailing coming from those whose finances might now be in the doldrums, but who had otherwise lived comfortably through the Nazi years, could succeed in bringing me to a point of near explosion.

'We who have so suffered, Frau Bielenberg, and are suffering now.' Suffered – suffering? My hat!!

Boys dying on far-flung battlefields had suffered – suffered in the desert and in the snows, and some were still suffering in Russian POW camps. What about the posters plastering the walls, the films from the concentration camps, the piles of starved skeletons, the gas chambers? This was no longer rumour, this was fact. To blazes with their complaints and their suffering! As far as I was concerned they could all take up their worthless share portfolios and go jump in the Rhine.

It soon became clear to me that, being not only underprivileged but constantly under their orders professionally, Peter had become almost hostile to the Allies. It just did not suit him to be an underdog and, in order to remain happy together, we decided that the allied occupation of his country should, if possible, remain a closed subject between us.

Our pact was not always easy to abide by, for clouds of misunderstanding threatened it from all sides. We managed fairly successfully until I was approached one evening in Kronberg by a gentleman whom I had seen there once before and not much liked. After drawing me aside he told me in a conspiratorial whisper that he had information to give me from an absolutely impeccable source which he felt I should know about.

It appeared that the British, instead of trying to feed their zone of occupation to the best of their ability, were allowing planeloads of food, particularly butter, to take off from Hamburg every day bound for London. Was he certain of his source? Indeed he was and if necessary could supply me with the times of their departure. I was deeply shocked, hardly able to believe that behind a smoke-screen of morality the British were behaving much like the French, who were systematically clearing their zone of wine and timber and anything else that they could profitably lay their hands on. The thought of those minute pats of butter at home flashed across my mind, but at least they turned up every morning, whereas I knew that even in the American zone many had not seen butter for months.

It was not easy to penetrate the security network with which the higher-ups in Military government surrounded themselves and the badge on my cap which betrayed my connection with Press and publicity was not helpful. So when I finally manoeuvred my way to my desired goal I was glad to meet a personable young officer who welcomed me to share his pot of tea. After the usual opening remarks about the weather, I asked him if he would perhaps tell me whether transport planes loaded with food were taking off from Hamburg or Bremen airfields every day. 'Oh yes, indeed they are,' came his prompt reply. 'Every day for the last fortnight,' – and their destination? Well, Berlin of course, had I not heard that conditions in the British Sector were far worse than in the American zone? 'We may have to step it up next week if I can get the Yanks to give us a hand with more supplies,' he added, obviously unable to fathom the look of profound relief which must have come over my face.

The sense of relief soon vanished; instead, long before I got back to Frankfurt, I was ready to explode.

I do not lose my temper very often but when I do I gather that it is better to keep out of my way, and allow me to bawl my head off for a while until I peter out. Only a year back this particular characteristic had come to my rescue just before my interrogation in Gestapo Headquarters when I'd been forced to witness a Gestapo woman slapping the face of an elderly prisoner sitting before her in chains. After that I had been scared no longer, but was able to bounce into my interrogation, borne on wings of rage.

Freda was cranking away at her ancient sewing-machine when I burst into the kitchen the following day. I was still on the rampage. 'Listen, Fredachen,' I announced in clarion tones, 'you may or may not have heard of the latest wild goose chase that stinker sent me on, but all I can say is I'm simply fed up. I've got to the stage of wishing I hadn't come, and I'm glad I'm going. OK, I can see from your face that you don't like him either – then why does he come here? Why does Peter have such bloody liars about the place? Why do I have to meet them and listen to their dreary complaints? Has he forgotten how it used to be? How can he surround himself with such second-raters? To listen to them

361

you'd think the Americans had started the whole business. I can assure you they don't want to be here either. They'd be far happier rocking on some porch in Ohio or some other damn place. Butter to London, for God's sake! Types like him would have been informers in the old days, ready to carry their snivelling little bits of information to the Gestapo.'

I sensed I was being unreasonable and probably also beginning to simmer down for I found myself adding more quietly, 'The real trouble is, Fredachen, Peter and I are drifting apart. I don't really understand anything any more. I know it's terrible to say so, but sometimes I don't care if I never see Germany again.'

Freda's machine had stopped its rhythmic clanking and she was sitting back, looking at me with eyes as clear blue as an autumn sky. She was also shaking her head as if she did not want to hear. 'Now, now, Chris,' she said. 'Take off your cap and sit down – that's better. Well now, let me do the talking for a bit. You've been here exactly a fortnight, and we were all just so happy to see you back but don't forget, Peter has been here for months without you, and although I know you both decided not to talk about what has been going on here in the meantime, I'm not so sure that it was such a wise thing to do after all.

'You see, Peter had to get a job of some kind and with his clean political record and his knowledge of English that was easy enough. I'm not sure whether he was already with the *Metallgesellschaft* before you left, but, if you remember, when I arrived on the scene he'd already been given the task of helping the Americans in what they were calling "de-Nazification". I know he took it on in good faith – you see, I think he feels as I do that anyone who has survived has a duty to do what they can – but I guess it was not long after you left before he wished he hadn't. I don't know if you have looked at the huge *Fragebogen* which has been doing the rounds since Christmas, well I have. It's a questionnaire which has to be filled out by everyone in the zone so that Military government can decide who has been a Nazi and who not.

'According to the answers received, the plan is then to divide the population into five categories from major offenders, lesser offenders, down to those who can be exonerated. Then the baddies will be punished, the goodies let off and that's that. It all sounds quite dotty to me – almost like trying to psychoanalyse a whole nation. Surely, Chrislein, you and I would have lost our touch if we couldn't spot a real Nazi if we met one, but no, they want it all in black and white. Listen to this one about religion. "With what church are you affiliated? Have you ever severed your connection with any church officially or unofficially? If so, give particulars and reasons." Oh dear, I remember that one because Furtwängler's Berlin housekeeper turned up here the other day and asked me to give her a hand with the questions as she couldn't make head or tail of most of them. She knew the answer to this one though and told me to write down, "I stopped going to church when an Allied bomb hit it and killed the parson". As you see, *Berlin bleibt Berlin*!

'But back to your poor Peter, he's in the middle of it, although he only has to deal with industrialists who either want to hang on to their businesses or start up new ones and can't do so unless they can prove a non-Nazi past. Let me tell you, dear, these are not friends about the place as we had in the old days – they died, Chris, they died, or are scattered to the winds. These I suppose could be called new acquaintances, most of them wanting Peter's help to start their lives over again and so long as they have a legitimate case he is willing to do so.

'One other thing which I only learned lately was that when the Americans occupied Italy they enrolled a whole lot of expatriate Italians into their administration and the result was fine. They could speak the language, they were glad to be back there and when it came to fiddling and diddling no one knew better than they how to cope with their former countrymen. So it soon became a very happy, not over-pedantic family set-up which functioned very well.

'I think they hoped to repeat the performance here in Germany with German expatriates but these were of course, unfortunately, mainly Jews. Well, you can't expect Jews to love us, Chris, and I guess you can't blame them if they throw their weight around. But the fact remains, most of them refuse to speak German and their English is as bad as my cooking. They expect Germans to stand to attention when spoken to, and they don't believe a word they say anyway.

'So think of your Peter, eager to get things right, who has never exactly been a paragon when it comes to patience, or for that matter being subordinate. Why he never even stood up when his interrogator came into his cell in Ravensbrück! "Stand up for that bastard, I just couldn't." Do you remember?

'I don't know if he told you about the incident the other day when he brought a case to whichever official was in charge of such things in Military government. I know he'd prepared it most carefully, all about some fellow who had joined the SS in the hope of protecting his half-Jewish wife and of keeping his brother-in-law's firm intact. He'd done nothing culpable and had succeeded in protecting his wife and her brother, but according to the *Fragebogen* the SS ticket was enough to deprive him of his livelihood and send him to jail.

'Anyway, this particular official listened to him in silence and said nothing even when he'd finished. So Peter suggested that if he couldn't understand English perhaps they'd better speak German. He told me he'd spoken very politely but somehow I doubt it. Anyway, at that the officer jumped to his feet and yelled "*Raus* – get out" – flung him out in fact, although I can't think he could have done much flinging as according to Peter he was small and round and looked as if he'd never worn a uniform in his life before. Peter left, but I'm afraid one of these days if something similar happens again he won't, he'll simply knock one of them over the head with his briefcase, and land himself in another detention camp – but an American one this time.

'So listen, dear, if you want my advice, here it is. Get him out, persuade him to get out if you can – and soonest.

'Just one last thing before I shut up. I think you should realize that there are plenty of love-sick females about the place just now and, except for the Americans, very few men. As you've doubtless noticed, Peter is very good looking, and if you are not around he's also, so to speak, available. I love you both but you can't expect me to remain a watchdog for ever.'

Freda had risen to her feet before delivering her ultimatum and was eyeing me sternly. But, even as she spoke, her expression changed from that of a miniature recording angel to one of amazement. I watched too, as, slowly yet purposefully, a strange, multi-coloured excrescence seemed to be pushing its way out from the innards of her rusty sewing-machine.

'It looks like a lump of squished cotton or something,' I said. 'We'll have to poke about a bit.'

But Freda was not listening. Instead she was banging the table and shouting quite as loudly as ever I had, 'Damn, damn, damn, damn! – damn this rotten machine – damn the Germans – damn

the Allies – damn the war, damn, well, damn everything!!'
Whereupon she sat down suddenly and burst into tears.

'OK, Freda – you win – I'll be back again after the holidays and
I'll try my best to get that exit permit for Peter even if it's only a
temporary one – my father's already doing all he can. I'm sure
there are others who'll give me a hand.'

I was trying with no success to be of some comfort until finally
all I could find to say was, 'Oh, do stop crying, or I'll start off too.'

So we mopped ourselves up with one of my brother's khaki
handkerchiefs and jabbed away together at that ridiculous lump
of cotton until it gave in. A minor mystery was solved when Freda
remarked casually that the eruption might have had something
to do with the scrapings off the frying-pan which, due to a lack
of oil, she had emptied into the contraption that morning. I defy
anyone to remain in the dumps after that piece of information,
and so it was not long before harmony was restored. As a result
of our combined efforts, the cogs and wheels were functioning as
smoothly as could ever be hoped for and we could rest assured
that with luck the fashion world need have no fears that Maison
Rechenberg's unique collection might suddenly go off the market.

Chapter Six

One journey which I knew I must make before leaving for England was to travel back to Rohrbach, even if I might feel rather foolish doing so in khaki regalia at the wheel of an American jeep. There was something about that small corner of Germany which I hoped might help to wipe away the artificial world I seemed to be living in and carry me back to simple sanity.

I wished I could have had Peter with me, but there was something about the French-occupied zone which he found uncomfortable. He was unable to communicate, and although he knew well how the Germans had behaved in France, it was not easy to experience revenge.

In the French zone little towns such as Furtwangen were still overladen with tricolours, but Spahis and Goumiers no longer roamed the streets, having been replaced by hordes of French civilians. This had come about because, as soon as the combat troops departed and the regular occupation forces took their place, they had been allowed to import their families: their wives, their children, their mothers, grandmothers, aunts, uncles, nephews, nieces – the lot. This pragmatic arrangement had possibly helped to solve the problems of food and housing shortages in France, but added an extra burden on those who were trying to live and make ends meet in occupied Germany.

Nonetheless I found the attitude of the Germans towards their conquerors healthier than in the other zones since they were not being asked to show a respect which they certainly did not feel. On the whole they seemed to take the view that 'we gave it to them, now they are giving it to us and no moral implications need be involved'.

Rohrbach itself had not changed at all, and except for the white table-cloth spread out in my honour over the Mayor's

Stammtisch (special table) and the wine glasses usually produced for weddings and funerals, the *Gaststube* in the Adler, which soon filled to overflowing, received me as one of its own again.

We had plenty to talk about although I had to re-accustom myself to the dialect in order to learn what had been going on in the valley since my departure. Sepp, in fulfilment of his prophecy as to his post-war activities made to me during the war, still mended shoes and manned the telephone, which he hoped might recover one day from the treatment it had received at the hands of the *Ingénieurs*.

The Mayor, whose re-election in spite of our intervention with the *Gouverneur* in Villingen had suffered a temporary set-back, had been forced into temporary retirement. But this was a problem soon solved by the villagers themselves who, by interpreting the newly established democratic process in their own way, soon had him back again at the head of their community.

Only Frau Muckle gave me cause for concern for she had aged considerably and lost weight, and her rheumatism seemed to plague her more than I could remember. Filled with hope, she still kept my cardboard Union Jack stuck up in the window, but after our departure this had not saved the Adler from being over-run with French troops. Some had behaved as soldiers sometimes do, spreading their bulky equipment all over the place, eating up her reserves, and were not averse to stealing.

I could tell that she missed us all, but my little son Christopher more than anyone else, for tears came to her eyes when she told me that in order never to forget, she and Martina had christened their latest kitten Christofli. As for Martina, she no longer talked of becoming a nun and I was certain that she would stay around feeding and caring for whatever livestock might be left to them, so long as Frau Muckle was in charge.

But for how long would that be? Only one boy from higher up the valley had returned from the wars to take up his craft as a wheelwright; no further news had reached her after that dreadful day when she heard that her son Ernst was 'missing' and I felt she had given up hope that he would ever return from Russia to take over the inn.

I wished for her so many things, even so far as wishing that I had a son old enough to carry on in Ernst's place.

But after two days I had to leave. I had a long journey before me back to the outside world, a different, for me almost unreal, world, which lay far over the horizon.

Halfway down the hill towards Schönenbach I pulled the jeep over to the side of the track and clambered out.

The snows had left the valley later than last year but cowslips were already pushing their way into the dark patches of pasture left behind.

After removing every spare part which might come in useful, the villagers had obviously shown no further interest in the crippled tanks and guns left behind by the retreating German army. Just below me lay one such deserted hulk and again it seemed that only a little bird found it useful for again this year it had decided to build its nest in the exhaust pipe.

As I steered my way down from the hills and back to so-called civilization, I was finding it increasingly hard to leave, so that by the time I reached Donaueschingen I decided to postpone my return for just a little longer and head towards Riedlingen and the nearby castle Wilflingen where I hoped to find Dölt and Camilla Stauffenberg, good friends from the Berlin days. Dölt was a cousin of Claus, whose bomb attempt on Hitler's life had so nearly succeeded and Camilla's family came from Northern Ireland; when I had last seen her she had been awaiting Dölt's return from England where he was a prisoner of war.

My transport in those days had been a bicycle and the journey had taken nearly a day, but now, behind the wheel of a jeep, I managed it in a couple of hours.

They were delighted to see me, particularly because Dölt, who had been released some days before, was enthusiastic about how he had been treated as a POW in England. It was only after my remarking that, in spite of all, I did not think that he was looking particularly healthy, that Camilla told me of his fate after leaving England. It would seem that along with other POWs, all of whom had been equally well treated before being sent back home, he had to pass through a British transit camp in Belgium. Here they had all been robbed of their few possessions, their watches, any money, and also practically starved, so that when they had arrived back by the trainload in Düsseldorf many were hardly able to walk. Camilla, in her quiet way, was obviously embarrassed at telling me this tale and as for me, I was frankly horrified.

On the long journey back to Frankfurt I found myself unable to keep it out of my mind, but as soon as I reached the Press Camp I thought I knew what I should do. I was, after all, supposed to be a journalist. How should I otherwise be tootling about in a jeep, waving and saluting, with a large golden 'C' on my silly cap? I had a story, I must contact my newspaper immediately.

I was no longer a complete beginner at the game, but I thought it best to make an initial, tentative approach in order to enquire if it was a story worth developing and, if so, whether they would trust me to carry it further.

If I had ever been in doubt, it was then that I became convinced of the supreme importance of a free press, not to mention in my case, a Foreign Editor bent on upholding liberal and democratic traditions. I was given the go-ahead immediately, and some days later was supplied with the number and location of this camp, the name of the Camp Commandant, and also that of a British Officer who knew of the circumstances and who, after being demobbed, had tried and failed to get any response from the War Office. I was also given an assurance that two Members of Parliament were lined up, ready to put down awkward questions in the House of Commons. One blank that still had to be filled in was to be provided by the War Camps Commission, whose Headquarters were in Berlin. My job was to listen, to record and to assure the Commission that whatever it had to say on the matter would also appear in print.

The Allied train left Frankfurt in the evening, rumbled through the night across what was left of Germany and arrived in Berlin the next morning. Somewhere near Hanover a substantial breakfast was served in a brightly lit restaurant car, and I was only too glad that curtaining covered the lower half of the window, so that those crowding the platforms of every station we passed through could not see what we had on our plates. Eighteen months previously I had been one of them, pushing and scrambling, overtired and hungry, and the journey had taken two days and two nights before we reached our destination. Now a uniform had somehow changed my status, but why that should be the case was sometimes beyond me, for underneath it all, I felt that I was still just me.

I was anxious to get to Berlin, firstly to see if anything was left of our little house in Dahlem, and secondly to discover if there were any friends still left alive in that reportedly devastated city.

As soon as the train reached its destination and came to a steaming halt, a motley crowd pushed forward to the doors and windows, hoping to earn a few cigarettes by carrying any baggage they could lay their hands on. As I stared out over the restless sea of grey faces, I noticed one who was smaller than the rest, less aggressive perhaps. He was wearing a German military cap turned back to front, on which was pinned a large cardboard identity number, very obviously of his own concoction. Despite this personal brain-wave, I could see that due to his size he was gradually losing ground and so, after waiting for the crowd to disperse, I stepped onto the platform and approached him with a request to carry my bag. '*Träger?*' I asked, and was reminded immediately and in no uncertain terms that I was back in Berlin. '*Träyer?*' he piped back as cocky as they come and in that unmistakable Berlin accent which my son John had not lost after months of living in the Black Forest. '*Träyer?* What do you mean? I have been promoted. I am now called, "Porter",' and his pronunciation of the word as he pocketed my packet of Luckys and whipped up my bag could not have been bettered had he been returning from a day's hunting in the Shires.

A message awaited me at the Press Camp that a car would be sent by the POW overlords to fetch me on the following day at eleven o'clock. I had the afternoon to myself and so I decided to make my way to Dahlem and spend some time in our little house there, alone with my memories.

It was summer and the unmistakable smell of pine trees from the Grunewald took me back very quickly to those years we spent in the Falkenried. As is often the case with memories, in spite of the bombs, the danger, the fears and the sorrows, it was only the happier ones which seemed to be waiting around ready to rise to the surface.

Our little house, which had managed to survive the final onslaught, looked shabby enough, but it was still intact. The garden gate hung askew from one rusty hinge, looking as if someone had given it an almighty kick, and the pathway to the front door was oozing with slippery brown moss. The house seemed to be occupied, however, as my knock was soon answered by an aggressive-looking character in shirt-sleeves, whose expression at the sight of my uniform changed immediately from one of hostility to that mixture of mistrust and servility which I had learned to dislike intensely. Mistrust predominated when I told him in German that I simply wanted to look around, as this had been my home.

From then on, a cloud of almost nightmarish quality went with me on my tour of inspection. When we had left Berlin many months – it seemed now decades – before, Peter and I had had to abandon most of our possessions: pictures, china, lamps, some furniture, pots and pans. In some way, we had both lost much feeling for possessions, but we were also naïve enough to hope that if a new family took over they would be appreciative of what they found, and take care.

A glance around our sitting-room put an abrupt end to such wishful thinking. It was bare of furniture except for a heavy oak sideboard and an equally heavy oak bridal chest, given to us by Peter's grandmother, peasant furniture from her homeland in Schleswig-Holstein. Highly polished matching suites in rose-wood and mahogany were all the rage when we married, but Peter and I loved different things and it seemed to me that there was something essentially reassuring about those sturdy pieces of oak. Wars and invasions had passed over them so often and now they had even succeeded in weathering this latest storm. For the rest, the parquet floors had been ripped up and doubtless used as firewood, and our small collection of Hamburg prints torn from the walls and slashed with knives. There seemed so little point in all this destruction that it was almost a relief to see from the window that our lawn had been dug over to make way for a patch of vegetables.

Meanwhile the man in shirt-sleeves, after shouting up the stairs that there were Americans about the place, had disappeared into our bedroom, which was on the ground floor, and locked the door behind him.

After leaving the sitting-room, I felt I'd almost had enough. But there was still the door to the cellar where we had stored apples and so often sat together trying to play Snakes and Ladders with the boys during the air-raids. So just in case something, a child's toy, anything really, might have managed to remain intact, I opened the door and peered down into the cellar. The stairs were strewn with broken glass and chips of china and at the bottom were the remains of what had once been our household goods and chattels, all smashed to smithereens. I went down the stone steps just in case, and came back up again with an egg cup and a breakfast plate which I wrapped up carefully in my handkerchief before leaving by one of the french windows and pulling shut the garden gate behind me.

An army car came to fetch me at exactly 10.45 a.m. the next morning. Our goal was the headquarters of the POW Commission. As we wound our way through the narrow canyons which had once been streets, I was given some idea of what had happened to Berlin during those last cataclysmic days when Hitler insisted that it should be defended to the last man.

'I guess the bloody bastard didn't realize what he'd started.' My driver came from Coventry and seemed to have some understanding for the ghostlike figures wandering aimlessly from one pile of rubble to the next. 'Some of the poor buggers don't seem to know where they're going,' he added, as he skilfully avoided one such sleep-walker heading straight for the bonnet of our car.

A pleasant young officer was awaiting our arrival at the bottom of a flight of stone steps which led into one of the few buildings left standing in the street. He escorted me to an antiquated lift which brought us to an upper floor. My hunch that I was being given VIP treatment was confirmed when the door was opened by a busy figure also in uniform; in fact, he was so busy being polite that he obviously did not realize that we had met before. This time he proffered a chair, asked me whether I would care for a cup of coffee, did I smoke, and finally cleared his throat and introduced me to three upright figures of obviously higher rank. They had risen to their feet as I came in and were standing, as if on parade, behind a trestle-table. The table was laden with three massive tomes, one of which was open.

Our conversation began with the usual remarks as to the weather and the pleasantness or otherwise of my journey, until one of the three came to the point and asked if and how they could be of help to me. So I proceeded with my tale, and on being asked if I could identify the camp, I was able to provide them with the details put at my disposal by the *Observer*.

I find there is something straightforward, almost simple, about a high-ranking soldier, from whichever nation he may come. Those before me were particularly good specimens, so that I almost felt sorry for them as they flipped back and forth through the pages of their massive tomes and finally came to rest at one in particular. My instinct told me then that they realized that the game was lost. One indeed asked if the camp were liquidated, would it not be possible for Lord Astor to forget about the whole thing, and here I had to deliver the final blow and tell them that the story would be published the following Sunday and that subsequent questions would be put to the House. Not being used to such things, I found it almost embarrassing to accept their gratitude for being granted space to provide their own version of the story.

Meanwhile, my own little side-show was progressing very favourably. The underling, who was plying me with coffee and cigarettes and had not been asked to take a chair, seemed suddenly to remember that he had seen me some place before. 'Surely, Mrs Bielenberg, we must know each other. I never forget a face,' he murmured in my ear as he put a match to my cigarette. 'Could it have been in London – Paris?' and I could answer coolly, before turning to his superiors, 'Oh yes, we have met, and it wasn't in London or Paris.'

The interview came to an end. 'Take Mrs Bielenberg to the lift, colonel, will you, and see her to her car.'

There is something similar, I discovered, in certain inter-national voices of command which expects immediate obedience and is used to getting it. My companion grabbed my briefcase and leaped for the door, and as he pattered beside me down the long passage which led to the lift, I could sense that he was in no way at ease. 'You know,' he insisted, 'you really have me worried, Mrs Bielenberg. I'm simply quite sure we have met before. Where could it have been?'

I am not by nature a vindictive person, but as I turned to look at him puffing along beside me carrying my briefcase, I could only wonder how often fate allows for such an unexpected day of reckoning.

'You should be worried,' I found myself replying. 'And don't bother to bring me to my car. It was Frankfurt, you see, some months ago, and at the time I was the poor fool who married a bloody German.'

My companion barely reached the lift and I was surely enjoying myself. As the old contraption descended to the ground floor and his head, stocky torso and his boots were cut off from view I realized that I was smiling; a sort of Cheshire Cat smile, and probably not a very nice one I could believe. For, beside my feeling that there was something theatrical about my uniform, I could also rest assured that my farewell message to the POW Camps Commission could be chalked up as a very effective closing line.

It was lunchtime when I returned to the Press Camp and the bar was crowded with journalists, some serious, some lighthearted, few able to speak German, many wearing service ribbons which showed where they had spent the last six years of their lives. They were also generous hearted, only too willing to help an obvious amateur bang the keys and file her story back to London in time for the following Sunday's edition.

'Have a G & T, Chris. You look a bit shattered.' I was not shattered. In fact, after downing a gin and tonic worthy of a confirmed alcoholic, I was decidedly elated. No longer a maverick but a Special Correspondent and, according to those experts, producing front-page stuff, which it proved to be. Now I could take an active part in a different world, perhaps, share the frustrations provided by sub-editors who, according to my companions, had nothing better to do than mangle the literary masterpieces they bashed out so diligently on their ancient typewriters day after day, night after night.

If I allowed my thoughts to wander to the scene outside, news stories were inadequate. Maybe one day I could go one bit further, try to explain and, if possible, make some sense of a theme which would probably never make total sense nor be explained away.

Before leaving Berlin, I had one further obligation to fulfil. It was to discover, if possible, the whereabouts of Alexander Werth. Alexander had been a loyal friend of Adam von Trott, working with him in the German Foreign Office. When a high-up Nazi was put in charge of their department and a bomb destroyed this gentleman's home, Alex offered to take him into his own flat, officially to show willingness, but unofficially to keep an eye on him. Alex himself avoided arrest after the Bomb Plot of 20th July, but fate caught up with him later when he was arrested by the Russians; he was now just another war criminal awaiting trial somewhere in some camp outside Berlin. I decided to try my luck with Alex right away.

It took me some time to persuade one of the taxi-drivers who waited with their ancient vehicles outside the Press Camp every day to take me to the Russian Sector of Berlin. The first one I asked flatly refused, saying that even if he didn't care that much about his life, he did value his taxi. The second seemed to wish that our Eastern Allies had remained on the far side of the Urals, and the third, after eyeing my proffered cigarettes, decided to chance it; at least, to get me there as long as I found my own way back. So, to the accompaniment of such ribald comments as 'See you again some day' and 'Hope you've got a few sandwiches with you', we set off for Karlshorst where the Russians had established their Headquarters.

We had hardly arrived at a large concrete structure, liberally decorated with hammers and sickles, before my taxi-driver, after wishing me luck, roared off and away in a cloud of dust, as if the devil were on his tail.

A lively throng of men and women in fur caps and shabby tunics were milling about in front of the building, laughing and talking, and as they did so, flashing at all and sundry an extraordinary supply of silver teeth. I did not know whether they were supposed to be guards, but if so, no one seemed to be taking their duty too seriously. In fact, had they been British soldiers, I reckoned only the inevitable football was missing.

Inside the gloomy interior, things seemed slightly more organized. A clerk lounging behind a desk appeared to understand why I was there and directed me up a stone staircase to a small office where an exceptionally good-looking young man with plenty of medals pinned to his tunic greeted me in excellent English. I had come about Alexander Werth, oh yes, he seemed acquainted with the case. He produced a pen made in Germany, offered me a cigarette made in America, listened carefully and proceeded to take down notes.

When I came to the end of my story, he rose to his feet, shook me warmly by the hand, and told me that he himself was not exactly the right person for me to deal with, but if I went along the passage and took the last door on the right, No. 225 – I could not miss it – I would be able to contact the exact official for my needs. I thanked him sincerely, wondering in truth why so much nonsense was being talked about Russian behaviour and inefficiency.

The room number at the end of the passage which he had given me proved to be a large hall completely void of furniture, except for rows of wooden chairs placed around the walls. They were occupied by chattering boys and girls, all in uniform, who seemed to move along in pairs from one chair to the next, until they reached the door at the far end when they disappeared behind it. After some minutes they reappeared through another door to be greeted with much laughter and back-slapping, so obviously delighted with each other's company.

There were no officials to be seen and, as everyone was speaking Russian, when I sat myself down at the end of the queue it took me some little time to make out what was going on. The wrong room? That could not be possible, for the handsome officer had definitely said the last one on the right and given me its number.

I was nearing the far door and the couple ahead of me were obviously becoming more excited and fidgety by the minute before I realized what might be happening and got up to leave. Whatever was going on behind that door had definitely nothing to do with Alexander Werth. In fact, I decided that it must be some kind of marriage registry and the absurd thought ran through my mind that if I stayed any longer I might find myself bigamously married to a Russian.

A quick visit back down the passage was enough to convince me that my self-appointed mission to help Alex had been a complete fiasco. No one was about; I was greeted with echoing silence, and the door to the office of my handsome Russian officer was firmly locked.

When I got outside the building an overcrowded tram was preparing to leave and a long queue was already forming, doubtless in the hope of getting the next one.

As we moved forward step by step I found myself standing beside a tall, slight girl who looked in some way different from the shapeless human bundles who were shuffling along beside us. She was not lugging the inevitable bulging sack, and her clothes were dark green; from Bavaria I could imagine for, although they were shabby and well worn, they were unmistakably well cut. 'I wish you had hurried along just that bit faster last year.' The voice beside me seemed to be directed at the ample back of the lady in front of us, but, to my surprise, was speaking English, which could only be meant for me. 'How do you mean? The Allies? The advance on Berlin? If so, I couldn't agree more,' I replied with some feeling, thinking of those days back in the Black Forest when we could only pray that the final storm would pass over us as soon as possible and leave us alive. The girl was now looking at me with a smile, a sad sort of half-smile, but she seemed to want to go on talking, to unburden herself maybe, in a language that only I could understand. 'Just another fifty kilometres, you see, and we could have welcomed everyone to my home. Instead—'

A tram came rattling down the track towards us and it was not until we found ourselves propelled inside and wedged in next to each other that she could continue. Instead – well, instead it had of course been the Russians, and her father could not bring himself to leave his lands. Her mother had died during the war and both her brothers had been killed on the Eastern Front. So, without his lands, without an heir, he had no particular reason for wanting to live anyway. No one had heard the shot with which her father had killed himself, for the Russians were practically at the gates by then and a lot of shooting was going on in the village. But a faithful gamekeeper had seen to it that the Herr Graf had a proper burial, whatever that might mean. 'Under one of his trees, I hope, I never had the courage to go and see.'

As for herself, she had been extraordinarily lucky. In true Prussian fashion, her parents always insisted that she spend certain days of the year in the kitchen quarters, learning to cook, learning to cope with the quantities of meat – hams and sausages – which needed smoking, and preparing to see the household through the winter; learning to get to know those who worked on the Estate, their *Leute*, their people, as she called them.

When the Russians finally burst in she retired to the kitchens, and although the work was hard enough, she was not molested, nor did she starve, for the cook was a natural martinet and soon managed to convince even the Russian soldiery of the need for orderly behaviour. 'No proper manners – no food' and that was that!

Luck, too, was on her side when the Russian commandant who held the rank of colonel moved in later with his wife and two children – a boy and a girl – and she was promoted to playing the rôle of governess. 'It was an extraordinary experience really, because although the children were not easy to teach – already somehow too spoilt – their parents were ardent learners and never failed to turn up every evening with their homework neatly completed.'

Her colonel and his family were now stationed in Berlin and had decided to bring her along with them. Beside the cooking and the cleaning and the supervising of their education, she was at present engaged in a rather bizarre extra task.

It would seem that one of the perks granted to a Russian officer was permission for his eldest son to wear an identical uniform, medals included, but, of course, in miniature. Father though had noticed that his offspring was not taking sufficient care of his get-up and came to the conclusion that the mess down the front must come about because of his son's habit of blowing his nose out of the window instead of using a handkerchief.

So *Fräulein* was summoned and expected to go into action. 'They didn't seem to have any handkerchiefs,' she explained, so, 'right nostril, foof – left nostril, faf.' My companion could not suppress a real laugh as she described her ultimate expertise in directing the seemingly endless flow of snot emitted by her charge; 'Out of the window, but not into the wind!' had been her solution.

The girl left the tram before it clattered its way out of the Russian Sector and into the British. As I watched her through the window, pushing her way resolutely along the crowded pavement, it occurred to me that although we had talked together in much harmony, I had not asked her name, nor she mine. Old habits die hard, for me as well as for her. We had been through so many years when mere acquaintanceship was simply not enough, could even be dangerous. It had to be friendship, real friendship, before the barriers fell.

After some months, Alex Werth was freed from captivity, and, being a truthful man, had to tell me that my visit had been of little help to him – in fact, to the contrary. The atmosphere between us and our Eastern Allies was no longer a warm one, it would seem, and in fact, my plea on his behalf had merely aroused extra suspicion.

Chapter Seven

It took several months before Freda's urgent advice to get Peter out soonest could materialize. My father was particularly active on our behalf which I found very touching, especially when I remembered his original anxiety about our marriage. Friends, too, helped wherever possible, but Allied directives were strict and the year was nearing its end before I could return to that Kronberg kitchen waving a travel permit to England for Peter H. W. Bielenberg, Doctor of Law. It was the first of its kind to be issued to a German civilian after hostilities ceased.

So much for the hopes of all those love-lorn German females Freda was so bothered about, that was a party! Hans and Ellen Eiche arrived with two bottles of superb Alsatian wine which they had discovered in father Eiche's cellar. They also had every reason to be cheerful because their little girl, Ursula, had recovered from meningitis after an American army doctor had provided me with penicillin which was otherwise unobtainable except on the black market, where the going rate per shot was an unobtainable ten kilos of butter. Bob Stephens of the *Observer*, Betty, Dick and Pat Nicholson, two other American officers and two from UNRRA, also armed with bottles, all seemed happy enough to forgo some PX meal and share with us an extraordinary mixture which Freda and I managed to cook up with everything we could find in the larder.

Some weeks earlier Peter had resigned from the De-Nazification Board without bloodshed and moved to the newly established Board of Trade, and, on hearing the good news, made a dash for the black market, spent a fortune and returned with a spectacular bottle of what was supposedly vintage brandy but which turned out to be cold tea. But nothing could dampen our spirits; even Hannes, Freda's husband, was persuaded to leave his philosophical studies in peace for an hour or so. He had been freed from jail in the summer after some effort I had made on his behalf and had since been banished to the attic along with a gim-crack typewriter which got on everyone's nerves but his own.

It was surely a good party and not without temporary drama for, doubtless due to those unaccustomed bottles, before it broke up there was some confusion as to the exact whereabouts of Peter's precious travel permit.

I knew that I could not stay in Frankfurt for long because just before leaving England a situation had arisen which I had seen coming all summer. Needless to say, it concerned my little son Christopher and his so-called watchdog Madi. Madi had managed to survive my absence in the spring but, on hearing that I might be away again and possibly for a week or so, she clutched her ample bosom and nearly had a heart attack on the spot.

My sister and I had done our best to postpone the day of decision by carting all the children off to Devonshire during the holidays in order to spend a fortnight by the sea in pouring rain. I would have preferred to take the children to Ireland, not because of the lashings of bacon and eggs and soda bread which were luring ration-weary Britons in droves to cross the Irish Sea, but simply because of my nostalgic memories of a happy-go-lucky island which belonged to my own carefree childhood. But back here in Codicote, having witnessed Madi chasing the little darling around the garden at lunchtime, teatime and bedtime, I was not really surprised when a week before I left she packed her bags and made her tearful goodbyes.

I know that I have a habit of leaving possible problems until the last moment, always hoping that some wonderful solution will come to my rescue but, beyond cutting myself in half, on this occasion I could find none. In fact, as the day for my departure drew nearer I was ready to stuff Christopher into my duffel bag and take him along with me, when my brother John, who had unbearable memories of public school, came up with a possible answer: A. S. Neill's boarding-school in Suffolk where the Founder and Headmaster was a pioneer in the science of education, allowing the pupils in his care to do more or less exactly as they liked whenever they pleased.

My interview with Mr Neill took place in his so-called office, seated on a three-legged sofa only kept on an even keel by a pile of books. He explained that the missing leg was the result of a minor revolution which had taken place in the school the term before, when some of the older boys had gone on the rampage, smashing windows, breaking crockery and chopping up their desks and beds. His response had been to provide panes of glass and planks of wood and leave them to repair the damage themselves which, as the days grew colder and their discomfort more acute, he assured me they had managed most successfully. He also assured me that the Junior School was still intact and on my rather dubious tour of inspection I found this to be the case: a warm, comfortable little house with plenty of toys about the place and a gentle nanny-like matron whom I trusted on first sight.

So Neill's school it was to be and thus Christopher took his first step on an unusual journey through eleven different schools before arriving sixteen years later at an Honours Degree in the Sciences at Trinity College, Dublin. I still wonder whether this unorthodox approach to a gratifying conclusion, although partly due to circumstances, did not also include my own indecision as a parent, after having the iniquity of the traditional educational system explained to me in much detail while sitting on a three-legged sofa in Suffolk.

But all this, as the Germans would say, was *Zukunftsmusik* – future music. For the time being it was 1946, I was in Frankfurt muddling my way along through clouds of uncertainties, and besides being the bearer of good tidings I had two further reasons for being there.

Firstly, as the weeks went by, it had become clear to all concerned that our fund to help the widows of the 20th July Bomb Plot was getting completely out of hand. Gritta could hardly get into her little office for the piles of parcels which were piling up daily, and poor Diana's typewriter was working overtime. We had asked Marion Dönhoff, a good friend of ours, to help from the German end, but she was starting up a newspaper and had hinted that she could no longer carry on. We would have to find someone else.

My second reason could become a little more complicated. It concerned a certain Gerhard Graf von Schwerin whom David had heard was in an American prison camp awaiting trial as a war criminal.

We had known Graf von Schwerin since before the war when, a young officer in the *Wehrmacht*, he crossed to England in order, as he hoped, to warn the British of what lay ahead should Hitler remain in power. He had not been alone in his belief that the British, instead of continuously negotiating *à la* Munich, should be persuaded to make some dramatic gesture. An envoy, preferably a general, should be sent by the King direct to Hitler in person, bypassing diplomatic channels, and carrying with him a simple message, 'One more move and it's war!'

It was, of course, questionable whether such a warning would have caused Hitler to hesitate, but there were many who thought it worth a try. Indeed, some days before war actually broke out, Peter had pocketed his call-up papers and set off for England carrying the same desperate, last-minute plea. Both Peter and Schwerin returned empty-handed: Schwerin, because the British High Command seemed to suspect something treacherous in his behaviour; Peter, because it was August and most responsible civil servants were away on holiday.

We had not seen much of Schwerin during the war as he seldom came to Berlin on leave, but it was not difficult to follow his career as he was transferred from battlefield to battlefield and was promoted to Major-General. This was because of the unofficial dispatches he sent to trusted friends on the home front. From Poland, from France, from Russia and finally from Italy, Schwerin minced no words describing conditions existing at the front, never attempting to hide his intense disapproval of excesses he believed to be prevailing behind the battle-lines. He was, in fact, one of those courageous and highly efficient professional soldiers who had found themselves caught in a dilemma, that of fighting for an overlord whose methods of warfare they knew to be despicable.

On his pre-war mission to England Schwerin had met with and sought help from David Astor, not so well known to me at the time, but someone I was learning to appreciate warmly as a friend who would never give up. David had trusted and liked Schwerin, who was now in Dachau, a former concentration camp transformed by the Americans into an internment camp for major war criminals awaiting trial.

There must be some mistake – something must be done. When it came to the value of friendship and to the possibility of injustice David was like a hound on the trail. So, although I could hardly believe that a practically unknown British war correspondent would find it easy to barge her way unaided into such a fortress and persuade whoever was in charge as to the wrongness of their ways, I knew the very least I could do was to give it a try.

When we discussed how best to start off on such a venture, Captain Register immediately came to mind and I remembered how he had stressed the importance of a rubber stamp when dealing with the Army; it was not long before David came up trumps with something even better. This was a letter of introduction and a request for assistance to my humble self, signed by Robert Murphy, Political Adviser to General Eisenhower.

This trip to Dachau had to be my first priority and as soon as Pat Nicholson could provide suitable transport, even including a chauffeur when she read my credentials and I told her of my goal, I left Frankfurt for Munich. By then, I was already armed with two further letters from amiable Generals who had taken note of Robert Murphy's signature and seen no harm in joining in.

My only experience of a concentration camp had been Ravensbrück where I had visited Peter in 1944. I was to discover that Dachau, even under new management, was just as sinister. The high wire fence with its watch-guard towers, the Nissen huts, all looked as if they had been there for a long time. Only guards in black battle-dress with MP blazoned in white on their steel helmets were more recent arrivals. As in Ravensbrück, the Camp Commandant had taken up residence outside the camp's perimeter and I experienced a strange sensation of *déjà vu* when I rang the doorbell of a neat villa and the door was opened by a short, fattish man with a cold blue eye and a shaven head. He was wearing a pair of the most highly polished army boots I had ever seen in my life. Why those boots and leather gaiters made such an impression I do not know, for it did not take long to discover that despite a certain swagger of authority, he was not too sure what to do with me once he had read my letters of introduction. His frequent, irresolute glances at the badge on my cap betrayed the typical response of all underlings whose common sense tells them to do one thing, but whose fear of reprimand from above causes them to do another. But it gave me much satisfaction that he did not seem to recognize the golden 'C' as being connected with the Press.

It would be wrong to pretend that my interview with Dachau's Camp Commandant caused me much misgiving. In fact, by the time he agreed to grant me a ten-minute interview with Schwerin, I was almost beginning to enjoy myself. It was hardly possible to believe that little more than a year had passed since I sat, numb with fear, awaiting my turn in the Prinz Albrechtstrasse Headquarters of the Gestapo; the scenario was so similar but the circumstances so very different. When we parted, a jeep manned by several guards was waiting to take me on my journey into the camp. Bulging rolls of barbed wire hedged us in as we wound our way from one narrow track to the next before arriving at what seemed the very centre of the enclosure. An open space, a parade ground perhaps, surrounded by the inevitable Nissen huts, with no sound coming from their boarded walls and wired-up windows, except from one where black-clad guards lounged about on the steps in the sun, and a radio squawked in the background.

The guards were obviously forewarned of my arrival, and the fact that one came forward to help me out of the jeep seemed to indicate that the commandant had failed to judge the insignificance of my rank or to make out the reason for my presence.

'Prisoner No. 75 will be over any moment,' I was told, and it was not long before an upright figure wearing one of those white sheepskin greatcoats provided (as often as not too late) for the German troops in Russia, emerged from between two of the distant huts and walked briskly towards us, carrying his cap under his arm.

'At last a general that looks like a general,' drawled one of the guards who was watching Schwerin's approach, and as he had just informed me that he sure liked my English brogue, I felt that things so far were not going too badly at all. However, one thing that I had not reckoned with was the profound shock my appearance would have on poor Gerhard. The last time we had met was in Berlin. He had been wearing civilian clothes which smelled strongly of mothballs and he had offered to hang them in the garden and borrow some things of Peter's for the afternoon. Now, having nodded to the guards and placed his cap (from which I noticed all insignia had been removed) on the table beside the door, his glance passed to me and he froze. For one dreadful moment I thought he might burst out, 'Chris! *Um Gottes Willen!*' or some such inappropriate greeting. But I suppose he had been a prisoner long enough, for he merely stood there silently, staring at me as if at a ghost, whilst sudden beads of perspiration appeared on his forehead, cheeks and chin.

'Ten minutes – OK?' The tension was broken by one of the

guards, and I could help out a little by addressing him formally in German.

'Graf Schwerin, I have been given ten minutes in which to discuss certain matters with you,' I said. Then, realizing that we might not be able to keep up this formality for long, and also that my confidence was growing by the minute, I turned to the guards and announced in my best 'English brogue' that I wished, of course, to speak with the General in private.

No one seemed to object, and we were ushered into a small adjoining room not much bigger than a cupboard, where the furniture consisted of a bench against the wall, and the décor was provided by a poster displaying two completely naked ladies laughing and waving, seated astride a bored-looking giraffe. The bench was needed by both of us because when Gerhard turned to take my hand, I realized that he was near to tears and his voice had almost deserted him. Finally, he managed to bring out, 'I'm sorry, Chris, what a welcome – but I had no warning – thought I was being summoned to an interrogation, and then you of all people – a friend and in British uniform. I'm really sorry.' Then, pulling himself together, he straightened his back and burst out, '*Um Gottes Willen!* Am I mad? What are you doing in this dump?'

'You're not a bit mad,' I assured him. 'It's just something that's wrong with the world.' And in order to give him time, I thought it well to repeat the remark the guard had made about him as he crossed the parade ground. Then, realizing that the precious minutes were passing, I hurried on to ask him whether in heaven's name he had any idea why he was there.

'I have none whatsoever,' he replied. 'I just know that I go from one interrogation to the next – no ill treatment, mind you – but just the same questions over and over again about places and happenings I know nothing about. I tell them so and I know they don't believe me. One of them even told me he'd like to meet the Kraut who knew anything about anything, and as far as he was concerned the whole race was a bunch of bloody liars. Now they've got stuck into a case where five hostages from some village near Brussels were shot on my express orders and I was never near the place. It's degrading – how could . . . ?' Gerhard jumped to his feet, and if the room had not been so small, I felt he would have started pacing up and down.

It was then that for me things started to fall into place. Gerhard was a professional soldier, equipped with all the nobler attributes of his class and profession and also some of the limitations. I could imagine that he was making a glorious mess of his interrogations because he knew he was telling the truth, was being dubbed a liar, and this was hitting him so hard that he was becoming almost incapable of defending himself.

'Listen, Gerhard,' I said. 'We're getting nowhere this way, and we haven't much time left. If you weren't where they think you were, are there any other Schwerins about the place?'

'Oh, yes,' he replied, 'there are lots of us around. We are a big clan.'

'No one in the SS, I suppose?' My innocent question almost seemed to make him jump, but he answered quietly, 'Yes, unfortunately, one.' And, as if still not understanding the importance of what he was saying, he added, 'I did not know him nor wish to know him. He may in fact be dead.'

'Good God, Gerhard!' Had it not been for the guards next door, I would have been shouting. 'Can't you see, dead or alive, he's the answer? Quickly – his name. It's mistaken identity.' I was almost stuttering with excitement as I gave him my notebook and he began to write down a name very slowly, much too slowly, as if almost ashamed at having to do so.

I could hear chairs being scraped back along the floor of the room next door as I opened my briefcase to stow away this precious document. It was then that I came across the five cartons of cigarettes I had brought with me in case of emergency. I had forgotten about them – how maddening – and now it was too late.

But I had not reckoned with a newly resurrected Graf von Schwerin, and it was my turn to be amazed.

'Quickly, can you . . .?'

'Can I not?' he answered briskly, and in a matter of seconds he stuffed two cartons down each sleeve of his sheepskin greatcoat and one into his belt and was standing before me as if he had not moved a muscle. As the door opened and a guard called out that our time was up, Gerhard was grinning like a schoolboy and managed, in spite of the stuffing, to bow and kiss my hand.

'Goodbye, Mrs Bielenberg, and thank you,' he said, and added in English, before leaving on what I felt might be a chancy crossing of the parade ground, 'at last a General who knows what he's doing.'

Some six weeks later, a long letter from Gerhard von Schwerin was left for me at the Press Camp. He had been released from Dachau and was driving trucks for the Americans. He seemed to think that I had played some part in saving his life, but I knew that without that inimitable rubber stamp, I would have got nowhere, and he might still be shut up in Dachau, wondering why.

After what I hoped had been a worthwhile effort I still had one more task to fulfil before I could leave Germany, and as Peter, too, had to sort some things out before retiring from the Board of Trade, I decided to head off for Hamburg and discuss the future of our 20th July Memorial Fund with Marion Dönhoff herself. I found her in fine fettle as her newspaper, *Die Zeit*, which appeared once a week was already becoming well established. The first edition had indeed been a complete sell-out and the enthusiasm of her colleagues was only slightly tempered when they were informed in true Hamburg fashion (Hamburg being a city where high spirits are not really approved of) that this initial success was not surprising as they happened to have chosen a day when the fish market was doing business and, wrapping paper being scarce or non-existent, they could reckon for themselves what use had been made of their literary efforts. The name she gave me was of a Graf Hardenberg who was the administrator of the Hohenzollern Estates. I was frankly a little surprised that such things still existed, for having been a small child in the First World War and having burned the effigy of the Kaiser every Guy Fawkes' Day during my childhood, I thought we must have got rid of the Hohenzollerns and their possessions for good and all. But it seemed that Graf Hardenberg's wife was showing lively interest in the 20th July Memorial Fund and the address Marion gave me in order to contact her was in Berlin, from whence it would seem her husband administered whatever remained of the Kaiser's goods and chattels. I decided, therefore, to make straight for Berlin before returning to Frankfurt.

In the *Reichstrümmerstadt* (State Rubble Town), after wandering up and down several nameless alleyways, unoccupied, except for where an unexpected chimney thrust its nose through the rubble, and drifting smoke seemed to indicate that human beings could be living underneath, searching for the address Marion had given me, I decided I must have been right about the Kaiser, or at least he must have moved house. I was, therefore, taken aback when, passing the shattered remains of a tree, I saw a neat notice pinned to its stump: No. 75. There could be no doubt about it, nor about the arrow pointing to the left at what seemed to be just another mountain of bricks and mortar.

On closer examination, I discovered that the arrow was pointing towards a narrow passage, skilfully cleared of rubble and laid down with paving stones from which every speck of dust had been brushed. By the time the twists and turns brought me to a highly polished door and a radiant brass plate indicated that I had reached my destination, I was ready for almost anything, although hardly for my tentative knock to be answered immediately by a spruce figure whose glossy shaven pate was devoid of hair except for a neat tuft on the top which was parted expertly down the middle. He was wearing some kind of uniform which included highly polished leather gaiters and white cotton gloves.

'The *gnädige Frau* is expected and is welcome,' he announced, addressing me in the third person, which I seemed to remember as being a somewhat out-dated procedure still preferred by the more die-hard members of German nobility when being spoken to by an underling.

'Would the *gnädige Frau* take a chair? Would she care for a cup of tea?' As he ushered me into a small dark room and steered me towards two chairs and a large refectory table which seemed to complete the furnishing, little did he know that he could have added, 'And would the *gnädige Frau* now like to get the shock of a lifetime?' For, when bustling off to a further door telling me that he intended alerting the *Herr Graf* of my arrival, he reached up in passing and pulled on a piece of cord which had the instant effect of flooding the room with bright light. The transformation did not come from above me, but, to my horror, from a full-length, fully illuminated wall portrait of *Seine Kaiserliche Hoheit* himself – Kaiser Bill – Big Willie, the bogeyman of my early childhood. There he was, just as I had known as a child he would be, with his golden eagle atop a brass helmet, his white uniform ablaze with coloured sashes and brassy medals, but, above all, his cadaverous face, his cold brown staring eyes and his moustache trimmed like the letter 'W'. No wonder I had never dared have a bath on my own in those days of my childhood for there was always that narrow space between the bath-tub and the wall, and who could promise me that one bath-night the dreaded monster might not manage to ooze his way up it, helmet and all, before I could grab my towel and make for the nursery!

A ghost was laid when Graf Hardenberg appeared and proved

to be a tall, slight, very gentle person. He did not look well fed, his clothes hung loosely about him and one empty sleeve was tucked into his jacket pocket. But he was genuinely grateful that such a fund as ours had been started, and for him it was nothing less than miraculous that the response from ordinary English people had been so immediate. He knew that his wife, who had many personal friends among the widows of those who had been hanged after the failure of the 20th July Plot, would be overjoyed to play her part. Such was his enthusiasm that when I got up to leave, I was convinced that our somewhat amateur venture at reconciliation was worthwhile, and almost felt like cocking a well-deserved snook at Big Willie, who, during our talk together, had remained immobile, staring sternly down over his countryman's shoulder, as if rigid with disapproval.

Graf Hardenberg took me to the door, apologizing for being unable to accompany me further. As we stood in the doorway, a shaft of evening sun lit up the ruins about us, casting weird silhouettes against the clear Berlin sky. A windowless wall, a rickety chimney stack like a hunchback cripple, looking down over huge grey boulders which might have belonged to some retreating mountain glacier. 'We Germans have got to calling this time, *Die Stunde Null* – zero hour,' my companion remarked as he kissed my hand and asked that God might bless our efforts. Then he added with a sudden smile, 'But maybe our meeting here has started something new. Let's call it from now on *Die Stunde Eins.*'

When I arrived back at the shattered tree stump, the sun had set, evening was closing in and a rather beautiful pink glow lit up the stark outlines of the rubble summits, last to catch the evening light against the still cloudless sky.

As I set off rather hesitantly back down the pathway I had come by, I was beginning to wonder how I was going to find my way out of this silent moon-world before darkness fell. I was therefore much relieved when movement of a kind, accompanied by a curious rhythmic clanking, materialized out of the shadows ahead of me. I quickened my step but had no need to hurry in order to catch up with a line of marching figures. It was difficult at first to tell if they were men or women for some were shouldering spades, some pick-axes, and shapeless sacking seemed to play a major rôle in whatever they were wearing. Nor would marching be the right word to describe their progress, although they seemed to be shuffling their way forward in some kind of rhythm, banging the buckets which formed part of their equipment against the path's side walls. I did not want to push past them and seeing that they were obviously heading for some place and I was lost, I decided to tag along behind and hope for the best.

We came to a second rather more important crossing where one or two broke away from the group and, murmuring something which sounded like, 'Good night – 'till tomorrow', they made off down one of the side-tracks of which I counted five in all. Five gaping holes in the rubble walls, five possibilities of taking a wrong turn – I decided that the moment had come for me to explain myself.

I was an alien in their midst, but I could speak German and my lack of any air of authority was so manifest that in spite of my uniform they gathered around me, obviously eager to be of help.

At close quarters there was no mistaking that my companions were all women. The drab headgear, caps and scarves and shapeless lumps of felt, and the rest of their rig-out – a hotch-potch of any old remnants capable of being used as protection against the elements – could have belonged to either sex, but their voices were women's voices, their hands were women's hands as they leaned on their shovels and proceeded to bombard me in a variety of dialects of which I could only recognize that of Berlin.

Where was I going? They, as I could see, were on their way to the Opera – *Rosenkavalier* – pass the chocolates, Irmgard! As usual it was a chirpy Berliner amongst them who was guaranteed to raise a laugh. The fact that I was billeted in a part of Berlin taken over by the British caused some confusion, and a waving of picks and shovels in all directions gave me to understand that they hadn't a clue how to get there. Confined as they were to their own bit of ground, the rest of Berlin was plainly unknown territory.

By the time a heated argument amongst themselves as to my future was well under way, some of the manifestly exhausted ladies were already giving themselves a much needed rest on their upturned buckets, others had flopped to the ground and, seated with their backs to the walls, were staring dully at their unwieldy old boots.

Something told me that this might be the moment to produce some cigarettes. The Kaiser had managed to keep me off them all day and with luck I had enough for all of us. 'Listen,' I said as loudly as I could above the clamour, 'you are just being too kind, too solicitous. Why don't I tag along with you until we meet up with a main road, and maybe a tram or a taxi or even a military vehicle might be passing and you can push me into it and get rid of me. But in the meantime, why don't we smoke a cigarette together?' 'A cigarette?' 'One each?' A deep, almost reverent silence descended immediately, not, I knew, because of my brilliant solving of their problem, but at the sound of that sacred word, cigarette – Holy Writ! – and as I went the rounds with my lighter, watching the look of complete contentment which came over one dusty face after another, I decided that in the future no one was going to persuade me that cigarettes were bad for you.

As we sat there puffing away in the half-light, watched over by the towering ruins, I was able to listen to some of the stories they had to tell. There were refugees from the East amongst them, some who could barely speak German, although most of them were from Berlin, and two came from Dresden. None of them seemed really young any more and the tales they told were grimly repetitive. The long trek westwards driven from their homes like cattle, husbands dead or missing, children lost, and then those final days and nights in Berlin, the howling shells, the seething flames, as they prayed in vain that the Allies would arrive before the Russians. Lastly, the violation, the rape, some not once, not twice, but many times. The Russians were being allowed to take their revenge and the sagas which unfolded were horrific, somehow made even more so by the absence of self-pity, the almost matter-of-fact way in which they were told.

Time was passing, cigarettes ceased to glow, although I noticed that the stubs were being carefully stowed away in apron pockets. The day was not yet over for my companions: some had to fetch children from friends or relatives who looked after them during the day, others to join long queues for possible food or firing for themselves and for others too old or too ill to manage. Each to her appointed task; they had learned the value of teamwork in the survival game.

The journey to the main road did not take too long. We seemed to be moving more swiftly and the faces about me suddenly looked much younger.

I have a theory that women, old school-friends, old buddies, when they get together and feel so inclined, are ready to cast their years and responsibilities to the winds and become quite juvenile. Why this should be I do not know, but it was so when one of us noticed that the jagged cliffs about us, if given some encouragement, could return a resounding echo and, before we knew quite what we were about, this had us cooing and crowing, booing and bawling and hardly able to control ourselves with laughter, waiting for the answer to float back at us from the non-existent roof-tops. We were thoroughly enjoying ourselves and the game would have gone on longer if one voice had not decided to shout, 'Heil!' and, as 'Heil' after 'Heil' came back at us, the fun was suddenly over and we were reduced to silence. So much for memories. 'Ein kleiner Schönheitsfehler – a bit of a mistake,' remarked my neighbour, wiping away the tears of laughter with her apron. 'I guess she meant to yell out Hölle (Hell).'

The driver and the conductor and most of the passengers on the rickety old tram which picked me up at the main road were also women, and after waving goodbye to the last few stalwarts who had insisted on coming with me to the tram stop, it occurred to me that during the time we had been together, talked and laughed together, hardly any mention had been made of the male sex. Distant memories of ladies' tea parties came flooding back to me when, 'I must ask my husband', was a constant battle squeak, and when over-worked fathers, equally over-worked husbands, and their resultant 'nerves' supplied an endless subject for conversation. I had been new to the rôle of Hausfrau then and it remained a mystery to me how German women, whose efficiency I envied, could succumb so easily to second-class citizenship.

Now, after six years of war and a year of so-called liberation, these same women had carried on scrimping and saving, foraging for food, managing to keep their families alive, the remains of their homes intact. Could it be they had discovered that they could do so quite successfully on their own? Soon what was left of their menfolk would be drifting homewards and I could only wonder if they would be allowed to slip back into their old-established roles as undisputed masters of the household.

Back in the comparatively supreme comfort of the Press Camp where we could indulge in plenty of complaints about the dullness of the NAAFI food, and the lumpy mattresses which reminded us all of boarding-school, I found my thoughts returning to those Trümmerfrauen – the Rubble Women. These were the German women whom Hitler had identified with his famous three 'Ks' – Kinder, Küche, Kirche – children, the kitchen and the church – and here they were, dusty and dishevelled but undaunted, replacing their missing menfolk, clearing up, starting again at the beginning. *Die Stunde Null*, zero hour. If ever there was to be a start somewhere, it seemed to me that with their dusty faces, calloused hands and ragged aprons, these women could certainly count themselves among the flag bearers of *Die Stunde Eins*.

Three days after my return to Frankfurt from Berlin, Peter and I left for England. Only allied personnel could travel by air and the rail route prescribed for us was via Hanover, Hamburg and Copenhagen. Just before leaving, an envelope marked 'On His Majesty's Service' was delivered at the Press Camp. My passport, and although I was described inside as a naturalized British subject of British birth and though I could not quite understand how I could have managed to become both, I was only too happy to welcome the lion and the unicorn back into my possession once more.

As soon as we crossed the Danish border I removed my uniform and became myself again, although I cannot pretend that the rather weary eight-year-old garment which I had brought with me from Kronberg would stamp me as travelling in the height of fashion.

In Copenhagen we headed for one of our pre-war favourite restaurants where Peter demolished a huge basin of *Bœuf Stroganoff* and I nearly managed to clear the most extensive platter of smoked salmon I had ever set eyes on.

I do not know why but, during the long train journey through devastated Germany and then Denmark, where the villages and little towns showed no bomb scars whatsoever, Graf Hardenberg's farewell words to me in Berlin kept recurring in my mind. *Die Stunde Null* – zero hour – was easy enough to translate, but what about *Die Stunde Eins*? It was only on the following morning when Peter and I were leaning on the ship's rails as dawn was breaking that I thought to have found an answer.

Die Stunde Eins, why try to translate the words? Let them simply remain a symbol of hope for two young human beings with lots of life before them, leaning over those railings in the early dawn and wondering what lay ahead as the ship left the North Sea storms behind and glided smoothly into the mouth of the Thames.

Chapter Eight

I have come to believe that as a lifetime progresses, it does so from one milestone to the next. You may think to be following a certain course, but unseen, unrecognizable as such at the time, events lie ahead waiting for you to come their way and stop short before passing by.

Thoughts such as these kept churning over in my mind as night after night I sat at Peter's bedside in the casualty ward of Selly Oak Hospital, in Birmingham, waiting and hoping for him to regain consciousness.

It seemed so useless to ask why this essential part of my life should have survived the war, the bombs, the dangers and months in a concentration camp and now lie here motionless, looking so young, breathing so lightly, maybe slipping away without protest into the unknown. Useless to ask why had it to be, that just as some kind of future, however uncertain, seemed to be dawning on our horizon, a motor cycle, a careless lorry driver and a fractured skull should have been allowed to block our path and bring us to possible finality, an unforeseen, inescapable cul-de-sac. The surgeon had asked me was Peter's heartbeat by nature very slow – an athlete's heart? – yes, yes, it was! My answer seemed to please him. He was an honest man, just out of the Army, and obviously accustomed to giving a forthright opinion. In that case he could raise my hopes from a 10 per cent to a 20 per cent chance of recovery. What exactly he meant by 'recovery' I had not dared to ask.

A hospital ward is an eerie place at night, when the rattling trolleys and all other daytime commotion have died away, when the lights are dimmed, and the nurses move from bed to bed like wraiths on their slippered feet. Only an occasional sigh, a whimper or perhaps a moan breaks the silence as one or other would-be survivor lies there struggling, however feebly, to cling on to life. When left so alone in a twilight world with no reliable future ahead of me, I found it easier to live with memories of the past. There was certainty, happiness, even a few absurdities about the past which were all safer to think about than a future which did not bear thought. I had many such memories to call upon.

There was, for instance, the tumultuous reception given to Peter by my family, all obviously determined to make it extra special. My father, returning from the cellar with some superb bottles and my mother, after clearing the garden of flowers, throwing her principles to the winds, and managing to rustle up a beef roast of pre-war dimensions. Peter, my brothers, my brother-in-law and a favourite cousin, not yet out of uniform, five young men all able to make nonsense of six years of bitter enmity by the warmth of their welcome and their obvious pleasure at still being alive and able to meet up with each other once again.

Then there was the day I set off for Neill's school in Suffolk to discover how Christopher was faring in his educational establishment. I went on my own as, after our long separation, I was not too certain whether Peter who, just as I had been months before, was being confronted by new impressions every day, might not find this particular phenomenon on the post-war English scene to be well beyond his understanding. True enough, I found Christopher squatting on the floor of a large bare gym hall amongst other little boys, some of whom were smoking cigarettes.

There are certain unforgettable moments in life and one must be when you know for certain that you are loved, loved with an innocent trusting love which can possibly only be offered to you by children. One such magic moment came when my little son pushed aside a mop of tousled hair and looked up to see me standing in the doorway. For a moment he seemed to think I was not of this world but just some longed-for dream-person. Then he scrambled to his feet and jumping over heads and legs, anything that might block his path, he flung himself into my arms.

Well, needless to say, that was quite enough for me. There were still some weeks of term to go but he took it for granted that he was leaving immediately and I was only too happy to go along with such a splendid notion. There was only one moment of hesitation when he suddenly remembered something which he had left behind in the gym hall. Cigarettes were scarce in Germany when he had left. He showed me a little tin half-filled with his friends' cigarette stubs which he had been collecting for his father.

Then again there was a chapter so recent that whenever I thought about it, I was uncertain whether I should feel pleased with myself or downright ashamed.

I had not been destined to stay long in Codicote after our arrival: barely a week had passed before news reached me of my favourite uncle, who was also my godfather. Since the death of his wife, my Uncle Cecil had lived alone in a mansion of enormous proportions overlooking Hyde Park, being cared for by an elderly retainer, formerly his butler, known to one and all as Mr Wilkins. The message amounted almost to an SOS telling me, to my dismay, that Mr Wilkins had died quite suddenly when preparing to proceed upstairs with my uncle's early morning cup of tea.

Uncle Cecil had been exceptionally generous to me for as long as I could remember and, on hearing of this, I suggested to his family that I should move in temporarily and try to arrange for new staff to look after him. Needless to say my offer was accepted with alacrity and after some weeks I could well understand why.

Lack of space, at least, was no longer to be a problem, for my uncle's mansion, No. 13 Hyde Park Gardens, could have housed a small army. It was equipped with a huge library, a ballroom, a dining hall, several drawing-rooms and, on upper floors, endless lofty bedrooms and bathrooms, while ten or twelve smaller bedrooms on the top floor completed the picture. All floors could be reached by an antiquated lift which was inclined to get stuck now and again and was provided with a strident whistle which, if the occupier got stuck, alerted a member of the household who then had to give one of its gates a mighty kick to start it on its way once again.

I had never actually penetrated the kitchen quarters before arriving to take up my temporary task, but soon learned that finding staff to replace Mr Wilkins looked like becoming the job of a lifetime. We had several answers to our advertisements in the newspapers and I interviewed a number of very suitable candidates who seemed favourably impressed with my uncle's financial intentions, but I could never complete a guided tour of the basement in which they were destined to live before being given to understand that to continue further would be a waste of time. Not surprising really, as I had discovered that the kitchen quarters could only be compared in size with, perhaps, Piccadilly

Circus Underground Station. A huge kitchen, quite capable of accommodating a full-sized bowling alley, was ruled over by a kitchen range which I felt would have had no trouble roasting an ox. Innumerable coal houses, sculleries and butler's pantries and three or four large empty cells, which my aunt had used as air-raid shelters, more or less completed the scene.

As the weeks passed, the children's school holidays came and went as did the artless victims I managed to lure into the basement, at most, for a day or so; my temporary stay looked like becoming a permanency.

In some ways our move to London had its brighter side in that Peter, never very adept at doing nothing, soon met up with an old friend, Werner von Simson, also married to an English girl and, who, after spending some time in an internment camp, was now bent on starting up a small export business. Werner was an asset anyway for besides being extremely astute, he was inclined to eye the goings-on in the world with much amusement; an attitude which I found could very easily become infectious. The centre of what he called his future industrial empire was a tiny office in Birmingham and he was content to overlook the fact that Peter's exit visa did not include a work permit, and to invite him to join in, so long as he could fit inside the door.

For my part I found that by living nearer to the centre of things I could play a more active rôle in our Memorial Fund, relieving the *Observer* of our presence and establishing our headquarters (consisting of two typewriters and a few cardboard boxes) in one of the many empty upstairs bedrooms. I could also meet more easily with such endlessly helpful friends as David Astor, Isobel Cripps and Victor Gollancz.

As for my uncle, he seemed to enjoy having the boys and the noise about him, and they were happy to have found a brand-new grandfather who studied their stamp collections with assiduous attention and did not seem to mind if they tore around his outsize veranda on their roller-skates. I, too, valued the evenings we spent together reading before the fire in the library or listening to the natural eloquence with which he could describe his career in the House of Commons and now the House of Lords. I realized that only one subject was definitely taboo, for it was then that he could betray a totally unexpected contradiction in an otherwise most equitable character. Quite simply he could not abide Jews. He never mentioned why, although rumour had it that during a period in the Foreign Office, some time long before the First World War, he had had some unpleasing experience with the machinations of certain Jewish diamond merchants in South Africa which, he insisted, had been the cause of the outbreak of the Boer War.

The day arrived when Victor Gollancz and I were lunching together at The Ivy, a favourite haunt of his, and I found him unusually down-hearted. It seemed that for some time he had known that his Trust Fund, 'Save Europe Now', would have to move house, as an unexploded bomb had been discovered underneath their offices in Covent Garden. He had procrastinated, but the authorities had now given him three days in which to clear the place and as yet he had found no new accommodation. He had every reason for sadness, for he had many plans, and a devoted staff, and he envisaged the winding-up of a venture which was very close to his heart.

I do not know when it was that the thought of those upstairs bedrooms at No. 13 flashed across my mind, but it was of necessity short-lived. Victor was a Jew and as far as my Uncle Cecil was concerned that would be that.

However, when I returned from the luncheon and stood in the echoing hallway, still thinking of Victor and his dilemma, one of my better ideas occurred to me. At least it seemed so at the time. Need I ask Uncle Cecil after all? Need he in fact know? The more I thought about it the clearer it became and it all seemed so simple.

Three days and the move forced upon him would bring Victor to Saturday, and on Saturdays my uncle retired to his country estate in Egham, returning only on Monday morning. On weekdays the household routine was extremely regular. At 9.00 a.m. the lift must be waiting at the second floor to bring my uncle down to breakfast; and at 7.00 p.m. on the ground floor to transport him upstairs to change for dinner. If Victor's faithful staff could arrive in the basement at 8.00 a.m., even travelling two at a time, they could all be at the top of the house before my uncle appeared and be back home again before the lift had to perform its evening mission.

The plan seemed fairly flawless and on the following weekend my uncle had hardly left for the country before the sound of the lift creaking up and down went on for what seemed a very long time – it could surely not take such ages to transport what I imagined to be a few typewriters. But when evening silence fell, and I travelled up to the attic, to my consternation, I found ten well-equipped offices, chairs, tables, filing cabinets, typewriters – the lot. Victor's faithful staff had achieved a miracle.

There would be no use pretending that I was not relieved when three weeks later a telephone call from Victor told me that all was well, he had found new accommodation and on the following Saturday the caravanserai could move out.

Saturday arrived and with it the appearance at breakfast of my Uncle Cecil holding on to a large white handkerchief. He had a little cold and had decided in the night that he would not leave for the country that day, but would prefer to stay for the weekend in London.

No amount of trying to persuade him that there was really nothing better for a cold than good fresh country air could move him an inch. His mind was made up; and as for fresh air, he might take a little stroll in the park during the day but that would be sufficient.

Two frantic telephone calls, unanswered, convinced me that my well-deserved fate was on its way and that there was little I could do about it beyond seating myself in the library hoping for the best, praying that Victor's exit might be swifter than his entrance or that my uncle might get lost in the park!

Fate was not on my side, for hardly had the heavy front door slammed behind my uncle, setting forth on his little stroll, before the well-remembered rumpus started up in the basement. Up and down – up and down – the lift, thoroughly overtaxed, creaked and groaned, emitting one whistle after another, and I was so busy wishing I had never been born that I did not notice the door to the library opening quietly until I looked up to see my uncle, still in hat, gloves and woolly scarf, standing in the doorway.

There was a slight pause and then – 'Chrismary,' he said (as a child I was always called Chrismary by the family in order to differentiate me from my mother). 'On returning from my walk a little earlier than usual, there being a mischievous nip in the air, I came across a large furniture van parked outside and some unusual-looking individuals – possibly Balkan terrorists – who seemed to be emptying my house of furniture. Would you have any idea what is afoot?'

Had I any idea? At that moment I could think of only one, which was to spill the beans, to mention his dislike of Jews, to tell him of Victor's plight and to confess to my own efforts at trying to deal with my conscience when it came to Victor's race. I was listened to in silence, only being interrupted once to be asked just how long had he entertained the uninvited guests.

'Three weeks?'

He made the words sound like three centuries and then added, 'Dear me, what an intolerable situation.'

To which I could only answer meekly that I quite agreed – intolerable.

After my narrative petered out there were several minutes of complete silence when I found myself examining the faded carpet about me with exaggerated intensity. Then Uncle Cecil rose to his feet and made for the door, but before leaving the library he turned and cleared his throat. Now I was in for it – I braced myself for the onslaught – but no! —

'Chrismary,' he said, 'at this moment I can think of nothing whatsoever to say, but may I make myself quite clear – let it never happen again.' Yes, indeed, just as much as I loved him I think my Uncle Cecil must have loved me – and he showed his love when a telephone call from Werner, closely followed by a visit from two policemen, arrived to tell me of the accident. I must leave for Birmingham immediately, he would see that Christopher was brought from his kindergarten and delivered to my sister safe and sound. Had I money? Taxis, train tickets, everything must be done to bring me soonest to Peter's bedside.

So my vigil had started and as the hours passed and darkness became dawn I learned how easy it is for thoughts to turn into fantasies.

A caring, soft-voiced Irish night nurse brought me cups of tea and took my place occasionally. She came from Connemara and she was homesick and we could talk together in whispers of her home on that far western coast. What had the surgeon in mind when he talked of recovery? If he awoke – no, *when* he awoke – would Peter ever be able to go back to a post-war rat race?

Many years ago, with Hitler heading for war, Peter and I had talked of Ireland and of farming there perhaps. At the time it was not to be, but now? Surely just fantasy, but the smell of those turf fires, the sound of the sea and of the wind blowing over heather-covered hills, sometimes allowed that little nurse and I to leave the ache of homesickness and the sorrow of separation behind us and carry us away together to a dream world all of our own.

400

At 5 o'clock in the morning of the seventh day Peter returned from his other world and opened his eyes. For a short while, he looked about at the walls, the ceiling, seemingly unsurprised at the strangeness of his surroundings and when he saw me sitting there he simply asked, 'Where have you been?' and added, 'I've been looking for you all over the place.' And I heard my voice answering, 'I don't really know where I've been, all over the place too I guess,' which, when I come to think of it, was not far from the truth.

PART II

Ireland

'The history of a nation is not in parliaments and battlefields, but in what the people say to each other on fair days and high days and in how they farm and quarrel and go on pilgrimage'

W. B. YEATS

Chapter Nine

Wait till I tell you! One does not have to live long in Ireland before recognizing that by accepting such an invitation to move in closer by the fireside, at the crossroads, indeed, anywhere you happen to be at the time, you are in for much enjoyment. For whether the tale you are about to listen to be tragic, hilarious or plain dubious, you can be assured of melodrama. 'Whisht on you! Mary, Mother of God, could you believe it? Honest to God, don't be talking!'; such are the enthusiastic interjections which help to urge things along to the inevitable climax. It could be a marriage – 'a grand poor fellow, but herself, thanks-be, with a plot of land'; or a funeral – 'no Will, God rest his soul, and couldn't you slate the roof with the uncles and cousins that turned up from across the water for the wake'. Perhaps even a law case, but surely best of all a possible scandal, with the parish priest giving-out fit to deafen the saints.

If I were to begin my own particular story, as again all Irish sagas mostly do, hidden somewhere in the mists of time, I would have to go back to the year of our Lord 1610 when two brothers, the younger sons of yeoman farmers from Shropshire in England, left their homeland and set sail for Ireland, choosing to settle in a far western corner of that turbulent island. Their names were Francis and Thomas Burton and it was not too difficult to discover their reason for choosing County Clare to be their future home.

At the end of the sixteenth century, when Clare was a kingdom, the O'Briens, most powerful of the clans, decided (with only the occasional back-slide) to link their fortunes with those of the English Crown. Their allegiance did them no harm, for their chieftain at the time was created Earl of Thomond and, unlike others within the new county, their lands were not confiscated.

Instead they were rewarded with added acres to their already large possessions. Indeed, in 1610 Donagh O'Brien, fourth Earl of Thomond, together with his brother, Daniel, Baron Inchiquin, doubtless in order to clinch matters, became Protestant converts and their lands stretched from Bunratty in the east of the county to Carrigaholt in the far south-west.

The West of Ireland had not yet been stripped of her famous Irish oak forests in order to build the English fleet, and, according to records of the time, you could travel the O'Brien lands, from one corner to the other, without seeing the sky.

I could believe that no lands, no fortified castles were secure in those days when other mighty clans like the O'Neills and the O'Donnells were ever ready to descend in their hordes, in the respectable cause of Irish freedom and independence, ravaging and plundering the countryside before returning to their northern fastnesses loaded with useful booty. It thus makes sense that in 1610 the O'Briens, Lords of Thomond, were only too happy to welcome as tenant settlers reliable fellow Protestants of sturdy English yeoman stock who could assist them in warding off such damaging forays.

It is said that Ireland has the ability to absorb her conquerors, so that those who would wish to impose their will, to alter a way of life which has survived the centuries, soon give up the hopeless task and settle down to become more Irish than the Irish themselves. But for those who leave her shores, there are always the dreams of *Tír na nÓg*, the golden land of eternal youth, or of *Tuath de Danaan*, the little people or the Banshee wail heralding approaching death. These myths lurking in the misty hedgerows, drifting wraith-like about the rounded summits of her ancient hills are siren songs which never allow them to forget the land from whence they came.

When I returned to live in Ireland, 337 years later, I had little knowledge and not much interest in my Anglo-Irish ancestry. Nor do I think that my attachment came from some inborn mythical urge, but rather that, having been brought up in England in a very orderly household, where meals appeared on the dot and bedtime was bedtime, and then in Germany where *Ordnung* was a compulsory fact of life, the Ireland of my memories was of joyous journeyings to a land where nothing whatsoever functioned as I had learned that it should.

My up-bringing, for instance, had included a very liberal

attitude towards religion, particularly when it came to church-going, but I only had to cross the Irish Sea to discover that religion played a serious rôle in the lives of my Irish relatives, all active supporters of their church – the Protestant Church of Ireland. Their loyalty was influenced a little, perhaps, by having to compare their small, isolated battalions, their elderly weather-beaten houses of prayer, with the colourful armies of 'Holy Romans' who poured forth every Sunday from their newly built, highly varnished, monoliths of cold grey stone.

The battle was an uneven one, but my Irish relatives did not falter, keeping up a useful rear-guard action with garden fêtes and sales of work, when home-made jams, books and discarded clothing, tinker tents and hoopla stands all contributed to keeping the roof intact and the old organ blowing in the church of their ancestors.

'Putting up a show, keeping up the side', these I could remember were expressions often used to underline the necessity for donning our Sunday best, swallowing our breakfasts and grabbing our hymn books, preparatory to joining the select band of local 'Prods' in the seldom very melodious worship of our God.

But, although in many ways hide-bound, steadfastly refusing to recognize that their rôle in Irish history had suffered a body blow with the founding of the Irish Free State, and still talking doggedly of Sackville Street, Queenstown, King's County and so on, they had also refused to abandon a happy capacity to look upon unorthodox behaviour as being quite normal and acceptable.

There was, for instance, my Uncle Ned, who was firmly convinced that no worthwhile roof had been constructed in Ireland since the end of the eighteenth century. The slates came then from Bangor in Wales, he explained, and the craftsmen in those days were artisans who had gone out with the dodo. He was considered rather mad later, as he carried this conviction a little too far, refusing to have his roof repaired when leaks appeared and finally ending his days sleeping under an umbrella in the dining-room. But I did not find him mad when as a child I sat with him on the banks of the Slaney and watched him pick out a suitable fly from his old tweed hat and cast it with unerring exactitude over the still pool of waters below. Nor when he led me by the hand through the jungle of his walled gardens to that distant corner where he tended his prize roses. He never got around to cultivating a particular rose which he had promised to name after me, but he always assured me that he had it in mind.

Then there was my cousin's wedding. I will call her Cousin Letitia and, at thirty-nine years of age, she seemed to me at the time a very elderly lady. There was, of course, general rejoicing when at last she got her man, for although he was no film star, whatever was missing so far as physical charm was concerned was made up for by the fact that he was gentry and owned two hundred acres of prime grazing land in County Meath.

In order to celebrate in a manner suited to the occasion a domestic hire service had been approached and a butler engaged to take command of the household staff, which normally consisted of two pretty little girls from the village, each aged about fourteen.

As is usual in Ireland, things were soon running late. The Reverend Canon, a relative of the bridegroom who had come over from England to conduct the wedding service, had somehow been unable to wind up his sermon, and afterwards those of the guests who had motor cars found themselves unable to start their engines. Nonetheless, late or no, as the guests finally made it to the bride's home, the noble presence of the hired butler certainly added an air of glamour to the proceedings, particularly as he and the little girls had obviously busied themselves filling every vase, bowl and bucket they could find with flowers, and spreading out the wedding presents most tastefully in the dining-room. Unfortunately, not quite so obviously, at least at the start, the butler had also spent some of the time at his disposal in opening bottles and sampling the champagne. I do not know when it was that he decided that the guests, Mr and Mrs So-and-So, the Reverend and Mrs Whats-it, were not really up to his usual standard and proceeded to add the odd title here and there. Anglo-Irish gentry are rather fond of titles but when Lieutenants and Captains became Colonels and even Generals, and anyone wearing a clerical collar was assured of at least a bishopric, it had to be acknowledged that something was amiss. The climax was reached when the butler, now well into his stride, cast caution to the winds and in stentorian tones announced, 'The Lord and Lady Inglenook'. The local auctioneer who then slipped in with his wife did not allow himself to look anything more than slightly surprised when so suddenly raised to the peerage, but his wife got a fit of the giggles which lasted for the rest of the afternoon.

If this had happened in England, a severe reprimand at least would have ensued. As for Germany, dear me! there would almost have been a revolution, certainly a law case, and the chorus of *'Unerhört'* and *'Mein Gott, was soll das?'* would have spoiled the festivities altogether. Instead I do not remember hearing one word of startled surprise, let alone of condemnation. On the contrary, as we pushed the bridal couple up the drive in their newly furbished Morris Minor, it was generally agreed that the wedding had been a splendid affair altogether.

Finally, already in my teens, I would stay with my close friend, Gwennie McCormack, at Moore Abbey, her home in County Kildare, and in the evenings we would gather around the piano in the drawing-room where her father, the world-renowned tenor, John McCormack, allowed us to sing with him – opera, *lieder* and haunting Irish melodies – which reduced us all, including himself, to tears. They were magical evenings which gave me the courage to become a singer myself, although Gwennie and I, when sharing a bedroom at night and able to have interminable discussions as to our futures, were both agreed that we would, of course, also get married one day. Seeing that she was spending her school days in a convent where she was not allowed to take a bath without donning a pair of black combinations, and I in an establishment where prowess on the lacrosse field was considered far more important than an awareness of life, it was not surprising that our conception of the married state never got much further than picturing ourselves duly veiled, in gorgeous white dresses, being swept down the aisle by an Adonis whom we had promised to look after for the rest of our lives.

After Peter's accident I was faced with realities. Selly Oak Hospital insisted that, if released from the casualty ward, he would have to spend at least seven more weeks in hospital in care and under surveillance. But this did not coincide with Peter's own opinion as to his future. Two weeks later, when I was hardly back in London, a telephone call from the surgeon told me that he was up and rampaging about the place, threatening to leave in his pyjamas if they did not return his clothes. 'He is still a very ill man, Mrs Bielenberg, and he needs medical care,' the surgeon told me, 'but we are not a prison and I will have to ask you to take him home.'

Whenever I read in the newspaper that people who are institutionalized would be far better off if cared for at home, I think of those weeks of Peter's convalescence and, to be honest, my sympathy lies with the home.

The following months were surely no easier for Peter than for anyone else trying to behave as if everything was as normal as before. We sympathized, tried to tread carefully, to bypass the ever-recurring monologues on the theme of his having to return forthwith to Germany where he was needed, and to overlook his explosions of helpless frustration when he found that he could not cross a London street without breaking out in a cold sweat. The surgeon had been correct of course about the state of his health and, although seemingly unable to do anything right, I listened and tried to produce words of encouragement, at the same time aware that the thought of returning to Germany was for me becoming an ever-increasing anathema. Worst of all, I could not ignore a creeping sensation that someone I loved and who had shared my life had suddenly become a stranger. It was not to be long before an occasional glance in the mirror was enough to let me know that Peter was not the only one who was looking the worse for wear.

It was when I had got as far as wondering whether all this might mean a parting of the ways, that my mother, in her own practical fashion, stepped into the breach.

Fresh country air being, in her opinion, a certain cure for all ills, both physical and psychic, and with Uncle Cecil, at least, temporarily catered for by a family of amateur retainers who seemed content in the cellars, we were back in Codicote, ensconced in her experimental house at the far end of the vegetable garden. She had grown very fond of Peter, admiring his energy and sharing with him a certain direct way of expressing an opinion; in simple terms, she usually called a spade a spade. An active person herself, she could also understand his frustration, although fully aware that he was not what she called 'his usual self'. Something similar had happened to my father after being shell-shocked in the First World War – 'difficult, dear, a little difficult' – but he had recovered as would Peter and she did not approve of giving in when things became a 'little difficult'. Although Germany must be a dreadful place, she could well understand his wanting to get back there and his not being happy in England, where Germans as a whole were not exactly popular just at present, and particularly when he had nothing to do now beyond wondering about his future health. To uproot the children all over again would be nonsense, as would be parting company. Some compromise must be found. Peter had once confided to her that one of his dreams as a boy had been to become a farmer and, before the war, when it looked as if Hitler had come to stay and war was imminent, had we not had some plan to leave for Ireland?

I knew that she herself felt no particular attachment to Ireland, viewing the scene there with, at best, amused incomprehension. Her orderly mind was not easily able to understand the rather haphazard lifestyle of my Irish relatives; as for the social conditions prevailing, 'Too many prelates for me, dear – far too many.'

But now, although she was not certain of having found a solution, dithering was not a solution either, so maybe it was worth giving it a try. She ended her little speech in very typical manner, by advising me to go over to Ireland first with the children; the summer holidays were upon us and these would probably drive Peter even further up the wall. 'Make up your mind, dear. I have lots of plans for the garden which will keep Peter busy for a few weeks. If you want my advice, do it now.'

So, in the summer of 1947, the children and I set off by train for the Fishguard Ferry in Wales, bound for Rosslare in County Wexford and for Kilmore Quay, a fishing village some fourteen miles down the coast to the south-west, where a guest-house had been highly recommended by several Irish relatives. Although the journey ahead of us was to be long and tedious, as soon as we arrived on the platform at Paddington Station I was immediately made aware, as in years gone by, that I had left England behind me and was surrounded by boisterous foreigners. Young men, old men, family parties, children galore, cloth caps worn over one eye, bulging sacks and cardboard suitcases only prevented from bursting apart by bits of old rope. These were the exiles returning home for a bit of a holiday after helping England to conquer the enemy in their own way.

When it finally drew in to the platform the train was filthy. It was as if the authorities were determined to ensure that this journey to their homeland should be made as unattractive as possible for the Irish. As we crowded on board though, my fellow passengers were in no mood to show resentment. Assorted possessions were soon stacked perilously on the luggage rack and overflowed into the corridors, and the train had hardly gathered speed before a number of bottles appeared from nowhere and started doing the rounds. What will it be? Would I care for a jar? Irish voices are particularly gentle and pleasant; Irish manners likewise, and although I was the only female in the compartment it would have been unmannerly to leave me out. For my part I remembered enough about Irish drinking etiquette to refuse. I had no alcohol with me and could therefore not manage 'my round' should it come to my turn to provide. 'A mineral, then, for the lads?' Their generosity knew no bounds, and as the train rattled along through the night, and the children were finally asleep on the floor, I closed my eyes, trying to doze off, but finding myself listening to the ceaseless chatter, drifting in and out of a different world from the one I had been accustomed to in Ireland. This one was not that of the happy-go-lucky, come-down-in-the-world Anglo-Irish gentry, but one in which the Mammy and the Da played an almost exaggerated rôle, where funerals were 'luvly' and teeth a nuisance. I sensed that a certain amount of showing off would be the order of the day, when these returning heroes arrived at the family hearth. For they had seen the world, Manchester, Birmingham, Coventry, one had fought 'them Germans' and all had been in air-raids. Another had even risked breaking a rigid law of his country and ventured inside a Protestant church – a funeral to be sure, but what a funeral, beautiful altogether, the music, the flowers – 'Jaysus, I am telling you, we are not buried at all over here' was a conclusion seemingly shared by all.

I must have slept for a little for when I awakened the bottles were empty and the sounds reverberating around the carriage were similar to those inclined to erupt when the pubs close in Kilburn. What England had done to them and what they were going to do in return was nobody's business. A poor young man called Kevin Barry was hanged from a gallows tree over and over again and the grey dawn never stopped breaking over Kathleen Mavourneen. As for Mother Macree, whatever happened to her became lost in dirge-like dronings and the occasional snore long before we got to Fishguard.

There, to my pleasant surprise, drawn up at the quay, awaiting the arrival of our train, was none other than an old friend, SS *Princess Maud*. It had always been of interest when travelling to Ireland to find out which boat had been laid on for the often stormy crossing of the Irish Sea. If it were 'the Princess', as she was fondly known to her crew, or simply 'the Maud' for those whose politics could not allow a hint of royal connection to cross their lips, one thing was certain: if the surface of the Irish Sea differed only slightly from plate-glass, *SS Princess Maud* behaved in a manner one could only describe as skittish. She had a certain corkscrew movement aft, almost a habit of kicking up her legs behind, which was guaranteed to send the most sea-worthy passengers reaching blindly for the paper bags which were supplied in abundance, or for those who had given up and merely wished to die, to heave up another basinful and really no longer care where it landed.

A further hazard when travelling aboard 'the Princess' was due to her advanced age. Launched decades ago before the First World War, she had battled her way back and forth across the Irish Sea so often that no one could object to her taking her time about it and allowing her, in spite of German submarines and possible torpedoes, to arrive the odd hour or so late. If the day were a weekday and her destination Rosslare Harbour, she docked at the end of a long sea wall which did duty as a pier. Here a small train would wait for her passengers to disembark and transport them to Wexford from whence they could travel on to Dublin or Cork City. If it were a Sunday though, or indeed a Holy Day, this was not always the case. Then the late arrival of the boat might mean that the engine driver would miss morning Mass in Wexford some ten miles up the track; a matter not so much of concern to his job, but to that of his ultimate salvation. On such occasions, therefore, he was wont to depart taking his train with him, leaving late arrivals to a long wait behind inadequate wind shelters or to what was known as 'chancing it'. To chance it, which I remembered to be a very Irish concept, meant lugging one's baggage along a rickety structure composed of planks and bits of rope attached to the windward side of the sea wall.

When, after some years of use this whole contraption collapsed into the sea one stormy night I imagine that the Rosslare Port Authorities were much relieved that it had not done so when loaded with 'chancers' on a Sunday or a Holy Day.

On arrival, I was delighted to find the *Princess Maud* unchanged – the gleaming brass fittings, the red plush bunks, the polished mahogany and even the stewardesses no longer in their first youth, with gentle, friendly faces and starched white aprons, waiting to welcome the passengers aboard, as if it were to their own home. The sea was to be only slight and, if I was not mistaken, there would still be that corner of the deck where we could stow ourselves away and avoid the unhappy drama which might soon unfold in the lounges and lavatories below.

My special corner was luckily unoccupied, so that before the Fishguard Harbour lights had faded into the darkness behind us, the children, well wrapped up in rugs, were nearly asleep again. I was unable to sleep but sat there with thoughts already travelling far ahead to a land that I had not seen for more than fifteen years. Would Ireland have changed as I had changed? I was married now and had three sons, and as for Ireland, she had not been at war, but remained a peaceful oasis with nothing much to complain about except the scarcity of tea. She had remained neutral, playing her cards adroitly – sometimes too adroitly for my taste, as when Prime Minister de Valera joined with the German ambassador in a telegram of condolence to the German people on the death of Adolf Hitler. I also had to remember those dubious individuals calling themselves Irish, and carefully to be avoided in Berlin, who were known to be lurking in the corridors of Hitler's Ministry of Propaganda. What were they doing there? They had faded into obscurity as soon as the war was over, but I was older now, more wary perhaps.

The Princess docked punctually at 7 a.m. and sure enough there was the little train, also unchanged, awaiting us at the end of the pier in order to travel some two hundred and fifty yards to Rosslare Harbour Station, where we hoped to be met by motor car. Before departing on this little trip, the guard went from carriage door to carriage door locking it firmly on the outside. I remembered once as a schoolgirl travelling alone, asking the guard why. 'To stop the folk from flying out of the window, me darlin" had been his explanation, which was, I suppose, as good a reason as any.

The journey accomplished and the carriage doors unlocked, I stood on the harbour platform looking about me. The coast-guards' cottages up on the cliff, the rusty old dredger in the bay, the fishing boats, the seagulls, the soft morning air; nothing had changed, except that the little stone-built waiting-room was sporting a new title and the adjoining public conveniences like-wise. No longer 'Ladies' and 'Gents', they were now 'Fir' and 'Mna' and here some confusion was already taking place as those not up to date with the Gaelic revival and uncertain whether they were 'Fir' or 'Mna' dodged in and swiftly out again having opted for the wrong one.

We had not long to wait before we were met by an extremely pleasant little man who introduced himself as Mick and who led us to the shell of a spacious motor car parked on the hill leading down to the harbour. A large piece of rock wedged under one of the front wheels had to be removed, the vehicle started to roll and the engine sprang into life just in time to prevent us hitting the harbour wall. We stopped twice before reaching Kilmore Quay, once to collect a newspaper and again to load up a large crate of Guinness which Mick explained was for a fellow guest who was in the position of not being able to do without it.

The guesthouse in Kilmore proved something of a surprise. It was situated at the far end of the village, overlooking the sea and consisted of a ramshackle bungalow, two caravans propped up rather perilously on some logs of wood and what looked like a converted hen-house. The hen-house was called the annexe and had been prepared for the children. The owner of the guesthouse, a Mrs Godfrey, greeted us in the doorway. She proved to be a lady of ample proportions, so ample in fact, as I learned later, that she had had to relinquish her rôle as Master of Hounds when she became too heavy for her horse. But I learned immediately that her voice had lost none of the carrying power usually associated with the hunting field for, on seeing us and before bidding us welcome, she bellowed into the darkness of the hallway behind her, where I suppose fellow guests had been discussing the implications of a name like Bielenberg, 'They are not Jews!'

Mick, too, was somewhat out of the ordinary, acting not only as the establishment's chauffeur, but also as the gardener, the housemaid, the parlourmaid and the kitchenmaid, although his main interest seemed to be his rôle as Honorary Secretary to the Life Boat Association.

At that time Britons in their hundreds were crossing the Irish Sea in order to escape for a week or so the conditions brought about by having won the war. The Wexford Chamber of Commerce decided that something must be done to exploit such a favourable opportunity. Bacon and eggs, soda bread, country butter, fish from the rivers and lobster from the sea were not, it seemed, enough to attract the more fastidious tourist, especially Americans, whose sole interest seemed to centre upon their Irish origins and the plumbing. The Chamber issued a decree, therefore, that each little house aspiring to accommodate paying guests must be possessed of a bath-tub and an indoor lavatory.

This ruling presented Kilmore with quite a problem. For though several cottages had applied for a licence to be registered, the only bath-tub for miles around was owned by Mrs Godfrey. I had, at first, been somewhat nonplussed to discover that this tub, which was of noble proportions with big shining taps and splendid drainage fittings, was not attached to any water supply. The reason for this became clear when the postman reported the imminent arrival of an inspector from Wexford who was doing the rounds to discover if those who had applied for a tourist licence had also complied with the ruling as to the plumbing.

On hearing this news the entire village moved into gear with spontaneous alacrity. Mrs Godfrey's, of course, must be his first visit where tea and hot scones and the bath-tub would await him. It was then for Mick to lead him off around the corner to the Life Boat House, considered to be another very potent tourist attraction. They were barely inside the building and I could imagine Mick waxing lyrical on the subject of his beloved life boat when a tractor and trailer appeared from nowhere. It drew up behind the hen-house and four sturdy young men moved quietly into the house and headed for the bathroom. In a matter of minutes the bath was out of the back door, through the gate, on to the trailer and away! It had four further visits to make and I could only imagine that either the inspector had been born in the district and joined in the game, or else something a good deal stronger than tea and scones was provided for his refreshment *en route.*

In the evening of that day, when the cortège returned, I was leaning over the sea-wall staring out towards the Saltee Islands and the sunset, listening to the familiar sea sounds of small waves lapping against the rocks and of boats chugging off to the fishing grounds with their retinue of clamouring sea gulls.

The tractor, the trailer, Mick and the bath had been joined by quite a few happy hangers-on and Mick assured me that all had gone well. The inspector had been a grand poor fellow altogether and before he had left had even given him a couple of shillings for the Life Boat.

I think it was then I came to a final decision. I knew that it was far too soon to think in finalities, that there were still too many obstacles along the path, but I seemed to have found a goal I must strive for. I must return to live in this strange, haphazard country, return and live out my days. There had been too much organization in my life so far, too much authority. Beautiful bath-tub, beautiful Kilmore, beautiful Ireland, could it be that I had found a corner of the world where those other outlandish concepts could never hope to survive?

On our return to England, it was a joy to discover that Peter's health had greatly improved. My mother's brand of 'care and surveillance' had obviously been far more successful than mine. To look after him she had engaged a daily lady whose interest in politics did not extend beyond the village, and whose Hertfordshire accent he could barely understand anyway. To remedy inactivity she had 'started him off' in the vegetable garden which he had transformed from a rough field into a chessboard of symmetrical exactitude.

So far so good, but in spite of Peter's return to comparative health, as the months passed and 1947 became 1948, there still seemed no glimmer of permanency in our lives. The path seemed to wind on ahead of us, but a sense of direction was missing. I do not, therefore, find it easy to pin-point any one particular event, any loosely shaped plan which might have influenced our progress one way or another.

It could have been when news reached us that Peter's mother was suffering from hunger oedema and, with the help of Lord Pakenham who now headed the British Control Commission in Germany, we could obtain a special visa for her to come and see us in England. She had sacrificed her health for her grandchildren and if we had any illusions as to the seriousness of the food situation in Germany we could learn from her at first hand of the conditions still prevailing there.

It could have been that, as travel regulations between Germany and England were eased and Peter could travel back to Frankfurt to learn that, belonging as he did to a missing generation, he need have no fear of not getting prestigious employment. But on this same journey he met Marion Dönhoff who, although involved with her newspaper, was lonely in Hamburg and still dreamed of wide open spaces, of those lost estates in East Prussia which had been in her family for hundreds of years. If we could collect visas for Ireland, or even Canada, for her scattered family and two good friends who were also expert in land management, why not pool our resources, form a co-operative, get back to the land, start life anew? Together they filled the air with new possibilities and doubtless added to Peter's own indecision. For I suppose that I, too, must have been hovering in the background. The *Observer* seemingly still had use for my services and I had been back and forth to Germany several times, privileged in being allowed to assist (which really meant learn from) their permanent correspondent – Sebastian Haffner, to my mind one of the great journalists of his day.

Maybe my sense of alienation which increased with each visit came about because I was in uniform and in some ways was cut off from the daily round. It had to be different for Peter. Germany was his country. I had tried it before and had been happy there, able to identify with so many others whose friendship I valued and whose ideals I could share. But Germany had simply slaughtered them and, for me, it was just like any country vigorously trying to forget the past and to concentrate on establishing a respectable, above all prosperous, future for itself. Somehow I could not contemplate trying to live there again.

I am inclined to agree with those who consider that an English up-bringing which enjoins bottling up the emotions and adopting a stiff upper lip when facing adversity is an uncomfortable fallacy. My Italian sister-in-law, who could bawl her head off for a few minutes and then double up with laughter, at least had it easier.

Psycho-somatism was an unknown concept to me in those days, although I had certainly experienced times when emotional upheaval sparked off acute physical pain; for instance, in Berlin, when I had felt obliged to tell a young Jewish couple that I could not harbour them in our house for longer than a few days or when I had heard of Peter's accident and was standing by his bedside in that Birmingham hospital. Now though, as 1948 moved into place, pain rather than being sporadic became constant and my health broke down completely.

I was sent off to Harley Street where various medical pundits looked extremely concerned and told me that I would have to have an operation. In fact they voiced their combined opinions in such doom-laden obscurity that they succeeded in putting the fear of God into me and I thought it wise to take a leaf in practical behaviour from my mother's book and make my Will. They also told me I needed 'building up' before they could take to their knives, and suggested Eastbourne as a possible venue.

Eastbourne? Where the hell was Eastbourne? Peter was now in charge. He knew of my love for the mountains and, before I realized what exactly was afoot, he had alerted a very good Swiss friend who was only too happy to send us official invitations and whisked me off to Switzerland, where after a fortnight of sun and snow the pundits, this time Swiss pundits, decided to do the deed. They removed my gall bladder and my Will could be relegated to the waste-paper basket.

I have recorded certain details of those months of indecision when it seemed to me that as a family we had become little more than privileged gypsies. It was a time when I had to hope that, while their parents were trying to sort out their lives, our three sons, although never certain as to where they would be spending their next school holidays, were doing likewise. The auspices seemed favourable: Nicky was soon to become Head Boy at Dane Court; Johnny was resigned to it, in spite of writing home that he now knew why it was called 'boring' school; and Christopher, in Bexhill-on-Sea at a little school recommended by a friend and approved of by her small daughter, was having his nails scrubbed, his teeth cleaned and his hair trimmed in office-boy style, none of which seemed to upset him unduly.

And I can record that Peter and I rode out these storms together, side by side, and finally arrived at the moment on 28th August 1948 which brought him on his first visit to Ireland. To be exact the moment when, once more astride his ancient motor cycle, he arrived before the door of an aunt of mine who lived near Athy in County Kildare.

Chapter Ten

I suppose it all really started when a lump of turf fell out of the fire in the sitting-room and burned a large hole in my aunt's hearthrug. The rug had surely seen better days, but after all she was insured and here was a chance to get a new one. My aunt had quite a reputation for making insurance claims, but usually got away with it because she was also most useful in getting new clients for the Insurance Company. So it was that the insurance agent, who was obviously a frequent visitor, turned up promptly to assess the damage. He was in a hurry that day though, for he had a difficult task ahead of him. One of his clients, who had failed to pay his bill for two years, had told him of his continued inability to pay in cash, but of his willingness to give him a horse instead. The agent had closed the deal before he had been given to understand that the horse was not waiting patiently to be collected from its stable, but had broken out some days before and had been seen contentedly grazing some bogland about ten miles away. The agent was nothing if not resourceful, and rather than lose a client he had borrowed a horse-box, hitched it to his motor car and set out to catch the horse before nightfall.

Here I must digress in order to describe another of my aunt's paying guests, and, to keep the record straight, declare that he was not the only one of his ilk helping to keep the wolf from the door in bleak mansions throughout Ireland. In my aunt's case, this important source of income came from a retired army officer who had succumbed to the bottle and whose relatives were willing to pay handsomely in order to keep him out of England. In former days he had risen to the rank of major in a prestigious British cavalry regiment and was known to the rest of the household as 'The Mage'. When he was sober, no one could have been more amiable, nor more polished, radiating that kind of honourable innocence often displayed by those who choose the Army for a career. When he was drunk there was no holding him. A short visit to a public house, of which there were many in the local town, a rapid downing of several outsize gins, and he would explode onto the pavement singing and dancing and ready to fling himself about the neck of any female who happened to get in his way. The Irish are adept at dealing with such situations, but after complaints arrived from the convent that when in this state he had shown himself unable to discriminate between ordinary housewives doing their bit of shopping and those who had taken the veil, my aunt's main concern was to keep him as near to her side as possible, whereas that of the Mage, of course, was to discover ways and means of evading her watchful eye.

Now at the mention of the word horse the ex-cavalry officer became very attentive, and from the glint in his eye I could tell that he was busy making several important calculations. 'See here, dear boy,' he said to the agent as smoothly as could be, 'this is where I can be of help. Dammit, I've lived with horses all my life. It's not that easy to catch a horse. Take me along with you and you'll need no horse-box. I'll catch the nag for you and ride it back here and we can put it up in the stable until you can sell it. What about that for a solution?'

The agent, who for diplomatic reasons had been kept in ignorance of the Mage's occasional escapades, looked highly relieved. 'Thank you, sir,' he said. 'In fact thanks a million, that is indeed an idea.' And the words were hardly out of his mouth before the Mage had nipped upstairs and returned, all spit and polish in riding boots and breeches.

My aunt was known in the district to be an ingenious character, but also one who could recognize a dilemma when it came her way. Now she knew herself to be in a fix, for nothing but trouble could arise if the Mage were let loose in the district – even if he were on horseback. On the other hand, the insurance money for the mat in the sitting-room had not yet reached the bank account and there was always that rusty ballcock in the water tank upstairs. If that got stuck again – as she often hoped it would – the staircase and the hallway would soon be awash, and they had needed redecorating for a long time. She decided to plump for letting the Mage go, hoping for the best, and at the same time asking Peter and my cousin please to go along on the expedition and to try their best to keep things in some sort of order.

Some three hours later they returned; at least Peter, the insurance agent and my cousin did so. They were very pleased with themselves and reported that the outing had been a complete success. They had taken some time to locate the whereabouts of the horse, but once having done so, the Mage had taken over with true professionalism, approaching it with care, coaxing and calling, and finally slipping a halter over its head with the greatest of ease.

But where was the Mage right now? Well, that was rather difficult to say. The last they had seen of him he was cantering along beside the road, an upright military presence heading purposefully for the next village. 'A grand man altogether,' declared the insurance agent in his innocence, and we sat down to wait for news of what we felt must be certain disaster.

It was now that Peter started talking to the insurance agent. We were in deep trouble. Our grand ideas of forming a co-operative with the Dönhoffs had fallen through. Marion had become increasingly involved in her newspaper and the others had decided to stay in Germany, all of them having found excellent farming jobs in the Bundesrepublik. Although I sometimes secretly worried about having been too pigheaded about returning to Germany, we had settled on trying to make a go of it on our own in Ireland. We had followed up every advertisement, scouring the countryside for weeks looking for a suitable farm to be purchased at a price we could afford. We had in fact very little capital at our disposal, £5,000 to be exact, and Peter, who spent much of his time studying a series of little volumes called *Teach Yourself Farming*, had assured himself that it was useless to spend every bean on buying the land as we would need more capital to equip and stock it.

I was not making things easier, for after trudging for miles looking for acres he considered workable, he would find me sitting on the motor cycle, a grumpy heap, declaring that I would not be seen dead in the horrible shack which went with them. On the other hand, if I found the house of my dreams, not too big, Georgian, Regency perhaps, with rooms of such happy proportions that I could visualize just how things would look when I moved in with an army of painters and decorators, I could be sure of hearing that the estate, described by the auctioneer in such glowing terms as the best of farming land, was mainly scrub or bog and utterly useless.

That evening the insurance agent listened sympathetically to our tale of woe, nodding his head, while keeping one ear cocked towards the window in the hope that the clatter of horse's hoofs would herald the arrival of the Mage.

He seemed hardly to hear when Peter mentioned that he must cover quite a lot of country in the course of his business. Had he not even heard of a place? Could he not perhaps . . .? No, not really, he could not think of anything for the moment – oh, well, but wait, he'd been over in a place called Tullow last week – had some business with an auctioneer over there, one Paddy Dawson, to his way of thinking one of the few honest auctioneers in the whole country, and he had told him of some place he'd been trying to sell for years. Up in the hills; it sounded a desperate sort of a place but he understood from Paddy that it would be going cheap.

A welcome commotion from the yard did not allow him to continue. It turned out to be a neighbouring farmer leading the horse and delivering the Mage, who was fast asleep in his ass-cart. But when the horse was safely bedded down in the stable, the Mage packed off to bed, and the insurance agent had departed with much gratitude, Peter and I sat down before a dying fire and took out our dog-eared old map so liberally spattered over with little red circles to remind us of the many 'gentleman's residences', the hundreds of derelict acres we had inspected with so much hope and left behind us with so much disappointment. Tullow, where was Tullow? Ah no, it was miles away: Athy, Carlow, Tullow; and our ration of petrol was nearing its end, and anyway the motor cycle had got to the stage when it had a puncture almost every day. It was sure to be another dud, just another waste of time and money. It was no use; perhaps farming was a silly idea anyway; perhaps we should have risked it and gone to Canada; perhaps I should not have been so stubborn in my attitude to post-war Germany.

It was then I truly believe that fate came to the conclusion that we had had enough and decided to take a hand in the game, for on the following morning my aunt returned from her shopping trip to town waving the local newspaper and telling us she had made up her mind. Made up her mind, that is, to sell every hen she had in the barnyard.

We had often wondered why she had not come to this decision before, as her birds seemed to suffer from a complete dearth of feathers. This we were led to understand came from the fact that they had developed a disease called 'the Pick' or 'the Peck' which drove them to go at each other hammer and tongs until they all ended up stark naked. It also seemed to inhibit them from laying a single egg.

Now, as a result of reading one of the smaller advertisements in the local newspaper, my aunt had decided on a change. She explained that all her life she had wanted to own Ancona hens, a rare breed; 'little dotes of birds', even their legs were covered with feathers, and now if there wasn't a woman from Newtownbarry who had twelve such birds for sale and they would go fast, so she intended to set off that very day in order to clinch the deal.

To set off for Newtownbarry that very day, a distance of at least thirty miles there and thirty miles back, was an almost impossible ambition. Our form of transport consisted of a motor cycle with a very boney pillion seat which I repeatedly decided never to mount again. It also had one of its usual punctures and the front tyre was as bald as an egg. My aunt's means of transport, a pre-war Morris Cowley which was only kept on the road by the ingenuity of her son, was in even worse condition in that it had developed a permanent leak in the roof and could only be driven in fine weather; the floor-boards, particularly those beneath the feet of the back-seat passengers, had simply rotted away.

As I have said though, my aunt was a determined character, her son was resourceful and in this case she had useful allies: only the day before we had seen the name Newtownbarry on the map and decided it could not be far from that place called Tullow, so Peter and I decided it could do no harm for us to go along with them.

As is usual in Ireland, the fact that something out of the ordinary was about to take place generated an unusual, brisk whirl of activity, a light-hearted certainty that although the auspices were surely hopeless, somehow or other they could be overcome.

It had rained during the night and my aunt's car leaked; due to the rotted floor-boards, those sitting on the back seats would not be able to rest their feet on the floor, for fear of finding themselves skittering perilously along the roadway beneath. But my cousin had an answer for everything. In the toolshed he had discovered a large tin of something he told us was liquid rubber solution. Although the directions for use stated firmly that the surface on which it should be painted must be dry he proceeded to plaster it all over the roof. As for the floor-boards he decided that the front doormat would at least protect the back-seat passengers from breaking their ankles or from being spattered from head to foot with mud. In no time at all every obstacle seemed to be overcome.

My aunt and I were installed in the back seat with our legs firmly pressed against the two seats in front in order to spare the doormat. Peter was clutching a piece of string which did duty as a choke, my cousin swung the starting handle once, twice and the little engine sputtered to life. We were off, all was well and perhaps would have remained so, if, halfway to Athy, a mother duck accompanied by her five ducklings had not appeared suddenly out of a ditch and, in no hurry whatsoever, set off across the road.

My cousin suddenly applied the brakes, equally suddenly the world ahead of the windscreen disappeared behind an opaque film of white rubber solution, and my aunt and I found ourselves with our feet resting squarely on the road. Worse still, large white blobs raining down on us, drip by sticky drip, convinced us there was more than one leak in the roof.

I think, had it not been for the hand of fate and my aunt's Ancona hens, we would have decided to call off the whole expedition, for otherwise I do not know why it never occurred to us to do anything of the kind. Instead, to hell with the leaking roof; there was a bundle of old newspapers behind the back seat. My aunt and I considered ourselves rather adept at making paper hats when the children needed them for dressing-up; and anyway perhaps the deluge down the windscreen would not repeat itself now that warm sunshine, as happens so often in Ireland, had suddenly replaced the rain.

Four splendid three-cornered paper hats, four paper capes, and enough newspaper left to cover our knees, and if our motor car had been a Rolls-Royce and the paper hats festooned with plumes, my aunt, at least, could almost have passed for an admiral of the fleet setting off for some investiture at Buckingham Palace! As it was, of course, we could not have looked more ridiculous and, as we progressed at a sedate twenty-five miles per hour – the maximum speed attainable – through Athy and Castledermot and on towards Tullow, meeting perhaps two cars on the road, I could only wonder at the tactful acceptance displayed by those who greeted us in passing. The sideways shake of the head, the friendly smile, the touch of the cap, those customary Irish ways behind which I often sensed a quiet, calculating assessment of any situation. In our case, the motor car – however decrepit – must belong to gentry. Ah well, was it paper hats they were after wanting to parade around in this time? Long centuries had taught them how to cope with gentry, and paper hats were surely one of the less harmful of their many strange notions . . .

As we neared Tullow the landscape about us changed. No longer the rich grasslands of County Kildare, this was wilder country with unkempt fields of gorse and fern rising to heather-covered hills ahead of us – the Wicklow Mountains, deep blue in colour, the rain having ceased, and near now, very near. On asking for directions we were told to pass over two humps in the road, and Mr Dawson's would be the first farmer's place on the left. There was slight delay here: as we approached the house, a loud hissing sound, billowing clouds of steam and a barrage of assorted curses seemed to be coming from the cow-house. But when Peter and my cousin leaped out of the car, certain that we had arrived just in time to avert a crisis, they were met at the door by a cheerful old man wielding an empty bucket. It was the milking machine, so it was, as obstinate, impenitent a class of a yoke as had ever plagued a Christian. We must not disturb ourselves, it caught fire once a week, but he was well able for it, himself and a couple of buckets of water. If we were looking for the boss, he would allow he was in his office in Tullow Town.

Tullow, when we arrived there, was a quiet little town with a few small shops, a bank, and a turf accountant, watched over by the usual mossy statue of some long-dead patriot: this time he seemed to be a priest. There was not a motor car to be seen, just the odd pony trap or ass-cart, tied up in the square waiting patiently for their owners to emerge from one or other of the inevitable public houses which completed the scene.

Two church towers dominated the township, one Catholic and one Church of Ireland, both projecting a certain air of solid granite well-being, very obviously not shared by the members of their flock.

Paddy Dawson, the auctioneer, proved to be what is known in Ireland as 'a lovely man, God bless him'. To be such a person need have nothing to do with physical good looks, which he had, but honesty, kindness of heart and quickness of wit are essential to qualify. With Paddy there was a bonus, in that he possessed a certain quizzical spark in the eye, a sudden side glance just to show that the world was an odd sort of a place and you should never quite believe the tales that were in it. We later learned that, together with a Mr Flynn who owned a garage, he was the uncrowned king of the district.

Mr Dawson explained to us that the property he had for sale was in the townlands of Munny, or Money, an anglicized version of the original Irish *Muinebeag*, denoting a small wood. It had once been part of the four thousand acre Fitzwilliam estate, which had been expropriated by the British and stretched from Shillelagh to the sea. Munny lands consisted of four hundred and eighty acres and had been owned for the last hundred years by a family called Lawrenson. While the father was alive, it had been a showplace, for he had been an outstanding man. He had constructed a water course from the hills behind with such ingenuity that all his machinery for butter-making or turnip-chopping could be driven by huge water wheels. The house and lands currently belonged to his son, who lived there with his two sisters and a younger brother. None of them had married, and they were now old and frail, and, as he explained, no longer able for it. It was no use pretending that it was a showplace any longer, for the lands had been let by conacre for years. Would it have a telephone perhaps? Ah now – electricity? – don't be talking. It was in fact a hardy sort of a place, but then Peter looked a hardy class of fellow.

We were so used to auctioneers waxing lyrical about the properties they had on their hands that Mr Dawson's description came as something of a relief, and since my aunt and my cousin had sputtered off towards Newtownbarry there seemed no harm in accepting his offer to drive us over and at least have a look at the place.

As we drove along the road to Shillelagh and turned off at a cluster of cottages called the Coolkenna cross, the road became a rough track. A further mile or so and we reached what Mr Dawson laughingly described as the 'great gates'. 'No longer in use,' he added rather unnecessarily, as it was hard to tell what could go on behind such a tangle of ivy and honeysuckle. A few yards further on, beside a high granite wall, there was a further entrance. No gates, great or small, this time, and after fifty yards or so the drive also petered out to become a muddy footpath. Ahead of us through bushes and undergrowth we could see a grey wall of battered stucco which we realized must be the house.

Mr Dawson left us here explaining that he wanted to warn the old people of our unexpected arrival. He would go around to the back as the front door had gone the way of the great gates and was no longer in use.

It would be no use my pretending that we approached that back door with anything other than misgiving. The house was larger than we anticipated, larger and also nearer to disintegration. There seemed to be two kitchens, in one of which a large, dark, rather menacing-looking figure sat on a wooden stool before an open fire, over which were suspended some large rusty iron pots. She did not turn her head when we stood in the doorway, but remained staring into the flames, immobile except for her right arm, rhythmically turning an iron wheel which seemed to function as some kind of bellows. The second and larger kitchen was a shambles, dominated at the far end by the wreckage of a huge black kitchen range which looked as if it had been hit by a hand grenade.

Our arrival seemed to have caused some excitement, for as we stood talking with a small birdlike old lady whom Mr Dawson introduced to us as Miss Lottie, I could hear hurried footsteps above us, doors being slammed, and shutters flung open. Finally we were joined by the remaining members of the family, equally elderly, rather breathless, who were referred to as Master Ralphy, Miss Maggie and Master Dick.

An hour and a half later we drove back to Tullow in silence. I was silent because on my guided tour through that lonely, empty house with its peeling walls and tattered curtainings, I thought to have seen a certain beauty hidden somewhere beneath the dust and decay. Peter, who meanwhile had walked over some of the lands, was also lost in thought, and I could believe that Mr Dawson's lack of any remark was due to his tact in allowing us time to get over the shock.

My aunt, my cousin, their motor car and the hens had not yet returned from Newtownbarry and it was not until Peter and I stood waiting for them in the town square, watched over by the benevolent eye of the local patriot, while the pony traps and the ass-carts dispersed to their various dwelling-places, that Peter put the question he had so often asked before: 'Well, what do you think of it?' The fact that I hesitated probably showed him that he was going to be spared the usual shattering reply. 'I don't know,' I answered tentatively enough. 'What do you?' 'I don't know either really,' he said, 'there's such an awful lot of land and one walk around is simply not enough.' Then with *Teach Yourself Farming* in mind, he added, 'I would have to take soil samples of course and – and, well, soil samples . . .'

We paid two further visits to Munny House, in spite of the fact that Mr Dawson told us that the lands had been over-exploited. They had been what is known as conacred for years, let for grazing on the eleven-month system: a deadly arrangement whereby local farmers removed all nourishment from the soil and nothing was ever given back to the land. We knew that this had come about because as Mr Dawson had explained the owners were simply 'not able for it', but as it proved they were still able to consume as much alcohol as the sale of their possessions could supply them with. When the furniture had gone and they were left with a table, four chairs, four beds, four trunks and a pony trap, they had cut down trees and sold them for firewood, and as soon as they learned that one Bangor slate could be exchanged for a bottle of Guinness they had immediately started on the roofs. When we arrived on the scene, however, they had luckily not progressed much further than part of the outhouses.

We knew, too, that because of Paddy Dawson's loyalty and also that of their old herd, Will Byrne, the property was not in the hands of the Bank – 'The Bank', which since Ireland's freedom had taken over the power once wielded by British landlords.

'It was and it wasn't,' had been Paddy Dawson's cryptic reply when we asked this all-important question. It was, on the one hand, because the Lawrensons owed £9,000 to the Bank; it wasn't, on the other hand, because whenever the Bank had tried to sell the property Will Byrne had stood resolutely at the entrance and warned any would-be buyers that no luck would go with it if they dared to open their mouths and make a bid. In Paddy Dawson's opinion the result was that the Bank was now also no longer able for it and might be only too willing to take a few hundred pounds in lieu of what they now recognized as being a hopelessly irretrievable debt.

In fact we had both fallen in love with the idea of buying Munny if, taking the soil tests and the state of the house and fencing into consideration, we could buy at a low enough price. But soil tested it had to be. Luckily Peter had met the son of a director of a big firm of maltsters who had studied agriculture. Peter asked him how one could set about taking and evaluating soil samples, a notion quite foreign to Ireland at the time. He told Peter that his father's firm employed such a man, Stephen Cullinan. With great enthusiasm, and delighted to be putting his science to practical use, Stephen worked very fast. After four days we had the result. The land was excessively acid, but it had a fair reserve of organic matter which could not rot to provide the necessary fertility because of the acidity. It needed vast quantities of lime and phosphate, but then it would produce anything. But the materials and the miles of new fencing needed would require a lot of money which we had to calculate as part of the purchase price.

Again we approached Paddy Dawson who, having had Munny on his books for some fifteen years, had no illusions about its value. He agreed to submit our offer of £4,500 to the owners who accepted without hesitation. We drew up the contract and made a down payment of a quarter of the price. We were to complete in February 1949.

On the day that we put down our deposit and after we left Paddy Dawson's office, awash with tea and warmed by messages of good luck, we decided to drive back towards Shillelagh and to have one more look at the home which would be ours if all the land deeds proved in order. We turned off at the Coolkenna crossroad and, as we approached the Munny lands, above the straggling hedgerows and the colourful boglands, I thought I saw one window of the old grey house peering down above the trees from the hill before us.

We turned in at the high grey wall and perforce stopped the motor cycle halfway up the track.

We did not wish to disturb the former owners but climbed over the fence and stood beneath a low wall which separated what must have once been a garden, from what we later knew to be the 'lawn field'.

As so often in Ireland, after a day of persistent rain, the sky was now cloudless as if washed clean, and the setting sun lit up the lands around us with an almost fluorescent radiance. Some of the great trees, the oaks and the elms, were already tinged with orange and with yellow, and stood out in meticulous detail against the purple background of the rolling Wicklow Mountains. In the far blue distance towered the highest peak of the Dublin Mountains, Lugnaquilla – 'mountain near the sun'.

Peter took my hand in his. 'Well, whatever the lands, whatever the poor old ruin,' he said, 'nothing, just nothing, can beat that view.'

Before leaving, I turned to look back towards the old grey house which we hoped would be our future home. Only that top dormer window could look back at me above the ragged yew trees and the tangled bushes, and I thought to myself, You've watched these trees being set in their places and you've watched them grow to such noble maturity, and you've watched the generations come and go; and now you've got a new lot to deal with, and I wonder what you think about it all.

Perhaps it was just a reflection of the setting sun, perhaps a simple reaction born of hope; but I thought to see a faint flicker of benevolence beam back at me over the bushes. Difficult to interpret really, except that, with luck, it might involve God's blessing; but then again being an Irish dormer window, it would equally include the equivocal after-thought that in this contrary world, whichever way it was, there would be divil a bit of harm in our chancing it.

Chapter Eleven

I had no clear idea of what 'chancing it' might involve when some weeks later I arrived once more in Ireland to take up residence, so to speak.

Off and away once more, intent on opening a further chapter in our lives; this time one which would include trying to bridge a gulf which divides urban living from that of the yeoman farmer.

The day I chose to travel was 17th March, the feast day of St Patrick, celebrated with a tremendous show of blarneyfied enthusiasm, even to the downing of gallons of green beer by the descendants of those who had 'taken to the boats' in the last century and managed to reach the shores of America.

My childhood recollection of 'Paddy's Day', as celebrated in the homeland, was of a more muted affair altogether. Nothing more exciting than a few drab floats passing down O'Connell Street in Dublin, followed by a motley procession of – to me – very old men in caps and raincoats, who never seemed quite able to march in step. A saffron-kilted band thumping out patriotic airs with bagpipes and drums made a brief impression, but even this cheerful din fell silent as the cavalcade passed by the General Post Office, the GPO, symbol of the abortive uprising against the British in 1916. There a row of top-hatted figures stood to attention, perched on a rickety-looking platform which had obviously been erected for the occasion.

I was twelve years old at the time and, much against her principles, a good-natured aunt had been persuaded to take me to see the show. She was able to point out at least one of those figures as being President de Valera; tall, austere, and dressed in sombre black, he surveyed the passing procession through steel-rimmed spectacles with unsmiling severity. Only the tinkers, peddling the national emblem, seemed to be enjoying themselves in the side-streets, especially when, instead of the miniature shamrock, they managed to palm off a bunch of ordinary field clover on some unsuspecting customer.

I could not tell whether with the years, when celebrating their patron saint, the Republic of Ireland had managed to adopt at least one of their former rulers' virtues, which was a capacity to put on a really good show. But one thing that was certain was that on that day, as many 'exiles' as could fill the boats crossed the Irish Sea heading for 'the auld sod'. So my journey from London via the Mailboat from Holyhead to Dun Laoghaire looked like becoming long and uncomfortable and, as ever, bibulous and vocal.

In order to escape the rumpus I found my way to the usual sheltered corner on one of the upper decks where only wind and sea sounds and the rhythmic chugging of the ferry's engines disturbed the darkness and the quietness of the night.

I needed to be alone because just before leaving my family in England, when the furniture van stood before the door filled with what my mother assured me were easily dispensable 'bits and pieces', I had had a bad attack of cold feet. It could have been due to a sudden flashback memory of a parting which had taken place ten years before with everyone trying to be so cheerful. 'Good luck, Chris', 'See you soon, darling', until the final 'Goodbye – goodbye', with the kisses and the hugs and the waving hands. Then I was leaving for Germany, war was pending, and it was to be six long years and too many other farewells before I saw them all again. Now, although self-analysis was not one of my usual habits, there must have been something about the regular chugging of those Mailboat engines which triggered off my apprehension. How would it be?

We would no longer be townsfolk whose means of transport could be a bus, a train, or a motor car, and whose daily needs could be supplied by the shop around the corner, who could head for the country at weekends to sniff the air and pause awhile to contemplate the peaceful scene of cows grazing lush green pastures or to watch little lambs frolicking in the fields under the watchful eye of their placid mothers. Instead, we would be joining up with those whose livelihoods depended on whether those lambs lived and thrived, or wilted and died, and on milking those cows rain or shine from Monday morning through to Sunday eve in order that others, referred to with scant respect

433

as 'townees', should find their morning milk in bottles on their doorsteps.

I could reckon that although our attitude towards life as farmers of the land was probably tinged with romanticism, we were all in good health and well equipped for our new venture. Except for my spell in the Black Forest, all that I knew of the country life was extreme comfort, with gardeners busy at the lawns and flowerbeds, and a household so well equipped with domestics that my mother, more honest than her pampered offspring, once declared that she wondered what we did all day.

Why the sudden panic? Simply perhaps that I was older now, beginning to recognize just how little I really knew about Ireland and that to remember it simply as a happy-go-lucky playground would not be enough. The regular chugging of the Mailboat's engines reminded me of a certain trait in my own make-up, my innate inability to maintain a rhythm of non-stop, undiluted purposefulness. Instead I found it all too easy to wander from a central theme, to stray from the path, searching the horizon for something new, curious to discover what could lie over the brow of any hill. *'A penny for your thoughts – pay attention, Christabel!'* It was surely a liability, but well compensated by a sturdy optimism, always ready to assure me that whatever awaited my wide-eyed arrival would probably be something rather nice.

The darkness was fading into a dawn glow and the ship's engines were gradually slowing down. Some time back I thought to have picked out a shadowy contour and sensed the nearness of land. One of the outer islands perhaps; could be Ireland's Eye.

But the morning was bitterly cold and for some time I had been regretting my decision to send my anorak off in the furniture van. Instead, for no reason I can think of, I had decided to doll myself up as if heading for some civic reception in black and pale blue, with a hat which, with some imagination, I felt made me look like Greta Garbo in her film, *Anna Karenina*. The result: I was simply freezing! So I made for the lower decks which I found to be already alive with the excitement of imminent arrival. Bundles and bags, babies in arms and rolls of bedding. When the Irish come home they do it in quantity and style, and to judge from the waving, welcoming crowds, half the island turns out on the quayside to greet them.

I could see my special bit of Ireland, standing almost head and shoulders above the rest, waiting quietly near the gang plank. It was almost a relief when after the warmest of welcomes one of the first things Peter asked me was whether I had remembered to bring with me a bag of something called cobalt, unobtainable in Ireland, but seemingly essential to our future livelihood. A relief, because even if I had not been able to answer with supreme confidence that the stuff was coming along in the furniture van, I could be reassured that the much-needed, non-stop, undiluted purposefulness part of the bargain was in good shape.

Over a splendid breakfast in a Victorian edifice which overlooked the harbour, a hotel which had undoubtedly given comfort to many a seasick traveller, and from the state of the décor possibly even to Queen Victoria herself, Greta Garbo hats were soon forgotten. I could see that, for the first time since his accident, Peter had become completely involved in what was still to me a new and unknown world.

While I was trying to fix up affairs in England, Peter was living in Munny together with its former owners, as the inimitable Paddy Dawson tried to find them a house suitable to their means. He had managed to do so a fortnight before my arrival, and, to celebrate their departure, a giant auction had taken place on the premises. Fair days and auctions, it would seem, along with church going and Mass on Sundays, were social occasions not to be missed by the scattered country folk who lived about us. There could not have been much to collect but just the same a cavalcade of bicycles, pony traps, ass-carts and even the odd ancient tractor turned up to join the fun and also doubtless take a look at 'them Germans', who were now the owners of 'the Big House'. Nothing much to collect, but urged on by Paddy Dawson, nuts and bolts, leaking buckets, ladders with missing rungs, tattered curtains and even some pots of paint and brushes which Peter had bought in the hope of doing some decorating before my arrival, were carted away, along with the *pièce de résistance*, in the form of a donkey. The donkey, it seemed, was a particular attraction in the district, as its task in life had been to take Kate, our predecessors' factotum, to Mass on Sundays. She seldom arrived on time, because whenever she was greeted on her journey by friendly neighbours well used to the game, it stopped stone dead. 'Grand day, Kate,' was enough, and it took at least ten minutes to get Kate, the ass-cart, and the donkey, into motion once again.

Peter could tell me that, to add to our assets, we now also had allies. There was Michael Noctor, whose parents had been with some of my relations as housekeeper and gardener, and had carried on stoically as the big house began to crumble and the garden threatened to become a wilderness. Michael, their second son, had decided to risk leaving the rich farmlands of Kildare and to join us in County Wicklow, which was to him a foreign country. With him had come the daughter of a neighbour, who warned us, accurately it was to prove, that her knowledge of cooking was 'anarchic'. But Molly, as was her name, had taken charge of the iron pots and pans suspended over the open fire and could produce what she called a 'cake of bread' from under the ashes, which Peter declared was the nearest thing to *Vollkornbrot* he had tasted since leaving Germany.

There was also the gallant Will Byrne who had spent his working life as herd to the former owners of Munny, and as they sank deeper into debt had kept prospective buyers at bay. Lastly, there was Stephen Cullinan. Stephen, who had taken the soil samples, came from one of those indomitable Irish families evicted to the West of Ireland, 'to hell or to Connaught', by English landowners. He was one of six sons and two daughters, all reared on the patch of rock and bogland which had been allotted to them. All had survived and made good. His brothers, those who had not 'taken to the boats' as the journey to America was known at the time, had become engineers and civil servants, his sisters nuns or nurses. Stephen himself had become an agricultural chemist, and when we met him he was living in cramped quarters in Athy, County Kildare, employed for a pittance by the firm of maltsters. In spite of his splendid looks, with his shock of curly dark hair and the green-blue eyes so often to be found in the West, Stephen's health was delicate, with bouts of asthma which were surely not alleviated by his mode of living. Nothing, however, could dim his enthusiasm. 'Look after the land and the land will look after you' was his dictum, learned at his father's knee, and as soon as he heard we were buying the derelict farm in the Wicklow Mountains, he volunteered to join us and advise us on how to proceed.

While filling me in on all the details, Peter was talking so much and at such speed that I was finding it quite hard to swallow my excellent breakfast. When he arrived at the result of Stephen's investigations, pH this and pH that, the chemical terms he used sounded most professional. But, as far as I could gather, they indicated that because of constant neglect, constant over-grazing and over-cropping, no fertility whatsoever was left in the soil we were supposed to till, reap and harvest. So I thought I had better eat up quickly as it looked as if it might be the last square meal I would have for months.

Leaving Dublin behind us, the van, devoid of a single spring, leaped boisterously from one pothole to the next, and Peter explained to me, between gasps, that when he left Munny at 5 o'clock that morning, he had not been too happy about the situation he had left behind.

All of our allies, including of course *Teach Yourself Farming*, had made it clear that in order to make a start on very little capital, we would have to invest in a herd of milking cows. Larger sums of money from beef and sheep and hoped-for corn crops would only reach the bank account at irregular intervals, whereas a milk cheque would arrive by the month and thus help pay the wages and keep us financially afloat.

It was this future milking herd that was causing Peter concern. He had bought about eight heifers, all in calf, and they had been delivered by lorry the previous day. During the night, he had heard curious noises coming from the cow-house, and before he left Michael confirmed that at least two of the expectant ladies had not enjoyed the cross-country journey by lorry, and were well on the way to producing their offspring. At 5 o'clock that morning Peter had had to leave Michael coping alone with the situation, and as we bounced up the drive and came to a dead stop outside the cow-house, even I could understand from the grunts and groans, the rattling of chains and the stamping of hoofs, that the situation inside might be out of hand. Peter leaped out of the van, dragged off his jacket, and, in spite of my finery, I thought best to follow suit.

Having been brought up in the aforementioned 'stiff upper lip' tradition, I shall describe the sight which met my eyes as I gingerly put my head round the cow-house only as a somewhat crude introduction to country life.

The straw strewn about the floor was a mass of blood mixed up with some shining mess which I afterwards learned was the afterbirth. Two of the row of animals before me obviously had their ordeal behind them and were busily licking their calves, one of which had already struggled to its feet and discovered the milk supply. The rest had decided to follow their good example, but had not as yet been so successful. They were, in fact, still hard at it, so that forefeet, heads, half-heads, and, in one case, something which looked rather like a tail, were vigorously trying to churn their way into the world. Poor Michael, also well spattered with blood and armed with a rope, was obviously exhausted, but as Peter pulled off his jacket and plunged into the fray, he managed to smile, bid me welcome, and remark that the way it was, it looked as if we were in for some class of a struggle.

According to Michael, it seemed that it was necessary to sprinkle salt on the heads of newly born calves in order to encourage their mothers to lick them dry, so, when Peter yelled for more salt, I was only too glad to retire hurriedly and see if I could find it up in the house. In truth, if the thought of myself standing there all dressed up and probably pea-green in the face had not suddenly struck me as extremely funny, the *mise-en-scène* before me, combined with the pungent smell of creation, was well on the way to making me feel extremely sick.

A narrow pathway, cleared of grass and undergrowth, led me to the house and to the front door, which only needed a sharp kick to push it open, and I found I was standing in the hallway which no longer seemed so dark as when I had been there before. Dark red with the occasional purple blotch had been the colour scheme favoured by our predecessors, but Peter must have used whatever paint he had managed to rescue from the farm auction, for the walls were now white. He had not managed the staircase, but no amount of dark brown veneer could hide its graceful curves as it wound its way up to the floor above. Only a row of assorted buckets, some half-filled with water, and lined up from one step to the next, made me pause a moment to conclude that they could only be explained away by the absence of so many slates from the roof.

As I stood there in the echoing, carpetless hallway, looking about me, my eyes wandering over the well-laid floor-boards, the fine mahogany doorways so liberally spattered with worm holes, a curious thought occurred to me. Could it have been some racial memory, some chance anecdote, some sudden reminiscence conjured up by my father when rustling through family papers, which had induced me to try and dress the part of châtelaine? How had they behaved, those Anglo-Irish ancestors of mine, during the various rebellions, the famines, the occupation of an island geographically so close at hand, racially so remote? Had there been pity when the native Irish died of hunger in their

438

thousands or left by the boatload for America? As I had never before actually lived here, I felt myself to be free of the 'Big House' syndrome. Bother the worm holes and the buckets on the stairs; for me, for us, I decided it was all going to be different.

It was Molly's gentle voice bidding me welcome, invoking God's blessing on us and the house which brought me back to the present realities, for she added that the kettle was boiling on the hob and she was 'allowing' the boss man and Michael would be needing a cup of tea when the performance outside was behind them.

Salt – of course, it was salt they needed, and, if my extra smart get-up had anything to do with ancestral memories, I felt this was the moment to cast them aside. To hell with worm holes!

A pair of Wellington boots and a raincoat seemed to be doing nothing useful in the hall, so I kicked off my shoes, discarded my black and pale blue ensemble, dropped my Greta Garbo hat into one of the empty buckets, and with my glowing desire to blaze a trail dimmed only temporarily, I followed Molly into the kitchen where she supplied me with a drum of salt and let me out of the back door into the yard.

Chapter Twelve

'A satisfactory term's work – Christabel is settling in nicely.' Anyone acquainted with the British educational system would recognize the well-worn phrasing as all over England children sentenced to boarding-school, when most of them would have been far happier at home, were doubtless trying to do just that. I had so often read the wording on my own, my sister's, brothers' and sons' school reports, and sometimes wondered if it had not been conceived by weary pedagogues simply to pacify anxious, possibly guilt-ridden parents.

The settling-in process at Munny was very different, involving nothing so passive as settling-down, but rather scenes which stand out in my memory like flash-light photographs, some surprising, some inspiring, some disconcerting, some hilarious; all milestones along our chosen road, as we advanced from cows to beef cattle and to sheep; from sparse crops of oats, cut with a binder, stooked and threshed, to respectable harvests of barley and wheat, blown into trailers by a combine harvester.

The school holidays in the spring of 1949 were, for me, a joyous prelude to all this activity. There must be an element of the broody hen in my make-up, for I was well aware that my main reason for happiness came from having all my family under one roof, something which had not been the case since bombs drove us out of Berlin. I could not excel myself in the garden, for when I wrote to my expert mother for advice, her reply was to wait awhile before planting to see what came up. The summer passed and nothing whatsoever did come up, except a forest of Jerusalem artichokes which could have provided us with enough soup to last a lifetime.

Nevertheless I remained deeply content, for the leaking roof I knew to be our very own, the bath-tub, our bath-tub, and the tangled scrub outside maybe our future garden. I could even imagine that the old grey mansion itself, with its glorious view over the hills, could be joining in the fun. It might be listening with pleasure to our irrepressible sons sliding down the banisters and clattering up and down its long carpetless passageways, or sharing our astonishment when we tried to run a bath and water flowed from those splendid taps but was accompanied by an assortment of incomplete frogs and a steady flow of tadpoles.

If I allowed my imagination to run wild, I could even picture those crumbling walls urging us on to greater effort, hoping perhaps to return one day to a long-lost eighteenth-century elegance.

While the boys were busy at what they called exploring everything and I at what Peter described as nest-building, he was applying himself with untiring energy to what was to become his 'Four-Year Plan'. Stephen Cullinan, Paddy Dawson and *Teach Yourself Farming* were his constant advisers.

Cows, well why not? The gay yodelling of cowherds and the delicate tinkle of cowbells returning from the high pastures in the Black Forest still echoed in my ears. And what about the 'Daisies', the 'Buttercups' and the 'Rosebuds', docile friends all eager to provide fresh milk and butter for the household?

Wait till I tell you! Anyone who might entertain romantic ideas as to the rôle of the cow in farming family life and who expects harmony to prevail would be wise to drop them forthwith. For there is something utterly dispiriting about milking a lot of cows morning and evening, Monday to Sunday, January to December.

In the nature of things, a cow's lactation does not go on for ever, so that, even if not overtaken by milk fever or mastitis, her supply of milk slowly dries up, the graph on the wall curves downwards, and the humour of the attendant cowman follows suit. When he then lugs increasingly fewer cans down the road, and heaves them onto the milk stand to await collection, he can only think with deepening gloom of that dwindling milk cheque. It cannot be long before such sympathetic noises as 'Oh dear – bad luck, never mind' soon dry up likewise.

As for a bull, although appreciating the necessity, I had visions of bull fighters being tossed about like discarded dolls; although not wishing to disturb the 'Four-Year Plan' I decided that no bull was going to rampage about our hedgeless, gateless, unprotected fields. I only relented when assured that this ferocious addition to our menagerie would be confined to just one paddock, so fenced in, so enclosed as to resemble an impregnable fortress. One of those impregnable fortresses you can read about no doubt, for it was only a matter of days before, called outside to consult with our local Garda about a gun licence, I and the bull met up with each other face to face. Obviously no heroine, I only had time to screech, 'The bull's out,' before scooting back into the house. Although I could not reach the roof, I still managed to arrive in record time at a top-floor window from whence I could witness our arm of the law, gun licence forgotten, pedalling his ancient bicycle away down the drive at break-neck speed, while my courageous, but surely doomed, husband, armed with a golf umbrella, somehow succeeded in bluffing the animal to retreat backwards into an outhouse.

My hunch about cows became conviction after Peter von Mentzingen joined our team for a full year and became as another son to us. Peter was strong and extremely handsome with a delightful sense of humour and as he was due to inherit an estate in Wurttemberg which, having a castle attached might include plenty of debts, he was well aware of the importance of the monthly milk cheque. It took some time for the cow-house to have its effect on this cheerful boy. For many weeks he entered into the spirit of the game, welcoming them in from the field, watching with amusement as they pushed their way into their favourite stalls, whistling to himself as he washed down their udders before applying the milking machine and driving them out again with an affectionate slap on the haunches. Yet one morning, as I passed through the yard, I found him leaning against the cow-house door staring disconsolately into the distance, with the usual river of liquid manure flowing round his boots. 'Bally old Brünhilde's let me down today, Chris,' he said and added, 'I'm afraid it'll have to be cows when I get back again to Germany. German cows, but I guess they are the same all over the world.'

I had to admit that I had no idea how German cows behaved, but could well believe that, rather than goose-stepping into the cow-house they would jostle and kick, get mastitis and lash out with their tails at exactly the wrong moment, just like every other cow. As we strolled back together to the house, although, as ever, not wishing to disturb my husband's 'Four-Year Plan', I knew I was on my way to coming to a firm decision. It might need a bit of time but a few hints, some more forceful than others, should do the trick as far as I was concerned: the cows, the chugging of the milking machine, all the paraphernalia required to put a bottle of milk on a stranger's doorstep would, as soon as we could afford it, be past history.

Peter von Mentzingen went back to Germany, inherited his castle and married a lovely girl. When we visited him we were able to report that our cows now reared their own calves, single suckling being the order of the day. We could also take note that Peter had taken to breeding horses. Bidding goodbye to our milking herd had been far easier than expected as by then we had all reached the stage of hardly being able to wait for our milk contract to expire. The first phase of the 'Four-Year Plan' had come to a successful end.

Something however had to make up for what even I was beginning to refer to as our cash flow. It was decided that it must be more grain growing and the addition of sheep which meant attending a sheep and cattle fair. Fair days in Tullow took place once a month, on a Monday, when the little town was invaded by local farmers and their families, accompanied by their means of livelihood. Prudent shopkeepers boarded up their doors and windows while cows, bullocks, heifers and calves, ponies and donkeys took over the main street, flooding it in no time with slithery rivers of greenish muck. No one allowed this to disturb the main business of the day, nor the general air of cheerful sociability, which I once heard described with enthusiasm as being 'as good as a wake'. In those days banks played little rôle in business deals as no one wished for 'them fellows in their shirts and ties' to be poking around in affairs that were private. Instead, a spit on the palm and a handshake were enough to seal a bargain, after which those shopkeepers who happened to have a 'Select Lounge' tucked away in their back premises came into their own. They could remove the barricade and be assured of profiting in their own fashion from the subsequent celebrations. In the evening of those market days a little cattle train chugged down the track towards Dublin and our town returned to normality once again.

My own experience of such a day in Tullow was unusual in that, still innocent of what might be outside the bounds of possibility, I chose to go to the hairdresser and was sitting under the drier reading peacefully when a disturbance made me glance in the mirror and I realized I was not alone in my cubicle: I had been joined by a bullock, or it could have been a heifer. The animal gazed at me placidly for a moment or two before retreating backwards through the curtains, seeming to understand that it had come to the wrong address. 'Mary, Mother of God – would you know,' laughed the hairdresser as she saw it off the premises, and I gathered that this was not the first time she had dealt with such an unusual client.

Peter's visit to the market was of more consequence, although the result was no less disconcerting when he returned home the proud and innocent owner of a certain breed of sheep known as 'Hornies'. Rural communication can surely only be equalled by the African drum-beat for everyone he met in the market square that day seemed to know he was 'after sheep'. Before long, he was approached by a persuasive old hand at the game, who soon convinced him that if he was looking for a real bargain, hardy, prolific, and above all, not too expensive, he could offer him the real thing. The fact that in order to inspect this attractive proposition he would have to accompany the owner to a distant hilltop, should, I suppose, have sounded an alarm signal. The farming world being what it is, it would have been unnatural for the owner to explain that his sheep were only suitable for mountain grazing and that hedges, fences and ditches, even five-bar gates, were child's play should one purposeful animal decide to break out. It would then be followed, almost immediately, by its baaing, bleating, companions, all heading for some unknown reason towards some other grazing ground.

'They're on the move,' became Peter's rallying cry, as the usual hullabaloo reached our ears and had us whooping and charging about the place, as often as not in our night-clothes, in an abortive effort to keep those hornies off our crops.

I suppose anyone brought up on the land could have told us that when dealing with sheep, whooping and charging around the place was a recipe for disaster, and that when lacking a sheep-dog, man should make a quiet, almost uninterested, approach. Patience, much patience, would then be needed before a leader made up its mind to venture off in the desired direction, when with luck the remainder of the flock would obediently follow suit. Quite simple really, but just one of those lessons to be learned the hard way by a former student of the Law and one clueless woman who had once prided herself on having won a scholarship to Oxford University.

I have to admit that by the time those hornies departed and were replaced by a less adventurous breed, my interest in sheep, apart from the financial virtues, had reached another low ebb. It was not their fault that, in my opinion, they possessed the dumbest, glummest faces on earth, but it was beyond me why they could not stay put. Why lie down and die at the drop of a hat, or, in snow, head with deadly purpose for the nearest snow-drift and allow themselves to be buried alive?

I suppose it is about time I admitted to not being a natural devotee of farm animals, and therefore needed occasional encouragement. It came my way on a glorious April day when the lambing season was in full swing.

She was lying near the gate, with Michael beside her, that yellow-eyed ewe who was struggling with a breech birth and whose efforts were getting weaker by the minute. It must have been the look she gave me. 'Don't just stand there,' she seemed to be pleading as her eyes glazed over in agony. 'You're a woman too, can't you see what I am going through? Give us a hand, for God's sake.'

I glanced at Michael standing helplessly by with his bucket of Jeyes Fluid and his lump of Pears soap and his dilemma came to me in a flash. He had tried to turn the lamb and bring it into the world right way round but his hand was too big. I glanced at my own and without quite knowing how I was to go about it, I found myself muttering, 'Come on, old girl, I'm with you,' as I rolled up my sleeve, delved my arm into the bucket, soaked it well and proceeded to go about my business. 'I'm with you,' but in truth once inside I had little idea where I was; from then on, the assortment of slithery heads and legs, fore and aft, was completely bewildering. I was lucky that day, as the ewe had been through it before and the head and forelegs I managed to get a grip on happened to belong to each other. A steady pull and the miracle happened. A lamb had been born and I was midwife. 'It could be twins, it could be triplets, mam, so it could!' Michael was smiling, too, as he wiped its face, held it upside down and smacked it smartly until it sneezed. Twins? – Triplets? I was ready for anything, and by the time I had delivered number three, that first-born was struggling to its feet nosing around for the milk supply.

Just a fleeting moment in time when the skies clear and mists are swept away. 'Carved in God's image or something, that's what

445

we both are, see?' I could assure my woolly companion rather breathlessly as we lay there resting up against each other in a pool of mud and blood.

I would like to be able to say that besides becoming rather an expert as a midwife, I played a significant rôle where further farming activities were concerned. Would I ever become a worthwhile farmer's wife? I had to doubt it, for to judge by some of our more professional neighbours, a farmer's wife needed to be a prodigy in order to consider herself worthy of her salt. Besides keeping her family fed and clothed, rearing the calves, possibly some piglets, tending the vegetable patch and hustling to the rescue when crises occurred, if she ever had time to sit down and read, she must learn how to bake special cakes, make special jams, so that the sight of an unripe tomato would be enough to ensure her directing what remained of her energy towards tasty pickles, preserves and chutneys.

But I was determined to make my contribution and decided to plump for hens, mainly, I think, because Christopher was still at an age when finding eggs in a nest is an exciting and satisfying experience. He was six when we came to Munny, and had left his days in boarding-school, temporarily at least, behind him. Much of his time was now spent trudging back and forth to the local school where a charming young teacher tried to instil some learning into a group of Protestant children between the ages of six and fourteen. As far as our son was concerned, she had not got much beyond persuading him to recite the Lord's Prayer, at the top of his voice, with a splendid Irish accent, and to knit me a golliwog for Christmas; but feeding those hens and collecting the eggs was a job he took very seriously.

It was, therefore, a major tragedy when a friend who had taken an early morning stroll returned to breakfast with downcast eye and advised me not to go near the hen paddock. A fox had obviously invaded my hen-run in the night, and except for a few mutilated corpses, there was no longer a hen to be seen.

I must have had some affection for those birds as it took me two days, and the removal of the bodies, before I could take Christopher by the hand and with him face up to their deserted home. As I looked about me, wondering why it should be that not only certain humans, but also animals seem to kill for fun, I heard a faint sound, the rustling of leaves, coming from an upper branch of one of the surrounding trees. There, sure enough, with head sunk in its feathers and somewhat rocky on its legs, was perched one of my hens, obviously a sole survivor. We were delighted to see her and Christopher was about to run off and fetch her some food when she fluttered to the ground, landed like a stone and suddenly let out a resounding whoop, a joyful crow, unmistakably that of a cock. 'Gosh! Mum, what's that?' Christopher stopped in his tracks, turned to me and seeing the expression on my face, burst out laughing. What's that? A good question, and certainly one for which I had no answer. *Teach Yourself Poultry* had certainly not mentioned that the fright of a lifetime could spark off a sex change for a hen.

We set about trying to woo our sole survivor back to becoming a hen again by sitting it on some eggs. It responded for a while, only to ruin its chance of ever rearing a family by forgetting about them every morning in order to greet the dawn with its newly discovered trumpet call. Thinking perhaps that it was lonely we introduced it to three ducks, but it was not long before they became fed up with its behaviour and fled in panic as soon as he/she approached them with a purposeful glint in its eye.

The veterinary profession provided no answer, and doubting if Herr Freud had ever applied himself to the problem of the bisexual hen, we finally left her to her bizarre lifestyle until she died a natural death. Only Christopher was satisfied at being able to inform a spellbound school audience that one of his charges up on the farm could surely qualify for a world record.

When my thoughts turn to those early years in Munny, one vivid memory chases another. I sit in comfort and warmth; I switch on the light and switch it off again; I go to the telephone and chat with a friend or a neighbour should I so wish. If I look back over my shoulder though, just behind me, is a small oil lamp casting weird shadows on the wall and beside it a fizzing, flaring 'Tilley', last witness to the only blazing row about our finances that Peter and I ever had, when I bought the wretched thing without first consulting his 'Four-Year Plan'!

Our initial introduction to what was known in those days as 'the Electric' came from someone who was known in the district as 'a great man with the wires'. He installed a generator, six old bus batteries and two extra light bulbs for the house. We were only plunged back into darkness when all available light was needed for the milking machine and as this could happen quite suddenly it was wise to keep a candle close at hand. The expert

447

with the wires made only one mistake when trying to extend his territory to include the pig-house, which contained two sows destined, along with their offspring, to make a fortune for our eldest son, Nicky.

On their way back to pasture, the cows had to pass the pig-house door and they had not done so more than twice when our cowman of the day declared he would no longer stay with us as the place was haunted. 'Lepping around, sir, and that scared as if the Divil had them by the tail,' he exclaimed and was about to launch into one of the many horror tales which are rife in all lonely country places, when Peter persuaded him to drive all the cows back again into the yard. Sure enough, as they passed the pig-house they launched themselves into what looked like a parody of some ritual dance, legs up, knees up, head down, tails up, a bovine jam session, which would have been awe-inspiring if some of the participants had not been in an obvious state of near panic. Needless to relate, wet hoofs, and too lightly insulated wiring laid just an inch below the ground, soon solved the mystery of our haunted farmyard.

The day came at last when rumour had it that the mains supply was described as advancing on us all the way from Dublin or it could be Cork, or might be Limerick; no matter, such was the enthusiasm that it was not easy to dissuade the Electricity Board from placing a huge pylon right beside our front door.

However, with tact, another crisis was avoided and we could switch those lights on and off, off and on, upstairs and downstairs, all over the place, transforming at will our not so stately home into a fairyland.

I was to discover that one of the many attractions of living in Ireland for anyone with a disorderly mind is the lack of need to waste time wondering if, how, why or when certain happenings, certain predictable events, will take place; they might so they might, but they also might not, you could never be quite sure.

For instance, I often wondered how many artless tourists, ignorant of the national game of playing about with signposts, and therefore much confused, have spent further hours trying to reach their destination by simply stopping and asking the way. Charmed then by the friendly solicitude of their informant, told to wheel this way, to wheel that, how could they know as they continued their journey smiling so gratefully, that a widespread difficulty in distinguishing the right hand from the left had more than likely sent them off once more in the wrong direction?

'A chara – mise le meas', after spending many useless hours in the grocer's store waiting for temperamental telephone calls, I used up my five words of Irish hoping to show enough respect to apply to the Department of Posts and Telegraphs for a private line. No one seemed much impressed with my patriotic effort but after several months I did receive a reply, letting me know that the installation of such a luxury would cost us an initial outlay of £350.00. We were not feeling too affluent at the time so decided with regret to postpone things for another day. Imagine my surprise, when, *en route* for the Post Office some days later, I passed a lively crew of postal engineers well equipped with ladders, wires and poles, digging holes and lopping off branches, obviously bent on bringing a telephone up to our door. Nor was that the end of it, for it was not to be too long before we were supplied with two telephones. The first was a period piece, with a crank handle, which when turned at speed alerted the postmistress into setting off on her voyage along the wires to whatever number we required. This was soon joined by another with a numbered dial. Ireland had joined the EEC, the 'dialling' was upon us, and we were assured that once the new arrival was fixed up and had settled down, we would find ourselves talking to 'the whole wide world'.

Sure enough, one year later, almost to the day, this information proved to be correct. Well, perhaps not quite correct, but by following the instructions sent to us in the post, by turning the dial slowly and methodically and by ignoring certain noises which made us wonder if the grandfather clock was advancing upon us from the kitchen, whichever way we dialled we could find ourselves talking to a host of people we had never met or heard of in our lives before.

Some seemed unduly upset at our intrusion into what might have been a business call of some urgency; others quite willing to pass a few minutes of the day in friendly chat with a stranger. Only one poor lady from Donegal hung up on us after declaring that the whole country was in a heap anyway and she was off to America. On a further occasion, having dialled as I thought a Dublin number, I was answered by the cheerful voice of our linesman 'working on the line,' he said, and we could even exchange witticisms, agreeing with each other whole-heartedly that he was not the only one who was 'up the pole'.

Why was it then that in spite of all this progress we felt a sense of loss when our old friend with the crank handle was declared redundant and we were given to understand that the friendly voice of the postmistress must also go off the air; nor when the line crackled, threatened to burst our eardrums and go dead as heretofore, could we sally forth with a long pole and bash away at the wires until we were on the air again.

We were not alone in our temporary fit of the dumps for I had to think of those many local ladies who kept the wheels of Irish rural industry turning; who sat unperturbed beside minute electric fires in back-room offices buffeted by gale-force draughts, and of the one who confessed it would be 'awful lonesome' once the dialling took over. No more heart-to-hearts for free with friends on the local switchboards, no more crossed lines to give one the opportunity of keeping abreast with local and even national affairs. For some progress just looked like being awful lonesome.

For me progress was a light bulb and some books, all luxuries I had been unable to indulge in simultaneously for years.

I would probably have been better occupied if I had followed Peter's good example, tried to stick to my present rôle as farmer's wife, and looked for a booklet entitled *Teach Yourself How To Love Cows, Sheep, Cats and Dogs*, but instead, I steered my lone course towards contemporary Irish history. Needless to say I was unaware of how many before me had tried to make sense of the subject and failed, nor was it to be long before I joined their bewildered ranks.

Chapter Thirteen

Ireland united Gaelic and Free. When surveying the events in Ireland of the 1950s and the 1960s the history books could proudly proclaim these decades as having witnessed the Republic's great leap forward from a small, partly dependent state, intimately, almost incestuously, involved with its own affairs, to a new, outward-looking Ireland freed from the last threads of British rule, outside the Commonwealth, eager to plan its own destiny and to play a rôle in international affairs.

Ulster, Munster, Leinster and Connaught, the 'Four Green Fields', the only cloud on such a glowing horizon being the awkward fact that one of those green fields still stubbornly refused to be drawn in, preferring with iron determination to remain outside the fence.

Why? Protestants to the North, Catholics to the South of a carelessly drawn borderline dividing neighbour from neighbour, farmhouse from farmlands, but, above all, dyed-in-the-wool Protestants from equally rigid Catholics. It was thus the so-called 'Troubles' had been born and as yet seemed to have found no solution.

There was no use denying that the Catholic Church, 'the Faith', had kept an educational ethic alive in Ireland in times of great hardship, providing the famous 'hedge schools' when the Irish were banned from schooling by their British overlords. In those times of worldly suffering, too, it had provided the escape route to a blissful hereafter. But now it held the stage and the bigotry displayed on each side of a straggling North–South border was beyond my comprehension.

This was the situation which had existed for so many decades in Ireland; one which I could not help fearing might ultimately tear the little country apart. It was one which I hoped at least to

451

clarify, ensconced in our only armchair with the written word and plenty of cigarettes to hand, and that almost audible silence about me which belongs to long winter evenings in the country. I soon discovered that I was not too well equipped for my self-appointed task, for my own liberal up-bringing in England had not included differentiating between Catholic and Protestant, Jew and Gentile, and my experience of Hitler's régime in Germany had given me a loathing of racial or religious discrimination of any kind. During those Nazi years the scenario had been so different. It was a time when the churches – Protestant and Catholic – were united against a common enemy.

There was Claus von Stauffenberg, a devout Catholic, who had asked for and been granted dispensation by his priest before setting off for Hitler's Army Headquarters in order to rid the world of a monster he believed to be an Anti-Christ. Both were to die, as was one of my heroes, Father Delp, who turned to his persecutors before being hanged and remarked with serenity, 'In a few minutes' time I will know for certain what many of you may be wondering about.'

There was Graf Galen, the Catholic Archbishop of Cologne (Münster), whose sermons and pastoral letters were passed avidly from ear to ear, from hand to hand, no matter whether Catholic or Protestant; and the Lutheran Pastors, Niemöller and Bonhœffer, whose messages from prison did likewise. To me all this had nothing to do with churches, statues or monuments, but signified the true strength of Christianity as I believed it should be.

I therefore found myself becoming increasingly dismayed to find that in this so-called 'free democracy', the ethics and moral teachings of one church – the Roman Catholic Church – represented by the hierarchy of bishops, could not only hold such powerful sway over the lives of their own Catholic flock, but that their authority extended to include everyone who happened to live in what had become the 'Republic of Ireland'.

Since 1937, a Censorship of Publications Act, which included theatrical plays and films, had reached the Statute Book, and Censorship Boards, mostly chaired by a member of the priesthood, were firmly entrenched, having succeeded in banning the works of many outstanding authors of the day. The quality of some judgements made could be measured when a learned tome on soil erosion, with the unfortunate title *Rape Around Our Shores*, never reached the bookshelves. When it came to films, a visit to the local cinema often included a challenge to the imagination, for as soon as the screen portrayed sex, even in its most innocent form, out came the censor's scissors. A snip, a blank, and a bewildered audience could find themselves transported post-haste to safer and less controversial territory. The Public Dance Hall Act of 1929 saw to it that such entertainment could only take place under the watchful eye of a priest, whose rôle was to convince himself, and his superiors, that, in between dances, the width of the dance floor divided the would-be revellers, the boys from the girls.

Divorce and birth control by any means other than abstinence were dealt with under a so-called Criminal Law Amendment Act, later to be enshrined in the Constitution. In the case of divorce, something had come unstuck: the State, by forbidding it under any circumstances, found itself limping along well behind the Church, which in certain cases could grant an annulment of marriage. It could do so by conveniently overlooking the paradoxical position of any children born to such a union, declaring quite simply that the marriage had never been consummated. For a Catholic to attend Trinity College, Dublin, the oldest university in the land, founded some four hundred years ago by Queen Elizabeth I, a known heretic, was seriously to sin. It was in fact to risk excommunication, as it was for a Catholic to be seen inside a Protestant church.

Personalities emerged in the telling, like Éamon de Valera, a towering figure who had occupied the stage almost continuously since the rebellion against the British in 1916, with his passionate aim for the uniting of the island, his skill as a negotiator, his success, in spite of outward pressures, in maintaining Ireland's neutrality during the war.

As I read on it seemed to me that the question should arise as to just how this inscrutable patriot of Spanish–American heritage had managed so successfully to steer his upward course and remain so firmly lodged on his pedestal, considering his rigid concern for the dominant rôle that Roman Catholic moral teaching should play in State affairs, and his seeming lack of such concern when it came to social progress, or consideration for religious minorities. Again, I was troubled by his mythical, almost Hitlerian, dream for Irish rural society where, instead of buxom, blond, blue-eyed Teutons thumping around dressed up

453

as peasants, it was to be innocent, nimble-footed Gaels dancing jigs and reels, singing and conversing in a language which few but themselves could understand. As I turned the pages I found myself asking, as had possibly many others, if de Valera's reign had not been over-long and thus successfully retarded not only Ireland's ultimate unity, but also her advance into the twentieth century.

So many sins, so much wickedness, so many pastoral warnings – but I had spent twelve years of my life in a country where real wickedness ruled the land and I could only wonder at the triviality of such authoritarian rules and regulations designed to keep the people of Ireland on a straight and narrow, but utterly cheerless, path.

As for a once all-powerful Protestant minority, they seemed to have opted out, content to play no further rôle in public life, sending their sons to school in England, later perhaps to die for England and her causes.

But then my disquiet began to wane, for I only had to venture abroad to detect a certain philosophical attitude not only towards the laws of the land, but also to the constant priestly exhortations. There had to be tragedies lurking beneath the surface of such a rigid régime; poverty, ignorance, unwanted pregnancies, and heart-rending farewells. But when I saw the ordinary folk around us going about their daily business, coming from their prayers, their weddings, even their funerals, chatting and laughing, flirting and joking, they did not look overburdened with wickedness, nor for that matter particularly penitent; a state of affairs I could believe to be most frustrating for their prelates, but to me a great relief.

If I were occasionally inclined to despair at the seemingly endless wrangle between Church and State, when the battalions drawn up on the one side seemed too entrenched and on the other too supine, where hopes for a slight degree of social advancement were silenced again and again in the interest of ecclesiastical sanctity, I was given cause for further relief when I first experienced the Irish electoral system. The countryside was disfigured for weeks beforehand, and for months afterwards, by huge posters portraying would-be statesmen, doing their utmost to look purposeful, honest and reliable. Determined to become a loyal Irish citizen, I changed my passport once again to one emblazoned with the Irish harp. I was in no position to write them all off as did a fellow voter, from whom I sought advice on my way to the polling station. 'Sons of their dead Da's, publicans, and the rest – nothing but holy chancers' was my companion's summing-up, pushing his cap to the back of his head, with no sign of rancour, as we moved inside preparatory to playing our part in the shaping of the country's future.

On such occasions, a farmhouse up the road did duty as a Polling Station, and as I stood in the makeshift cabin set up in the parlour, pencil in hand, studying a list of names, none of which made sense to me, and listened to the rattling of tea cups from the kitchen next door where our local Garda – our arm of the law – was ensconced with some neighbours beside a cosy turf fire, my thoughts inevitably drifted back to the last time I recorded my vote in 1937. 'Heil Hitler, your name, please,' Nazi flags, brown shirts, pillbox hats, shining boots and clicking heels, and one blank square, just one, in which to express your opinion. '*Ja* – *Nein*', 'Yes – No', and the eerie sensation that my hand holding the pencil was being very carefully studied by a pair of very attentive eyes.

So much for the history books and my amateur attempt to make head or tail of so much that was contradictory in the land in which we now lived. It could have been inertia, it could also have come from a certain sense of sadness which seemed to pervade those pages, but it was more likely the arrival of spring, when the days grew longer and one glorious sunrise after another lit up the eastern sky, which encouraged me to lay books aside, and turn to another source. It was a hidden source, nearer to home, more manageable, which as folk were dying, memories fading, and television and the motor car were fast invading the land, could soon be gone for ever.

The facts had been carefully recorded in deeds and documents and meticulously confirmed by statistical survey. The lands of 'Munny' or 'Money', an anglicized version from the Gaelic '*Muine*, to denote a copse, a group of trees, consisted of four hundred and fifty statute acres of Irish land not to be mistaken for Irish acres of a larger dimension. These were spurious measurements created by Cromwell when he parcelled out Irish land to his victorious soldiery. In 1949 they were still in use, but the reason for their usage had not been forgotten by the descendants of the dispossessed. These acres were now entrusted to us to do with as we willed. We could either allow the gorse and ferns to creep in further, and the rushes to advance at will, or see to it that each separate field be allowed to develop its own personality, changing its character from season to season, from year to year, to become a shifting patchwork of greens and golds.

I had my own kingdom and had not yet explored its boundaries: The Rath, The Moate and the hidden corners sheltering ivy-covered ruins – *sibíní* or *tigíní*, small, tiny roofless homesteads where once big families were born and reared in bygone days.

I also had my historians to hand. Will Byrne, our herdsman, lived across the hill and had spent all his working life with the former owners of the land; he knew every hump and hollow of his kingdom. From him we learned that each field had its name. The Rathfield, with its scrap of circular scrubland and a blackthorn tree, insignificant enough if you were not in the know, but a certain sure landmark indicating what must be a ruined homestead beneath. His advice was 'Best not to meddle with it' nor with the grassy hummock planted with tall trees and known as 'The Moate', a place of burial perhaps. 'Best not to meddle with that either,' for it was known that the souls of departed Druids sometimes took a notion to return to such places, and no luck would come the way of any temporary custodian who might think to tidy up, to flatten such hindrances, and thus cause the rightful original owners much inconvenience.

The Mistress's Bog – Miss Kitty's Grove – The Racecourse. Who was that unknown lady who gave her name to a windflower-covered swamp? Who was Miss Kitty, who must have wandered through her grove? Did she wander alone?

My informant was uncertain as to the identity of 'The Mistress', except for knowing that there was a time when, in years past, the Lord Fitzwilliam oft-times came to visit, and it was he who in old age installed the graceful staircase whose shallow steps were fashioned so that the mistress of the house, older now too and troubled with rheumatism, could ascend to her chamber nice and easy.

As for Miss Kitty, she was a poor one, gave her heart to a handsome local priest, and was only able to tell of her love by way of the confessional. The way it was, little notes passed back and forth by way of the dividing grid. All went well until one day it was a stranger who sat before her in the darkness, and it was he who received the scrap of paper and thought to tell his superiors of such an obvious mortal sin.

As Will took a long draw on his pipe, I was beginning to fear he was about to launch into another tragedy. Poor Miss Kitty could have had it, gone into a decline or whatever love-sick ladies did in those days, but luckily, not at all. It would seem a certain confusion set in here, as some said the priest was banished to another parish, others that he left straight away for America, but all were agreed that he returned to his Miss Kitty, and one dark night they left together, destination unknown. As neither of us could suppress happy smiles, I could gather that both Will and I were much content with this solution, he adding, 'God forgive them,' just to make quite sure.

The Big Stone Field yielded up its full story when a local stonemason arrived in the yard telling me that he'd heard that the Boss Man wished to clear the land of some larger rocks using dynamite, and he'd come to make enquiries. After offering the usual opening remarks as to the weather which, in Ireland, is usually 'grand', 'soft', or 'barbarous', he hesitated before coming to the subject and then explained that the way it was when accepting the job, he had failed to ask Peter what he intended doing about the big stone in the Stone Field. 'Would the Boss Man be thinking of meddling with it?' was how he expressed himself, and, recognizing that key word, it was not difficult for me to reassure him about the big stone, as I was certain it would have needed all the dynamite in his possession to blow even a small hole in it. When he showed relief, and assured me he would be along the next morning, I could not help asking the reason for his initial hesitation. He seemed surprised at my ignorance, but was also very happy and willing to launch into his story, which, as he explained after first leading me to the front of the house, began on the heights of Aghold Hill before us. He presumed that I, of course, knew that St Kevin was often inclined to wander in the Wicklow Mountains, but maybe it was a new one on me that one day he stood up there with the wind to his back, threw his cloak in the air and called into the wind that where it fell to earth, there he would build his church. 'And the Holy Man kept his word,' said the stonemason, 'for there, can you not see, it still stands.'

For a moment I could not see why a small roofless church, built more than a thousand years ago, could have much to do with dynamite, but the stonemason was in full flight, caught up in the natural eloquence of his race.

'Centuries passed,' he said, 'and the Holy Man's little chapel became a meeting place for all those who would not desert the Faith and when a wee bell called them, they would flock along the Mass paths, the hidden ways, to worship before the altar of St Kevin. Then came one dark night, when the wind was again blowing strongly from the west, and the bell did toll no more. What would I say to that?' he asked, and I could only look at him expectantly, knowing that there was more to come. 'It was thieves, you see,' he said, 'and them dragging the bell over the fields, when a mighty flash lit up the sky and there was a powerful rumbling and they turned to see a rock break away from the hillside and come at them. And whichever way they turned and twisted, wheeled and stumbled, it came after them until they reached the field before us, and they could run no further, and they let loose the bell and fled, and the big stone rolled on and over it, and stopped where it is today.'

The stonemason had been pointing out the route taken by the thieves as if it had all happened last week and when his outstretched arm fell to his side, I thought he had come to the end of his tale, but – 'Every seven years, they do be saying – the old ones, that is – that they can hear the wee bell tolling and then if you have an ear for it, comes the rustling and the whispering along the Mass paths. I don't know, it may be so, it may not be so, but whichever way it is, I wouldn't meddle with it,' he concluded, as he bade me good day until the morrow.

The mystery as to why water came through the roof by the gallon had been easily solved: after all, one Bangor slate was worth one bottle of Guinness, and our predecessors had preferred Guinness. Why I often shared my bath with a few tadpoles puzzled me quite a lot until, here again, Will Byrne came to the rescue when he told us of the Watercourse and what he called 'the grandeur of it'. Grand indeed had been its conception in the mid-nineteenth century; grand also the achievement of bringing water from the hills to flow for miles between cut granite banks in sufficient volume to move huge water wheels which drove the rugged machines which churned and chopped, thrashed and pulped the produce of the Munny Estate when it was in its heyday at the turn of the century.

Not so grand, I would say, for those smallholders who, for fear of eviction, laboured for a pittance in its construction, but who, had they known it, could bide their time awaiting the inevitable decline of their Protestant landlord's power over their lives. For as one Land Act followed another, and as the twentieth century progressed, a World War, a successful rebellion, and the declaration of an Irish Free State finally and successfully upset the former social structure of their island.

There were surely some landlords less profligate, less defeated, than our predecessors and perhaps it was too much to ask of former tenantry to show enthusiasm for an emblem of the past in which they had played little rôle except as under-dog. Nonetheless, when we took over with our hopes for the future, years of neglect had allowed the granite dykes to collapse into the water so that cattle could splash their way along the stream unheeded and an ingenious sluice gate used to control the flow had disappeared beneath a slimy green carpet of water weeds. At the end of the line the rusted water wheels with rotting flails now hung motionless on their axles.

Ireland, Ireland – burdened with so many abandoned projects, so many dilapidated grandeurs. On the upper reaches of the flow, the usual intrigues were soon to follow; fields flooded here, a sudden dearth there, and no one around on whom to lay the blame. For us at least, with the discovery of a well in the woods behind the house, the Watercourse and the 'grandeur of it' had come to its end and with it the tadpoles in the bath-tub.

Chapter Fourteen

I have told of those early years when Peter and I left his country in ruins behind us, and of how we turned a corner to find ourselves carrying on in uncharted territory.

We were not alone in our venture, for we had our three sons with us and for them holidays became sheer hard work. In spite of a few guaranteed flea bites, a visit to the local cinema was mind-blowing entertainment and two whole pound notes a month could be looked upon as a princely wage. Hedging, ditching, stooking, stacking, the daily slog when farming the land; Peter and his 'Four-Year Plan' would have been hard put without their loyal involvement.

Progress, progress, cattle and sheep, more cattle, more sheep, hardly any debts, and in spite of dire warnings that only oats could ever prosper on our exhausted Munny lands, Peter had signed a contract with Messrs Guinness to grow barley, considered at the time to be a far more lucrative crop.

In those days no local farmer had learned to apply limestone to acid soil such as ours and soon many a cautious neighbour could be seen leaning over our gates watching for the emergence of that first crop of barley, until one day it was once more Will Byrne who could finally declare that whatever Peter was putting into his 'bag stuff' the crop was growing apace and looked like surviving. Limestone was a key which had obviously unlocked an infinite supply of unused fertility and Peter's much groaned-about 'Four-Year Plan' with Stephen Cullinan's and Paddy Dawson's enthusiastic cooperation had come of age and laid the foundation for what looked like becoming a flourishing enterprise.

The farming cycle maintains a slow inevitable rhythm all of its own – the ploughing, the sowing, the greening and ripening finally reaching a climax, the crest of the wave, on that final day of the harvest when after the crows, the rabbits and the weather have all been defied, the gate can be closed on that very last field to be cleared of its crop.

It is hard to describe the jubilant sense of accomplishment which follows that ultimate trailer load of corn as it trundles off down the road heading for the loft, the silo or the corn merchant.

The harvesting days in Munny were unusual, maybe even unique, for our sons were joined each year by a team of extra hands (almost able to lay claim to being a miniature community of nations). They were the sons and daughters of friends and relatives, particularly from England and Germany, but also from France and Italy and as far afield as Botswana – Christian and Otto, Fritz, Elke, Pierre and Winfried, Leapeetswe and Sekgoma, their goal was doubtless to learn English but language seemed no barrier as they rode the tractors, lugged and loaded the sacks or relaxed together leaning up against the banks and hedgerows.

My particular rôle in the harvest ritual was to 'bring up the tea'. On hearing that the activity in the field might go on well into the night, I would then appear at 6 o'clock with my equally international retinue of 'home-helps' and enough sustenance to keep things going for a few more hours; Puppi and Angela, Verena and Adi, Renate and Rixi, and as I had long decided that I must be one of the least-efficient housewives in the business, I could only hope their mothers had not expected that, besides English, under my tutelage they might also pick up a few hints as to how a large household should be run.

I do not remember, however, that a lack of confidence was ever one of my failings, and so as the sun disappeared behind the hills and the mugs of tea and doorstep sandwiches did the rounds, I could sit back with them amongst the bulging sacks listening to their laughter and their cheerful misuse of the English language and think that maybe this journey to Ireland was giving these children something more important. They belonged to a new generation unburdened by impending war as we had been, and hopefully could remain undisturbed by race or colour, never again having even to contemplate sallying forth to kill each other.

As the years flowed by, I learned, too, that a certain pattern seems to emerge in the life of a family. In the beginning two people, strangers to each other so far, meet by chance and joyfully set off on a journey together, as yet unaware of what lies ahead of them. When children join the scene they set a family routine in motion – nursery days – school days – university – and suddenly, they are no longer children but, grown to adulthood, are off and away as is their right. One hopes that the family ties will remain intact, but close family involvement in their affairs inevitably loosens. In practical terms the family bank account looks far more cheerful, but the landscape without those loved landmarks lies curiously deserted.

I learned that it had to be, but did not find it easy to cast aside a protective rôle and accept that children belong to the future, a tomorrow country filled with surprises, adventure and also suffering as it had been for me when I left England for Germany so many years before. Fortunately the hiatus in our family did not last for too long. A year, two years or so, then came the grandchildren, and prams and cots and teddy bears could re-emerge from retirement to take up their duties once again. Nor was I destined to spend too long moping about the place, sadly aware of favourite haunts deserted and prize possessions abandoned; a tree house in the woods, an old bag of golf clubs, even a stray pair of football boots proving sometimes enough to set me off.

I was freed of such attacks of nostalgia when I heard from David Astor that a plan was afoot for a British author to produce a biography on the life of Adam von Trott, whose effort to hinder the outbreak of war in 1939 and to convince the British government of a German opposition to Hitler had proved to no avail.

Adam had been a Rhodes scholar at Oxford during the 1930s and my mandate was to help the author by conducting some re-search into that period of his life. I was glad to do so for Adam had been a close friend of ours during the war; in fact it was he, an ardent anti-Nazi, who persuaded us not to emigrate to Ireland in 1938, but to join with him and others in opposition to Hitler and his régime.

On my return to England I had heard rumours that his failure to convince had come about because doubts as to his bona fides had been circulated by former university contemporaries. Many of them had since become eminent scholars in their various fields and unfortunately their voices had been listened to.

Germany had nothing to be proud of during Hitler's reign, but there were two outstanding exceptions. Firstly, the courage and tenacity of her soldiers when, inadequately equipped, they ultimately found themselves defending their country against the whole world. Secondly, the 20th July Bomb Plot, when those who had taken part so nearly succeeded in ridding their country of a monster who had ruled over them for eleven years and who claimed their lives when it failed.

Unlike the British, the Germans I found were slow to honour their real heroes. I often had to think of those tattered, shattered remains of the mighty German army whom I had seen in 1945 in Frankfurt, squatting on the pavements, sheltering in doorways with their begging bowls beside them, and found myself comparing their plight with that of the British Expeditionary Force which was given such a joyous heartwarming welcome when, equally defeated, they returned home to England from France in 1940. Different, so different, and it seemed to me not only appropriate, but rather typical, that Adam's heroic story should be one of the first to be told in English by an English author.

I had not been back to Oxford since my 'deb' days in 1929, somehow not daring to do so in case this very beautiful seat of learning might shake my resolve to abandon a scholarship and to study music in Germany instead.

As I proceeded from one noble precinct, one interview, one thimbleful of sherry to the next, it became clear that as a student in Balliol, three years older than themselves, Adam had played a dramatic rôle in many of these people's lives. Although only one learned scholar admitted to remorse at having spread false rumours, not one could understand why Adam had not trusted their friendship and come clean as to his true attitude to Nazism. In 1959 I spent ten days listening, trying and failing to explain how impossible this would have been if he wished to return to his country. As it was, news of my own humble arrival was already busy doing the rounds of this cloistered community, and friendship or no friendship, I could easily calculate just how long Adam's possible confession as to his true political thinking would have taken to reach official Nazi ears.

By the time my visit came to an end I realized that by wishing to help an author I had gone a long way to clearing my own mind. Intellectual achievement, I decided, rests on very narrow and immature emotional foundations. To study history was an intellectual exercise; to live it was beyond my listeners' comprehension. No one could understand what it was like to live under a dictatorship unless they had experienced it themselves.

Before leaving, I had just one more interview to complete, this time with a noted don, and an historian I much admired. After I had delivered my usual impassioned earful he remarked quietly, 'Well, my dear, it looks to me as if there is a missing book. If you feel so strongly about it, why don't you write it yourself?'

The train journey back to London passed quickly because, in spite of the pile of notes I had collected for my mission, I knew that the final interview had been for me the most momentous. When the train jolted to a halt in Paddington Station I had made up my mind to accept the challenge.

I was staying with my mother at the time who, to escape the loneliness of my father's death, had moved to a little house near to my elder brother in St John's Wood, and always came to us in Ireland for the summer months. When I burst in on her, bringing with me my newly discovered ambition, I was surprised, almost overcome, by the instant enthusiasm with which she greeted what could still be a pipe dream.

Her own literary efforts had never reached much beyond an occasional postcard; potent enough postcards though, giving her advice in the briefest possible terms, but conveying also how often she had helped us ride out the storm financially: 'Let's go a bust and get an Aga', 'Hope the new harvester is doing its stuff', 'Love to Peter and thanks for cheque'. In her day, as she often explained, education was reserved for sons, and she was the youngest of the Harmsworth clan with eleven brothers lined up ahead of her. Her particular determined personality saw to it, however, that she more than held her own. In a day or so she had a room upstairs ready for me, equipped with a writing table, pencils and paper. Whenever I should be in London the order of the day was to leave me in peace.

For some years peace was not the word I would have chosen to describe my state of mind for it meant confronting sad memories packed neatly away in a corner of the mind and not to be disturbed with comfort. There were some days when words seemed to flow faster than a pen could cover the paper, and others when the well ran dry, the page remained a blank, and I just wished that some celestial being would float in and tell me firmly that enough was enough. The only such being whose judgement I felt I could trust was my cousin, Cecil King, who rang me up after reading the first two chapters and let me know in true Cecil fashion that if I did not continue he would never speak to me again.

It is a long and harrowing journey until the moment comes when the publisher hands you back your story which has miraculously become a book with its pages neatly bound and its cover decked out, ready to face the world. It was 1968 before Ian Parsons of Chatto & Windus, after apologizing for a delay which had occurred in its production, handed it to me most gently, almost lovingly, and said, 'Here it is at last, dear Chris, and if I may say so it is my opinion that we may have a classic in our hands.'

The delay in publishing saddened me for I had much hoped that my mother could have shared in its possible success. It was not to be, for she died shortly before the publication. It did not seem fair, for I could not tell her that when it came to choosing a title I had needed help, and that, when sorting forlornly through her possessions, I came across her little Victorian Birthday Book; birthdays of family and friends had been faithfully recorded and to each date belonged a small quotation from the works of Robert Louis Stevenson. I turned instinctively to a date which meant as much to me as many a birthday – 20th July – and the quotation beneath from Stevenson's *Tales of the Road* read: 'The future is nothing, but the past is myself, my own history, the seed of my present thoughts, the mould of my present disposition.'

The Past is Myself, my book had its title, and I was comforted because in a roundabout way I felt my mother's clear voice had not yet been stilled.

Epilogue

One of the many problems confronting anyone who has decided to risk writing an autobiography must be to decide when that life story should be allowed to reach a certain conclusion. In simple terms, to know very definitely where and when to stop. If your life happens to have been eventful a further problem must arise as to what should be included and what left out.

I could and should have told more of Leapeetswe and Sekgoma Khama, who dropped in for three days on their way to school in Ireland and stayed for four years – Peachy and Secky, 'the two black lads' as they came to be known to the townsfolk of Tullow – and of the letter Peachy wrote to me after his father died and he had to leave Trinity College to return to Botswana and take his place as paramount chief of his tribe. 'Madre' – by then we had adopted each other and I was very sad to see my black lad go – 'Madre,' he wrote, 'you cannot know what it is like to have the door to knowledge opened a small way and then slammed shut.'

I could have told of the Peace Rallies and of how one day we all arrived with our banners on the southern bank of the River Boyne, and the silence we met with until a sea-mist lying over the river lifted – and they were there, the Northern women in equal numbers – and the cries of joy which greeted us as we flooded across the bridge. Laughter, hugs and kisses, a heart-warming welcome and agreement later over endless cups of tea that it was surely nonsense to allow men to run the affairs of the world.

Maybe I should have told of my association with the Peace People, and their charismatic leaders, Betty Williams and Mairead Corrigan, of my experience and growing admiration for the sturdy self-reliance of those other Northern women, and of my enthusiasm after joining those rallies when women from the North and South of Ireland crossed the divide together and convinced me that if peace and ceasing of bloodshed were to come to this small divided island it would be brought about by the women.

Then if my ambition was to provide a grand finale, what could be more dramatic than finding myself in the Great Hall, the Aula Maxima of Heidelberg University, perched on a platform with Betty Williams by my side? My rôle was to be that of interpreter, but although the hall was crowded it did not look as if we were to have much success with our peace message. As soon as Betty opened her mouth she was greeted by howling groups of well-trained rowdies, obviously made in Germany, whose chorused protests amounted to yells of 'Up ze Repoblik' and 'Get ze Brits out of Doblin'.

The police were moving in to our rescue when Betty stepped down from the platform, approached one of the ringleaders, took him firmly by the shoulders, plonked him on a chair and announced in clarion tones, 'Sit there, 'till I tell ye to get up. I'm going to speak and you're going to listen, d'y hear me, y' wee fucker!' From then on the stupefied yob sat transfixed while Betty returned to continue her piece to a silent, spellbound audience. I sat beside her doing my stuff, relieved that no interpreter had been needed to translate that particular piece of good, sound Belfast rhetoric.

After some thought I finally decided that I would shut up shop, close the shutters, in the summer of 1979 when I celebrated my seventieth birthday.

There are one or two advantages in reaching the age of seventy when still more or less in right mind. Not many I would say, just one or two.

Firstly perhaps that with luck you have reached a comforting conclusion that to forget certain happenings and events is so usual that for one's peace of mind it is best taken for granted. Then, a certain leaning towards eccentricity is permissible and most of the time looked upon with tolerant amusement.

It need not go so far as a charming old lady I encountered one day when the two of us were looking in a window of Harrods. She was wearing a neat little toque and a short fur jacket with a scrap of some animal about her neck which used to be known as a tippet. I spoke to her because I felt that someone should let her know that she had forgotten to put on her skirt. 'Thank you, my dear, thank you,' she said showing no sign of embarrassment. 'In that case perhaps I had better make for home.'

There are also what might be called tricks of the trade, as I learned when wedged between two senior citizens on a flight between Dublin and Heathrow. My neighbours were two cheerful old ladies who had obviously travelled extensively, for they were soon chatting of Hong Kong, Australia, the Caribbean, as if such places were just around the corner. It was also obvious that the paraphernalia of travel, the complexities involved in the crossing of national frontiers left them undaunted, for they were loaded down with duty-free goods and seemed to have plenty of baggage in the hold. Both were agreed that an air of helplessness was essential if fellow travellers were to be encouraged to show more than usual consideration, or for officialdom a benevolent side to their nature.

'Everyone is so kind,' beamed the one. 'And I haven't been caught once!' boasted the other.

As we downed our whiskies together the lady to my right admitted to having occasionally gone to the extreme of putting one arm into a sling and that she always carried one with her – 'just in case' – but she to my left declared that she found a slight limp and a walking-stick to be quite sufficient.

As I listened, fascinated by their exploits, I began to believe in the existence of some kind of Mafia designed exclusively for oldies. In fact it only needed a second whisky before I found little harm in such behaviour and my initial unease turned to admiration. After all, it is not so long ago that elderly ladies were expected to wear constant mourning and to live in the hope of finding someone to push them around in a bath chair. Instead, my companions were off and away defying old age, bent on enjoying themselves and filled with warm appreciation of human nature at its best.

So, to my own birthday: 18th June to be exact. It was a date I could easily remember, not only because I arrived in the world on that midsummer's day in 1909, but because the Battle of Waterloo was won on the same day in 1815.

It happened that one of the earlier arguments I had with Peter concerned that particular battle, because at school our history teacher, doubtless a true patriot, had provided me with the rather puzzling piece of information that this great British victory was 'fought and won on the playing fields of Eton'. Peter, however, could only remember from his history class that as the battle dragged on Wellington prayed, 'Would that it were eve and the Prussians were here.' And sure enough they arrived in the nick of time. So much for history lessons; a timely warning to both of us when we were trying to feel our way towards a deeper under-standing between our two countries.

Now, half a century later, with the exploding of many such national myths behind us, our family had multiplied to include daughters-in-law and a host of grandchildren, and they were of the opinion that as I was the first amongst them to arrive at such a venerable plateau, just one party to celebrate my Seventieth would not be enough. In their enthusiasm they decided that the festivities should last a whole weekend commencing in Munny on the evening of the day before. This, being Ireland, was an assurance that they would continue until long after midnight and last well on into my birthday. Then, if I was still able for it, a dinner party would take place in a nearby schoolhouse which had been skilfully converted into a restaurant. Due to an abundance of 'acceptances with pleasure' the home celebrations would perforce have to overflow into the garden. Seeing that it had rained ceaselessly for weeks beforehand this seemed to me a particularly brave decision.

But now the prospects did not look so dire. In spite of those weeks of so-called 'soft weather', the forecasters had stuck their necks out far enough to predict that a ridge of high pressure developing even into an anti-cyclone might be making its way towards us across the Atlantic. For once they proved right, for on the day before our own particular 'hooley' was to take place, the hills emerged from behind their clouds, the mists drifted away down the valley and the sun rose at dawn to move warmly across a cloudless sky until one of Ireland's miraculous sunsets set the western sky ablaze.

Such unexpected good fortune galvanized everyone around me into immediate action. Peter, off to Kilmore Quay to fetch lobsters; Heather, a daughter-in-law, with Cis, my faithful house-keeper, and Elke, a good friend, to start preparing the cold buffet supper; grandchildren to set about mowing the lawns and clipping the hedges; my brother John from Switzerland who, having cast his expert eye over my dishevelled flowerbeds, to decide that what he called 'instant gardening' was the only

469

solution. This involved his making tracks for the nearest garden centre to equip himself with shrubs and plants in full flower. Not exactly the Sissinghurst routine perhaps, but the result, he assured us, would be electrifying. The instructions given to me by my family and friends were to relax and do nothing.

So it happened that, with plenty of hustle and bustle going on around me, I found myself sitting alone on a deck-chair in the sun; alone with my thoughts and my years in what had once been my vegetable garden until I gave up the unequal struggle with slugs and weeds and we went berserk and installed a swimming-pool.

The swimming-pool garden then, a quiet green place now, with just the pool and the lawn surrounded by grey stone walls covered with rambling roses. A thick laurel hedge to one side protected it from the north winds which could blow in from the Wicklow Mountains. Very quiet, very green, and as I sat there in the peace, the warmth and the silence, I found my thoughts wandering away on their own.

Thirty-three years had slipped by since I stood leaning on a low wall in Kilmore Quay looking out over the sea to the Saltee Islands. Small waves were lapping at the rocks below me and the cry of many seagulls rang in my ears as they followed the fishing boats out to the fishing grounds. On that day I had come to a tentative conclusion to live out my days if possible in this beautiful and unpredictable island. And this we had done, whilst Peter built up what was now considered to be a flourishing farm. Munny House, too, had become a home and, to judge from those who had travelled far to be with us this weekend, a home for many besides ourselves. Children of those who had been killed by Hitler, coming for the holidays and always returning; our own sons growing up here, married now, and nine grandchildren. I would like to think that Peter and I had managed to build something on the ruins we had left behind us. Something perhaps demanded of us by the very fact that we had survived. I would like to believe that we had provided a centre, a never-changing reality which they could look back upon and hold in their hearts with happiness as they grew up to face an ever-changing world.

Ireland, too, had changed in those thirty-three years. Ireland now had television, Ireland had supermarkets. Ass-carts and horse-drawn tinkers' caravans were now only there for the tourists, for Ireland now had motor cars, and Virgin Marys and teddy bears no longer bobbed about in their rear windows 'just in case'. Perhaps the peak of modern convenience known as 'family planning' had not yet reached the statute books, but there was always the possibility of slipping across the Irish Sea in order to stock up or, if need be, avoid the consequences. The birthrate was not quite what it used to be, dear God, so it wasn't.

A breath of wind rustled the leaves of the copper-beech tree which overhung the garden and a swallow swooped over me, skimmed the surface of the pool and shot up to join a group of its frolicking companions. The swallows had returned to their nests in the rafters early this year, and they were flying high. Another good omen for the weather to come.

I tried to concentrate on the only task allotted to me which was to decide on the seating arrangements for the dinner to take place on the following day. A carefully prepared list of participants had been thrust into my hand and I had shown a degree of enthusiasm to be of help at least in some small way. But now with my eye running down from one name to the next, David Astor, Sekgoma Khama, Betty Williams, I found myself wondering was it so important where they sat themselves down? They knew each other after all, would fit themselves in anywhere, each in their own way slipping without fuss into their allotted place in the jigsaw pattern of my life.

The sun was high and warm above me and the shape of my chair becoming more congenial by the minute, so that I suspected that it would not be long before I fell asleep.

I have never discovered the exact moment when sleep and dreams take over from reality. As a child I could tell more or less, because of the advent too often of an ever-recurring nightmare. Myself very small and alone surrounded by a huge and silent emptiness until distant walls began to close in around me and as they moved in nearer I could hear voices, many voices, increasing in volume until the chattering became strident screeching. It was then, when I could bear it no longer, that I usually awoke screaming equally noisily and in need of much comfort.

Today I would doubtless have been taken to visit a psychiatrist, but in those days the explanation given was that I must have eaten something for supper which had disagreed with me and if I wished to avoid a dose of castor oil I would have to find my own solution. I did so one night when I turned on those threatening walls and burst out laughing. To my joy they were silenced immediately. They were defeated and I awoke with a childlike conviction that horrors cannot survive ridicule.

A passer-by could be forgiven if he thought to recognize an elderly lady comfortably ensconced in the sun, hands folded in lap, eyes closed, just about to nod off. But Christabel was not asleep, at least she did not think she was, although it was certainly a little odd to find that she was no longer alone in her garden and that the granite, rose-covered walls seemed to have melted away into the woodlands behind them, where oak trees had become conifers; giant Christmas trees swaying and sighing in the wind as they had done in the Black Forest when they freed themselves from the winter snows.

Nor was this all, for there was movement in the depths of the woods and she could hear voices. They were not strident human cacklings as in her childhood, but friendly gentle sounds and there was laughter in the air.

Had there been some mention of a birthday party? Could it be about to start? She tried to stand up and move towards a colourful throng, a sudden sparkling river which seemed to flow towards her out of the shadows into the sunlight. But she could not stir, could not join them. It was as if she were rooted to the earth and could only watch silently as one familiar being after another passed her by. Her father, her mother, a much-loved brother, Freda, Adam, Lexi, Frau Muckle – this was no ordinary gathering, these were never-to-be-forgotten people, their faces as clear and as dearly loved as when they left her years back to travel along the rest of her road without them.

Splash – a sound like a pistol shot rang out and echoed through my head, shattering the silence, scattering my dream people. I awoke with a start to find myself staring over the edge of the swimming-pool into the laughing face of – could it be my son? – no, it must be my grandson. Why is it that in photographs people are always smiling, in dreams they never grow old? 'I'm sorry, Chris,' he said, turning and diving like a dolphin to reappear at the far end of the pool and call back, 'Please don't ever be seventy again, Grandma, your lawns look super, but I'm pooped!'

Whereupon he proceeded to thresh up and down the pool at what to me seemed almost the speed of sound. I could not help smiling at his effort to belie his state of exhaustion and stood watching him for a while for he was surely showing off a bit too, which I knew to be no fun at all unless someone is there looking on.

On rounding the corner of the house I could hear the bees busily working away under the slates of the roof. They had been there for several years now and there must be gallons of honey awaiting anyone who was willing to risk dismantling part of the house.

Before going indoors I stood for a short while on the steps leading up to the front door, newly painted for the occasion, and looked about me. There were sheep grazing half-heartedly in the lawn field, and down in the valley a drifting pool of sunlight picked out St Kevin's little roofless ivy-covered church. I was only going to be seventy after all, but watched over by the rounded heather-covered hills of Aghold and Aghade, it had braved the elements for seven centuries.

Maybe there was something uncanny in the sultry air; perhaps my strange dream still held me in its spell for, as I stood there, looking about me, able to recognize every hill and hollow, for a moment in time it seemed to me that I now belonged to those hills and they to me for ever – in eternity.

So it was that, a little off-balance, but still eager to be of some help, I retreated into the cool, welcoming half-light of the house.

THE END

APPENDIX

CONTENTS

PREFACE

Christabel Bielenberg was in her late fifties when she sat in an upstairs room in Munny House, Co. Carlow, to write *The Past is Myself*, first published in 1968. With Germany devastated by war and England a difficult prospect for her husband, Peter, she and her family had moved to Ireland in 1949. They established a farm on the Carlow/Wicklow border, and the story of the life that unfolded there is told in *The Road Ahead*. Peter died in March 2001, Christabel in November 2003 at the age of ninety-four.

As a family we welcomed the opportunity offered by Brenda Kimber at Transworld to combine the two books in one edition, and to publish it for a new generation of readers. This coincided with the discovery amongst Christabel's papers of unpublished chapters of the two books, a moving and fascinating collection of letters, and a number of diary entries dating from 20 July 1944 onwards, which may go some way to explaining the immediacy and vividness of a book written fully twenty years after the events it describes. Dorothea Depner is to be thanked for this; her Ph.D. thesis led her to Munny House and to Christabel's papers. She has written a perceptive introduction to the additional chapters, which follows here, and has transcribed and footnoted the diary entries and letters. Together we selected the letters to be included, and I am extremely grateful for her help and resourcefulness throughout.

Christabel herself was not a natural archivist. In her later years, failing eyesight and her age prevented her from climbing the stairs to her former workroom, where her letters and papers were kept. Instead, her sustained act for posterity was to talk: to her sons, grandchildren and great-grandchildren, to friends, and at length. The experiences of her time in Germany and the people she and Peter knew there informed each day of the rest of their long lives.

KATHARINA BIELENBERG
July 2011

INTRODUCTION

When Christabel Bielenberg began drafting *The Past is Myself* in the early 1960s, she wanted to write a missing book: an account by a witness of day-to-day life in Nazi Germany, with all its compromises and horrors. As a survivor of Hitler's regime, she felt a responsibility to leave a record for later generations and trusted that her English background would give her credibility with her readers. *The Past is Myself* made such a lasting impact. It remains a point of reference for many works on the Third Reich, and as recently as 1995 Christabel was voted one of '100 Women Who Shook the World' by readers of the *Observer*. In remembering and writing about her past, however, Christabel also underwent a personal catharsis. Even the memoir's title, *The Past is Myself* – a quotation she found in her mother's Victorian birthday book for the all-important date of 20 July – allows us a glimpse of the struggle behind her attempt to establish continuity between her former and her present self, between memories salvaged from the ruins of the war and the re-rooting of her family in Ireland. The material in this appendix to a new edition of Christabel's works gives readers an opportunity to better understand the pivotal events in her life during, and just after, the Second World War. It brings together a range of documents, recently discovered among the author's papers, which both reinforce and broaden the image of the strong and spirited woman conveyed in Christabel's writing, adding further nuance to the legacy she created.

Among the sources reproduced in this volume are two previously unpublished chapters, one from *The Past is Myself* and one from *The Road Ahead*. The first, called 'A Luncheon Party, Summer 1940', throws light on the author's association with German resistance circles at the beginning of the war. Christabel feared that its omission from *The Past is Myself* would disturb the flow of her story. Instead, it contributed to the conventional image of Christabel as an English mother and spouse trapped in Nazi Germany, who courageously succeeded in persuading the Gestapo of her husband's innocence following his arrest in August 1944. The previously unpublished chapter shows, however, that long before her intervention on Peter's behalf, Christabel had played an active part in a daring plan devised by her close friend Adam von Trott zu Solz.

The second chapter published here for the first time is dedicated to Christabel's mother, who died a year before the publication of *The Past is Myself*.* As Virginia Woolf observed in *A Room of One's Own*, 'we think back through our mothers if we are women'. Christabel took great pride in sharing her mother's first name and in the steadfastness of her mother's convictions, as well as her practical attitude in social and religious matters. The documents in this appendix emphasize that Christabel the daughter possessed many of these qualities herself: her letters to her parents and to her Swedish friend, Elsa von Rosen, during the war show her remarkable determination not to let homesickness and despair dominate her life. They also give us an early taste of the wry humour and self-deprecating understatement that are so characteristic of her later writing.

Without doubt, the most exciting discovery among Christabel's papers is a few loose pages, inserted in a German notebook, containing her handwritten diary notes from July to September 1944. These are published here for the first time in a transcript which allows readers to experience Christabel's immediate reactions to the failed bomb plot of 20 July, her anguish at not receiving any news from Peter in the weeks that followed, and, after hearing of his arrest, her instant decision to act in order to save his life. A second transcript reproduces the diary notes entered on the pages still attached to the actual notebook. The later record begins, in mid-sentence, with the departure of the German army from Rohrbach in April 1945. Christabel's entries from that time capture the chaos and fatigue that followed, her liberation by the French army, and her condemnation of the

---

*In the chapter reproduced here, Christabel recalls her mother's death occurred in 1968, the same year her memoir was published, although she died on 11 June 1967 (*The Times*, 13 June 1967: 18).

terror wreaked by French troops on civilians, and on women in particular. The last entry dates from 8 July 1945, and, true to form, combines her impulse to record events as she witnessed them with darkly humorous reflections on the appetite of the French occupying forces for loot. It was written just before her departure for Frankfurt, where she would establish contact with home and organize her children's and her own repatriation. Where her diary notes end, her correspondence resumes, allowing readers to share in her growing excitement ahead of the eventual reunion with her family in England. The letters which conclude this selection were written by Christabel to Peter during their year of separation. Along with perceptive comments on the changes the war had worked in London society and in her own family, they offer us an insight into the difficulties Christabel and Peter faced together in order to attempt a new beginning in a new home in Ireland.

DOROTHEA DEPNER
18 February 2011

A LUNCHEON PARTY

(Summer 1940)

This chapter was originally written for inclusion in The Past is Myself, *and would have appeared before the chapter entitled 'A DINNER PARTY (Autumn 1940)' on p. 83.*

The Garde Kavallerie Club in Berlin was to be found in the Bendlerstrasse, not far from the War Office. If it had been transplanted to St James' in London, it could have settled down quite comfortably as a poorer, but equally proud relation of Boodles, Whites, or indeed the Cavalry Club, for it possessed all the family characteristics. It had, however, one distinctive feature all its own, in that in spite of the Third Reich, it had managed to hold on to its identity, and also to the exclusiveness of its membership list; in spite of war, it had also succeeded in keeping up a high standard of cuisine and was therefore very popular at lunchtime. There was hardly a member who had not the prefix 'von' before his name, and although this was no passport to political respectability, at least within the precincts of the Club, those who had 'taken the wrong turning' could be more easily identified. It was said that if one lunched there, one did not have to read the daily *Wehrmachtsbericht*, because if a certain princeling was to be seen lunching with, for instance, Herr Schacht, matters at the front did not look so rosy, whereas if all was going well, then that same princeling might be found lunching with Herr von Doernberg, Hitler's Chief of Protocol.

It was here that arrangements had been made for me to meet my first Nazi bigwig, Ambassador Hewel, Ribbentrop's own Special Ambassador to the Reichs Chancellery, who, because of the Foreign Minister's terror of being pushed out on a lonely limb, had to spend most of his time as near to the Führer as possible, in order to be able to report back to his superior on the latter's every change of mood.

As I bumped along the roads towards my goal in the old M bus which, in deference to so many victories, was sporting a couple of flags on her bonnet, it seemed to me that my forthcoming meeting with Hewel could only make real sense in the confused atmosphere which had succeeded Hitler's crazy little dance of triumph before a railway carriage in the woods of Compiègne. Until then, the successful overthrow of his regime had seemed well within the bounds of possibility, but it would have needed a more resilient nature than mine to take courage when, after the defeat of France, the illustrated papers published pictures of our Generals lined up like skittles, awaiting presentation by their Führer of their bejewelled Field Marshal's batons. Only Goering going one better by getting himself promoted to *Reichsmarschall*, State Marshal, whatever that might be.

'Germans, unfurl the flags, let the church bells ring, let highest honour be given to the greatest Warlord of all time.' Out they came, of course, those flags, and the church bells duly clattered away for hours on end, but still I found it hard to classify my fellow citizens of Berlin, the other occupants of my bus, for instance, as confident world conquerors. In fact, I decided that I could detect nothing really invincible about them except, the day being hot, the smell of well-worn clothing washed with war-time soap. They stared out of the windows over mounds of bursting shopping nets and clambered off and onto the bus, seemingly utterly indifferent to those gaudy sheets which fluttered and flapped and plastered the walls. They gave no indication as to whether Hitler's victories had meant for them the triumphant fulfilment of an age-old dream, had aroused amazed, perhaps even unwilling admiration, consternation or despair. There was room, I knew, in Hitler's Reich for the whole gamut of such emotions. But it mattered very little what they thought, for the simple fact remained that similar flags were fluttering and flapping and plastering the walls from the north of Norway to the coast of Brittany; and many of their husbands, or their brothers, or their sons, were waving those flags. The fact remained, too, that a landing in England must be imminent and that, judging by what had gone before, England would be occupied and the same gruesome story would repeat itself all over again.

I tried to concentrate on what Adam had told me of Hewel's past, which as far as I could gather had taken the same devious course as that of most of the other stars in Hitler's firmament. He had joined the Party in its very early days and had then disappeared to Australia where he had met up not only with Rudolf Hess, but also with a distant cousin of Adam's. Together they had made one or two unsuccessful attempts to pile up a fortune. Hewel had to wait until 1933, though, before getting on to a really good thing, for then, recalling to memory his Party allegiance and encouraged by his friend Hess, he had returned to Germany. And from then on his career had been meteoric.

Although reputedly not in possession of much of a head for the heights, he was not considered to be a thug and, contrary to his direct superior, Herr von Ribbentrop, he was basically an anglophile, nostalgic almost for those golden years spent bumming around the outposts of Empire. He had been known to help Jews get out of the country and had also been of great help to Adam when he needed official backing for his trip to England a year ago, and again for his mission to America. He was in fact Adam's Nazi, not to be confided in, but not to be ignored, rather to be used with circumspection whenever the need arose. The reason he had been asked to meet me had something to do with a sturdy effort to readjust ourselves to a completely new and unexpected situation. After the defeat of France, all thought, all hope of a possible putsch had to be put to one side. It was no use churning over the whys and the wherefores, for whatever the reason, a chance had been missed. Yet things could not stand still, some *modus vivendi* had to be found. Not by me, I was just a hotchpotch of emotions, with nothing very steadfast about me beyond a rather childish longing to get back among my own people. I could only be grateful for any tentative suggestion when it came. Alright, if England were occupied, then the fight must be taken up from there. The German Foreign Office was enlarging its special department for dealing with English affairs. It must be infiltrated with as many reliables as could be found, in the hope that Himmler and his cohorts would not be the only arrivals in England after the victorious invaders. Friends had to be there too, ready and willing to warn, to succour where possible, to make intelligible the workings of a system under which we had lived for years and which must be a new and terrifying phenomenon for any country which had not yet experienced it; and above all to unite, if possible, with like-minded Englishmen in continued opposition. Neither Peter nor Adam nor many others who wangled their way onto the so-called 'England Committee' could pretend that they relished the thought of such an equivocal assignment. As for me, knowing my England – shades of Mrs Pleydell-Bouverie – it was not surprising that I felt nothing more nor less than intense gratitude, and a deep desire to help where I could.

Luncheon at the Garde Kavallerie Club was to be served at one o'clock in a private room, and I found myself sitting next to a large, rather handsome man, with smooth brown hair brushed straight back from his pale forehead. In spite of his grey-green uniform (which I learned later had been specially designed by Herr von Ribbentrop for members of his staff), my neighbour was not at his ease and it was up to me to put him so. By the time we had reached the meat course, therefore, I had progressed favourably enough for us to be talking English together – he with a pronounced Australian accent – and I had got so far as to calling him an Aussie at heart, which seemed to please him immensely: 'tew trew' had been his comment. The rest of Adam's guests kept up a rather feverish background chatter as our dialogue flourished. Hewel had a fund of excellent stories about his efforts to make his pile and told them much as my brother-in-law Charles might have done. Soft drinks had been one fiasco, bubbly soft drinks, he had hoped to corner the market, but the bloody drought, the bloody heat, something to do with the bloody corks, poof! the bloody bottles had bloody well exploded before they even reached the bloody wholesalers! I found myself laughing a lot, relaxed and indeed enjoying myself. We were tucking into some yellow 'crème', which tasted rather like sweetened soap suds, when we came to talk of Hitler. Except for my Uncle Rothermere, who had dropped his voice and spoke of him as being 'a very, very great man', I had never met anyone who had managed to get within spitting distance of the greatest warlord of all time and I had been trying to bring the conversation round that way for a while.

'The Leader, *Gnädige Frau*, is the genius of our time, of that there is no doubt, he is more than human, he is in fact superhuman and it is an honour to serve him.'

Hewel's expression changed suddenly as he spoke and an odd, fanatical, almost humble glow lit up his pale face. He also started speaking German, which I thought was perhaps as well, since he might otherwise have found himself referring to his 'bloody Führer'.

'I could give you so many instances of His unsurpassed powers, *Gnädige Frau*, His uncanny intuitions.' – 'The Russo German Pact for instance, which you must agree was a diplomatic *tour de force*. I was privileged to be there in the Berghof, when the seed of that masterstroke was sown in the Führer's mind. We were watching films – the Führer finds his sole recreation in watching films – and we were watching a news reel of Stalin reviewing the Russian troops on May Day. The Führer insisted that the film should be run through again and again, and each time, when the close-up appeared of Stalin's face, he ordered that the film should be stopped. STALIN – HALT! Stalin – Halt! It was most dramatic. After about the tenth run-through, the Führer held up his hand. "Enough," he said, "enough, that is a real man; with him I will make a Pact."' – The expression on Hewel's face could not have been more devout had the words been 'Let there be light.' – 'Let me tell you of another time, *gnädige Frau*,' he went on, 'we were sitting on the terrace of the Berghof, last October it must have been, someone remarked on a rose which was still blooming in the garden, and the Leader said quietly, almost as if to himself, "strange to think that when the roses are next in bloom" – there was a moment's pause – "I shall be in Paris."' 'He is doubtless a prophet,' I said, not quite certain whether I should have eaten that 'crème', and since we had progressed so far I thought I could ask him, would he know, had the Leader ever mentioned, what were his feelings with regard to England. Hewel hesitated before answering and then said that in his opinion Hitler had no quarrel with England; the British Empire had been conquest on the grand scale, and was an entity which the Leader respected, and had repeatedly assured the British that he did not want to destroy. His particular respect for the Empire came from the fact that it was held together by sea power, and the sea was an element with which the Leader felt little *rapport*. The Empire had been established to provide living space for a virile nation, and he found it impossible to understand why the British had chosen to risk losing it in order to try and deny just that right to another equally virile race.

By the time coffee had done the rounds, the Ambassador had in spirit at least discarded his grey-green uniform and once more donned his sweat shirt. We were back in Australia, outbacking, as far as I was concerned in every sense of the word.

We parted company at the foot of the stairs, shook hands heartily and expressed mutual hope that we would meet again. Clausewitz, Carl von (1780–1831), Gneisenau, August Wilhelm von (1760–1831) – before I left I glanced up at their portraits adorning the hallway and they returned my glance with unswerving disapproval. As I stood outside blinking in the sunlight, wondering what on earth my luncheon party could have to do with the fate of nations, I decided that they probably had every right to do so.

This untitled chapter, about Christabel's mother, Christabel Rose Burton, née Harmsworth, would have been written for inclusion in The Road Ahead. *Some of its content appears in compressed form in the few paragraphs that precede the Epilogue.*

No chronicle of mine would be complete without telling of my mother, who after my father's death became very much part of our lives in Ireland. Until then she had shown no particular attachment to the country as a whole, viewing the scene with, at best, amused incomprehension. The rather haphazard lifestyle of my father's Irish relatives was not easily understood by her orderly mind, and as for the social conditions prevailing, 'Too many prelates for me, dear, far too many,' was her verdict on the goings on there.

It was therefore quite a breakthrough when it became her custom to arrive in early summer to stay for as long as she liked, once recording in our Visitors Book how happy she was to be in Munny and that she hoped to stay until she was 'pushed out'. When she finally returned to London in the autumn, she filled the gap by answering my letters by return of post, nearly always using her favourite form of communication, which was a postcard. She was thus able to witness and also take part as our derelict lands became a flourishing farm and our ramshackle mansion a home, an achievement which would have been hardly possible without her enthusiastic involvement and her financial support.

My mother died in the sixties, in 1968 to be exact. She had out-lived my father by seventeen years and her dying left an aching void in all of our lives.

We had all married long before the death of my father. My elder brother firstly to a Russian, and then to a French girl, my sister to an Australian and my younger brother to an Italian. Seeing that I had chosen a German, it was perhaps not surprising that my father found it hard to understand why one of us at least had not attached ourselves to something nearer home. 'Nothing but a cockeyed League of Nations, that's what we are,' he would announce occasionally, somewhat at a loss when the chattering around the dining table bounced about from one language to another.

It was surely an unusual state of affairs, possibly even a cockeyed one, but by identifying us all with the League he perhaps subconsciously paid tribute to my mother, who, clearheaded and straightforward, down to earth, in her later years very wise, became the firm friend and confidante of sons, daughters and assorted in-laws alike. Her influence reached out to her grandchildren and to many of her numerous nieces and nephews, all drawn I could believe by her lively participation in their problems, as well as those of the day, and by the precision with which she was wont to give her opinion and advice.

'Come along, dear, tidy up.' As I sat alone in my mother's London sitting room, staring forlornly out of the window at the flower bed of roses she had planted the year before, I do not think I could have faced up to the necessary task of sorting through her private papers and possessions had I not thought to hear a clear voice telling me to get moving.

Her flower room had been easy enough, for it could only remind me of her genius with flowers and her care in choosing the exact shape of vase capable of bringing her garden into the house. But now there was her sitting room, in some way not yet deserted by her personality, with the chaise longue to which she had been mainly confined in latter months, and also her beautiful writing desk with its many drawers and cubby holes and those two familiar black steel boxes, one sealed, both locked. In spite of a bunch of keys neatly labelled, I found it impossible to avoid a feeling that I was intruding, a certain hesitation at suddenly being allowed to rummage about in parts of my mother's life which she might have wished to remain hers alone.

Nevertheless I felt as though I had been given my instructions – 'Tidy up!' – but unfortunately tidiness is not a virtue for which I have ever shown the least promise, whereas I felt I could rely on a song unsung to arouse whatever talent I could call upon. So I decided to interpret my mother's bidding in my own way. Tidy up as best I could, call upon my memories, round off some ragged edges, fill in some of the blurred contours and perhaps be able to reveal a picture of a loved human being who was not the most publicly renowned member of her family, but in terms of purpose and personality well able to hold her own.

Many scribes, some benevolent, some less so, have tried their hand at recording the rise to power and wealth of the Harmsworth family; of the Lords Northcliffe and Rothermere, the first of the so-called Barons of Fleet Street, who when still young men recognized the significance of the Elementary Education Act of 1870. From then on illiteracy in England was to be a thing of the past, which for them became a clear indication that by the turn of the century a brand-new class of newspaper readership would have arrived on the scene, for whom a more lively, less costly form of communication could be found.

Carefully preserved in one of my mother's writing-table drawers I discovered a first copy of the *Daily Mail*, priced at one halfpenny, dated 4th May, 1896. It reminded me of my mother's telling of the occasion when her eldest brother Alfred burst into their none-too-prosperous little villa in Maida Vale, at breakfast time, with a bundle under his arm. Fresh from the printing presses, one copy for each member of the family, and for my grandmother a kiss on the top of her head and the assurance that in the opinion of her first born, her family was sitting on a goldmine.

My mother was the youngest but one of this family. She had eleven brothers and two sisters and grew to young womanhood in what she called 'the rich days', when beside a host of national newspapers the family owned large houses in London as well as country estates, and when an assortment of titles was also beginning to come their way. She had not consciously experienced 'the poor days', only hearing of these from her mother, a staunch Ulster Protestant who, because of her fear of Fenian riots, persuaded her husband to leave Ireland and a modest but secure position as a schoolteacher in Dublin. She must have been a very determined lady, for it was she who planned for him to study law, then gathered up the first two instalments of what was to become her prolific brood and set off across the Irish Sea for London and a most uncertain future.

My mother always regretted not having really known her father, who died when she was seven years old. Having made his name as a barrister at law he became an alcoholic, but she often remembered her mother looking at his portrait with a gentle eye and saying that her heart would leap for joy when she heard his step on the stairs. She could remember, too, a certain lightening in the otherwise rather sombre atmosphere of her home whenever her father was around. It would appear that he kept a little monkey as a pet, and she could still hear his burst of laughter when on trooping into the dining room the family discovered his monkey seated on the Sunday roast, doubtless enjoying the warmth. So when ardent biographers of Harmsworth family history recorded her father's weakness for the bottle, she could lay these tomes aside and remark: 'I don't know, perhaps he did drink a little too much, but he had a lovely laugh.' It was he, too, a supporter of women's suffrage and a staunch admirer of the Pankhurst family, who had decided that his youngest daughter should be called Christabel; a name passed on to me as a tribute to Christabel Pankhurst, who was in jail around the time of my birth.*

In family photograph albums, amongst the many scenes recording Harmsworths at play, dressed in the height of contemporary fashion, boating on rivers, posed playing croquet on spacious lawns, horses and carriages, even muffled to the ears aboard ancient motor cars, I discovered one of a solemn-faced little girl, seated alone on a wall, hands folded in her lap, her button boots barely touching the ground. The inscription beneath: 'Me, C.R.H. Aged 12.' It was the contrasting simplicity and also the solitude reflected by this picture which seemed to confirm that my mother's early youth was, as she remembered, a very lonely one. No proper schooling for her, as her elders (and there were so many of them) were unanimous in their opinion that it was quite sufficient for girls to be able to read and write; having first filled the role of beautiful daughter, they were hopefully destined to marry anyway, a calling which needed no formal education whatsoever. I think one would have to take a further look at that photograph, noting the little girl's steady gaze fixed resolutely on the camera's lens, to venture a fairly safe bet that behind the demure exterior, something resembling quiet but very determined revolt might already have been brewing. Revolt, I could believe, against so many of the hidebound certainties, the well-entrenched convictions of her time and generation.

*It is possible that Christabel, born in 1909, was named after Christabel Pankhurst, but her mother could not have been, as she and Christabel Pankhurst were born in the same year, 1880. This was, however, apparently a deeply held belief which was referred to on more than one occasion, and a point of pride. (ed.)

Turn the pages and the little girl is now a bride. Top hats and morning coats, a billowing surround of bridesmaids and my handsome father by her side, looking extremely pleased with himself. No more button boots, all is now elegance, even the cardboard box marked 'My wedding petticoat' contains a glorious creation in satin and lace. Happiness is there as befits the occasion, but again it is the bride's clear, unwavering look which catches the attention.

As I sat before her writing table, progressing from one drawer, from one cubby hole to the next, I began to wonder if it was not too daring a task for a daughter, another Christabel, to venture into the past and to speculate as to the circumstances which contributed to the development of such a vivid personality. But I soon discovered that my mother had been far better prepared to leave us than we were to have her go.

A neatly stacked parcel of cheque stubs reminded me of one strict ruling which remained with her all her life, which was her insistence, almost amounting to compulsion, on paying all debts 'on the dot'. Hardly had a bill arrived in the post before my mother could be found seated at this desk, signing a cheque. Perhaps some subconscious urge left over from those early days in London when her mother had sometimes found it hard enough to pay the milkman, but it was a habit which stood her in good stead after we moved to a rambling Elizabethan manor house near Hatfield. A leaking tap, a slate slithering from the roof and – 'I must telephone with Mr Laing.' Seeing that Mr Laing was then chairman of one of England's largest construction consortiums, such a pronouncement could have seemed somewhat incongruous. Not at all: within an hour or so a team would arrive to repair the damage, sometimes accompanied by Mr Laing himself. 'There's nothing that can kill a small man easier than unpaid bills – bad debts. When I was starting up in Whetstone, large or small, your mother always paid me immediately and I'm only too happy to have the chance to thank her,' was the reason he gave for his constant prompt attention.

Born in the 'poor days', already grown up when the rich days came along, my mother doubtless inherited something of the flair for the accumulation of wealth exhibited by her Harmsworth brethren, although her attitude towards her money affairs was hers alone. She was for instance of the firm conviction, almost revolutionary in her day, that if possible no woman should ever have to be financially dependent on her husband – a situation which she considered degrading. She therefore set about forming a trust fund with monies inherited from her brother Northcliffe, which provided my sister and myself with a certain private income, then deciding to include my brothers and even my father in the deal in order to satisfy her sense of what she called 'fair dos'. No point in waiting until after she died when we might be too old to enjoy it, or well enough off not to need it. 'I'll do it now, dears, and the way you wish to spend it is your own affair.'

In spreading her wings outside of the family circle, again her attitude was simple enough. If you were comfortably off, you had a duty towards those who were not so lucky. She did not approve of the Lady Bountiful act. I do not know if Victorian novels read in girlhood had influenced her opinion, but the thought of ladies in carriages swooping about, delivering largesse to curtsying peasantry was to her 'quite dreadful'. Nonetheless, the social conditions prevailing amongst the poor, particularly in towns, could not escape her clear blue eye. So together with Eleanor Rathbone, a Member of Parliament whom she recognized as a kindred soul, she pursued and succeeded in a plan to provide free milk for ill-nourished schoolchildren in council schools throughout England. A further plan to provide for them a hot and nourishing midday meal for sixpence was her next escapade. As before, she first experimented on her own as to costings – 'You can bet they'll all start by saying it can't be done, the country can't afford it or some such nonsense as they won't drink milk' – so firstly to the local school, then to a canteen in London, the venue provided by her brother Rothermere in Coram's Fields, where they did drink milk and the sixpences rolled in, and she could thus provide Dame Eleanor with all the information and the weaponry she required to push such a measure through the House.

A letter indicating the successful outcome of the free milk scheme, written on House of Commons notepaper and signed by Dame Eleanor, ends with the message, 'Bravo. We've done it!', and this must have given my mother much quiet satisfaction.

I am not sure why the word quiet seems to come to mind when thinking of my mother's activities, for although she was in no way as ebullient as my Irish father, she was far from being a passive person. Never one for the barricades perhaps, but simply

494

holding fast to certain moral values, certain liberal views, and a determination to get things done, which came as naturally to her as breathing. So that when occasions arose which she considered needed her involvement, she could remark, 'It looks as if I'll have to get a move on,' and proceed without much fuss to do just that.

If I wish to complete my picture, I am conscious that flashbacks from my childhood should be included, but here I find myself at a loss. Photographs abound, set pieces of solemn, wide-eyed little mortals all dressed in their best for the occasion. But memories of my mother's role are nebulous and I can only conclude that we shared a certain emotional timidity or that I belonged to a class and generation where nannies and governesses, the nursery and boarding school, managed to intervene, and that we did not go to parents for comfort or enlightenment. Sufficient that they provided us with a sure and safe, all-is-right-within-the-world background as we muddled our way towards adulthood.

So to Ireland, and to a far closer relationship with a small upright figure busy at her tapestry needlework, having placed herself whenever possible between open door and open window in a howling draught which she insisted was merely fresh air. Here, unless kept at a distance by a fear of instantly developing pneumonia, she could be assured of an audience. Peter would drop in for a cup of coffee, and I would listen to their chat and laughter knowing that they were fast becoming a mutual admiration society, with her approval of his good looks, sheer physical energy and sense of purpose, and his respect for her integrity, her youthful clarity of mind and her capacity for hitting the nail on the head. As for the next generation – 'I think I'll go and have a gas with Granny,' and a subsequent murmur of voices indicated that it was no duty call. Even our local parson seemed always ready to come back for more, although when hoping for some contribution to the Missions Overseas, I heard him being told that she had never seen much point in trying to turn good Muslims into bad Christians, or again, on churchgoing, she often wondered if God really enjoyed so much 'serenading!' 'Your mother is like a breath of fresh air,' he beamed at me as he left after his last visit, adding with a sigh, as his thoughts perhaps strayed to his more docile but none too musical congregation, 'one could only wish there were more of her like around.' In saying so he echoed another remark made to me by the splendid matron of Queen Charlotte's Maternity Hospital after my mother retired from its board of governors. 'I will miss her enormously,' she said, 'because as soon as she arrived at our meetings, I could rely on an end to waffling and we could get on with the business of running the hospital.'

I knew what she meant, having once overheard a telephone call between my mother and her stockbroker, who obviously had many plans for rearranging her portfolio. He knew the rules as to companies associated with alcohol or armaments, but her particular objection to those whose board of directors was loaded down with elderly peers of the realm or retired Generals had obviously escaped him. Already well into her seventies, she was busy writing off their Lordships as being far too old, and as for those others, 'they had difficulty enough fighting wars, why they should know anything about running a business is beyond me!'

I mentioned the postcard as my mother's chosen form of communication. Back in Munny after she died I came across some of these, and was moved and also surprised to discover how, in spite of their brevity, they could conjure up the past with startling clarity. True, when she sometimes overdid the verbal economy some of her dispatches were a little difficult to interpret. 'No dear, no' for instance, or 'Yes, excellent, I quite agree.' But there were others which reminded me of the beauty of my home in England and of her skill as a gardener, and of my gratitude that she could turn her lively mind to our tangled wilderness. 'Wait until the spring, dear, and see what comes up' – or, 'Doesn't sound too good to me, try Rhododendrons and Azaleas.' This last doubtless a reply to my letting her know that I had indeed waited in expectation, and nothing whatsoever had come up except plenty of weeds and for some reason or other loads of Jerusalem artichokes. Nothing could dim her enthusiasm, however, as she moved postcard-wise from the non-existent garden into the house: 'One sink useless will pay for No 2 – birthday!' 'Let's all go abust and make it an Aga.' Then an exception in the shape of a letter telling us that she had planned for furniture (list provided), which had been kept in storage since our home in England was sold, and was now to be shipped to Ireland with her love and a request to care for it.

With the instalment of our telephone, even though its performance was eccentric, those postcards arrived less frequently. 'Lovely to hear your voice, darling. Couldn't understand a word. Arrival at 4.30 p.m. Aer Lingus. Much looking forward. Have bought a new hat. Love Mum,' was perhaps my mother's last message to Ireland. She had postponed her visit that year because Esmond Rothermere, one of her favourite nephews, had invited her to be Guest of Honour at the opening of the Ideal Home Exhibition. 'Dearest Aunt, do come, you will be the belle of the ball!' A personal note from Esmond was pinned to the invitation and marked, 'Yes, with pleasure, C.R.B.' The new hat might have indicated that she had every intention of accepting. But she could not attend and did not come to us again, for she fell ill and some months later died. She was the last of that Harmsworth clan which had left Ireland behind them one hundred years before and succeeded in founding a first great empire of the Press.

I would wish that she had been so honoured by her family; I would have liked for her to share the success of my own first venture into writing. I would wish – I would wish. So many wishes, but it is too late.

My mother's house is to be sold and her writing table leaves for Switzerland where my Italian sister-in-law will, I know, look after it with care. So best now close those empty drawers and leave. A last glance out of the window where a shaft of evening sun lights up her roses as if defying sorrow. Then close the door gently and finally behind me, for I do not want to return when the walls are bare and new occupants have inevitably replaced a particular ambience which still fills her room. In her Will, my mother asked that her ashes be strewn over a garden, but if that proved a 'nuisance' then together with my father in some country churchyard. So she lies in Hertfordshire, in Totteridge, where she lived, where she married, and where we were all born. Nearby lies the verger, the lady who played the organ in the church, our doctor, our gardener, the sisters who kept the sweetshop and other congenial village companions. So I think she will be at home there.

If obituaries, inscriptions on tombstones or graveside orations could be trusted, the world would be overflowing with an unending supply of paragons of wisdom and virtue. Such hymns of praise would not have appealed to my mother, but I think she would have enjoyed a remark made to me by a small boy playing with his building blocks. A great-grandchild this time, with a tangle of fair hair and blue eyes not so very unlike her own. 'You know, Chris, I really do miss Granny,' he said quite suddenly and out of the blue, then adding with a short sigh before returning to the job in hand: 'You see, I think she was just super.'

Schreibblock

Liniert — mit Löschblatt

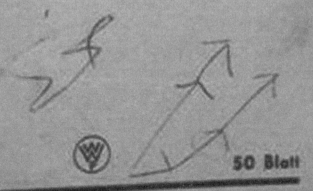

Nr. 23

50 Blatt

TRANSCRIPT OF CHRISTABEL BIELENBERG'S DIARY NOTES

July–September 1944

July 20th: Summer weather at last. Suddenly this afternoon Frau Koff came running down to the Adler saying 'Turn on the radio, turn on the radio. They've thrown a bomb at that Hitler!' 'Yes, and, have they succeeded?' I nearly yelled. 'I don't know, but it's all being said on the radio.' I hurried into the Wirtsstube* and felt my heart bumping. Goebbels was speaking. I knew as soon as I heard his voice that it had failed. He said a few names of Generals I'd heard of but didn't know. I found myself praying that it wasn't the same as Adam's plan? Perhaps it was really only a few officers of the army. I had written a long letter to A. though and it was waiting to leave with the post. I went over to the post and retrieved it. The incoming post had just arrived bringing a letter from Peter posted on July 14th and addressed to Tante Ulla: 'Dear Ulla, I heard from Chris that you always take over the children when she is not there and now I want to thank you for this and to beg you to continue to play ersatz mother to our little family. Above all I think it wise to separate up in various houses our supplies which we have collected during the years and to have them looked after by trustworthy peasants. Great changes may be coming in the near future and everything at the moment is slightly unclear. Please look after my family.'

I read it and felt myself go cold. So Peter had known this was the end of our planning. But still I have hope that perhaps Adam will be able to keep in the background.

*Bar.

July 26th: The first list of names of the collaborators has been published. Peter Yorck and von Haeften are amongst them. It is quite impossible that Adam, and through him Peter, should not be implicated. I have had flu for the last few days and have never felt as ill in my life. The whole weight of these happenings came down over me and I felt pain as never before. I can't believe that it has not succeeded. Those splendid men have planned and plotted in spite of air raids and continual danger of imprisonment and now it is finished, Stauffenberg (Dölt's cousin) is dead. Only last week Camilla told me how charming he was. I must write to Camilla or now I'd better go over there, her letters will probably be controlled now. I would rather go to Berlin and see if I can see Adam, but it would probably not help him to have an Englishwoman looking around.

August 2nd: Nicky's birthday and still no news of Peter. I have sent letter after letter and today a telegram. As the days go by I have sort of got quieter. Adam is so clever, perhaps he'll diddle them. As yet there is no news in the paper that anyone has been imprisoned. Peter is quite mad not to give me any news. Reckling that fat ass came over this evening and said in ponderous tones that he and some *massgebend** people from Strassling† had all come to the conclusion that it would have been a catastrophe for Germany if Hitler had died on the 20th. These Germans sometimes make me spitting mad. They are such political fools that they don't deserve anything better than to be regimented around by the Gestapo and probably sooner or later by the Allies or Russians. And then I look around this valley and see the patient peasants, simple, kindly, in each farm a missing son or father or husband. They are bringing in the hay now, the old men and women who should have peace, and the children working away in the fields. The orderliness everywhere.

August 8th: A letter from Peter at last. Adam was arrested on the 25th of July. Peter writes 'I can't imagine why.' So he seems to reckon with his letters being watched. Yesterday I came back from Wilflingen. The whole family have been arrested. I didn't go

---

*Influential, important.
†It remains unclear to which locality this place name refers.

to the castle in case of a control. It is worse than anything having to wait down here doing nothing but I can only do harm by going to Berlin.

August 30th: The days have clipped by but I have been too worried to write this diary. Have no news of Peter whatsoever. Even a telegram has remained unanswered. Last week they published the names of the main collaborators who were to have taken over the Government when H. was dead. Adam was amongst the eight. They are to be hanged. It is like living in an awful dream. I sometimes feel it can't be true. The English radio tells of a wave of arrests which are going over Berlin. But thank God for the Allies, they are pushing daily nearer. The breakthrough has succeeded and they are coming up to the Rhine. Here the peasants have all been called up to dig trenches and tank holes. A pathetic sight to see these old men and boys shouldering their spades and marching off. Let's pray that the Rhine doesn't hold them up. We are not much worried by planes these days. They need them all in France I suppose. As usual the British and Canadians seem to be doing all the slogging, while the Americans tear ahead in their tanks. Clever of the Allies to arrange it that way, because the British are no doubt the toughest and need no praise or success to make the fight doggedly. Whereas the American must have success and cover ground, otherwise he gets dissatisfied. The German soldiers who pass through confirm that, saying that the American only fights when the air force has cleared the way first. First he comes feeling along with his tanks and when he meets opposition he stops and telephones for air support. Over come the planes and drop a carpet or two,* then the tanks try again, if there is still a German gun shooting they send for more planes. After that the tanks usually just have to mop up. Well, I don't care how they do it as long as they hurry. Please God make them hurry.

September 2nd: The news I dreaded has come. I had a letter from Mabel dated August 25th telling me that Peter was arrested

---

*Nicholas Bielenberg observed that his mother must have picked up the term 'carpet bombing' from secretly listening to the BBC, as it would not have featured in the English vocabulary before the war.

in Graudenz on August 7th. They had only heard the news on August 23rd and she hoped he would soon be out again etc. etc. It is no use writing what I feel, but there is one thing that I have learned. There is a stage beyond pain just as in physical pain there is a borderline beyond which one becomes unconscious. So there is a boundary to psychical pain, beyond which a sort of numbness sets in. If P. is in prison and A. probably hanged, what of our other friends Langbehn Roloff Moltke? I have decided to leave for Berlin tomorrow. The Americans are coming daily nearer and the journey is long and dangerous and perhaps I shall be cut off from the children but I must go. The last time I was in G. [Graudenz] Peter showed me those Gestapo brutes up there and said they were after his blood. I know they've got him. There is no thinking what they may do to him. I think I will go first to Munich and see Seiler. And then up to Berlin. Let's hope no alarms. There is of course a chance that I'll be arrested too. I have written to Mummy and Pom in case. I want the children to go to England if anything happens to us. I have decided that should I find out that they have definite proof on Peter then I must try to bribe Lange. If he forgets P's *Akte*,* then I will see if I can help him after the war. I think the end must be near now, and he must know it too. There is of course the chance that he will arrest me too, but I must risk that. Sometimes I find myself wishing I didn't know so much. I have no idea how I will react to third degree or those injections. The best thing I think is to read and soak myself in *Völkischer Beobachter*† until I talk N. Socialism in my sleep.

The journey to Munich and then on to Berlin was a pretty good nightmare. Weather good and planes plentiful. I sat on my suitcases in the corridor for two days and two nights. In Munich, Seiler told me that A. had been hanged. He said it in such a vile way, that I wanted to hit him. Instead I had to pretend we hardly knew him and had never discussed politics together. Forgive me, Adam, if you are really dead, you know how much I meant it.

*File.
†Official newspaper of the NSDAP (National Socialist German Workers' Party).

September 8th: I am back again now in Rohrbach and Berlin seems far away. The visit to our little house, with no Peter, is over. Berlin is a terrible town now. Over and above the air raids which are slowly battering it to pieces, is the more awful shadow of the Gestapo. The usual old M bus clattered past A.'s flat and I saw the closed shutters. The air was full of autumn and I remembered the last time we were there together. Adam saying 'You know it's almost embarrassing to be still going around without a uniform. One gets quite a lot of nasty looks, but you mustn't think we're doing nothing, Chris. Things are really getting a move on now although it's almost too late.' And my saying, 'It's never too late, the main thing is it happens.'

April–July 1945

[. . .] I wished them good luck and left them. In Rohrbach everything was in an upheaval preparing to leave. Everything was being destroyed and Ellen and Hans and everyone in the village was collecting what they could. Food, loot, car parts, telephones, wireless, cigarettes in thousands. The cars were being burned, everything else smashed. A terrible sight. I said goodbye to my friends. They seemed confident of breaking through but it's easy for them to talk, they have a car. I think of that slow-moving stream down the road. As the sun went down they left, and a sudden stillness came to the village only broken by the crackling of flames as the cars burned and an occasional crack and munition went off in the flames. Nothing but destruction is everywhere. Dirt, filth and destruction. Our sitting room is full of junk. For the children a sort of glorified Christmas. We are all completely exhausted. P. came out of hiding and we all felt rather dotty.

April 25th: Mam's birthday and we are sitting in a sort of vacuum. Peasants are coming with oxen and fetch the cars away. The village idiot has three lovely limousines and a lorry. We are trying to tidy a little, but everything is so dirty that I don't know where to start. We wander around in a sort of dream. There is a lot to collect still. We heard the French had entered Furtwangen. Blacks apparently. Peter is going to have a look tomorrow.

503

April 25th: Yes the blacks are in Furtwangen. Peter went over and found a well-equipped cavalry division standing around. Their welcome was very friendly. Everyone is delighted that the chance of an air raid is over.

April 29th: I went shopping again, more or less out of curiosity. The first thing I saw on the main road was an empty packet of Lucky Strikes. Well, they are here. Then the troops all black in British uniform and on perfect horses. They look rather like a pirate crew but I suppose alright.

May 1st: The poor people in the valley went through a terrible night. The blacks went around the lonely farmhouses plundering and assaulting. Old women and young children. Really awful. They smashed everything looking as they said for German soldiers. There are of course many of these wandering around in strange, ill-fitting civil clothes. We gave two men some of Peter's clothes. His suit from Charles' Aussee tailor. They hope to get to Lahr.

May 5th: Since last week we have been getting going. It began with a French sergeant asking Peter for his papers. As he had none I had to explain everything and although he wasn't very impressed that P. had been in a concentration camp ('Everybody could tell that story,' he said, 'and if one must believe every story then every second German was Jewish or had been in a camp.') he believed me and the next day came in and asked me to *dolmetsch** for him.

Two obvious German soldiers he had caught. He ate here and then I asked him to take us to Villingen. He agreed and off we went at terrible speed after he had taken all sorts of parts out of other cars and screwed them into ours. It was all very French. During the drive they suddenly sprang out and shot at a telegraph pole, just for fun and to try out a newly stolen pistol. To cut a long story short, we managed (a certain amount of cheek on our part) to see the Town Commandant of Villingen a big fine-looking Frenchman who speaks perfect English. I told our story and he was most polite and friendly and asked Peter to help him by informing him about Furtwangen. We walked about V.

*Interpret.

504

without white armbands and after 7 in the evening. He occupies the *Rathaus** which is draped in the Tricolour, the Stars and Stripes and a strange-looking business which is supposed to be the Union Jack. Masses of rather badly dressed policemen lolled about, now and again a car tore up hooted itself silly and tore off again. The Germans with the white armbands looked on apathetically. They aren't to be moved by anything after 12 years of Nazi rule. Even the sight of a Jewish Brigade swaggering past didn't move them. Peter suffered considerably, but I couldn't stop laughing. Frenchmen always have that effect on me. We left M. le Capitaine and promised to return a few days later with news of Furtwangen.

May 5th: Peter and Hans have been going around collecting petrol. Now that there is something to be done they are like children. They have decided to try and get a car together. They went off with a nail hammer and a bucket and managed to squeeze about 8 litres of petrol out of the wrecks lying around here. We left today by car for Villingen and having spoken to the Commandant we returned. The biggest bit of cheek yet. A sentry on the roads examined our papers and saluted smartly as we drove away. The war seems to be ending.

May 26th: I haven't written for some time because everything that I have done has left a nasty taste. My honest feeling is that I want to get up and tell all these rotten Frenchmen that the quicker they get to hell out of here the better. Everywhere large notices that plundering will be punished with death, and the glorious French army and lots of highfalutin baloney, and the result French soldiers, officers, Russians, Spahis, everyone plundering as well as they can, women raped (in our little village six cases, Wilflingen 20) when one old man tried to save his 60-year-old wife he was shot. It would be easier if they said that they've only come for that, but they then seem horrified at what the Germans did in France and are doing exactly the same. The Moroccans are probably the worst because they attack anything female between the age of 15 and 70. Women and chickens are their main sport. Women at night and chickens during the day. When

*Town Hall.

a patrol rides through, they halt, ask for arms, ogle the women, and then off after the chickens. They then ride off with each one or two squawking birds hanging from their saddlebags. La grande armée. At night the frightened peasant women and girls in the lonely farms are as easy to get as the chickens. It is really bad luck that this quiet peaceful Catholic part of Germany should have this plague. It has never been very Nazi here. They deserved it more in Thuringen–Saxony, where you heard Heil Hitler all day.

As for ourselves, we made some efforts to get law and order and then decided to play their game and cheat as well as we can. We have learned it well under the Nazis.

Some nice days stand out in my memory. The day of days when the British liaison officer Capt. Register came to see me. He arrived with three lorries and a smart Mercedes and suddenly stood in the room breathing England. I only then realized how I <u>love</u> and <u>miss</u> my country. It came over me like a terrific pain. We got coffee ready and he asked if the drivers of the lorries could come in too. I would have welcomed the whole British army. The whole four of them were so nice that the short visit went like lightning. A Canadian who had heard Charles' planes droning over his home in Canada, bound for Europe. A North of England man with a simple wee English face and Register himself big blond laughing at himself the war the French army, liaison officer who doesn't speak a word of French or German. We smoked Lucky's and I felt I was in another world.

May 26th: Peter left for Hamburg yesterday on his motorcycle. With his ski blouse and gaiters he looked like a French soldier. He was excited to leave, and I can imagine the joy of his mother and sister when he arrives. I wish I could go too. I can't wait now until I hear some news from home. Sitting here and doing housework is sort of hard on my patience. Frau M. is so frightened that I can hardly leave the house. When Moroccans come, I stand there and chat away about 'Anglaise, poulets anglaises, maison anglaise' and when they ask where my husband is, I always say he is with the Commandant and will be back any minute. Being large and fat the blacks seem to have a particular liking for me which makes things rather difficult. One of the funny things is that the oldest and stringiest of the females in the village are the most frightened of being raped. Aged spinsters and grandmothers barricade themselves in everywhere. Tante Ulla is certain they'll

506

have a go at her one day and Ellen's mother won't stay alone in the house.

July 8th: The interests of the French army have widened from chickens and women to clocks. Clocks clocks and more clocks. The least important soldier to the grandest general they all scramble for clocks. I think if Hitler had waited until the French army was over the Rhine and then let off a lot of alarm clocks on the Alsatian bank the whole of the Grande Armée du Rhin et du Danube would have turned and fought its way back over the river to get an alarm. They all have the most splendid wrist watches and yesterday I went into the *Rathaus* and in a sideroom I saw some fat colonels squabbling over some kitchen clocks which would have cost about 3/6 before the war.

A SELECTION OF LETTERS WRITTEN
BETWEEN 1940 AND 1946

Card from Christabel to her parents.

15th April, 1940

My darlingest Pom & Mam,

I do hope this reaches you in time for Mam's birthday. I had so hoped you would get some flowers from me on the day, but I only wrote to Elsa* a few days ago & I'm rather afraid now that my letter may not arrive in time. But if you don't get any flowers darlings, you may be sure that our thoughts will be with you if possible more than ever on the day & we shall be sending you so much love & so many wishes.

It is lovely having P. back again & we have long talks together. His views about the garden† etc. so absolutely coincide with mine. I do so wish that we could just see each other for a bit, my darlings. I miss you all sometimes so much that I don't know what to do. But now I believe is the time to learn & we <u>must</u> try to learn & see that we are bigger people when this is past. My dearest love to all of you to Bas, Bar & John.‡

Ever your devoted Chris

We are all very well.

*Her Swedish friend, Elsa von Rosen. At different points during the war, Christabel used the help of various friends in Sweden (Elsa and Outram Mott) and Switzerland (Jenny Thurneysen and André de Blonay) to communicate with her parents. However, only Christabel's letters to Elsa survive.
†A veiled reference to their shared political views?
‡Christabel's two brothers, Basil and John, and her sister, Barbara.

Copy of a letter from Christabel to Elsa von Rosen (nicknamed Johnnie) from her first lodgings in Rohrbach in the Black Forest, before she moved the family into Gasthaus Adler.

12th June, 1943

My dearest Johnnie,

I was so awfully happy to get your news that all was well with the B. [Burton] family. I have thought so much of the boys and knew somehow in my bones where they were. Peter as you know was on his way there when he was recalled.

We have been here now for exactly two days and it is perfectly awful. We came down to look at it last summer and found it very nice and clean and the peasants seemed very nice. But the wife has been ill during the winter and everything has gone to rack and ruin and it is so dirty that I can't put Christopher down anywhere. We arrived after a very long and tiring journey and thought to spend our time here until the end of the war. But I think that in spite of lovely scenery I shall go slowly bats if I stay here long. My nurse has of course struck anyway, and left before we came here so I am alone with my three sons. Nicky informed me on my first day he would rather be bombed than be here, and although I wouldn't go as far as that, I am busy looking for something else. It is rather difficult to find anything nice but perhaps we shall have luck.

Dear Johnny how I wish I could come to you in Koberg* – that would be the nicest of all. I was looking at the photographs which we took on our lovely holiday there so many years ago it seems now. But I'm afraid it is not to be yet awhile. Perhaps before long – what do you think?

Sometimes I get so homesick I don't know what I am going to do. I think of all the lovely times we had and remember every detail. Playing golf with Pom at Porters, or going up to town with Mam, and the flowers Mam always put in our rooms when we arrived, or wandering over to see Bar, and the talks with Bas and John – it was all so good – it must come back. You must excuse me blowing off to you like this Johnny, but you know perhaps the way it is. Sometimes one feels like bursting. The children are a great help though and are really very sweet. Nicholas is a complete school

---

*Koberg Castle, Sweden, home of Elsa's parents, the Silfverschiölds.

boy and rather clever. He is very understanding and sensible and is beginning to get to the stage of being embarrassed when he or anyone else says or does anything out of the ordinary. Everything must be as ordinary as possible otherwise his 'friends' at school might laugh and that's the most awful thing that could happen!! John is quite the opposite – dreamy, imaginative, can't sleep alone at night. He goes to school this year and it will probably be hard work because if he is thinking of something else, nothing in the wide world can disturb him. He is long and thin and (says fond Mama) very nice looking, still very fair with big grey eyes. Nicky is dark with very blue eyes and Christopher who is just a fat pet is almost the sweetest looking of the lot. He beams all day and looks exactly like Bas used to look. So you see, Gunilla* has a nice assortment to choose from! I've done my best for you Johnny.

As I am writing this I am sitting in a barely furnished room with the walls covered with pictures of ancestors of the peasants. They are none of them beautiful and some of them hideous. Some of them are in groups at weddings etc. and have 'God bless the married pair' written underneath. I think of my nice little house and could weep.

Since starting this letter I have had an invitation from a very nice friend of mine to spend the winter in their castle not far from here.† I felt like sending a telegram of acceptance but have restrained myself and sent a letter.

So Johnnie, this is a long and rather boring letter but you know the way one feels nowadays, sort of flat and wishing the time would go quicker. Please God I see you all again soon.

> My love to everyone my dear,
> Ever your,
> Chris

---

*Elsa's daughter.
†The invitation is probably to Schloss Wilflingen, where her friend Camilla Schenk von Stauffenberg, née Acheson, daughter of the 5th Earl of Gosford, lived. Her husband, Dölt Schenk von Stauffenberg, was a cousin of Claus Graf Schenk von Stauffenberg, who carried out the bomb attack on Hitler on 20 July, 1944.

Letter from Christabel to Elsa von Rosen.

Rohrbach
November 1943

My dearest Johnnie,

I was so happy to get your letter & hear your news. I have been meaning to answer it for some time but somehow the days go by here, and although nothing very thrilling happens, I find it is evening before I know where I am. I have become so completely countrified that at nine o'clock I begin to yawn and at ten o'clock if I am still up, I can hardly look out of my eyes. There is quite a lot to do too, because I have quite a nice, but terribly lazy nurse, whose one idea is to sit in her room & write to her boyfriends. She is Dutch & looks rather like a cheese, but has apparently hidden charm. Added to this I have John not so well. He has grown so fast that he is sort of overstrained & has some inflammation of the lung glands. So he has to rest half the day & must be frightfully carefully looked after.

We are settling down to a pretty hard winter up here now. Snow is thick everywhere & the storms are simply terrific. We are about 2700 feet above sea level & well you know what the country is like. Black woods on the hills & long green valleys.

I suppose my dear that I should send you now all my loving wishes for Christmas. It seems so early to start thinking of it, but in three or four weeks it will be there. The longer this war lasts the more homesick I get. This is the fifth Christmas, & it seems like yesterday & sometimes like another life that we were all together.

I went up north to our little house last month & meant to go again this week, but decided not to after all. Peter was coming there too & we had decided to have a few days together. But everything is in a complete muddle & now I can't get hold of him to tell him not to come. Johnny dear I suppose you couldn't get permission to send me a box of Christmas tree candles. It seems a funny wish my dear & if you have any trouble with it just don't. But I try to keep things as normal as possible at least for the children & my store of candles consists of three red ones nearly used up!

For the children it is rather ideal here. The eldest both have skis & can ski quite well. Christopher is inclined to sit down rather a lot, but I still have the old snow suits belonging to the others, &

with enormous take-ins & seams they fit him quite well. I wish I could send you a picture of him, but I can't find anyone who will develop & print my films. He looks exactly like Basil used to look & is too sweet for words.

6th December Johnnie my dear, a pause for me to get pneumonia & get over it. Yes you may laugh but I am now lying in hospital recovering from pneumonia. I had a pretty nasty three or four days but am now getting on very well. I kept having to think of the time Mummy had it too & how worried we all were. They luckily have wonderful means of fighting it now though, & in three days I had the crisis behind me. I am indeed lucky that I had it here in this little country town & not in one of the big towns. We have luck too in that our doctor has turned out to have been with Peter at the university. He came to visit Christopher one day & saw Peter's photograph & nearly popped with joy at meeting his children in this funny out of the world little place. I hope to get out of hospital at the end of next week, and Peter hopes to come on the 18th so that we have Christmas together. He telephoned me the day I got ill that our house is still braving the storms, one of the few. It is full of friends who look after it with loving care, & have made it a matter of honour that it shouldn't burn down!

Now I must stop & get this sent off. Christmas is not so far off & I want you to get it on time.

My dearest love to you & to everyone Johnnie. I shall think so much of everyone this Christmas. If one could only have television & see what they are all doing, bless them.

> A kiss for Gunilla
> Ever your
> Chris

Letter from Christabel to Elsa von Rosen written after Christmas 1943.

My dearest Johnnie,
I was overjoyed to get your letter with Christmas wishes. It is a lonely Christmas when no news comes. I would have written before but we have had a series of illnesses which kept one on the run. Firstly John then Nicholas then John again & finally Christopher. All more or less harmless colds, coughs, tonsillitis & earache but it meant sleepless nights. Then to crown it all, I

went down myself with pneumonia, & was carted off to hospital. I suppose I got it hopping in & out of bed in this unheated house. I managed to get out before Christmas & Peter came down for a few days which was very good. He came laden with as many household goods as he could pack onto himself & we had a laugh. Our house still stands & is full of friends who live a sort of happy-go-lucky existence. When they get hold of alcohol they all get drunk & if someone has cigarettes they all smoke themselves silly. They all have a feeling that nothing can happen to them under my roof! & I send my nightly blessing to them I must say.

From now on Peter is going to be there too & I pray that my blessing holds good. I bet you get about as fed up with Umea as I with Rohrbach. The winter is long & hard up here, & very lonely indeed. Snow, snow & more snow & a wind blows up or down the valley which nearly knocks you down. Nicholas stands the climate very well & is tall & strong & healthy. John is tall too but has continued colds & ear trouble. I hope he grows out of it. Little Christopher is a pet & is healthy too.

Can you imagine my joy Johnnie at getting a letter from Pom today. I nearly burst with pleasure. He sounded full of beans. Told me that Bill & Marie were staying with them. Should you see them please give them my very best love. I drank his, Pom's & his wife's health in real coffee, I was so excited!

My dear I would so love to see you & little Gunilla. I bet I would love her, & it must be fun for your parents having her at Koberg. I don't know what I would do without my three sons. They are so completely different from each other & take my mind off most of the other troubles in the world. It is of course ideal for them here, they are outside most of the day on skis or sledges & if I want to know any village gossip I just have to ask Nicky who knows everything about 5 minutes after it's happened. Last night the whole sky was lit up, & it was obvious that a fire was burning over the hill. Some people thought it was a forest fire, other a farm. Very soon Nicky came strolling in (he had mysteriously disappeared) & informed us all that the fire was the cowshed & part of the house a certain peasant (he named the name). He had been down to the village shop & he & the shop owner had telephoned around to find out where it was. He is great friends with the shop owner who at the moment has nothing whatsoever to sell which could interest Nicky, but I found that he was spending all his weekly money on fly papers. I remonstrated at the waste of money, but Nicky informed me that he was buying up all the fly papers he could at 5 ore* a piece, now, in winter, when nobody needed fly papers & in summer there would be no more fly papers in the village & he would be able to sell out at 10 ore per fly paper. So you see he has a sound business head!

Johnnie my dear I must stop now & go to bed. I still have to be rather careful of myself & I try to get to bed as early as possible. At the moment my nurse is ill too, so that I have lots to do. Please give my love to everyone, & a special greeting to all the very thrilling officers' wives that I bet live in Umea.

>Ever your loving
>Chris

Note from Peter to his mother after she visited him in Ravensbrück concentration camp, translated here from German.

>19th November, 1944

My dear Mum,
I am so grateful for your visit which I enjoyed <u>so</u> much. At first I had wanted to dissuade you from coming, as the circumstances of our meeting again are rather disagreeable. But if it wasn't too much trouble for you, it really was worth it, because it gave me huge pleasure to see you.

Yesterday I already received your three Christmas packages. Thanks a million. I shall put up the light with the apple and the spruce and think of all of you with all my heart. Then I shall feel as if we were together. – Everything still seems like a bad dream to me – except it's all too real. The Christmas holidays are soon upon us and there seems to be no hope unless a miracle happens.

[...]

I have to hand in the post now. To all of you, my sincere and heartfelt thanks and all my best wishes for Christmas and the New Year.

>To you, dear mother, a loving kiss
>from your
>Peter

*Swedish currency; a Krona consists of one hundred ores.

Copy of a letter from Capt. Pecquet to Christabel's parents.

11th July, 1945
Germany

Dear Mr & Mrs Burton,

Today for the second time I saw your daughter and her husband. The day before yesterday they had arrived from the Black Forest where they left their three children. All three children are in good health. Your daughter and husband are staying at Mr. Peterson's home near Frankfurt am Main. You could always get in touch with them c/o Director Peterson, Metallgesellschaft, Frankfurt am Main. The building is easy to find as it is one of the few not in ruins.

Peter is probably going to get a job with the Chamber of Commerce, Frankfurt. As he speaks excellent English it ought not to be too difficult. Mr Peterson is head of the Chamber of Commerce. For his role in the 20th July coup, Peter spent 9 months in a concentration camp. During the war, for a while, he was in Poland and Norway. In Norway he had trouble with the Gestapo. Treated his Russians too well. Because of his anti-Nazi activities he is lucky to be alive.

Chris is in excellent health. Had travelled from the Black Forest on a motor-bicycle. The food situation is good. And now the behaviour of the French colonial troops is much better. The house in Berlin still stands but has been looted. As far as I know the house in Hamburg is all right.

For six years your daughter has had no news. She hopes and prays you are well. For a while, in the Black Forest, she was under Gestapo surveillance.

Right now I guess it is all I have to say. Please write to me as per address on envelope.

Yours truly,
(Sgd.) Andre E. Pecquet (Capt.)

Letter sent by Christabel to her Swiss friend André de Blonay from Frankfurt am Main in the American zone, to forward to her family in England

26th July, 1945

My dear André,

You can perhaps imagine my joy at getting your letters. The first news of you for such a long time, and then two at the same time. I didn't know what I was doing with excitement. It came at a perfect time because I was just getting more than bothered at lack of news. It is really almost too good to be true that every single member of the family is well. How I would love to see you all. Mam writes that Bar is just the same & Bar writes Mam and Pom are just the same, so now it's up to me. I hope I'm as charming as ever!

Peter and I have been here for three weeks now. It's all rather a muddle, but Peter seems to be going to get a job in the Chamber of Commerce. We are staying now at the President's house. He is a brother of the Mr Peterson who is Mayor of Hamburg. (you remember him.) The difficulty is to get a roof over our heads. The RAF having removed most of them here in Frankfurt. I have left the children in the Black Forest, & came up here mainly to contact you. Now at last I seem to see daylight. I hope to know tomorrow just how long it will take before I can come over, & if I can bring the children. I left them awfully well indeed but am going down this weekend to see them. As hardly any trains & no post or telephone are working, they are very cut off down in the French zone, & to get down there is a work of art. But I want to be there on Nicky's birthday, with Peter, because last year I heard of his arrest on that day, & the birthday was rather a flop.

Darling Mam, I am delighted to hear that you have such stacks of furniture! We possess nothing whatsoever, not even a sauce-pan. It is a strange feeling, but if we come along & look all poor & refugee you must just help us!

July 30th I went yesterday to the Consul here & he told me that Pom had made a request for us to come home. He gave me lots of papers to fill out & said he thought it would last about 4-6 weeks. So we'll have to see darlings. I shall bring the children here to Frankfurt as soon as possible & then await results. I think it would be a good idea if Pom kept things moving from your side,

517

& I shall do the same here. Have you really got such an elastic house that you can take in so many people?

At the moment it's not quite clear how we should be able to get back. But Peter is really very sweet & says the main thing is, we go & see each other all again & then we can see what happens. He'll muddle along somehow in the meantime.

We have with our usual luck found a little house here, & some friends are going to lend us some furniture, so I think I shall bring the children as soon as possible. Food is slightly difficult, but I'm not an Irishwoman for nothing, & the last six years have given me good practice!

Well my darlings I stop now because this letter must leave. Does Pom know anyone over here in the American or British Military Government? If so give me his name & I could look them up. I have to go up to the British zone when I get back from the Black Forest.

My love to all of you & please tell Bar I'm <u>longing</u> to see her children so much. Nicky remembers Carley absolutely, I have started speaking English with my children. Nicky & John try their best, but Christopher just dies with laughter every time I say a word of English.

Once more all love
Chris

Letter from Christabel to her parents, anticipating her repatriation.

Schönberg / Frankfurt
5 Hindenburgstrasse
10th October, 1945

My darlingest Mam & Pom,

Since my last letter to you a very definite ray of light has reached us. Last Sunday a jeep drew up at the door & some sort of angels of God got out & asked for me. They had with them a letter from Johnnie (?) Bond to a General Morgan & from you Pom to Johnnie. They turned out to be people from UNRRA* & one of them was a <u>very</u> nice Mr Pichard who was leaving for England last Tuesday. He was going to ring you up when he got home. They came again

---

*United Nations Relief and Rehabilitation Administration.

in the evening & it was rather like a terrific Christmas for us & the children. Chocolate, cigarettes, soap!, matches, tea, toothpaste, shoe cream, a bottle of brandy, tinned things & a case of rations. Things we hadn't seen for years. It was really awfully sweet to see Nick & John's faces. They went to sleep chewing gum, each with a bar of chocolate saved up for the morning. One of the most happy things for me was to read from your letter that the prospects for my journey to you seem to be so bright. I do hope & pray that it will soon happen. But anyway now that we are in the hands of UNRRA, I feel quite different. I think the problem of keeping the children healthy until I leave is thereby solved. They (UNRRA) have been so completely kind & I know that through them I shall be in connection with you. I cannot explain darlings what a relief it is. I had begun to think I had done wrong to bring the children up here, away from cows & chickens etc. But my feeling was that we were so cut off in the French zone that we would never get in touch.

Mr Pichard has probably told you how we are living & that you needn't worry about us <u>at all</u>. I even thought afterwards that I wished I hadn't said about our clothes, because I don't want you to think you have to send us anything. I don't expect it's so marvellous in England that you have so much over. So please don't send any thing if it means the <u>least</u> sacrifice. We can get along quite well on what we have. Peter is still not sure if he will stay in his job here. He is in the Chamber of Commerce & has the denazification under him. He would rather be in some business though, & vaguely thinks of returning to his old firm, which belongs to Unilever. Well we'll see, the main thing is that Adolf has gone to Walhalla for good & all. I have got used to sitting & waiting for something to turn up.

We are having the most lovely autumn weather, & the trees here in the hills are simply lovely. The nicest thing about our house is the view which is very lovely just now.

Unfortunately John seems to have used my pen & ruined it, so please excuse this muddled letter, darlings. It is punctuated with cursing at my pen & pulling bits of fur out of it.

Peter wanted very much to add a few words to this but it looks as if he won't be back in time.

My dear love to all of you & bless you
ever your own
Chris

Incomplete letter from Christabel to her parents, apparently written the same day as the previous one.

Schönberg,
10th October , 1945

My darlings,

Just a short & <u>very</u> grateful note. Pat Erskine came here straight from his plane dragging a large bag with J. Burton on it. He just brought you all into the room with it. Peter & I had been having a long discussion & had just come to the conclusion that a farm in Ireland would be the thing for us or some firm with connections in England & in came Pat, bursting with news of you all. We sat & talked until late into the night & I felt really quite sick to see you all. It is strange & good Pom that you have been working along the same line as to our future. We must talk it all over when I come. P. is willing to do anything, & I think something will come along, don't you? As to the children I am not worried either now. In fact after hearing Pat's news of you I just feel on air. The contents of John's bag were <u>marvellous</u>. Particularly the pullovers for the children & I nearly wept when I saw Bas' bear coat coming out. It fits Peter as if made for him. I think Bas a major is too good for words. If Pom had been told that ten [. . .]

Letter from Christabel to Peter written just after her return to England, exploring the possibility of purchasing a farm in Ireland.

Codicote, Herts
13th December, 1945

My darling Peter,

I am writing to you on your birthday & wondering so much what you are doing. It is 11.15 at night, & I picture you being gay some place. I do hope that Freda is now better & that you are drinking my health in *schnapps*. [. . .]

I have put Ernest Harpur on the Irish business. He is going there at Christmas & knows several lads over there. He himself is battling with a similar problem. He has been offered to take over the whole of transport in the British zone of Germany but must sign on for seven years, & also a job in Ireland, & doesn't know which to do. At the moment the prices there are very moderate but unfortunately many English are getting the idea that it's a good place to go to. So no doubt prices will go up as a result. [. . .]

Charles* has returned from Ireland unfortunately without your stuff. But I hope to get lots of coupons & will then send you something. I'm afraid this letter is rather muddled, but this house is just packed with people & it's hard to get a quiet corner. I thought I'd got it now, but Charley is now switching from one American radio station to another on a superb radio that he has. Bar's house is going to be ready to move into after Christmas & then there will be some moving space. Charles is taking a fly-boat down to Buenos Aires on Thursday. He is just the same as ever with the same good common sense, & utterly irregular ways.

In fact the only one who has changed lots is little Mam, not so much in her looks as her ways. The war has been hard for her. John was apparently missing for months before reported POW, & then rather a lot of V1 & V2 fell in this neighbourhood. The most refreshing thing over here is the sort of sturdiness of everyone's point of view. Their attitude to America is that America needs them as much as they need America & rather than go under they will go through years of austerity. America can't take austerity & will get all balled up sooner or later if she doesn't get more sensible. The state of health over here is as good as never before. The children look marvellous. They have all got frightfully cheap orange juice, cod liver oil & free milk in the schools. This was because all mothers were at work. Anything like the conscription here I have never seen. Everyone almost has to work. They are letting up slightly now but during the war it must have been terrific. As there are no maids, and wives are working too, men with huge incomes are used to getting their own breakfasts, brushing shoes & doing household jobs. [. . .] I stop now or this will go on forever darling. Please write again soon.

> All love to you
> Chris

*Barbara's husband, Christabel's brother-in-law.

Letter from Christabel to Peter.

Codicote
23rd January, 1946

My darling Pete,

Still without news from you, but as the Gestapo no longer exists, I anyway needn't bother about you in that respect. I don't know whether you have got my last letters & parcels but hope you have.

I am now slowly getting things going over here I hope. I lunched with David [Astor] & his new wife the day before yesterday. He leaves for Switzerland today to fetch Clarita* over on a short trip. I lunch next week with the Stafford Cripps. My talk with D. which lasted many hours was very moving, I think as well for him as for me, as he wrote me a long letter afterwards which arrived this morning. He told me a thing which I had much feared, that Adam's reports at the time never reached their destination but were pigeonholed in the Foreign Office.† There were strong powers working against A. over here, so that when Cripps on D's request went to Eden (during the war after his successful return from Moscow) & told him what he knew of A. & how he trusted him, Eden sent for A's dossier & told Cripps the case against him was very black. Apparently A's camouflage behind Bose was not trusted.

When D. came back from the army he went at once to Bevin &

---

*Adam von Trott's widow.

†A Rhodes scholar in Oxford between 1931 and 1933, Adam von Trott zu Solz had met and impressed many eminent English scholars and personalities (A. L. Rowse, Isaiah Berlin, Christopher Hill, David Astor, Sheila Grant Duff, Maurice Bowra among others), and even leading politicians (Lord Halifax, Neville Chamberlain and Sir Richard Stafford Cripps). His decision to return to Nazi Germany at the end of his scholarship in order to support 'the other Germany' baffled many of his English friends, and his later attempts to put out 'peace feelers' and to influence the Allies' position favourably to the inner opposition against Hitler met with incomprehension and suspicion on their side. While participating in a conference at the Institute of Pacific Relations in the United States in late 1939, early 1940, Adam drafted a memorandum of the German opposition with the help of John Wheeler-Bennett, who was to convey it to President Roosevelt and to Lord Lothian. However, in a report written in 1943 for the Political Warfare Executive, entitled 'Adam von Trott and Peace Feelers', Wheeler-Bennett revised his previous supportive position and rejected co-operation with von Trott, who he claimed was a nationalist and therefore not to be trusted.

told him what he knew of A's story & mentioned that you were his best friend & he knew that you were living still. He then sent B. a written request that Clarita should be allowed a short visit in this country. A report of A's speech for his defence has since arrived in this country & has made an impression. Bevin, who is seemingly a perfectly marvellous old fellow, sent apparently for A's dossier & on the strength of D's report & although he did not know A., the result is Clarita's visa, which is quite unprecedented. I think this is a very hopeful start. Next week I meet the Cripps & then we must see further. A good piece of news is that Fritz* has got a huge job in G.C.C. Berlin. He has been given British nationality & leaves soon for Berlin. He will have the whole economics of the British zone under him. Muschi† is expecting a baby in May/June but hopes to come to Germany in August.

I myself have had bad luck in that I fell down some ice-covered steps yesterday & have sprained my ankle so badly that I shall be on sticks for six weeks. At the moment I have lots of pain but hope it will go off soon. [. . .]

I am trying now to get your tweed & flannel through Ralph & Ernest in Ireland but if they can't do it, I will get some on coupons here.

Well darling I stop now & send this off & pack up some cigs for you. I miss you lots my Pete & hope that all my efforts to make some sort of future for us will not be fruitless.

> Bless you sweet
> Chris

Letter from Christabel to Peter after her return to England following her first stint as a special correspondent for the Observer *in Germany in spring/summer 1946.*

30th July, 1946

Darlingest Pete,
I am sending you this via Peter B. in the hopes that it will reach you more quickly. I expect by now you will have seen Mabel & heard my news as from there. My journey back was bumpy but

---

*Fritz Schumacher (1911–1977), economic thinker whose 1973 book *Small is Beautiful* was among the *Times Literary Supplement*'s 100 most influential books since the Second World War.
†Shumacher's wife.

we landed safely. Bar had arrived from Argentina on the day before. Charles has landed a good job out there and they are off in September. It must be a heavenly place. Just everything you can want.

Today I met Werner von S. for the first time. He was quite charming & is longing for you to come. He thinks that trade will be opening very soon with Germany & particularly wants you to keep your Metallgesellschaft connections. He thought you were with the Metallgesellschaft & as I was not sure how you stand, I did not contradict him. I told him P. had offered you the Köln job but that you had not been able to decide to take it because of you coming here. He doesn't think much of old Petersen (Alfred), but hopes to do business with Metallgesellschaft Lübeck. He thanked for report as it was all he wanted to know. As Sir Wilfred Eady is not yet back from the Argentine (expected in a fortnight) I got Pom to enquire at Home Office how we stand. The answer, your case was being handled at a high level, & as yet no decision. I think it wiser for Eady to make further enquiries when he returns. Should answer be no, I will go straight to Dulanty. If yes I will wire P.B. or Vaughan, so that you can get on with exit permit. Please excuse scrawl but I'm in bed with flu of all things, & my head is thumping slightly.

You will laugh to hear Nicky won nearly everything at his school sports, & was proclaimed Junior Athletic Champion. You will wonder what the others were like & it's true that the fact of him being just under 11 years old helped some. But he has certainly improved enormously & has a grand turn of speed & a huge amount of determination. His face was a picture as he just won the relay race, running last against the fastest boy in the school. The rest of his side had helped him to a certain start, & he tore along with the big boy catching up on him at every stride. I am afraid his fond Mamma nearly popped with excitement & Bar & I yelled ourselves silly.

Vaughan has just rung to say he will be going to Germany on Tuesday. So I will post this to him, & hope you get it even quicker.

Everyone sends fondest love, & so do I darling & bless you
    Chris

Letter from Christabel to Peter prior to her second trip to Germany as a special correspondent for the Observer *and shortly before Peter's arrival in England.*

The White House
Codicote
Herts
29th August, 1946

My darling Pete,
Your letter written on August 2nd arrived today. I was so glad to hear from you darling. By now you know the good news about the visa, & can make your plans accordingly. I am so longing for you to come, as I am missing you enormously, & am completely fed up with this state of affairs. But I feel we did and are doing the right thing in backing this horse, although I expect we have some funny times ahead of us. But I don't mind a bit as long as we are all together darling, & as our star hasn't looked after us so badly so far, maybe it will continue to do so. We are leaving here at the beginning of next week for home. We have had very bad weather, but the children have enjoyed themselves and are looking splendid. They unfortunately do not return to school until September 20th. So that I cannot leave for Germany until the 21st. However I think it will take no time from then onwards. If you could have a car it would be marvellous, as we could set your mother up for the winter and generally tool around a bit. Could you get me the ages and sexes of Schlabrendorffs'* children. I would like to bring as much as I can and Bar has things which may help. Also ask Muschi† how she is off for shoes. If the situation is very bad I would spend my own coupons on

---

*Fabian von Schlabrendorff (1907–1980) was an officer involved in several attempts on Hitler's life. He was arrested after the failed bomb plot on 20 July 1944 and was repeatedly tortured by the Gestapo. He miraculously escaped a certain death sentence when a bomb hit the *Volksgerichtshof* in February 1945, shortly before his trial, and killed his judge, the notorious Ronald Freisler. Schlabrendorff spent the last months of the war in several concentration camps and was eventually liberated by American troops on 4 May 1945. After the war, he published the first account on the German military resistance against Hitler (*Offiziere gegen Hitler – Officers against Hitler*) and served as judge on the Federal Republic's Constitutional Court between 1967 and 1975.
†Peter's sister.

getting them, but if Ulla has brought stuff with her, & if it's not so bad, I would rather not, as we are not <u>so</u> well off with coupons ourselves. Please send me the sizes of their feet though because I might get some off Pom who has stacks of shoes which I am sure he never wears. Could you answer this if possible via Blake darling, because I would like to have the reply before I leave.

Freda writes that you are off to Bavaria. I am so glad for you and hope you have a good time. How I would love to be coming with you, & just be with you without always others knocking around. Perhaps some day we shall have some time together, in some lovely place.

I think it would be a good idea if we visited Ireland when you come. In fact I think we will have to. I thought to go to the High Commissioner when we get back, and tell him that you have this visa now for England, as you wanted first to discuss possibilities with Pom & friends over here etc. I do not want him to feel rebuffed in any way, because he was so really charming about everything. When you come we can go and see him together. It is really lovely to be able to write 'when you come' & to know that it is now certain. The horrible failure of all our plans after 20th of July makes one always surprised if anything succeeds, & has given me a sort of complex almost about it. I suppose deep down we have taken a big knock which will take years to recover from. But it is no use grumbling or getting depressed, we have just got to build up again, & try to learn from our despair. I don't think that that would be possible for us in Germany because we would be continually chafing against the stupidity either of the occupying power or else of the remnants of the second class Germans who will be running the show. I dread to think of this winter in Germany. When you are with your mother you could perhaps find out from those lodgers upstairs what the peasants want for wood. I could bring bicycle tyres & inner tubes, or shoe leather, or in fact many odd things which aren't food or clothing. Get him to ask around so that we could do some deals for wood & potatoes. We would otherwise have to do it in the Frankfurt district & take it up to them. We must get them O.K. before leaving.

I enclose a cutting from the newspaper about the girl who was in camp with you & called herself Mrs Churchill. Puppy wrote to me some time ago & told me that Samson* was her real name. She was obviously one of the top Resistance people & pretended she was married to Churchill to hide his real reason for being in France. She was lucky to get home alright. Perhaps you can go and see her when you come. I have not heard anything from Frau Langbehn's parents. I wonder where the hitch is. I wonder did anything happen about the Swiss business. Would you also let me know if Botho Wussow† is out yet. I would very much like to help him if I can, this time when I come. When I think that A.K. is out & about & others still in, it just bothers me to put it mildly.

Well darling please answer this as soon as possible, via Peter B. or Vaughan Jones.

My dear love to you from
your own
Chris (who misses you!)

Peter was able to leave Germany a few months later and the Bielenberg family was reunited in England. The stamp in his Military Exit Permit indicates his departure took place on 14th November, 1946, from Flensburg railway station in northern Germany. His destination is entered as Eire (Athy), but a three-month visa for the United Kingdom is stamped on the back of his travel document. The stated object of his journey was simply 'TO LIVE WITH FAMILY'.

*Odette Samson (1912–1995), a French-born English agent who worked in Nazi-occupied France. When she and her supervisor, Peter Churchill, were caught, she successfully convinced the Gestapo that he was a nephew of Sir Winston Churchill and her husband, which saved their lives.
†Botho von Wussow (1901–1971), a German diplomat involved with the resistance circles and husband of Chris's friend Mary, née Pilcher. Following the denunciation of his wife in January 1942 – Chris relates the event which led to this in the chapter 'A Dangerous Tea Party' in The Past is Myself – the couple was transferred to Lisbon for their own safety, where they lived until the end of the war.